NCERT EXEMPLAR

Problems-Solutions

Mathematics

Detailed Explanation to all Objective & Subjective Problems

CLASS

XII

NCERT EXEMPLAR

Problems-Solutions

Mathematics

Detailed Explanation to all Objective & Subjective Problems

CLASS

XII

Ankesh Kumar Singh

arihant

Arihant Prakashan (School Division Series)

arihant

Arihant Prakashan (School Division Series)

卐 **Administrative & Production Offices**

Regd. Office

'Ramchhaya' 4577/15, Agarwal Road, Darya Ganj, New Delhi -110002
Tele: 011- 47630600, 43518550

卐 **Head Office**

Kalindi, TP Nagar, Meerut (UP) - 250002
Tel: 0121-7156203, 7156204

卐 **Sales & Support Offices**

Agra, Ahmedabad, Bengaluru, Bareilly, Chennai, Delhi, Guwahati, Hyderabad, Jaipur, Jhansi, Kolkata, Lucknow, Nagpur & Pune.

卐 **ISBN** 978-93-27197-47-1

PO No : TXT-XX-XXXXXXX-X-XX

Published by Arihant Publications (India) Ltd.

For further information about the books published by Arihant, log on to www.arihantbooks.com or e-mail at info@arihantbooks.com

Follow us on

PREFACE

The Department of Education in Science & Mathematics (DESM) & National Council of Educational Research & Training (NCERT) developed **Exemplar Problems** in Science and Mathematics for Secondary and Senior Secondary Classes with the objective to provide the students a large number of quality problems in various forms and format *viz*. Multiple Choice Questions, Short Answer Questions, Long Answer Questions etc., with varying levels of difficulty.

NCERT Exemplar Problems are very important for both; School & Board Examinations as well as competitive examinations like Engineering Entrances. The questions given in exemplar book are mainly of higher difficulty order by practicing these problems, you will able to manage with the margin between a good score and a very good or an excellent score.

Approx 20% problems asked in any Board Examination or Entrance Examinations are of higher difficulty order, exemplar problems will make you ready to solve these difficult problems.

This book **NCERT Exemplar Problems-Solutions Mathematics XII** contains Explanatory & Accurate Solutions to all the questions given in NCERT Exemplar Mathematics book.

For the overall benefit of the students' we have made unique this book in such a way that it presents not only hints and solutions but also detailed and authentic explanations. Through these detailed explanations, students can learn the concepts which will enhance their thinking and learning abilities.

We have introduced some additional features with the solutions which are as follows :

- **Thinking Process** Along with the solutions to questions we have given thinking process that tell how to approach to solve a problem. Here, we have tried to cover all the loopholes which may lead to confusion. All formulae and hints are discussed in detail.
- **Note** We have provided notes also to solutions in which special points are mentioned which are of great value for the students.

With the hope that this book will be of great help to the students,
I wish great success to my readers.

Author

CONTENTS

1

Relations and Functions

Short Answer Type Questions

Q. 1 Let $A = \{a, b, c\}$ and the relation R be defined on A as follows

$$R = \{(a, a), (b, c), (a, b)\}$$

Then, write minimum number of ordered pairs to be added in R to make R reflexive and transitive.

Sol. Given relation, $R = \{(a, a), (b, c), (a, b)\}$.

To make R is reflexive we must add (b, b) and (c, c) to R. Also, to make R is transitive we must add (a, c) to R.

So, minimum number of ordered pair is to be added are (b, b), (c, c), (a, c).

Q. 2 Let D be the domain of the real valued function f defined by $f(x) = \sqrt{25 - x^2}$. Then, write D.

Sol. Given function is, $f(x) = \sqrt{25 - x^2}$

For real valued of $f(x)$ $\quad 25 - x^2 \geq 0$

$$x^2 \leq 25$$

$$-5 \leq x \leq +5$$

$\therefore \quad D = [-5, 5]$

Q. 3 If $f, g : R \rightarrow R$ be defined by $f(x) = 2x + 1$ and $g(x) = x^2 - 2$, $\forall\, x \in R$, respectively. Then, find gof.

Thinking Process

If $f, g : R \rightarrow R$ be two functions, then $gof(x) = g\{f(x)\}\ \forall x \in R$.

Sol. Given that, $\quad f(x) = 2x + 1$ and $g(x) = x^2 - 2$, $\forall x \in R$

$$\therefore \quad gof = g\{f(x)\}$$

$$= g(2x + 1) = (2x + 1)^2 - 2$$

$$= 4x^2 + 4x + 1 - 2$$

$$= 4x^2 + 4x - 1$$

Q. 4 Let $f : R \rightarrow R$ be the function defined by $f(x) = 2x - 3, \forall\ x \in R$. Write f^{-1}.

Sol. Given that, $f(x) = 2x - 3, \forall\ x \in R$

Now, let
$$y = 2x - 3$$
$$2x = y + 3$$
$$x = \frac{y+3}{2}$$
$$\therefore \quad f^{-1}(x) = \frac{x+3}{2}$$

Q. 5 If $A = \{a, b, c, d\}$ and the function $f = \{(a, b), (b, d), (c, a), (d, c)\}$, write f^{-1}.

Sol. Given that, $A = \{a, b, c, d\}$

and $f = \{(a, b), (b, d), (c, a), (d, c)\}$
$$f^{-1} = \{(b, a), (d, b), (a, c), (c, d)\}$$

Q. 6 If $f : R \rightarrow R$ is defined by $f(x) = x^2 - 3x + 2$, write $f\{f(x)\}$.

Thinking Process

To solve this problem use the formula i.e., $(a+b+c)^2 = (a^2 + b^2 + c^2 + 2ab + 2bc + 2ca)$

Sol. Given that, $f(x) = x^2 - 3x + 2$
$$\therefore \quad f\{f(x)\} = f(x^2 - 3x + 2)$$
$$= (x^2 - 3x + 2)^2 - 3(x^2 - 3x + 2) + 2$$
$$= x^4 + 9x^2 + 4 - 6x^3 - 12x + 4x^2 - 3x^2 + 9x - 6 + 2$$
$$= x^4 + 10x^2 - 6x^3 - 3x$$
$$f\{f(x)\} = x^4 - 6x^3 + 10x^2 - 3x$$

Q. 7 Is $g = \{(1, 1), (2, 3), (3, 5), (4, 7)\}$ a function? If g is described by $g(x) = \alpha x + \beta$, then what value should be assigned to α and β?

Sol. Given that, $g = \{(1, 1), (2, 3), (3, 5), (4, 7)\}$.

Here, each element of domain has unique image. So, g is a function.

Now given that, $g(x) = \alpha x + \beta$
$$g(1) = \alpha + \beta$$
$$\alpha + \beta = 1 \quad \ldots(i)$$
$$g(2) = 2\alpha + \beta$$
$$2\alpha + \beta = 3 \quad \ldots(ii)$$

From Eqs. (i) and (ii),
$$2(1 - \beta) + \beta = 3$$
$$\Rightarrow \quad 2 - 2\beta + \beta = 3$$
$$\Rightarrow \quad 2 - \beta = 3$$
$$\beta = -1$$

If $\beta = -1$, then $\alpha = 2$
$$\alpha = 2,\ \beta = -1$$

Q. 8 Are the following set of ordered pairs functions? If so examine whether the mapping is injective or surjective.

(i) $\{(x, y) : x$ is a person, y is the mother of $x\}$.

(ii) $\{(a, b) : a$ is a person, b is an ancestor of $a\}$.

Sol. **(i)** Given set of ordered pair is $\{(x, y) : x$ is a person, y is the mother of $x\}$.

It represent a function. Here, the image of distinct elements of x under f are not distinct, so it is not a injective but it is a surjective.

(ii) Set of ordered pairs $= \{(a, b) : a$ is a person, b is an ancestor of $a\}$

Here, each element of domain does not have a unique image. So, it does not represent function.

Q. 9 If the mappings f and g are given by $f = \{(1, 2), (3, 5), (4, 1)\}$ and $g = \{(2, 3), (5, 1), (1, 3)\}$, write fog.

Sol. Given that, $f = \{(1, 2), (3, 5), (4, 1)\}$

and $g = \{(2, 3), (5, 1), (1, 3)\}$

Now,
$$fog(2) = f\{g(2)\} = f(3) = 5$$
$$fog(5) = f\{g(5)\} = f(1) = 2$$
$$fog(1) = f\{g(1)\} = f(3) = 5$$
$$fog = \{(2, 5), (5, 2), (1, 5)\}$$

Q. 10 Let C be the set of complex numbers. Prove that the mapping $f : C \to R$ given by $f(z) = |z|, \forall z \in C$, is neither one-one nor onto.

Sol. The mapping $f : C \to R$

Given,
$$f(z) = |z|, \forall z \in C$$
$$f(1) = |1| = 1$$
$$f(-1) = |-1| = 1$$
$$f(1) = f(-1)$$

But $1 \neq -1$

So, $f(z)$ is not one-one. Also, $f(z)$ is not onto as there is no pre-image for any negative element of R under the mapping $f(z)$.

Q. 11 Let the function $f : R \to R$ be defined by $f(x) = \cos x, \forall x \in R$. Show that f is neither one-one nor onto.

Sol. Given function, $f(x) = \cos x, \forall x \in R$

Now,
$$f\left(\frac{\pi}{2}\right) = \cos\frac{\pi}{2} = 0$$

$\Rightarrow$
$$f\left(\frac{-\pi}{2}\right) = \cos\frac{\pi}{2} = 0$$

$\Rightarrow$
$$f\left(\frac{\pi}{2}\right) = f\left(\frac{-\pi}{2}\right)$$

But
$$\frac{\pi}{2} \neq \frac{-\pi}{2}$$

So, $f(x)$ is not one-one.

Now, $f(x) = \cos x, \forall x \in R$ is not onto as there is no pre-image for any real number. Which does not belonging to the intervals $[-1, 1]$, the range of $\cos x$.

Q. 12 Let $X = \{1, 2, 3\}$ and $Y = \{4, 5\}$. Find whether the following subsets of $X \times Y$ are functions from X to Y or not.

(i) $f = \{(1, 4), (1, 5), (2, 4), (3, 5)\}$ (ii) $g = \{(1, 4), (2, 4), (3, 4)\}$
(iii) $h = \{(1, 4), (2, 5), (3, 5)\}$ (iv) $k = \{(1, 4), (2, 5)\}$

Sol. Given that, $X = \{1, 2, 3\}$ and $Y = \{4, 5\}$

$$X \times Y = \{(1, 4), (1, 5), (2, 4), (2, 5), (3, 4), (3, 5)\}$$

(i) $f = \{(1, 4), (1, 5), (2, 4), (3, 5)\}$
f is not a function because f has not unique image.

(ii) $g = \{(1, 4), (2, 4), (3, 4)\}$
Since, g is a function as each element of the domain has unique image.

(iii) $h = \{(1, 4), (2, 5), (3, 5)\}$
It is clear that h is a function.

(iv) $k = \{(1, 4), (2, 5)\}$
k is not a function as 3 has not any image under the mapping.

Q. 13 If functions $f : A \to B$ and $g : B \to A$ satisfy $gof = I_A$, then show that f is one-one and g is onto.

Sol. Given that,

$$f : A \to B \text{ and } g : B \to A \text{ satisfy } gof = I_A$$

$\because$ $gof = I_A$

$\Rightarrow$ $gof\{f(x_1)\} = gof\{f(x_2)\}$

$\Rightarrow$ $g(x_1) = g(x_2)$ $[\because gof = I_A]$

$\therefore$ $x_1 = x_2$

Hence, f is one-one and g is onto.

Q. 14 Let $f : R \to R$ be the function defined by $f(x) = \dfrac{1}{2 - \cos x}$, $\forall\, x \in R$. Then, find the range of f.

Thinking Process

Range of $f = \{y \in Y : y = f(x) : \text{for some in } x\}$ and use range of $\cos x$ is $[-1, 1]$

Sol. Given function, $f(x) = \dfrac{1}{2 - \cos x}$, $\forall\, x \in R$

Let $y = \dfrac{1}{2 - \cos x}$

$\Rightarrow$ $2y - y\cos x = 1$

$\Rightarrow$ $y\cos x = 2y - 1$

$\Rightarrow$ $\cos x = \dfrac{2y - 1}{y} = 2 - \dfrac{1}{y} \Rightarrow \cos x = 2 - \dfrac{1}{y}$

$\Rightarrow$ $-1 \le \cos x \le 1 \Rightarrow -1 \le 2 - \dfrac{1}{y} \le 1$

$\Rightarrow$ $-3 \le -\dfrac{1}{y} \le -1 \Rightarrow 1 \le \dfrac{1}{y} \le 3$

$\Rightarrow$ $\dfrac{1}{3} \le \dfrac{1}{y} \le 1$

So, y range is $\left[\dfrac{1}{3}, 1\right]$.

Q. 15 **Let n be a fixed positive integer. Define a relation R in Z as follows $\forall\ a, b \in Z$, aRb if and only if $a - b$ is divisible by n. Show that R is an equivalence relation.**

Sol. Given that, $\forall\ a, b \in Z$, aRb if and only if $a - b$ is divisible by n.
Now,

I. **Reflexive**

$aRa \Rightarrow (a - a)$ is divisible by n, which is true for any integer a as 'O' is divisible by n.
Hence, R is reflexive.

II. **Symmetric**

aRb
$\Rightarrow$ $a - b$ is divisible by n.
$\Rightarrow$ $-b + a$ is divisible by n.
$\Rightarrow$ $-(b - a)$ is divisible by n.
$\Rightarrow$ $(b - a)$ is divisible by n.
$\Rightarrow$ bRa

Hence, R is symmetric.

III. **Transitive**

Let aRb and bRc
$\Rightarrow$ $(a - b)$ is divisible by n and $(b - c)$ is divisible by n
$\Rightarrow$ $(a - b) + (b - c)$ is divisibly by n
$\Rightarrow$ $(a - c)$ is divisible by n
$\Rightarrow$ aRc

Hence, R is transitive.
So, R is an equivalence relation.

Long Answer Type Questions

Q. 16 **If $A = \{1, 2, 3, 4\}$, define relations on A which have properties of being**

(i) reflexive, transitive but not symmetric.
(ii) symmetric but neither reflexive nor transitive.
(iii) reflexive, symmetric and transitive.

Sol. Given that, $A = \{1, 2, 3, 4\}$

(i) Let $R_1 = \{(1, 1), (1, 2), (2, 3), (2, 2), (1, 3), (3, 3)\}$
R_1 is reflexive, since, (1, 1) (2, 2) (3, 3) lie in R_1.
Now, $(1, 2) \in R_1, (2, 3) \in R_1 \Rightarrow (1, 3) \in R_1$
Hence, R_1 is also transitive but $(1, 2) \in R_1 \Rightarrow (2, 1) \notin R_1$.
So, it is not symmetric.

(ii) Let $R_2 = \{(1, 2), (2, 1)\}$
Now, $(1, 2) \in R_2, (2, 1) \in R_2$
So, it is symmetric.

(iii) Let $R_3 = \{(1, 2), (2, 1), (1, 1), (2, 2), (3, 3), (1, 3), (3, 1), (2, 3)\}$
Hence, R_3 is reflexive, symmetric and transitive.

Q. 17 **Let R be relation defined on the set of natural number N as follows, $R = \{(x, y) : x \in N, y \in N, 2x + y = 41\}$. Find the domain and range of the relation R. Also verify whether R is reflexive, symmetric and transitive.**

Sol. Given that, $R = \{(x, y) : x \in N, y \in N, 2x + y = 41\}$.

$$\text{Domain} = \{1, 2, 3, \ldots, 20\}$$
$$\text{Range} = \{1, 3, 5, 7, \ldots, 39\}$$
$$R = \{(1, 39), (2, 37), (3, 35), \ldots, (19, 3), (20, 1)\}$$

R is not reflexive as $(2, 2) \notin R$

$$2 \times 2 + 2 \neq 41$$

So, R is not symmetric.

As $(1, 39) \in R$ but $(39, 1) \notin R$

So, R is not transitive.

As $(11, 19) \in R, (19, 3) \in R$

But $(11, 3) \notin R$

Hence, R is neither reflexive, nor symmetric and nor transitive.

Q. 18 **Given, $A = \{2, 3, 4\}$, $B = \{2, 5, 6, 7\}$. Construct an example of each of the following**

(i) an injective mapping from A to B.

(ii) a mapping from A to B which is not injective.

(iii) a mapping from B to A.

Sol. Given that, $A = \{2, 3, 4\}, B = \{2, 5, 6, 7\}$

(i) Let $f : A \to B$ denote a mapping

$$f = \{(x, y) : y = x + 3\}$$

i.e., $f = \{(2, 5), (3, -6), (4, 7)\}$, which is an injective mapping.

(ii) Let $g : A \to B$ denote a mapping such that $g = \{(2, 2), (3, 5), (4, 5)\}$, which is not an injective mapping.

(iii) Let $h : B \to A$ denote a mapping such that $h = \{(2, 2), (5, 3), (6, 4), (7, 4)\}$, which is a mapping from B to A.

Q. 19 **Give an example of a map**

(i) which is one-one but not onto.

(ii) which is not one-one but onto.

(iii) which is neither one-one nor onto.

Sol. **(i)** Let $f : N \to N$, be a mapping defined by $f(x) = 2x$ which is one-one.

For $f(x_1) = f(x_2)$

$\Rightarrow$ $2x_1 = 2x_2$

$$x_1 = x_2$$

Further f is not onto, as for $1 \in N$, there does not exist any x in N such that $f(x) = 2x + 1$.

(ii) Let $f : N \to N$, given by $f(1) = f(2) = 1$ and $f(x) = x - 1$ for every $x > 2$ is onto but not one-one. f is not one-one as $f(1) = f(2) = 1$. But f is onto.

(iii) The mapping $f : R \to R$ defined as $f(x) = x^2$, is neither one-one nor onto.

Q. 20 Let $A = R - \{3\}$, $B = R - \{1\}$. If $f : A \to B$ be defined by $f(x) = \frac{x-2}{x-3}$, $\forall\, x \in A$. Then, show that f is bijective.

Thinking Process

A function $f : x \to y$ is said to be bijective, if f is both one-one and onto.

Sol. Given that, $A = R - \{3\},\ B = R - \{1\}$.

$f : A \to B$ is defined by $f(x) = \frac{x-2}{x-3}, \forall\, x \in A$

For injectivity

Let $f(x_1) = f(x_2) \Rightarrow \frac{x_1 - 2}{x_1 - 3} = \frac{x_2 - 2}{x_2 - 3}$

$\Rightarrow \quad (x_1 - 2)(x_2 - 3) = (x_2 - 2)(x_1 - 3)$

$\Rightarrow \quad x_1x_2 - 3x_1 - 2x_2 + 6 = x_1x_2 - 3x_2 - 2x_1 + 6$

$\Rightarrow \quad -3x_1 - 2x_2 = -3x_2 - 2x_1$

$\Rightarrow \quad -x_1 = -x_2 \Rightarrow x_1 = x_2$

So, $f(x)$ is an injective function.

For surjectivity

Let $y = \frac{x-2}{x-3} \Rightarrow x - 2 = xy - 3y$

$\Rightarrow \quad x(1-y) = 2 - 3y \Rightarrow x = \frac{2-3y}{1-y}$

$\Rightarrow \quad x = \frac{3y-2}{y-1} \in A, \forall\, y \in B$ [codomain]

So, $f(x)$ is surjective function.

Hence, $f(x)$ is a bijective function.

Q. 21 Let $A = [-1, 1]$, then, discuss whether the following functions defined on A are one-one onto or bijective.

(i) $f(x) = \frac{x}{2}$ (ii) $g(x) = |x|$

(iii) $h(x) = x|x|$ (iv) $k(x) = x^2$

Sol. Given that, $A = [-1, 1]$

(i) $f(x) = \frac{x}{2}$

Let $f(x_1) = f(x_2)$

$\Rightarrow \quad \frac{x_1}{2} = \frac{x_2}{2} \Rightarrow x_1 = x_2$

So, $f(x)$ is one-one.

Now, let $y = \frac{x}{2}$

$\Rightarrow \quad x = 2y \notin A, \forall\, y \in A$

As for $y = 1 \in A, x = 2 \notin A$

So, $f(x)$ is not onto.

Also, $f(x)$ is not bijective as it is not onto.

(ii) $g(x) = |x|$

Let $g(x_1) = g(x_2)$

$\Rightarrow$ $|x_1| = |x_2| \Rightarrow x_1 = \pm x_2$

So, $g(x)$ is not one-one.

Now, $y = |x| \Rightarrow x = \pm y \notin A, \forall y \in A$

So, $g(x)$ is not onto, also, $g(x)$ is not bijective.

(iii) $h(x) = x|x|$

Let $h(x_1) = h(x_2)$

$\Rightarrow$ $x_1|x_1| = x_2|x_2| \Rightarrow x_1 = x_2$

So, $h(x)$ is one-one.

Now, let $y = x|x|$

$\Rightarrow$ $y = x^2 \in A, \forall x \in A$

So, $h(x)$ is onto also, $h(x)$ is a bijective.

(iv) $k(x) = x^2$

Let $k(x_1) = k(x_2)$

$\Rightarrow$ $x_1^2 = x_2^2 \Rightarrow x_1 = \pm x_2$

Thus, $k(x)$ is not one-one.

Now, let $y = x^2$

$\Rightarrow$ $x = \sqrt{y} \notin A, \forall y \in A$

As for $y = -1$, $x = \sqrt{-1} \notin A$

Hence, $k(x)$ is neither one-one nor onto.

Q. 22 Each of the following defines a relation of N

(i) x is greater than y, $x, y \in N$.

(ii) $x + y = 10$, $x, y \in N$.

(iii) xy is square of an integer $x, y \in N$.

(iv) $x + 4y = 10$, $x, y \in N$

Determine which of the above relations are reflexive, symmetric and transitive.

Sol. **(i)** x is greater than y, $x, y \in N$

$(x, x) \in R$

For xRx $x > x$ is not true for any $x \in N$.

Therefore, R is not reflexive.

Let $(x, y) \in R \Rightarrow xRy$

$x > y$

but $y > x$ is not true for any $x, y \in N$

Thus, R is not symmetric.

Let xRy and yRz

$x > y$ and $y > z \Rightarrow x > z$

$\Rightarrow$ xRz

So, R is transitive.

(ii) $x + y = 10,\ x, y \in N$

$$R = \{(x, y);\ x + y = 10,\ x, y \in N\}$$

$$R = \{(1, 9), (2, 8), (3, 7), (4, 6), (5, 5), (6, 4), (7, 3), (8, 2), (9, 1)\}\ (1, 1) \notin R$$

So, R is not reflexive.

$$(x, y) \in R \Rightarrow (y, x) \in R$$

Therefore, R is symmetric.

$$(1, 9) \in R, (9, 1) \in R \Rightarrow (1, 1) \notin R$$

Hence, R is not transitive.

(iii) Given xy, is square of an integer $x, y \in N$.

$\Rightarrow$ $$R = \{(x, y) : xy \text{ is a square of an integer } x, y \in N\}$$

$$(x, x) \in R,\ \forall\, x \in N$$

As x^2 is square of an integer for any $x \in N$.

Hence, R is reflexive.

If $$(x, y) \in R \Rightarrow (y, x) \in R$$

Therefore, R is symmetric.

If $$(x, y) \in R, (y, z) \in R$$

So, xy is square of an integer and yz is square of an integer.

Let $xy = m^2$ and $yz = n^2$ for some $m, n \in Z$

$$x = \frac{m^2}{y} \text{ and } z = \frac{x^2}{y}$$

$$xz = \frac{m^2n^2}{y^2}, \text{ which is square of an integer.}$$

So, R is transitive.

(iv) $$x + 4y = 10,\ x, y \in N$$

$$R = \{(x, y) : x + 4y = 10,\ x, y \in N\}$$

$$R = \{(2, 2), (6, 1)\}$$

$$(1, 1), (3, 3), \ldots, \notin R$$

Thus, R is not reflexive.

$$(6, 1) \in R \text{ but } (1, 6) \notin R$$

Hence, R is not symmetric.

$$(x, y) \in R \Rightarrow x + 4y = 10 \text{ but } (y, z) \in R$$

$$y + 4z = 10 \Rightarrow (x, z) \in R$$

So, R is transitive.

Q. 23 Let $A = \{1, 2, 3, \ldots, 9\}$ and R be the relation in $A \times A$ defined by $(a, b)\ R\ (c, d)$ if $a + d = b + c$ for $(a, b), (c, d)$ in $A \times A$. Prove that R is an equivalence relation and also obtain the equivalent class $[(2, 5)]$.

Sol. Given that, $A = \{1, 2, 3, \ldots, 9\}$ and $(a, b)\ R(c, d)$ if $a + d = b + c$ for $(a, b) \in A \times A$ and $(c, d) \in A \times A$.

Let $(a, b)\ R\ (a, b)$

$\Rightarrow$ $$a + b = b + a,\ \forall\, a, b \in A$$

which is true for any $a, b \in A$.

Hence, R is reflexive.

Let $(a, b)\ R\ (c, d)$ $$a + d = b + c$$

$$c + b = d + a \Rightarrow (c, d)\ R\ (a, b)$$

So, R is symmetric.

Let $\quad (a, b) R (c, d)$ and $(c, d) R (e, f)$

$$a + d = b + c \text{ and } c + f = d + e$$
$$a + d = b + c \text{ and } d + e = c + f$$
$$(a + d) - (d + e) = (b + c) - (c + f)$$
$$(a - e) = b - f$$
$$a + f = b + e$$
$$(a, b) R (e, f)$$

So, R is transitive.

Hence, R is an equivalence relation.

Now, equivalence class containing [(2, 5)] is {(1, 4), (2, 5), (3, 6), (4, 7), (5, 8), (6, 9)}.

Q. 24 Using the definition, prove that the function $f : A \rightarrow B$ is invertible if and only if f is both one-one and onto.

Sol. A function $f : X \rightarrow Y$ is defined to be invertible, if there exist a function $g = Y \rightarrow X$ such that $gof = I_X$ and $fog = I_Y$. The function is called the inverse of f and is denoted by f^{-1}.

A function $f = X \rightarrow Y$ is invertible iff f is a bijective function.

Q. 25 Functions $f, g : R \rightarrow R$ are defined, respectively, by $f(x) = x^2 + 3x + 1$, $g(x) = 2x - 3$, find

(i) fog (ii) gof (iii) fof (iv) gog

Sol. Given that, $f(x) = x^2 + 3x + 1, g(x) = 2x - 3$

(i)
$$fog = f\{g(x)\} = f(2x - 3)$$
$$= (2x - 3)^2 + 3(2x - 3) + 1$$
$$= 4x^2 + 9 - 12x + 6x - 9 + 1 = 4x^2 - 6x + 1$$

(ii)
$$gof = g\{f(x)\} = g(x^2 + 3x + 1)$$
$$= 2(x^2 + 3x + 1) - 3$$
$$= 2x^2 + 6x + 2 - 3 = 2x^2 + 6x - 1$$

(iii)
$$fof = f\{f(x)\} = f(x^2 + 3x + 1)$$
$$= (x^2 + 3x + 1)^2 + 3(x^2 + 3x + 1) + 1$$
$$= x^4 + 9x^2 + 1 + 6x^3 + 6x + 2x^2 + 3x^2 + 9x + 3 + 1$$
$$= x^4 + 6x^3 + 14x^2 + 15x + 5$$

(iv)
$$gog = g\{g(x)\} = g(2x - 3)$$
$$= 2(2x - 3) - 3$$
$$= 4x - 6 - 3 = 4x - 9$$

Q. 26 Let * be the binary operation defined on Q. Find which of the following binary operations are commutative

(i) $a * b = a - b, \forall a, b \in Q$ (ii) $a * b = a^2 + b^2, \forall a, b \in Q$

(iii) $a * b = a + ab, \forall a, b \in Q$ (iv) $a * b = (a - b)^2, \forall a, b \in Q$

Sol. Given that * be the binary operation defined on Q.

(i) $a * b = a - b, \forall a, b \in Q$ and $b * a = b - a$

So, $\quad a * b \neq b * a \quad [\because b - a \neq a - b]$

Hence, * is not commutative.

(ii) $a * b = a^2 + b^2$

$b * a = b^2 + a^2$

So, $*$ is commutative. [since, '+' is on rational is commutative]

(iii) $a * b = a + ab$

$b * a = b + ab$

Clearly, $a + ab \neq b + ab$

So, $*$ is not commutative.

(iv) $a * b = (a - b)^2, \forall a, b \in Q$

$b * a = (b - a)^2$

$\because \quad (a - b)^2 = (b - a)^2$

Hence, $*$ is commutative.

Q. 27 If $*$ be binary operation defined on R by $a * b = 1 + ab, \forall a, b \in R$. Then, the operation $*$ is

(i) commutative but not associative.

(ii) associative but not commutative.

(iii) neither commutative nor associative.

(iv) both commutative and associative.

Sol. (i) Given that, $a * b = 1 + ab, \forall a, b \in R$

$a * b = ab + 1 = b * a$

So, $*$ is a commutative binary operation.

Also, $a * (b * c) = a * (1 + bc) = 1 + a(1 + bc)$

$a * (b * c) = 1 + a + abc$ ...(i)

$(a * b) * c = (1 + ab) * c$

$= 1 + (1 + ab)c = 1 + c + abc$ ...(ii)

From Eqs. (i) and (ii),

$$a * (b * c) \neq (a * b) * c$$

So, $*$ is not associative

Hence, $*$ is commutative but not associative.

Objective Type Questions

Q. 28 Let T be the set of all triangles in the Euclidean plane and let a relation R on T be defined as aRb, if a is congruent to b, $\forall a, b \in T$. Then, R is

(a) reflexive but not transitive
(b) transitive but not symmetric
(c) equivalence
(d) None of these

Sol. *(c)* Consider that aRb, if a is congruent to b, $\forall a, b \in T$.

Then, $aRa \Rightarrow a \cong a$,

which is true for all $a \in T$

So, R is reflexive, ...(i)

Let $aRb \Rightarrow a \cong b$

$\Rightarrow b \cong a \Rightarrow b \cong a$

$\Rightarrow bRa$

So, R is symmetric. ...(ii)

Let aRb and bRc

$\Rightarrow a \cong b$ and $b \cong c$

$\Rightarrow a \cong c \Rightarrow aRc$

So, R is transitive. ...(iii)

Hence, R is equivalence relation.

Q. 29 Consider the non-empty set consisting of children in a family and a relation R defined as aRb, if a is brother of b. Then, R is

(a) symmetric but not transitive

(b) transitive but not symmetric

(c) neither symmetric nor transitive

(d) both symmetric and transitive

Sol. ***(b)*** Given, $aRb \Rightarrow a$ is brother of b

$\therefore aRa \Rightarrow a$ is brother of a, which is not true.

So, R is not reflexive.

$aRb \Rightarrow a$ is brother of b.

This does not mean b is also a brother of a and b can be a sister of a.

Hence, R is not symmetric.

$aRb \Rightarrow a$ is brother of b

and $bRc \Rightarrow b$ is a brother of c.

So, a is brother of c.

Hence, R is transitive.

Q. 30 The maximum number of equivalence relations on the set $A = \{1, 2, 3\}$ are

(a) 1 (b) 2 (c) 3 (d) 5

Sol. ***(d)*** Given that, $A = \{1, 2, 3\}$

Now, number of equivalence relations as follows

$$R_1 = \{(1, 1), (2, 2), (3, 3)\}$$
$$R_2 = \{(1, 1), (2, 2), (3, 3), (1, 2), (2, 1)\}$$
$$R_3 = \{(1, 1), (2, 2), (3, 3), (1, 3), (3, 1)\}$$
$$R_4 = \{(1, 1), (2, 2), (3, 3), (2, 3), (3, 2)\}$$
$$R_5 = \{(1, 2, 3) \Leftrightarrow A \times A = A^2\}$$

$\therefore$ Maximum number of equivalence relation on the set $A = \{1, 2, 3\} = 5$

Q. 31 If a relation R on the set $\{1, 2, 3\}$ be defined by $R = \{(1, 2)\}$, then R is

(a) reflexive (b) transitive (c) symmetric (d) None of these

Sol. ***(b)*** R on the set $\{1, 2, 3\}$ be defined by $R = \{(1, 2)\}$

It is clear that R is transitive.

Q. 32 Let us define a relation R in R as aRb if $a \geq b$. Then, R is

(a) an equivalence relation
(b) reflexive, transitive but not symmetric
(c) symmetric, transitive but not reflexive
(d) neither transitive nor reflexive but symmetric

Sol. *(b)* Given that, aRb if $a \geq b$

$\Rightarrow \quad aRa \Rightarrow a \geq a$ which is true.

Let aRb, $a \geq b$, then $b \geq a$ which is not true R is not symmetric.

But aRb and $b\,R\,c$

$$\Rightarrow \quad a \geq b \text{ and } b \geq c$$

$$\Rightarrow \quad a \geq c$$

Hence, R is transitive.

Q. 33 If $A = \{1, 2, 3\}$ and consider the relation

$$R = \{(1, 1), (2, 2), (3, 3), (1, 2), (2, 3), (1, 3)\}$$

Then, R is

(a) reflexive but not symmetric (b) reflexive but not transitive
(c) symmetric and transitive (d) neither symmetric nor transitive

Sol. *(a)* Given that, $A = \{1, 2, 3\}$

and $R = \{(1, 1), (2, 2), (3, 3), (1, 2), (2, 3), (1, 3)\}$

$\because \quad (1, 1), (2, 2), (3, 3) \in R$

Hence, R is reflexive.

$$(1, 2) \in R \text{ but } (2, 1) \notin R$$

Hence, R is not symmetric.

$$(1, 2) \in R \text{ and } (2, 3) \in R$$

$$\Rightarrow \quad (1, 3) \in R$$

Hence, R is transitive.

Q. 34 The identity element for the binary operation $*$ defined on $Q - \{0\}$ as $a * b = \frac{ab}{2}, \forall\, a, b \in Q - \{0\}$ is

(a) 1 (b) 0 (c) 2 (d) None of these

Thinking Process

For given binary operation $* : A \times A \to A$, an element $e \in A$, if it exists, is called identity for the operation $*$, if $a * e = a = e * a, \forall\, a \in A$.

Sol. *(c)* Given that, $a * b = \frac{ab}{2}, \forall\, a, b \in Q - \{0\}$.

Let e be the identity element for $*$.

$$\therefore \quad a * e = \frac{ae}{2}$$

$$\Rightarrow \quad a = \frac{ae}{2} \Rightarrow e = 2$$

Q. 35 If the set A contains 5 elements and the set B contains 6 elements, then the number of one-one and onto mappings from A to B is

(a) 720 (b) 120 (c) 0 (d) None of these

Sol. *(c)* We know that, if A and B are two non-empty finite set containing m and n elements respectively, then the number of one-one and onto mapping from A to B is

$$n!, \text{ if } m = n$$
$$0, \text{ if } m \neq n$$

Given that, $m = 5$ and $n = 6$

$\therefore$ $m \neq n$

Number of mapping = 0

Q. 36 If $A = \{1, 2, 3, \ldots, n\}$ and $B = \{a, b\}$. Then, the number of surjections from A into B is

(a) ${}^nP_2$ (b) $2^n - 2$ (c) $2^n - 1$ (d) None of these

Sol. *(d)* Given that, $A = \{1, 2, 3, \ldots, n\}$ and $B = \{a, b\}$.

We know that, if A and B are two non-empty finite sets containing m and n elements respectively, then the number of surjection from A into B is

$$^nC_m \times m!, \text{ if } n \geq m$$
$$0, \text{ if } n < m$$

Here, $m = 2$

$\therefore$ Number of surjection from A into B is ${}^nC_2 \times 2! = \dfrac{n!}{2!(n-2)!} \times 2!$

$$= \frac{n(n-1)(n-2)!}{2 \times 1(n-2)} \times 2! = n^2 - n$$

Q. 37 If $f : R \to R$ be defined by $f(x) = \dfrac{1}{x}$, $\forall\, x \in R$. Then, f is

(a) one-one (b) onto (c) bijective (d) f is not defined

Thinking Process

In the given function at $x = 0$, $f(x) = \infty$. So, the function is not define.

Sol. *(d)* Given that, $f(x) = \dfrac{1}{x}$, $\forall\, x \in R$

For $x = 0$,

$f(x)$ is not defined.

Hence, $f(x)$ is a not define function.

Q. 38 If $f : R \to R$ be defined by $f(x) = 3x^2 - 5$ and $g : R \to R$ by $g(x) = \dfrac{x}{x^2 + 1}$. Then, gof is

(a) $\dfrac{3x^2 - 5}{9x^4 - 30x^2 + 26}$ (b) $\dfrac{3x^2 - 5}{9x^4 - 6x^2 + 26}$

(c) $\dfrac{3x^2}{x^4 + 2x^2 - 4}$ (d) $\dfrac{3x^2}{9x^4 + 30x^2 - 2}$

Sol. ***(a)*** Given that, $f(x) = 3x^2 - 5$ and $g(x) = \dfrac{x}{x^2 + 1}$

$$gof = g\{f(x)\} = g(3x^2 - 5)$$
$$= \frac{3x^2 - 5}{(3x^2 - 5)^2 + 1} = \frac{3x^2 - 5}{9x^4 - 30x^2 + 25 + 1}$$
$$= \frac{3x^2 - 5}{9x^4 - 30x^2 + 26}$$

Q. 39 Which of the following functions from Z into Z are bijections?

(a) $f(x) = x^3$ (b) $f(x) = x + 2$ (c) $f(x) = 2x + 1$ (d) $f(x) = x^2 + 1$

Sol. ***(b)*** Here,

$$f(x) = x + 2 \Rightarrow f(x_1) = f(x_2)$$
$$x_1 + 2 = x_2 + 2 \Rightarrow x_1 = x_2$$

Let $y = x + 2$

$$x = y - 2 \in Z, \forall y \in x$$

Hence, $f(x)$ is one-one and onto.

Q. 40 If $f : R \to R$ be the functions defined by $f(x) = x^3 + 5$, then $f^{-1}(x)$ is

(a) $(x + 5)^{\frac{1}{3}}$ (b) $(x - 5)^{\frac{1}{3}}$ (c) $(5 - x)^{\frac{1}{3}}$ (d) $5 - x$

Sol. ***(b)*** Given that, $f(x) = x^3 + 5$

Let $y = x^3 + 5 \Rightarrow x^3 = y - 5$

$$x = (y - 5)^{\frac{1}{3}} \Rightarrow f(x)^{-1} = (x - 5)^{\frac{1}{3}}$$

Q. 41 If $f : A \to B$ and $g : B \to C$ be the bijective functions, then $(gof)^{-1}$ is

(a) $f^{-1}og^{-1}$ (b) fog (c) $g^{-1}of^{-1}$ (d) gof

Sol. ***(a)*** Given that, $f : A \to B$ and $g : B \to C$ be the bijective functions.

$$(gof)^{-1} = f^{-1}og^{-1}$$

Q. 42 If $f : R - \left\{\frac{3}{5}\right\} \to R$ be defined by $f(x) = \dfrac{3x + 2}{5x - 3}$, then

(a) $f^{-1}(x) = f(x)$ (b) $f^{-1}(x) = -f(x)$ (c) $(fof)x = -x$ (d) $f^{-1}(x) = \dfrac{1}{19}f(x)$

Sol. ***(a)*** Given that, $f(x) = \dfrac{3x + 2}{5x - 3}$

Let $y = \dfrac{3x + 2}{5x - 3}$

$$3x + 2 = 5xy - 3y \Rightarrow x(3 - 5y) = -3y - 2$$
$$x = \frac{3y + 2}{5y - 3} \Rightarrow f^{-1}(x) = \frac{3x + 2}{5x - 3}$$

$\therefore$ $f^{-1}(x) = f(x)$

Q. 43 If $f:[0, 1] \to [0, 1]$ be defined by $f(x) = \begin{cases} x, & \text{if } x \text{ is rational} \\ 1-x, & \text{if } x \text{ is irrational} \end{cases}$

then $(fof)x$ is

(a) constant (b) $1+x$ (c) x (d) None of these

Sol. *(c)* Given that, $f: [0, 1] \to [0, 1]$ be defined by

$$f(x) = \begin{cases} x, & \text{if } x \text{ is rational} \\ 1-x, & \text{if } x \text{ is irrational} \end{cases}$$

$\therefore$ $(fof)x = f(f(x)) = x$

Q. 44 If $f:[2, \infty) \to R$ be the function defined by $f(x) = x^2 - 4x + 5$, then the range of f is

(a) R (b) $[1, \infty)$ (c) $[4, \infty)$ (d) $[5, \infty)$

Thinking Process

Range of $f = \{y \in Y : y = f(x)$ for some in $X\}$

Sol. *(b)* Given that, $f(x) = x^2 - 4x + 5$

Let $y = x^2 - 4x + 5$

$\Rightarrow$ $y = x^2 - 4x + 4 + 1 = (x-2)^2 + 1$

$\Rightarrow$ $(x-2)^2 = y - 1 \Rightarrow x - 2 = \sqrt{y-1}$

$\Rightarrow$ $x = 2 + \sqrt{y-1}$

$\therefore$ $y - 1 \ge 0, y \ge 1$

Range $= [1, \infty)$

Q. 45 If $f: N \to R$ be the function defined by $f(x) = \frac{2x-1}{2}$ and $g: Q \to R$ be another function defined by $g(x) = x + 2$. Then, $(gof)\frac{3}{2}$ is

(a) 1 (b) 1 (c) $\frac{7}{2}$ (d) None of these

Sol. *(d)* Given that, $f(x) = \frac{2x-1}{2}$ and $g(x) = x + 2$

$$(gof)\frac{3}{2} = g\left[f\left(\frac{3}{2}\right)\right] = g\left(\frac{2 \times \frac{3}{2} - 1}{2}\right)$$

$$= g(1) = 1 + 2 = 3$$

Q. 46 If $f: R \rightarrow R$ be defined by $f(x) = \begin{cases} 2x : x > 3 \\ x^2 : 1 < x \leq 3 \\ 3x : x \leq 1 \end{cases}$

Then, $f(-1) + f(2) + f(4)$ is

(a) 9 (b) 14 (c) 5 (d) None of these

Sol. *(a)* Given that, $f(x) = \begin{cases} 2x : x > 3 \\ x^2 : 1 < x \leq 3 \\ 3x : x \leq 1 \end{cases}$

$$f(-1) + f(2) + f(4) = 3(-1) + (2)^2 + 2 \times 4$$
$$= -3 + 4 + 8 = 9$$

Q. 47 If $f: R \rightarrow R$ be given by $f(x) = \tan x$, then $f^{-1}(1)$ is

(a) $\frac{\pi}{4}$ (b) $\left\{n\pi + \frac{\pi}{4} : n \in Z\right\}$

(c) Does not exist (d) None of these

Sol. *(a)* Given that, $f(x) = \tan x$

Let $y = \tan x \Rightarrow x = \tan^{-1} y$

$\Rightarrow f^{-1}(x) = \tan^{-1} x \Rightarrow f^{-1}(1) = \tan^{-1} 1$

$\Rightarrow = \tan^{-1}\tan\frac{\pi}{4} = \frac{\pi}{4}$ $\left[\because \tan\frac{\pi}{4} = 1\right]$

Fillers

Q. 48 Let the relation R be defined in N by aRb, if $2a + 3b = 30$. Then, $R = \ldots\ldots$.

Sol. Given that,

$$2a + 3b = 30$$
$$3b = 30 - 2a$$
$$b = \frac{30 - 2a}{3}$$

For

$$a = 3, b = 8$$
$$a = 6, b = 6$$
$$a = 9, b = 4$$
$$a = 12, b = 2$$
$$R = \{(3, 8), (6, 6), (9, 4), (12, 2)\}$$

Q. 49 If the relation R be defined on the set $A = \{1, 2, 3, 4, 5\}$ by $R = \{(a, b) : |a^2 - b^2| < 8\}$. Then, R is given by ....

Sol. Given,

$A = \{1, 2, 3, 4, 5\}$,

$R = \{(a, b) : |a^2 - b^2| < 8\}$

$R = \{(1, 1), (1, 2), (2, 1), (2, 2), (2, 3), (3, 2), (3, 3), (4, 3), (3, 4), (4, 4), (5, 5)\}$

Q. 50 If $f = \{(1, 2), (3, 5), (4, 1)\}$ and $g = \{(2, 3), (5, 1), (1, 3)\}$, then $gof = \dots\dots\dots$ and $fog = \dots\dots\dots$.

Sol. Given that, $f = \{(1, 2), (3, 5), (4, 1)\}$ and $g = \{(2, 3), (5, 1), (1, 3)\}$

$$gof(1) = g\{f(1)\} = g(2) = 3$$
$$gof(3) = g\{f(3)\} = g(5) = 1$$
$$gof(4) = g\{f(4)\} = g(1) = 3$$
$$gof = \{(1, 3), (3, 1), (4, 3)\}$$

Now,
$$fog(2) = f\{g(2)\} = f(3) = 5$$
$$fog(5) = f\{g(5)\} = f(1) = 2$$
$$fog(1) = f\{g(1)\} = f(3) = 5$$
$$fog = \{(2, 5), (5, 2), (1, 5)\}$$

Q. 51 If $f : R \to R$ be defined by $f(x) = \dfrac{x}{\sqrt{1 + x^2}}$, then $(fofof)(x) = \dots\dots\dots$.

Sol. Given that, $f(x) = \dfrac{x}{\sqrt{1 + x^2}}$

$$(fofof)(x) = f[f\{f(x)\}]$$
$$= f\left[f\left(\frac{x}{\sqrt{1+x^2}}\right)\right] = f\left(\frac{\dfrac{x}{\sqrt{1+x^2}}}{\sqrt{1+\dfrac{x^2}{1+x^2}}}\right)$$
$$= f\left[\frac{x\sqrt{1+x^2}}{\sqrt{1+x^2}(\sqrt{2x^2}+1)}\right] = f\left(\frac{x}{\sqrt{1+2x^2}}\right)$$
$$= \frac{\dfrac{x}{\sqrt{1+2x^2}}}{\sqrt{1+\dfrac{x^2}{1+2x^2}}} = \frac{x\sqrt{1+2x^2}}{\sqrt{1+2x^2}\sqrt{1+3x^2}}$$
$$= \frac{x}{\sqrt{1+3x^2}} = \frac{x}{\sqrt{3x^2+1}}$$

Q. 52 If $f(x) = [4 - (x - 7)^3]$, then $f^{-1}(x) = \dots\dots\dots$.

Sol. Given that, $f(x) = \{4 - (x - 7)^3\}$

Let $y = [4 - (x - 7)^3]$
$$(x - 7)^3 = 4 - y$$
$$(x - 7) = (4 - y)^{1/3}$$
$\Rightarrow$ $x = 7 + (4 - y)^{1/3}$
$$f^{-1}(x) = 7 + (4 - x)^{1/3}$$

True/False

Q. 53 Let $R = \{(3, 1), (1, 3), (3, 3)\}$ be a relation defined on the set $A = \{1, 2, 3\}$. Then, R is symmetric, transitive but not reflexive.

Sol. ***False***

Given that, $R = \{(3, 1), (1, 3), (3, 3)\}$ be defined on the set $A = \{1, 2, 3\}$

$$(1, 1) \notin R$$

So, R is not reflexive. $\quad (3, 1) \in R, (1, 3) \in R$

Hence, R is symmetric.

Since, $\quad (3, 1) \in R, (1, 3) \in R$

But $\quad (1, 1) \notin R$

Hence, R is not transitive.

Q. 54 If $f : R \to R$ be the function defined by $f(x) = \sin(3x + 2)\ \forall\ x \in R$. Then, f is invertible.

Sol. ***False***

Given that, $f(x) = \sin(3x + 2),\ \forall\ x \in R$ is not one-one function for all $x \in R$.

So, f is not invertible.

Q. 55 Every relation which is symmetric and transitive is also reflexive.

Sol. ***False***

Let R be a relation defined by

$$R = \{(1, 2), (2, 1), (1, 1), (2, 2)\} \text{ on the set } A = \{1, 2, 3\}$$

It is clear that $(3, 3) \notin R$. So, it is not reflexive.

Q. 56 An integer m is said to be related to another integer n, if m is a integral multiple of n. This relation in Z is reflexive, symmetric and transitive.

Sol. ***False***

The given relation is reflexive and transitive but not symmetric.

Q. 57 If $A = \{0, 1\}$ and N be the set of natural numbers. Then, the mapping $f : N \to A$ defined by $f(2n - 1) = 0,\ f(2n) = 1,\ \forall\ n \in N$, is onto.

Sol. ***True***

Given, $\quad A = \{0, 1\}$

$$f(2n - 1) = 0,\ f(2n) = 1,\ \forall\ n \in N$$

So, the mapping $f : N \to A$ is onto.

Q. 58 The relation R on the set $A = \{1, 2, 3\}$ defined as $R = \{(1, 1), (1, 2), (2, 1), (3, 3)\}$ is reflexive, symmetric and transitive.

Sol. ***False***

Given that, $\quad R = \{(1, 1), (1, 2), (2, 1), (3, 3)\}$

$$(2, 2) \notin R$$

So, R is not reflexive.

Q. 59 The composition of function is commutative.

Sol. ***False***

Let $f(x) = x^2$

and $g(x) = x + 1$

$$fog(x) = f\{g(x)\} = f(x+1)$$
$$= (x+1)^2 = x^2 + 2x + 1$$
$$gof(x) = g\{f(x)\} = g(x^2) = x^2 + 1$$

$\therefore$ $fog(x) \neq gof(x)$

Q. 60 The composition of function is associative.

Sol. ***True***

Let $f(x) = x, g(x) = x + 1$

and $h(x) = 2x - 1$

Then, $fo\{goh(x)\} = f[g\{h(x)\}]$

$$= f\{g(2x-1)\}$$
$$= f(2x - 1 + 1)$$
$$= f(2x) = 2x$$

$\therefore$ $(fog)oh(x) = (fog)\{h(x)\}$

$$= (fog)(2x-1)$$
$$= f\{g(2x-1)\}$$
$$= f(2x - 1 + 1)$$
$$= f(2x) = 2x$$

Q. 61 Every function is invertible.

Sol. ***False***

Only bijective functions are invertible.

Q. 62 A binary operation on a set has always the identity element.

Sol. ***False***

'+' is a binary operation on the set N but it has no identity element.

2

Inverse Trigonometric Functions

Short Answer Type Questions

Q. 1 Find the value of $\tan^{-1}\left(\tan\dfrac{5\pi}{6}\right)+\cos^{-1}\left(\cos\dfrac{13\pi}{6}\right)$.

Thinking Process

Use the property, $\tan^{-1}\tan x = x,\ x \in \left(-\dfrac{\pi}{2},\dfrac{\pi}{2}\right)$ *and* $\cos^{-1}(\cos x) = x,\ x \in [0,\pi]$ *to get the answer.*

Sol. We know that, $\tan^{-1}\tan x = x;\ x \in \left(-\dfrac{\pi}{2},\dfrac{\pi}{2}\right)$ and $\cos^{-1}\cos x = x;\ x\in[0,\pi]$

$$\therefore \quad \tan^{-1}\left(\tan\frac{5\pi}{6}\right)+\cos^{-1}\left(\cos\frac{13\pi}{6}\right)$$

$$= \tan^{-1}\left[\tan\left(\pi-\frac{\pi}{6}\right)\right]+\cos^{-1}\left[\cos\left(\pi+\frac{7\pi}{6}\right)\right]$$

$$= \tan^{-1}\left(-\tan\frac{\pi}{6}\right)+\cos^{-1}\left(-\cos\frac{7\pi}{6}\right) \qquad [\because \cos(\pi+\theta) = -\cos\theta]$$

$$= -\tan^{-1}\left(\tan\frac{\pi}{6}\right)+\pi-\left[\cos^{-1}\cos\left(\frac{7\pi}{6}\right)\right]$$

$$\{\because \tan^{-1}(-x) = -\tan^{-1}x;\ x\in R \text{ and } \cos^{-1}(-x) = \pi-\cos^{-1}x;\ x\in[-1,1]\}$$

$$= -\tan^{-1}\left(\tan\frac{\pi}{6}\right)+\pi-\cos^{-1}\left[\cos\left(\pi+\frac{\pi}{6}\right)\right]$$

$$= -\tan^{-1}\left(\tan\frac{\pi}{6}\right)+\pi-\left[\cos^{-1}\left(-\cos\frac{\pi}{6}\right)\right] \qquad [\because \cos(\pi+\theta) = -\cos\theta]$$

$$= -\tan^{-1}\left(\tan\frac{\pi}{6}\right)+\pi-\pi+\cos^{-1}\left(\cos\frac{\pi}{6}\right) \qquad [\because \cos^{-1}(-x) = \pi-\cos^{-1}x]$$

$$= -\frac{\pi}{6}+0+\frac{\pi}{6} = 0$$

Note *Remember that,* $\tan^{-1}\left(\tan\dfrac{5\pi}{6}\right)\neq\dfrac{5\pi}{6}$ *and* $\cos^{-1}\left(\cos\dfrac{13\pi}{6}\right)\neq\dfrac{13\pi}{6}$

Since, $\dfrac{5\pi}{6}\notin\left(-\dfrac{\pi}{2},\dfrac{\pi}{2}\right)$ *and* $\dfrac{13\pi}{6}\notin[0,\pi]$

Q. 2 Evaluate $\cos\left[\cos^{-1}\left(\frac{-\sqrt{3}}{2}\right)+\frac{\pi}{6}\right]$.

Sol. We have, $\cos\left[\cos^{-1}\left(\frac{-\sqrt{3}}{2}\right)+\frac{\pi}{6}\right]=\cos\left[\cos^{-1}\left(\cos\frac{5\pi}{6}\right)+\frac{\pi}{6}\right]$ $\left[\because \cos\frac{5\pi}{6}=\frac{-\sqrt{3}}{2}\right]$

$$=\cos\left(\frac{5\pi}{6}+\frac{\pi}{6}\right) \qquad \{\because \cos^{-1}\cos x = x;\ x\in[0,\pi]\}$$

$$=\cos\left(\frac{6\pi}{6}\right)$$

$$=\cos(\pi)=-1$$

Q. 3 Prove that $\cot\left(\frac{\pi}{4}-2\cot^{-1}3\right)=7$.

Sol. We have to prove, $\cot\left(\frac{\pi}{4}-2\cot^{-1}3\right)=7$

$\Rightarrow$ $\left(\frac{\pi}{4}-2\cot^{-1}3\right)=\cot^{-1}7$

$\Rightarrow$ $(2\cot^{-1}3)=\frac{\pi}{4}-\cot^{-1}7$

$\Rightarrow$ $2\tan^{-1}\frac{1}{3}=\frac{\pi}{4}-\tan^{-1}\frac{1}{7}$

$\Rightarrow$ $2\tan^{-1}\frac{1}{3}+\tan^{-1}\frac{1}{7}=\frac{\pi}{4}$

$\Rightarrow$ $\tan^{-1}\frac{2/3}{1-(1/3)^2}+\tan^{-1}\frac{1}{7}=\frac{\pi}{4}$

$\Rightarrow$ $\tan^{-1}\frac{2/3}{8/9}+\tan^{-1}\frac{1}{7}=\frac{\pi}{4}$

$\Rightarrow$ $\tan^{-1}\frac{3}{4}+\tan^{-1}\frac{1}{7}=\frac{\pi}{4}$

$\Rightarrow$ $\tan^{-1}\frac{\frac{3}{4}+\frac{1}{7}}{1-\frac{3}{4}\cdot\frac{1}{7}}=\frac{\pi}{4}$

$\Rightarrow$ $\tan^{-1}\frac{(21+4)/28}{(28-3)/28}=\frac{\pi}{4}$

$\Rightarrow$ $\tan^{-1}\frac{25}{25}=\frac{\pi}{4}$

$\Rightarrow$ $1=\tan\frac{\pi}{4}$

$\Rightarrow$ $1=1$

$\Rightarrow$ LHS = RHS **Hence proved.**

Q. 4 Find the value of $\tan^{-1}\left(-\frac{1}{\sqrt{3}}\right)+\cot^{-1}\left(\frac{1}{\sqrt{3}}\right)+\tan^{-1}\left[\sin\left(\frac{-\pi}{2}\right)\right]$.

Sol. We have, $\tan^{-1}\left(-\frac{1}{\sqrt{3}}\right)+\cot^{-1}\left(\frac{1}{\sqrt{3}}\right)+\tan^{-1}\left[\sin\left(\frac{-\pi}{2}\right)\right]$

$$= \tan^{-1}\left(\tan\frac{5\pi}{6}\right)+\cot^{-1}\left(\cot\frac{\pi}{3}\right)+\tan^{-1}(-1)$$

$$= \tan^{-1}\left[\tan\left(\pi-\frac{\pi}{6}\right)\right]+\cot^{-1}\left[\cot\left(\frac{\pi}{3}\right)\right]+\tan^{-1}\left[\tan\left(\pi-\frac{\pi}{4}\right)\right]$$

$$= \tan^{-1}\left(-\tan\frac{\pi}{6}\right)+\cot^{-1}\left(\cot\frac{\pi}{3}\right)+\tan^{-1}\left(-\tan\frac{\pi}{4}\right)$$

$\left[\because \tan^{-1}(\tan x)=x,\ x\in\left(-\frac{\pi}{2},\frac{\pi}{2}\right),\ \cot^{-1}(\cot x)=x, x\in(0,\pi) \text{ and } \tan^{-1}(-x)=-\tan^{-1}x\right]$

$$= -\frac{\pi}{6}+\frac{\pi}{3}-\frac{\pi}{4}=\frac{-2\pi+4\pi-3\pi}{12}$$

$$= \frac{-5\pi+4\pi}{12}=-\frac{\pi}{12}$$

Q. 5 Find the value of $\tan^{-1}\left(\tan\frac{2\pi}{3}\right)$.

Sol. We have, $\tan^{-1}\left(\tan\frac{2\pi}{3}\right)=\tan^{-1}\tan\left(\pi-\frac{\pi}{3}\right)$

$$= \tan^{-1}\left(-\tan\frac{\pi}{3}\right) \qquad [\because \tan^{-1}(-x)=-\tan^{-1}x]$$

$$= -\tan^{-1}\tan\frac{\pi}{3}=-\frac{\pi}{3} \qquad \left[\because \tan^{-1}(\tan x)=x,\ x\in\left(\frac{-\pi}{2},\frac{\pi}{2}\right)\right]$$

Note *Remember that,* $\tan^{-1}\left(\tan\frac{2\pi}{3}\right)\neq\frac{2\pi}{3}$

Since, $\tan^{-1}(\tan x)=x$, *if* $x\in\left(-\frac{\pi}{2},\frac{\pi}{2}\right)$ *and* $\frac{2\pi}{3}\notin\left(\frac{-\pi}{2},\frac{\pi}{2}\right)$

Q. 6 Show that $2\tan^{-1}(-3)=\frac{-\pi}{2}+\tan^{-1}\left(\frac{-4}{3}\right)$.

Sol. $\text{LHS}=2\tan^{-1}(-3)=-2\tan^{-1}3 \qquad [\because \tan^{-1}(-x)=-\tan^{-1}x, x\in R]$

$$= -\left[\cos^{-1}\frac{1-3^2}{1+3^2}\right] \qquad \left[\because 2\tan^{-1}x=\cos^{-1}\frac{1-x^2}{1+x^2}, x\geq 0\right]$$

$$= -\left[\cos^{-1}\left(\frac{-8}{10}\right)\right]=-\left[\cos^{-1}\left(\frac{-4}{5}\right)\right]$$

$$= -\left[\pi-\cos^{-1}\left(\frac{4}{5}\right)\right] \qquad \{\because \cos^{-1}(-x)=\pi-\cos^{-1}x, x\in[-1,1]\}$$

$$= -\pi+\cos^{-1}\left(\frac{4}{5}\right) \qquad \left[\text{let } \cos^{-1}\left(\frac{4}{5}\right)=\theta \Rightarrow \cos\theta=\frac{4}{5}\Rightarrow \tan\theta=\frac{3}{4}\Rightarrow \theta=\tan^{-1}\frac{3}{4}\right]$$

$$= -\pi + \tan^{-1}\left(\frac{3}{4}\right) = -\pi + \left[\frac{\pi}{2} - \cot^{-1}\left(\frac{3}{4}\right)\right]$$

$$= -\frac{\pi}{2} - \cot^{-1}\frac{3}{4} = -\frac{\pi}{2} - \tan^{-1}\frac{4}{3}$$

$$= -\frac{\pi}{2} + \tan^{-1}\left(\frac{-4}{3}\right) \qquad [\because \tan^{-1}(-x) = -\tan^{-1}x]$$

= RHS **Hence proved.**

Q. 7 Find the real solution of

$$\tan^{-1}\sqrt{x(x+1)} + \sin^{-1}\sqrt{x^2+x+1} = \frac{\pi}{2}.$$

Thinking Process

Convert the $\sin^{-1}\sqrt{x^2+x+1}$ *into inverse of tangent function and then use the property* $\tan^{-1}x + \tan^{-1}y = \tan^{-1}\left(\frac{x+y}{1-xy}\right)$.

Sol. We have, $\tan^{-1}\sqrt{x(x+1)} + \sin^{-1}\sqrt{x^2+x+1} = \frac{\pi}{2}$ ...(i)

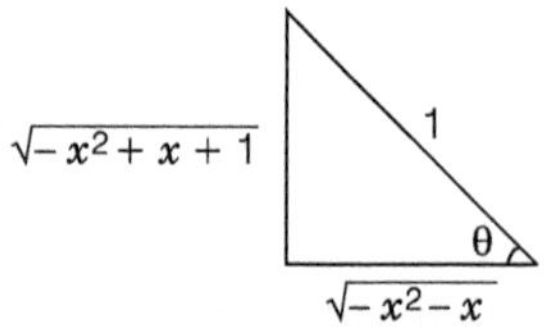

Let $\sin^{-1}\sqrt{x^2+x+1} = \theta$

$$\Rightarrow \quad \sin\theta = \sqrt{\frac{x^2+x+1}{1}}$$

$$\Rightarrow \quad \tan\theta = \frac{\sqrt{x^2+x+1}}{\sqrt{-x^2-x}} \qquad \left[\because \tan\theta = \frac{\sin\theta}{\cos\theta}\right]$$

$$\because \quad \theta = \tan^{-1}\frac{\sqrt{x^2+x+1}}{\sqrt{-x^2-x}}$$

$$= \sin^{-1}\sqrt{x^2+x+1}$$

On putting the value of θ in Eq. (i), we get

$$\tan^{-1}\sqrt{x(x+1)} + \tan^{-1}\frac{\sqrt{x^2+x+1}}{\sqrt{-x^2-x}} = \frac{\pi}{2}$$

We know that, $\tan^{-1}x + \tan^{-1}y = \tan^{-1}\left(\frac{x+y}{1-xy}\right),\ xy < 1$

$$\therefore \quad \tan^{-1}\left[\frac{\sqrt{x(x+1)} + \sqrt{\frac{x^2+x+1}{-x^2-x}}}{1 - \sqrt{x(x+1)}\cdot\sqrt{\frac{x^2+x+1}{-x^2-x}}}\right] = \frac{\pi}{2}$$

$$\Rightarrow \quad \tan^{-1}\left[\frac{\sqrt{x^2+x} + \sqrt{\frac{x^2+x+1}{-1(x^2+x)}}}{1 - \sqrt{(x^2+x)\cdot\frac{(x^2+x+1)}{-1(x^2+x)}}}\right] = \frac{\pi}{2}$$

$$\Rightarrow \quad \frac{x^2+x+\sqrt{-(x^2+x+1)}}{[1-\sqrt{-(x^2+x+1]}\sqrt{(x^2+x)}} = \tan\frac{\pi}{2} = \frac{1}{0}$$

$$\Rightarrow \quad [1-\sqrt{-(x^2+x+1)}]\sqrt{(x^2+x)}=0$$

$$\Rightarrow \quad -(x^2+x+1)=1 \text{ or } x^2+x=0$$

$$\Rightarrow \quad -x^2-x-1=1 \text{ or } x(x+1)=0$$

$$\Rightarrow \quad x^2+x+2=0 \text{ or } x(x+1)=0$$

$$\therefore \quad x=\frac{-1\pm\sqrt{1-4\times 2}}{2}$$

$$\Rightarrow \quad x=0 \text{ or } x=-1$$

For real solution, we have $x = 0, -1$.

Q. 8 Find the value of $\sin\left(2\tan^{-1}\frac{1}{3}\right)+\cos(\tan^{-1}2\sqrt{2})$.

Sol. We have, $\sin\left(2\tan^{-1}\frac{1}{3}\right)+\cos(\tan^{-1}2\sqrt{2})$

$$=\sin\left[\sin^{-1}\left\{\frac{2\times\frac{1}{3}}{1+\left(\frac{1}{3}\right)^2}\right\}\right]+\cos\left(\cos^{-1}\frac{1}{3}\right) \qquad \left[\because \tan^{-1}x=\cos^{-1}\frac{1}{\sqrt{1+x^2}}\right]$$

$$\left[\because 2\tan^{-1}x=\sin^{-1}\frac{2x}{1+x^2}, -1\le x\le 1 \text{ and } \tan^{-1}(2\sqrt{2})=\cos^{-1}\frac{1}{3}\right]$$

$$=\sin\left[\sin^{-1}\left(\frac{\frac{2}{3}}{1+\frac{1}{9}}\right)\right]+\frac{1}{3} \qquad \{\because \cos(\cos^{-1}x)=x;\ x\in[-1,1]\}$$

$$=\sin\left[\sin^{-1}\left(\frac{2\times 9}{3\times 10}\right)\right]+\frac{1}{3}=\sin\left[\sin^{-1}\left(\frac{3}{5}\right)\right]+\frac{1}{3} \qquad [\because \sin(\sin^{-1}x)=x]$$

$$=\frac{3}{5}+\frac{1}{3}=\frac{9+5}{15}=\frac{14}{15}$$

Q. 9 If $2\tan^{-1}(\cos\theta)=\tan^{-1}(2\operatorname{cosec}\theta)$, then show that $\theta=\frac{\pi}{4}$, where n is any integer.

Thinking Process

Use the property, $2\tan^{-1}x=\tan^{-1}\left(\frac{2x}{1-x^2}\right)$ to prove the desired result.

Sol. We have, $2\tan^{-1}(\cos\theta)=\tan^{-1}(2\operatorname{cosec}\theta)$

$$\Rightarrow \quad \tan^{-1}\left(\frac{2\cos\theta}{1-\cos^2\theta}\right)=\tan^{-1}(2\operatorname{cosec}\theta)$$

$$\left[\because 2\tan^{-1}x=\tan^{-1}\left(\frac{2x}{1-x^2}\right)\right]$$

$$\Rightarrow \quad \left(\frac{2\cos\theta}{\sin^2\theta}\right)=(2\operatorname{cosec}\theta)$$

$$\Rightarrow \quad (\cot\theta\cdot 2\operatorname{cosec}\theta)=(2\operatorname{cosec}\theta) \Rightarrow \cot\theta=1$$

$$\Rightarrow \quad \cot\theta=\cot\frac{\pi}{4} \Rightarrow \theta=\frac{\pi}{4}$$

Q. 10 Show that $\cos\left(2\tan^{-1}\frac{1}{7}\right)=\sin\left(4\tan^{-1}\frac{1}{3}\right)$.

Thinking Process

Use the property $2\tan^{-1}x=\cos^{-1}\frac{1-x^2}{1+x^2}$ *and* $2\tan^{-1}x=\tan^{-1}\frac{2x}{1-x^2}$, *to prove LHS = RHS.*

Sol. We have, $\cos\left(2\tan^{-1}\frac{1}{7}\right)=\sin\left(4\tan^{-1}\frac{1}{3}\right)$

$$\Rightarrow \cos\left[\cos^{-1}\left(\frac{1-\left(\frac{1}{7}\right)^2}{1+\left(\frac{1}{7}\right)^2}\right)\right]=\sin\left[2\cdot 2\tan^{-1}\frac{1}{3}\right] \qquad \left[\because 2\tan^{-1}x=\cos^{-1}\left(\frac{1-x^2}{1+x^2}\right)\right]$$

$$\Rightarrow \cos\left[\cos^{-1}\left(\frac{\frac{48}{49}}{\frac{50}{49}}\right)\right]=\sin\left[2\cdot\left(\tan^{-1}\frac{\frac{2}{3}}{1-\left(\frac{1}{3}\right)^2}\right)\right] \qquad \left[\because 2\tan^{-1}x=\tan^{-1}\left(\frac{2x}{1-x^2}\right)\right]$$

$$\Rightarrow \cos\left[\cos^{-1}\left(\frac{48\times 49}{50\times 49}\right)\right]=\sin\left[2\tan^{-1}\left(\frac{18}{24}\right)\right]$$

$$\Rightarrow \cos\left[\cos^{-1}\left(\frac{24}{25}\right)\right]=\sin\left(2\tan^{-1}\frac{3}{4}\right)$$

$$\Rightarrow \cos\left[\cos^{-1}\left(\frac{24}{25}\right)\right]=\sin\left(\sin^{-1}\frac{2\times\frac{3}{4}}{1+\frac{9}{16}}\right) \qquad \left[\because 2\tan^{-1}x=\sin^{-1}\frac{2x}{1+x^2}\right]$$

$$\Rightarrow \frac{24}{25}=\sin\left(\sin^{-1}\frac{3/2}{25/16}\right)$$

$$\Rightarrow \frac{24}{25}=\frac{48}{50} \Rightarrow \frac{24}{25}=\frac{24}{25}$$

$\therefore$ LHS = RHS **Hence proved.**

Q. 11 Solve the equation $\cos(\tan^{-1}x)=\sin\left(\cot^{-1}\frac{3}{4}\right)$.

Sol. We have, $\cos(\tan^{-1}x)=\sin\left(\cot^{-1}\frac{3}{4}\right)$

$$\Rightarrow \cos\left(\cos^{-1}\frac{1}{\sqrt{x^2+1}}\right)=\sin\left(\sin^{-1}\frac{4}{5}\right)$$

Let $\tan^{-1}x=\theta_1 \Rightarrow \tan\theta_1=\frac{x}{1}$

$\Rightarrow \cos\theta_1=\frac{1}{\sqrt{x^2+1}} \Rightarrow \theta_1=\cos^{-1}\frac{1}{\sqrt{x^2+1}}$

and $\cot^{-1}\frac{3}{4}=\theta_2 \Rightarrow \cot\theta_2=\frac{3}{4}$

$\Rightarrow \sin\theta_2=\frac{4}{5} \Rightarrow \theta_2=\sin^{-1}\frac{4}{5}$

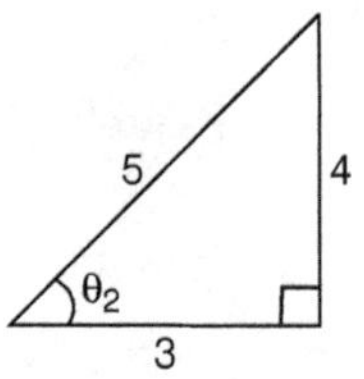

$$\Rightarrow \quad \frac{1}{\sqrt{x^2+1}} = \frac{4}{5}$$

$\{\because \cos(\cos^{-1}x) = x, x \in [-1, 1]$ and $\sin(\sin^{-1}x) = x, x \in [-1, 1]\}$

On squaring both sides, we get

$$16(x^2+1) = 25$$

$$\Rightarrow \quad 16x^2 = 9$$

$$\Rightarrow \quad x^2 = \left(\frac{3}{4}\right)^2$$

$$\therefore \quad x = \pm\frac{3}{4} = \frac{-3}{4}, \frac{3}{4}$$

Long Answer Type Questions

Q. 12 Prove that $\tan^{-1}\left(\dfrac{\sqrt{1+x^2}+\sqrt{1-x^2}}{\sqrt{1+x^2}-\sqrt{1-x^2}}\right) = \dfrac{\pi}{4} + \dfrac{1}{2}\cos^{-1}x^2.$

Sol. We have,

$$\tan^{-1}\left(\frac{\sqrt{1+x^2}+\sqrt{1-x^2}}{\sqrt{1+x^2}-\sqrt{1-x^2}}\right) = \frac{\pi}{4} + \frac{1}{2}\cos^{-1}x^2$$

$$\therefore \quad \text{LHS} = \tan^{-1}\left(\frac{\sqrt{1+x^2}+\sqrt{1-x^2}}{\sqrt{1+x^2}-\sqrt{1-x^2}}\right) \quad \ldots(i)$$

$[\text{let } x^2 = \cos 2\theta = (\cos^2\theta - \sin^2\theta) = 1 - 2\sin^2\theta = 2\cos^2\theta - 1]$

$$\Rightarrow \quad \cos^{-1}x^2 = 2\theta \Rightarrow \theta = \frac{1}{2}\cos^{-1}x^2$$

$$\therefore \quad \sqrt{1+x^2} = \sqrt{1+\cos 2\theta}$$

$$= \sqrt{1+2\cos^2\theta - 1} = \sqrt{2}\cos\theta$$

and

$$\sqrt{1-x^2} = \sqrt{1-\cos 2\theta}$$

$$= \sqrt{1-1+2\sin^2\theta} = \sqrt{2}\sin\theta$$

$$\therefore \quad \text{LHS} = \tan^{-1}\left(\frac{\sqrt{2}\cos\theta + \sqrt{2}\sin\theta}{\sqrt{2}\cos\theta - \sqrt{2}\sin\theta}\right)$$

$$= \tan^{-1}\left(\frac{\cos\theta + \sin\theta}{\cos\theta - \sin\theta}\right)$$

$$= \tan^{-1}\left(\frac{1+\tan\theta}{1-\tan\theta}\right) = \tan^{-1}\left(\frac{\tan\frac{\pi}{4} + \tan\theta}{1 - \tan\frac{\pi}{4}\cdot\tan\theta}\right)$$

$$= \tan^{-1}\left[\tan\left(\frac{\pi}{4} + \theta\right)\right] \quad \left[\because \tan(x+y) = \frac{\tan x + \tan y}{1 - \tan x \cdot \tan y}\right]$$

$$= \frac{\pi}{4} + \theta = \frac{\pi}{4} + \frac{1}{2}\cos^{-1}x^2$$

$= \text{RHS}$ **Hence proved.**

Q. 13 Find the simplified form of

$$\cos^{-1}\left(\frac{3}{5}\cos x+\frac{4}{5}\sin x\right), \text{ where } x\in\left[\frac{-3\pi}{4},\frac{\pi}{4}\right].$$

Sol. We have, $\cos^{-1}\left[\frac{3}{5}\cos x+\frac{4}{5}\sin x\right], x\in\left[\frac{-3\pi}{4},\frac{\pi}{4}\right]$

Let $\cos y=\frac{3}{5}$

$\Rightarrow$ $\sin y=\frac{4}{5}$

$\Rightarrow$ $y=\cos^{-1}\frac{3}{5}=\sin^{-1}\frac{4}{5}=\tan^{-1}\left(\frac{4}{3}\right)$

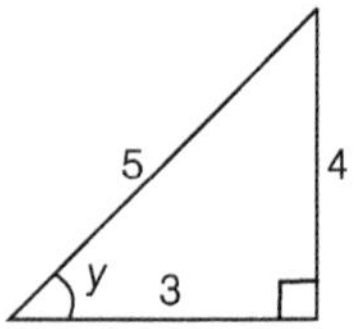

$\therefore$ $\cos^{-1}[\cos y\cdot\cos x+\sin y\cdot\sin x]$

$=\cos^{-1}[\cos(y-x)]$ $[\because \cos(A-B)=\cos A\cdot\cos B+\sin A\cdot\sin B]$

$=y-x=\tan^{-1}\frac{4}{3}-x$ $\left[\because y=\tan^{-1}\frac{4}{3}\right]$

Q. 14 Prove that $\sin^{-1}\frac{8}{17}+\sin^{-1}\frac{3}{5}=\sin^{-1}\frac{77}{85}$.

Sol. We have, $\sin^{-1}\frac{8}{17}+\sin^{-1}\frac{3}{5}=\sin^{-1}\frac{77}{85}$

$\therefore$ $\text{LHS}=\sin^{-1}\frac{8}{17}+\sin^{-1}\frac{3}{5}$

$=\tan^{-1}\frac{8}{15}+\tan^{-1}\frac{3}{4}$

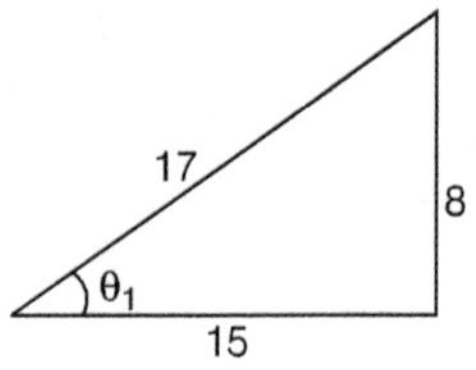

Let $\sin^{-1}\frac{8}{17}=\theta_1 \Rightarrow \sin\theta_1=\frac{8}{17}$

$\Rightarrow$ $\tan\theta_1=\frac{8}{15} \Rightarrow \theta_1=\tan^{-1}\frac{8}{15}$

and $\sin^{-1}\frac{3}{5}=\theta_2 \Rightarrow \sin\theta_2=\frac{3}{5}$

$\Rightarrow$ $\tan\theta_2=\frac{3}{4} \Rightarrow \theta_2=\tan^{-1}\frac{3}{4}$

$=\tan^{-1}\left[\dfrac{\frac{8}{15}+\frac{3}{4}}{1-\frac{8}{15}\times\frac{3}{4}}\right]$ $\left[\because \tan^{-1}x+\tan^{-1}y=\tan^{-1}\left(\frac{x+y}{1-xy}\right)\right]$

$=\tan^{-1}\left[\dfrac{\frac{32+45}{60}}{\frac{60-24}{60}}\right]=\tan^{-1}\left(\frac{77}{36}\right)$

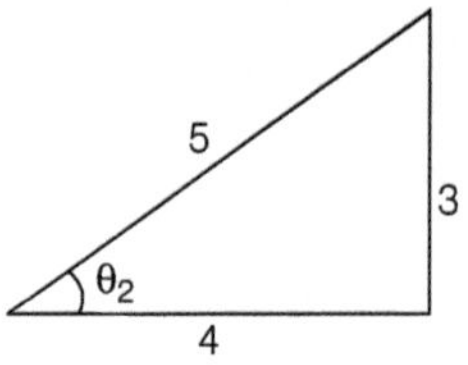

Let $\theta_3=\tan^{-1}\frac{77}{36} \Rightarrow \tan\theta_3=\frac{77}{36}$

$\Rightarrow$ $\sin\theta_3=\frac{77}{\sqrt{5929+1296}}=\frac{77}{85}$

$\therefore$ $\theta_3=\sin^{-1}\frac{77}{85}$

$=\sin^{-1}\frac{77}{85}=\text{RHS}$ **Hence proved.**

Alternate Method

To prove, $\sin^{-1}\frac{8}{17}+\sin^{-1}\frac{3}{5}=\sin^{-1}\frac{77}{85}$

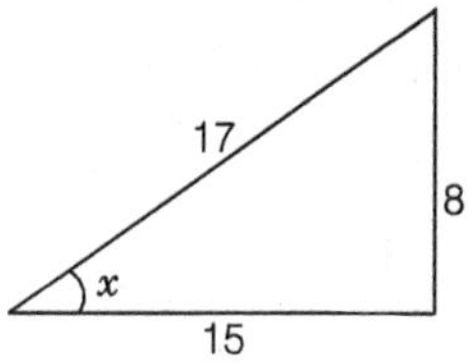

Let $\sin^{-1}\frac{8}{17}=x$

$\Rightarrow$ $\sin x=\frac{8}{17}$

$\Rightarrow$ $\cos x=\sqrt{1-\sin^2 x}=\sqrt{1-\left(\frac{8}{17}\right)^2}$

$=\sqrt{\frac{289-64}{289}}=\sqrt{\frac{225}{289}}=\frac{15}{17}$

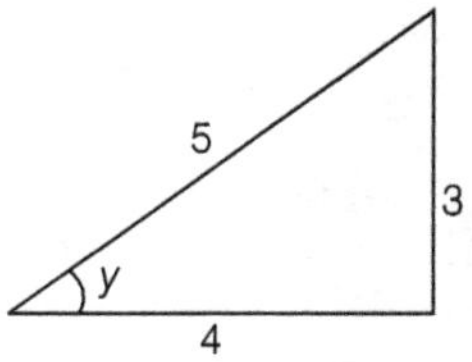

Let $\sin^{-1}\frac{3}{5}=y$

$\Rightarrow$ $\sin y=\frac{3}{5}\Rightarrow \sin^2 y=\frac{9}{25}$

$\therefore$ $\cos^2 y=1-\frac{9}{25}$

$\Rightarrow$ $\cos^2 y=\left(\frac{4}{5}\right)^2\Rightarrow \cos y=\frac{4}{5}$

Now, $\sin(x+y)=\sin x\cdot\cos y+\cos x\cdot\sin y$

$=\frac{8}{17}\cdot\frac{4}{5}+\frac{15}{17}\cdot\frac{3}{5}$

$=\frac{32}{85}+\frac{45}{85}=\frac{77}{85}$

$\Rightarrow$ $(x+y)=\sin^{-1}\left(\frac{77}{85}\right)$

$\Rightarrow$ $\sin^{-1}\frac{8}{17}+\sin^{-1}\frac{3}{5}=\sin^{-1}\frac{77}{85}$

Q. 15 Show that $\sin^{-1}\frac{5}{13}+\cos^{-1}\frac{3}{5}=\tan^{-1}\frac{63}{16}$.

Sol. We have, $\sin^{-1}\frac{5}{13}+\cos^{-1}\frac{3}{5}=\tan^{-1}\frac{63}{16}$ ...(i)

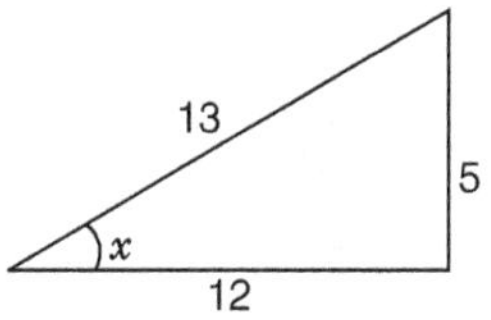

Let $\sin^{-1}\frac{5}{13}=x$

$\Rightarrow$ $\sin x=\frac{5}{13}$

and $\cos^2 x=1-\sin^2 x$

$=1-\frac{25}{169}=\frac{144}{169}$

$\Rightarrow$ $\cos x=\sqrt{\frac{144}{169}}=\frac{12}{13}$

$\therefore$ $\tan x=\frac{\sin x}{\cos x}=\frac{5/13}{12/13}=\frac{5}{12}$ ...(ii)

$\Rightarrow$ $\tan x=5/12$ ...(iii)

Again, let $\cos^{-1}\frac{3}{5} = y \Rightarrow \cos y = \frac{3}{5}$

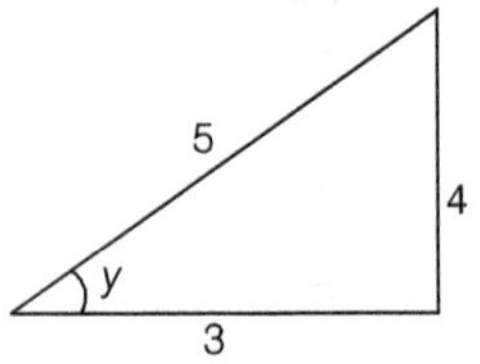

$$\therefore \quad \sin y = \sqrt{1-\cos^2 y}$$

$$= \sqrt{1-\left(\frac{3}{5}\right)^2} = \sqrt{1-\frac{9}{25}}$$

$$\sin y = \sqrt{\frac{16}{25}} = \frac{4}{5}$$

$$\Rightarrow \quad \tan y = \frac{\sin y}{\cos y} = \frac{4/5}{3/5} = \frac{4}{3} \quad \text{...(iii)}$$

We know that,

$$\tan(x+y) = \frac{\tan x + \tan y}{1-\tan x \cdot \tan y}$$

$$\Rightarrow \quad \tan(x+y) = \frac{\frac{5}{12}+\frac{4}{3}}{1-\frac{5}{12}\cdot\frac{4}{3}} \Rightarrow \tan(x+y) = \frac{\frac{15+48}{36}}{\frac{36-20}{36}}$$

$$\Rightarrow \quad \tan(x+y) = \frac{63/36}{16/36}$$

$$\Rightarrow \quad \tan(x+y) = \frac{63}{16}$$

$$\Rightarrow \quad x+y = \tan^{-1}\frac{63}{16}$$

$$\Rightarrow \quad \tan^{-1}\frac{5}{12} + \tan^{-1}\frac{4}{3} = \tan^{-1}\frac{63}{16}$$

Hence proved.

Q. 16 **Prove that $\tan^{-1}\frac{1}{4} + \tan^{-1}\frac{2}{9} = \sin^{-1}\frac{1}{\sqrt{5}}$.**

Sol. We have, $\tan^{-1}\frac{1}{4} + \tan^{-1}\frac{2}{9} = \sin^{-1}\frac{1}{\sqrt{5}}$ ...(i)

Let $\tan^{-1}\frac{1}{4} = x$

$$\Rightarrow \quad \tan x = \frac{1}{4}$$

$$\Rightarrow \quad \tan^2 x = \frac{1}{16}$$

$$\Rightarrow \quad \sec^2 x - 1 = \frac{1}{16}$$

$$\Rightarrow \quad \sec^2 x = 1 + \frac{1}{16} = \frac{17}{16}$$

$$\Rightarrow \quad \frac{1}{\cos^2 x} = \frac{17}{16}$$

$$\Rightarrow \quad \cos^2 x = \frac{16}{17}$$

$$\Rightarrow \quad \cos x = \frac{4}{\sqrt{17}}$$

$$\Rightarrow \quad \sin^2 x = 1-\cos^2 x = 1-\frac{16}{17} = \frac{1}{17}$$

$$\Rightarrow \quad \sin x = \frac{1}{\sqrt{17}} \quad \text{...(ii)}$$

Again, let $\tan^{-1}\frac{2}{9} = y$

$\Rightarrow \quad \tan y = \frac{2}{9} \Rightarrow \tan^2 y = \frac{4}{81}$

$\Rightarrow \quad \sec^2 y - 1 = \frac{4}{81}$

$\Rightarrow \quad \sec^2 y = \frac{4}{81} + 1 = \frac{85}{81}$

$\Rightarrow \quad \cos^2 y = \frac{81}{85} \Rightarrow \cos y = \frac{9}{\sqrt{85}}$

$\Rightarrow \quad \sin^2 y = 1 - \cos^2 y = 1 - \frac{81}{85} = \frac{4}{85}$

$\Rightarrow \quad \sin y = \frac{2}{\sqrt{85}}$ ...(iii)

We know that, $\sin(x+y) = \sin x \cdot \cos y + \cos x \cdot \sin y$

$$= \frac{1}{\sqrt{17}} \cdot \frac{9}{\sqrt{85}} + \frac{4}{\sqrt{17}} \cdot \frac{2}{\sqrt{85}}$$

$$= \frac{17}{\sqrt{17} \cdot \sqrt{85}} = \frac{\sqrt{17}}{\sqrt{17} \cdot \sqrt{5}} = \frac{1}{\sqrt{5}}$$

$\Rightarrow \quad (x+y) = \sin^{-1}\frac{1}{\sqrt{5}}$

$\Rightarrow \quad \tan^{-1}\frac{1}{4} + \tan^{-1}\frac{2}{9} = \sin^{-1}\frac{1}{\sqrt{5}}$ **Hence proved.**

Q. 17 Find the value of $4\tan^{-1}\frac{1}{5} - \tan^{-1}\frac{1}{239}$.

Thinking Process

Use the properties $2\tan^{-1}x = \tan^{-1}\left(\frac{2x}{1-x^2}\right)$ *and* $\tan^{-1}x + \tan^{-1}y = \tan^{-1}\left(\frac{x-y}{1+xy}\right)$ *to get the desired value.*

Sol. We have, $4\tan^{-1}\frac{1}{5} - \tan^{-1}\frac{1}{239}$

$$= 2 \cdot 2\tan^{-1}\frac{1}{5} - \tan^{-1}\frac{1}{239}$$

$$= 2 \cdot \left[\tan^{-1}\frac{\frac{2}{5}}{1-\left(\frac{1}{5}\right)^2}\right] - \tan^{-1}\frac{1}{239} \qquad \left[\because 2\tan^{-1}x = \tan^{-1}\left(\frac{2x}{1-x^2}\right)\right]$$

$$= 2 \cdot \left[\tan^{-1}\left(\frac{\frac{2}{5}}{1-\frac{1}{25}}\right)\right] - \tan^{-1}\frac{1}{239}$$

$$= 2 \cdot \left[\tan^{-1}\left(\frac{2/5}{24/25}\right)\right] - \tan^{-1}\frac{1}{239}$$

$$= 2\tan^{-1}\frac{5}{12} - \tan^{-1}\frac{1}{239}$$

$$= \tan^{-1} \frac{2 \cdot \frac{5}{12}}{1 - \left(\frac{5}{12}\right)^2} - \tan^{-1} \frac{1}{239} \quad \left[\because 2\tan^{-1} x = \tan^{-1}\left(\frac{2x}{1-x^2}\right)\right]$$

$$= \tan^{-1} \left(\frac{\frac{5}{6}}{1 - \frac{25}{144}} \right) - \tan^{-1} \frac{1}{239}$$

$$= \tan^{-1} \left(\frac{144 \times 5}{119 \times 6} \right) - \tan^{-1} \frac{1}{239}$$

$$= \tan^{-1} \left(\frac{120}{119} \right) - \tan^{-1} \frac{1}{239}$$

$$= \tan^{-1} \left(\frac{\frac{120}{119} - \frac{1}{239}}{1 + \frac{120}{119} \cdot \frac{1}{239}} \right) \quad \left[\because \tan^{-1} x - \tan^{-1} y = \tan^{-1}\left(\frac{x-y}{1+xy}\right)\right]$$

$$= \tan^{-1} \left(\frac{120 \times 239 - 119}{119 \times 239 + 120} \right)$$

$$= \tan^{-1} \left[\frac{28680 - 119}{28441 + 120} \right] = \tan^{-1} \frac{28561}{28561}$$

$$= \tan^{-1}(1) = \tan^{-1}\left(\tan\frac{\pi}{4}\right) = \frac{\pi}{4}$$

Q. 18 Show that $\tan\left(\frac{1}{2}\sin^{-1}\frac{3}{4}\right) = \frac{4-\sqrt{7}}{3}$ and justify why the other value $\frac{4+\sqrt{7}}{3}$ is ignored?

Sol. We have, $\tan\left(\frac{1}{2}\sin^{-1}\frac{3}{4}\right) = \frac{4-\sqrt{7}}{3}$

$\therefore$ $\text{LHS} = \tan\left[\frac{1}{2}\sin^{-1}\left(\frac{3}{4}\right)\right]$

Let $\frac{1}{2}\sin^{-1}\frac{3}{4} = \theta \Rightarrow \sin^{-1}\frac{3}{4} = 2\theta$

$\Rightarrow$ $\sin 2\theta = \frac{3}{4} \Rightarrow \frac{2\tan\theta}{1+\tan^2\theta} = \frac{3}{4}$

$\Rightarrow$ $3 + 3\tan^2\theta = 8\tan\theta$

$\Rightarrow$ $3\tan^2\theta - 8\tan\theta + 3 = 0$

Let $\tan\theta = y$

$\therefore$ $3y^2 - 8y + 3 = 0$

$\Rightarrow$ $y = \frac{+8 \pm \sqrt{64 - 4 \times 3 \times 3}}{2 \times 3} = \frac{8 \pm \sqrt{28}}{6}$

$= \frac{2[4 \pm \sqrt{7}]}{2 \cdot 3}$

$\Rightarrow$ $\tan\theta = \frac{4 \pm \sqrt{7}}{3}$

$$\Rightarrow \quad \theta = \tan^{-1}\left[\frac{4 \pm \sqrt{7}}{3}\right]$$

$$\left\{\text{but } \frac{4+\sqrt{7}}{3} > \frac{1}{2}\cdot\frac{\pi}{2}, \text{ since max}\left[\tan\left(\frac{1}{2}\sin^{-1}\frac{3}{4}\right)\right] = 1\right\}$$

$$\therefore \quad \text{LHS} = \tan\tan^{-1}\left(\frac{4-\sqrt{7}}{3}\right) = \frac{4-\sqrt{7}}{3} = \text{RHS}$$

Note *Since,*

$$-\frac{\pi}{2} \le \sin^{-1}\frac{3}{4} \le \pi/2$$

$$\Rightarrow \quad \frac{-\pi}{4} \le \frac{1}{2}\sin^{-1}\frac{3}{4} \le \pi/4$$

$$\therefore \quad \tan\left(\frac{-\pi}{4}\right) \le \tan\frac{1}{2}\left(\sin^{-1}\frac{3}{4}\right) \le \tan\frac{\pi}{4}$$

$$\Rightarrow \quad -1 \le \tan\left(\frac{1}{2}\sin^{-1}\frac{3}{4}\right) \le 1$$

Q. 19 If $a_1, a_2, a_3, \ldots, a_n$ is an arithmetic progression with common difference d, then evaluate the following expression.

$$\tan\left[\tan^{-1}\left(\frac{d}{1+a_1a_2}\right) + \tan^{-1}\left(\frac{d}{1+a_2a_3}\right) + \tan^{-1}\left(\frac{d}{1+a_3a_4}\right) + \ldots + \tan^{-1}\left(\frac{d}{1+a_{n-1}\,a_n}\right)\right]$$

Sol. We have, $a_1 = a,\ a_2 = a + d,\ a_3 = a + 2d$

and $d = a_2 - a_1 = a_3 - a_2 = a_4 - a_3 = \ldots = a_n - a_{n-1}$

Given that,

$$\tan\left[\tan^{-1}\left(\frac{d}{1+a_1a_2}\right) + \tan^{-1}\left(\frac{d}{1+a_2a_3}\right) + \tan^{-1}\left(\frac{d}{1+a_3a_4}\right) + \ldots + \tan^{-1}\left(\frac{d}{1+a_{n-1}\cdot a_n}\right)\right]$$

$$= \tan\left[\tan^{-1}\frac{a_2 - a_1}{1 + a_2 \cdot a_1} + \tan^{-1}\frac{a_3 - a_2}{1 + a_3 \cdot a_2} + \ldots + \tan^{-1}\frac{a_n - a_{n-1}}{1 + a_n \cdot a_{n-1}}\right]$$

$$= \tan\left[(\tan^{-1}a_2 - \tan^{-1}a_1) + (\tan^{-1}a_3 - \tan^{-1}a_2) + \ldots + (\tan^{-1}a_n - \tan^{-1}a_{n-1})\right]$$

$$= \tan[\tan^{-1}a_n - \tan^{-1}a_1]$$

$$= \tan\left[\tan^{-1}\frac{a_n - a_1}{1 + a_n \cdot a_1}\right] \qquad \left[\because \tan^{-1}x - \tan^{-1}y = \tan^{-1}\left(\frac{x-y}{1+xy}\right)\right]$$

$$= \frac{a_n - a_1}{1 + a_n \cdot a_1} \qquad [\because \tan(\tan^{-1}x) = x]$$

Objective Type Questions

Q. 20 Which of the following is the principal value branch of $\cos^{-1} x$?

(a) $\left[-\dfrac{\pi}{2}, \dfrac{\pi}{2}\right]$ (b) $(0, \pi)$ (c) $[0, \pi]$ (d) $(0, \pi) - \left\{\dfrac{\pi}{2}\right\}$

Sol. *(c)* We know that, the principal value branch of $\cos^{-1} x$ is $[0, \pi]$.

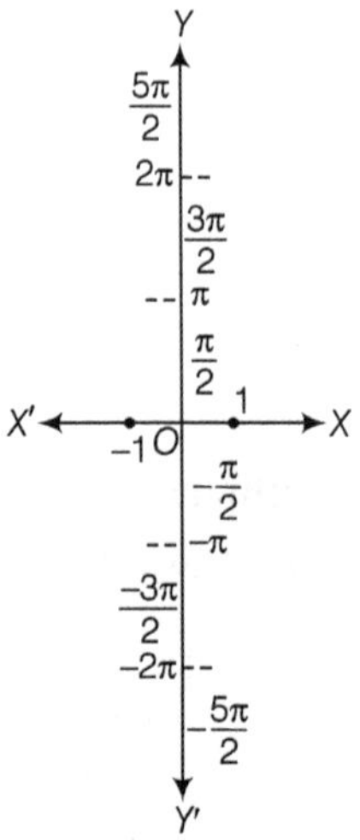

$\therefore$ $y = \cos^{-1} x$

Q. 21 Which of the following is the principal value branch of $\text{cosec}^{-1} x$?

(a) $\left(\dfrac{-\pi}{2}, \dfrac{\pi}{2}\right)$ (b) $[0, \pi] - \left\{\dfrac{\pi}{2}\right\}$ (c) $\left[\dfrac{\pi}{2}, \dfrac{\pi}{2}\right]$ (d) $\left[\dfrac{-\pi}{2}, \dfrac{\pi}{2}\right] - [0]$

Sol. *(d)* We know that, the principal value branch of $\text{cosec}^{-1} x$ is $\left[\dfrac{-\pi}{2}, \dfrac{\pi}{2}\right] - 0$.

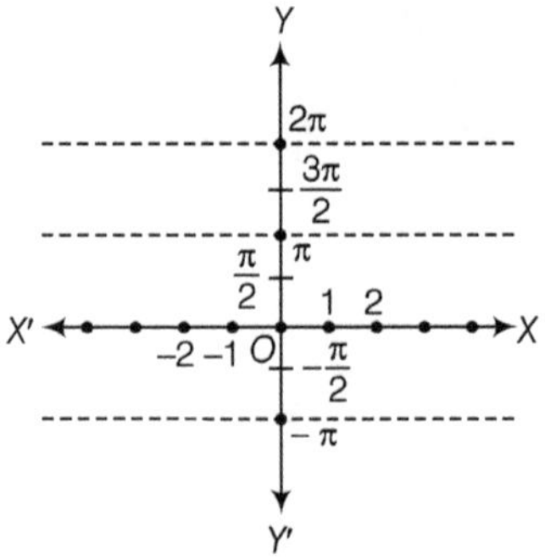

$\therefore$ $y = \text{cosec}^{-1} x$

Q. 22 If $3\tan^{-1} x + \cot^{-1} x = \pi$, then x equals to

(a) 0 (b) 1 (c) −1 (d) $\frac{1}{2}$

Sol. *(b)* Given that, $3\tan^{-1} x + \cot^{-1} x = \pi$ ...(i)

$$\Rightarrow \quad 2\tan^{-1} x + \tan^{-1} x + \cot^{-1} x = \pi$$

$$\Rightarrow \quad 2\tan^{-1} x = \pi - \frac{\pi}{2} \qquad \left[\because \tan^{-1} x + \cot^{-1} x = \frac{\pi}{2}\right]$$

$$\Rightarrow \quad 2\tan^{-1} x = \frac{\pi}{2}$$

$$\Rightarrow \quad \tan^{-1}\frac{2x}{1-x^2} = \frac{\pi}{2} \qquad \left[\because 2\tan^{-1} x = \tan^{-1}\frac{2x}{1-x^2}, \forall x \in (-1, 1)\right]$$

$$\Rightarrow \quad \frac{2x}{1-x^2} = \tan\frac{\pi}{2}$$

$$\Rightarrow \quad \frac{2x}{1-x^2} = \frac{1}{0} \Rightarrow 1 - x^2 = 0$$

$$\Rightarrow \quad x^2 = 1 \Rightarrow x = \pm 1 \Rightarrow x = 1$$

Hence, only $x = 1$ satisfies the given equation.

Note *Here, putting $x = -1$ in the given equation, we get*

$$3\tan^{-1}(-1) + \cot^{-1}(-1) = \pi$$

$$\Rightarrow \quad 3\tan^{-1}\left[\tan\left(\frac{-\pi}{4}\right)\right] + \cot^{-1}\left[\cot\left(\frac{-\pi}{4}\right)\right] = \pi$$

$$\Rightarrow \quad 3\tan^{-1}\left(-\tan\frac{\pi}{4}\right) + \cot^{-1}\left(-\cot\frac{\pi}{4}\right) = \pi$$

$$\Rightarrow \quad -3\tan^{-1}\left(\tan\frac{\pi}{4}\right) + \pi - \cot^{-1}\left(\cot\frac{\pi}{4}\right) = \pi$$

$$\Rightarrow \quad -3\cdot\frac{\pi}{4} + \pi - \frac{\pi}{4} = \pi$$

$$\Rightarrow \quad -\pi + \pi = \pi \Rightarrow 0 \neq \pi$$

Hence, $x = -1$ does not satisfy the given equation.

Q. 23 The value of $\sin^{-1}\left[\cos\left(\frac{33\pi}{5}\right)\right]$ is

(a) $\frac{3\pi}{5}$ (b) $\frac{-7\pi}{5}$ (c) $\frac{\pi}{10}$ (d) $\frac{-\pi}{10}$

Sol. *(d)* We have,

$$\sin^{-1}\left(\cos\frac{33\pi}{5}\right) = \sin^{-1}\left[\cos\left(6\pi + \frac{3\pi}{5}\right)\right] = \sin^{-1}\left[\cos\left(\frac{3\pi}{5}\right)\right] \qquad [\because \cos(2n\pi + \theta) = \cos\theta]$$

$$= \sin^{-1}\left[\cos\left(\frac{\pi}{2} + \frac{\pi}{10}\right)\right] = \sin^{-1}\left(-\sin\frac{\pi}{10}\right)$$

$$= -\sin^{-1}\left(\sin\frac{\pi}{10}\right) \qquad [\because \sin^{-1}(-x) = -\sin^{-1} x]$$

$$= -\frac{\pi}{10} \qquad \left[\because \sin^{-1}(\sin x) = x, x \in \left(\frac{-\pi}{2}, \frac{\pi}{2}\right)\right]$$

Q. 24 The domain of the function $\cos^{-1}(2x-1)$ is

(a) [0, 1] (b) [−1, 1] (c) (−1, 1) (d) $[0, \pi]$

Sol. *(a)* We have, $f(x) = \cos^{-1}(2x-1)$

$$\therefore \quad -1 \le 2x - 1 \le 1$$
$$\Rightarrow \quad 0 \le 2x \le 2$$
$$\Rightarrow \quad 0 \le x \le 1$$
$$\therefore \quad x \in [0, 1]$$

Q. 25 The domain of the function defined by $f(x) = \sin^{-1}\sqrt{x-1}$ is

(a) [1, 2] (b) [−1, 1] (c) [0, 1] (d) None of these

Sol. *(a)* $\because \quad f(x) = \sin^{-1}\sqrt{x-1}$

$$\Rightarrow \quad 0 \le x - 1 \le 1 \quad \left[\because \sqrt{x-1} \ge 0 \text{ and } -1 \le \sqrt{x-1} \le 1\right]$$
$$\Rightarrow \quad 1 \le x \le 2$$
$$\therefore \quad x \in [1, 2]$$

Q. 26 If $\cos\left(\sin^{-1}\frac{2}{5} + \cos^{-1}x\right) = 0$, then x is equal to

(a) $\frac{1}{5}$ (b) $\frac{2}{5}$ (c) 0 (d) 1

Sol. *(b)* We have, $\cos\left(\sin^{-1}\frac{2}{5} + \cos^{-1}x\right) = 0$

$$\Rightarrow \quad \sin^{-1}\frac{2}{5} + \cos^{-1}x = \cos^{-1}0$$
$$\Rightarrow \quad \sin^{-1}\frac{2}{5} + \cos^{-1}x = \cos^{-1}\cos\frac{\pi}{2}$$
$$\Rightarrow \quad \sin^{-1}\frac{2}{5} + \cos^{-1}x = \frac{\pi}{2}$$
$$\Rightarrow \quad \cos^{-1}x = \frac{\pi}{2} - \sin^{-1}\frac{2}{5}$$
$$\Rightarrow \quad \cos^{-1}x = \cos^{-1}\frac{2}{5} \quad \left[\because \cos^{-1}x + \sin^{-1}x = \frac{\pi}{2}\right]$$
$$\therefore \quad x = \frac{2}{5}$$

Q. 27 The value of $\sin[2\tan^{-1}(0.75)]$ is

(a) 0.75 (b) 1.5 (c) 0.96 (d) sin 1.5

Sol. *(c)* We have, $\sin[2\tan^{-1}(0.75)] = \sin\left(2\tan^{-1}\frac{3}{4}\right) \quad \left[\because 0.75 = \frac{75}{100} = \frac{3}{4}\right]$

$$= \sin\left(\sin^{-1}\frac{2\cdot\frac{3}{4}}{1+\frac{9}{16}}\right) = \sin\left[\sin^{-1}\frac{3/2}{25/16}\right]$$
$$= \sin\left[\sin^{-1}\left(\frac{48}{50}\right)\right] = \sin\left[\sin^{-1}\left(\frac{24}{25}\right)\right] = \frac{24}{25} = 0.96$$

Q. 28 The value of $\cos^{-1}\left(\cos\frac{3\pi}{2}\right)$ is

(a) $\frac{\pi}{2}$ (b) $\frac{3\pi}{2}$ (c) $\frac{5\pi}{2}$ (d) $\frac{7\pi}{2}$

Sol. *(a)* We have, $\cos^{-1}\left(\cos\frac{3\pi}{2}\right)$

$$= \cos^{-1}\cos\left(2\pi - \frac{\pi}{2}\right) \qquad \left[\because \cos\left(2\pi - \frac{\pi}{2}\right) = \cos\frac{\pi}{2}\right]$$

$$= \cos^{-1}\cos\left(\frac{\pi}{2}\right) = \frac{\pi}{2} \qquad \{\because \cos^{-1}(\cos x) = x,\ x \in [0, \pi]\}$$

Note *Remember that,* $\cos^{-1}\left(\cos\frac{3\pi}{2}\right) \neq \frac{3\pi}{2}$

$\because \quad \frac{3\pi}{2} \notin (0, \pi)$

Q. 29 The value of $2\sec^{-1}2 + \sin^{-1}\left(\frac{1}{2}\right)$ is

(a) $\frac{\pi}{6}$ (b) $\frac{5\pi}{6}$ (c) $\frac{7\pi}{6}$ (d) 1

Sol. *(b)* We have, $2\sec^{-1}2 + \sin^{-1}\frac{1}{2} = 2\sec^{-1}\sec\frac{\pi}{3} + \sin^{-1}\sin\frac{\pi}{6}$

$$= 2\cdot\frac{\pi}{3} + \frac{\pi}{6} \qquad [\because \sec^{-1}(\sec x) = x \text{ and } \sin^{-1}(\sin x) = x]$$

$$= \frac{4\pi + \pi}{6} = \frac{5\pi}{6}$$

Q. 30 If $\tan^{-1}x + \tan^{-1}y = \frac{4\pi}{5}$, then $\cot^{-1}x + \cot^{-1}y$ equals to

(a) $\frac{\pi}{5}$ (b) $\frac{2\pi}{5}$ (c) $\frac{3\pi}{5}$ (d) π

Sol. *(a)* We have, $\tan^{-1}x + \tan^{-1}y = \frac{4\pi}{5}$

$$\Rightarrow \frac{\pi}{2} - \cot^{-1}x + \frac{\pi}{2} - \cot^{-1}y = \frac{4\pi}{5}$$

$$\Rightarrow -(\cot^{-1}x + \cot^{-1}y) = \frac{4\pi}{5} - \pi \qquad \left[\because \tan^{-1}x + \cot^{-1}x = \frac{\pi}{2}\right]$$

$$\Rightarrow \cot^{-1}x + \cot^{-1}y = -\left(-\frac{\pi}{5}\right)$$

$$\Rightarrow \cot^{-1}x + \cot^{-1}y = \frac{\pi}{5}$$

Q. 31 If $\sin^{-1}\left(\frac{2a}{1+a^2}\right)+\cos^{-1}\left(\frac{1-a^2}{1+a^2}\right)=\tan^{-1}\left(\frac{2x}{1-x^2}\right)$, where $a, x \in]0, 1[$, then the value of x is

(a) 0 (b) $\frac{a}{2}$ (c) a (d) $\frac{2a}{1-a^2}$

Sol. *(d)* We have, $\sin^{-1}\left(\frac{2a}{1+a^2}\right)+\cos^{-1}\left(\frac{1-a^2}{1+a^2}\right)=\tan^{-1}\left(\frac{2x}{1-x^2}\right)$

Let $a=\tan\theta \Rightarrow \theta=\tan^{-1}a$

$$\therefore \quad \sin^{-1}\left(\frac{2\tan\theta}{1+\tan^2\theta}\right)+\cos^{-1}\left(\frac{1-\tan^2\theta}{1+\tan^2\theta}\right)=\tan^{-1}\frac{2x}{1-x^2}$$

$$\Rightarrow \quad \sin^{-1}\sin 2\theta+\cos^{-1}\cos 2\theta=\tan^{-1}\frac{2x}{1-x^2}$$

$$\Rightarrow \quad 2\theta+2\theta=\tan^{-1}\frac{2x}{1-x^2}$$

$$\Rightarrow \quad 4\tan^{-1}a=\tan^{-1}\frac{2x}{1-x^2}$$

$$\Rightarrow \quad 2\cdot 2\tan^{-1}a=\tan^{-1}\frac{2x}{1-x^2}$$

$$\Rightarrow \quad 2\cdot\tan^{-1}\frac{2a}{1-a^2}=\tan^{-1}\frac{2x}{1-x^2} \qquad \left[\because 2\tan^{-1}x=\tan^{-1}\frac{2x}{1-x^2}\right]$$

$$\Rightarrow \quad \tan^{-1}\frac{2\cdot\left(\frac{2a}{1-a^2}\right)}{1-\left(\frac{2a}{1-a^2}\right)^2}=\tan^{-1}\left(\frac{2x}{1-x^2}\right)$$

$$\therefore \quad x=\frac{2a}{1-a^2}$$

Q. 32 The value of $\cot\left[\cos^{-1}\left(\frac{7}{25}\right)\right]$ is

(a) $\frac{25}{24}$ (b) $\frac{25}{7}$ (c) $\frac{24}{25}$ (d) $\frac{7}{24}$

Sol. *(d)* We have, $\cot\left[\cos^{-1}\left(\frac{7}{25}\right)\right]$

Let $\cos^{-1}\frac{7}{25}=x$

$$\Rightarrow \quad \cos x=\frac{7}{25}$$

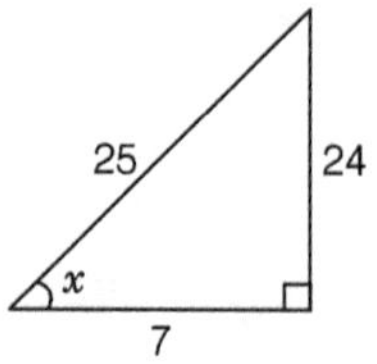

$$\therefore \quad \sin x=\sqrt{1-\cos^2 x}=\sqrt{1-\left(\frac{7}{25}\right)^2}$$

$$=\sqrt{\frac{625-49}{625}}=\frac{24}{25}$$

$$\therefore \qquad \cot x = \frac{\cos x}{\sin x} = \frac{\frac{7}{25}}{\frac{24}{25}} = \frac{7}{24} \qquad \text{...(i)}$$

$$\Rightarrow \qquad x = \cot^{-1}\left(\frac{7}{24}\right) = \cos^{-1}\left(\frac{7}{25}\right)$$

$$\therefore \qquad \cot\left(\cos^{-1}\frac{7}{25}\right) = \cot\left(\cot^{-1}\frac{7}{24}\right) = \frac{7}{24} \qquad \left[\because \cot^{-1}\frac{7}{24} = \cos^{-1}\frac{7}{25}\right]$$

Q. 33 The value of $\tan\left(\frac{1}{2}\cos^{-1}\frac{2}{\sqrt{5}}\right)$ is

(a) $2+\sqrt{5}$ (b) $\sqrt{5}-2$ (c) $\frac{\sqrt{5}+2}{2}$ (d) $5+\sqrt{2}$

Sol. ***(b)*** We have, $\tan\left(\frac{1}{2}\cos^{-1}\frac{2}{\sqrt{5}}\right)$

Let $\frac{1}{2}\cos^{-1}\frac{2}{\sqrt{5}} = \theta$

$$\Rightarrow \qquad \cos^{-1}\frac{2}{\sqrt{5}} = 2\theta \Rightarrow \cos 2\theta = \frac{2}{\sqrt{5}}$$

$$\therefore \qquad (1-2\sin^2\theta) = \frac{2}{\sqrt{5}}$$

$$\Rightarrow \qquad 2\sin^2\theta = 1 - \frac{2}{\sqrt{5}}$$

$$\Rightarrow \qquad \sin^2\theta = \frac{1}{2} - \frac{1}{\sqrt{5}}$$

$$\Rightarrow \qquad \sin\theta = \sqrt{\frac{1}{2} - \frac{1}{\sqrt{5}}}$$

$$\therefore \qquad \cos^2\theta = 1 - \sin^2\theta$$

$$= 1 - \frac{1}{2} + \frac{1}{\sqrt{5}} = \frac{1}{2} + \frac{1}{\sqrt{5}}$$

$$\Rightarrow \qquad \cos\theta = \sqrt{\frac{1}{2} + \frac{1}{\sqrt{5}}}$$

$$\therefore \qquad \tan\theta = \sqrt{\frac{\frac{1}{2} - \frac{1}{\sqrt{5}}}{\frac{1}{2} + \frac{1}{\sqrt{5}}}} = \sqrt{\frac{\sqrt{5}-2}{\sqrt{5}+2}} \qquad \left[\because \tan\theta = \frac{\sin\theta}{\cos\theta}\right]$$

$$\Rightarrow \qquad \theta = \tan^{-1}\sqrt{\frac{\sqrt{5}-2}{\sqrt{5}+2}} = \frac{1}{2}\cos^{-1}\frac{2}{\sqrt{5}}$$

$$\therefore \qquad \tan\left(\frac{1}{2}\cos^{-1}\frac{2}{\sqrt{5}}\right) = \tan\tan^{-1}\sqrt{\frac{\sqrt{5}-2}{\sqrt{5}+2}}$$

$$= \sqrt{\frac{\sqrt{5}-2}{\sqrt{5}+2}\cdot\frac{\sqrt{5}-2}{\sqrt{5}-2}}$$

$$= \sqrt{\frac{(\sqrt{5}-2)^2}{5-4}} = \sqrt{5}-2$$

Q. 34 If $|x| \le 1$, then $2\tan^{-1} x + \sin^{-1}\left(\dfrac{2x}{1+x^2}\right)$ is equal to

(a) $4\tan^{-1} x$ (b) 0 (c) $\dfrac{\pi}{2}$ (d) π

Sol. *(a)* We have, $2\tan^{-1} x + \sin^{-1}\dfrac{2x}{1+x^2}$

Let $x = \tan\theta$

$\therefore$ $2\tan^{-1}\tan\theta + \sin^{-1}\dfrac{2\tan\theta}{1+\tan^2\theta}$ $[\because \tan^{-1}(\tan x) = x]$

$= 2\theta + \sin^{-1}\sin 2\theta$ $\left[\because \sin 2\theta = \dfrac{2\tan\theta}{1+\tan^2\theta}\right]$

$= 2\theta + 2\theta$ $[\because \sin^{-1}(\sin x) = x]$

$= 4\theta$ $[\because \theta = \tan^{-1} x]$

$= 4\tan^{-1} x$

Q. 35 If $\cos^{-1}\alpha + \cos^{-1}\beta + \cos^{-1}\gamma = 3\pi$, then $\alpha(\beta+\gamma) + \beta(\gamma+\alpha) + \gamma(\alpha+\beta)$ equals to

(a) 0 (b) 1 (c) 6 (d) 12

Sol. *(c)* We have, $\cos^{-1}\alpha + \cos^{-1}\beta + \cos^{-1}\gamma = 3\pi$

We know that, $0 \le \cos^{-1} x \le \pi$

$\Rightarrow$ $\cos^{-1}\alpha + \cos^{-1}\beta + \cos^{-1}\gamma = 3\pi$

If and only if, $\cos^{-1}\alpha = \cos^{-1}\beta = \cos^{-1}\gamma = \pi$

$\Rightarrow$ $\cos\pi = \alpha = \beta = \gamma$

$\Rightarrow$ $-1 = \alpha = \beta = \gamma$

$\Rightarrow$ $\alpha = \beta = \gamma = -1$

$\therefore$ $\alpha(\beta+\gamma) + \beta(\gamma+\alpha) + \gamma(\alpha+\beta)$

$= -1(-1-1) - 1(-1-1) - 1(-1-1)$

$= 2 + 2 + 2 = 6$

Q. 36 The number of real solutions of the equation

$$\sqrt{1+\cos 2x} = \sqrt{2}\cos^{-1}(\cos x) \text{ in } \left[\frac{\pi}{2}, \pi\right] \text{ is}$$

(a) 0 (b) 1 (c) 2 (d) ∞

Sol. *(a)* We have, $\sqrt{1+\cos 2x} = \sqrt{2}\cos^{-1}(\cos x), \left[\dfrac{\pi}{2}, \pi\right]$

$\Rightarrow$ $\sqrt{1+2\cos^2 x - 1} = \sqrt{2}\cos^{-1}(\cos x)$

$\Rightarrow$ $\sqrt{2}\cos x = \sqrt{2}\cos^{-1}(\cos x)$

$\Rightarrow$ $\cos x = \cos^{-1}(\cos x)$

$\Rightarrow$ $\cos x = x$ $[\because \cos^{-1}(\cos x) = x]$

which is not true for any real value of x.

Hence, there is no solution possible for the given equation.

Q. 37 If $\cos^{-1} x > \sin^{-1} x$, then

(a) $\frac{1}{\sqrt{2}} < x \le 1$ (b) $0 \le x < \frac{1}{\sqrt{2}}$ (c) $-1 \le x < \frac{1}{\sqrt{2}}$ (d) $x > 0$

Sol. *(c)* We have, $\cos^{-1} x > \sin^{-1} x$, where $x \in [-1, 1]$

$\Rightarrow \quad x < \cos(\sin^{-1} x)$

$\Rightarrow \quad x < \cos[\cos^{-1}\sqrt{1-x^2}] \quad \left[\text{let } \sin^{-1} x = \theta \Rightarrow \sin\theta = \frac{x}{1}\right]$

$\left[\because \cos\theta = \sqrt{1-\sin^2\theta} = \sqrt{1-x^2} \Rightarrow \theta = \cos^{-1}\sqrt{1-x^2}\right]$

$\Rightarrow \quad x < \sqrt{1-x^2}$

$\Rightarrow \quad x^2 < 1 - x^2 \Rightarrow 2x^2 < 1$

$\Rightarrow \quad x^2 < \frac{1}{2} \Rightarrow x < \pm\left(\frac{1}{\sqrt{2}}\right)$ ...(i)

Also, $\quad -1 \le x \le 1$ ...(ii)

$\therefore \quad -1 \le x \le \frac{1}{\sqrt{2}}$

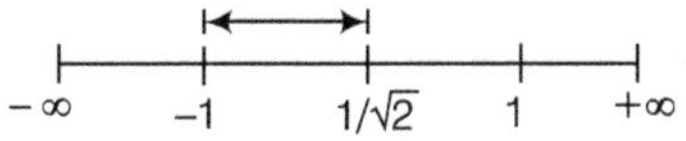

Alternate Method

$$\frac{\pi}{2} - \sin^{-1} x > \sin^{-1} x$$

$$\frac{\pi}{2} > 2\sin^{-1} x \Rightarrow \frac{\pi}{4} > \sin^{-1} x$$

$$\frac{1}{\sqrt{2}} > x \Rightarrow \frac{1}{\sqrt{2}} < x \le 1$$

We know that, $\quad \sin^{-1} x \in \left[\frac{-\pi}{2}, \frac{\pi}{2}\right]$

Fillers

Q. 38 The principal value of $\cos^{-1}\left(-\frac{1}{2}\right)$ is ....

Sol. $\because \quad 0 \le \cos^{-1} x \le \pi$

$$\cos^{-1}\left(-\frac{1}{2}\right) = \cos^{-1}\left(\cos\frac{2\pi}{3}\right) = \frac{2\pi}{3}$$

Q. 39 The value of $\sin^{-1}\left(\sin\frac{3\pi}{5}\right)$ is ....

Sol. $\because \quad -\frac{\pi}{2} \le \sin^{-1} x \le \frac{\pi}{2}$

$\therefore \quad \sin^{-1}\left(\sin\frac{3\pi}{5}\right) = \sin^{-1}\sin\left(\pi - \frac{2\pi}{5}\right) = \sin^{-1}\left(\sin\frac{2\pi}{5}\right) = \frac{2\pi}{5}$

Q. 40 If $\cos(\tan^{-1} x + \cot^{-1}\sqrt{3}) = 0$, then the value of x is ....

Sol. We have, $\cos(\tan^{-1} x + \cot^{-1}\sqrt{3}) = 0$

$\Rightarrow \tan^{-1} x + \cot^{-1}\sqrt{3} = \cos^{-1} 0$

$\Rightarrow \tan^{-1} x + \cot^{-1}\sqrt{3} = \cos^{-1}\cos\frac{\pi}{2}$

$\Rightarrow \tan^{-1} x + \cot^{-1}\sqrt{3} = \frac{\pi}{2}$

$\Rightarrow \tan^{-1} x = \frac{\pi}{2} - \cot^{-1}\sqrt{3}$

$\Rightarrow \tan^{-1} x = \tan^{-1}\sqrt{3}$ $\left[\because \tan^{-1} x + \cot^{-1} x = \frac{\pi}{2}\right]$

$\therefore x = \sqrt{3}$

Q. 41 The set of values of $\sec^{-1}\frac{1}{2}$ is ....

Sol. Since, domain of $\sec^{-1} x$ is $R - (-1, 1)$.

$\Rightarrow (-\infty, -1] \cup [1, \infty)$

So, there is no set of values exist for $\sec^{-1}\frac{1}{2}$.

So, ϕ is the answer.

Q. 42 The principal value of $\tan^{-1}\sqrt{3}$ is ....

Sol. $\because \tan^{-1}\sqrt{3} = \tan^{-1}\tan\left(\frac{\pi}{3}\right)$ $\left[\because \tan^{-1}(\tan x) = x, x \in \left(-\frac{\pi}{2}, \frac{\pi}{2}\right)\right]$

$= \left(\frac{\pi}{3}\right)$

Q. 43 The value of $\cos^{-1}\left(\cos\frac{14\pi}{3}\right)$ is ....

Sol. We have, $\cos^{-1}\left(\cos\frac{14\pi}{3}\right) = \cos^{-1}\cos\left(4\pi + \frac{2\pi}{3}\right)$

$= \cos^{-1}\cos\frac{2\pi}{3}$ $[\because \cos(2n\pi + \theta) = \cos\theta]$

$= \frac{2\pi}{3}$ $\{\because \cos^{-1}(\cos x) = x, x \in [0, \pi]\}$

Note *Remember that,* $\cos^{-1}\left(\cos\frac{14\pi}{3}\right) \neq \frac{14\pi}{3}$

Since, $\frac{14\pi}{3} \notin [0, \pi]$

Q. 44 The value of $\cos(\sin^{-1} x + \cos^{-1} x)$, where $|x| \le 1$, is ....

Sol. $\cos(\sin^{-1} x + \cos^{-1} x)$

$= \cos\frac{\pi}{2} = 0$ $\left[\because \sin^{-1} x + \cos^{-1} x = \frac{\pi}{2}\right]$

Q. 45 The value of $\tan\left(\frac{\sin^{-1}x+\cos^{-1}x}{2}\right)$, when $x=\frac{\sqrt{3}}{2}$, is ....

Sol. $\because$ $\tan\left(\frac{\sin^{-1}x+\cos^{-1}x}{2}\right)=\tan\left(\frac{\pi/2}{2}\right)$ $\left[\because \sin^{-1}x+\cos^{-1}x=\frac{\pi}{2}\right]$

$$=\tan\frac{\pi}{4}=1$$

Q. 46 If $y=2\tan^{-1}x+\sin^{-1}\left(\frac{2x}{1+x^2}\right)$, then .... $< y <$ ....

Sol. We have, $y=2\tan^{-1}x+\sin^{-1}\frac{2x}{1+x^2}$

$\therefore$ $y=2\tan^{-1}\tan\theta+\sin^{-1}\frac{2\tan\theta}{1+\tan^2\theta}$ [let $x=\tan\theta$]

$\Rightarrow$ $y=2\theta+\sin^{-1}\sin 2\theta$ $\left[\because \sin 2\theta=\frac{2\tan\theta}{1+\tan^2\theta}\right]$

$\Rightarrow$ $y=2\theta+2\theta=4\theta$ [$\because \theta=\tan^{-1}x$]

$\Rightarrow$ $y=4\tan^{-1}x$

$\because$ $-\pi/2<\tan^{-1}x<\pi/2$

$\therefore$ $-\frac{4\pi}{2}<4\tan^{-1}x<4\pi/2$

$\Rightarrow$ $-2\pi<4\tan^{-1}x<2\pi$

$\Rightarrow$ $-2\pi<y<2\pi$ [$\because y=4\tan^{-1}x$]

Q. 47 The result $\tan^{-1}x-\tan^{-1}y=\tan^{-1}\left(\frac{x-y}{1+xy}\right)$ is true when the value of xy is ....

Sol. We know that, $\tan^{-1}x-\tan^{-1}y=\tan^{-1}\left(\frac{x-y}{1+xy}\right)$

where, $xy>-1$

Q. 48 The value of $\cot^{-1}(-x)$ $x\in R$ in terms of $\cot^{-1}x$ is ....

Sol. We know that,

$$\cot^{-1}(-x)=\pi-\cot^{-1}x,\ x\in R$$

True/False

Q. 49 All trigonometric functions have inverse over their respective domains.

Sol. *False*

We know that, all trigonometric functions have inverse over their restricted domains.

Q. 50 The value of the expression $(\cos^{-1} x)^2$ is equal to $\sec^2 x$.

Sol. ***False***

$$\because \quad [\cos^{-1} x]^2 = \left[\sec^{-1}\frac{1}{x}\right]^2 \neq \sec^2 x$$

Q. 51 The domain of trigonometric functions can be restricted to any one of their branch (not necessarily principal value) in order to obtain their inverse functions.

Sol. ***True***

We know that, the domain of trigonometric functions are restricted in their domain to obtain their inverse functions.

Q. 52 The least numerical value, either positive or negative of angle θ is called principal value of the inverse trigonometric function.

Sol. ***True***

We know that, the smallest numerical value, either positive or negative of θ is called the principal value of the function.

Q. 53 The graph of inverse trigonometric function can be obtained from the graph of their corresponding function by interchanging X and Y-axes.

Sol. ***True***

We know that, the graph of an inverse function can be obtained from the corresponding graph of original function as a mirror image (*i.e.*, reflection) along the line $y = x$.

Q. 54 The minimum value of n for which $\tan^{-1}\frac{n}{\pi} > \frac{\pi}{4}$, $n \in N$, is valid is 5.

Sol. ***False***

$$\because \quad \tan^{-1}\frac{n}{\pi} > \frac{\pi}{4} \Rightarrow \frac{n}{\pi} > \tan\frac{\pi}{4}$$

$$\Rightarrow \quad \frac{n}{\pi} > 1 \qquad \left[\because \tan\frac{\pi}{4} = 1\right]$$

$$\Rightarrow \quad n > \pi$$

So, the minimum value of n is 4. $[\because n \in N \text{ and } \pi = 3.14...]$

Q. 55 The principal value of $\sin^{-1}\left[\cos\left(\sin^{-1}\frac{1}{2}\right)\right]$ is $\frac{\pi}{3}$.

Sol. ***True***

Given that, $$\sin^{-1}\left[\cos\left(\sin^{-1}\frac{1}{2}\right)\right] = \sin^{-1}\left[\cos \sin^{-1}\left(\sin\frac{\pi}{6}\right)\right]$$

$$= \sin^{-1}\left[\cos\frac{\pi}{6}\right] \qquad [\because \sin^{-1}(\sin x) = x]$$

$$= \sin^{-1}\frac{\sqrt{3}}{2}$$

$$= \sin^{-1}\sin\frac{\pi}{3} = \frac{\pi}{3}$$

3

Matrices

Short Answer Type Questions

Q. 1 If a matrix has 28 elements, what are the possible orders it can have? What if it has 13 elements?

Sol. We know that, if a matrix is of order $m \times n$, it has mn elements, where m and n are natural numbers.

We have, $m \times n = 28$

$\Rightarrow \quad (m, n) = \{(1, 28), (2, 14), (4, 7), (7, 4), (14, 2), (28, 1)\}$

So, the possible orders are $1 \times 28, 2 \times 14, 4 \times 7, 7 \times 4, 14 \times 2, 28 \times 1$.

Also, if it has 13 elements, then $m \times n = 13$

$\Rightarrow \quad (m, n) = \{(1,13), (13,1)\}$

Hence, the possible orders are $1 \times 13, 13 \times 1$.

Q. 2 In the matrix $A = \begin{bmatrix} a & 1 & x \\ 2 & \sqrt{3} & x^2 - y \\ 0 & 5 & \frac{-2}{5} \end{bmatrix}$, write

(i) the order of the matrix A.

(ii) the number of elements.

(iii) elements a_{23}, a_{31} and a_{12}.

Sol. We have,
$$A = \begin{bmatrix} a & 1 & x \\ 2 & \sqrt{3} & x^2 - y \\ 0 & 5 & \frac{-2}{5} \end{bmatrix}$$

(i) the order of matrix $A = 3 \times 3$

(ii) the number of elements $= 3 \times 3 = 9$

[since, the number of elements in an $m \times n$ matrix will be equal to $m \times n = mn$]

(iii) $a_{23} = x^2 - y$, $a_{31} = 0$, $a_{12} = 1$

[since, we know that a_{ij}, is a representation of element lying in the ith row and jth column]

Q. 3 Construct $a_{2\times 2}$ matrix, where

(i) $a_{ij} = \dfrac{(i-2j)^2}{2}$ (ii) $a_{ij} = |-2i+3j|$

Sol. We know that, the notation, namely $A = [a_{ij}]_{m\times n}$ indicates that A is a matrix of order $m\times n$, also $1\le i\le m, 1\le j\le n;\ i, j \in N$.

(i) Here, $A = [a_{ij}]_{2\times 2}$

$$\Rightarrow \quad A = \frac{(i-2j)^2}{2}, 1\le i\le 2;1\le j\le 2 \quad \ldots(i)$$

$$\therefore \quad a_{11} = \frac{(1-2)^2}{2} = \frac{1}{2}$$

$$a_{12} = \frac{(1-2\times 2)^2}{2} = \frac{9}{2}$$

$$a_{21} = \frac{(2-2\times 1)^2}{2} = 0$$

$$a_{22} = \frac{(2-2\times 2)^2}{2} = 2$$

Thus,
$$A = \begin{bmatrix} \frac{1}{2} & \frac{9}{2} \\ 0 & 2 \end{bmatrix}_{2\times 2}$$

(ii) Here, $A = [a_{ij}]_{2\times 2} = |-2i+3j|, 1\le i\le 2; 1\le j\le 2$

$$\therefore \quad a_{11} = |-2\times 1+3\times 1| = 1$$

$$a_{12} = |-2\times 1+3\times 2| = 4 \quad [\because |-1| = 1]$$

$$a_{21} = |-2\times 2+3\times 1| = 1$$

$$a_{22} = |-2\times 2+3\times 2| = 2$$

$$\therefore \quad A = \begin{vmatrix} 1 & 4 \\ 1 & 2 \end{vmatrix}_{2\times 2}$$

Q. 4 Construct a 3×2 matrix whose elements are given by $a_{ij} = e^{i\cdot x} = \sin jx$.

Sol. Since, $A = [a_{ij}]_{m\times n}$ $1\le i\le m$ and $1\le j\le n, i,j \in N$

$$\therefore \quad A = [e^{i\cdot x}\sin jx]_{3\times 2};\ 1\le i\le 3;\ 1\le j\le 2$$

$$\Rightarrow \quad a_{11} = e^{1\cdot x}\cdot\sin 1\cdot x = e^x \sin x$$

$$a_{12} = e^{1\cdot x}\cdot\sin 2\cdot x = e^x \sin 2x$$

$$a_{21} = e^{2\cdot x}\cdot\sin 1\cdot x = e^{2x}\sin x$$

$$a_{22} = e^{2\cdot x}\cdot\sin 2\cdot x = e^{2x}\sin 2x$$

$$a_{31} = e^{3\cdot x}\cdot\sin 1\cdot x = e^{3x}\sin x$$

$$a_{32} = e^{3\cdot x}\cdot\sin 2\cdot x = e^{3x}\sin 2x$$

$$\therefore \quad A = \begin{bmatrix} e^x\sin x & e^x\sin 2x \\ e^{2x}\sin x & e^{2x}\sin 2x \\ e^{3x}\sin x & e^{3x}\sin 2x \end{bmatrix}_{3\times 2}$$

Also, $A^2 = A \cdot A$

$$= \begin{bmatrix} 0 & 1 \\ 1 & 1 \end{bmatrix} \cdot \begin{bmatrix} 0 & 1 \\ 1 & 1 \end{bmatrix}$$

$$= \begin{bmatrix} 0+1 & 0+1 \\ 0+1 & 1+1 \end{bmatrix} = \begin{bmatrix} 1 & 1 \\ 1 & 2 \end{bmatrix}$$

and $B^2 = B \cdot B$ $= \begin{bmatrix} 0 & -1 \\ 1 & 0 \end{bmatrix} \cdot \begin{bmatrix} 0 & -1 \\ 1 & 0 \end{bmatrix}$

$$= \begin{bmatrix} 0-1 & 0+0 \\ 0+0 & -1+0 \end{bmatrix} = \begin{bmatrix} -1 & 0 \\ 0 & -1 \end{bmatrix}$$

$\therefore$ $A^2 - B^2 = \begin{bmatrix} 1 & 1 \\ 1 & 2 \end{bmatrix} - \begin{bmatrix} -1 & 0 \\ 0 & -1 \end{bmatrix} = \begin{bmatrix} 2 & 1 \\ 1 & 3 \end{bmatrix}$ ...(ii)

Thus, we see that

$(A+B) \cdot (A-B) \neq A^2 - B^2$ [using Eqs. (i) and (ii)]

$\Rightarrow$ $\begin{bmatrix} 0 & 0 \\ 0 & 5 \end{bmatrix} \neq \begin{bmatrix} 2 & 1 \\ 1 & 3 \end{bmatrix}$ **Hence proved.**

Q. 10 Find the value of x, if $[1\ x\ 1] \begin{bmatrix} 1 & 3 & 2 \\ 2 & 5 & 1 \\ 15 & 3 & 2 \end{bmatrix} \begin{bmatrix} 1 \\ 2 \\ x \end{bmatrix} = 0$.

Sol. We have, $[1\ x\ 1]_{1\times 3} \begin{bmatrix} 1 & 3 & 2 \\ 2 & 5 & 1 \\ 15 & 3 & 2 \end{bmatrix}_{3\times 3} \begin{bmatrix} 1 \\ 2 \\ x \end{bmatrix}_{3\times 1} = 0$

$\Rightarrow$ $[1+2x+15 \quad 3+5x+3 \quad 2+x+2]_{1\times 3} \begin{bmatrix} 1 \\ 2 \\ x \end{bmatrix}_{3\times 1} = 0$

$\Rightarrow$ $[16+2x \quad 5x+6 \quad x+4]_{1\times 3} \begin{bmatrix} 1 \\ 2 \\ x \end{bmatrix}_{3\times 1} = 0$

$\Rightarrow$ $[16+2x+(5x+6)\cdot 2+(x+4)\cdot x]_{1\times 1} = 0$

$\Rightarrow$ $[16+2x+10x+12+x^2+4x] = 0$

$\Rightarrow$ $[x^2+16x+28] = 0$

$\Rightarrow$ $[x^2+2x+14x+28] = 0$

$\Rightarrow$ $(x+2)(x+14) = 0$

$\therefore$ $x = -2, -14$

Q. 11 Show that $A = \begin{bmatrix} 5 & 3 \\ -1 & -2 \end{bmatrix}$ satisfies the equation $A^2 - 3A - 7I = 0$ and hence find the value of A^{-1}.

Sol. We have, $A = \begin{bmatrix} 5 & 3 \\ -1 & -2 \end{bmatrix}$

$\therefore$ $A^2 = A \cdot A = \begin{bmatrix} 5 & 3 \\ -1 & -2 \end{bmatrix} \cdot \begin{bmatrix} 5 & 3 \\ -1 & -2 \end{bmatrix}$

$$= \begin{bmatrix} 25-3 & 15-6 \\ -5+2 & -3+4 \end{bmatrix} = \begin{bmatrix} 22 & 9 \\ -3 & 1 \end{bmatrix}$$

$$3A = 3\begin{bmatrix} 5 & 3 \\ -1 & -2 \end{bmatrix} = \begin{bmatrix} 15 & 9 \\ -3 & -6 \end{bmatrix}$$

and $$7I = 7\begin{bmatrix} 1 & 0 \\ 0 & 1 \end{bmatrix} = \begin{bmatrix} 7 & 0 \\ 0 & 7 \end{bmatrix}$$

$\therefore$ $$A^2 - 3A - 7I = \begin{bmatrix} 22 & 9 \\ -3 & 1 \end{bmatrix} - \begin{bmatrix} 15 & 9 \\ -3 & -6 \end{bmatrix} - \begin{bmatrix} 7 & 0 \\ 0 & 7 \end{bmatrix}$$

$$= \begin{bmatrix} 22-15-7 & 9-9-0 \\ -3+3-0 & 1+6-7 \end{bmatrix}$$

$$= \begin{bmatrix} 0 & 0 \\ 0 & 0 \end{bmatrix}$$

$$= 0$$ **Hence proved.**

Since, $$A^2 - 3A - 7I = 0$$

$\Rightarrow$ $$A^{-1}[(A^2) - 3A - 7I] = A^{-1}0$$

$\Rightarrow$ $$A^{-1}A \cdot A - 3A^{-1}A - 7A^{-1}I = 0 \quad [\because A^{-1}0 = 0]$$

$\Rightarrow$ $$IA - 3I - 7A^{-1} = 0 \quad [\because A^{-1}A = I]$$

$\Rightarrow$ $$A - 3I - 7A^{-1} = 0 \quad [\because A^{-1}I = A^{-1}]$$

$\Rightarrow$ $$-7A^{-1} = -A + 3I$$

$$= \begin{bmatrix} -5 & -3 \\ 1 & 2 \end{bmatrix} + \begin{bmatrix} 3 & 0 \\ 0 & 3 \end{bmatrix} = \begin{bmatrix} -2 & -3 \\ 1 & 5 \end{bmatrix}$$

$\therefore$ $$A^{-1} = \frac{-1}{7}\begin{bmatrix} -2 & -3 \\ 1 & 5 \end{bmatrix}$$

Q. 12 Find the matrix A satisfying the matrix equation

$$\begin{bmatrix} 2 & 1 \\ 3 & 2 \end{bmatrix} A \begin{bmatrix} -3 & 2 \\ 5 & -3 \end{bmatrix} = \begin{bmatrix} 1 & 0 \\ 0 & 1 \end{bmatrix}.$$

Thinking Process

We know that, if two matrices A and B of order $m \times n$ and $p \times q$ respectively are multiplied, then necessity condition to multiplication of $A \cdot B$ is $n = p$. So, by taking a matrix of correct order we can get the desired elements of the required matrix.

Sol. We have, $$\begin{bmatrix} 2 & 1 \\ 3 & 2 \end{bmatrix}_{2\times 2} A \cdot \begin{bmatrix} -3 & 2 \\ 5 & -3 \end{bmatrix}_{2\times 2} = \begin{bmatrix} 1 & 0 \\ 0 & 1 \end{bmatrix}_{2\times 2}$$

Let $$A = \begin{bmatrix} a & b \\ c & d \end{bmatrix}_{2\times 2}$$

$\therefore$ $$\begin{bmatrix} 2 & 1 \\ 3 & 2 \end{bmatrix}\begin{bmatrix} a & b \\ c & d \end{bmatrix}\begin{bmatrix} -3 & 2 \\ 5 & -3 \end{bmatrix} = \begin{bmatrix} 1 & 0 \\ 0 & 1 \end{bmatrix}$$

$\Rightarrow$ $$\begin{bmatrix} 2a+c & 2b+d \\ 3a+2c & 3b+2d \end{bmatrix}\begin{bmatrix} -3 & 2 \\ 5 & -3 \end{bmatrix} = \begin{bmatrix} 1 & 0 \\ 0 & 1 \end{bmatrix}$$

$\Rightarrow$ $$\begin{bmatrix} -6a-3c+10b+5d & 4a+2c-6b-3d \\ -9a-6c+15b+10d & 6a+4c-9b-6d \end{bmatrix} = \begin{bmatrix} 1 & 0 \\ 0 & 1 \end{bmatrix}$$

$\Rightarrow$ $$-6a-3c+10b+5d = 1 \quad \ldots(\text{i})$$

$$\Rightarrow \quad 4a + 2c - 6b - 3d = 0 \quad \text{...(ii)}$$

$$\Rightarrow \quad -9a - 6c + 15b + 10d = 0 \quad \text{...(iii)}$$

$$\Rightarrow \quad 6a + 4c - 9b - 6d = 1 \quad \text{...(iv)}$$

On adding Eqs. (i) and (iv), we get

$$c + b - d = 2 \Rightarrow d = c + b - 2 \quad \text{...(v)}$$

On adding Eqs. (ii) and (iii), we get

$$-5a - 4c + 9b + 7d = 0 \quad \text{...(vi)}$$

On adding Eqs. (vi) and (iv), we get

$$a + 0 + 0 + d = 1 \Rightarrow d = 1 - a \quad \text{...(vii)}$$

From Eqs. (v) and (vii),

$$c + b - 2 = 1 - a \Rightarrow a + b + c = 3 \quad \text{...(viii)}$$

$$\Rightarrow \quad a = 3 - b - c$$

Now, using the values of a and d in Eq. (iii), we get

$$-9(3 - b - c) - 6c + 15b + 10(-2 + b + c) = 0$$

$$\Rightarrow \quad -27 + 9b + 9c - 6c + 15b - 20 + 10b + 10c = 0$$

$$\Rightarrow \quad 34b + 13c = 47 \quad \text{...(ix)}$$

Now, using the values of a and d in Eq. (ii), we get

$$4(3 - b - c) + 2c - 6b - 3(b + c - 2) = 0$$

$$\Rightarrow \quad 12 - 4b - 4c + 2c - 6b - 3b - 3c + 6 = 0$$

$$\Rightarrow \quad -13b - 5c = -18 \quad \text{...(x)}$$

On multiplying Eq. (ix) by 5 and Eq. (x) by 13, then adding, we get

$$\begin{array}{r} -169b - 65c = -234 \\ \underline{170b + 65c = 235} \\ b = 1 \end{array}$$

$$\Rightarrow \quad -13 \times 1 - 5c = -18 \quad \text{[from Eq. (x)]}$$

$$\Rightarrow \quad -5c = -18 + 13 = -5 \Rightarrow c = 1$$

$$\therefore \quad a = 3 - 1 - 1 = 1 \text{ and } d = 1 - 1 = 0$$

$$\therefore \quad A = \begin{bmatrix} 1 & 1 \\ 1 & 0 \end{bmatrix}$$

Q. 13 Find A, if $\begin{bmatrix} 4 \\ 1 \\ 3 \end{bmatrix} A = \begin{bmatrix} -4 & 8 & 4 \\ -1 & 2 & 1 \\ -3 & 6 & 3 \end{bmatrix}$.

Sol. We have,

$$\begin{bmatrix} 4 \\ 1 \\ 3 \end{bmatrix}_{3 \times 1} A = \begin{bmatrix} -4 & 8 & 4 \\ -1 & 2 & 1 \\ -3 & 6 & 3 \end{bmatrix}_{3 \times 3}$$

Let $\quad A = [x\, y\, z]$

$$\therefore \quad \begin{bmatrix} 4 \\ 1 \\ 3 \end{bmatrix}_{3 \times 1} [x \; y \; z]_{1 \times 3} = \begin{bmatrix} -4 & 8 & 4 \\ -1 & 2 & 1 \\ -3 & 6 & 3 \end{bmatrix}_{3 \times 3}$$

$$\Rightarrow \quad \begin{bmatrix} 4x & 4y & 4z \\ x & y & z \\ 3x & 3y & 3z \end{bmatrix} = \begin{bmatrix} -4 & 8 & 4 \\ -1 & 2 & 1 \\ -3 & 6 & 3 \end{bmatrix}$$

$\Rightarrow \quad 4x = -4 \Rightarrow x = -1,\ 4y = 8$

$\Rightarrow \quad y = 2$ and $4z = 4$

$\Rightarrow \quad z = 1$

$\therefore \quad A = [-1\ 2\ 1]$

Q. 14 If $A\begin{bmatrix} 3 & -4 \\ 1 & 1 \\ 2 & 0 \end{bmatrix}$ and $B = \begin{bmatrix} 2 & 1 & 2 \\ 1 & 2 & 4 \end{bmatrix}$, then verify $(BA)^2 \neq B^2 A^2$.

Sol. We have, $A = \begin{bmatrix} 3 & -4 \\ 1 & 1 \\ 2 & 0 \end{bmatrix}_{3\times2}$ and $B = \begin{bmatrix} 2 & 1 & 2 \\ 1 & 2 & 4 \end{bmatrix}_{2\times3}$

$$\therefore \quad BA = \begin{bmatrix} 2 & 1 & 2 \\ 1 & 2 & 4 \end{bmatrix}_{2\times3} \begin{bmatrix} 3 & -4 \\ 1 & 1 \\ 2 & 0 \end{bmatrix}_{3\times2}$$

$$= \begin{bmatrix} 6+1+4 & -8+1+0 \\ 3+2+8 & -4+2+0 \end{bmatrix} = \begin{bmatrix} 11 & -7 \\ 13 & -2 \end{bmatrix}$$

and $$(BA)\cdot(BA) = \begin{bmatrix} 11 & -7 \\ 13 & -2 \end{bmatrix}\begin{bmatrix} 11 & -7 \\ 13 & -2 \end{bmatrix}$$

$$\Rightarrow \quad (BA)^2 = \begin{bmatrix} 121-91 & -77+14 \\ 143-26 & -91+4 \end{bmatrix} = \begin{bmatrix} 30 & -63 \\ 117 & -87 \end{bmatrix} \quad \text{...(i)}$$

Also, $$B^2 = B\cdot B = \begin{bmatrix} 2 & 1 & 2 \\ 1 & 2 & 4 \end{bmatrix}_{2\times3} \begin{bmatrix} 2 & 1 & 2 \\ 1 & 2 & 4 \end{bmatrix}_{2\times3}$$

So, B^2 is not possible, since the B is not a square matrix.
Hence, $(BA)^2 \neq B^2 A^2$.

Q. 15 If possible, find the value of BA and AB, where

$$A = \begin{bmatrix} 2 & 1 & 2 \\ 1 & 2 & 4 \end{bmatrix} \text{ and } B = \begin{bmatrix} 4 & 1 \\ 2 & 3 \\ 1 & 2 \end{bmatrix}.$$

Sol. We have, $A = \begin{bmatrix} 2 & 1 & 2 \\ 1 & 2 & 4 \end{bmatrix}_{2\times3}$ and $B = \begin{bmatrix} 4 & 1 \\ 2 & 3 \\ 1 & 2 \end{bmatrix}_{3\times2}$

So, AB and BA both are possible.
[since, in both $A\cdot B$ and $B\cdot A$, the number of columns of first is equal to the number of rows of second.]

$$\therefore \quad AB = \begin{bmatrix} 2 & 1 & 2 \\ 1 & 2 & 4 \end{bmatrix}_{2\times3} \cdot \begin{bmatrix} 4 & 1 \\ 2 & 3 \\ 1 & 2 \end{bmatrix}_{3\times2}$$

$$= \begin{bmatrix} 8+2+2 & 2+3+4 \\ 4+4+4 & 1+6+8 \end{bmatrix} = \begin{bmatrix} 12 & 9 \\ 12 & 15 \end{bmatrix}$$

and $$BA = \begin{bmatrix} 4 & 1 \\ 2 & 3 \\ 1 & 2 \end{bmatrix}_{3 \times 2} \begin{bmatrix} 2 & 1 & 2 \\ 1 & 2 & 4 \end{bmatrix}_{2 \times 3}$$

$$= \begin{bmatrix} 4 \times 2 + 1 & 4+2 & 8+4 \\ 4+3 & 2+6 & 4+12 \\ 2+2 & 1+4 & 2+8 \end{bmatrix} = \begin{bmatrix} 9 & 6 & 12 \\ 7 & 8 & 16 \\ 4 & 5 & 10 \end{bmatrix}$$

Q. 16 **Show by an example that for $A \neq 0$, $B \neq 0$ and $AB = 0$.**

Sol. Let $$A = \begin{bmatrix} 0 & -4 \\ 0 & 2 \end{bmatrix} \neq 0 \text{ and } B = \begin{bmatrix} 3 & 5 \\ 0 & 0 \end{bmatrix} \neq 0$$

$\therefore$ $$AB = \begin{bmatrix} 0 & 0 \\ 0 & 0 \end{bmatrix} = 0$$ **Hence proved.**

Q. 17 **Given, $A = \begin{bmatrix} 2 & 4 & 0 \\ 3 & 9 & 6 \end{bmatrix}$ and $B = \begin{bmatrix} 1 & 4 \\ 2 & 8 \\ 1 & 3 \end{bmatrix}$. is $(AB)' = B'A'$?**

Sol. We have, $A = \begin{bmatrix} 2 & 4 & 0 \\ 3 & 9 & 6 \end{bmatrix}_{2\times3}$ and $B = \begin{bmatrix} 1 & 4 \\ 2 & 8 \\ 1 & 3 \end{bmatrix}_{3\times2}$

$\therefore$ $$AB = \begin{bmatrix} 2+8+0 & 8+32+0 \\ 3+18+6 & 12+72+18 \end{bmatrix} = \begin{bmatrix} 10 & 40 \\ 27 & 102 \end{bmatrix}$$

and $$(AB)' = \begin{bmatrix} 10 & 27 \\ 40 & 102 \end{bmatrix} \quad \ldots(i)$$

Also, $$B' = \begin{bmatrix} 1 & 2 & 1 \\ 4 & 8 & 3 \end{bmatrix}_{2\times3} \text{ and } A' = \begin{bmatrix} 2 & 3 \\ 4 & 9 \\ 0 & 6 \end{bmatrix}_{3\times2}$$

$\therefore$ $$B'A' = \begin{bmatrix} 2+8+0 & 3+18+6 \\ 8+32+0 & 12+72+18 \end{bmatrix} = \begin{bmatrix} 10 & 27 \\ 40 & 102 \end{bmatrix} \quad \ldots(ii)$$

Thus, we see that, $(AB)' = B'A'$ [using Eqs. (i) and (ii)]

Q. 18 **Solve for x and y, $x\begin{bmatrix} 2 \\ 1 \end{bmatrix} + y\begin{bmatrix} 3 \\ 5 \end{bmatrix} + \begin{bmatrix} -8 \\ -11 \end{bmatrix} = 0$.**

Sol. We have, $$x\begin{bmatrix} 2 \\ 1 \end{bmatrix} + y\begin{bmatrix} 3 \\ 5 \end{bmatrix} + \begin{bmatrix} -8 \\ -11 \end{bmatrix} = 0$$

$\Rightarrow$ $$\begin{bmatrix} 2x \\ x \end{bmatrix} + \begin{bmatrix} 3 \cdot y \\ 5 \cdot y \end{bmatrix} + \begin{bmatrix} -8 \\ -11 \end{bmatrix} = 0$$

$\Rightarrow$ $$\begin{bmatrix} 2x & 3y & -8 \\ x & 5y & -11 \end{bmatrix} = \begin{bmatrix} 0 \\ 0 \end{bmatrix}$$

$\therefore$ $$2x + 3y - 8 = 0$$

$\Rightarrow$ $$4x + 6y = 16 \quad \ldots(i)$$

and $$x + 5y - 11 = 0$$

$\Rightarrow$ $$4x + 20y = 44 \quad \ldots(ii)$$

On subtracting Eq. (i) from Eq. (ii), we get

$$14y = 28 \Rightarrow y = 2$$

$\therefore$ $$2x + 3\times 2 - 8 = 0$$

$\Rightarrow$ $$2x = 2 \Rightarrow x = 1$$

$\therefore$ $$x = 1 \text{ and } y = 2$$

Q. 19 If X and Y are 2×2 matrices, then solve the following matrix equations for X and Y

$$2X + 3Y = \begin{bmatrix} 2 & 3 \\ 4 & 0 \end{bmatrix}, 3X + 2Y = \begin{bmatrix} -2 & 2 \\ 1 & -5 \end{bmatrix}.$$

Sol. We have,

$$2X + 3Y = \begin{bmatrix} 2 & 3 \\ 4 & 0 \end{bmatrix} \quad \text{...(i)}$$

and $$3X + 2Y = \begin{bmatrix} -2 & 2 \\ 1 & -5 \end{bmatrix} \quad \text{...(ii)}$$

On subtracting Eq. (i) from Eq. (ii), we get

$\therefore$ $$(3X + 2Y) - (2X + 3Y) = \begin{bmatrix} -2-2 & 2-3 \\ 1-4 & -5-0 \end{bmatrix}$$

$$(X - Y) = \begin{bmatrix} -4 & -1 \\ -3 & -5 \end{bmatrix} \quad \text{...(iii)}$$

On adding Eqs. (i) and (ii), we get

$$(5X + 5Y) = \begin{bmatrix} 0 & 5 \\ 5 & -5 \end{bmatrix}$$

$\Rightarrow$ $$(X + Y) = \frac{1}{5}\begin{bmatrix} 0 & 5 \\ 5 & -5 \end{bmatrix} = \begin{bmatrix} 0 & 1 \\ 1 & -1 \end{bmatrix} \quad \text{...(iv)}$$

On adding Eqs. (iii) and (iv), we get

$$(X - Y) + (X + Y) = \begin{bmatrix} -4 & 0 \\ -2 & -6 \end{bmatrix}$$

$\Rightarrow$ $$2X = 2\begin{bmatrix} -2 & 0 \\ -1 & -3 \end{bmatrix}$$

$\therefore$ $$X = \begin{bmatrix} -2 & 0 \\ -1 & -3 \end{bmatrix}$$

From Eq. (iv),

$$\begin{bmatrix} -2 & 0 \\ -1 & -3 \end{bmatrix} + Y = \begin{bmatrix} 0 & 1 \\ 1 & -1 \end{bmatrix}$$

$\therefore$ $$Y = \begin{bmatrix} 2 & 1 \\ 2 & 2 \end{bmatrix} \text{ and } X = \begin{bmatrix} -2 & 0 \\ -1 & -3 \end{bmatrix}$$

Q. 20 **If $A = [3 \ 5]$ and $B = [7 \ 3]$, then find a non-zero matrix C such that $AC = BC$.**

Sol. We have, $A = [3 \ 5]_{1\times 2}$ and $B = [7 \ 3]_{1\times 2}$

Let $C = \begin{bmatrix} x \\ y \end{bmatrix}_{2\times 1}$ is a non-zero matrix of order 2×1.

$$\therefore \quad AC = [3 \ 5]\begin{bmatrix} x \\ y \end{bmatrix} = [3x + 5y]$$

$$\text{and} \quad BC = [7 \ 3]\begin{bmatrix} x \\ y \end{bmatrix} = [7x + 3y]$$

For $AC = BC$,

$$[3x + 5y] = [7x + 3y]$$

On using equality of matrix, we get

$$3x + 5y = 7x + 3y$$

$$\Rightarrow \quad 4x = 2y$$

$$\Rightarrow \quad x = \frac{1}{2}y$$

$$\Rightarrow \quad y = 2x$$

$$\therefore \quad C = \begin{bmatrix} x \\ 2x \end{bmatrix}$$

We see that on taking C of order $2 \times 1, 2 \times 2, 2 \times 3, \ldots$, we get

$$C = \begin{bmatrix} x \\ 2x \end{bmatrix}, \begin{bmatrix} x & x \\ 2x & 2x \end{bmatrix}, \begin{bmatrix} x & x & x \\ 2x & 2x & 2x \end{bmatrix} \ldots$$

In general,

$$C = \begin{bmatrix} k \\ 2k \end{bmatrix}, \begin{bmatrix} k & k \\ 2k & 2k \end{bmatrix} \text{etc...}$$

where, k is any real number.

Q. 21 **Give an example of matrices A, B and C, such that $AB = AC$, where A is non-zero matrix but $B \neq C$.**

Sol. Let $$A = \begin{bmatrix} 1 & 0 \\ 0 & 0 \end{bmatrix}, B = \begin{bmatrix} 2 & 3 \\ 4 & 0 \end{bmatrix} \text{ and } C = \begin{bmatrix} 2 & 3 \\ 4 & 4 \end{bmatrix} \quad [\because B \neq C]$$

$$\therefore \quad AB = \begin{bmatrix} 1 & 0 \\ 0 & 0 \end{bmatrix}\begin{bmatrix} 2 & 3 \\ 4 & 0 \end{bmatrix} = \begin{bmatrix} 2 & 3 \\ 0 & 0 \end{bmatrix} \quad \ldots(i)$$

$$\text{and} \quad AC = \begin{bmatrix} 1 & 0 \\ 0 & 0 \end{bmatrix} \cdot \begin{bmatrix} 2 & 3 \\ 4 & 4 \end{bmatrix} = \begin{bmatrix} 2 & 3 \\ 0 & 0 \end{bmatrix} \quad \ldots(ii)$$

Thus, we see that $AB = AC$ [using Eqs. (i) and (ii)]

where, A is non-zero matrix but $B \neq C$.

Q. 22 If $A=\begin{bmatrix}1 & 2\\-2 & 1\end{bmatrix}$, $B=\begin{bmatrix}2 & 3\\3 & -4\end{bmatrix}$ and $C=\begin{bmatrix}1 & 0\\-1 & 0\end{bmatrix}$, verify

(i) $(AB)\,C=A(BC)$.

(ii) $A\,(B+C)=AB+AC$.

Sol. We have, $A=\begin{bmatrix}1 & 2\\-2 & 1\end{bmatrix}$, $B=\begin{bmatrix}2 & 3\\3 & -4\end{bmatrix}$ and $C=\begin{bmatrix}1 & 0\\-1 & 0\end{bmatrix}$

(i) $(AB)=\begin{bmatrix}1 & 2\\-2 & 1\end{bmatrix}\begin{bmatrix}2 & 3\\3 & -4\end{bmatrix}=\begin{bmatrix}2+6 & 3-8\\-4+3 & -6-4\end{bmatrix}=\begin{bmatrix}8 & -5\\-1 & -10\end{bmatrix}$

and $(AB)C=\begin{bmatrix}8 & -5\\-1 & -10\end{bmatrix}\begin{bmatrix}1 & 0\\-1 & 0\end{bmatrix}$

$=\begin{bmatrix}8+5 & 0\\-1+10 & 0\end{bmatrix}=\begin{bmatrix}13 & 0\\9 & 0\end{bmatrix}$ ...(i)

Again, $(BC)=\begin{bmatrix}2 & 3\\3 & -4\end{bmatrix}\begin{bmatrix}1 & 0\\-1 & 0\end{bmatrix}$

$=\begin{bmatrix}2-3 & 0\\3+4 & 0\end{bmatrix}=\begin{bmatrix}-1 & 0\\7 & 0\end{bmatrix}$

and $A\,(BC)=\begin{bmatrix}1 & 2\\-2 & 1\end{bmatrix}\begin{bmatrix}-1 & 0\\7 & 0\end{bmatrix}$

$=\begin{bmatrix}-1+14 & 0\\+2+7 & 0\end{bmatrix}=\begin{bmatrix}13 & 0\\9 & 0\end{bmatrix}$ ...(ii)

$\therefore$ $(AB)\,C=A(BC)$ [using Eqs. (i) and (ii)]

(ii) $(B+C)=\begin{bmatrix}2 & 3\\3 & -4\end{bmatrix}+\begin{bmatrix}1 & 0\\-1 & 0\end{bmatrix}=\begin{bmatrix}3 & 3\\2 & -4\end{bmatrix}$

and $A\cdot(B+C)=\begin{bmatrix}1 & 2\\-2 & 1\end{bmatrix}\begin{bmatrix}3 & 3\\2 & -4\end{bmatrix}$

$=\begin{bmatrix}3+4 & 3-8\\-6+2 & -6-4\end{bmatrix}=\begin{bmatrix}7 & -5\\-4 & -10\end{bmatrix}$ ...(iii)

Also, $AB=\begin{bmatrix}1 & 2\\-2 & 1\end{bmatrix}\cdot\begin{bmatrix}2 & 3\\3 & -4\end{bmatrix}$

$=\begin{bmatrix}2+6 & 3-8\\-4+3 & -6-4\end{bmatrix}=\begin{bmatrix}8 & -5\\-1 & -10\end{bmatrix}$

and $AC=\begin{bmatrix}1 & 2\\-2 & 1\end{bmatrix}\begin{bmatrix}1 & 0\\-1 & 0\end{bmatrix}=\begin{bmatrix}1-2 & 0\\-2-1 & 0\end{bmatrix}=\begin{bmatrix}-1 & 0\\-3 & 0\end{bmatrix}$

$\therefore$ $AB+AC=\begin{bmatrix}8 & -5\\-1 & -10\end{bmatrix}+\begin{bmatrix}-1 & 0\\-3 & 0\end{bmatrix}$

$\Rightarrow$ $AB+AC=\begin{bmatrix}7 & -5\\-4 & -10\end{bmatrix}$ ...(iv)

From Eqs. (iii) and (iv),

$A\,(B+C)=AB+AC$

Q. 23 If $P = \begin{bmatrix} x & 0 & 0 \\ 0 & y & 0 \\ 0 & 0 & z \end{bmatrix}$ and $Q = \begin{bmatrix} a & 0 & 0 \\ 0 & b & 0 \\ 0 & 0 & c \end{bmatrix}$, then prove that

$$PQ = \begin{bmatrix} xa & 0 & 0 \\ 0 & yb & 0 \\ 0 & 0 & zc \end{bmatrix} = QP.$$

Sol. $PQ = \begin{bmatrix} x & 0 & 0 \\ 0 & y & 0 \\ 0 & 0 & z \end{bmatrix} \begin{bmatrix} a & 0 & 0 \\ 0 & b & 0 \\ 0 & 0 & c \end{bmatrix} = \begin{bmatrix} xa & 0 & 0 \\ 0 & yb & 0 \\ 0 & 0 & zc \end{bmatrix}$ ...(i)

and $QP = \begin{bmatrix} a & 0 & 0 \\ 0 & b & 0 \\ 0 & 0 & c \end{bmatrix} \begin{bmatrix} x & 0 & 0 \\ 0 & y & 0 \\ 0 & 0 & z \end{bmatrix} = \begin{bmatrix} ax & 0 & 0 \\ 0 & by & 0 \\ 0 & 0 & zc \end{bmatrix}$ ...(ii)

Thus, we see that, $PQ = QP$ [using Eqs. (i) and (ii)]

Hence proved.

Q. 24 If $\begin{bmatrix} 2 & 1 & 3 \end{bmatrix} \begin{bmatrix} -1 & 0 & -1 \\ -1 & 1 & 0 \\ 0 & 1 & 1 \end{bmatrix} \begin{bmatrix} 1 \\ 0 \\ -1 \end{bmatrix} = A$, then find the value of A.

Sol. We have, $[2\ 1\ 3] \begin{bmatrix} -1 & 0 & -1 \\ -1 & 1 & 0 \\ 0 & 1 & 1 \end{bmatrix} \begin{bmatrix} 1 \\ 0 \\ -1 \end{bmatrix} = A$

$\therefore$ $[2\,1\,3] \begin{bmatrix} -1 & 0 & -1 \\ -1 & 1 & 0 \\ 0 & 1 & 1 \end{bmatrix} = [-2-1+0 \quad 0+1+3 \quad -2+0+3]$

$= [-3 \quad 4 \quad 1]$

Now, $[-3\,4\,1] \begin{bmatrix} 1 \\ 0 \\ -1 \end{bmatrix} = A$

$\therefore$ $A = [-3\,4\,1] \begin{bmatrix} 1 \\ 0 \\ -1 \end{bmatrix}$

$= [-3 + 0 - 1] = [-4]$

Q. 25 If $A = [2\ 1]$, $B = \begin{bmatrix} 5 & 3 & 4 \\ 8 & 7 & 6 \end{bmatrix}$ and $C = \begin{bmatrix} -1 & 2 & 1 \\ 1 & 0 & 2 \end{bmatrix}$, then verify that $A(B + C) = (AB + AC)$.

Sol. We have to verify that, $A(B + C) = AB + AC$

We have, $A = [2 \quad 1]$, $B = \begin{bmatrix} 5 & 3 & 4 \\ 8 & 7 & 6 \end{bmatrix}$ and $C = \begin{bmatrix} -1 & 2 & 1 \\ 1 & 0 & 2 \end{bmatrix}$

$$\therefore \quad A(B+C) = [2\ \ 1]\begin{bmatrix} 5-1 & 3+2 & 4+1 \\ 8+1 & 7+0 & 6+2 \end{bmatrix}$$

$$= [2\ 1]\begin{bmatrix} 4 & 5 & 5 \\ 9 & 7 & 8 \end{bmatrix}$$

$$= [8+9\ \ 10+7\ \ 10+8]$$

$$= [17\ 17\ 18] \quad \text{...(i)}$$

Also,

$$AB = [2\ 1]\begin{bmatrix} 5 & 3 & 4 \\ 8 & 7 & 6 \end{bmatrix}$$

$$= [10+8\ \ 6+7\ \ 8+6] = [18\ \ 13\ \ 14]$$

and

$$AC = [2\ 1]\begin{bmatrix} -1 & 2 & 1 \\ 1 & 0 & 2 \end{bmatrix}$$

$$= [-2+1\ \ 4+0\ \ 2+2] = [-1\ \ 4\ \ 4]$$

$$\therefore \quad AB + AC = [18\ \ 13\ \ 14] + [-1\ \ 4\ \ 4]$$

$$= [17\ \ 17\ \ 18] \quad \text{...(ii)}$$

$$\therefore \quad A(B+C) = (AB + AC) \quad \text{[using Eqs. (i) and (ii)]}$$

Hence proved.

Q. 26 If $A = \begin{bmatrix} 1 & 0 & -1 \\ 2 & 1 & 3 \\ 0 & 1 & 1 \end{bmatrix}$, then verify that $A^2 + A = (A + I)$, where I is 3×3 unit matrix.

Sol. We have,

$$A = \begin{bmatrix} 1 & 0 & -1 \\ 2 & 1 & 3 \\ 0 & 1 & 1 \end{bmatrix}$$

$$\therefore \quad A^2 = A \cdot A$$

$$= \begin{bmatrix} 1 & 0 & -1 \\ 2 & 1 & 3 \\ 0 & 1 & 1 \end{bmatrix}\begin{bmatrix} 1 & 0 & -1 \\ 2 & 1 & 3 \\ 0 & 1 & 1 \end{bmatrix} = \begin{bmatrix} 1 & -1 & -2 \\ 4 & 4 & 4 \\ 2 & 2 & 4 \end{bmatrix}$$

$$\therefore \quad A^2 + A = \begin{bmatrix} 1 & -1 & -2 \\ 4 & 4 & 4 \\ 2 & 2 & 4 \end{bmatrix} + \begin{bmatrix} 1 & 0 & -1 \\ 2 & 1 & 3 \\ 0 & 1 & 1 \end{bmatrix}$$

$$= \begin{bmatrix} 2 & -1 & -3 \\ 6 & 5 & 7 \\ 2 & 3 & 5 \end{bmatrix} \quad \text{...(i)}$$

Now,

$$A + I = \begin{bmatrix} 1 & 0 & -1 \\ 2 & 1 & 3 \\ 0 & 1 & 1 \end{bmatrix} + \begin{bmatrix} 1 & 0 & 0 \\ 0 & 1 & 0 \\ 0 & 0 & 1 \end{bmatrix} = \begin{bmatrix} 2 & 0 & -1 \\ 2 & 2 & 3 \\ 0 & 1 & 2 \end{bmatrix}$$

and

$$A(A + I) = \begin{bmatrix} 1 & 0 & -1 \\ 2 & 1 & 3 \\ 0 & 1 & 1 \end{bmatrix} \cdot \begin{bmatrix} 2 & 0 & -1 \\ 2 & 2 & 3 \\ 0 & 1 & 2 \end{bmatrix} = \begin{bmatrix} 2 & -1 & -3 \\ 6 & 5 & 7 \\ 2 & 3 & 5 \end{bmatrix} \quad \text{...(ii)}$$

Thus, we see that $A^2 + A = A(A + I)$ [using Eqs. (i) and (ii)]

Q. 27 If $A = \begin{bmatrix} 0 & -1 & 2 \\ 4 & 3 & -4 \end{bmatrix}$ and $B = \begin{bmatrix} 4 & 0 \\ 1 & 3 \\ 2 & 6 \end{bmatrix}$, then verify that

(i) $(A')' = A$

(ii) $(AB)' = B'A'$

(iii) $(kA)' = (kA')$.

Sol. We have, $A = \begin{bmatrix} 0 & -1 & 2 \\ 4 & 3 & -4 \end{bmatrix}$ and $B = \begin{bmatrix} 4 & 0 \\ 1 & 3 \\ 2 & 6 \end{bmatrix}$

(i) We have to verify that, $A' = A$

$$\therefore \quad A' = \begin{bmatrix} 0 & 4 \\ -1 & 3 \\ 2 & -4 \end{bmatrix}$$

and $$A' = \begin{bmatrix} 0 & -1 & 2 \\ 4 & 3 & -4 \end{bmatrix} = A$$ **Hence proved.**

(ii) We have to verify that, $AB' = B'A'$

$$\therefore \quad AB = \begin{bmatrix} 3 & 9 \\ 11 & -15 \end{bmatrix}$$

$$\Rightarrow \quad (AB)' = \begin{bmatrix} 3 & 11 \\ 9 & -15 \end{bmatrix}$$

and $$B'A' = \begin{bmatrix} 4 & 1 & 2 \\ 0 & 3 & 6 \end{bmatrix} \begin{bmatrix} 0 & 4 \\ -1 & 3 \\ 2 & -4 \end{bmatrix} = \begin{bmatrix} 3 & 11 \\ 9 & -15 \end{bmatrix}$$

$$= (AB)'$$ **Hence proved.**

(iii) We have to verify that, $(kA)' = (kA')$

Now, $$(kA) = \begin{bmatrix} 0 & -k & 2k \\ 4k & 3k & -4k \end{bmatrix}$$

and $$(kA)' = \begin{bmatrix} 0 & 4k \\ -k & 3k \\ 2k & -4k \end{bmatrix}$$

Also, $$kA' = \begin{bmatrix} 0 & 4k \\ -k & 3k \\ 2k & -4k \end{bmatrix}$$

$$= (kA)'$$ **Hence proved.**

Q. 28 If $A=\begin{bmatrix}1 & 2\\4 & 1\\5 & 6\end{bmatrix}$ and $B=\begin{bmatrix}1 & 2\\6 & 4\\7 & 3\end{bmatrix}$, then verify that

(i) $(2A+B)'=2AA+B'$.

(ii) $(A-B)'=A'-B'$.

Sol. We have, $A=\begin{bmatrix}1 & 2\\4 & 1\\5 & 6\end{bmatrix}$ and $B=\begin{bmatrix}1 & 2\\6 & 4\\7 & 3\end{bmatrix}$

(i) $\therefore$ $(2A+B)=\begin{bmatrix}2 & 4\\8 & 2\\10 & 12\end{bmatrix}+\begin{bmatrix}1 & 2\\6 & 4\\7 & 3\end{bmatrix}=\begin{bmatrix}3 & 6\\14 & 6\\17 & 15\end{bmatrix}$

and $(2A+B)'=\begin{bmatrix}3 & 14 & 17\\6 & 6 & 15\end{bmatrix}$

Also, $2A'+B'=2\begin{bmatrix}1 & 4 & 5\\2 & 1 & 6\end{bmatrix}+\begin{bmatrix}1 & 6 & 7\\2 & 4 & 3\end{bmatrix}$

$=\begin{bmatrix}3 & 14 & 17\\6 & 6 & 15\end{bmatrix}=(2A+B)'$ **Hence proved.**

(ii) $(A-B)=\begin{bmatrix}1 & 2\\4 & 1\\5 & 6\end{bmatrix}-\begin{bmatrix}1 & 2\\6 & 4\\7 & 3\end{bmatrix}=\begin{bmatrix}0 & 0\\-2 & -3\\-2 & 3\end{bmatrix}$

and $(A-B)'=\begin{bmatrix}0 & -2 & -2\\0 & -3 & 3\end{bmatrix}$

Also, $A'-B'=\begin{bmatrix}1 & 4 & 5\\2 & 1 & 6\end{bmatrix}-\begin{bmatrix}1 & 6 & 7\\2 & 4 & 3\end{bmatrix}$

$=\begin{bmatrix}0 & -2 & -2\\0 & -3 & 3\end{bmatrix}$

$=(A-B)'$ **Hence proved.**

Q. 29 Show that $A'A$ and AA' are both symmetric matrices for any matrix A.

Thinking Process

We know that, for a matrix A to be symmetric matrix, $A'=A$. Also by using the result $(AB)'=BA'$, we can prove that $A'A$ and AA' are both symmetric matrices for any matrix A.

Sol. Let $P=A'A$

$\therefore$ $P'=(AA')'$

$=A'(A')'$ $[\because (AB')'=B'A']$

$=A'A=P$

So, $A'A$ is symmetric matrix for any matrix A.

Similarly, let $Q=AA'$

$\therefore$ $Q'=(AA')'=(A')'(A)'$

$=A(A')'=Q$

So, AA' is symmetric matrix for any matrix A.

Q. 30 Let A and B be square matrices of the order 3×3. Is $(AB)^2 = A^2B^2$? Give reasons.

Sol. Since, A and B are square matrices of order 3×3.

$$\therefore \quad AB^2 = AB \cdot AB$$
$$= ABAB$$
$$= AABB \quad [\because AB = BA]$$
$$= A^2B^2$$

So, $AB^2 = A^2B^2$ is true when $AB = BA$.

Q. 31 Show that, if A and B are square matrices such that $AB = BA$, then $(A+B)^2 = A^2 + 2AB + B^2$.

Sol. Since, A and B are square matrices such that $AB = BA$.

$$\therefore \quad (A+B)^2 = (A+B)\cdot(A+B)$$
$$= A^2 + AB + BA + B^2$$
$$= A^2 + AB + AB + B^2 \quad [\because AB = BA]$$
$$= A^2 + 2AB + B^2$$

Hence proved.

Q. 32 If $A = \begin{bmatrix} 1 & 2 \\ -1 & 3 \end{bmatrix}$, $B = \begin{bmatrix} 4 & 0 \\ 1 & 5 \end{bmatrix}$, $C = \begin{bmatrix} 2 & 0 \\ 1 & -2 \end{bmatrix}$, $a = 4$, and $b = -2$, then show that

(i) $A + (B + C) = (A + B) + C$

(ii) $A\,(BC) = (AB)\,C$

(iii) $(a + b)B = aB + bB$

(iv) $a\,(C - A) = aC - aA$

(v) $(A^T)^T = A$

(vi) $(bA)^T = b\,A^T$

(vii) $(AB)^T = B^T A^T$

(viii) $(A - B)C = AC - BC$

(ix) $(A - B)^T = A^T - B^T$

Sol. We have,

$$A = \begin{bmatrix} 1 & 2 \\ -1 & 3 \end{bmatrix}, B = \begin{bmatrix} 4 & 0 \\ 1 & 5 \end{bmatrix}$$
$$C = \begin{bmatrix} 2 & 0 \\ 1 & -2 \end{bmatrix} \text{ and } a = 4,\ b = -2$$

(i) $A + (B + C) = \begin{bmatrix} 1 & 2 \\ -1 & 3 \end{bmatrix} + \begin{bmatrix} 6 & 0 \\ 2 & 3 \end{bmatrix} = \begin{bmatrix} 7 & 2 \\ 1 & 6 \end{bmatrix}$

and $\quad (A + B) + C = \begin{bmatrix} 5 & 2 \\ 0 & 8 \end{bmatrix} + \begin{bmatrix} 2 & 0 \\ 1 & -2 \end{bmatrix}$

$$= \begin{bmatrix} 7 & 2 \\ 1 & 6 \end{bmatrix} = A + (B + C)$$

Hence proved.

(ii) $(BC) = \begin{bmatrix} 4 & 0 \\ 1 & 5 \end{bmatrix}\begin{bmatrix} 2 & 0 \\ 1 & -2 \end{bmatrix} = \begin{bmatrix} 8 & 0 \\ 7 & -10 \end{bmatrix}$

and $A\,(BC) = \begin{bmatrix} 1 & 2 \\ -1 & 3 \end{bmatrix}\begin{bmatrix} 8 & 0 \\ 7 & -10 \end{bmatrix}$

$= \begin{bmatrix} 8+14 & 0-20 \\ -8+21 & 0-30 \end{bmatrix} = \begin{bmatrix} 22 & -20 \\ 13 & -30 \end{bmatrix}$

Also, $(AB) = \begin{bmatrix} 1 & 2 \\ -1 & 3 \end{bmatrix} \cdot \begin{bmatrix} 4 & 0 \\ 1 & 5 \end{bmatrix} = \begin{bmatrix} 6 & 10 \\ -1 & 15 \end{bmatrix}$

$(AB)\,C = \begin{bmatrix} 6 & 10 \\ -1 & 15 \end{bmatrix}\begin{bmatrix} 2 & 0 \\ 1 & -2 \end{bmatrix}$

$= \begin{bmatrix} 22 & -20 \\ 13 & -30 \end{bmatrix} = A(BC)$ **Hence proved.**

(iii) $(a+b)\,B = (4-2)\begin{bmatrix} 4 & 0 \\ 1 & 5 \end{bmatrix}$ $[\because a = 4, b = -2]$

$= \begin{bmatrix} 8 & 0 \\ 2 & 10 \end{bmatrix}$

and $aB + bB = 4B - 2B$

$= \begin{bmatrix} 16 & 0 \\ 4 & 20 \end{bmatrix} - \begin{bmatrix} 8 & 0 \\ 2 & 10 \end{bmatrix}$

$= \begin{bmatrix} 8 & 0 \\ 2 & 10 \end{bmatrix}$

$= (a+b)B$ **Hence proved.**

(iv) $(C - A) = \begin{bmatrix} 2-1 & 0-2 \\ 1+1 & -2-3 \end{bmatrix} = \begin{bmatrix} 1 & -2 \\ 2 & -5 \end{bmatrix}$

and $a(C - A) = \begin{bmatrix} 4 & -8 \\ 8 & -20 \end{bmatrix}$ $[\because a = 4]$

Also, $aC - aA = \begin{bmatrix} 8 & 0 \\ 4 & -8 \end{bmatrix} - \begin{bmatrix} 4 & 8 \\ -4 & 12 \end{bmatrix} = \begin{bmatrix} 4 & -8 \\ 8 & -20 \end{bmatrix}$

$= a(C - A)$ **Hence proved.**

(v) $A^T = \begin{bmatrix} 1 & 2 \\ -1 & 3 \end{bmatrix}^T = \begin{bmatrix} 1 & -1 \\ 2 & 3 \end{bmatrix}$

Now, $(A^T)^T = \begin{bmatrix} 1 & 2 \\ -1 & 3 \end{bmatrix}^T$

$= A$ **Hence proved.**

(vi) $(bA)^T = \begin{bmatrix} -2 & -4 \\ 2 & -6 \end{bmatrix}^T$ $[\because b = -2]$

$= \begin{bmatrix} -2 & 2 \\ -4 & -6 \end{bmatrix}$

and $A^T = \begin{bmatrix} 1 & -1 \\ 2 & 3 \end{bmatrix}$

$\therefore$ $bA^T = \begin{bmatrix} -2 & 2 \\ -4 & -6 \end{bmatrix} = (bA)^T$ **Hence proved.**

(vii) $AB = \begin{bmatrix} 1 & 2 \\ -1 & 3 \end{bmatrix}\begin{bmatrix} 4 & 0 \\ 1 & 5 \end{bmatrix} = \begin{bmatrix} 4+2 & 0+10 \\ -4+3 & 0+15 \end{bmatrix} = \begin{bmatrix} 6 & 10 \\ -1 & 15 \end{bmatrix}$

$\therefore \quad (AB)^T = \begin{bmatrix} 6 & -1 \\ 10 & 15 \end{bmatrix}$

Now, $B^T A^T = \begin{bmatrix} 4 & 1 \\ 0 & 5 \end{bmatrix}\begin{bmatrix} 1 & -1 \\ 2 & 3 \end{bmatrix} = \begin{bmatrix} 6 & -1 \\ 10 & 15 \end{bmatrix}$

$= (AB)^T$ **Hence proved.**

(viii) $(A-B) = \begin{bmatrix} 1-4 & 2-0 \\ -1-1 & 3-5 \end{bmatrix} = \begin{bmatrix} -3 & 2 \\ -2 & -2 \end{bmatrix}$

$(A-B)\ C = \begin{bmatrix} -3 & 2 \\ -2 & -2 \end{bmatrix}\begin{bmatrix} 2 & 0 \\ 1 & -2 \end{bmatrix} = \begin{bmatrix} -4 & -4 \\ -6 & 4 \end{bmatrix}$ ...(i)

Now, $AC = \begin{bmatrix} 1 & 2 \\ -1 & 3 \end{bmatrix}\begin{bmatrix} 2 & 0 \\ 1 & -2 \end{bmatrix} = \begin{bmatrix} 4 & -4 \\ 1 & -6 \end{bmatrix}$ ...(ii)

and $BC = \begin{bmatrix} 4 & 0 \\ 1 & 5 \end{bmatrix}\begin{bmatrix} 2 & 0 \\ 1 & -2 \end{bmatrix} = \begin{bmatrix} 8 & 0 \\ 7 & -10 \end{bmatrix}$ ...(iii)

$\therefore \quad AC - BC = \begin{bmatrix} 4-8 & -4-0 \\ 1-7 & -6+10 \end{bmatrix}$ [using Eqs. (ii) and (iii)]

$= \begin{bmatrix} -4 & -4 \\ -6 & 4 \end{bmatrix}$

$= (A-B)C$ [using Eq. (i)] **Hence proved.**

(ix) $(A-B)^T = \begin{bmatrix} 1-4 & 2-0 \\ -1-1 & 3-5 \end{bmatrix}^T$

$= \begin{bmatrix} -3 & 2 \\ -2 & -2 \end{bmatrix}^T = \begin{bmatrix} -3 & -2 \\ 2 & -2 \end{bmatrix}$

$A^T - B^T = \begin{bmatrix} 1 & -1 \\ 2 & 3 \end{bmatrix} - \begin{bmatrix} 4 & 1 \\ 0 & 5 \end{bmatrix}$

$= \begin{bmatrix} -3 & -2 \\ 2 & -2 \end{bmatrix} = (A-B)^T$ **Hence proved.**

Q. 33 If $A = \begin{bmatrix} \cos q & \sin q \\ -\sin q & \cos q \end{bmatrix}$, then show that $A^2 = \begin{bmatrix} \cos 2q & \sin 2q \\ -\sin 2q & \cos 2q \end{bmatrix}$.

Sol. We have, $A = \begin{bmatrix} \cos q & \sin q \\ -\sin q & \cos q \end{bmatrix}$

$\therefore \quad A^2 = A \cdot A = \begin{bmatrix} \cos q & \sin q \\ -\sin q & \cos q \end{bmatrix} \cdot \begin{bmatrix} \cos q & \sin q \\ -\sin q & \cos q \end{bmatrix}$

$= \begin{bmatrix} \cos^2 q - \sin^2 q & \cos q \cdot \sin q + \sin q \cos q \\ -\sin q \cos q - \cos q \sin q & -\sin^2 q + \cos^2 q \end{bmatrix}$

$= \begin{bmatrix} \cos 2q & 2\sin q \cos q \\ -2\sin q \cos q & \cos 2q \end{bmatrix}$ $[\because \cos^2\theta - \sin^2\theta = \cos 2\theta]$

$= \begin{bmatrix} \cos 2q & \sin 2q \\ -\sin 2q & \cos 2q \end{bmatrix}$ $[\because \sin 2\theta = 2\sin\theta \cdot \cos\theta]$ **Hence proved.**

Q. 34 If $A=\begin{bmatrix}0 & -x\\ x & 0\end{bmatrix}$, $B=\begin{bmatrix}0 & 1\\ 1 & 0\end{bmatrix}$ and $x^2=-1$, then show that $(A+B)^2=A^2+B^2$.

Sol. We have, $A=\begin{bmatrix}0 & -x\\ x & 0\end{bmatrix}$, $B=\begin{bmatrix}0 & 1\\ 1 & 0\end{bmatrix}$ and $x^2=-1$

$\therefore$ $(A+B)=\begin{bmatrix}0 & -x+1\\ x+1 & 0\end{bmatrix}$

and $(A+B)^2=\begin{bmatrix}0 & -x+1\\ x+1 & 0\end{bmatrix}\begin{bmatrix}0 & -x+1\\ x+1 & 0\end{bmatrix}$

$=\begin{bmatrix}1-x^2 & 0\\ 0 & 1-x^2\end{bmatrix}$ ...(i)

Also, $A^2=A\cdot A=\begin{bmatrix}0 & -x\\ x & 0\end{bmatrix}\begin{bmatrix}0 & -x\\ x & 0\end{bmatrix}=\begin{bmatrix}-x^2 & 0\\ 0 & -x^2\end{bmatrix}$

and $B^2=B\cdot B=\begin{bmatrix}0 & 1\\ 1 & 0\end{bmatrix}\begin{bmatrix}0 & 1\\ 1 & 0\end{bmatrix}=\begin{bmatrix}1 & 0\\ 0 & 1\end{bmatrix}$

Now, $A^2+B^2=\begin{bmatrix}-x^2+1 & 0\\ 0 & -x^2+1\end{bmatrix}=\begin{bmatrix}1-x^2 & 0\\ 0 & 1-x^2\end{bmatrix}$ [using Eq. (i)]

$=(A+B)^2$ **Hence proved.**

Q. 35 Verify that $A^2=I$, when $A=\begin{bmatrix}0 & 1 & -1\\ 4 & -3 & 4\\ 3 & -3 & 4\end{bmatrix}$.

Sol. We have, $A=\begin{bmatrix}0 & 1 & -1\\ 4 & -3 & 4\\ 3 & -3 & 4\end{bmatrix}$

$\therefore$ $A^2=\begin{bmatrix}0 & 1 & -1\\ 4 & -3 & 4\\ 3 & -3 & 4\end{bmatrix}\cdot\begin{bmatrix}0 & 1 & -1\\ 4 & -3 & 4\\ 3 & -3 & 4\end{bmatrix}$ $[\because A^2=A\cdot A]$

$=\begin{bmatrix}1 & 0 & 0\\ 0 & 1 & 0\\ 0 & 0 & 1\end{bmatrix}=I$ **Hence proved.**

Q. 36 Prove by mathematical induction that $(A')^n=(A^n)'$ where $n\in N$ for any square matrix A.

Sol. Let $P(n): (A')^n=(A^n)'$

$\therefore$ $P(1): (A')^1=(A)'$

$\Rightarrow$ $A'=A' \Rightarrow P(1)$ is true.

Now, $P(k): (A')^k=(A^k)'$,

where $k\in N$

and $P(k+1): (A')^{k+1}=(A^{k+1})'$

where $P(k+1)$ is true whenever $P(k)$ is true.

$$\therefore \quad P(k+1): (A')^k . (A')^1 = [A^{k+1}]'$$
$$(A^k)'. (A)' = [A^{k+1}]'$$
$$(A \cdot A^k)' = [A^{k+1}]' \qquad [\because (A')^k = (A^k)' \text{ and } (AB) = B'A']$$
$$(A^{k+1})' = [A^{k+1}]'$$

Hence proved.

Q. 37 Find inverse, by elementary row operations (if possible), of the following matrices.

(i) $\begin{bmatrix} 1 & 3 \\ -5 & 7 \end{bmatrix}$ (ii) $\begin{bmatrix} 1 & -3 \\ -2 & 6 \end{bmatrix}$

Thinking Process

To find the inverse of a matrix A, we know that A = IA is used for elementary row operations. So, with the help of this method we can get the desired result.

Sol. (i) Let $A = \begin{bmatrix} 1 & 3 \\ -5 & 7 \end{bmatrix}$

In order to use elementary row operations we may write $A = IA$.

$$\therefore \quad \begin{bmatrix} 1 & 3 \\ -5 & 7 \end{bmatrix} = \begin{bmatrix} 1 & 0 \\ 0 & 1 \end{bmatrix} A$$

$$\Rightarrow \quad \begin{bmatrix} 1 & 3 \\ 0 & 22 \end{bmatrix} = \begin{bmatrix} 1 & 0 \\ 5 & 1 \end{bmatrix} A \qquad [\because R_2 \to R_2 + 5R_1]$$

$$\Rightarrow \quad \begin{bmatrix} 1 & 3 \\ 0 & 1 \end{bmatrix} = \begin{bmatrix} 1 & 0 \\ 5/22 & 1/22 \end{bmatrix} A \qquad \left[\because R_2 \to \frac{1}{22} R_2\right]$$

$$\Rightarrow \quad \begin{bmatrix} 1 & 0 \\ 0 & 1 \end{bmatrix} = \begin{bmatrix} 7/22 & -3/22 \\ 5/22 & 1/22 \end{bmatrix} A \qquad [\because R_1 \to R_1 - 3R_2]$$

$$\Rightarrow \quad \begin{bmatrix} 1 & 0 \\ 0 & 1 \end{bmatrix} = \frac{1}{22} \begin{bmatrix} 7 & -3 \\ 5 & 1 \end{bmatrix} A$$

$\Rightarrow I = BA$, where B is the inverse of A.

$$\therefore \quad B = \frac{1}{22} \begin{bmatrix} 7 & -3 \\ 5 & -1 \end{bmatrix}$$

(ii) Let $A = \begin{bmatrix} 1 & -3 \\ -2 & 6 \end{bmatrix}$

In order to use elementary row operations, we write $A = IA$

$$\Rightarrow \quad \begin{bmatrix} 1 & -3 \\ -2 & 6 \end{bmatrix} = \begin{bmatrix} 1 & 0 \\ 0 & 1 \end{bmatrix} A$$

$$\Rightarrow \quad \begin{bmatrix} 1 & -3 \\ 0 & 0 \end{bmatrix} = \begin{bmatrix} 1 & 0 \\ 2 & 1 \end{bmatrix} A \qquad [\because R_2 \to R_2 + 2R_1]$$

Since, we obtain all zeroes in a row of the matrix A on LHS, so A^{-1} does not exist.

Q. 38 If $\begin{bmatrix} xy & 4 \\ z+6 & x+y \end{bmatrix} = \begin{bmatrix} 8 & w \\ 0 & 6 \end{bmatrix}$, then find the values of x, y, z and w.

Sol. We have, $\begin{bmatrix} xy & 4 \\ z+6 & x+y \end{bmatrix} = \begin{bmatrix} 8 & w \\ 0 & 6 \end{bmatrix}$

By equality of matrix, $x + y = 6$ and $xy = 8$

$\Rightarrow$ $x = 6 - y$ and $(6 - y) \cdot y = 8$

$\Rightarrow$ $y^2 - 6y + 8 = 0$

$\Rightarrow$ $y^2 - 4y - 2y + 8 = 0$

$\Rightarrow$ $(y - 2)(y - 4) = 0$

$\Rightarrow$ $y = 2$ or $y = 4$

$\therefore$ $x = 6 - 2 = 4$

or $x = 6 - 4 = 2$ $[\because x = 6 - y]$

Also, $z + 6 = 0$

$\Rightarrow$ $z = -6$ and $w = 4$

$\therefore$ $x = 2, y = 4$ or $x = 4, y = 2, z = -6$ and $w = 4$

Q. 39 If $A = \begin{bmatrix} 1 & 5 \\ 7 & 12 \end{bmatrix}$ and $B = \begin{bmatrix} 9 & 1 \\ 7 & 8 \end{bmatrix}$, then find a matrix C such that $3A + 5B + 2C$ is a null matrix.

Sol. We have, $A = \begin{bmatrix} 1 & 5 \\ 7 & 12 \end{bmatrix}$ and $B = \begin{bmatrix} 9 & 1 \\ 7 & 8 \end{bmatrix}$

Let $C = \begin{bmatrix} a & b \\ C & d \end{bmatrix}$

$\therefore$ $3A + 5B + 2C = 0$

$\Rightarrow$ $\begin{bmatrix} 3 & 15 \\ 21 & 36 \end{bmatrix} + \begin{bmatrix} 45 & 5 \\ 35 & 40 \end{bmatrix} + \begin{bmatrix} 2a & 2b \\ 2c & 2d \end{bmatrix} = \begin{bmatrix} 0 & 0 \\ 0 & 0 \end{bmatrix}$

$\Rightarrow$ $\begin{bmatrix} 48 + 2a & 20 + 2b \\ 56 + 2c & 76 + 2d \end{bmatrix} = \begin{bmatrix} 0 & 0 \\ 0 & 0 \end{bmatrix}$

$\Rightarrow$ $2a + 48 = 0 \Rightarrow a = -24$

Also, $20 + 2b = 0 \Rightarrow b = -10$

$56 + 2c = 0 \Rightarrow c = -28$

and $76 + 2d = 0 \Rightarrow d = -38$

$\therefore$ $C = \begin{bmatrix} -24 & -10 \\ -28 & -38 \end{bmatrix}$

Q. 40 If $A = \begin{bmatrix} 3 & -5 \\ -4 & 2 \end{bmatrix}$, then find $A^2 - 5A - 14I$. Hence, obtain A^3.

Sol. We have, $A = \begin{bmatrix} 3 & -5 \\ -4 & 2 \end{bmatrix}$ ...(i)

$\therefore$ $A^2 = A \cdot A = \begin{bmatrix} 3 & -5 \\ -4 & 2 \end{bmatrix} \begin{bmatrix} 3 & -5 \\ -4 & 2 \end{bmatrix}$

$= \begin{bmatrix} 29 & -25 \\ -20 & 24 \end{bmatrix}$ ...(ii)

$$\therefore \quad A^2 - 5A - 14I = \begin{bmatrix} 29 & -25 \\ -20 & 24 \end{bmatrix} - \begin{bmatrix} 15 & -25 \\ -20 & 10 \end{bmatrix} - \begin{bmatrix} 14 & 0 \\ 0 & 14 \end{bmatrix}$$

$$= \begin{bmatrix} 0 & 0 \\ 0 & 0 \end{bmatrix}$$

Now, $A^2 - 5A - 14I = 0$

$\Rightarrow \quad A \cdot A^2 - 5A \cdot A - 14AI = 0$

$\Rightarrow \quad A^3 - 5A^2 - 14A = 0$ $\quad [\because AI = A]$

$\Rightarrow \quad A^3 = 5A^2 = 14A$

$$= 5\begin{bmatrix} 29 & -25 \\ -20 & 24 \end{bmatrix} + 14\begin{bmatrix} 3 & -5 \\ -4 & 2 \end{bmatrix} \quad \text{[using Eqs. (i) and (ii)]}$$

$$= \begin{bmatrix} 145 & -125 \\ -100 & 120 \end{bmatrix} + \begin{bmatrix} 42 & -70 \\ -56 & 28 \end{bmatrix}$$

$$= \begin{bmatrix} 187 & -195 \\ -156 & 148 \end{bmatrix}$$

Q. 41 Find the values of a, b, c and d, if

$$3\begin{bmatrix} a & b \\ c & d \end{bmatrix} = \begin{bmatrix} a & 6 \\ -1 & 2d \end{bmatrix} + \begin{bmatrix} 4 & a+b \\ c+d & 3 \end{bmatrix} z.$$

Sol. We have,

$$3\begin{bmatrix} a & b \\ c & d \end{bmatrix} = \begin{bmatrix} a & 6 \\ -1 & 2d \end{bmatrix} + \begin{bmatrix} 4 & a+b \\ c+d & 3 \end{bmatrix}$$

$$\Rightarrow \quad \begin{bmatrix} 3a & 3b \\ 3c & 3d \end{bmatrix} = \begin{bmatrix} a+4 & 6+a+b \\ c+d-1 & 3+2d \end{bmatrix}$$

$\Rightarrow \quad 3a = a + 4 \Rightarrow a = 2;$

$3b = 6 + a + b$

$\Rightarrow \quad 3b - b = 8 \Rightarrow b = 4;$

$3d = 3 + 2d \Rightarrow d = 3$

and $\Rightarrow \quad 3c = c + d - 1$

$\Rightarrow \quad 2c = 3 - 1 \; c = 1$

$\therefore \quad a = 2, \; b = 4, \; c = 1$ and $d = 3$

Q. 42 Find the matrix A such that $\begin{bmatrix} 2 & -1 \\ 1 & 0 \\ -3 & 4 \end{bmatrix} A = \begin{bmatrix} -1 & -8 & -10 \\ 1 & -2 & -5 \\ 9 & 22 & 15 \end{bmatrix}$.

Sol. We have, $\begin{bmatrix} 2 & -1 \\ 1 & 0 \\ -3 & 4 \end{bmatrix}_{3 \times 2} A = \begin{bmatrix} -1 & -8 & -10 \\ 1 & -2 & -5 \\ 9 & 22 & 15 \end{bmatrix}_{3 \times 3}$

From the given equation, it is clear that order of A should be 2×3.

Let $A = \begin{bmatrix} a & b & c \\ d & e & f \end{bmatrix}$

$$\therefore \quad \begin{bmatrix} 2 & -1 \\ 1 & 0 \\ -3 & 4 \end{bmatrix}\begin{bmatrix} a & b & c \\ d & e & f \end{bmatrix} = \begin{bmatrix} -1 & -8 & -10 \\ 1 & -2 & -5 \\ 9 & 22 & 15 \end{bmatrix}$$

$$\Rightarrow \quad \begin{bmatrix} 2a-d & 2b-e & 2c-f \\ a+0d & b+0\cdot e & c+0\cdot f \\ -3a+4d & -3b+4e & -3c+4f \end{bmatrix} = \begin{bmatrix} -1 & -8 & -10 \\ 1 & -2 & -5 \\ 9 & 22 & 15 \end{bmatrix}$$

$$\Rightarrow \quad \begin{bmatrix} 2a-d & 2b-e & 2c-f \\ a & b & c \\ -3a+4d & -3b+4e & -3c+4f \end{bmatrix} = \begin{bmatrix} -1 & -8 & -10 \\ 1 & -2 & -5 \\ 9 & 22 & 15 \end{bmatrix}$$

By equality of matrices, we get

$$a = 1, b = -2, c = -5$$

and $\quad 2a - d = -1 \Rightarrow d = 2a + 1 = 3;$

$\Rightarrow \quad 2b - e = -8 \Rightarrow e = 2(-2) + 8 = 4$

$$2c - f = -10 \Rightarrow f = 2c + 10 = 0$$

$$\therefore \quad A = \begin{bmatrix} 1 & -2 & -5 \\ 3 & 4 & 0 \end{bmatrix}$$

Q. 43 If $A = \begin{bmatrix} 1 & 2 \\ 4 & 1 \end{bmatrix}$, then find $A^2 + 2A + 7I$.

Sol. We have, $A = \begin{bmatrix} 1 & 2 \\ 4 & 1 \end{bmatrix}$

$$\therefore \quad A^2 = \begin{bmatrix} 1 & 2 \\ 4 & 1 \end{bmatrix}\begin{bmatrix} 1 & 2 \\ 4 & 1 \end{bmatrix} \qquad [\because A^2 = A \cdot A]$$

$$= \begin{bmatrix} 1+8 & 2+2 \\ 4+4 & 8+1 \end{bmatrix} = \begin{bmatrix} 9 & 4 \\ 8 & 9 \end{bmatrix}$$

$$\therefore \quad A^2 + 2A + 7I = \begin{bmatrix} 9 & 4 \\ 8 & 9 \end{bmatrix} + \begin{bmatrix} 2 & 4 \\ 8 & 2 \end{bmatrix} + \begin{bmatrix} 7 & 0 \\ 0 & 7 \end{bmatrix} = \begin{bmatrix} 18 & 8 \\ 16 & 18 \end{bmatrix}$$

Q. 44 If $A = \begin{bmatrix} \cos\alpha & \sin\alpha \\ -\sin\alpha & \cos\alpha \end{bmatrix}$ and $A^{-1} = A'$, then find the value of α.

Sol. We have,

$$A = \begin{bmatrix} \cos a & \sin a \\ -\sin a & \cos a \end{bmatrix} \text{ and } A' = \begin{bmatrix} \cos a & -\sin a \\ \sin a & \cos a \end{bmatrix}$$

Also, $\quad A^{-1} = A'$

$\Rightarrow \quad AA^{-1} = AA'$

$$\Rightarrow \quad I = \begin{bmatrix} \cos\alpha & \sin\alpha \\ -\sin\alpha & \cos\alpha \end{bmatrix}\begin{bmatrix} \cos\alpha & -\sin\alpha \\ \sin\alpha & \cos\alpha \end{bmatrix}$$

$$\Rightarrow \quad \begin{bmatrix} 1 & 0 \\ 0 & 1 \end{bmatrix} = \begin{bmatrix} \cos^2\alpha + \sin^2\alpha & 0 \\ 0 & \sin^2\alpha + \cos^2\alpha \end{bmatrix}$$

By using equality of matrices, we get

$$\cos^2\alpha + \sin^2\alpha = 1$$

which is true for all real values of α.

Q. 45 **If matrix** $\begin{bmatrix} 0 & a & 3 \\ 2 & b & -1 \\ c & 1 & 0 \end{bmatrix}$ **is a skew-symmetric matrix, then find the values of** a, b **and** c.

Thinking Process

We know that, a matrix A is skew-symmetric matrix, if A′= – A, so by using this we can get the values of a, b and c.

Sol. Let $A = \begin{bmatrix} 0 & a & 3 \\ 2 & b & -1 \\ c & 1 & 0 \end{bmatrix}$

Since, A is skew-symmetric matrix.

$$\therefore \quad A' = -A$$

$$\Rightarrow \begin{bmatrix} 0 & 2 & c \\ a & b & 1 \\ 3 & -1 & 0 \end{bmatrix} = -\begin{bmatrix} 0 & a & 3 \\ 2 & b & -1 \\ c & 1 & 0 \end{bmatrix}$$

$$\Rightarrow \begin{bmatrix} 0 & 2 & c \\ a & b & 1 \\ 3 & -1 & 0 \end{bmatrix} = \begin{bmatrix} 0 & -a & -3 \\ -2 & -b & +1 \\ -c & -1 & 0 \end{bmatrix}$$

By equality of matrices, we get

$$a = -2, c = -3 \text{ and } b = -b \Rightarrow b = 0$$

$$\therefore \quad a = -2, b = 0 \text{ and } c = -3$$

Q. 46 **If** $P(x) = \begin{bmatrix} \cos x & \sin x \\ -\sin x & \cos x \end{bmatrix}$, **then show that** $P(x) \cdot P(y) = P(x + y) = P(y) \cdot P(x)$.

Sol. We have,

$$P(x) = \begin{bmatrix} \cos x & \sin x \\ -\sin x & \cos x \end{bmatrix}$$

$$\therefore \quad P(y) = \begin{bmatrix} \cos y & \sin y \\ -\sin y & \cos y \end{bmatrix}$$

Now, $$P(x) \cdot P(y) = \begin{bmatrix} \cos x & \sin x \\ -\sin x & \cos x \end{bmatrix} \begin{bmatrix} \cos y & \sin y \\ -\sin y & \cos y \end{bmatrix}$$

$$= \begin{bmatrix} \cos x \cdot \cos y - \sin x \cdot \sin y & \cos x \cdot \sin y + \sin x \cdot \cos y \\ -\sin x \cdot \cos y - \cos x \cdot \sin y & -\sin x \cdot \sin y + \cos x \cdot \cos y \end{bmatrix}$$

$$= \begin{bmatrix} \cos (x + y) & \sin (x + y) \\ -\sin (x + y) & \cos (x + y) \end{bmatrix} \quad \text{...(i)}$$

$$\left[\because \cos (x + y) = \cos x \cdot \cos y - \sin x \cdot \sin y \text{ and } \sin (x + y) = \sin x \cdot \cos y + \cos x \cdot \sin y \right]$$

and $$P(x + y) = \begin{bmatrix} \cos (x + y) & \sin (x + y) \\ -\sin (x + y) & \cos (x + y) \end{bmatrix} \quad \text{...(ii)}$$

Also, $P(y) \cdot P(x) = \begin{bmatrix} \cos y & \sin y \\ -\sin y & \cos y \end{bmatrix} \begin{bmatrix} \cos x & \sin x \\ -\sin x & \cos x \end{bmatrix}$

$$= \begin{bmatrix} \cos y \cdot \cos x - \sin y \cdot \sin x & \cos y \cdot \sin x + \sin y \cdot \cos x \\ -\sin y \cdot \cos x - \sin x \cdot \cos y & -\sin y \cdot \sin x + \cos y \cdot \cos x \end{bmatrix}$$

$$= \begin{bmatrix} \cos(x+y) & \sin(x+y) \\ -\sin(x+y) & \cos(x+y) \end{bmatrix} \quad \text{...(iii)}$$

Thus, we see from the Eqs. (i), (ii) and (iii) that,

$$P(x) \cdot P(y) = P(x+y) = P(y) \cdot P(x)$$ **Hence proved.**

Q. 47 If A is square matrix such that $A^2 = A$, then show that $(I + A)^3 = 7A + I$.

Sol. Since, $A^2 = A$ and $(I+A) \cdot (I+A) = I^2 + IA + AI + A^2$

$$= I^2 + 2AI + A^2$$
$$= I + 2A + A = I + 3A$$

and $(I + A) \cdot (I + A)(I + A) = (I + A)(I + 3A)$

$$= I^2 + 3AI + AI + 3A^2$$
$$= I + 4AI + 3A$$
$$= I + 7A = 7A + I$$ **Hence proved.**

Q. 48 If A, B are square matrices of same order and B is a skew-symmetric matrix, then show that $A'BA$ is skew-symmetric.

Sol. Since, A and B are square matrices of same order and B is a skew-symmetric matrix *i.e.*, $B' = -B$.

Now, we have to prove that $A'BA$ is a skew-symmetric matrix.

$\therefore$ $A'BA' = A'BA' = BA'A'$ $[\because AB' = B'A']$

$$= A'B'A = A'-BA = -A'BA$$

Hence, $A'BA$ is a skew-symmetric matrix.

Long Answer Type Questions

Q. 49 If $AB = BA$ for any two square matrices, then prove by mathematical induction that $(AB)^n = A^n B^n$.

Sol. Let $P(n) : (AB)^n = A^n B^n$

$\therefore$ $P(1) : (AB)^1 = A^1 B^1 \Rightarrow AB = AB$

So, $P(1)$ is true.

Now, $P(k) : (AB)^k = A^k B^k, k \in N$

So, $P(K)$ is true, whenever $P(k+1)$ is true.

$\therefore$ $P(K+1 : AB)^{k+1} = A^{k+1} B^{k+1}$ ...(i)

$\Rightarrow$ $AB^k \cdot AB^1$ $[\because AB = BA]$

$\Rightarrow$ $A^k B^k \cdot BA \Rightarrow A^k B^{k+1} A$

$\Rightarrow$ $A^k \cdot A \cdot B^{k+1} \Rightarrow A^{k+1} B^{k+1}$

$\Rightarrow$ $(A \cdot B)^{k+1} = A^{k+1} B^{k+1}$

So, $P(k + 1)$ is true for all $n \in N$, whenever $P(k)$ is true.

By mathematical induction $(AB) = A^n B^n$ is true for all $n \in N$.

Q. 50 Find x, y and z, if $A = \begin{bmatrix} 0 & 2y & z \\ x & y & -z \\ x & -y & z \end{bmatrix}$ satisfies $A' = A^{-1}$.

Sol. We have, $A = \begin{bmatrix} 0 & 2y & z \\ x & y & -z \\ x & -y & z \end{bmatrix}$ and $A' = \begin{bmatrix} 0 & x & x \\ 2y & y & -y \\ z & -z & z \end{bmatrix}$

By using elementary row transformations, we get

$$A = IA$$

$$\Rightarrow \begin{bmatrix} 0 & 2y & z \\ x & y & -z \\ x & -y & z \end{bmatrix} = \begin{bmatrix} 1 & 0 & 0 \\ 0 & 1 & 0 \\ 0 & 0 & 1 \end{bmatrix} A$$

$$\Rightarrow \begin{bmatrix} 0 & 2y & z \\ x & y & -z \\ 0 & -2y & 2z \end{bmatrix} = \begin{bmatrix} 1 & 0 & 0 \\ 0 & 1 & 0 \\ 0 & -1 & 1 \end{bmatrix} A \qquad [\because R_3 \to R_3 - R_2]$$

$$\Rightarrow \begin{bmatrix} 0 & 2y & z \\ x & 3y & 0 \\ 0 & 0 & 3z \end{bmatrix} = \begin{bmatrix} 1 & 0 & 0 \\ 1 & 1 & 0 \\ 1 & -1 & 1 \end{bmatrix} A \qquad \begin{bmatrix} \because R_3 \to R_3 + R_1 \\ \text{and } R_2 \to R_2 + R_1 \end{bmatrix}$$

$$\Rightarrow \begin{bmatrix} -x & -y & z \\ x & 3y & 0 \\ 0 & 0 & z \end{bmatrix} = \begin{bmatrix} 0 & -1 & 0 \\ 1 & 1 & 0 \\ \frac{1}{3} & \frac{-1}{3} & \frac{1}{3} \end{bmatrix} A \qquad \begin{bmatrix} \because R_1 \to R_1 - R_2 \\ \text{and } R_3 \to \frac{1}{3}R_3 \end{bmatrix}$$

$$\Rightarrow \begin{bmatrix} -x & -y & 0 \\ x & 3y & 0 \\ 0 & 0 & z \end{bmatrix} = \begin{bmatrix} \frac{-1}{3} & \frac{-2}{3} & \frac{-1}{3} \\ 1 & 1 & 0 \\ \frac{1}{3} & \frac{-1}{3} & \frac{1}{3} \end{bmatrix} A \qquad [\because R_1 \to R_1 - R_3]$$

$$\Rightarrow \begin{bmatrix} -x & -y & 0 \\ 0 & 2y & 0 \\ 0 & 0 & z \end{bmatrix} = \begin{bmatrix} \frac{-1}{3} & \frac{-2}{3} & \frac{-1}{3} \\ \frac{2}{3} & \frac{1}{3} & \frac{-1}{3} \\ \frac{1}{3} & \frac{-1}{3} & \frac{1}{3} \end{bmatrix} A \qquad [\because R_2 \to R_2 + R_1]$$

$$\Rightarrow \begin{bmatrix} -x & 0 & 0 \\ 0 & 2y & 0 \\ 0 & 0 & z \end{bmatrix} = \begin{bmatrix} 0 & \frac{-1}{2} & \frac{-1}{2} \\ \frac{2}{3} & \frac{1}{3} & \frac{-1}{3} \\ \frac{1}{3} & \frac{-1}{3} & \frac{1}{3} \end{bmatrix} A \qquad \left[\because R_1 \to R_1 + \frac{1}{2}R_2\right]$$

$$\Rightarrow \begin{bmatrix} 1 & 0 & 0 \\ 0 & 1 & 0 \\ 0 & 0 & 1 \end{bmatrix} = \begin{bmatrix} 0 & \frac{1}{2x} & \frac{1}{2x} \\ \frac{1}{3y} & \frac{1}{6y} & \frac{-1}{6y} \\ \frac{1}{3z} & \frac{-1}{3z} & \frac{1}{3z} \end{bmatrix} A \qquad \begin{bmatrix} \because R_1 \to \frac{-1}{x}R_1, \\ R_2 \to \frac{1}{2y}R_2 \\ \text{and } R_3 \to \frac{1}{z}R_3 \end{bmatrix}$$

$$\therefore \qquad A^{-1} = \begin{bmatrix} 0 & \frac{1}{2x} & \frac{1}{2x} \\ \frac{1}{3y} & \frac{1}{6y} & \frac{-1}{6y} \\ \frac{1}{3z} & \frac{-1}{3z} & \frac{1}{3z} \end{bmatrix} = \begin{bmatrix} 0 & x & x \\ 2y & y & -y \\ z & -z & z \end{bmatrix}$$

$$\Rightarrow \qquad \frac{1}{2x} = x \Rightarrow \; = \pm\frac{1}{\sqrt{2}}$$

$$\Rightarrow \qquad \frac{1}{6y} = y \Rightarrow y = \pm\frac{1}{\sqrt{6}}$$

and $$\frac{1}{3z} = z \Rightarrow z = \pm\frac{1}{\sqrt{3}}$$

Alternate Method

We have,

$$A = \begin{bmatrix} 0 & 2y & z \\ x & y & -z \\ x & -y & z \end{bmatrix} \text{ and } A' = \begin{bmatrix} 0 & x & x \\ 2y & y & -y \\ z & -z & z \end{bmatrix}$$

Also, $$A' = A^{-1}$$

$$\Rightarrow \qquad AA' = AA^{-1} \qquad [\because AA^{-1} = I]$$

$$\Rightarrow \qquad AA' = I$$

$$\Rightarrow \qquad \begin{bmatrix} 0 & 2y & z \\ x & y & -z \\ x & -y & z \end{bmatrix}\begin{bmatrix} 0 & x & x \\ 2y & y & -y \\ z & -z & z \end{bmatrix} = \begin{bmatrix} 1 & 0 & 0 \\ 0 & 1 & 0 \\ 0 & 0 & 1 \end{bmatrix}$$

$$\Rightarrow \qquad \begin{bmatrix} 4y^2 + z^2 & 2y^2 - z^2 & -2y^2 + z^2 \\ 2y^2 - z^2 & x^2 + y^2 + z^2 & x^2 - y^2 - z^2 \\ -2y^2 + z^2 & x^2 - y^2 - z^2 & x^2 + y^2 + z^2 \end{bmatrix} = \begin{bmatrix} 1 & 0 & 0 \\ 0 & 1 & 0 \\ 0 & 0 & 1 \end{bmatrix}$$

$$\Rightarrow \qquad 2y^2 - z^2 = 0 \Rightarrow 2y^2 = z^2$$

$$\Rightarrow \qquad 4y^2 + z^2 = 1$$

$$\Rightarrow \qquad 2 \cdot z^2 + z^2 = 1$$

$$z = \pm\frac{1}{\sqrt{3}}$$

$$\therefore \qquad y^2 = \frac{z^2}{2} \Rightarrow y = \pm\frac{1}{\sqrt{6}}$$

Also, $$x^2 + y^2 + z^2 = 1$$

$$\Rightarrow \qquad x^2 = 1 - y^2 - z^2 = 1 - \frac{1}{6} - \frac{1}{3}$$

$$= 1 - \frac{3}{6} = \frac{1}{2}$$

$$\Rightarrow \qquad x = \pm\frac{1}{\sqrt{2}}$$

$$\therefore \qquad x = \pm, \frac{1}{\sqrt{2}}, y = \pm\frac{1}{\sqrt{6}}$$

and $$z = \pm\frac{1}{\sqrt{3}}$$

Q. 51 If possible, using elementary row transformations, find the inverse of the following matrices.

(i) $\begin{bmatrix} 2 & -1 & 3 \\ -5 & 3 & 1 \\ -3 & 2 & 3 \end{bmatrix}$ (ii) $\begin{bmatrix} 2 & 3 & -3 \\ -1 & -2 & 2 \\ 1 & 1 & -1 \end{bmatrix}$

(iii) $\begin{bmatrix} 2 & 0 & -1 \\ 5 & 1 & 0 \\ 0 & 1 & 3 \end{bmatrix}$

Sol. For getting the inverse of the given matrix A by row elementary operations we may write the given matrix as

$$A = IA$$

(i) $\because \begin{bmatrix} 2 & -1 & 3 \\ -5 & 3 & 1 \\ -3 & 2 & 3 \end{bmatrix} = \begin{bmatrix} 1 & 0 & 0 \\ 0 & 1 & 0 \\ 0 & 0 & 1 \end{bmatrix} A$

$$\Rightarrow \begin{bmatrix} 2 & -1 & 3 \\ -3 & 2 & 4 \\ -3 & 2 & 3 \end{bmatrix} = \begin{bmatrix} 1 & 0 & 0 \\ 1 & 1 & 0 \\ 0 & 0 & 1 \end{bmatrix} A \quad [\because R_2 \to R_2 + R_1]$$

$$\Rightarrow \begin{bmatrix} 2 & -1 & 3 \\ -3 & 2 & 4 \\ 0 & 0 & -1 \end{bmatrix} = \begin{bmatrix} 1 & 0 & 0 \\ 1 & 1 & 0 \\ -1 & -1 & 1 \end{bmatrix} A \quad [\because R_3 \to R_3 - R_2]$$

$$\Rightarrow \begin{bmatrix} -1 & 1 & 7 \\ -3 & 2 & 4 \\ 0 & 0 & -1 \end{bmatrix} = \begin{bmatrix} 2 & 1 & 0 \\ 1 & 1 & 0 \\ -1 & -1 & 1 \end{bmatrix} A \quad [\because R_1 \to R_1 + R_2]$$

$$\Rightarrow \begin{bmatrix} -1 & 1 & 7 \\ 0 & -1 & -17 \\ 0 & 0 & -1 \end{bmatrix} = \begin{bmatrix} 2 & 1 & 0 \\ -5 & -2 & 0 \\ -1 & -1 & 1 \end{bmatrix} A \quad [\because R_2 \to R_2 - 3R_1]$$

$$\Rightarrow \begin{bmatrix} -1 & 0 & -10 \\ 0 & -1 & -17 \\ 0 & 0 & 1 \end{bmatrix} = \begin{bmatrix} -3 & -1 & 0 \\ -5 & -2 & 0 \\ 1 & 1 & -1 \end{bmatrix} A \quad \begin{bmatrix} \because R_1 \to R_1 + R_2 \\ \text{and } R_3 \to -1 \cdot R_3 \end{bmatrix}$$

$$\Rightarrow \begin{bmatrix} -1 & 0 & 0 \\ 0 & -1 & 0 \\ 0 & 0 & 1 \end{bmatrix} = \begin{bmatrix} 7 & 9 & -10 \\ 12 & 15 & -17 \\ 1 & 1 & -1 \end{bmatrix} A \quad \begin{bmatrix} \because R_1 \to R_1 + 10R_3 \\ \text{and } R_2 \to R_2 + 17R_3 \end{bmatrix}$$

$$\Rightarrow \begin{bmatrix} 1 & 0 & 0 \\ 0 & 1 & 0 \\ 0 & 0 & 1 \end{bmatrix} = \begin{bmatrix} -7 & -9 & 10 \\ -12 & -15 & 17 \\ 1 & 1 & -1 \end{bmatrix} A \quad \begin{bmatrix} \because R_1 \to -1R_1 \\ \text{and } R_2 \to -1R_2 \end{bmatrix}$$

So, the inverse of A is $\begin{bmatrix} -7 & -9 & 10 \\ -12 & -15 & 17 \\ 1 & 1 & -1 \end{bmatrix}$.

(ii) $\therefore$
$$\begin{bmatrix}2 & 3 & -3\\-1 & -2 & 2\\1 & 1 & -1\end{bmatrix}=\begin{bmatrix}1 & 0 & 0\\0 & 1 & 0\\0 & 0 & 1\end{bmatrix}A$$

$$\Rightarrow \begin{bmatrix}0 & 1 & -1\\0 & -1 & 1\\1 & 1 & -1\end{bmatrix}=\begin{bmatrix}1 & 0 & -2\\0 & 1 & 1\\0 & 0 & 1\end{bmatrix}A \quad \begin{bmatrix}\because R_2 \to R_2 + R_3\\ \text{and } R_1 \to R_1 - 2R_3\end{bmatrix}$$

$$\Rightarrow \begin{bmatrix}0 & 1 & -1\\0 & 0 & 0\\1 & 1 & 1\end{bmatrix}=\begin{bmatrix}1 & 0 & -2\\2 & 1 & -2\\0 & 0 & 1\end{bmatrix}A \quad [\because R_2 \to R_2 + R_1]$$

Since, second row of the matrix A on LHS is containing all zeroes, so we can say that inverse of matrix A does not exist.

(iii) $\therefore$
$$\begin{bmatrix}2 & 0 & -1\\5 & 1 & 0\\0 & 1 & 3\end{bmatrix}=\begin{bmatrix}1 & 0 & 0\\0 & 1 & 0\\0 & 0 & 1\end{bmatrix}A$$

$$\Rightarrow \begin{bmatrix}2 & 0 & -1\\3 & 1 & 1\\0 & 1 & 3\end{bmatrix}=\begin{bmatrix}1 & 0 & 0\\-1 & 1 & 0\\0 & 0 & 1\end{bmatrix}A \quad [\because R_2 \to R_2 - R_1]$$

$$\Rightarrow \begin{bmatrix}2 & 0 & -1\\1 & 1 & 2\\2 & 1 & 2\end{bmatrix}=\begin{bmatrix}1 & 0 & 0\\-2 & 1 & 0\\1 & 0 & 1\end{bmatrix}A \quad \begin{bmatrix}\because R_2 \to R_2 - R_1\\ \text{and } R_3 \to R_3 + R_1\end{bmatrix}$$

$$\Rightarrow \begin{bmatrix}2 & 0 & -1\\0 & 1 & \frac{5}{2}\\4 & 1 & 1\end{bmatrix}=\begin{bmatrix}1 & 0 & 0\\\frac{-5}{2} & 1 & 0\\2 & 0 & 1\end{bmatrix}A \quad \begin{bmatrix}\because R_3 \to R_3 + R_1\\ \text{and } R_2 \to R_2 - \frac{1}{2}R_1\end{bmatrix}$$

$$\Rightarrow \begin{bmatrix}2 & 0 & -1\\0 & 1 & \frac{5}{2}\\0 & 1 & 3\end{bmatrix}=\begin{bmatrix}1 & 0 & 0\\\frac{-5}{2} & 1 & 0\\0 & 0 & 1\end{bmatrix}A \quad [\because R_3 \to R_3 - 2R_1]$$

$$\Rightarrow \begin{bmatrix}2 & 0 & -1\\0 & 1 & \frac{5}{2}\\0 & 0 & \frac{1}{2}\end{bmatrix}=\begin{bmatrix}1 & 0 & 0\\\frac{-5}{2} & 1 & 0\\\frac{5}{2} & -1 & 1\end{bmatrix}A \quad [\because R_3 \to R_3 - R_2]$$

$$\Rightarrow \begin{bmatrix}1 & 0 & \frac{-1}{2}\\0 & 1 & \frac{5}{2}\\0 & 0 & 1\end{bmatrix}=\begin{bmatrix}\frac{1}{2} & 0 & 0\\\frac{-5}{2} & 1 & 0\\5 & -2 & 2\end{bmatrix}A \quad \begin{bmatrix}\because R_1 \to \frac{1}{2}R_1\\ \text{and} R_3 \to 2R_3\end{bmatrix}$$

$$\Rightarrow \begin{bmatrix}1 & 0 & 0\\0 & 1 & 0\\0 & 0 & 1\end{bmatrix}=\begin{bmatrix}3 & -1 & 1\\-15 & 6 & -5\\5 & -2 & 2\end{bmatrix}A \quad \begin{bmatrix}\because R_1 \to R_1 + \frac{1}{2}R_3\\ \text{and } R_2 \to R_2 - \frac{5}{2}R_3\end{bmatrix}$$

Hence, $\begin{bmatrix}3 & -1 & 1\\-15 & 6 & -5\\5 & -2 & 2\end{bmatrix}$ is the inverse of given matrix A.

Q. 52 Express the matrix $\begin{bmatrix} 2 & 3 & 1 \\ 1 & -1 & 2 \\ 4 & 1 & 2 \end{bmatrix}$ as the sum of a symmetric and a skew-symmetric matrix.

Thinking Process

We know that, any square matrix A can be expressed as the sum of a symmetric matrix and skew-symmetric matrix, i.e., $A = \dfrac{A+A'}{2} + \dfrac{A-A'}{2}$, *where* $A + A'$ *and* $A - A'$ *are a symmetric matrix and a skew-symmetric matrix, respectively.*

Sol. We have,
$$A = \begin{bmatrix} 2 & 3 & 1 \\ 1 & -1 & 2 \\ 4 & 1 & 2 \end{bmatrix}$$

$\therefore$
$$A' = \begin{bmatrix} 2 & 1 & 4 \\ 3 & -1 & 1 \\ 1 & 2 & 2 \end{bmatrix}$$

Now,
$$\frac{A+A'}{2} = \frac{1}{2}\begin{bmatrix} 4 & 4 & 5 \\ 4 & -2 & 3 \\ 5 & 3 & 4 \end{bmatrix} = \begin{bmatrix} 2 & 2 & \frac{5}{2} \\ 2 & -1 & \frac{3}{2} \\ \frac{5}{2} & \frac{3}{2} & 2 \end{bmatrix}$$

and
$$\frac{A-A'}{2} = \frac{1}{2}\begin{bmatrix} 0 & 2 & -3 \\ -2 & 0 & 1 \\ 3 & -1 & 0 \end{bmatrix} = \begin{bmatrix} 0 & 1 & \frac{-3}{2} \\ -1 & 0 & \frac{1}{2} \\ \frac{3}{2} & \frac{-1}{2} & 0 \end{bmatrix}$$

$\therefore$
$$\frac{A+A'}{2} + \frac{A-A'}{2} = \begin{bmatrix} 2 & 2 & \frac{5}{2} \\ 2 & -1 & \frac{3}{2} \\ \frac{5}{2} & \frac{3}{2} & 2 \end{bmatrix} + \begin{bmatrix} 0 & 1 & \frac{-3}{2} \\ -1 & 0 & \frac{1}{2} \\ \frac{3}{2} & \frac{-1}{2} & 0 \end{bmatrix}$$

which is the required expression.

Objective Type Questions

Q. 53 The matrix $P = \begin{bmatrix} 0 & 0 & 4 \\ 0 & 4 & 0 \\ 4 & 0 & 0 \end{bmatrix}$ is a

(a) square matrix
(b) diagonal matrix
(c) unit matrix
(d) None of these

Sol. *(a)* We know that, in a square matrix number of rows are equal to the number of columns, so the matrix $P = \begin{bmatrix} 0 & 0 & 4 \\ 0 & 4 & 0 \\ 4 & 0 & 0 \end{bmatrix}$ is a square matrix.

Q. 54 Total number of possible matrices of order 3×3 with each entry 2 or 0 is

(a) 9
(b) 27
(c) 81
(d) 512

Sol. *(d)* Total number of possible matrices of order 3×3 with each entry 2 or 0 is 2^9 *i.e.*, 512.

Q. 55 $\begin{bmatrix} 2x + y & 4x \\ 5x - 7 & 4x \end{bmatrix} = \begin{bmatrix} 7 & 7y - 13 \\ y & x + 6 \end{bmatrix}$, then the value of $x + y$ is

(a) $x = 3, y = 1$
(b) $x = 2, y = 3$
(c) $x = 2, y = 4$
(d) $x = 3, y = 3$

Sol. *(b)* We have, $4x = x + 6 \Rightarrow x = 2$

and $4x = 7y - 13 \Rightarrow 8 = 7y - 13$

$\Rightarrow 7y = 21 \Rightarrow y = 3$

$\therefore x + y = 2 + 3 = 5$

Q. 56 If $A = \dfrac{1}{\pi}\begin{bmatrix} \sin^{-1}(x\pi) & \tan^{-1}\left(\dfrac{x}{\pi}\right) \\ \sin^{-1}\left(\dfrac{x}{\pi}\right) & \cot^{-1}(\pi x) \end{bmatrix}$ and $B = \dfrac{1}{\pi}\begin{bmatrix} -\cos^{-1}(x\pi) & \tan^{-1}\left(\dfrac{x}{\pi}\right) \\ \sin^{-1}\left(\dfrac{x}{\pi}\right) & -\tan^{-1}(\pi x) \end{bmatrix}$,

then $A - B$ is equal to

(a) I
(b) 0
(c) $2I$
(d) $\dfrac{1}{2}I$

Sol. *(d)* We have, $A = \begin{bmatrix} \dfrac{1}{\pi}\sin^{-1} x\pi & \dfrac{1}{\pi}\tan^{-1}\dfrac{x}{\pi} \\ \dfrac{1}{\pi}\sin^{-1}\dfrac{x}{\pi} & \dfrac{1}{\pi}\cot^{-1}\pi x \end{bmatrix}$

and $B = \begin{bmatrix} \dfrac{-1}{\pi}\cos^{-1} x\pi & \dfrac{1}{\pi}\tan^{-1}\dfrac{x}{\pi} \\ \dfrac{1}{\pi}\sin^{-1}\dfrac{x}{\pi} & \dfrac{-1}{\pi}\tan^{-1}\pi x \end{bmatrix}$

$$\therefore \quad A-B=\begin{bmatrix}\frac{1}{\pi}(\sin^{-1}x\pi+\cos^{-1}x\pi) & \frac{1}{\pi}\left(\tan^{-1}\frac{x}{\pi}-\tan^{-1}\frac{x}{\pi}\right)\\ \frac{1}{\pi}\left(\sin^{-1}\frac{x}{\pi}-\sin^{-1}\frac{x}{\pi}\right) & \frac{1}{\pi}\cot^{-1}\pi x+\tan^{-1}\pi x\end{bmatrix}$$

$$=\begin{bmatrix}\frac{1}{\pi}\cdot\frac{\pi}{2} & 0\\ 0 & \frac{1}{\pi}\cdot\frac{\pi}{2}\end{bmatrix} \qquad \left[\because \sin^{-1}x+\cos^{-1}x=\frac{\pi}{2} \text{ and } \tan^{-1}x+\cot^{-1}x=\frac{\pi}{2}\right]$$

$$=\frac{1}{2}\begin{bmatrix}1 & 0\\ 0 & 1\end{bmatrix}$$

$$=\frac{1}{2}I$$

Q. 57 If A and B are two matrices of the order $3\times m$ and $3\times n$, respectively and $m=n$, then order of matrix $(5A-2B)$ is

(a) $m\times 3$ (b) 3×3
(c) $m\times n$ (d) $3\times n$

Sol. *(d)* $A_{3\times m}$ and $B_{3\times n}$ are two matrices. If $m=n$, then A and B have same orders as $3\times n$ each, so the order of $(5A-2B)$ should be same as $3\times n$.

Q. 58 If $A=\begin{bmatrix}0 & 1\\ 1 & 0\end{bmatrix}$, then A^2 is equal to

(a) $\begin{bmatrix}0 & 1\\ 1 & 0\end{bmatrix}$ (b) $\begin{bmatrix}1 & 0\\ 1 & 0\end{bmatrix}$ (c) $\begin{bmatrix}0 & 1\\ 0 & 1\end{bmatrix}$ (d) $\begin{bmatrix}1 & 0\\ 0 & 1\end{bmatrix}$

Sol. *(d)* $\because A^2=A\cdot A=\begin{bmatrix}0 & 1\\ 1 & 0\end{bmatrix}\cdot\begin{bmatrix}0 & 1\\ 1 & 0\end{bmatrix}=\begin{bmatrix}1 & 0\\ 0 & 1\end{bmatrix}$

Q. 59 If matrix $A=[a_{ij}]_{2\times 2}$, where $a_{ij}=1$, if $i\neq j=0$ and if $i=j$, then A^2 is equal to

(a) I (b) A
(c) 0 (d) None of these

Sol. *(a)* We have, $A=[a_{ij}]_{2\times 2}$, where $a_{ij}=1$, if $i\neq j=0$ and if $i=j$

$$\therefore \quad A=\begin{bmatrix}0 & 1\\ 1 & 0\end{bmatrix}$$

and

$$A^2=\begin{bmatrix}0 & 1\\ 1 & 0\end{bmatrix}\begin{bmatrix}0 & 1\\ 1 & 0\end{bmatrix}=\begin{bmatrix}1 & 0\\ 0 & 1\end{bmatrix}=I$$

Q. 60 The matrix $\begin{bmatrix}1 & 0 & 0\\ 0 & 2 & 0\\ 0 & 0 & 4\end{bmatrix}$ is a

(a) identity matrix (b) symmetric matrix
(c) skew-symmetric matrix (d) None of these

Sol. *(b)* Let

$$A = \begin{bmatrix} 1 & 0 & 0 \\ 0 & 2 & 0 \\ 0 & 0 & 4 \end{bmatrix}$$

$\therefore$

$$A' = \begin{bmatrix} 1 & 0 & 0 \\ 0 & 2 & 0 \\ 0 & 0 & 4 \end{bmatrix} = A$$

So, the given matrix is a symmetric matrix.

[since, in a square matrix A, if $A' = A$, then A is called symmetric matrix]

Q. 61 The matrix $\begin{bmatrix} 0 & -5 & 8 \\ 5 & 0 & 12 \\ -8 & -12 & 0 \end{bmatrix}$ is a

(a) diagonal matrix
(b) symmetric matrix
(c) skew-symmetric matrix
(d) scalar matrix

Sol. *(c)* We know that, in a square matrix, if $b_{ij} = 0$, when $i \neq j$, then it is said to be a diagonal matrix. Here, $b_{12}, b_{13}, \ldots \neq 0$, so the given matrix is not a diagonal matrix.

Now,
$$B = \begin{bmatrix} 0 & -5 & 8 \\ 5 & 0 & 12 \\ -8 & -12 & 0 \end{bmatrix}$$

$\therefore$
$$B' = \begin{bmatrix} 0 & 5 & -8 \\ -5 & 0 & -12 \\ 8 & 12 & 0 \end{bmatrix} = -\begin{bmatrix} 0 & -5 & 8 \\ 5 & 0 & 12 \\ -8 & -12 & 0 \end{bmatrix} = -B$$

So, the given matrix is a skew-symmetric matrix, since we know that in a square matrix B, if $B' = -B$, then it is called skew-symmetric matrix.

Q. 62 If A is matrix of order $m \times n$ and B is a matrix such that AB' and $B'A$ are both defined, then order of matrix B is

(a) $m \times m$
(b) $n \times n$
(c) $n \times m$
(d) $m \times n$

Sol. *(d)* Let $A = [a_{ij}]_{m \times n}$ and $B = [b_{ij}]_{p \times q}$

$\therefore$ $B' = [b_{ji}]_{q \times p}$

Now, AB' is defined, so $n = q$

and $B'A$ is also defined, so $p = m$

$\therefore$ Order of $B' = [b_{ji}]_{n \times m}$

and order of $B = [b_{ij}]_{m \times n}$

Q. 63 If A and B are matrices of same order, then $(AB' - BA')$ is a

(a) skew-symmetric matrix
(b) null matrix
(c) symmetric matrix
(d) unit matrix

Sol. *(a)* We have matrices A and B of same order.

Let $P = (AB' - BA')$

Then,
$$P' = (AB' - BA')' = (AB')' - (BA')'$$
$$= (B')'(A)' - (A')'B' = BA' - AB'$$
$$= -(AB' - BA') = -P$$

Hence, $(AB' - BA')$ is a skew-symmetric matrix.

Q. 64 If A is a square matrix such that $A^2 = I$, then $(A - I)^3 + (A + I)^3 - 7A$ is equal to

(a) A (b) $I - A$ (c) $I + A$ (d) $3A$

Sol. *(a)* We have, $A^2 = I$

$$\therefore (A - I)^3 + (A + I)^3 - 7A = [(A - I) + (A + I)\{(A - I)^2 + (A + I)^2 - (A - I)(A + I)\}] - 7A$$

$[\because a^3 + b^3 = (a + b)(a^2 + b^2 - ab)]$

$$= [(2A)\{A^2 + I^2 - 2AI + A^2 + I^2 + AI - (A^2 - I^2)\}] - 7A$$
$$= 2A[I + I^2 + I + I^2 - A^2 + I^2] - 7A \quad [\because A^2 = AI]$$
$$= 2A[5I - I] - 7A$$
$$= 8AI - 7AI \quad [\because A = AI]$$
$$= AI = A$$

Q. 65 For any two matrices A and B, we have

(a) $AB = BA$ (b) $AB \neq BA$ (c) $AB = O$ (d) None of these

Sol. *(d)* For any two matrices A and B, we may have $AB = BA = I$, $AB \neq BA$ and $AB = O$ but it is not always true.

Q. 66 On using elementary column operations $C_2 \to C_2 - 2C_1$ in the following matrix equation $\begin{bmatrix} 1 & -3 \\ 2 & 4 \end{bmatrix} = \begin{bmatrix} 1 & -1 \\ 0 & 1 \end{bmatrix}\begin{bmatrix} 3 & 1 \\ 2 & 4 \end{bmatrix}$, we have

(a) $\begin{bmatrix} 1 & -5 \\ 0 & 4 \end{bmatrix} = \begin{bmatrix} 1 & -1 \\ -2 & 2 \end{bmatrix}\begin{bmatrix} 3 & -5 \\ 2 & 0 \end{bmatrix}$ (b) $\begin{bmatrix} 1 & -5 \\ 0 & 4 \end{bmatrix} = \begin{bmatrix} 1 & -1 \\ 0 & 1 \end{bmatrix}\begin{bmatrix} 3 & -5 \\ -0 & 2 \end{bmatrix}$

(c) $\begin{bmatrix} 1 & -5 \\ 2 & 0 \end{bmatrix} = \begin{bmatrix} 1 & -3 \\ 0 & 1 \end{bmatrix}\begin{bmatrix} 3 & 1 \\ -2 & 4 \end{bmatrix}$ (d) $\begin{bmatrix} 1 & -5 \\ 2 & 0 \end{bmatrix} = \begin{bmatrix} 1 & -1 \\ 0 & 1 \end{bmatrix}\begin{bmatrix} 3 & -5 \\ 2 & 0 \end{bmatrix}$

Sol. *(d)* Given that, $\begin{bmatrix} 1 & -3 \\ 2 & 4 \end{bmatrix} = \begin{bmatrix} 1 & -1 \\ 0 & 1 \end{bmatrix}\begin{bmatrix} 3 & 1 \\ 2 & 4 \end{bmatrix}$

On using $C_2 \to C_2 - 2C_1$, $\begin{bmatrix} 1 & -5 \\ 2 & 0 \end{bmatrix} = \begin{bmatrix} 1 & -1 \\ 0 & 1 \end{bmatrix}\begin{bmatrix} 3 & -5 \\ 2 & 0 \end{bmatrix}$

Since, on using elementary column operation on $X = AB$, we apply these operations simultaneously on X and on the second matrix B of the product AB on RHS.

Q. 67 On using elementary row operation $R_1 \to R_1 - 3R_2$ in the following matrix equation $\begin{bmatrix} 4 & 2 \\ 3 & 3 \end{bmatrix} = \begin{bmatrix} 1 & 2 \\ 0 & 3 \end{bmatrix}\begin{bmatrix} 2 & 0 \\ 1 & 1 \end{bmatrix}$, we have

(a) $\begin{bmatrix} -5 & -7 \\ 3 & 3 \end{bmatrix} = \begin{bmatrix} 1 & -7 \\ 0 & 3 \end{bmatrix}\begin{bmatrix} 2 & 0 \\ 1 & 1 \end{bmatrix}$ (b) $\begin{bmatrix} -5 & -7 \\ 3 & 3 \end{bmatrix} = \begin{bmatrix} 1 & 2 \\ 0 & 3 \end{bmatrix}\begin{bmatrix} -1 & -3 \\ 1 & 1 \end{bmatrix}$

(c) $\begin{bmatrix} -5 & -7 \\ 3 & 3 \end{bmatrix} = \begin{bmatrix} 1 & 2 \\ 1 & -7 \end{bmatrix}\begin{bmatrix} 2 & 0 \\ 1 & 1 \end{bmatrix}$ (d) $\begin{bmatrix} 4 & 2 \\ -5 & -7 \end{bmatrix} = \begin{bmatrix} 1 & 2 \\ -3 & -3 \end{bmatrix}\begin{bmatrix} 2 & 0 \\ 1 & 1 \end{bmatrix}$

Sol. *(a)* We have, $\begin{bmatrix} 4 & 2 \\ 3 & 3 \end{bmatrix} = \begin{bmatrix} 1 & 2 \\ 0 & 3 \end{bmatrix} \begin{bmatrix} 2 & 0 \\ 1 & 1 \end{bmatrix}$

Using elementary row operation $R_1 \to R_1 - 3R_2$,

$$\begin{bmatrix} -5 & -7 \\ 3 & 3 \end{bmatrix} = \begin{bmatrix} 1 & -7 \\ 0 & 3 \end{bmatrix} \begin{bmatrix} 2 & 0 \\ 1 & 1 \end{bmatrix}$$

Since, on using elementary row operation on $X = AB$, we apply these operation simultaneously on X and on the first matrix A of the product AB on RHS.

Fillers

Q. 68 ……… matrix is both symmetric and skew-symmetric matrix.

Sol. Null matrix is both symmetric and skew-symmetric matrix.

Q. 69 Sum of two skew-symmetric matrices is always ……… matrix.

Sol. Let A is a given matrix, then $(-A)$ is a skew-symmetric matrix.
Similarly, for a given matrix $-B$ is a skew-symmetric matrix.
Hence, $-A - B = -(A + B) \Rightarrow$ sum of two skew-symmetric matrices is always skew-symmetric matrix.

Q. 70 The negative of a matrix is obtained by multiplying it by ……… .

Sol. Let A is a given matrix.

$$\therefore \quad -A = -1[A]$$

So, the negative of a matrix is obtained by multiplying it by -1.

Q. 71 The product of any matrix by the scalar ……… is the null matrix.

Sol. The product of any matrix by the scalar 0 is the null matrix. *i.e.,* $0 \cdot A = 0$.
[where, A is any matrix]

Q. 72 A matrix which is not a square matrix is called a ……… matrix.

Sol. A matrix which is not a square matrix is called a rectangular matrix. For example a rectangular matrix is $A = [a_{ij}]_{m \times n}$, where $m \neq n$.

Q. 73 Matrix multiplication is …… over addition.

Sol. Matrix multiplication is distributive over addition.
e.g., For three matrices A, B and C,

(i) $A(B + C) = AB + AC$

(ii) $(A + B)C = AC + BC$

Q. 74 If A is a symmetric matrix, then A^3 is a .... matrix.

Sol. If A is a symmetric matrix, then A^3 is a symmetric matrix.

$\because \quad A' = A$

$\therefore \quad (A^3)' = A'^3$

$= A^3 \qquad [\because (A')^n = (A^n)']$

Q. 75 If A is a skew-symmetric matrix, then A^2 is a ....

Sol. If A is a skew-symmetric matrix, then A^2 is a symmetric matrix.

$\because \quad A' = -A$

$\therefore \quad (A^2)' = (A')^2$

$= (-A)^2 \qquad [\because A' = -A]$

$= A^2$

So, A^2 is a symmetric matrix.

Q. 76 If A and B are square matrices of the same order, then

(i) $(AB)' =$ ....

(ii) $(kA)' =$ .... (where, k is any scalar)

(iii) $[k(A - B)]' =$ ....

Sol. **(i)** $(AB)' = B'A'$

(ii) $(kA)' = kA'$

(iii) $[k(A - B)]' = k(A' - B')$

Q. 77 If A is a skew-symmetric, then kA is a .... (where, k is any scalar).

Sol. If A is a skew-symmetric, then kA is a skew-symmetric matrix (where, k is any scalar).

$[\because A' = -A \Rightarrow (kA)' = k(A)' = -(kA)]$

Q. 78 If A and B are symmetric matrices, then

(i) $AB - BA$ is a ....

(ii) $BA - 2AB$ is a ....

Sol. **(i)** $AB - BA$ is a skew-symmetric matrix.

Since, $\quad [AB - BA]' = (AB)' - (BA)'$

$= B'A' - A'B' \qquad [\because (AB)' = B'A']$

$= BA - AB \qquad [\because A' = A \text{ and } B' = B]$

$= -[AB - BA]$

So, $[AB - BA]$ is a skew-symmetric matrix.

(ii) $[BA - 2AB]$ is a neither symmetric nor skew-symmetric matrix.

$\therefore \quad (BA - 2AB)' = (BA)' - 2(AB)'$

$= A'B' - 2B'A'$

$= AB - 2BA$

$= -(2BA - AB)$

So, $[BA - 2AB]$ is neither symmetric nor skew-symmetric matrix.

Q. 79 If A is symmetric matrix, then $B'AB$ is ....

Sol. If A is a symmetric matrix, then $B'AB$ is a symmetric metrix.

$$\because \quad [B'AB]' = [B'(AB)]'$$
$$= (AB)'(B')' \quad [\because (AB)' = B'A']$$
$$= B'A'B$$
$$= [B'A'B] \quad [\because A' = A]$$

So, $B'AB$ is a symmetric matrix.

Q. 80 If A and B are symmetric matrices of same order, then AB is symmetric if and only if......... .

Sol. If A and B are symmetric matrices of same order, then AB is symmetric if and only if $AB = BA$.

$$\therefore \quad (AB)'$$
$$= B'A' = BA$$
$$= AB \quad [\because AB = BA]$$

Q. 81 In applying one or more row operations while finding A^{-1} by elementary row operations, we obtain all zeroes in one or more, then A^{-1} ....

Sol. In applying one or more row operations while finding A^{-1} by elementary row operations, we obtain all zeroes in one or more, then A^{-1} does not exist.

True/False

Q. 82 A matrix denotes a number.

Sol. ***False***

A matrix is an ordered rectangular array of numbers or functions.

Q. 83 Matrices of any order can be added.

Sol. ***False***

Two matrices are added, if they are of the same order.

Q. 84 Two matrices are equal, if they have same number of rows and same number of columns.

Sol. ***False***

If two matrices have same number of rows and same number of columns, then they are said to be square matrix and if two square matrices have same elements in both the matrices, only then they are called equal.

Q. 85 Matrices of different order cannot be subtracted.

Sol. ***True***

Two matrices of same order can be subtracted

Q. 86 Matrix addition is associative as well as commutative.

Sol. ***True***

Matrix addition is associative as well as commutative *i.e.*,
$(A + B) + C = A + (B + C)$ and $A + B = B + A$, where A, B and C are matrices of same order.

Q. 87 Matrix multiplication is commutative.

Sol. ***False***

Since, $AB \neq BA$ is possible when AB and BA are both defined.

Q. 88 A square matrix where every element is unity is called an identity matrix.

Sol. ***False***

Since, in an identity matrix, the diagonal elements are all one and rest are all zero.

Q. 89 If A and B are two square matrices of the same order, then $A + B = B + A$.

Sol. ***True***

Since, matrix addition is commutative *i.e.*, $A + B = B + A$, where A and B are two square matrices.

Q. 90 If A and B are two matrices of the same order, then $A - B = B - A$.

Sol. ***False***

Since, the addition of two matrices of same order are commutative.

$$\therefore \quad A + (-B) = A - B = -[B - A] \neq B - A$$

Q. 91 If matrix $AB = 0$, then $A = 0$ or $B = 0$ or both A and B are null matrices.

Sol. ***False***

Since, for two non-zero matrices A and B of same order, it can be possible that $A \cdot B = 0 =$ null matrix

Q. 92 Transpose of a column matrix is a column matrix.

Sol. ***False***

Transpose of a column matrix is a row matrix.

Q. 93 If A and B are two square matrices of the same order, then $AB = BA$.

Sol. ***False***

For two square matrices of same order it is not always true that $AB = BA$.

Q. 94 If each of the three matrices of the same order are symmetric, then their sum is a symmetric matrix.

Sol. ***True***

Let A, B and C are three matrices of same order

$$\therefore \quad A' = A, B' = B \text{ and } C' = C$$

$$\therefore \quad (A + B + C)' = A' + B' + C'$$

$$= (A + B + C)$$

Q. 95 If A and B are any two matrices of the same order, then $(AB)' = A'B'$.

Sol. ***False***

$\because \quad (AB)' = B'A'$

Q. 96 If $(AB)' = B'A'$, where A and B are not square matrices, then number of rows in A is equal to number of columns in B and number of columns in A is equal to number of rows in B.

Sol. ***True***

Let A is of order $m \times n$ and B is of order $p \times q$.

Since, $\quad (AB)' = B'A'$

$\therefore \quad A_{(m \times n)} B_{(p \times q)}$ is defined $\Rightarrow n = p$ ...(i)

and AB is of order $m \times q$.

$\Rightarrow \quad (AB)'$ is of order $q \times m$ ...(ii)

Also, B' is of order $q \times p$ and A' is of order $n \times m$

$\therefore \quad B'A'$ is defined $\Rightarrow p = n$

and $\quad B'A'$ is of order $q \times m$. ...(iii)

Also, equality of matrices $(AB)' = B'A'$, we get the given statement as true.

e.g., If A is of order (3×1) and B is of order (1×3), we get

Order of $(AB)'$ = Order of $(B'A') = 3 \times 3$

Q. 97 If A, B and C are square matrices of same order, then $AB = AC$ always implies that $B = C$.

Sol. ***False***

If $AB = AC = 0$, then it can be possible that B and C are two non-zero matrices such that $B \neq C$.

$\therefore \quad A \cdot B = 0 = A \cdot C$

Let $\quad A = \begin{bmatrix} 1 & 0 \\ 0 & 0 \end{bmatrix}, B = \begin{bmatrix} 0 & 0 \\ 1 & 3 \end{bmatrix}$

and $\quad C = \begin{bmatrix} 0 & 0 \\ 3 & 1 \end{bmatrix}$

$\therefore \quad AB = \begin{bmatrix} 1 & 0 \\ 0 & 0 \end{bmatrix} \begin{bmatrix} 0 & 0 \\ 1 & 3 \end{bmatrix} = \begin{bmatrix} 0 & 0 \\ 0 & 0 \end{bmatrix}$

and $\quad AC = \begin{bmatrix} 1 & 0 \\ 0 & 0 \end{bmatrix} \cdot \begin{bmatrix} 0 & 0 \\ 3 & 1 \end{bmatrix} = \begin{bmatrix} 0 & 0 \\ 0 & 0 \end{bmatrix}$

$\Rightarrow \quad AB = AC$ but $B \neq C$

Q. 98 AA' is always a symmetric matrix for any matrix A.

Sol. ***True***

$\because [AA']' = (A')' A' = [AA']$

Q. 99 If $A = \begin{vmatrix} 2 & 3 & -1 \\ 1 & 4 & 2 \end{vmatrix}$ and $B = \begin{vmatrix} 2 & 3 \\ 4 & 5 \\ 2 & 1 \end{vmatrix}$, then AB and BA are defined and equal.

Sol. ***False***

Since, AB is defined.

$$\therefore \quad AB = \begin{bmatrix} 2 & 3 & -1 \\ 1 & 4 & 2 \end{bmatrix} \begin{bmatrix} 2 & 3 \\ 4 & 5 \\ 2 & 1 \end{bmatrix} = \begin{bmatrix} 14 & 20 \\ 22 & 25 \end{bmatrix}$$

Also, BA is defined.

$$\therefore \quad BA = \begin{bmatrix} 2 & 3 \\ 4 & 5 \\ 2 & 1 \end{bmatrix} \begin{bmatrix} 2 & 3 & -1 \\ 1 & 4 & 2 \end{bmatrix}$$

$$= \begin{bmatrix} 7 & 18 & 4 \\ 13 & 32 & 6 \\ 5 & 10 & 0 \end{bmatrix}$$

$$\therefore \quad AB \neq BA$$

Q. 100 If A is skew-symmetric matrix, then A^2 is a symmetric matrix.

Sol. ***True***

$$\because \quad [A^2]' = [A']^2$$

$$= [-A]^2 \qquad [\because A' = -A]$$

$$= A^2$$

Hence, A^2 is symmetric matrix.

Q. 101 $(AB)^{-1} = A^{-1} \cdot B^{-1}$, where A and B are invertible matrices satisfying commutative property with respect to multiplication.

Sol. ***True***

We know that, if A and B are invertible matrices of the same order, then

$$(AB)^{-1} = (BA)^{-1} \qquad [\because AB = BA]$$

Here, $(AB)^{-1} = (AB)^{-1}$

$$\Rightarrow \quad B^{-1}A^{-1} = A^{-1}B^{-1}$$

[since, A and B are satisfying commutative property with respect to multiplications].

4

Determinants

Short Answer Type Questions

Q. 1 $\begin{vmatrix} x^2 - x + 1 & x - 1 \\ x + 1 & x + 1 \end{vmatrix}$

Sol. We have, $\begin{vmatrix} x^2 - x + 1 & x - 1 \\ x + 1 & x + 1 \end{vmatrix} = \begin{vmatrix} x^2 - 2x + 2 & x - 1 \\ 0 & x + 1 \end{vmatrix}$ $[\because C_1 \to C_1 - C_2]$

$$= (x^2 - 2x + 2) \cdot (x + 1) - (x - 1) \cdot 0$$
$$= x^3 - 2x^2 + 2x + x^2 - 2x + 2$$
$$= x^3 - x^2 + 2$$

Q. 2 $\begin{vmatrix} a + x & y & z \\ x & a + y & z \\ x & y & a + z \end{vmatrix}$

Sol. We have, $\begin{vmatrix} a + x & y & z \\ x & a + y & z \\ x & y & a + z \end{vmatrix} = \begin{vmatrix} a & -a & 0 \\ 0 & a & -a \\ x & y & a + z \end{vmatrix}$ $\left[\begin{matrix} \because R_1 \to R_1 - R_2 \\ \text{and } R_2 \to R_2 - R_3 \end{matrix}\right]$

$$= \begin{vmatrix} a & 0 & 0 \\ 0 & a & -a \\ x & x + y & a + z \end{vmatrix} \quad [\because C_2 \to C_2 + C_1]$$

$$= a (a^2 + az + ax + ay)$$
$$= a^2 (a + z + x + y)$$

Q. 3 $\begin{vmatrix} 0 & xy^2 & xz^2 \\ x^2y & 0 & yz^2 \\ x^2z & zy^2 & 0 \end{vmatrix}$

Sol. We have, $\begin{vmatrix} 0 & xy^2 & xz^2 \\ x^2y & 0 & yz^2 \\ x^2z & zy^2 & 0 \end{vmatrix} = x^2y^2z^2 \begin{vmatrix} 0 & x & x \\ y & 0 & y \\ z & z & 0 \end{vmatrix}$

[taking x^2, y^2 and z^2 common from C_1, C_2 and C_3, respectively]

$$= x^2y^2z^2 \begin{vmatrix} 0 & 0 & x \\ y & -y & y \\ z & z & 0 \end{vmatrix} \qquad [\because C_2 \to C_2 - C_3]$$

$$= x^2y^2z^2 \, [x\,(yz + yz)]$$

$$= x^2y^2z^2 \cdot 2xyz = 2x^3y^3z^3$$

Q. 4 $\begin{vmatrix} 3x & -x+y & -x+z \\ x-y & 3y & z-y \\ x-z & y-z & 3z \end{vmatrix}$

Sol. We have, $\begin{vmatrix} 3x & -x+y & -x+z \\ x-y & 3y & z-y \\ x-z & y-z & 3z \end{vmatrix}$

Applying, $C_1 \to C_1 + C_2 + C_3$,

$$= \begin{vmatrix} x+y+z & -x+y & -x+z \\ x+y+z & 3y & z-y \\ x+y+z & y-z & 3z \end{vmatrix}$$

$$= (x+y+z) \begin{vmatrix} 1 & -x+y & -x+z \\ 1 & 3y & z-y \\ 1 & y-z & 3z \end{vmatrix}$$

[taking $(x+y+z)$ common from column C_1]

$$= (x+y+z) \begin{vmatrix} 1 & -x+y & -x+z \\ 0 & 2y+x & x-y \\ 0 & x-z & 2z+x \end{vmatrix}$$

[$\because$ $R_2 \to R_2 - R_1$ and $R_3 \to R_3 - R_1$]

Now, expanding along first column, we get

$$(x+y+z) \cdot 1\,[(2y+x)(2z+x) - (x-y)(x-z)]$$

$$= (x+y+z)\,(4yz + 2yx + 2xz + x^2 - x^2 + xz + yx - yz)$$

$$= (x+y+z)\,(3yz + 3yx + 3xz)$$

$$= 3\,(x+y+z)(yz + yx + xz)$$

Q. 5 $\begin{vmatrix} x+4 & x & x \\ x & x+4 & x \\ x & x & x+4 \end{vmatrix}$

Sol. We have, $\begin{vmatrix} x+4 & x & x \\ x & x+4 & x \\ x & x & x+4 \end{vmatrix} = \begin{vmatrix} 2x+4 & 2x+4 & 2x \\ x & x+4 & x \\ x & x & x+4 \end{vmatrix}$ $[\because R_1 \to R_1 + R_2]$

$$= \begin{vmatrix} 2x & 2x & 2x \\ x & x+4 & x \\ x & x & x+4 \end{vmatrix} + \begin{vmatrix} 4 & 4 & 0 \\ x & x+4 & x \\ x & x & x+4 \end{vmatrix}$$

[here, given determinant is expressed in sum of two determinants]

$$= 2x \begin{vmatrix} 1 & 1 & 1 \\ x & x+4 & x \\ x & x & x+4 \end{vmatrix} + 4 \begin{vmatrix} 1 & 1 & 0 \\ x & x+4 & x \\ x & x & x+4 \end{vmatrix}$$

[taking $2x$ common from first row of first determinant and 4 from first row of second determinant]

Applying $C_1 \to C_1 - C_3$ and $C_2 \to C_2 - C_3$ in first and applying $C_1 \to C_1 - C_2$ in second, we get

$$= 2x \begin{vmatrix} 0 & 0 & 1 \\ 0 & 4 & x \\ -4 & -4 & x+4 \end{vmatrix} + 4 \begin{vmatrix} 0 & 1 & 0 \\ -4 & x+4 & x \\ 0 & x & x+4 \end{vmatrix}$$

Expanding both the along first column, we get

$$2x\,[-4(-4)] + 4\,[4\,(x+4-0)]$$
$$= 2x \times 16 + 16\,(x+4)$$
$$= 32x + 16x + 64$$
$$= 16\,(3x+4)$$

Q. 6 $\begin{vmatrix} a-b-c & 2a & 2a \\ 2b & b-c-a & 2b \\ 2c & 2c & c-a-b \end{vmatrix}$

Sol. Wehave, $\begin{vmatrix} a-b-c & 2a & 2a \\ 2b & b-c-a & 2b \\ 2c & 2c & c-a-b \end{vmatrix}$

$$= \begin{vmatrix} a+b+c & a+b+c & a+b+c \\ 2b & b-c-a & 2b \\ 2c & 2c & c-a-b \end{vmatrix} \quad [\because R_1 \to R_1 + R_2 + R_3]$$

$$= (a+b+c) \begin{vmatrix} 1 & 1 & 1 \\ 2b & b-c-a & 2b \\ 2c & 2c & c-a-b \end{vmatrix}$$

[taking $(a+b+c)$common from the first row]

$$= (a+b+c) \begin{vmatrix} 0 & 0 & 1 \\ 0 & -(a+b+c) & 2b \\ (a+b+c) & (a+b+c) & (c-a-b) \end{vmatrix}$$

$[\because C_1 \to C_1 - C_3$ and $C_2 \to C_2 - C_3]$

Expanding along R_1,

$$= (a+b+c)[1\{0+(a+b+c^2\}]$$
$$= (a+b+c)[(a+b+c)^2]$$
$$= (a+b+c)^3$$

Q. 7 $\begin{vmatrix} y^2z^2 & yz & y+z \\ z^2x^2 & zx & z+x \\ x^2y^2 & xy & x+y \end{vmatrix} = 0$

Sol. We have to prove,

$$\begin{vmatrix} y^2z^2 & yz & y+z \\ z^2x^2 & zx & z+x \\ x^2y^2 & xy & x+y \end{vmatrix} = 0$$

$\therefore$ $$\text{LHS} = \begin{vmatrix} y^2z^2 & yz & y+z \\ z^2x^2 & zx & z+x \\ x^2y^2 & xy & x+y \end{vmatrix} = \frac{1}{xyz}\begin{vmatrix} xy^2z^2 & xyz & xy+xz \\ x^2yz^2 & xyz & yz+xy \\ x^2y^2z & xyz & xz+yz \end{vmatrix}$$

$[\because R_1 \to xR_1, R_2 \to yR_2, R_3 \to zR_3]$

$$= \frac{1}{xyz}(xyz)^2\begin{vmatrix} yz & 1 & xy+xz \\ xz & 1 & yz+xy \\ xy & 1 & xz+yz \end{vmatrix}$$

[taking (xyz) common from C_1 and C_2]

$$= xyz\begin{vmatrix} yz & 1 & xy+yz+zx \\ xz & 1 & xy+yz+zx \\ xy & 1 & xy+yz+zx \end{vmatrix} \quad [C_3 \to C_3 + C_1]$$

$$= xyz(xy+yz+zx)\begin{vmatrix} yz & 1 & 1 \\ xz & 1 & 1 \\ xy & 1 & 1 \end{vmatrix}$$

[taking $(xy+yz+zx)$ common from C_3]

$= 0$ [since, C_2 and C_3 are identicals]

$=$ RHS **Hence proved.**

Q. 8 $\begin{vmatrix} y+z & z & y \\ z & z+x & x \\ y & x & x+y \end{vmatrix} = 4xyz$

Thinking Process

First in LHS use $C_1 \to C_1 + C_2 + C_3$ and then by using $C_1 \to C_1 - C_2$ and $R_1 \to R_1 - R_3$, we can get two zeroes in column 1 and then by simplification we will get the desired result.

Sol. We have to prove,

$$\begin{vmatrix} y+z & z & y \\ z & z+x & x \\ y & x & x+y \end{vmatrix} = 4xyz$$

$$\therefore \quad \text{LHS} = \begin{vmatrix} y+z & z & y \\ z & z+x & x \\ y & x & x+y \end{vmatrix}$$

$$= \begin{vmatrix} y+z+z+y & z & y \\ z+z+x+x & z+x & x \\ y+x+x+y & x & x+y \end{vmatrix} \quad [\because C_1 \to C_1 + C_2 + C_3]$$

$$= 2\begin{vmatrix} (y+z) & z & y \\ (z+x) & z+x & x \\ (x+y) & x & x+y \end{vmatrix} \quad [\text{taking 2 common from } C_1]$$

$$= 2\begin{vmatrix} y & z & y \\ 0 & z+x & x \\ y & x & x+y \end{vmatrix} \quad [\because C_1 \to C_1 - C_2]$$

$$= 2\begin{vmatrix} 0 & z-x & -x \\ 0 & z+x & x \\ y & x & x+y \end{vmatrix} \quad [\because R_1 \to R_1 - R_3]$$

$$= 2\,[y(xz - x^2 + xz + x^2)]$$

$$= 4xyz = \text{RHS}$$

Hence proved.

Q. 9 $\begin{vmatrix} a^2+2a & 2a+1 & 1 \\ 2a+1 & a+2 & 1 \\ 3 & 3 & 1 \end{vmatrix} = (a-1)^3$

Thinking Process

Here, by using $R_1 \to R_1 - R_2$ and $R_2 \to R_2 - R_3$ in LHS, we can easily get the desired result.

Sol. We have to prove,

$$= \begin{vmatrix} a^2+2a & 2a+1 & 1 \\ 2a+1 & a+2 & 1 \\ 3 & 3 & 1 \end{vmatrix} = (a-1)^3$$

$$\therefore \quad \text{LHS} = \begin{vmatrix} a^2+2a & 2a+1 & 1 \\ 2a+1 & a+2 & 1 \\ 3 & 3 & 1 \end{vmatrix}$$

$$= \begin{vmatrix} a^2+2a-2a-1 & 2a+1-a-2 & 0 \\ 2a+1-3 & a+2-3 & 0 \\ 3 & 3 & 1 \end{vmatrix}$$

$[\because R_1 \to R_1 - R_2$ and $R_2 \to R_2 - R_3]$

$$= \begin{vmatrix} (a-1)(a+1) & (a-1) & 0 \\ 2(a-1) & (a-1) & 0 \\ 3 & 3 & 1 \end{vmatrix} = (a-1)^2 \begin{vmatrix} (a+1) & 1 & 0 \\ 2 & 1 & 0 \\ 3 & 3 & 1 \end{vmatrix}$$

[taking $(a-1)$ common from R_1 and R_2 each]

$$= (a-1)^2[1(a+1) - 2] = (a-1)^3$$

$$= \text{RHS}$$

Hence proved.

Q. 10 If $A+B+C=0$, then prove that $\begin{vmatrix} 1 & \cos C & \cos B \\ \cos C & 1 & \cos A \\ \cos B & \cos A & 1 \end{vmatrix} = 0.$

Thinking Process

We have, given $A+B+C=0$, so on solving the determinant by expansion, we can use $\cos(A+B)=\cos(-C)$ and similarly after simplification this expansion we will get the desired result.

Sol. We have to prove, $\begin{vmatrix} 1 & \cos C & \cos B \\ \cos C & 1 & \cos A \\ \cos B & \cos A & 1 \end{vmatrix} = 0$

$$\therefore \quad \text{LHS} = \begin{vmatrix} 1 & \cos C & \cos B \\ \cos C & 1 & \cos A \\ \cos B & \cos A & 1 \end{vmatrix}$$

$$= 1(1-\cos^2 A) - \cos C(\cos C - \cos A\cdot\cos B) + \cos B(\cos C\cdot\cos A - \cos B)$$

$$= \sin^2 A - \cos^2 C + \cos A\cdot\cos B\cdot\cos C + \cos A\cdot\cos B\cdot\cos C - \cos^2 B$$

$$= \sin^2 A - \cos^2 B + 2\cos A\cdot\cos B\cdot\cos C - \cos^2 C$$

$$= -\cos(A+B)\cdot\cos(A-B) + 2\cos A\cdot\cos B\cdot\cos C - \cos^2 C$$

$$[\because \cos^2 B - \sin^2 A = \cos(A+B)\cdot\cos(A-B)]$$

$$= -\cos(-C)\cdot\cos(A-B) + \cos C(2\cos A\cdot\cos B - \cos C) \quad [\because \cos(-\theta) = \cos\theta]$$

$$= -\cos C(\cos A\cdot\cos B + \sin A\cdot\sin B - 2\cos A\cdot\cos B + \cos C)$$

$$= \cos C(\cos A\cdot\cos B - \sin A\cdot\sin B - \cos C)$$

$$= \cos C[\cos(A+B) - \cos C]$$

$$= \cos C(\cos C - \cos C) = 0 = \text{RHS}$$

Hence proved.

Q. 11 If the coordinates of the vertices of an equilateral triangle with sides of length 'a' are $(x_1, y_1), (x_2, y_2)$ and (x_3, y_3), then

$$\begin{vmatrix} x_1 & y_1 & 1 \\ x_2 & y_2 & 1 \\ x_3 & y_3 & 1 \end{vmatrix}^2 = \frac{3a^4}{4}.$$

Sol. Since, we know that area of a triangle with vertices (x_1, y_1), (x_2, y_2) and (x_3, y_3), is given by

$$\Delta = \frac{1}{2}\begin{vmatrix} x_1 & y_1 & 1 \\ x_2 & y_2 & 1 \\ x_3 & y_3 & 1 \end{vmatrix}$$

$$\Rightarrow \quad \Delta^2 = \frac{1}{4}\begin{vmatrix} x_1 & y_1 & 1 \\ x_2 & y_2 & 1 \\ x_3 & y_3 & 1 \end{vmatrix}^2 \quad \text{...(i)}$$

We know that, area of an equilateral triangle with side a,

$$\Delta = \frac{1}{2}\left(\frac{\sqrt{3}}{2}\right)a^2 = \frac{\sqrt{3}}{4}a^2$$

$$\Rightarrow \quad \Delta^2 = \frac{3}{16}a^4 \quad \text{...(ii)}$$

From Eqs. (i) and (ii), $\dfrac{3}{16}a^4 = \dfrac{1}{4}\begin{vmatrix} x_1 & y_1 & 1 \\ x_2 & y_2 & 1 \\ x_3 & y_3 & 1 \end{vmatrix}^2$

$\Rightarrow \begin{vmatrix} x_1 & y_1 & 1 \\ x_2 & y_2 & 1 \\ x_3 & y_3 & 1 \end{vmatrix}^2 = \dfrac{3}{4}a^4$ **Hence proved.**

Q. 12 Find the value of θ satisfying $\begin{bmatrix} 1 & 1 & \sin 3\theta \\ -4 & 3 & \cos 2\theta \\ 7 & -7 & -2 \end{bmatrix} = 0$

Sol. We have, $\begin{vmatrix} 1 & 1 & \sin 3\theta \\ -4 & 3 & \cos 2\theta \\ 7 & -7 & -2 \end{vmatrix} = 0$

$\Rightarrow \begin{vmatrix} 0 & 1 & \sin 3\theta \\ -7 & 3 & \cos 2\theta \\ 14 & -7 & -2 \end{vmatrix} = 0$ $[\because C_1 \to C_1 - C_2]$

$\Rightarrow 7\begin{vmatrix} 0 & 1 & \sin 3\theta \\ -1 & 3 & \cos 2\theta \\ 2 & -7 & -2 \end{vmatrix} = 0$ [taking 7 common from C_1]

$\Rightarrow 7[0 - 1(2 - 2\cos 2\theta) + \sin 3\theta(7 - 6)] = 0$ [expanding along R_1]

$\Rightarrow 7[-2(1 - \cos 2\theta) + \sin 3\theta] = 0$

$\Rightarrow -14 + 14\cos 2\theta + 7\sin 3\theta = 0$

$\Rightarrow 14\cos 2\theta + 7\sin 3\theta = 14$

$\Rightarrow 14(1 - 2\sin^2\theta) + 7(3\sin\theta - 4\sin^3\theta) = 14$

$\Rightarrow -28\sin^2\theta + 14 + 21\sin\theta - 28\sin^3\theta = 14$

$\Rightarrow -28\sin^2\theta - 28\sin^3\theta + 21\sin\theta = 0$

$\Rightarrow 28\sin^3\theta + 28\sin^2\theta - 21\sin\theta = 0$

$\Rightarrow 4\sin^3\theta + 4\sin^2\theta - 3\sin\theta = 0$

$\Rightarrow \sin\theta(4\sin^2\theta + 4\sin\theta - 3) = 0$

$\Rightarrow$ Either $\sin\theta = 0$,

$\Rightarrow \theta = n\pi$ or $4\sin^2\theta + 4\sin\theta - 3 = 0$

$\therefore \sin\theta = \dfrac{-4 \pm \sqrt{16 + 48}}{8} = \dfrac{-4 \pm \sqrt{64}}{8}$

$= \dfrac{-4 \pm 8}{8} = \dfrac{4}{8}, \dfrac{-12}{8}$

$\sin\theta = \dfrac{1}{2}, \dfrac{-3}{2}$

If $\sin\theta = \dfrac{1}{2} = \sin\dfrac{\pi}{6}$, then

$\theta = n\pi + (-1)^n \dfrac{\pi}{6}$

Hence, $\sin\theta = \dfrac{-3}{2}$ [not possible because $-1 \le \sin\theta \le 1$]

Q. 13 If $\begin{bmatrix} 4-x & 4+x & 4+x \\ 4+x & 4-x & 4+x \\ 4+x & 4+x & 4-x \end{bmatrix} = 0$, then find the value of x.

Sol. Given,
$$\begin{vmatrix} 4-x & 4+x & 4+x \\ 4+x & 4-x & 4+x \\ 4+x & 4+x & 4-x \end{vmatrix} = 0$$

$$\Rightarrow \begin{vmatrix} 12+x & 12+x & 12+x \\ 4+x & 4-x & 4+x \\ 4+x & 4+x & 4-x \end{vmatrix} = 0 \quad [\because R_1 \to R_1 + R_2 + R_3]$$

$$\Rightarrow (12+x)\begin{vmatrix} 1 & 1 & 1 \\ 4+x & 4-x & 4+x \\ 4+x & 4+x & 4-x \end{vmatrix} = 0 \quad [\text{taking } (12+x) \text{ common from } R_1]$$

$$\Rightarrow (12+x)\begin{vmatrix} 0 & 0 & 1 \\ 0 & 8 & 4+x \\ 2x & 8 & 4-x \end{vmatrix} = 0 \quad [\because C_1 \to C_1 - C_3 \text{ and } C_2 \to C_2 + C_3]$$

$$\Rightarrow (12+x)[1 \cdot (-16x)] = 0$$
$$\Rightarrow (12+x)(-16x) = 0$$
$$\therefore x = -12, 0$$

Q. 14 If $a_1, a_2, a_3, \ldots, a_r$ are in GP, then prove that the determinant $\begin{vmatrix} a_{r+1} & a_{r+5} & a_{r+9} \\ a_{r+7} & a_{r+11} & a_{r+15} \\ a_{r+11} & a_{r+17} & a_{r+21} \end{vmatrix}$ is independent of r.

Thinking Process

We know that, nth term of a GP has value ar^{n-1}, where a = first term and r = common ratio. So, by using this result, we can prove the given determinant as independent of r.

Sol. We know that, $a_{r+1} = AR^{(r+1)-1} = AR^r$

where r = r th term of a GP, A = First term of a GP and R = Common ratio of GP

We have,
$$\begin{vmatrix} a_{r+1} & a_{r+5} & a_{r+9} \\ a_{r+7} & a_{r+11} & a_{r+15} \\ a_{r+11} & a_{r+17} & a_{r+21} \end{vmatrix}$$
$$= \begin{vmatrix} AR^r & AR^{r+4} & AR^{r+8} \\ AR^{r+6} & AR^{r+10} & AR^{r+14} \\ AR^{r+10} & AR^{r+16} & AR^{r+20} \end{vmatrix}$$
$$= AR^r \cdot AR^{r+6} \cdot AR^{r+10} \begin{vmatrix} 1 & AR^4 & AR^8 \\ 1 & AR^4 & AR^8 \\ 1 & AR^6 & AR^{10} \end{vmatrix}$$

[taking AR^r, AR^{r+6} and AR^{r+10} common from R_1, R_2 and R_3, respectively]

$= 0$ [since, R_1 and R_2 are identicals]

Q. 15 Show that the points $(a+5, a-4)$, $(a-2, a+3)$ and (a, a) do not lie on a straight line for any value of a.

Thinking Process

We know that, if three points lie in a straight line, then area formed by these points will be equal to zero. So, by showing area formed by these points other than zero, we can prove the result.

Sol. Given, the points are $(a+5, a-4)$, $(a-2, a+3)$ and (a, a).

$$\therefore \quad \Delta = \frac{1}{2}\begin{vmatrix} a+5 & a-4 & 1 \\ a-2 & a+3 & 1 \\ a & a & 1 \end{vmatrix}$$

$$= \frac{1}{2}\begin{vmatrix} 5 & -4 & 0 \\ -2 & 3 & 0 \\ a & a & 1 \end{vmatrix} \quad [\because R_1 \to R_1 - R_3 \text{ and } R_2 \to R_2 - R_3]$$

$$= \frac{1}{2}[1(15-8)]$$

$$\Rightarrow \quad = \frac{7}{2} \neq 0$$

Hence, given points form a triangle *i.e.*, points do not lie in a straight line.

Q. 16 Show that ΔABC is an isosceles triangle, if the determinant

$$\Delta = \begin{vmatrix} 1 & 1 & 1 \\ 1+\cos A & 1+\cos B & 1+\cos C \\ \cos^2 A + \cos A & \cos^2 B + \cos B & \cos^2 C + \cos C \end{vmatrix} = 0.$$

Sol. We have, $\Delta = \begin{vmatrix} 1 & 1 & 1 \\ 1+\cos A & 1+\cos B & 1+\cos C \\ \cos^2 A + \cos A & \cos^2 B + \cos B & \cos^2 C + \cos C \end{vmatrix} = 0$

$$\Delta = \begin{vmatrix} 0 & 0 & 1 \\ \cos A - \cos C & \cos B - \cos C & 1+\cos C \\ \cos^2 A + \cos A - \cos^2 C - \cos C & \cos^2 B + \cos B - \cos^2 C - \cos C & \cos^2 C + \cos C \end{vmatrix} = 0$$

$$[\because C_1 \to C_1 - C_3 \text{ and } C_2 \to C_2 - C_3]$$

$$\Rightarrow (\cos A - \cos C)\cdot(\cos B - \cos C)\begin{vmatrix} 0 & 0 & 1 \\ 1 & 1 & 1+\cos C \\ \cos A + \cos C + 1 & \cos B + \cos C + 1 & \cos^2 C + \cos C \end{vmatrix} = 0$$

[taking $(\cos A - \cos C)$ common from C_1 and $(\cos B - \cos C)$ common from C_2]

$$\Rightarrow (\cos A - \cos C)\cdot(\cos B - \cos C)[(\cos B + \cos C + 1) - (\cos A + \cos C + 1)] = 0$$

$$\Rightarrow (\cos A - \cos C)\cdot(\cos B - \cos C)(\cos B + \cos C + 1 - \cos A - \cos C - 1) = 0$$

$$\Rightarrow (\cos A - \cos C)\cdot(\cos B - \cos C)(\cos B - \cos A) = 0$$

i.e., $\cos A = \cos C$ or $\cos B = \cos C$ or $\cos B = \cos A$

$\Rightarrow A = C$ or $B = C$ or $B = A$

Hence, ABC is an isosceles triangle.

Q. 17 Find A^{-1}, if $A=\begin{vmatrix}0&1&1\\1&0&1\\1&1&0\end{vmatrix}$ and show that $A^{-1}=\dfrac{A^2-3I}{2}$.

Sol. We have, $A=\begin{vmatrix}0&1&1\\1&0&1\\1&1&0\end{vmatrix}$

$\therefore$ $A_{11}=-1, A_{12}=1, A_{13}=1, A_{21}=1, A_{22}=-1, A_{23}=1, A_{31}=1, A_{32}=1$ and $A_{33}=-1$

$$\therefore \quad \text{adj } A=\begin{vmatrix}-1&1&1\\1&-1&1\\1&1&-1\end{vmatrix}^T=\begin{vmatrix}-1&1&1\\1&-1&1\\1&1&-1\end{vmatrix}$$

and $|A|=-1(-1)+1\cdot1=2$

$$\therefore \quad A^{-1}=\frac{\text{adj } A}{|A|}=\frac{1}{2}\begin{bmatrix}-1&1&1\\1&-1&1\\1&1&-1\end{bmatrix} \quad \text{...(i)}$$

$$\text{and} \quad A^2=\begin{bmatrix}0&1&1\\1&0&1\\1&1&0\end{bmatrix}\cdot\begin{bmatrix}0&1&1\\1&0&1\\1&1&0\end{bmatrix}=\begin{bmatrix}2&1&1\\1&2&1\\1&1&2\end{bmatrix} \quad \text{...(ii)}$$

$$\therefore \quad \frac{A^2-3I}{2}=\frac{1}{2}\left\{\begin{vmatrix}2&1&1\\1&2&1\\1&1&2\end{vmatrix}-\begin{vmatrix}3&0&0\\0&3&0\\0&0&3\end{vmatrix}\right\}=\frac{1}{2}\begin{vmatrix}-1&1&1\\1&-1&1\\1&1&-1\end{vmatrix}$$

$$=A^{-1}$$

[using Eq. (i)]
Hence proved.

Long Answer Type Questions

Q. 18 If $A=\begin{vmatrix}1&2&0\\-2&-1&-2\\0&-1&1\end{vmatrix}$, then find the value of A^{-1}.

Using A^{-1}, solve the system of linear equations $x-2y=10$, $2x-y-z=8$ and $-2y+z=7$.

Sol. We have, $A=\begin{vmatrix}1&2&0\\-2&-1&-2\\0&-1&1\end{vmatrix}$ ...(i)

$\therefore$ $|A|=1(-3)-2(-2)+0=1\neq 0$

Now, $A_{11}=-3, A_{12}=2, A_{13}=2, A_{21}=-2, A_{22}=1, A_{23}=1, A_{31}=-4, A_{32}=2$ and $A_{33}=3$

$$\therefore \quad \text{adj }(A)=\begin{vmatrix}-3&2&2\\-2&1&1\\-4&2&3\end{vmatrix}^T=\begin{vmatrix}-3&-2&-4\\2&1&2\\2&1&3\end{vmatrix}$$

$$\therefore \qquad A^{-1} = \frac{\text{adj } A}{|A|}$$

$$= \frac{1}{1}\begin{vmatrix} -3 & -2 & -4 \\ 2 & 1 & 2 \\ 2 & 1 & 3 \end{vmatrix}$$

$$\Rightarrow \qquad A^{-1} = \begin{vmatrix} -3 & -2 & -4 \\ 2 & 1 & 2 \\ 2 & 1 & 3 \end{vmatrix} \qquad \text{...(ii)}$$

Also, we have the system of linear equations as

$$x - 2y = 10,$$

$$2x - y - z = 8$$

and $$-2y + z = 7$$

In the form of $CX = D$,

$$\begin{bmatrix} 1 & 2 & 0 \\ 2 & -1 & -1 \\ 0 & -2 & 1 \end{bmatrix}\begin{bmatrix} x \\ y \\ z \end{bmatrix} = \begin{bmatrix} 10 \\ 8 \\ 7 \end{bmatrix}$$

where, $$C = \begin{bmatrix} 1 & -2 & 0 \\ 2 & -1 & -1 \\ 0 & -2 & 1 \end{bmatrix}, X = \begin{bmatrix} x \\ y \\ z \end{bmatrix} \text{ and } D = \begin{bmatrix} 10 \\ 8 \\ 7 \end{bmatrix}$$

We know that, $$(A^T)^{-1} = (A^{-1})^T$$

$$\therefore \qquad C^T = \begin{vmatrix} 1 & 2 & 0 \\ -2 & -1 & -2 \\ 0 & -1 & 1 \end{vmatrix} = A \qquad \text{[using Eq. (i)]}$$

$$\therefore \qquad X = C^{-1} D$$

$$\Rightarrow \qquad \begin{bmatrix} x \\ y \\ z \end{bmatrix} = \begin{bmatrix} -3 & 2 & 2 \\ -2 & 1 & 1 \\ -4 & 2 & 3 \end{bmatrix}\begin{bmatrix} 10 \\ 8 \\ 7 \end{bmatrix}$$

$$= \begin{bmatrix} -30 + 16 + 14 \\ -20 + 8 + 7 \\ -40 + 16 + 21 \end{bmatrix} = \begin{bmatrix} 0 \\ -5 \\ -3 \end{bmatrix}$$

$$\therefore \qquad x = 0, y = -5 \text{ and } z = -3$$

Q. 19 Using matrix method, solve the system of equations $3x + 2y - 2z = 3$, $x + 2y + 3z = 6$ and $2x - y + z = 2$.

Thinking Process

We know that, for given system of equations in the matrix form, we get $AX = B \Rightarrow X = A^{-1}B$, where $A^{-1} = \frac{\text{adj}(A)}{|A|}$ and then by getting inverse of A and determinant of A, we can get the desired result.

Sol. Given system of equations is

$$3x + 2y - 2z = 3,$$

$$x + 2y + 3z = 6$$

and $$2x - y + z = 2$$

In the form of $AX = B$,

$$\begin{bmatrix} 3 & 2 & -2 \\ 1 & 2 & 3 \\ 2 & -1 & 1 \end{bmatrix}\begin{bmatrix} x \\ y \\ z \end{bmatrix} = \begin{bmatrix} 3 \\ 6 \\ 2 \end{bmatrix}$$

For A^{-1}, $$|A| = |3(5) - 2(1-6) + (-2)(-5)|$$
$$= |15 + 10 + 10| = |35| \neq 0$$

$\therefore \quad A_{11} = 5, A_{12} = 5, A_{13} = -5, \quad A_{21} = 0, A_{22} = 7, A_{23} = 7, \quad A_{31} = 10, A_{32} = -11$ and $A_{33} = 4$

$$\therefore \qquad \text{adj } A = \begin{vmatrix} 5 & 5 & -5 \\ 0 & 7 & 7 \\ 10 & -11 & 4 \end{vmatrix}^T = \begin{vmatrix} 5 & 0 & 10 \\ 5 & 7 & -11 \\ -5 & 7 & 4 \end{vmatrix}$$

Now, $$A^{-1} = \frac{\text{adj } A}{|A|} = \frac{1}{35}\begin{vmatrix} 5 & 0 & 10 \\ 5 & 7 & -11 \\ -5 & 7 & 4 \end{vmatrix}$$

For $X = A^{-1}B$,

$$\begin{bmatrix} x \\ y \\ z \end{bmatrix} = \frac{1}{35}\begin{bmatrix} 5 & 0 & 10 \\ 5 & 7 & -11 \\ -5 & 7 & 4 \end{bmatrix}\begin{bmatrix} 3 \\ 6 \\ 2 \end{bmatrix}$$

$$= \frac{1}{35}\begin{bmatrix} 15 + 20 \\ 15 + 42 - 22 \\ -15 + 42 + 8 \end{bmatrix} = \frac{1}{35}\begin{bmatrix} 35 \\ 35 \\ 35 \end{bmatrix} = \begin{bmatrix} 1 \\ 1 \\ 1 \end{bmatrix}$$

$\therefore \qquad x = 1, y = 1$ and $z = 1$

Q. 20 **If** $A = \begin{vmatrix} 2 & 2 & -4 \\ -4 & 2 & -4 \\ 2 & -1 & 5 \end{vmatrix}$ **and** $B = \begin{vmatrix} 1 & -1 & 0 \\ 2 & 3 & 4 \\ 0 & 1 & 2 \end{vmatrix}$**, then find** BA **and use this to solve the system of equations** $y + 2z = 7$, $x - y = 3$ **and** $2x + 3y + 4z = 17$.

Sol. We have, $$A = \begin{vmatrix} 2 & 2 & -4 \\ -4 & 2 & -4 \\ 2 & -1 & 5 \end{vmatrix} \text{ and } B = \begin{vmatrix} 1 & -1 & 0 \\ 2 & 3 & 4 \\ 0 & 1 & 2 \end{vmatrix}$$

$$\therefore \qquad BA = \begin{vmatrix} 1 & -1 & 0 \\ 2 & 3 & 4 \\ 0 & 1 & 2 \end{vmatrix}\begin{vmatrix} 2 & 2 & -4 \\ -4 & 2 & -4 \\ 2 & -1 & 5 \end{vmatrix} = \begin{vmatrix} 6 & 0 & 0 \\ 0 & 6 & 0 \\ 0 & 0 & 6 \end{vmatrix} = 6I$$

$$\therefore \qquad B^{-1} = \frac{A}{6} = \frac{1}{6}A = \frac{1}{6}\begin{vmatrix} 2 & 2 & -4 \\ -4 & 2 & -4 \\ 2 & -1 & 5 \end{vmatrix} \qquad \text{...(i)}$$

Also, $$x - y = 3, 2x + 3y + 4z = 17 \text{ and } y + 2z = 7$$

$$\Rightarrow \qquad \begin{bmatrix} 1 & -1 & 0 \\ 2 & 3 & 4 \\ 0 & 1 & 2 \end{bmatrix}\begin{bmatrix} x \\ y \\ z \end{bmatrix} = \begin{bmatrix} 3 \\ 17 \\ 7 \end{bmatrix}$$

$$\therefore \quad \begin{bmatrix} x \\ y \\ z \end{bmatrix} = \begin{bmatrix} 1 & -1 & 0 \\ 2 & 3 & 4 \\ 0 & 1 & 2 \end{bmatrix}^{-1} \begin{bmatrix} 3 \\ 17 \\ 7 \end{bmatrix}$$

$$= \frac{1}{6}\begin{bmatrix} 2 & 2 & -4 \\ -4 & 2 & -4 \\ 2 & -1 & 5 \end{bmatrix} \begin{bmatrix} 3 \\ 17 \\ 7 \end{bmatrix} \quad \text{[using Eq. (i)]}$$

$$= \frac{1}{6}\begin{bmatrix} 6+34-28 \\ -12+34-28 \\ 6-17+35 \end{bmatrix} = \frac{1}{6}\begin{bmatrix} 12 \\ -6 \\ 24 \end{bmatrix} = \begin{bmatrix} 2 \\ -1 \\ 4 \end{bmatrix}$$

$\therefore \quad x = 2, y = -1$ and $z = 4$

Q. 21 If $a + b + c \neq 0$ and $\begin{vmatrix} a & b & c \\ b & c & a \\ c & a & b \end{vmatrix} = 0$, then prove that $a = b = c$.

Sol. Let $A = \begin{vmatrix} a & b & c \\ b & c & a \\ c & a & b \end{vmatrix}$

$$= \begin{vmatrix} a+b+c & a+b+c & a+b+c \\ b & c & a \\ c & a & b \end{vmatrix} \quad [\because R_1 \to R_1 + R_2 + R_3]$$

$$= (a+b+c)\begin{vmatrix} 1 & 1 & 1 \\ b & c & a \\ c & a & b \end{vmatrix}$$

$$= (a+b+c)\begin{vmatrix} 0 & 0 & 1 \\ b-a & c-a & a \\ c-b & a-b & b \end{vmatrix} \quad [\because C_1 \to C_1 - C_3 \text{ and } C_2 \to C_2 - C_3]$$

Expanding along R_1,

$$= (a+b+c)\,[1\,(b-a)(a-b) - (c-a)(c-b)]$$

$$= (a+b+c)\,(ba - b^2 - a^2 + ab - c^2 + cb + ac - ab)$$

$$= \frac{-1}{2}(a+b+c) \times (-2)\,(-a^2 - b^2 - c^2 + ab + bc + ca)$$

$$= \frac{-1}{2}(a+b+c)[a^2 + b^2 + c^2 - 2ab - 2bc - 2ca + a^2 + b^2 + c^2]$$

$$= -\frac{1}{2}(a+b+c)[a^2 + b^2 - 2ab + b^2 + c^2 - 2bc + c^2 + a^2 - 2ac]$$

$$= \frac{-1}{2}(a+b+c)\,[(a-b)^2 + (b-c)^2 + (c-a)^2]$$

Also, $\quad A = 0$

$$= \frac{-1}{2}(a+b+c)\,[(a-b)^2 + (b-c)^2 + (c-a)^2] = 0$$

$$(a-b)^2 + (b-c)^2 + (c-a)^2 = 0 \quad [\because a + b + c \neq 0, \text{ given}]$$

$$\Rightarrow \quad a - b = b - c = c - a = 0$$

$$a = b = c$$

Hence proved.

Q. 22 Prove that $\begin{vmatrix} bc-a^2 & ca-b^2 & ab-c^2 \\ ca-b^2 & ab-c^2 & bc-a^2 \\ ab-c^2 & bc-a^2 & ca-b^2 \end{vmatrix}$ is divisible by $(a+b+c)$ and find the quotient.

Sol. Let
$$\Delta = \begin{vmatrix} bc-a^2 & ca-b^2 & ab-c^2 \\ ca-b^2 & ab-c^2 & bc-a^2 \\ ab-c^2 & bc-a^2 & ca-b^2 \end{vmatrix}$$

$$= \begin{vmatrix} bc-a^2-ca+b^2 & ca-b^2-ab+c^2 & ab-c^2 \\ ca-b^2-ab+c^2 & ab-c^2-bc+a^2 & bc-a^2 \\ ab-c^2-bc+a^2 & bc-a^2-ca+b^2 & ca-b^2 \end{vmatrix}$$

$[\because C_1 \to C_1 - C_2 \text{ and } C_2 \to C_2 - C_3]$

$$= \begin{vmatrix} (b-a)(a+b+c) & (c-b)(a+b+c) & ab-c^2 \\ (c-b)(a+b+c) & (a-c)(a+b+c) & bc-a^2 \\ (a-c)(a+b+c) & (b-a)(a+b+c) & ca-b^2 \end{vmatrix}$$

$$= (a+b+c)^2 \begin{vmatrix} b-a & c-b & ab-c^2 \\ c-b & a-c & bc-a^2 \\ a-c & b-a & ca-b^2 \end{vmatrix}$$

[taking $(a+b+c)$ common from C_1 and C_2 each]

$$= (a+b+c)^2 \begin{vmatrix} 0 & 0 & ab+bc+ca-(a^2+b^2+c^2) \\ c-b & a-c & bc-a^2 \\ a-c & b-a & ca-b^2 \end{vmatrix}$$

$[\because R_1 \to R_1 + R_2 + R_3]$

Now, expanding along R_1,

$$= (a+b+c)^2 [ab+bc+ca-(a^2+b^2+c^2)][(c-b)(b-a)-(a-c)^2]$$

$$= (a+b+c)^2 (ab+bc+ca-a^2-b^2-c^2)$$
$$(cb-ac-b^2+ab-a^2-c^2+2ac)$$

$$= (a+b+c)^2 (a^2+b^2+c^2-ab-bc-ca)$$
$$(a^2+b^2+c^2-ac-ab-bc)$$

$$= \frac{1}{2}(a+b+c)[(a+b+c)(a^2+b^2+c^2-ab-bc-ca)]$$
$$[(a-b)^2+(b-c)^2+(c-a)^2]$$

$$= \frac{1}{2}(a+b+c)(a^3+b^3+c^3-3abc)[(a-b)^2+(b-c)^2+(c-a)^2]$$

Hence, given determinant is divisible by $(a+b+c)$ and quotient is
$$(a^3+b^3+c^3-3abc)[(a-b)^2+(b-c)^2+(c-a)^2].$$

Q. 23 If $x+y+z=0$, then prove that $\begin{vmatrix} xa & yb & zc \\ yc & za & xb \\ zb & xc & ya \end{vmatrix} = xyz\begin{vmatrix} a & b & c \\ c & a & b \\ b & c & a \end{vmatrix}$.

Thinking Process

We have, given $x+y+z=0 \Rightarrow x^3+y^3+z^3=3xyz$. So, by using this in solving the given determinant from both the sides, we can equate the obtained result from both the sides to desired result.

Sol. Since, $x+y+z=0$, also we have to prove

$$\begin{vmatrix} xa & yb & zc \\ yc & za & xb \\ zb & xc & ya \end{vmatrix} = xyz\begin{vmatrix} a & b & c \\ c & a & b \\ b & c & a \end{vmatrix}$$

$\therefore$
$$\text{LHS} = \begin{vmatrix} xa & yb & zc \\ yc & za & xb \\ zb & xc & ya \end{vmatrix}$$

$$= xa(za\cdot ya - xb\cdot xc) - yb(yc\cdot ya - xb\cdot zb) + zc(yc\cdot xc - za\cdot zb)$$
$$= xa(a^2yz - x^2bc) - yb(y^2ac - b^2xz) + zc(c^2xy - z^2ab)$$
$$= xyza^3 - x^3abc - y^3abc + b^3xyz + c^3xyz - z^3abc$$
$$= xyz(a^3+b^3+c^3) - abc(x^3+y^3+z^3)$$
$$= xyz(a^3+b^3+c^3) - abc(3xyz)$$
$$[\because x+y+z=0 \Rightarrow x^3+y^3+z^3-3xyz]$$
$$= xyz(a^3+b^3+c^3-3abc) \quad \text{...(i)}$$

Now,
$$\text{RHS} = xyz\begin{vmatrix} a & b & c \\ c & a & b \\ b & c & a \end{vmatrix} = xyz\begin{vmatrix} a+b+c & b & c \\ a+b+c & a & b \\ a+b+c & c & a \end{vmatrix} \quad [\because C_1 \to C_1 + C_2 + C_3]$$

$$= xyz(a+b+c)\begin{vmatrix} 1 & b & c \\ 1 & a & b \\ 1 & c & a \end{vmatrix} \quad [\text{taking } (a+b+c) \text{ common from } C_1]$$

$$= xyz(a+b+c)\begin{vmatrix} 0 & b-c & c-a \\ 0 & a-c & b-a \\ 1 & c & a \end{vmatrix}$$
$$[\because R_1 \to R_1 - R_3 \text{ and } R_2 \to R_2 - R_3]$$

Expanding along C_1,

$$= xyz(a+b+c)[1(b-c)(b-a) - (a-c)(c-a)]$$
$$= xyz(a+b+c)(b^2 - ab - bc + ac + a^2 + c^2 - 2ac)$$
$$= xyz(a+b+c)(a^2+b^2+c^2-ab-bc-ca)$$
$$= xyz(a^3+b^3+c^3-3abc) \quad \text{...(ii)}$$

From Eqs. (i) and (ii),

$$\text{LHS} = \text{RHS}$$

$$\Rightarrow \begin{vmatrix} xa & yb & zc \\ yc & za & xb \\ zb & xc & ya \end{vmatrix} = xyz\begin{vmatrix} a & b & c \\ c & a & b \\ b & c & a \end{vmatrix}$$

Hence proved.

Objective Type Questions

Q. 24 If $\begin{vmatrix} 2x & 5 \\ 8 & x \end{vmatrix} = \begin{vmatrix} 6 & -2 \\ 7 & 3 \end{vmatrix}$, then the value of x is

(a) 3 (b) ± 3 (c) ± 6 (d) 6

Sol. *(c)* $\because$ $\begin{vmatrix} 2x & 5 \\ 8 & x \end{vmatrix} = \begin{vmatrix} 6 & -2 \\ 7 & 3 \end{vmatrix}$

$\Rightarrow$ $2x^2 - 40 = 18 + 14$

$\Rightarrow$ $2x^2 = 32 + 40$

$\Rightarrow$ $x^2 = \frac{72}{2} = 36$

$\therefore$ $x = \pm 6$

Q. 25 The value of $\begin{vmatrix} a-b & b+c & a \\ b-a & c+a & b \\ c-a & a+b & c \end{vmatrix}$ is

(a) $a^3 + b^3 + c^3$ (b) $3bc$

(c) $a^3 + b^3 + c^3 - 3abc$ (d) None of these

Sol. *(d)* We have,

$$\begin{vmatrix} a-b & b+c & a \\ b-a & c+a & b \\ c-a & a+b & c \end{vmatrix} = \begin{vmatrix} a+c & b+c+a & a \\ b+c & c+a+b & b \\ c+b & a+b+c & c \end{vmatrix} \quad [\because C_1 \to C_1 + C_2 \text{ and } C_2 \to C_2 + C_3]$$

$$= (a+b+c)\begin{vmatrix} a+c & 1 & a \\ b+c & 1 & b \\ c+b & 1 & c \end{vmatrix} \quad [\text{taking } (a+b+c) \text{ common from } C_2]$$

$$= (a+b+c)\begin{vmatrix} a-b & 0 & a-c \\ 0 & 0 & b-c \\ c+b & 1 & c \end{vmatrix} \quad [\because R_2 \to R_2 - R_3 \text{ and } R_1 \to R_1 - R_3]$$

$$= (a+b+c)[-(b-c)\cdot(a-b)] \quad [\text{expanding along } R_2]$$

$$= (a+b+c)(c-b)(a-b)$$

Q. 26 If the area of a triangle with vertices $(-3, 0)$, $(3, 0)$ and $(0, k)$ is 9 sq units. Then, the value of k will be

(a) 9 (b) 3 (c) -9 (d) 6

Sol. *(b)* We know that, area of a triangle with vertices (x_1, y_1), (x_2, y_2) and (x_3, y_3) is given by

$$\Delta = \frac{1}{2}\begin{vmatrix} x_1 & y_1 & 1 \\ x_2 & y_2 & 1 \\ x_3 & y_3 & 1 \end{vmatrix}$$

$\therefore$ $$\Delta = \frac{1}{2}\begin{vmatrix} -3 & 0 & 1 \\ 3 & 0 & 1 \\ 0 & k & 1 \end{vmatrix}$$

Expanding along R_1,

$$9 = \frac{1}{2}[-3(-k) - 0 + 1(3k)]$$

$$\Rightarrow \quad 18 = 3k + 3k = 6k$$

$$\therefore \quad k = \frac{18}{6} = 3$$

Q. 27 The determinant

$$\begin{vmatrix} b^2 - ab & b - c & bc - ac \\ ab - a^2 & a - b & b^2 - ab \\ bc - ac & c - a & ab - a^2 \end{vmatrix} \text{ equals to}$$

(a) $abc(b - c)(c - a)(a - b)$ (b) $(b - c)(c - a)(a - b)$

(c) $(a + b + c)(b - c)(c - a)(a - b)$ (d) None of these

Sol. *(d)* We have,

$$\begin{vmatrix} b^2 - ab & b - c & bc - ac \\ ab - a^2 & a - b & b^2 - ab \\ bc - ac & c - a & ab - a^2 \end{vmatrix} = \begin{vmatrix} b(b - a) & b - c & c(b - a) \\ a(b - a) & a - b & b(b - a) \\ c(b - a) & c - a & a(b - a) \end{vmatrix}$$

$$= (b - a)^2 \begin{vmatrix} b & b - c & c \\ a & a - b & b \\ c & c - a & a \end{vmatrix}$$

[on taking $(b - a)$ common from C_1 and C_3 each]

$$= (b - a)^2 \begin{vmatrix} b - c & b - c & c \\ a - b & a - b & b \\ c - a & c - a & a \end{vmatrix} \qquad [\because C_1 \to C_1 - C_3]$$

$$= 0$$

[since, two columns C_1 and C_2 are identical, so the value of determinant is zero]

Q. 28 The number of distinct real roots of $\begin{vmatrix} \sin x & \cos x & \cos x \\ \cos x & \sin x & \cos x \\ \cos x & \cos x & \sin x \end{vmatrix} = 0$ in the interval $-\frac{\pi}{4} \le x \le \frac{\pi}{4}$ is

(a) 0 (b) 2 (c) 1 (d) 3

Sol. *(c)* We have,

$$\begin{vmatrix} \sin x & \cos x & \cos x \\ \cos x & \sin x & \cos x \\ \cos x & \cos x & \sin x \end{vmatrix} = 0$$

Applying $C_1 \to C_1 + C_2 + C_3$,

$$\begin{vmatrix} 2\cos x + \sin x & \cos x & \cos x \\ 2\cos x + \sin x & \sin x & \cos x \\ 2\cos x + \sin x & \cos x & \sin x \end{vmatrix} = 0$$

On taking $(2\cos x + \sin x)$ common from C_1, we get

$$\Rightarrow \quad (2\cos x + \sin x)\begin{vmatrix} 1 & \cos x & \cos x \\ 1 & \sin x & \cos x \\ 1 & \cos x & \sin x \end{vmatrix} = 0$$

$$\Rightarrow \quad (2\cos x + \sin x)\begin{vmatrix} 1 & \cos x & \cos x \\ 0 & \sin x - \cos x & 0 \\ 0 & 0 & (\sin x - \cos x) \end{vmatrix} = 0$$

[$\because R_2 \to R_2 - R_1$ and $R_3 \to R_3 - R_1$]

Expanding along C_1,

$$(2\cos x + \sin x)[1 \cdot (\sin x - \cos x)^2] = 0$$

$$\Rightarrow \quad (2\cos x + \sin x)(\sin x - \cos x)^2 = 0$$

Either $\quad 2\cos x = -\sin x$

$$\Rightarrow \quad \cos x = -\frac{1}{2}\sin x$$

$$\Rightarrow \quad \tan x = -2 \quad \text{...(i)}$$

But here for $-\frac{\pi}{4} \le x \le \frac{\pi}{4}$, we get $-1 \le \tan x \le 1$ so, no solution possible

and for $\quad (\sin x - \cos x)^2 = 0, \sin x = \cos x$

$$\Rightarrow \quad \tan x = 1 = \tan\frac{\pi}{4}$$

$$\therefore \quad x = \frac{\pi}{4}$$

So, only one distinct real root exist.

Q. 29 If A, B and C are angles of a triangle, then the determinant $\begin{vmatrix} -1 & \cos C & \cos B \\ \cos C & -1 & \cos A \\ \cos B & \cos A & -1 \end{vmatrix}$ is equal to

(a) 0 (b) -1 (c) 1 (d) None of these

Sol. *(a)* We have, $\begin{vmatrix} -1 & \cos C & \cos B \\ \cos C & -1 & \cos A \\ \cos B & \cos A & -1 \end{vmatrix}$

Applying $C_1 \to aC_1 + bC_2 + cC_3$,

$$\begin{vmatrix} -a + b\cos C + c\cos B & \cos C & \cos B \\ a\cos C - b + c\cos A & -1 & \cos A \\ a\cos B + b\cos A - c & \cos A & -1 \end{vmatrix}$$

Also, by projection rule in a triangle, we know that

$$a = b\cos C + c\cos B, b = c\cos A + a\cos C \text{ and } c = a\cos B + b\cos A$$

Using above equation in column first, we get

$$\begin{vmatrix} -a + a & \cos C & \cos B \\ b - b & -1 & \cos A \\ c - c & \cos A & -1 \end{vmatrix} = \begin{vmatrix} 0 & \cos C & \cos B \\ 0 & -1 & \cos A \\ 0 & \cos A & -1 \end{vmatrix} = 0$$

[since, determinant having all elements of any column or row gives value of determinant as zero]

Q. 30 If $f(t) = \begin{bmatrix} \cos t & t & 1 \\ 2\sin t & t & 2t \\ \sin t & t & t \end{bmatrix}$, then $\lim\limits_{t \to 0} \dfrac{f(t)}{t^2}$ is equal to

(a) 0 (b) –1 (c) 2 (d) 3

Sol. *(a)* We have,

$$f(t) = \begin{vmatrix} \cos t & t & 1 \\ 2\sin t & t & 2t \\ \sin t & t & t \end{vmatrix}$$

Expanding along C_1,

$$= \cos t\,(t^2 - 2t^2) - 2\sin t\,(t^2 - t) + \sin t\,(2t^2 - t)$$
$$= -t^2 \cos t - (t^2 - t)2\sin t + (2t^2 - t)\sin t$$
$$= -t^2 \cos t - t^2 \cdot 2\sin t + t \cdot 2\sin t + 2t^2 \sin t$$
$$= -t^2 \cos t + 2t \sin t$$

$$\therefore \quad \lim_{t \to 0} \frac{f(t)}{t^2} = \lim_{t \to 0} \frac{(-t^2 \cos t)}{t^2} + \lim_{t \to 0} \frac{2t \sin t}{t^2}$$
$$= -\lim_{t \to 0} \cos t + 2 \cdot \lim_{t \to 0} \frac{\sin t}{t}$$
$$= -1 + 1 \qquad \left[\because \lim_{t \to 0} \frac{\sin t}{t} = 1 \text{ and } \cos 0 = 1\right]$$
$$= 0$$

Q. 31 The maximum value of

$$\Delta = \begin{vmatrix} 1 & 1 & 1 \\ 1 & 1 + \sin\theta & 1 \\ 1 + \cos\theta & 1 & 1 \end{vmatrix}$$ is (where, θ is real number)

(a) $\frac{1}{2}$ (b) $\frac{\sqrt{3}}{2}$ (c) $\sqrt{2}$ (d) $\frac{2\sqrt{3}}{4}$

Sol. *(a)* Since,

$$\Delta = \begin{vmatrix} 1 & 1 & 1 \\ 1 & 1 + \sin\theta & 1 \\ 1 + \cos\theta & 1 & 1 \end{vmatrix}$$
$$= \begin{vmatrix} 0 & 0 & 1 \\ 0 & \sin\theta & 1 \\ \cos\theta & 0 & 1 \end{vmatrix} \qquad [\because C_1 \to C_1 - C_3 \text{ and } C_2 \to C_2 - C_3]$$
$$= 1(\sin\theta \cdot \cos\theta)$$
$$= \frac{1}{2} \cdot 2\sin\theta\cos\theta = \frac{1}{2}\sin 2\theta$$

Since, the maximum value of $\sin 2\theta$ is 1. So, for maximum value of θ should be 45°.

$$\therefore \quad \Delta = \frac{1}{2}\sin 2 \cdot 45^\circ$$
$$= \frac{1}{2}\sin 90^\circ = \frac{1}{2} \cdot 1 = \frac{1}{2}$$

Q. 32 If $f(x)=\begin{vmatrix} 0 & x-a & x-b \\ x+a & 0 & x-c \\ x+b & x+c & 0 \end{vmatrix}$, then

(a) $f(a)=0$ (b) $f(b)=0$ (c) $f(0)=0$ (d) $f(1)=0$

Sol. *(c)* We have,

$$f(x)=\begin{vmatrix} 0 & x-a & x-b \\ x+a & 0 & x-c \\ x+b & x+c & 0 \end{vmatrix}$$

$$\Rightarrow \quad f(a)=\begin{vmatrix} 0 & 0 & a-b \\ 2a & 0 & a-c \\ a+b & a+c & 0 \end{vmatrix}$$

$$=[(a-b)\{2a\cdot(a+c)\}]\neq 0$$

$$\therefore \quad f(b)=\begin{vmatrix} 0 & b-a & 0 \\ b+a & 0 & b-c \\ 2b & b+c & 0 \end{vmatrix}$$

$$=-(b-a)[2b(b-c)]$$

$$=-2b(b-a)(b-c)\neq 0$$

$$\therefore \quad f(0)=\begin{vmatrix} 0 & -a & -b \\ a & 0 & -c \\ b & c & 0 \end{vmatrix}$$

$$=a(bc)-b(ac)$$

$$=abc-abc=0$$

Q. 33 If $A=\begin{vmatrix} 2 & \lambda & -3 \\ 0 & 2 & 5 \\ 1 & 1 & 3 \end{vmatrix}$, then A^{-1} exists, if

(a) $\lambda=2$ (b) $\lambda\neq 2$
(c) $\lambda\neq -2$ (d) None of these

Sol. *(d)* We have,

$$A=\begin{vmatrix} 2 & \lambda & -3 \\ 0 & 2 & 5 \\ 1 & 1 & 3 \end{vmatrix}$$

Expanding along R_1,

$$|A|=2(6-5)-\lambda(-5)-3(-2)=2+5\lambda+6$$

We know that, A^{-1} exists, if A is non-singular matrix *i.e.*, $|A|\neq 0$.

$$\therefore \quad 2+5\lambda+6\neq 0$$

$$\Rightarrow \quad 5\lambda\neq -8$$

$$\therefore \quad \lambda\neq\frac{-8}{5}$$

So, A^{-1} exists if and only if $\lambda\neq\frac{-8}{5}$.

Q. 34 If A and B are invertible matrices, then which of the following is not correct?

(a) $\text{adj } A = |A| \cdot A^{-1}$ (b) $\det (A)^{-1} = [\det (A)]^{-1}$
(c) $(AB)^{-1} = B^{-1} A^{-1}$ (d) $(A + B)^{-1} = B^{-1} + A^{-1}$

Sol. *(d)* Since, A and B are invertible matrices. So, we can say that

$$(AB)^{-1} = B^{-1} A^{-1} \quad \text{...(i)}$$

Also, $$A^{-1} = \frac{1}{|A|} (\text{adj } A)$$

$\Rightarrow$ $$\text{adj } A = |A| \cdot A^{-1} \quad \text{...(ii)}$$

Also, $$\det (A)^{-1} = [\det (A)]^{-1}$$

$\Rightarrow$ $$\det (A)^{-1} = \frac{1}{[\det (A)]}$$

$\Rightarrow$ $$\det (A) \cdot \det (A)^{-1} = 1 \quad \text{...(iii)}$$

which is true.

Again, $$(A + B)^{-1} = \frac{1}{|(A + B)|} \text{adj } (A + B)$$

$\Rightarrow$ $$(A + B)^{-1} \neq B^{-1} + A^{-1} \quad \text{...(iv)}$$

So, only option (d) is incorrect.

Q. 35 If x, y and z are all different from zero and $\begin{vmatrix} 1+x & 1 & 1 \\ 1 & 1+y & 1 \\ 1 & 1 & 1+z \end{vmatrix} = 0$, then the value of $x^{-1} + y^{-1} + z^{-1}$ is

(a) xyz (b) $x^{-1}y^{-1}z^{-1}$ (c) $-x - y - z$ (d) -1

Sol. *(d)* We have, $$\begin{vmatrix} 1+x & 1 & 1 \\ 1 & 1+y & 1 \\ 1 & 1 & 1+z \end{vmatrix} = 0$$

Applying $C_1 \to C_1 - C_3$ and $C_2 \to C_2 - C_3$,

$\Rightarrow$ $$\begin{vmatrix} x & 0 & 1 \\ 0 & y & 1 \\ -z & -z & 1+z \end{vmatrix} = 0$$

Expanding along R_1,

$$x [y (1 + z) + z] - 0 + 1 (yz) = 0$$

$\Rightarrow$ $$x (y + yz + z) + yz = 0$$

$\Rightarrow$ $$xy + xyz + xz + yz = 0$$

$\Rightarrow$ $$\frac{xy}{xyz} + \frac{xyz}{xyz} + \frac{xz}{xyz} + \frac{yz}{xyz} = 0 \quad \text{[on dividing } (xyz) \text{ from both sides]}$$

$\Rightarrow$ $$\frac{1}{x} + \frac{1}{y} + \frac{1}{z} + 1 = 0$$

$\Rightarrow$ $$\frac{1}{x} + \frac{1}{y} + \frac{1}{z} = -1$$

$\therefore$ $$x^{-1} + y^{-1} + z^{-1} = -1$$

Q. 36 The value of $\begin{vmatrix} x & x+y & x+2y \\ x+2y & x & x+y \\ x+y & x+2y & x \end{vmatrix}$ is

(a) $9x^2(x+y)$
(b) $9y^2(x+y)$
(c) $3y^2(x+y)$
(d) $7x^2(x+y)$

Sol. *(b)* We have,

$$\begin{vmatrix} x & x+y & x+2y \\ x+2y & x & x+y \\ x+y & x+2y & x \end{vmatrix}$$

$$= \begin{vmatrix} 3(x+y) & x+y & y \\ 3(x+y) & x & y \\ 3(x+y) & x+2y & -2y \end{vmatrix} \quad [\because C_1 \to C_1 + C_2 + C_3 \text{ and } C_3 \to C_3 - C_2]$$

$$= 3(x+y)\begin{vmatrix} 1 & (x+y) & y \\ 1 & x & y \\ 1 & (x+2y) & -2y \end{vmatrix} \quad [\text{taking } 3(x+y) \text{ common from first column}]$$

$$= 3(x+y)\begin{vmatrix} 0 & y & 0 \\ 1 & x & y \\ 1 & (x+2y) & -2y \end{vmatrix} \quad [\because R_1 \to R_1 - R_2]$$

Expanding along R_1,

$$= 3(x+y)[-y(-2y-y)]$$
$$= 3y^2 \cdot 3(x+y) = 9y^2(x+y)$$

Q. 37 If there are two values of a which makes determinant,

$$\Delta = \begin{vmatrix} 1 & -2 & 5 \\ 2 & a & -1 \\ 0 & 4 & 2a \end{vmatrix} = 86,$$ then the sum of these number is

(a) 4
(b) 5
(c) – 4
(d) 9

Sol. *(c)* We have,

$$\Delta = \begin{vmatrix} 1 & -2 & 5 \\ 2 & a & -1 \\ 0 & 4 & 2a \end{vmatrix} = 86$$

$\Rightarrow \quad 1(2a^2 + 4) - 2(-4a - 20) + 0 = 86 \quad$ [expanding along first column]

$\Rightarrow \quad 2a^2 + 4 + 8a + 40 = 86$

$\Rightarrow \quad 2a^2 + 8a + 44 - 86 = 0$

$\Rightarrow \quad a^2 + 4a - 21 = 0$

$\Rightarrow \quad a^2 + 7a - 3a - 21 = 0$

$\Rightarrow \quad (a+7)(a-3) = 0$

$a = -7$ and 3

$\therefore \quad$ Required sum $= -7 + 3 = -4$

Fillers

Q. 38 If A is a matrix of order 3×3, then $|3A|$ is equal to ....

Sol. If A is a matrix of order 3×3, then $|3A| = 3 \times 3 \times 3|A| = 27|A|$

Q. 39 If A is invertible matrix of order 3×3, then $|A^{-1}|$ is equal to ....

Sol. If A is invertible matrix of order 3×3, then $|A^{-1}| = \dfrac{1}{|A|}$. [since, $|A| \cdot |A^{-1}| = 1$]

Q. 40 If $x, y, z \in R$, then the value of $\begin{vmatrix} (2^x + 2^{-x})^2 & (2^x - 2^{-x})^2 & 1 \\ (3^x + 3^{-x})^2 & (3^x - 3^{-x})^2 & 1 \\ (4^x + 4^{-x})^2 & (4^x - 4^{-x})^2 & 1 \end{vmatrix}$ is

Sol. We have,

$$\begin{vmatrix} (2^x + 2^{-x})^2 & (2^x - 2^{-x})^2 & 1 \\ (3^x + 3^{-x})^2 & (3^x - 3^{-x})^2 & 1 \\ (4^x + 4^{-x})^2 & (4^x - 4^{-x})^2 & 1 \end{vmatrix}$$

$$= \begin{vmatrix} (2 \cdot 2^x)(2 \cdot 2^{-x}) & (2^x - 2^{-x})^2 & 1 \\ (2 \cdot 3^x)(2 \cdot 3^{-x}) & (3^x - 3^{-x})^2 & 1 \\ (2 \cdot 4^x)(2 \cdot 4^{-x}) & (4^x - 4^{-x})^2 & 1 \end{vmatrix} \qquad [\because (a+b)^2 - (a-b)^2 = 4ab] \; [\because C_1 \to C_1 - C_2]$$

$$= \begin{vmatrix} 4 & (2^x - 2^{-x})^2 & 1 \\ 4 & (3^x - 3^{-x})^2 & 1 \\ 4 & (4^x - 4^{-x})^2 & 1 \end{vmatrix} = 0$$ [since, C_1 and C_3 are proportional to each other]

Q. 41 If $\cos 2\theta = 0$, then $\begin{vmatrix} 0 & \cos\theta & \sin\theta \\ \cos\theta & \sin\theta & 0 \\ \sin\theta & 0 & \cos\theta \end{vmatrix}^2$ is equal to ....

Sol. Since, $\cos 2\theta = 0$

$\Rightarrow \quad \cos 2\theta = \cos\dfrac{\pi}{2} \Rightarrow 2\theta = \dfrac{\pi}{2}$

$\Rightarrow \quad \theta = \dfrac{\pi}{4}$

$\therefore \quad \sin\dfrac{\pi}{4} = \dfrac{1}{\sqrt{2}}$ and $\cos\dfrac{\pi}{4} = \dfrac{1}{\sqrt{2}}$

$$\therefore \quad \begin{vmatrix} 0 & \frac{1}{\sqrt{2}} & \frac{1}{\sqrt{2}} \\ \frac{1}{\sqrt{2}} & \frac{1}{\sqrt{2}} & 0 \\ \frac{1}{\sqrt{2}} & 0 & \frac{1}{\sqrt{2}} \end{vmatrix}^2$$

Expanding along R_1,

$$= \left[-\frac{1}{\sqrt{2}}\left(\frac{1}{2}\right) + \frac{1}{\sqrt{2}}\left(-\frac{1}{2}\right)\right]^2 = \left[\frac{-2}{2\sqrt{2}}\right]^2 = \left(\frac{-1}{\sqrt{2}}\right)^2 = \frac{1}{2}$$

Q. 42 If A is a matrix of order 3×3, then $(A^2)^{-1}$ is equal to ....

Sol. If A is a matrix of order 3×3, then $(A^2)^{-1} = (A^{-1})^2$.

Q. 43 If A is a matrix of order 3×3, then the number of minors in determinant of A are ....

Sol. If A is a matrix of order 3×3, then the number of minors in determinant of A are 9. [since, in a 3×3 matrix, there are 9 elements]

Q. 44 The sum of products of elements of any row with the cofactors of corresponding elements is equal to ....

Sol. The sum of products of elements of any row with the cofactors of corresponding elements is equal to value of the determinant.

$$\text{Let } \Delta = \begin{vmatrix} a_{11} & a_{12} & a_{13} \\ a_{21} & a_{22} & a_{23} \\ a_{31} & a_{32} & a_{33} \end{vmatrix}$$

Expanding along R_1,

$$\Delta = a_{11}A_{11} + a_{12}A_{12} + a_{13}A_{13}$$

= Sum of products of elements of R_1 with their corresponding cofactors

Q. 45 If $x = -9$ is a root of $\begin{vmatrix} x & 3 & 7 \\ 2 & x & 2 \\ 7 & 6 & x \end{vmatrix} = 0$, then other two roots are ....

Sol. Since, $\begin{vmatrix} x & 3 & 7 \\ 2 & x & 2 \\ 7 & 6 & x \end{vmatrix} = 0$

Expanding along R_1,

$$x(x^2 - 12) - 3(2x - 14) + 7(12 - 7x) = 0$$

$$\Rightarrow \quad x^3 - 12x - 6x + 42 + 84 - 49x = 0$$

$$\Rightarrow \quad x^3 - 67x + 126 = 0 \quad \text{...(i)}$$

Here, $126 \times 1 = 9 \times 2 \times 7$

For $x = 2$, $2^3 - 67 \times 2 + 126 = 134 - 134 = 0$

Hence, $x = 2$ is a root.

For $x = 7$, $7^3 - 67 \times 7 + 126 = 469 - 469 = 0$

Hence, $x = 7$ is also a root.

Q. 46 $\begin{vmatrix} 0 & xyz & x-z \\ y-x & 0 & y-z \\ z-x & z-y & 0 \end{vmatrix}$ is equal to ....

Sol. We have, $\begin{vmatrix} 0 & xyz & x-z \\ y-x & 0 & y-z \\ z-x & z-y & 0 \end{vmatrix} = \begin{vmatrix} z-x & xyz & x-z \\ z-x & 0 & y-z \\ z-x & z-y & 0 \end{vmatrix}$ $[\because C_1 \to C_1 - C_3]$

$$= (z-x)\begin{vmatrix} 1 & xyz & x-z \\ 1 & 0 & y-z \\ 1 & z-y & 0 \end{vmatrix}$$

[taking $(z-x)$ common from column 1]

Expanding along R_1,

$= (z-x)[1 \cdot \{-(y-z)(z-y)\} - xyz(z-y) + (x-z)(z-y)]$
$= (z-x)(z-y)\ (-y+z-xyz+x-z)$
$= (z-x)(z-y)(x-y-xyz)$
$= (z-x)(y-z)(y-x+xyz)$

Q. 47 If $f(x) = \begin{vmatrix} (1+x)^{17} & (1+x)^{19} & (1+x)^{23} \\ (1+x)^{23} & (1+x)^{29} & (1+x)^{34} \\ (1+x)^{41} & (1+x)^{43} & (1+x)^{47} \end{vmatrix}$

$= A + Bx + Cx^2 + \ldots$, then A is equal to ....

Sol. Since,

$$f(x) = (1+x)^{17}(1+x)^{23}(1+x)^{41}\begin{vmatrix} 1 & (1+x)^2 & (1+x)^6 \\ 1 & (1+x)^6 & (1+x)^{11} \\ 1 & (1+x)^2 & (1+x)^6 \end{vmatrix} = 0$$

[since, R_1 and R_3 are identical]

$\therefore \quad A = 0$

True/False

Q. 48 $(A^3)^{-1} = (A^{-1})^3$, where A is a square matrix and $|A| \neq 0$.

Sol. ***True***

Since, $(A^n)^{-1} = (A^{-1})^n$, where $n \in N$.

Q. 49 $(aA)^{-1} = \frac{1}{a}A^{-1}$, where a is any real number and A is a square matrix.

Sol. ***False***

Since, we know that, if A is a non-singular square matrix, then for any scalar a (non-zero), aA is invertible such that

$$(aA)\left(\frac{1}{a}A^{-1}\right) = \left(a \cdot \frac{1}{a}\right)(A \cdot A^{-1})$$
$$= I$$

i.e., (aA) is inverse of $\left(\frac{1}{a}A^{-1}\right)$ or $(aA)^{-1} = \frac{1}{a}A^{-1}$, where a is any non-zero scalar.

In the above statement a is any real number. So, we can conclude that above statement is false.

Q. 50 $|A^{-1}| \neq |A|^{-1}$, where A is a non-singular matrix.

Sol. ***False***

$|A^{-1}| = |A|^{-1}$, where A is a non-singular matrix.

Q. 51 If A and B are matrices of order 3 and $|A| = 5$, $|B| = 3$, then $|3AB| = 27 \times 5 \times 3 = 405$.

Sol. ***True***

We know that, $|AB| = |A| \cdot |B|$

$\therefore$ $|3AB| = 27|AB|$

$= 27|A| \cdot |B|$

$= 27 \times 5 \times 3 = 405$

Q. 52 If the value of a third order determinant is 12, then the value of the determinant formed by replacing each element by its cofactor will be 144.

Sol. ***True***

Let A is the determinant.

$\therefore$ $|A| = 12$

Also, we know that, if A is a square matrix of order n, then $|\text{adj } A| = |A|^{n-1}$

For $n = 3$, $|\text{adj } A| = |A|^{3-1} = |A|^2$

$= (12)^2 = 144$

Q. 53 $\begin{vmatrix} x+1 & x+2 & x+a \\ x+2 & x+3 & x+b \\ x+3 & x+4 & x+c \end{vmatrix} = 0$, where a, b and c are in AP.

Sol. ***True***

Since, a, b and c are in AP, then $2b = a + c$

$$\therefore \quad \begin{vmatrix} x+1 & x+2 & x+a \\ x+2 & x+3 & x+b \\ x+3 & x+4 & x+c \end{vmatrix} = 0$$

$$\Rightarrow \quad \begin{vmatrix} 2x+4 & 2x+6 & 2x+a+c \\ x+2 & x+3 & x+b \\ x+3 & x+4 & x+c \end{vmatrix} = 0 \quad [\because R_1 \to R_1 + R_3]$$

$$\Rightarrow \quad \begin{vmatrix} 2(x+2) & 2(x+3) & 2(x+b) \\ x+2 & x+3 & x+b \\ x+3 & x+4 & x+c \end{vmatrix} = 0 \quad [\because 2b = a + c]$$

$\Rightarrow \quad 0 = 0$ [since, R_1 and R_2 are in proportional to each other]

Hence, statement is true.

Q. 54 $|\text{adj } A| = |A|^2$, where A is a square matrix of order two.

Sol. ***False***

If A is a square matrix of order n, then

$$|\text{adj } A| = |A|^{n-1}$$

$$\Rightarrow \quad |\text{adj } A| = |A|^{2-1} = |A| \quad [\because n = 2]$$

Q. 55 The determinant $\begin{vmatrix} \sin A & \cos A & \sin A + \cos B \\ \sin B & \cos A & \sin B + \cos B \\ \sin C & \cos A & \sin C + \cos B \end{vmatrix}$ is equal to zero.

Sol. ***True***

Since, $\begin{vmatrix} \sin A & \cos A & \sin A + \cos B \\ \sin B & \cos A & \sin B + \cos B \\ \sin C & \cos A & \sin C + \cos B \end{vmatrix} = \begin{vmatrix} \sin A & \cos A & \sin A \\ \sin B & \cos A & \sin B \\ \sin C & \cos A & \sin C \end{vmatrix} + \begin{vmatrix} \sin A & \cos A & \cos B \\ \sin B & \cos A & \cos B \\ \sin C & \cos A & \cos B \end{vmatrix}$

$$= 0 + \begin{vmatrix} \sin A & \cos A & \cos B \\ \sin B & \cos A & \cos B \\ \sin C & \cos A & \cos B \end{vmatrix}$$

[since, in first determinant C_1 and C_3 are identicals]

$$= \cos A \cdot \cos B \begin{vmatrix} \sin A & 1 & 1 \\ \sin B & 1 & 1 \\ \sin C & 1 & 1 \end{vmatrix}$$

[taking $\cos A$ common from C_2 and $\cos B$ common from C_3]

$= 0$ [since, C_2 and C_3 are identicals]

Q. 56 If the determinant $\begin{vmatrix} x+a & p+u & l+f \\ y+b & q+v & m+g \\ z+c & r+w & n+h \end{vmatrix}$ splits into exactly k determinants of order 3, each element of which contains only one term, then the value of k is 8.

Sol. ***True***

Since,
$$\begin{vmatrix} x+a & p+u & l+f \\ y+b & q+v & m+g \\ z+c & r+w & n+h \end{vmatrix}$$
$$= \begin{vmatrix} x & p & l \\ y+b & q+v & m+g \\ z+c & r+w & n+h \end{vmatrix} + \begin{vmatrix} a & u & f \\ y+b & q+v & m+g \\ z+c & r+w & n+h \end{vmatrix} \quad \text{[splitting first row]}$$
$$= \begin{vmatrix} x & p & l \\ y & q & m \\ z+c & r+m & n+h \end{vmatrix} + \begin{vmatrix} x & p & l \\ b & v & g \\ z+c & r+w & n+h \end{vmatrix}$$
$$+ \begin{vmatrix} a & u & f \\ y & q & m \\ z+c & r+w & n+h \end{vmatrix} + \begin{vmatrix} a & u & f \\ b & v & g \\ z+c & r+w & n+h \end{vmatrix} \quad \text{[splitting second row]}$$

Similarly, we can split these 4 determinants in 8 determinants by splitting each one in two determinants further. So, given statement is true.

Q. 57 If $\Delta = \begin{vmatrix} a & p & x \\ b & q & y \\ c & r & z \end{vmatrix} = 16$, then $\Delta_1 = \begin{vmatrix} p+x & a+x & a+p \\ q+y & b+y & b+q \\ r+z & c+z & c+r \end{vmatrix} = 32$.

Sol. ***True***

We have,
$$\Delta = \begin{vmatrix} a & p & x \\ b & q & y \\ c & r & z \end{vmatrix} = 16$$

and we have to prove,
$$\Delta_1 = \begin{vmatrix} p+x & a+x & a+p \\ q+y & b+y & b+q \\ r+z & c+z & c+r \end{vmatrix} = 32$$
$$\Delta_1 = \begin{vmatrix} 2p+2x+2a & a+x & a+p \\ 2q+2y+2b & b+y & b+q \\ 2r+2z+2c & c+z & c+r \end{vmatrix} \quad [\because C_1 \to C_1 + C_2 + C_3]$$
$$= 2\begin{vmatrix} p & x-p & a+p \\ q & y-q & b+q \\ r & z-r & c+r \end{vmatrix}$$

[taking 2 common from C_1 and then $C_1 \to C_1 - C_2$, $C_2 \to C_2 - C_3$]

$$= 2\left[\begin{vmatrix} p & x & a+p \\ q & y & b+q \\ r & z & c+r \end{vmatrix} - \begin{vmatrix} p & p & a+p \\ q & q & b+q \\ r & r & c+r \end{vmatrix}\right]$$

$$= 2\begin{vmatrix} p & x & a+p \\ q & y & b+q \\ r & z & c+r \end{vmatrix} - 0$$

[since, two columns C_1 and C_2 are identicals]

$$= 2\begin{vmatrix} p & x & a \\ q & y & b \\ r & z & c \end{vmatrix} + 2\begin{vmatrix} p & x & p \\ q & y & q \\ r & z & r \end{vmatrix}$$

$$= 2\begin{vmatrix} a & p & x \\ b & q & y \\ c & r & z \end{vmatrix} + 0$$

[since, C_1 and C_3 are identical in second determinant and in first determinant, $C_1 \leftrightarrow C_2$ and then $C_1 \leftrightarrow C_3$]

$= 2 \times 16$ [$\because \Delta = 16$]

$= 32$ **Hence proved.**

Q. 58 The maximum value of $\begin{vmatrix} 1 & 1 & 1 \\ 1 & 1+\sin\theta & 1 \\ 1 & 1 & 1+\cos\theta \end{vmatrix}$ is $\frac{1}{2}$.

Sol. ***True***

Since, $\begin{vmatrix} 1 & 1 & 1 \\ 0 & \sin\theta & 0 \\ 0 & 0 & \cos\theta \end{vmatrix}$ [$\because R_2 \to R_2 - R_1$ and $R_3 \to R_3 - R_1$]

On expanding along third row, we get the value of the determinant

$$= \cos\theta \cdot \sin\theta = \frac{1}{2}\sin 2\theta = \frac{1}{2}$$

[when θ is 45° which gives maximum value]

5

Continuity and Differentiability

Short Answer Type Questions

Q. 1 Examine the continuity of the function $f(x) = x^3 + 2x^2 - 1$ at $x = 1$.

Thinking Process

We know that, function f will be continuous at $x = a$, if $\lim_{x \to a^-} f(x) = \lim_{x \to a^+} f(x) = f(a)$.

Sol. We have, $f(x) = x^3 + 2x^2 - 1$ at $x = 1$.

$$\therefore \quad \lim_{x \to 1^+} f(x) = \lim_{h \to 0} (1 + h)^3 + 2(1 + h)^2 - 1 = 2$$

and $$\lim_{x \to 1^-} f(x) = \lim_{h \to 0} (1 - h)^3 + 2(1 - h)^2 - 1 = 2$$

$$\therefore \quad \lim_{x \to 1^+} f(x) = \lim_{x \to 1^-} f(x)$$

and $$f(1) = 1 + 2 - 1 = 2$$

So, $f(x)$ is continuous at $x = 1$.

Note *Every polynomial function is continuous at any real point.*

Q. 2 $f(x) = \begin{cases} 3x + 5, & \text{if } x \geq 2 \\ x^2, & \text{if } x < 2 \end{cases}$ at $x = 2$.

Sol. We have, $$f(x) = \begin{cases} 3x + 5, & \text{if } x \geq 2 \\ x^2, & \text{if } x < 2 \end{cases} \text{ at } x = 2.$$

At $x = 2$, $$\text{LHL} = \lim_{x \to 2^-} (x)^2$$

$$= \lim_{h \to 0} (2 - h)^2 = \lim_{h \to 0} (4 + h^2 - 4h) = 4$$

and $$\text{RHL} = \lim_{x \to 2^+} (3x + 5)$$

$$= \lim_{h \to 0} [3(2 + h) + 5] = 11$$

Since, $\text{LHL} \neq \text{RHL}$ at $x = 2$

So, $f(x)$ is discontinuous at $x = 2$.

Q. 3 $f(x)=\begin{cases}\dfrac{1-\cos 2x}{x^2}, & \text{if } x\neq 0\\ 5, & \text{if } x=0\end{cases}$ at $x=0$.

Sol. We have, $f(x)=\begin{cases}\dfrac{1-\cos 2x}{x^2}, & \text{if } x\neq 0\\ 5, & \text{if } x=0\end{cases}$ at $x=0$.

At $x=0$,

$$\text{LHL}=\lim_{x\to 0^-}\frac{1-\cos 2x}{x^2}$$

$$=\lim_{h\to 0}\frac{1-\cos 2(0-h)}{(0-h)^2}$$

$$=\lim_{h\to 0}\frac{1-\cos 2h}{h^2} \qquad [\because \cos(-\theta)=\cos\theta]$$

$$=\lim_{h\to 0}\frac{1-1+2\sin^2 h}{h^2} \qquad [\because \cos 2\theta=1-2\sin^2\theta]$$

$$=\lim_{h\to 0}\frac{2(\sin h)^2}{(h)^2} \qquad \left[\because \lim_{h\to 0}\frac{\sin h}{h}=1\right]$$

$$=2$$

$$\text{RHL}=\lim_{x\to 0^+}\frac{1-\cos 2x}{x^2}$$

$$=\lim_{h\to 0}\frac{1-\cos 2(0+h)}{(0+h)^2}$$

$$=\lim_{h\to 0}\frac{2\sin^2 h}{h^2}=2 \qquad \left[\because \lim_{h\to 0}\frac{\sin h}{h}=1\right]$$

and $f(0)=5$

Since, $\text{LHL}=\text{RHL}\neq f(0)$

Hence, $f(x)$ is not continuous at $x=0$.

Q. 4 $f(x)=\begin{cases}\dfrac{2x^2-3x-2}{x-2}, & \text{if } x\neq 2\\ 5, & \text{if } x=2\end{cases}$ at $x=2$.

Sol. We have, $f(x)=\begin{cases}\dfrac{2x^2-3x-2}{x-2}, & \text{if } x\neq 2\\ 5, & \text{if } x=2\end{cases}$ at $x=2$.

At $x=2$,

$$\text{LHL}=\lim_{x\to 2^-}\frac{2x^2-3x-2}{x-2}$$

$$=\lim_{h\to 0}\frac{2(2-h)^2-3(2-h)-2}{(2-h)-2}$$

$$=\lim_{h\to 0}\frac{8+2h^2-8h-6+3h-2}{-h}$$

$$=\lim_{h\to 0}\frac{2h^2-5h}{-h}=\lim_{h\to 0}\frac{h(2h-5)}{-h}=5$$

$$\text{RHL}=\lim_{x\to 2^+}\frac{2x^2-3x-2}{x-2}$$

$$= \lim_{h \to 0} \frac{2(2+h)^2 - 3(2+h) - 2}{(2+h) - 2}$$

$$= \lim_{h \to 0} \frac{8 + 2h^2 + 8h - 6 - 3h - 2}{h}$$

$$= \lim_{h \to 0} \frac{2h^2 + 5h}{h} = \lim_{h \to 0} \frac{h(2h+5)}{h} = 5$$

and $f(2) = 5$

$\therefore$ LHL = RHL = $f(2)$

So, $f(x)$ is continuous at $x = 2$.

Q. 5 $f(x) = \begin{cases} \dfrac{|x-4|}{2(x-4)}, & \text{if } x \neq 4 \\ 0, & \text{if } x = 4 \end{cases}$ **at $x = 4$.**

Sol. We have, $f(x) = \begin{cases} \dfrac{|x-4|}{2(x-4)}, & \text{if } x \neq 4 \\ 0, & \text{if } x = 4 \end{cases}$ at $x = 4$.

At $x = 4$,

$$\text{LHL} = \lim_{x \to 4^-} \frac{|x-4|}{2(x-4)}$$

$$= \lim_{h \to 0} \frac{|4-h-4|}{2[(4-h)-4]} = \lim_{h \to 0} \frac{|0-h|}{(8-2h-8)}$$

$$= \lim_{h \to 0} \frac{h}{-2h} = \frac{-1}{2} \quad \text{and} \quad f(4) = 0 \neq \text{LHL}$$

So, $f(x)$ is discontinuous at $x = 4$.

Q. 6 $f(x) = \begin{cases} |x| \cos \dfrac{1}{x}, & \text{if } x \neq 0 \\ 0, & \text{if } x = 0 \end{cases}$ **at $x = 0$.**

Sol. We have, $f(x) = \begin{cases} |x| \cos \dfrac{1}{x}, & \text{if } x \neq 0 \\ 0, & \text{if } x = 0 \end{cases}$ at $x = 0$

At $x = 0$,

$$\text{LHL} = \lim_{x \to 0^-} |x| \cos \frac{1}{x} = \lim_{h \to 0} |0-h| \cos \frac{1}{0-h}$$

$$= \lim_{h \to 0} h \cos \left(\frac{-1}{h}\right)$$

$$= 0 \times [\text{an oscillating number between } -1 \text{ and } 1] = 0$$

$$\text{RHL} = \lim_{x \to 0^+} |x| \cos \frac{1}{x}$$

$$= \lim_{h \to 0} |0+h| \cos \frac{1}{(0+h)}$$

$$= \lim_{h \to 0} h \cos \frac{1}{h}$$

$$= 0 \times [\text{an oscillating number between } -1 \text{ and } 1] = 0$$

and $f(0) = 0$

Since, LHL = RHL = $f(0)$

So, $f(x)$ is continuous at $x = 0$.

Q. 7 $f(x)=\begin{cases}|x-a|\sin\dfrac{1}{x-a}, & \text{if } x\neq 0\\ 0, & \text{if } x=a\end{cases}$ at $x=a$.

Sol. We have, $f(x)=\begin{cases}|x-a|\sin\dfrac{1}{x-a}, & \text{if } x\neq 0\\ 0, & \text{if } x=a\end{cases}$ at $x=a$

At $x=a$,

$$\text{LHL}=\lim_{x\to a^-}|x-a|\sin\frac{1}{x-a}$$
$$=\lim_{h\to 0}|a-h-a|\sin\left(\frac{1}{a-h-a}\right)$$
$$=\lim_{h\to 0}-h\sin\left(\frac{1}{h}\right) \qquad [\because \sin(-\theta)=-\sin\theta]$$
$= 0\times$ [an oscillating number between -1 and 1] $=0$

$$\text{RHL}=\lim_{x\to a^+}|x-a|\sin\left(\frac{1}{x-a}\right)$$
$$=\lim_{h\to 0}|a+h-a|\sin\left(\frac{1}{a+h-a}\right)=\lim_{h\to 0}h\sin\frac{1}{h}$$
$= 0\times$ [an oscillating number between -1 and 1] $=0$

and $f(a)=0$

$\therefore$ LHL = RHL = $f(a)$

So, $f(x)$ is continuous at $x=a$.

Q. 8 $f(x)=\begin{cases}\dfrac{e^{1/x}}{1+e^{1/x}}, & \text{if } x\neq 0\\ 0, & \text{if } x=0\end{cases}$ at $x=0$.

Sol. We have, $f(x)=\begin{cases}\dfrac{e^{1/x}}{1+e^{1/x}}, & \text{if } x\neq 0\\ 0, & \text{if } x=0\end{cases}$ at $x=0$

At $x=0$,

$$\text{LHL}=\lim_{x\to 0^-}\frac{e^{1/x}}{1+e^{1/x}}=\lim_{h\to 0}\frac{e^{1/0-h}}{1+e^{1/0-h}}$$
$$=\lim_{h\to 0}\frac{e^{-1/h}}{1+e^{-1/h}}=\lim_{h\to 0}\frac{1}{e^{1/h}(1+e^{-1/h})}$$
$$=\lim_{h\to 0}\frac{1}{e^{1/h}+1}=\frac{1}{e^{\infty}+1}=\frac{1}{\infty+1} \qquad [\because e^{\infty}=\infty]$$
$$=\frac{1}{\frac{1}{0}}=0$$

$$\text{RHL}=\lim_{x\to 0^+}\frac{e^{1/x}}{1+e^{1/x}}$$
$$=\lim_{h\to 0}\frac{e^{1/0+h}}{1+e^{1/0+h}}=\lim_{h\to 0}\frac{e^{1/h}}{1+e^{1/h}}$$

$$= \lim_{h \to 0} \frac{1}{e^{-1/h} + 1} = \frac{1}{e^{-\infty} + 1}$$

$$= \frac{1}{0+1} = 1 \qquad [\because e^{-\infty} = 0]$$

Hence, LHL $\neq$ RHL at $x = 0$.

So, $f(x)$ is discontinuous at $x = 0$.

Q. 9 $f(x) = \begin{cases} \dfrac{x^2}{2}, & \text{if } 0 \le x \le 1 \\ 2x^2 - 3x + \dfrac{3}{2}, & \text{if } 1 < x \le 2 \end{cases}$ **at $x = 1$.**

Sol. We have, $f(x) = \begin{cases} \dfrac{x^2}{2}, & \text{if } 0 \le x \le 1 \\ 2x^2 - 3x + \dfrac{3}{2}, & \text{if } 1 < x \le 2 \end{cases}$ at $x = 1$

At $x = 1$,

$$\text{HL} = \lim_{x \to 1^-} \frac{x^2}{2} = \lim_{h \to 0} \frac{(1-h)^2}{2}$$

$$= \lim_{h \to 0} \frac{1 + h^2 - 2h}{2} = \frac{1}{2}$$

$$\text{RHL} = \lim_{x \to 1^+} \left(2x^2 - 3x + \frac{3}{2}\right)$$

$$= \lim_{h \to 0} \left[2(1+h)^2 - 3(1+h) + \frac{3}{2}\right]$$

$$= \lim_{h \to 0} \left(2 + 2h^2 + 4h - 3 - 3h + \frac{3}{2}\right) = -1 + \frac{3}{2} = \frac{1}{2}$$

and $f(1) = \dfrac{1^2}{2} = \dfrac{1}{2}$

$\therefore$ LHL = RHL = $f(1)$

Hence, $f(x)$ is continuous at $x = 1$.

Q. 10 $f(x) = |x| + |x - 1|$ **at $x = 1$.**

Sol. We have, $f(x) = |x| + |x - 1|$ at $x = 1$

At $x = 1$,

$$\text{LHL} = \lim_{x \to 1^-} [|x| + |x - 1|]$$

$$= \lim_{h \to 0} [|1 - h| + |1 - h - 1|] = 1 + 0 = 1$$

and

$$\text{RHL} = \lim_{x \to 1^-} [|x| + |x - 1|]$$

$$= \lim_{h \to 0} [|1 + h| + |1 + h - 1|] = 1 + 0 = 1$$

and $f(1) = |1| + |0| = 1$

$\therefore$ LHL = RHL = $f(1)$

Hence, $f(x)$ is continuous at $x = 1$.

Note *Every modulus function is a continuous function at any real point.*

Q. 11 $f(x)=\begin{cases}3x-8, \text{if } x\le 5\\ 2k, \quad \text{if } x>5\end{cases}$ at $x=5$.

Sol. We have, $f(x)=\begin{cases}3x-8, \text{ if } x\le 5\\ 2k, \quad \text{ if } x>5\end{cases}$ at $x=5$

Since, $f(x)$ is continuous at $x=5$.

$\therefore \quad \text{LHL} = \text{RHL} = f(5)$

Now, $\text{LHL} = \lim_{x\to 5^-}(3x-8) = \lim_{h\to 0}[3(5-h)-8]$

$= \lim_{h\to 0}[15-3h-8] = 7$

$\text{RHL} = \lim_{x\to 5^+} 2k = \lim_{h\to 0} 2k = 2k = 7$ $\quad [\because \text{LHL} = \text{RHL}]$

and $f(5) = 3\times 5 - 8 = 7$

$\therefore \quad 2k = 7 \Rightarrow k = \frac{7}{2}$

Q. 12 $f(x)=\begin{cases}\dfrac{2^{x+2}-16}{4^x-16}, & \text{if } x\ne 2\\ k, & \text{if } x=2\end{cases}$ at $x=2$.

Sol. We have, $f(x)=\begin{cases}\dfrac{2^{x+2}-16}{4^x-16}, & \text{if } x\ne 2\\ k, & \text{if } x=2\end{cases}$ at $x=2$

Since, $f(x)$ is continuous at $x=2$.

$\therefore \quad \text{LHL} = \text{RHL} = f(2)$

At $x=2$, $\lim_{x\to 2}\frac{2^x\cdot 2^2-2^4}{4^x-4^2} = \lim_{x\to 2}\frac{4\cdot(2^x-4)}{(2^x)^2-(4)^2}$

$= \lim_{x\to 2}\frac{4\cdot(2^x-4)}{(2^x-4)(2^x+4)}$ $\quad [\because a^2-b^2=(a+b)(a-b)]$

$= \lim_{x\to 2}\frac{4}{2^x+4} = \frac{4}{8} = \frac{1}{2}$

But $f(2) = k$

$\therefore \quad k = \frac{1}{2}$

Q.13 $f(x)=\begin{cases}\dfrac{\sqrt{1+kx}-\sqrt{1-kx}}{x}, & \text{if } -1\le x<0\\ \dfrac{2x+1}{x-1}, & \text{if } 0\le x\le 1\end{cases}$ at $x=0$.

Sol. We have, $f(x)=\begin{cases}\dfrac{\sqrt{1+kx}-\sqrt{1-kx}}{x}, & \text{if } -1\le x<0\\ \dfrac{2x+1}{x-1}, & \text{if } 0\le x\le 1\end{cases}$ at $x=0$.

$\therefore$ $$\text{LHL} = \lim_{x \to 0^-} \frac{\sqrt{1+kx} - \sqrt{1-kx}}{x}$$

$$= \lim_{x \to 0^-} \left(\frac{\sqrt{1+kx} - \sqrt{1-kx}}{x}\right) \cdot \left(\frac{\sqrt{1+kx} + \sqrt{1-kx}}{\sqrt{1+kx} + \sqrt{1-kx}}\right)$$

$$= \lim_{x \to 0^-} \frac{1+kx-1+kx}{x[\sqrt{1+kx} + \sqrt{1-kx}]}$$

$$= \lim_{x \to 0^-} \frac{2kx}{x\sqrt{1+kx} + \sqrt{1-kx}}$$

$$= \lim_{h \to 0} \frac{2k}{\sqrt{1+k(0-h)} + \sqrt{1-k(0-h)}}$$

$$= \lim_{h \to 0} \frac{2k}{\sqrt{1-kh} + \sqrt{1+kh}} \qquad = \frac{2k}{2} = k$$

and $$f(0) = \frac{2 \times 0 + 1}{0-1} = -1$$

$\Rightarrow$ $k = -1$ $\quad [\because \text{LHL} = \text{RHL} = f(0)]$

Q. 14 $f(x) = \begin{cases} \dfrac{1-\cos kx}{x \sin x}, & \text{if } x \neq 0 \\ \dfrac{1}{2}, & \text{if } x = 0 \end{cases}$ **at $x = 0$.**

Sol. We have, $f(x) = \begin{cases} \dfrac{1-\cos kx}{x \sin x}, & \text{if } x \neq 0 \\ \dfrac{1}{2}, & \text{if } x = 0 \end{cases}$ at $x = 0$

At $x = 0$, $$\text{LHL} = \lim_{x \to 0^-} \frac{1-\cos kx}{x \sin x} = \lim_{h \to 0} \frac{1-\cos k(0-h)}{(0-h)\sin(0-h)}$$

$$= \lim_{h \to 0} \frac{1-\cos(-kh)}{-h\sin(-h)}$$

$$= \lim_{h \to 0} \frac{1-\cos kh}{h \sin h} \qquad [\because \cos(-\theta) = \cos\theta, \sin(-\theta) = -\sin\theta]$$

$$= \lim_{h \to 0} \frac{1-1+2\sin^2 \frac{kh}{2}}{h \sin h} \qquad \left[\because \cos\theta = 1 - 2\sin^2\frac{\theta}{2}\right]$$

$$= \lim_{h \to 0} \frac{2\sin^2 \frac{kh}{2}}{h \sin h}$$

$$= \lim_{h \to 0} \frac{2\sin\frac{kh}{2}}{\frac{kh}{2}} \cdot \frac{\sin\frac{kh}{2}}{\frac{kh}{2}} \cdot \frac{1}{\frac{\sin h}{h}} \cdot \frac{k^2h/4}{h}$$

$$= \frac{2k^2}{4} = \frac{k^2}{2} \qquad \left[\because \lim_{h \to 0} \frac{\sin h}{h} = 1\right]$$

Also, $$f(0) = \frac{1}{2} \Rightarrow \frac{k^2}{2} = \frac{1}{2} \Rightarrow k = \pm 1$$

Q. 15 Prove that the function f defined by $f(x)=\begin{cases}\dfrac{x}{|x|+2x^2}, & \text{if } x\neq 0\\ k, & \text{if } x=0\end{cases}$

remains discontinuous at $x=0$, regardless the choice of k.

Sol. We have, $$f(x)=\begin{cases}\dfrac{x}{|x|+2x^2}, & \text{if } x\neq 0\\ k, & \text{if } x=0\end{cases}$$

At $x=0$, $$\text{LHL}=\lim_{x\to 0^-}\frac{x}{|x|+2x^2}=\lim_{h\to 0}\frac{(0-h)}{|0-h|+2(0-h)^2}$$
$$=\lim_{h\to 0}\frac{-h}{h+2h^2}=\lim_{h\to 0}\frac{-h}{h(1+2h)}=-1$$
$$\text{RHL}=\lim_{x\to 0^+}\frac{x}{|x|+2x^2}=\lim_{h\to 0}\frac{0+h}{|0+h|+2(0+h)^2}$$
$$=\lim_{h\to 0}\frac{h}{h+2h^2}=\lim_{h\to 0}\frac{h}{h(1+2h)}=1$$

and $f(0)=k$

Since, LHL $\neq$ RHL for any value of k.

Hence, $f(x)$ is discontinuous at $x=0$ regardless the choice of k.

Q. 16 Find the values of a and b such that the function f defined by
$$f(x)=\begin{cases}\dfrac{x-4}{|x-4|}+a, & \text{if } x<4\\ a+b, & \text{if } x=4\\ \dfrac{x-4}{|x-4|}+b, & \text{if } x>4\end{cases}$$

is a continuous function at $x=4$.

Sol. We have, $$f(x)=\begin{cases}\dfrac{x-4}{|x-4|}+a, & \text{if } x<4\\ a+b, & \text{if } x=4\\ \dfrac{x-4}{|x-4|}+b, & \text{if } x>4\end{cases}$$

At $x=4$, $$\text{LHL}=\lim_{x\to 4^-}\frac{x-4}{|x-4|}+a$$
$$=\lim_{h\to 0}\frac{4-h-4}{|4-h-4|}+a=\lim_{h\to 0}\frac{-h}{h}+a$$
$$=-1+a$$
$$\text{RHL}=\lim_{x\to 4^+}\frac{x-4}{|x-4|}+b$$
$$=\lim_{h\to 0}\frac{4+h-4}{|4+h-4|}+b=\lim_{h\to 0}\frac{h}{h}+b=1+b$$
$$f(4)=a+b\Rightarrow -1+a=1+b=a+b$$

$\Rightarrow$ $-1+a=a+b$ and $1+b=a+b$

$\therefore$ $b=-1$ and $a=1$

Q. 17 If the function $f(x) = \frac{1}{x+2}$, then find the points of discontinuity of the composite function $y = f\{f(x)\}$.

Sol. We have,

$$f(x) = \frac{1}{x+2}$$

$\therefore$

$$y = f\{f(x)\}$$

$$= f\left(\frac{1}{x+2}\right) = \frac{1}{\frac{1}{x+2} + 2}$$

$$= \frac{1}{1 + 2x + 4} \cdot (x+2) = \frac{(x+2)}{(2x+5)}$$

So, the function y will not be continuous at those points, where it is not defined as it is a rational function.

Therefore, $y = \frac{x+2}{(2x+5)}$ is not defined, when $2x + 5 = 0$

$\therefore$

$$x = \frac{-5}{2}$$

Hence, y is discontinuous at $x = \frac{-5}{2}$.

Q. 18 Find all points of discontinuity of the function $f(t) = \frac{1}{t^2 + t - 2}$, where $t = \frac{1}{x-1}$.

Sol. We have,

$$f(t) = \frac{1}{t^2 + t - 2} \text{ and } t = \frac{1}{x-1}$$

$\therefore$

$$f(t) = \frac{1}{\left(\frac{1}{x^2 + 1 - 2x}\right) + \left(\frac{1}{x-1}\right) - \frac{2}{1}}$$

$$= \frac{1}{\left(\frac{1 + x - 1 + [-2(x-1)^2]}{(x^2 + 1 - 2x)}\right)}$$

$$= \frac{x^2 + 1 - 2x}{x - 2x^2 - 2 + 4x}$$

$$= \frac{x^2 + 1 - 2x}{-2x^2 + 5x - 2}$$

$$= \frac{(x-1)^2}{-(2x^2 - 5x + 2)}$$

$$= \frac{(x-1)^2}{(2x-1)(2-x)}$$

So, $f(t)$ is discontinuous at $2x - 1 = 0 \Rightarrow x = 1/2$

and $2 - x = 0 \Rightarrow x = 2$.

Q. 19 Show that the function $f(x) = |\sin x + \cos x|$ is continuous at $x = \pi$.

Sol. We have, $f(x) = |\sin x + \cos x|$ at $x = \pi$

Let $g(x) = \sin x + \cos x$

and $h(x) = |x|$

$\therefore$
$$hog(x) = h[g(x)] = h(\sin x + \cos x) = |\sin x + \cos x|$$

Since, $g(x) = \sin x + \cos x$ is a continuous function as it is forming with addition of two continuous functions $\sin x$ and $\cos x$.

Also, $h(x) = |x|$ is also a continuous function. Since, we know that composite functions of two continuous functions is also a continuous function.

Hence, $f(x) = |\sin x + \cos x|$ is a continuous function everywhere.

So, $f(x)$ is continuous at $x = \pi$.

Q. 20 Examine the differentiability of f, where f is defined by

$$f(x) = \begin{cases} x[x], & \text{if } 0 \le x < 2 \\ (x-1)x, & \text{if } 2 \le x < 3 \end{cases} \text{ at } x = 2.$$

Thinking Process

We know that, a function f is differentiable at a point a in its domain, if both $Lf'(a)$ and $Rf'(a)$ are finite and equal, where $Lf'(c) = \lim_{h \to 0} \frac{f(a-h) - f(a)}{-h}$ and $Rf'(c) = \lim_{h \to 0} \frac{f(a+h) - f(a)}{h}$.

Sol. We have,
$$f(x) = \begin{cases} x[x], & \text{if } 0 \le x < 2 \\ (x-1)x & \text{if } 2 \le x < 3 \end{cases} \text{ at } x = 2.$$

At $x = 2$,
$$Lf'(2) = \lim_{h \to 0} \frac{f(2-h) - f(2)}{-h}$$
$$= \lim_{h \to 0} \frac{(2-h)[2-h] - (2-1)2}{-h}$$

$\{\because [a-h] = [a-1], \text{where } a \text{ is any positive number}\}$

$$= \lim_{h \to 0} \frac{(2-h)(1) - 2}{-h}$$
$$= \lim_{h \to 0} \frac{2-h-2}{-h} = \lim_{h \to 0} \frac{-h}{-h} = 1$$
$$Rf'(2) = \lim_{h \to 0} \frac{f(2+h) - f(2)}{h}$$
$$= \lim_{h \to 0} \frac{(2+h-1)(2+h) - (2-1) \cdot 2}{h}$$
$$= \lim_{h \to 0} \frac{(1+h)(2+h) - 2}{h}$$
$$= \lim_{h \to 0} \frac{2+h+2h+h^2-2}{h}$$
$$= \lim_{h \to 0} \frac{h^2+3h}{h} = \lim_{h \to 0} \frac{h(h+3)}{h} = 3$$

$\therefore$ $Lf'(2) \ne Rf'(2)$

So, $f(x)$ is not differentiable at $x = 2$.

Q. 21 $f(x) = \begin{cases} x^2 \sin \dfrac{1}{x}, & \text{if } x \neq 0 \\ 0, & \text{if } x = 0 \end{cases}$ at $x = 0$.

Sol. We have, $f(x) = \begin{cases} x^2 \sin \dfrac{1}{x}, & \text{if } x \neq 0 \\ 0, & \text{if } x = 0 \end{cases}$ at $x = 0$

For differentiability at $x = 0$,

$$Lf'(0) = \lim_{x \to 0^-} \frac{f(x) - f(0)}{x - 0} = \lim_{x \to 0^-} \frac{x^2 \sin \frac{1}{x} - 0}{x - 0}$$

$$= \lim_{h \to 0} \frac{(0-h)^2 \sin \left(\frac{1}{0-h}\right)}{0-h} = \lim_{h \to 0} \frac{h^2 \sin \left(\frac{-1}{h}\right)}{-h}$$

$$= \lim_{h \to 0} + h \sin \left(\frac{1}{h}\right) \qquad [\because \sin(-\theta) = -\sin\theta]$$

$$= 0 \times [\text{an oscillating number between } -1 \text{and} 1] = 0$$

$$Rf'(0) = \lim_{x \to 0^+} \frac{f(x) - f(0)}{x - 0} = \lim_{x \to 0^+} \frac{x^2 \sin \frac{1}{x} - 0}{x - 0}$$

$$= \lim_{h \to 0} \frac{(0+h)^2 \sin \left(\frac{1}{0+h}\right)}{0+h} = \lim_{h \to 0} \frac{h^2 \sin(1/h)}{h}$$

$$= \lim_{h \to 0} h \sin(1/h)$$

$$= 0 \times [\text{an oscillating number between } -1 \text{ and } 1] = 0$$

$\because \quad Lf'(0) = Rf'(0)$

So, $f(x)$ is differentiable at $x = 0$.

Q. 22 $f(x) = \begin{cases} 1 + x, & \text{if } x \leq 2 \\ 5 - x, & \text{if } x > 2 \end{cases}$ at $x = 2$.

Sol. We have, $f(x) = \begin{cases} 1 + x, \text{ if } x \leq 2 \\ 5 - x, \text{ if } x > 2 \end{cases}$ at $x = 2$.

For differentiability at $x = 2$,

$$Lf'(2) = \lim_{x \to 2^-} \frac{f(x) - f(2)}{x - 2} = \lim_{x \to 2^-} \frac{(1+x) - (1+2)}{x - 2}$$

$$= \lim_{h \to 0} \frac{(1 + 2 - h) - 3}{2 - h - 2} = \lim_{h \to 0} \frac{-h}{-h} = 1$$

$$Rf'(2) = \lim_{x \to 2^+} \frac{f(x) - f(2)}{x - 2} = \lim_{x \to 2^+} \frac{(5-x) - 3}{x - 2}$$

$$= \lim_{h \to 0} \frac{5 - (2+h) - 3}{2 + h - 2}$$

$$= \lim_{h \to 0} \frac{5 - 2 - h - 3}{h} = \lim_{h \to 0} \frac{-h}{+h}$$

$$= -1$$

$\because \quad Lf'(2) \neq Rf'(2)$

So, $f(x)$ is not differentiable at $x = 2$.

Q. 23 Show that $f(x) = |x - 5|$ is continuous but not differentiable at $x = 5$.

Sol. We have,
$$f(x) = |x - 5|$$
$$\therefore \quad f(x) = \begin{cases} -(x-5), & \text{if } x < 5 \\ x - 5, & \text{if } x \geq 5 \end{cases}$$

For continuity at $x = 5$,
$$\text{LHL} = \lim_{x \to 5^-} (-x + 5)$$
$$= \lim_{h \to 0} [-(5 - h) + 5] = \lim_{h \to 0} h = 0$$
$$\text{RHL} = \lim_{x \to 5^+} (x - 5)$$
$$= \lim_{h \to 0} (5 + h - 5) = \lim_{h \to 0} h = 0$$
$$\therefore \quad f(5) = 5 - 5 = 0$$
$$\Rightarrow \quad \text{LHL} = \text{RHL} = f(5)$$

Hence, $f(x)$ is continuous at $x = 5$.

Now,
$$Lf'(5) = \lim_{x \to 5^-} \frac{f(x) - f(5)}{x - 5}$$
$$= \lim_{x \to 5^-} \frac{-x + 5 - 0}{x - 5} = -1$$
$$Rf'(5) = \lim_{x \to 5^+} \frac{f(x) - f(5)}{x - 5}$$
$$= \lim_{x \to 5^+} \frac{x - 5 - 0}{x - 5} = 1$$
$$\therefore \quad Lf'(5) \neq Rf'(5)$$

So, $f(x) = |x - 5|$ is not differentiable at $x = 5$.

Q. 24 A function $f : R \to R$ satisfies the equation $f(x + y) = f(x) \cdot f(y)$ for all $x, y \in R$, $f(x) \neq 0$. Suppose that the function is differentiable at $x = 0$ and $f'(0) = 2$, then prove that $f'(x) = 2f(x)$.

Sol. Let $f : R \to R$ satisfies the equation $f(x + y) = f(x) \cdot f(y)$, $\forall x, y \in R$, $f(x) \neq 0$.

Let $f(x)$ is differentiable at $x = 0$ and $f'(0) = 2$.
$$\Rightarrow \quad f'(0) = \lim_{x \to 0} \frac{f(x) - f(0)}{x - 0}$$
$$\Rightarrow \quad 2 = \lim_{x \to 0} \frac{f(x) - f(0)}{x}$$
$$\Rightarrow \quad 2 = \lim_{h \to 0} \frac{f(0 + h) - f(0)}{0 + h}$$
$$\Rightarrow \quad 2 = \lim_{h \to 0} \frac{f(0) \cdot f(h) - f(0)}{h}$$
$$\Rightarrow \quad 2 = \lim_{h \to 0} \frac{f(0)[f(h) - 1]}{h} \quad [\because f(0) = f(h)] \ldots \text{(i)}$$

Also,
$$f'(x) = \lim_{h \to 0} \frac{f(x + h) - f(x)}{h}$$
$$= \lim_{h \to 0} \frac{f(x) \cdot f(h) - f(x)}{h} \quad [\because f(x + y) = f(x) \cdot f(y)]$$
$$= \lim_{h \to 0} \frac{f(x)[f(h) - 1]}{h} = 2f(x) \quad [\text{using Eq. (i)}]$$
$$\therefore \quad f'(x) = 2f(x)$$

Q. 25 $2^{\cos^2 x}$

Sol. Let $$y = 2^{\cos^2 x}$$

$\therefore$ $$\log y = \log 2^{\cos^2 x} = \cos^2 x \cdot \log 2$$

On differentiating w.r.t. x, we get

$$\frac{d}{dy}\log y.\frac{dy}{dx} = \frac{d}{dx}\log 2 \cdot \cos^2 x$$

$$\Rightarrow \quad \frac{1}{y}\cdot\frac{dy}{dx} = \log 2 \frac{d}{dx}(\cos x)^2$$

$$\Rightarrow \quad \frac{1}{y}\cdot\frac{dy}{dx} = \log 2 \cdot [2\cos x]\cdot\frac{d}{dx}\cos x$$

$$= \log 2 \cdot 2\cos x \cdot (-\sin x)$$

$$= \log 2 \cdot [-(\sin 2x)]$$

$$\therefore \quad \frac{dy}{dx} = -y \cdot \log 2\,(\sin 2x)$$

$$= -2^{\cos^2 x}\cdot \log 2\,(\sin 2x)$$

Q. 26 $\dfrac{8^x}{x^8}$

Sol. Let $$y = \frac{8^x}{x^8} \Rightarrow \log y = \log \frac{8^x}{x^8}$$

$$\Rightarrow \quad \frac{d}{dy}\log y\cdot\frac{dy}{dx} = \frac{d}{dx}[\log 8^x - \log x^8]$$

$$\Rightarrow \quad \frac{1}{y}\cdot\frac{dy}{dx} = \frac{d}{dx}[x\cdot\log 8 - 8\cdot\log x]$$

On differentiating w.r.t. x, we get

$$\frac{1}{y}\cdot\frac{dy}{dx} = \log 8 \cdot 1 - 8\cdot\frac{1}{x}$$

$$\Rightarrow \quad \frac{1}{y}\cdot\frac{dy}{dx} = \log 8 - \frac{8}{x}$$

$$\therefore \quad \frac{dy}{dx} = y\left(\log 8 - \frac{8}{x}\right) = \frac{8^x}{x^8}\left(\log 8 - \frac{8}{x}\right)$$

Q. 27 $\log(x + \sqrt{x^2 + a})$

Sol. Let $$y = \log(x + \sqrt{x^2 + a})$$

$$\therefore \quad \frac{dy}{dx} = \frac{d}{dx}\log(x + \sqrt{x^2 + a})$$

$$= \frac{1}{(x + \sqrt{x^2 + a})}\cdot\frac{d}{dx}[x + \sqrt{x^2 + a}]$$

$$= \frac{1}{(x + \sqrt{x^2 + a})}\left[1 + \frac{1}{2}(x^2 + a)^{-1/2}\cdot 2x\right]$$

$$= \frac{1}{(x + \sqrt{x^2 + a})}\cdot\left(1 + \frac{x}{\sqrt{x^2 + a}}\right)$$

$$= \frac{(\sqrt{x^2 + a} + x)}{(x + \sqrt{x^2 + a})(\sqrt{x^2 + a})} = \frac{1}{(\sqrt{x^2 + a})}$$

Q. 28 $\log[\log(\log x^5)]$

Sol. Let $y = \log[\log(\log x^5)]$

$$\therefore \quad \frac{dy}{dx} = \frac{d}{dx}[\log(\log \log x^5)]$$

$$= \frac{1}{\log \log x^5} \cdot \frac{d}{dx}(\log \cdot \log x^5)$$

$$= \frac{1}{\log \log x^5} \cdot \left(\frac{1}{\log x^5}\right) \cdot \frac{d}{dx} \log x^5$$

$$= \frac{1}{\log \log x^5} \cdot \frac{1}{\log x^5} \cdot \frac{d}{dx}(5 \log x) = \frac{5}{x \cdot \log(\log x^5) \cdot \log(x^5)}$$

Q. 29 $\sin\sqrt{x} + \cos^2\sqrt{x}$

Sol. Let $y = \sin\sqrt{x} + (\cos\sqrt{x})^2$

$$\therefore \quad \frac{dy}{dx} = \frac{d}{dx}\sin(x^{1/2}) + \frac{d}{dx}[\cos(x^{1/2})]^2$$

$$= \cos x^{1/2} \cdot \frac{d}{dx} x^{1/2} + 2\cos(x^{1/2}) \frac{d}{dx}[\cos(x^{1/2})]$$

$$= \cos(x^{1/2}) \frac{1}{2} x^{-1/2} + 2 \cdot \cos(x^{1/2}) \cdot \left[-\sin(x^{1/2}) . \frac{d}{dx} x^{1/2}\right]$$

$$= \cos\sqrt{x} \cdot \frac{1}{2\sqrt{x}} [-2\cos(x^{1/2})] \cdot \sin x^{1/2} \cdot \frac{1}{2\sqrt{x}}$$

$$= \frac{1}{2\sqrt{x}} [\cos(\sqrt{x}) - \sin(2\sqrt{x})]$$

Q. 30 $\sin^n(ax^2 + bx + c)$

Sol. Let $y = \sin^n(ax^2 + bx + c)$

$$\therefore \quad \frac{dy}{dx} = \frac{d}{dx}[\sin(ax^2 + bx + c)]^n$$

$$= n \cdot [\sin(ax^2 + bx + c)]^{n-1} \cdot \frac{d}{dx} \sin(ax^2 + bx + c)$$

$$= n \cdot \sin^{n-1}(ax^2 + bx + c) \cdot \cos(ax^2 + bx + c) . \frac{d}{dx}(ax^2 + bx + c)$$

$$= n \cdot \sin^{n-1}(ax^2 + bx + c) \cdot \cos(ax^2 + bx + c) \cdot (2ax + b)$$

$$= n \cdot (2ax + b) \cdot \sin^{n-1}(ax^2 + bx + c) \cdot \cos(ax^2 + bx + c)$$

Q. 31 $\cos(\tan\sqrt{x+1})$

Sol. Let $y = \cos(\tan\sqrt{x+1})$

$$\therefore \quad \frac{dy}{dx} = \frac{d}{dx}\cos(\tan\sqrt{x+1}) = -\sin(\tan\sqrt{x+1}) \cdot \frac{d}{dx}(\tan\sqrt{x+1})$$

$$= -\sin(\tan\sqrt{x+1}) \cdot \sec^2\sqrt{x+1} \cdot \frac{d}{dx}(x+1)^{1/2} \qquad \left[\because \frac{d}{dx}(\tan x) = \sec^2 x\right]$$

$$= -\sin(\tan\sqrt{x+1}) \cdot (\sec\sqrt{x+1})^2 \cdot \frac{1}{2}(x+1)^{-1/2} \cdot \frac{d}{dx}(x+1)$$

$$= \frac{-1}{2\sqrt{x+1}} \cdot \sin(\tan\sqrt{x+1}) \cdot \sec^2(\sqrt{x+1})$$

Q. 32 $\sin x^2 + \sin^2 x + \sin^2 (x^2)$

Sol. Let $y = \sin x^2 + \sin^2 x + \sin^2 (x^2)$

$\therefore \quad \dfrac{dy}{dx} = \dfrac{d}{dx} \sin (x^2) + \dfrac{d}{dx} (\sin x)^2 + \dfrac{d}{dx} (\sin x^2)^2$

$= \cos (x^2) \dfrac{d}{dx} (x^2) + 2 \sin x \cdot \dfrac{d}{dx} \sin x + 2 \sin x^2 \cdot \dfrac{d}{dx} \sin x^2$

$= \cos x^2 2x + 2 \cdot \sin x \cdot \cos x + 2 \sin x^2 \cos x^2 \cdot \dfrac{d}{dx} x^2$

$= 2x \cos (x)^2 + 2 \cdot \sin x \cdot \cos x + 2 \sin x^2 \cdot \cos x^2 \cdot 2x$

$= 2x \cos (x)^2 + \sin 2x + \sin 2 (x)^2 \cdot 2x$

$= 2x \cos (x^2) + 2x \cdot \sin 2 (x^2) + \sin 2x$

Q. 33 $\sin^{-1} \dfrac{1}{\sqrt{x+1}}$

Sol. Let $y = \sin^{-1} \dfrac{1}{\sqrt{x + 1}}$

$\therefore \quad \dfrac{dy}{dx} = \dfrac{d}{dx} \sin^{-1} \dfrac{1}{\sqrt{x + 1}}$

$= \dfrac{1}{\sqrt{1 - \left(\dfrac{1}{\sqrt{x+1}}\right)^2}} \cdot \dfrac{d}{dx} \dfrac{1}{(x + 1)^{1/2}} \qquad \left[\because \dfrac{d}{dx} (\sin^{-1} x) = \dfrac{1}{\sqrt{1 - x^2}}\right]$

$= \dfrac{1}{\sqrt{\dfrac{x + 1 - 1}{x + 1}}} \cdot \dfrac{d}{dx} \cdot (x + 1)^{-1/2}$

$= \sqrt{\dfrac{x + 1}{x}} \cdot \dfrac{-1}{2} (x + 1)^{-\frac{1}{2} - 1} \cdot \dfrac{d}{dx} (x + 1)$

$= \dfrac{(x + 1)^{1/2}}{x^{1/2}} \cdot \left(-\dfrac{1}{2}\right) (x + 1)^{-3/2} = \dfrac{-1}{2\sqrt{x}} \cdot \left(\dfrac{1}{x + 1}\right)$

Q. 34 $(\sin x)^{\cos x}$

Sol. Let $y = (\sin x)^{\cos x}$

$\Rightarrow \quad \log y = \log (\sin x)^{\cos x} = \cos x \log \sin x$

$\therefore \quad \dfrac{d}{dy} \log y \cdot \dfrac{dy}{dx} = \dfrac{d}{dx} (\cos x \cdot \log \sin x)$

$\Rightarrow \quad \dfrac{1}{y} \cdot \dfrac{dy}{dx} = \cos x \cdot \dfrac{d}{dx} \log \sin x + \log \sin x \cdot \dfrac{d}{dx} \cos x$

$= \cos x \cdot \dfrac{1}{\sin x} \cdot \dfrac{d}{dx} \sin x + \log \sin x \cdot (-\sin x)$

$= \cot x \cdot \cos x - \log (\sin x) \cdot \sin x \qquad \left[\because \cot x = \dfrac{\cos x}{\sin x}\right]$

$\therefore \quad \dfrac{dy}{dx} = y \left[\dfrac{\cos^2 x}{\sin x} - \sin x \cdot \log (\sin x)\right]$

$= \sin x^{\cos x} \left[\dfrac{\cos^2 x}{\sin x} - \sin x \cdot \log (\sin x)\right]$

Q. 35 $\sin^m x \cdot \cos^n x$

Sol. Let $y = \sin^m x \cdot \cos^n x$

$$\therefore \quad \frac{dy}{dx} = \frac{d}{dx}[(\sin x)^m \cdot (\cos x)^n]$$

$$= (\sin x)^m \cdot \frac{d}{dx}(\cos x)^n + (\cos x)^n \cdot \frac{d}{dx}(\sin x)^m$$

$$= (\sin x)^m \cdot n(\cos x)^{n-1} \cdot \frac{d}{dx}\cos x + (\cos x)^n\, m(\sin x)^{m-1} \cdot \frac{d}{dx}\sin x$$

$$= (\sin x)^m \cdot n(\cos x)^{n-1}(-\sin x) + (\cos x)^n \cdot m(\sin x)^{m-1}\cos x$$

$$= -n\sin^m x \cdot \cos^{n-1} x \cdot (\sin x) + m\cos^n x \cdot \sin^{m-1} x \cdot \cos x$$

$$= -n \cdot \sin^m x \cdot \sin x \cdot \cos^n x \cdot \frac{1}{\cos x} + m \cdot \sin^m x. \frac{1}{\sin x} \cdot \cos^n x \cdot \cos x$$

$$= -n \cdot \sin^m x \cdot \cos^n x \cdot \tan x + m\sin^m x \cdot \cos^n x \cdot \cot x$$

$$= \sin^m x \cdot \cos^n x[-n\tan x + m\cot x]$$

Q. 36 $(x+1)^2(x+2)^3(x+3)^4$

Sol. Let $y = (x+1)^2(x+2)^3(x+3)^4$

$$\therefore \quad \log y = \log\{(x+1)^2 \cdot (x+2)^3(x+3)^4\}$$

$$= \log(x+1)^2 + \log(x+2)^3 + \log(x+3)^4$$

and
$$\frac{d}{dy}\log y \cdot \frac{dy}{dx} = \frac{d}{dx}[2\log(x+1)] + \frac{d}{dx}[3\log(x+2)] + \frac{d}{dx}[4\log(x+3)]$$

$$\frac{1}{y} \cdot \frac{dy}{dx} = \frac{2}{(x+1)} \cdot \frac{d}{dx}(x+1) + 3 \cdot \frac{1}{(x+2)} \cdot \frac{d}{dx}(x+2)$$

$$+ 4 \cdot \frac{1}{(x+3)} \cdot \frac{d}{dx}(x+3) \qquad \left[\because \frac{d}{dx}(\log x) = \frac{1}{x}\right]$$

$$= \left[\frac{2}{x+1} + \frac{3}{x+2} + \frac{4}{x+3}\right]$$

$$\therefore \quad \frac{dy}{dx} = y\left[\frac{2}{(x+1)} + \frac{3}{(x+2)} + \frac{4}{(x+3)}\right]$$

$$= (x+1)^2 \cdot (x+2)^3 \cdot (x+3)^4\left[\frac{2}{(x+1)} + \frac{3}{(x+2)} + \frac{4}{(x+3)}\right]$$

$$= (x+1)^2 \cdot (x+2)^3 \cdot (x+3)^4 \left[\frac{2(x+2)(x+3) + 3(x+1)(x+3) + 4(x+1)(x+2)}{(x+1)(x+2)(x+3)}\right]$$

$$= \frac{(x+1)^2(x+2)^3(x+3)^4}{(x+1)(x+2)(x+3)}[2(x^2+5x+6) + 3(x^2+4x+3) + 4(x^2+3x+2)]$$

$$= (x+1)(x+2)^2(x+3)^3[2x^2 + 10x + 12 + 3x^2 + 12x + 9 + 4x^2 + 12x + 8]$$

$$= (x+1)(x+2)^2(x+3)^3[9x^2 + 34x + 29]$$

Q. 37 $\cos^{-1}\left(\dfrac{\sin x+\cos x}{\sqrt{2}}\right), -\dfrac{\pi}{4}<x<\dfrac{\pi}{4}$

Sol. Let $$y=\cos^{-1}\left(\frac{\sin x+\cos x}{\sqrt{2}}\right)$$

$$\therefore \quad \frac{dy}{dx}=\frac{d}{dx}\cos^{-1}\left(\frac{\sin x+\cos x}{\sqrt{2}}\right)$$

$$=\frac{-1}{\sqrt{1-\left(\frac{\sin x+\cos x}{\sqrt{2}}\right)^2}}\cdot\frac{d}{dx}\left(\frac{\sin x+\cos x}{\sqrt{2}}\right)$$

$$\left[\because \frac{d}{dx}(\cos x)=-\frac{1}{\sqrt{1-x^2}}\right]$$

$$=\frac{-1}{\sqrt{4-\frac{(\sin^2 x+\cos^2 x+2\sin x\cdot\cos x)}{2}}}\cdot\frac{1}{\sqrt{2}}(\cos x-\sin x)$$

$$=\frac{-1\cdot\sqrt{2}}{\sqrt{1-\sin 2x}}\cdot\frac{1}{\sqrt{2}}(\cos x-\sin x)$$

$$[\because 1-\sin 2x=(\cos x-\sin x)^2=\cos^2 x+\sin^2 x-2\sin x\cos x]$$

$$=\frac{-1(\cos x-\sin x)}{(\cos x-\sin x)}=-1$$

Q. 38 $\tan^{-1}\sqrt{\dfrac{1-\cos x}{1+\cos x}}, -\dfrac{\pi}{4}<x<\dfrac{\pi}{4}$

Sol. Let $$y=\tan^{-1}\sqrt{\frac{1-\cos x}{1+\cos x}}$$

$$\therefore \quad \frac{dy}{dx}=\frac{d}{dx}\tan^{-1}\sqrt{\frac{1-\cos x}{1+\cos x}}$$

$$=\frac{1}{1+\sqrt{\left(\frac{1-\cos x}{1+\cos x}\right)^2}}\cdot\frac{d}{dx}\left[\frac{1-\cos x}{1+\cos x}\right]^{1/2} \qquad \left[\because \frac{d}{dx}(\tan^{-1}x)=\frac{1}{1+x^2}\right]$$

$$=\frac{1}{1+\frac{1-\cos x}{1+\cos x}}\cdot\frac{1}{2}\left[\frac{1-\cos x}{1+\cos x}\right]^{-1/2}\cdot\frac{d}{dx}\left(\frac{1-\cos x}{1+\cos x}\right)$$

$$=\frac{1}{\frac{1+\cos x+1-\cos x}{1+\cos x}}\cdot\frac{1}{2}\left[\frac{(1-\cos x)}{(1+\cos x)}\cdot\frac{(1-\cos x)}{(1-\cos x)}\right]^{-1/2}$$

$$\cdot\frac{(1+\cos x)\cdot\sin x+(1-\cos x)\cdot\sin x}{(1+\cos x)^2}$$

$$=\frac{(1+\cos x)}{2}\cdot\frac{1}{2}\left[\frac{(1-\cos x)^2}{(1-\cos^2 x)}\right]^{-1/2}\left[\frac{\sin x\,(1+\cos x+1-\cos x)}{(1+\cos x)^2}\right]$$

$$=\frac{(1+\cos x)}{2}\cdot\frac{1}{2}\left[\frac{(1-\cos x)^2}{(1-\cos^2 x)}\right]^{-1/2}\left[\frac{\sin x\,(1+\cos x+1-\cos x)}{(1+\cos x)^2}\right]$$

$$= \frac{(1+\cos x)}{2} \cdot \frac{1}{2}\left[\frac{(1-\cos x)^2}{\sin x}\right]^{-1/2} \cdot \frac{2\sin x}{(1+\cos x)^2}$$

$$= \frac{(1+\cos x)}{2} \cdot \frac{1}{2} \cdot \frac{\sin x}{(1-\cos x)} \cdot \frac{2\sin x}{(1+\cos x)^2}$$

$$= \frac{2\sin^2 x}{4(1+\cos x)(1-\cos x)} = \frac{1}{2} \cdot \frac{\sin^2 x}{(1-\cos^2 x)}$$

$$= \frac{1}{2} \cdot \frac{\sin^2 x}{\sin^2 x} = \frac{1}{2}$$

Alternate Method

Let $\quad y = \tan^{-1}\left(\sqrt{\frac{1-\cos x}{1+\cos x}}\right)$

$$= \tan^{-1}\left(\sqrt{\frac{1-1+2\sin^2 \frac{x}{2}}{1+2\cos^2 \frac{x}{2} - 1}}\right) \qquad \left[\because \cos x = 1 - 2\sin^2 \frac{x}{2} = 2\cos^2 \frac{x}{2} - 1\right]$$

$$= \tan^{-1}\left(\tan \frac{x}{2}\right) = \frac{x}{2}$$

On differentiating w.r.t. x, we get

$$\frac{dy}{dx} = \frac{1}{2}$$

Q. 39 $\tan^{-1}(\sec x + \tan x), \frac{-\pi}{2} < x < \frac{\pi}{2}$

Sol. Let $\quad y = \tan^{-1}(\sec x + \tan x)$

$$\therefore \quad \frac{dy}{dx} = \frac{d}{dx}\tan^{-1}(\sec x + \tan x)$$

$$= \frac{1}{1+(\sec x + \tan x)^2} \cdot \frac{d}{dx}(\sec x + \tan x) \qquad \left[\because \frac{d}{dx}(\tan^{-1} x) = \frac{1}{1+x^2}\right]$$

$$= \frac{1}{1+\sec^2 x + \tan^2 x + 2\sec x \cdot \tan x} \cdot [\sec x \cdot \tan x + \sec^2 x]$$

$$= \frac{1}{(\sec^2 x + \sec^2 x + 2\sec x \cdot \tan x)} \cdot \sec x \cdot (\sec x + \tan x)$$

$$= \frac{1}{2\sec x(\tan x + \sec x)} \cdot \sec x(\sec x + \tan x) = \frac{1}{2}$$

Q. 40 $\tan^{-1}\left(\frac{a\cos x - b\sin x}{b\cos x + a\sin x}\right), \frac{-\pi}{2} < x < \frac{\pi}{2}$ and $\frac{a}{b}\tan x > -1$.

Sol. Let $\quad y = \tan^{-1}\left(\frac{a\cos x - b\sin x}{b\cos x + a\sin x}\right)$

$$= \tan^{-1}\left[\frac{\frac{a\cos x}{b\cos x} - \frac{b\sin x}{b\cos x}}{\frac{b\cos x}{b\cos x} + \frac{a\sin x}{b\cos x}}\right] = \tan^{-1}\left[\frac{\frac{a}{b} - \tan x}{1 + \frac{a}{b}\tan x}\right]$$

$$= \tan^{-1}\frac{a}{b} - \tan^{-1}\tan x \qquad \left[\because \tan^{-1} x - \tan^{-1} y = \tan^{-1}\left(\frac{x-y}{1+xy}\right)\right]$$

$$= \tan^{-1}\frac{a}{b} - x$$

$$\therefore \quad \frac{dy}{dx} = \frac{d}{dx}\left(\tan^{-1}\frac{a}{b}\right) - \frac{d}{dx}(x)$$

$$= 0 - 1 \qquad \left[\because \frac{d}{dx}\left(\frac{a}{b}\right) = 0\right]$$

$$= -1$$

Q. 41 $\sec^{-1}\left(\dfrac{1}{4x^3 - 3x}\right), 0 < x < \dfrac{1}{\sqrt{2}}$

Sol. Let $\quad y = \sec^{-1}\left(\dfrac{1}{4x^3 - 3x}\right) \qquad \ldots(i)$

On putting $x = \cos\theta$ in Eq. (i), we get

$$y = \sec^{-1}\frac{1}{4\cos^3\theta - 3\cos\theta}$$

$$= \sec^{-1}\frac{1}{\cos 3\theta}$$

$$= \sec^{-1}(\sec 3\theta) = 3\theta$$

$$= 3\cos^{-1}x \qquad [\because \theta = \cos^{-1}x]$$

$$\therefore \quad \frac{dy}{dx} = \frac{d}{dx}(3\cos^{-1}x)$$

$$= 3\cdot\frac{-1}{\sqrt{1-x^2}}$$

Q. 42 $\tan^{-1}\left(\dfrac{3a^2 x - x^3}{a^3 - 3ax^2}\right), \dfrac{-1}{\sqrt{3}} < \dfrac{x}{a} < \dfrac{1}{\sqrt{3}}$

Sol. Let $\quad y = \tan^{-1}\left(\dfrac{3a^2 x - x^3}{a^3 - 3ax^2}\right)$

Put $\quad x = a\tan\theta \Rightarrow \theta = \tan^{-1}\dfrac{x}{a}$

$$\therefore \quad y = \tan^{-1}\left[\frac{3\tan\theta - \tan^3\theta}{1 - 3\tan^2\theta}\right] \qquad \left[\because \tan 3\theta = \frac{3\tan\theta - \tan^3\theta}{1 - 3\tan^2\theta}\right]$$

$$= \tan^{-1}(\tan 3\theta) = 3\theta$$

$$= 3\tan^{-1}\frac{x}{a} \qquad \left[\because \theta = \tan^{-1}\frac{x}{a}\right]$$

$$\therefore \quad \frac{dy}{dx} = 3\cdot\frac{d}{dx}\tan^{-1}\frac{x}{a} = 3\cdot\left[\frac{1}{1+\frac{x^2}{a^2}}\right]\cdot\frac{d}{dx}\cdot\left(\frac{x}{a}\right)$$

$$= 3\cdot\frac{a^2}{a^2 + x^2}\cdot\frac{1}{a} = \frac{3a}{a^2 + x^2}$$

Q. 43 $\tan^{-1}\left[\dfrac{\sqrt{1+x^2}+\sqrt{1-x^2}}{\sqrt{1+x^2}-\sqrt{1-x^2}}\right], -1 < x < 1, x \neq 0$

Sol. Let $$y = \tan^{-1}\left[\frac{\sqrt{1+x^2}+\sqrt{1-x^2}}{\sqrt{1+x^2}-\sqrt{1-x^2}}\right]$$

Put $$x^2 = \cos 2\theta$$

$\therefore$
$$y = \tan^{-1}\left(\frac{\sqrt{1+\cos 2\theta}+\sqrt{1-\cos 2\theta}}{\sqrt{1+\cos 2\theta}-\sqrt{1-\cos 2\theta}}\right)$$
$$= \tan^{-1}\left(\frac{\sqrt{1+2\cos^2\theta-1}+\sqrt{1-1+2\sin^2\theta}}{\sqrt{1+2\cos^2\theta-1}-\sqrt{1-1+2\sin^2\theta}}\right)$$
$$= \tan^{-1}\left(\frac{\sqrt{2}\cos\theta+\sqrt{2}\sin\theta}{\sqrt{2}\cos\theta-\sqrt{2}\sin\theta}\right) = \tan^{-1}\left[\frac{\sqrt{2}(\cos\theta+\sin\theta)}{\sqrt{2}(\cos\theta-\sin\theta)}\right]$$
$$= \tan^{-1}\left(\frac{\cos\theta+\sin\theta}{\cos\theta-\sin\theta}\right) = \tan^{-1}\left(\frac{\dfrac{\cos\theta+\sin\theta}{\cos\theta}}{\dfrac{\cos\theta-\sin\theta}{\cos\theta}}\right)$$
$$= \tan^{-1}\left(\frac{1+\tan\theta}{1-\tan\theta}\right)$$
$$= \tan^{-1}\tan\left(\frac{\pi}{4}+\theta\right) \qquad \left[\because \tan(a+b) = \frac{\tan a+\tan b}{1-\tan a\cdot\tan b}\right]$$
$$= \frac{\pi}{4}+\theta = \frac{\pi}{4}+\frac{1}{2}\cos^{-1}x^2 \qquad \left[\because 2\theta = \cos^{-1}x^2 \Rightarrow \theta = \frac{1}{2}\cos^{-1}x^2\right]$$

$\therefore$
$$\frac{dy}{dx} = \frac{d}{dx}\left(\frac{\pi}{4}\right)+\frac{d}{dx}\left(\frac{1}{2}\cos^{-1}x^2\right)$$
$$= 0+\frac{1}{2}\cdot\frac{-1}{\sqrt{1-x^4}}\cdot\frac{d}{dx}x^2 = \frac{1}{2}\cdot\frac{-2x}{\sqrt{1-x^4}} = \frac{-x}{\sqrt{1-x^4}}$$

Find $\dfrac{dy}{dx}$ of each of the functions expressed in parametric form.

Q. 44 $x = t+\dfrac{1}{t},\ y = t-\dfrac{1}{t}$

Sol. $\because$ $$x = t+\frac{1}{t} \text{ and } y = t-\frac{1}{t}$$

$\therefore$ $$\frac{dx}{dt} = \frac{d}{dt}\left(t+\frac{1}{t}\right) \quad\text{and}\quad \frac{dy}{dt} = \frac{d}{dt}\left(t-\frac{1}{t}\right)$$

$\Rightarrow$ $$\frac{dx}{dt} = 1+(-1)t^{-2} \quad\text{and}\quad \frac{dy}{dt} = 1-(-1)t^{-2}$$

$\Rightarrow$ $$\frac{dx}{dt} = 1-\frac{1}{t^2} \quad\text{and}\quad \frac{dy}{dt} = 1+\frac{1}{t^2}$$

$\Rightarrow$ $$\frac{dx}{dt} = \frac{t^2-1}{t^2} \quad\text{and}\quad \frac{dy}{dt} = \frac{t^2+1}{t^2}$$

$\therefore$ $$\frac{dy}{dx} = \frac{dy/dt}{dx/dt} = \frac{t^2+1/t^2}{t^2-1/t^2} = \frac{t^2+1}{t^2-1}$$

Q. 45 $x = e^{\theta}\left(\theta + \frac{1}{\theta}\right), y = e^{-\theta}\left(\theta - \frac{1}{\theta}\right)$

Sol. $\because$ $x = e^{\theta}\left(\theta + \frac{1}{\theta}\right)$ and $y = e^{-\theta}\left(\theta - \frac{1}{\theta}\right)$

$\therefore$
$$\frac{dx}{d\theta} = \frac{d}{d\theta}\left[e^{\theta}\cdot\left(\theta + \frac{1}{\theta}\right)\right]$$
$$= e^{\theta}\cdot\frac{d}{d\theta}\left(\theta + \frac{1}{\theta}\right) + \left(\theta + \frac{1}{\theta}\right)\cdot\frac{d}{d\theta}e^{\theta}$$
$$= e^{\theta}\left(1 - \frac{1}{\theta^2}\right) + \left(\theta + \frac{1}{\theta}\right)e^{\theta}$$
$$= e^{\theta}\left(1 - \frac{1}{\theta^2} + \theta + \frac{1}{\theta}\right)$$
$$= e^{\theta}\left(\frac{\theta^2 - 1 + \theta^3 + \theta}{\theta^2}\right) \quad \text{...(i)}$$

and
$$\frac{dy}{d\theta} = \frac{d}{d\theta}\left[e^{-\theta}\cdot\left(\theta - \frac{1}{\theta}\right)\right]$$
$$= e^{-\theta}\cdot\frac{d}{d\theta}\left(\theta - \frac{1}{\theta}\right) + \frac{d}{d\theta}e^{-\theta}\left(\theta - \frac{1}{\theta}\right)$$
$$= e^{-\theta}\left(1 + \frac{1}{\theta^2}\right) + \left(\theta - \frac{1}{\theta}\right)e^{-\theta}\cdot\frac{d}{d\theta}(-\theta)$$
$$= e^{-\theta}\left[\frac{\theta^2 + 1}{\theta^2} - \frac{\theta^2 - 1}{\theta}\right] = e^{-\theta}\left[\frac{\theta^2 + 1 - \theta^3 + \theta}{\theta^2}\right] \quad \text{...(ii)}$$

$\therefore$
$$\frac{dy}{dx} = \frac{dy/d\theta}{dx/d\theta} = \frac{e^{-\theta}\left(\frac{\theta^2 + 1 - \theta^3 + \theta}{\theta^2}\right)}{e^{\theta}\left(\frac{\theta^2 - 1 + \theta^3 + \theta}{\theta^2}\right)}$$
$$= e^{-2\theta}\left(\frac{-\theta^3 + \theta^2 + \theta + 1}{\theta^3 + \theta^2 + \theta - 1}\right)$$

Q. 46 $x = 3\cos\theta - 2\cos^3\theta, y = 3\sin\theta - 2\sin^3\theta$

Sol. $\because$ $x = 3\cos\theta - 2\cos^3\theta$ and $y = 3\sin\theta - 2\sin^3\theta$

$\therefore$
$$\frac{dx}{d\theta} = \frac{d}{d\theta}(3\cos\theta) - \frac{d}{d\theta}(2\cos^3\theta)$$
$$= 3\cdot(-\sin\theta) - 2\cdot 3\cos^2\theta\cdot\frac{d}{d\theta}\cdot\cos\theta$$
$$= -3\sin\theta + 6\cos^2\theta\sin\theta$$

and
$$\frac{dy}{d\theta} = 3\cos A - 2\cdot 3\sin^2\theta\cdot\frac{d}{d\theta}\cdot\sin\theta$$
$$= 3\cos\theta - 6\sin^2\theta\cdot\cos\theta$$

Now,
$$\frac{dy}{dx} = \frac{dy/d\theta}{dx/d\theta} = \frac{3\cos\theta - 6\sin^2\theta\cos\theta}{-3\sin\theta + 6\cos^2\theta\sin\theta}$$
$$= \frac{3\cos\theta(1 - 2\sin^2\theta)}{3\sin\theta(-1 + 2\cos^2\theta)} = \cot\theta\cdot\frac{\cos 2\theta}{\cos 2\theta} = \cot\theta$$

Q. 47 $\sin x = \dfrac{2t}{1+t^2}, \tan y = \dfrac{2t}{1-t^2}$

Sol. $\because$

$$\sin x = \frac{2t}{1+t^2} \quad \text{...(i)}$$

and

$$\tan y = \frac{2t}{1-t^2} \quad \text{...(ii)}$$

$$\therefore \quad \frac{d}{dx}\sin x \cdot \frac{dx}{dt} = \frac{d}{dt}\left(\frac{2t}{1+t^2}\right)$$

$$\Rightarrow \quad \cos x \frac{dx}{dt} = \frac{(1+t^2)\cdot \frac{d}{dt}(2t) - (2t)\cdot \frac{d}{dt}(1+t^2)}{(1+t^2)^2}$$

$$= \frac{2(1+t^2) - 2t \cdot 2t}{(1+t^2)^2} = \frac{2+2t^2-4t^2}{(1+t^2)^2}$$

$$\Rightarrow \quad \frac{dx}{dt} = \frac{2(1-t^2)}{(1+t^2)^2} \cdot \frac{1}{\cos x}$$

$$\Rightarrow \quad \frac{dx}{dt} = \frac{2(1-t^2)}{(1+t^2)^2} \cdot \frac{1}{\sqrt{1-\sin^2 x}} = \frac{2(1-t^2)}{(1+t^2)^2} \cdot \frac{1}{\sqrt{1-\left(\frac{2t}{1+t^2}\right)^2}}$$

$$\Rightarrow \quad \frac{dx}{dt} = \frac{2(1-t^2)}{(1+t^2)^2} \cdot \frac{(1+t^2)}{(1-t^2)} = \frac{2}{1+t^2} \quad \text{...(iii)}$$

Also,

$$\frac{d}{dy}\tan y \cdot \frac{dy}{dt} = \frac{d}{dt}\left(\frac{2t}{1-t^2}\right)$$

$$\sec^2 y \frac{dy}{dt} = \frac{(1-t^2)\frac{d}{dt}\cdot(2t) - 2t \cdot \frac{d}{dt}(1-t^2)}{(1-t^2)^2}$$

$$\frac{dy}{dt} = \frac{2-2t^2+4t^2}{(1-t^2)^2} \cdot \frac{1}{\sec^2 y}$$

$$= \frac{2(1+t^2)}{(1-t^2)^2} \cdot \frac{1}{(1+\tan^2 y)} = \frac{2(1+t^2)}{(1-t^2)^2} \cdot \frac{1}{1+\frac{4t^2}{(1-t^2)^2}}$$

$$= \frac{2(1+t^2)}{(1-t^2)^2} \cdot \frac{(1-t^2)^2}{(1+t^2)^2} = \frac{2}{1+t^2} \quad \text{...(iv)}$$

$$\therefore \quad \frac{dy}{dx} = \frac{dy/dt}{dx/dt} = \frac{2/1+t^2}{2/1+t^2} = 1 \quad \text{[from Eqs. (iii) and (iv)]}$$

Q. 48 $x = \dfrac{1+\log t}{t^2}, y = \dfrac{3+2\log t}{t}$

Sol. $\because$

$$x = \frac{1+\log t}{t^2} \text{ and } y = \frac{3+2\log t}{t}$$

$$\therefore \quad \frac{dx}{dt} = \frac{t^2 . \frac{d}{dt}(1+\log t) - (1+\log t). \frac{d}{dt}t^2}{(t^2)^2}$$

$$= \frac{t^2 \cdot \frac{1}{t} - (1+\log t)\cdot 2t}{t^4} = \frac{t - (1+\log t)\cdot 2t}{t^4}$$

$$= \frac{t}{t^4}[1 - 2(1+\log t) = \frac{-1-2\log t}{t^3} \quad \text{... (i)}$$

and $$\frac{dy}{dt} = \frac{t.\frac{d}{dt}(3+2\log t) - (3+2\log t).\frac{d}{dt}t}{t^2}$$

$$= \frac{t \cdot 2 \cdot \frac{1}{t} - (3+2\log t)\cdot 1}{t^2}$$

$$= \frac{2-3-2\log t}{t^2} = \frac{-1-2\log t}{t^2} \quad \text{...(ii)}$$

$\therefore$ $$\frac{dy}{dx} = \frac{dy/dt}{dx/dt} = \frac{-1-2\log t/t^2}{-1-2\log t/t^3} = t$$

Q. 49 **If $x = e^{\cos 2t}$ and $y = e^{\sin 2t}$, then prove that $\frac{dy}{dx} = -\frac{y \log x}{x \log y}$.**

Sol. $\because$ $$x = e^{\cos 2t} \text{ and } y = e^{\sin 2t}$$

$\therefore$ $$\frac{dx}{dt} = \frac{d}{dt}e^{\cos 2t} = e^{\cos 2t}.\frac{d}{dt}\cos 2t$$

$$= e^{\cos 2t} \cdot (-\sin 2t) \cdot \frac{d}{dt}(2t)$$

$$\frac{dx}{dt} = -2e^{\cos 2t} \cdot \sin 2t \quad \text{...(i)}$$

and $$\frac{dy}{dt} = \frac{d}{dt}e^{\sin 2t} = e^{\sin 2t}.\frac{d}{dt}\sin 2t$$

$$= e^{\sin 2t}\cos 2t \cdot \frac{d}{dt}2t$$

$$= 2e^{\sin 2t}.\cos 2t \quad \text{...(ii)}$$

$\therefore$ $$\frac{dy}{dx} = \frac{dy/dt}{dx/dt} = \frac{2e^{\sin 2t}\cdot\cos 2t}{-2e^{\cos 2t}\cdot\sin 2t}$$

$$= \frac{e^{\sin 2t}\cdot\cos 2t}{e^{\cos 2t}\cdot\sin 2t} \quad \text{...(iii)}$$

We know that, $$\log x = \cos 2t \cdot \log e = \cos 2t \quad \text{...(iv)}$$

and $$\log y = \sin 2t \cdot \log e = \sin 2t \quad \text{...(v)}$$

$\therefore$ $$\frac{dy}{dx} = \frac{-y\log x}{x\log y}$$

[using Eqs. (iv) and (v) in Eq. (iii) and $x = e^{\cos 2t}$, $y = e^{\sin 2t}$]

Hence proved.

Q. 50 **If $x = a\sin 2t(1+\cos 2t)$ and $y = b\cos 2t(1-\cos 2t)$, then show that $\left(\frac{dy}{dx}\right)_{t=\pi/4} = \frac{b}{a}$.**

Sol. $\because$ $$x = a\sin 2t(1+\cos 2t) \text{ and } y = b\cos 2t(1-\cos 2t)$$

$\therefore$ $$\frac{dx}{dt} = a\left[\sin 2t \cdot \frac{d}{dt}(1+\cos 2t) + (1+\cos 2t)\cdot\frac{d}{dt}\sin 2t\right]$$

$$= a\left[\sin 2t\cdot(-\sin 2t)\cdot\frac{d}{dt}2t + (1+\cos 2t)\cdot\cos 2t\cdot\frac{d}{dt}2t\right]$$

$$= -2a\sin^2 2t + 2a\cos 2t\,(1+\cos 2t)$$

$\Rightarrow$ $$\frac{dx}{dt} = -2a\,[\sin^2 2t - \cos 2t\,(1+\cos 2t)] \quad \text{...(i)}$$

and $$\frac{dy}{dt} = b\left[\cos 2t\cdot\frac{d}{dt}(1-\cos 2t) + (1-\cos 2t)\cdot\frac{d}{dt}\cos 2t\right]$$

$$= b\left[\cos 2t\cdot(\sin 2t)\frac{d}{dt}2t + (1-\cos 2t)(-\sin 2t)\cdot\frac{d}{dt}2t\right]$$

$$= b\,[2\sin 2t\cdot\cos 2t + 2\,(1-\cos 2t)(-\sin 2t)]$$

$$= 2b\,[\sin 2t\cdot\cos 2t - (1-\cos 2t)\sin 2t] \quad \text{...(ii)}$$

$\therefore$ $$\frac{dy}{dx} = \frac{dy/dt}{dx/dt} = \frac{-2b\,[-\sin 2t\cdot\cos 2t + (1-\cos 2t)\sin 2t]}{-2a\,[\sin^2 2t - \cos 2t\,(1+\cos 2t)]}$$

$\Rightarrow$ $$\left(\frac{dy}{dx}\right)_{t=\pi/4} = \frac{b}{a}\,\frac{\left[-\sin\frac{\pi}{2}\cos\frac{\pi}{2} + \left(1-\cos\frac{\pi}{2}\right)\sin\frac{\pi}{2}\right]}{\left[\sin^2\frac{\pi}{2} - \cos\frac{\pi}{2}\left(1+\cos\frac{\pi}{2}\right)\right]}$$

$$= \frac{b}{a}\cdot\frac{(0+1)}{(1-0)} \qquad \left[\because \sin\frac{\pi}{2} = 1 \text{ and } \cos\frac{\pi}{2} = 0\right]$$

$$= \frac{b}{a}$$

Hence proved.

Q. 51 If $x = 3\sin t - \sin 3t$, $y = 3\cos t - \cos 3t$, then find $\frac{dy}{dx}$ at $t = \frac{\pi}{3}$.

Sol. $\because$ $$x = 3\sin t - \sin 3t \text{ and } y = 3\cos t - \cos 3t$$

$\therefore$ $$\frac{dx}{dt} = 3\cdot\frac{d}{dt}\sin t - \frac{d}{dt}\sin 3t$$

$$= 3\cos t - \cos 3t\cdot\frac{d}{dt}3t = 3\cos t - 3\cos 3t \quad \text{...(i)}$$

and $$\frac{dy}{dt} = 3\cdot\frac{d}{dt}\cos t - \frac{d}{dt}\cos 3t$$

$$= -3\sin t + \sin 3t\cdot\frac{d}{dt}3t$$

$$\frac{dy}{dt} = 3\sin 3t - 3t\sin t \quad \text{...(ii)}$$

$\therefore$ $$\frac{dy}{dx} = \frac{dy/dt}{dx/dt} = \frac{3(\sin 3t - \sin t)}{3(\cos t - \cos 3t)}$$

Now, $$\left(\frac{dy}{dx}\right)_{t=\pi/3} = \frac{\sin\frac{3\pi}{3} - \sin\frac{\pi}{3}}{\left(\cos\frac{\pi}{3} - \cos 3\frac{\pi}{3}\right)} = \frac{0-\sqrt{3}/2}{\frac{1}{2}-(-1)}$$

$$= \frac{-\sqrt{3}/2}{3/2} = \frac{-\sqrt{3}}{3} = \frac{-1}{\sqrt{3}}$$

Q. 52 Differentiate $\dfrac{x}{\sin x}$ w.r.t. $\sin x$.

Sol. Let $u = \dfrac{x}{\sin x}$ and $v = \sin x$

$$\therefore \quad \frac{du}{dx} = \frac{\sin x \cdot \frac{d}{dx} x - x \cdot \frac{d}{dx} \sin x}{(\sin x)^2}$$

$$= \frac{\sin x - x \cos x}{\sin^2 x} \quad \text{...(i)}$$

and $$\frac{dv}{dx} = \frac{d}{dx} \sin x = \cos x \quad \text{...(ii)}$$

$$\therefore \quad \frac{du}{dv} = \frac{du/dx}{dv/dx} = \frac{\sin x - x \cos x / \sin^2 x}{\cos x}$$

$$= \frac{\sin x - x \cos x}{\sin^2 x \cos x} = \frac{\dfrac{\sin x - x \cos x}{\cos x}}{\dfrac{\sin^2 x \cos x}{\cos x}}$$

[dividing by $\cos x$ in both numerator and denominator]

$$= \frac{\tan x - x}{\sin^2 x}$$

Q. 53 Differentiate $\tan^{-1} \dfrac{\sqrt{1 + x^2} - 1}{x}$ w.r.t. $\tan^{-1} x$, when $x \neq 0$.

Sol. Let $u = \tan^{-1} \dfrac{\sqrt{1 + x^2} - 1}{x}$ and $v = \tan^{-1} x$

$$\therefore \quad x = \tan \theta$$

$$\Rightarrow \quad u = \tan^{-1} \frac{\sqrt{1 + \tan^2 \theta} - 1}{\tan \theta}$$

$$= \tan^{-1} \frac{(\sec \theta - 1) \cos \theta}{\sin \theta}$$

$$= \tan^{-1} \left(\frac{1 - \cos \theta}{\sin \theta} \right)$$

$$= \tan^{-1} \left[\frac{1 - 1 + 2 \sin^2 \theta/2}{2 \sin \theta/2 \cdot \cos \theta/2} \right] \quad [\because \cos \theta = 1 - 2 \sin^2 \theta]$$

$$= \tan^{-1} \left[\tan \frac{\theta}{2} \right]$$

$$= \frac{\theta}{2} = \frac{1}{2} \tan^{-1} x$$

$$\therefore \quad \frac{du}{dx} = \frac{1}{2} \frac{d}{dx} \tan^{-1} x = \frac{1}{2} \cdot \frac{1}{1 + x^2} \quad \text{...(i)}$$

and $$\frac{dv}{dx} = \frac{d}{dx} \tan^{-1} x = \frac{1}{1 + x^2} \quad \text{...(ii)}$$

$$\therefore \quad \frac{du}{dv} = \frac{du/dx}{dv/dx}$$

$$= \frac{1/2\,(1 + x^2)}{1/(1 + x^2)} = \frac{(1 + x^2)}{2(1 + x^2)} = \frac{1}{2}$$

Find $\frac{dy}{dx}$ when x and y are connected by the relation given.

Q. 54 $\sin(xy) + \frac{x}{y} = x^2 - y$

Sol. We have, $\sin(xy) + \frac{x}{y} = x^2 - y$

On differentiating both sides w.r.t. x, we get

$$\frac{d}{dx}(\sin xy) + \frac{d}{dx}\left(\frac{x}{y}\right) = \frac{d}{dx}x^2 - \frac{d}{dx}y$$

$$\Rightarrow \quad \cos xy \cdot \frac{d}{dx}(xy) + \frac{y\frac{d}{dx}x - x \cdot \frac{d}{dx}y}{y^2} = 2x - \frac{dy}{dx}$$

$$\Rightarrow \quad \cos xy \cdot \left[x \cdot \frac{d}{dx}y + y \cdot \frac{d}{dx} \cdot x\right] + \frac{y - x\frac{dy}{dx}}{y^2} = 2x - \frac{dy}{dx}$$

$$\Rightarrow \quad x\cos xy \cdot \frac{dy}{dx} + y\cos xy + \frac{y}{y^2} - \frac{x}{y^2}\frac{dy}{dx} = 2x - \frac{dy}{dx}$$

$$\Rightarrow \quad \frac{dy}{dx}\left[x\cos xy - \frac{x}{y^2} + 1\right] = 2x - y\cos xy - \frac{y}{y^2}$$

$$\therefore \quad \frac{dy}{dx} = \left[\frac{2xy - y^2\cos xy - 1}{y}\right]\left[\frac{y^2}{xy^2\cos xy - x + y^2}\right]$$

$$= \frac{(2xy - y^2\cos xy - 1)\,y}{(xy^2\cos xy - x + y^2)}$$

Q. 55 $\sec(x + y) = xy$

Sol. We have, $\sec(x + y) = xy$

On differentiating both sides w.r.t. x, we get

$$\frac{d}{dx}\sec(x + y) = \frac{d}{dx}(xy)$$

$$\Rightarrow \quad \sec(x + y) \cdot \tan(x + y) \cdot \frac{d}{dx}(x + y) = x \cdot \frac{d}{dx}y + y \cdot \frac{d}{dx}x$$

$$\Rightarrow \quad \sec(x + y) \cdot \tan(x + y) \cdot \left(1 + \frac{dy}{dx}\right) = x\frac{dy}{dx} + y$$

$$\Rightarrow \quad \sec(x + y)\tan(x + y) + \sec(x + y) \cdot \tan(x + y) \cdot \frac{dy}{dx} = x\frac{dy}{dx} + y$$

$$\Rightarrow \quad \frac{dy}{dx}[\sec(x + y) \cdot \tan(x + y) - x] = y - \sec(x + y) \cdot \tan(x + y)$$

$$\therefore \quad \frac{dy}{dx} = \frac{y - \sec(x + y) \cdot \tan(x + y)}{\sec(x + y) \cdot \tan(x + y) - x}$$

Q. 56 $\tan^{-1}(x^2 + y^2) = a$

Sol. We have, $\tan^{-1}(x^2 + y^2) = a$

On differentiating both sides w.r.t. x, we get

$$\frac{d}{dx}\tan^{-1}(x^2 + y^2) = \frac{d}{dx}(a)$$

$$\Rightarrow \quad \frac{1}{1+(x^2 + y^2)^2}\cdot\frac{d}{dx}(x^2 + y^2) = 0$$

$$\Rightarrow \quad 2x + \frac{d}{dy}y^2\cdot\frac{dy}{dx} = 0$$

$$\Rightarrow \quad 2y\cdot\frac{dy}{dx} = -2x$$

$$\therefore \quad \frac{dy}{dx} = \frac{-2x}{2y} = \frac{-x}{y}$$

Q. 57 $(x^2 + y^2)^2 = xy$

Sol. We have, $(x^2 + y^2)^2 = xy$

On differentiating both sides w.r.t. x, we get

$$\frac{d}{dx}(x^2 + y^2)^2 = \frac{d}{dx}(xy)$$

$$\Rightarrow \quad 2(x^2 + y^2)\cdot\frac{d}{dx}(x^2 + y^2) = x\cdot\frac{d}{dx}y + y\cdot\frac{d}{dx}x$$

$$\Rightarrow \quad 2(x^2 + y^2)\cdot\left(2x + 2y\frac{dy}{dx}\right) = x\frac{dy}{dx} + y$$

$$\Rightarrow \quad 2x^2\cdot 2x + 2x^2\cdot 2y\frac{dy}{dx} + 2y^2\cdot 2x + 2y^2\cdot 2y\frac{dy}{dx} = x\frac{dy}{dx} + y$$

$$\Rightarrow \quad \frac{dy}{dx}[4x^2y + 4y^3 - x] = y - 4x^3 - 4xy^2$$

$$\therefore \quad \frac{dy}{dx} = \frac{(y - 4x^3 - 4xy^2)}{(4x^2y + 4y^3 - x)}$$

Q. 58 If $ax^2 + 2hxy + by^2 + 2gx + 2fy + c = 0$, then show that $\dfrac{dy}{dx}\cdot\dfrac{dx}{dy} = 1$.

Sol. We have, $ax^2 + 2hxy + by^2 + 2gx + 2fy + c = 0$ ...(i)

On differentiating both sides w.r.t. x, we get

$$\frac{d}{dx}(ax^2) + \frac{d}{dx}(2hxy) + \frac{d}{dx}(by^2) + \frac{d}{dx}(2gx) + \frac{d}{dx}(2fy) + \frac{d}{dx}(c) = 0$$

$$\Rightarrow \quad 2ax + 2h\left(x\cdot\frac{dy}{dx} + y\cdot 1\right) + b\cdot 2y\frac{dy}{dx} + 2g + 2f\frac{dy}{dx} + 0 = 0$$

$$\Rightarrow \quad \frac{dy}{dx}[2hx + 2by + 2f] = -2ax - 2hy - 2g$$

$$\Rightarrow \quad \frac{dy}{dx} = \frac{-2(ax + hy + g)}{2(hx + by + f)}$$

$$= \frac{-(ax + hy + g)}{(hx + by + f)} \quad \text{...(ii)}$$

Now, differentiating Eq. (i) w.r.t. y, we get

$$\frac{d}{dy}(ax^2)+\frac{d}{dy}(2hxy)+\frac{d}{dy}(by^2)+\frac{d}{dy}(2gx)+\frac{d}{dy}(2fy)+\frac{d}{dy}(c)=0$$

$$\Rightarrow \quad a\cdot 2x\cdot\frac{dx}{dy}+2h\cdot\left(x\cdot\frac{d}{dy}y+y\cdot\frac{d}{dy}x\right)+b\cdot 2y+2g\cdot\frac{dx}{dy}+2f+0=0$$

$$\Rightarrow \quad \frac{dx}{dy}[2ax+2hy+2g]=-2hx-2by-2f$$

$$\Rightarrow \quad \frac{dx}{dy}=\frac{-2(hx+by+f)}{2(ax+hy+g)}=\frac{-(hx+by+f)}{(ax+hy+g)} \qquad \text{... (iii)}$$

$$\therefore \quad \frac{dy}{dx}\cdot\frac{dx}{dy}=\frac{-(ax+hy+g)}{(hx+by+f)}\cdot\frac{-(hx+by+f)}{(ax+hy+g)} \qquad \text{[using Eqs. (ii) and (iii)]}$$

$$=1=\text{RHS}$$

Hence proved.

Q. 59 If $x=e^{x/y}$, then prove that $\dfrac{dy}{dx}=\dfrac{x-y}{x\log x}$.

Sol. We have, $x=e^{x/y}$

$$\therefore \quad \frac{d}{dx}x=\frac{d}{dx}e^{x/y}$$

$$\Rightarrow \quad 1=e^{x/y}\cdot\frac{d}{dx}(x/y)$$

$$\Rightarrow \quad 1=e^{x/y}\cdot\left[\frac{y\cdot 1-x\cdot dy/dx}{y^2}\right]$$

$$\Rightarrow \quad y^2=y\cdot e^{x/y}-x\cdot\frac{dy}{dx}\cdot e^{x/y}$$

$$\Rightarrow \quad x\cdot\frac{dy}{dx}\cdot e^{x/y}=ye^{x/y}-y^2$$

$$\therefore \quad \frac{dy}{dx}=\frac{y(e^{x/y}-y)}{x\cdot e^{x/y}}$$

$$=\frac{(e^{x/y}-y)}{e^{x/y}\cdot\frac{x}{y}} \qquad \left[\because x=e^{x/y}\Rightarrow \log x=\frac{x}{y}\right]$$

$$=\frac{x-y}{x\cdot\log x}$$

Hence proved.

Q. 60 If $y^x=e^{y-x}$, then prove that $\dfrac{dy}{dx}=\dfrac{(1+\log y)^2}{\log y}$.

Sol. We have, $y^x=e^{y-x}$

$$\Rightarrow \quad \log y^x=\log e^{y-x}$$

$$\Rightarrow \quad x\log y=y-x\cdot\log_e=(y-x) \qquad [\because \log_e=1]$$

$$\Rightarrow \quad \log y=\frac{(y-x)}{x} \qquad \text{...(i)}$$

Now, differentiating w.r.t. x, we get

$$\frac{d}{dy}\log y\cdot\frac{dy}{dx}=\frac{d}{dx}\frac{(y-x)}{x}$$

$$\Rightarrow \quad \frac{1}{y}\cdot\frac{dy}{dx} = \frac{x\cdot\frac{d}{dx}(y-x) - (y-x)\cdot\frac{d}{dx}\cdot x}{x^2}$$

$$\Rightarrow \quad \frac{1}{y}\frac{dy}{dx} = \frac{x\left(\frac{dy}{dx}-1\right) - (y-x)}{x^2}$$

$$\Rightarrow \quad \frac{x^2}{y}\cdot\frac{dy}{dx} = x\frac{dy}{dx} - x - y + x$$

$$\Rightarrow \quad \frac{dy}{dx}\left(\frac{x^2}{y} - x\right) = -y$$

$$\therefore \quad \frac{dy}{dx} = \frac{-y^2}{x^2 - xy} = \frac{-y^2}{x(x-y)}$$

$$= \frac{y^2}{x(y-x)}\cdot\frac{x}{x} = \frac{y^2}{x^2}\cdot\frac{1}{\frac{(y-x)}{x}}$$

$$= \frac{(1+\log y)^2}{\log y} \quad \left[\because \log y = \frac{y-x}{x} \ \log y = \frac{y}{x} - 1 \Rightarrow 1 + \log y = \frac{y}{x}\right]$$

Hence proved.

Q. 61 If $y = (\cos x)^{(\cos x)^{(\cos x)^{\cdots\infty}}}$, then show that $\dfrac{dy}{dx} = \dfrac{y^2 \tan x}{y \log \cos x - 1}$.

Sol. We have,

$$y = (\cos x)^{(\cos x)^{(\cos x)^{\cdots\infty}}}$$

$$\Rightarrow \quad y = (\cos x)^y$$

$$\therefore \quad \log y = \log (\cos x)^y$$

$$\Rightarrow \quad \log y = y \log \cos x$$

On differentiating w.r.t. x, we get

$$\frac{1}{y}\cdot\frac{dy}{dx} = y\cdot\frac{d}{dx}\log \cos x + \log \cos x\cdot\frac{dy}{dx}$$

$$\Rightarrow \quad \frac{1}{y}\cdot\frac{dy}{dx} = \frac{y}{\cos x}\cdot\frac{d}{dx}\cos x + \log \cos x\cdot\frac{dy}{dx}$$

$$\Rightarrow \quad \frac{dy}{dx}\left[\frac{1}{y} - \log \cos x\right] = \frac{-y\sin x}{\cos x} = -y\tan x$$

$$\therefore \quad \frac{dy}{dx} = \frac{-y^2 \tan x}{(1 - y\log \cos x)}$$

$$= \frac{y^2 \tan x}{y \log \cos x - 1}$$

Hence proved.

Q. 62 If $x\sin(a+y) + \sin a\cdot\cos(a+y) = 0$, then prove that

$$\frac{dy}{dx} = \frac{\sin^2(a+y)}{\sin a}.$$

Sol. We have,

$$x\sin(a+y) + \sin a\cdot\cos(a+y) = 0$$

$$\Rightarrow \quad x\sin(a+y) = -\sin a\cdot\cos(a+y)$$

$$\Rightarrow \quad x = \frac{-\sin a\cdot\cos(a+y)}{\sin(a+y)}$$

$$\Rightarrow \quad x = -\sin a \cdot \cot(a+y)$$

$$\therefore \quad \frac{dx}{dy} = -\sin a \cdot [-\operatorname{cosec}^2(a+y)] \cdot \frac{d}{dy}(a+y)$$

$$= \sin a \cdot \frac{1}{\sin^2(a+y)} \cdot 1$$

$$= \frac{\sin^2(a+y)}{\sin a}$$

Hence proved.

Q. 63 If $\sqrt{1-x^2}+\sqrt{1-y^2}=a(x-y)$, then prove that $\frac{dy}{dx}=\sqrt{\frac{1-y^2}{1-x^2}}$.

Sol. We have,

$$\sqrt{1-x^2}+\sqrt{1-y^2}=a(x-y)$$

On putting $x = \sin\alpha$ and $y = \sin\beta$, we get

$$\sqrt{1-\sin^2\alpha}+\sqrt{1-\sin^2\beta}=a(\sin\alpha-\sin\beta)$$

$$\Rightarrow \quad \cos\alpha+\cos\beta=a(\sin\alpha-\sin\beta)$$

$$\Rightarrow \quad 2\cos\frac{\alpha+\beta}{2}.\cos\frac{\alpha-\beta}{2}=a\left(2\cos\frac{\alpha+\beta}{2}.\sin\frac{\alpha-\beta}{2}\right)$$

$$\Rightarrow \quad \cos\frac{\alpha-\beta}{2}=a\sin\frac{\alpha-\beta}{2}$$

$$\Rightarrow \quad \cot\frac{\alpha-\beta}{2}=a$$

$$\Rightarrow \quad \frac{\alpha-\beta}{2}=\cot^{-1}a$$

$$\Rightarrow \quad \alpha-\beta=2\cot^{-1}a$$

$$\Rightarrow \quad \sin^{-1}x-\sin^{-1}y=2\cot^{-1}a \qquad [\because x=\sin\alpha \text{ and } y=\sin\beta]$$

On differentiating both sides w.r.t. x, we get

$$\frac{1}{\sqrt{1-x^2}}-\frac{1}{\sqrt{1-y^2}}\frac{dy}{dx}=0$$

$$\therefore \quad \frac{dy}{dx}=\frac{\sqrt{1-y^2}}{\sqrt{1-x^2}}=\sqrt{\frac{1-y^2}{1-x^2}}$$

Hence proved.

Q. 64 If $y=\tan^{-1}x$, then find $\frac{d^2y}{dx^2}$ in terms of y alone.

Sol. We have,

$$y=\tan^{-1}x \qquad \text{[on differentiating w.r.t. } x]$$

$$\therefore \quad \frac{dy}{dx}=\frac{1}{1+x^2} \qquad \text{[again differentiating w.r.t. } x]$$

Now,

$$\frac{d^2y}{dx^2}=\frac{d}{dx}(1+x^2)^{-1}$$

$$=-1(1+x^2)^{-2}.\frac{d}{dx}(1+x^2)$$

$$=-\frac{1}{(1+x^2)^2}\cdot 2x$$

$$=\frac{-2\tan y}{(1+\tan^2 y)^2} \qquad [\because y=\tan^{-1}x \Rightarrow \tan y = x]$$

$$= \frac{-2\tan y}{(\sec^2 y)^2}$$

$$= -2\frac{\sin y}{\cos y}\cdot\cos^2 y\cdot\cos^2 y$$

$$= -\sin 2y\cdot\cos^2 y \qquad [\because \sin 2x = 2\sin x\cos x]$$

Verify the Rolle's theorem for each of the functions in following questions.

Q. 65 $f(x) = x(x-1)^2$ in [0,1]

Thinking Process

We know that, Rolle's theorem states that, if f be a real valued function, defined in the closed interval [a, b], such that (i) f is continuous on [a, b]. (ii) f is differentiable on]a, b[.(iii) f(a) = f(b).

Then, there exists a real number c in the open interval] a, b [, such that f′(c) = 0′. Here, we shall verify the Rolle's theorem for the given function.

Sol. We have, $f(x) = x(x-1)^2$ in [0, 1].

(i) Since, $f(x) = x(x-1)^2$ is a polynomial function.

So, it is continuous in [0, 1].

(ii) Now,

$$f'(x) = x\cdot\frac{d}{dx}(x-1)^2 + (x-1)^2\frac{d}{dx}x$$

$$= x\cdot 2(x-1)\cdot 1 + (x-1)^2$$

$$= 2x^2 - 2x + x^2 + 1 - 2x$$

$$= 3x^2 - 4x + 1 \text{ which exists in } (0, 1).$$

So, $f(x)$ is differentiable in (0, 1).

(iii) Now, $f(0) = 0$ and $f(1) = 0 \Rightarrow f(0) = f(1)$

f satisfies the above conditions of Rolle's theorem.

Hence, by Rolle's theorem $\exists\, c \in (0, 1)$ such that

$$f'(c) = 0$$

$$\Rightarrow \quad 3c^2 - 4c + 1 = 0$$

$$\Rightarrow \quad 3c^2 - 3c - c + 1 = 0$$

$$\Rightarrow \quad 3c(c-1) - 1(c-1) = 0$$

$$\Rightarrow \quad (3c-1)(c-1) = 0$$

$$\Rightarrow \quad c = \frac{1}{3}, 1 \Rightarrow \frac{1}{3} \in (0, 1)$$

Thus, we see that there exists a real number c in the open interval (0, 1).

Hence, Rolle's theorem has been verified.

Q. 66 $f(x) = \sin^4 x + \cos^4 x$ in $\left[0, \frac{\pi}{2}\right]$

Sol. We have, $f(x) = \sin^4 x + \cos^4 x$ in $\left[0, \frac{\pi}{2}\right]$ ...(i)

(i) $f(x)$ is continuous in $\left[0, \frac{\pi}{2}\right]$

[since, $\sin^4 x$ and $\cos^4 x$ are continuous functions and we know that, if g and h be continuous functions, then $(g + h)$ is a continuous function.]

(ii) $f'(x) = 4(\sin x)^3 \cdot \cos x + 4(\cos x)^3 \cdot (-\sin x)$

$= 4\sin^3 x \cdot \cos x - 4\sin x \cdot \cos^3 x$

$= 4\sin x \cos x\,(\sin^2 x - \cos^2 x)$ which exists in $\left(0, \frac{\pi}{2}\right)$ ...(ii)

Hence, $f(x)$ is differentiable in $\left(0, \frac{\pi}{2}\right)$.

(iii) Also, $f(0) = 0 + 1 = 1$ and $f\left(\frac{\pi}{2}\right) = 1 + 0 = 1$

$\Rightarrow \quad f(0) = f\left(\frac{\pi}{2}\right)$

Conditions of Rolle's theorem are satisfied.

Hence, there exists atleast one $c \in \left(0, \frac{\pi}{2}\right)$ such that $f'(c) = 0$.

$\therefore \quad 4\sin c \cos c\,(\sin^2 c - \cos^2 c) = 0$

$\Rightarrow \quad 4\sin c \cos c\,(-\cos 2c) = 0$

$\Rightarrow \quad -2\sin 2c \cdot \cos 2c = 0$

$\Rightarrow \quad -\sin 4c = 0$

$\Rightarrow \quad \sin 4c = 0$

$\Rightarrow \quad 4c = \pi$

$\Rightarrow \quad c = \frac{\pi}{4}$

and $\quad \frac{\pi}{4} \in \left(0, \frac{\pi}{2}\right)$

Hence, Rolle's theorem has been verified.

Q. 67 $f(x) = \log(x^2 + 2) - \log 3$ in $[-1, 1]$

Sol. We have, $f(x) = \log(x^2 + 2) - \log 3$.

(i) Logarithmic functions are continuous in their domain.

Hence, $f(x) = \log(x^2 + 2) - \log 3$ is continuous in $[-1, 1]$.

(ii) $f'(x) = \frac{1}{x^2 + 2} \cdot 2x - 0$

$= \frac{2x}{x^2 + 2}$, which exists in $(-1, 1)$.

Hence, $f(x)$ is differentiable in $(-1, 1)$.

(iii) $f(-1) = \log[(-1)^2 + 2] - \log 3 = \log 3 - \log 3 = 0$ and

$f(1) = \log(1^2 + 2) - \log 3 = \log 3 - \log 3 = 0$

$\Rightarrow \quad f(-1) = f(1)$

Conditions of Rolle's theorem are satisfied.

Hence, there exists a real number c such that

$$f'(c) = 0.$$

$$\Rightarrow \quad \frac{2c}{c^2 + 2} = 0$$

$$\Rightarrow \quad c = 0 \in (-1, 1)$$

Hence, Rolle's theorem has been verified.

Q. 68 $f(x) = x(x+3)e^{-x/2}$ **in** $[-3, 0]$

Sol. We have, $\quad f(x) = x(x + 3)e^{-x/2}$

(i) $f(x)$ is a continuous function. [since, it is a combination of polynomial functions $x(x + 3)$ and an exponential function $e^{-x/2}$ which are continuous functions]

So, $f(x) = x(x + 3)e^{-x/2}$ is continuous in $[-3, 0]$.

(ii) $\therefore$

$$f'(x) = (x^2 + 3x)\cdot\frac{d}{dx}e^{-x/2} + e^{-x/2}\cdot\frac{d}{dx}(x^2 + 3x)$$

$$= (x^2 + 3x)\cdot e^{-x/2}\cdot\left(-\frac{1}{2}\right) + e^{-x/2}\cdot(2x + 3)$$

$$= e^{-x/2}\left[2x + 3 - \frac{1}{2}\cdot(x^2 + 3x)\right]$$

$$= e^{-x/2}\left[\frac{4x + 6 - x^2 - 3x}{2}\right]$$

$$= e^{-x/2}\cdot\frac{1}{2}[-x^2 + x + 6]$$

$$= \frac{-1}{2}e^{-x/2}[x^2 - x - 6]$$

$$= \frac{-1}{2}e^{-x/2}[x^2 - 3x + 2x - 6]$$

$$= \frac{-1}{2}e^{-x/2}[(x + 2)(x - 3)] \text{ which exists in } (-3, 0).$$

Hence, $f(x)$ is differentiable in $(-3, 0)$.

(iii) $\therefore$

$$f(-3) = -3(-3 + 3)e^{-3/2} = 0$$

and

$$f(0) = 0(0 + 3)e^{-0/2} = 0$$

$$\Rightarrow \quad f(-3) = f(0)$$

Since, conditions of Rolle's theorem are satisfied.

Hence, there exists a real number c such that $f'(c) = 0$

$$\Rightarrow \quad -\frac{1}{2}e^{-c/2}(c + 2)(c - 3) = 0$$

$$\Rightarrow \quad c = -2, 3, \text{ where } -2 \in (-3, 0)$$

Therefore, Rolle's theorem has been verified.

Q. 69 $f(x) = \sqrt{4 - x^2}$ in $[-2, 2]$

Sol. We have, $f(x) = \sqrt{4 - x^2} = (4 - x^2)^{1/2}$

(i) $f(x) = \sqrt{4 - x^2}$ is a continuous function.

[since every polynomial function is a continuous function]

Hence, $f(x)$ is continuous in $[-2, 2]$.

(ii) $f'(x) = \frac{1}{2}(4 - x^2)^{-1/2} \cdot (-2x)$

$= -x \cdot \frac{1}{\sqrt{4 - x^2}}$, which exists everywhere except at $x = \pm 2$.

Hence, $f(x)$ is differentiable in $(-2, 2)$.

(iii) $f(-2) = \sqrt{(4 - 4)} = 0$ and $f(2) = \sqrt{(4 - 4)} = 0$

$\Rightarrow \quad f(-2) = f(2)$

conditions of Rolle's theorem are satisfied.

Hence, there exists a real number c such that $f'(c) = 0$.

$\Rightarrow \quad -c \frac{1}{\sqrt{4 - c^2}} = 0$

$\Rightarrow \quad c = 0 \in (-2, 2)$

Hence, Rolle's theorem has been verified.

Q. 70 Discuss the applicability of Rolle's theorem on the function given by

$$f(x) = \begin{cases} x^2 + 1, & \text{if } 0 \le x \le 1 \\ 3 - x, & \text{if } 1 \le x \le 2 \end{cases}$$

Sol. We have, $f(x) = \begin{cases} x^2 + 1, \text{ if } 0 \le x \le 1 \\ 3 - x, \text{ if } 1 \le x \le 2 \end{cases}$

We know that, polynomial function is everywhere continuous and differentiability.
So, $f(x)$ is continuous and differentiable at all points except possibly at $x = 1$.
Now, check the differentiability at $x = 1$,
At $x = 1$,

$$\text{LDH} = \lim_{x \to 1^-} \frac{f(x) - f(1)}{x - 1}$$

$$= \lim_{x \to 1} \frac{(x^2 + 1) - (1 + 1)}{x - 1} \quad [\because f(x) = x^2 + 1, \forall\, 0 \le x \le 1]$$

$$= \lim_{x \to 1} \frac{x^2 - 1}{x - 1} = \lim_{x \to 1} \frac{(x + 1)(x - 1)}{x - 1}$$

$$= 2$$

and
$$\text{RDH} = \lim_{x \to 1^+} \frac{f(x) - f(1)}{x - 1} = \lim_{x \to 1} \frac{(3 - x) f(1 + 1)}{(x - 1)}$$

$$= \lim_{x \to 1} \frac{3 - x - 2}{x - 1} = \lim_{x \to 1} \frac{-(x - 1)}{x - 1} = -1$$

$\therefore \quad \text{LHD} \ne \text{RHD}$

So, $f(x)$ is not differentiable at $x = 1$.
Hence, polle's theorem is not applicable on the interval [0, 2].

Q. 71 **Find the points on the curve $y = (\cos x - 1)$ in $[0, 2\pi]$, where the tangent is parallel to X-axis.**

Thinking Process

We know that, if f be a real valued function defined in the closed interval $[a, b]$ such that it follows all the three conditions of Rolle's theorem, then $f'(c) = 0$ shows that the tangent to the curve at $x = c$ has a slope 0, i.e., it is parallel to the X-axis. So, by getting the value of c' we can get the required point.

Sol. The equation of the curve is $y = \cos x - 1$.

Now, we have to find a point on the curve in $[0, 2\pi]$,

where the tangent is parallel to X-axis *i.e.,* the tangent to the curve at $x = c$ has a slope o, where $c \in]0, 2\pi[$.

Let us apply Rolle's theorem to get the point.

(i) $y = \cos x - 1$ is a continuous function in $[0, 2\pi]$.

[since it is a combination of cosine function and a constant function]

(ii) $y' = -\sin x$, which exists in $(0, 2\pi)$.

Hence, y is differentiable in $(0, 2\pi)$.

(iii) $y(0) = \cos 0 - 1 = 0$ and $y(2\pi) = \cos 2\pi - 1 = 0$,

$\therefore \quad y(0) = y(2\pi)$

Since, conditions of Rolle's theorem are satisfied.

Hence, there exists a real number c such that

$$f'(c) = 0$$

$$\Rightarrow \quad -\sin c = 0$$

$$\Rightarrow \quad c = \pi \text{ or } 0, \text{ where } \pi \in (0, 2\pi)$$

$$\Rightarrow \quad x = \pi$$

$$\therefore \quad y = \cos \pi - 1 = -2$$

Hence, the required point on the curve, where the tangent drawn is parallel to the X-axis is $(\pi, -2)$.

Q. 72 **Using Rolle's theorem, find the point on the curve $y = x(x-4)$, $x \in [0, 4]$, where the tangent is parallel to X-axis.**

Sol. We have, $y = x(x-4)$, $x \in [0, 4]$

(i) y is a continuous function since $x(x-4)$ is a polynomial function.

Hence, $y = x(x-4)$ is continuous in $[0, 4]$.

(ii) $y' = (x-4)\cdot 1 + x \cdot 1 = 2x - 4$ which exists in $(0, 4)$.

Hence, y is differentiable in $(0, 4)$.

(iii) $y(0) = 0(0-4) = 0$

and $\quad y(4) = 4(4-4) = 0$

$\Rightarrow \quad y(0) = y(4)$

Sicne, conditions of Rolle's theorem are satisfied.

Hence, there exists a point c such that

$$f'(c) = 0 \text{ in } (0, 4) \qquad [\because f'(x) = y']$$

$$\Rightarrow \quad 2c - 4 = 0$$

$$\Rightarrow \quad c = 2$$

$$\Rightarrow \quad x = 2;\ y = 2(2-4) = -4$$

Thus, $(2, -4)$ is the point on the curve at which the tangent drawn is parallel to X-axis.

Verify mean value theorem for each of the functions.

Q. 73 $f(x)=\dfrac{1}{4x-1}$ in [1, 4]

Thinking Process

We know that, mean value theorem states that, if f be a real function such that
(i) $f(x)$ is continuous on [a,b]
(ii) $f(x)$ is differentiable on]a,b[
Then, there exists a real number $c \in]a,b[$ such that $f'(c)=\dfrac{f(b)-f(a)}{b-a}$, thus we can verify it for given function.

Sol. We have, $f(x)=\dfrac{1}{4x-1}$ in [1, 4]

(i) $f(x)$ is continuous in [1, 4].
Also, at $x=\dfrac{1}{4}$, $f(x)$ is discontinuous.
Hence, $f(x)$ is continuous in [1, 4].

(ii) $f'(x)=-\dfrac{4}{(4x-1)^2}$, which exists in (1, 4).

Since, conditions of mean value theorem are satisfied.
Hence, there exists a real number $c \in]1, 4[$ such that

$$f'(c)=\frac{f(4)-f(1)}{4-1}$$

$$\Rightarrow \quad \frac{-4}{(4c-1)^2}=\frac{\frac{1}{16-1}-\frac{1}{4-1}}{4-1}=\frac{\frac{1}{15}-\frac{1}{3}}{3}$$

$$\Rightarrow \quad \frac{-4}{(4c-1)^2}=\frac{1-5}{45}=\frac{-4}{45}$$

$$\Rightarrow \quad (4c-1)^2=45$$

$$\Rightarrow \quad 4c-1=\pm 3\sqrt{5}$$

$$\Rightarrow \quad c=\frac{3\sqrt{5}+1}{4}\in(1,4) \quad \text{[neglecting (– ve) value]}$$

Hence, mean value theorem has been verified.

Q. 74 $f(x)=x^3-2x^2-x+3$ in [0, 1]

Sol. We have, $f(x)=x^3-2x^2-x+3$ in [0, 1]

(i) Since, $f(x)$ is a polynomial function.
Hence, $f(x)$ is continuous in [0, 1].

(ii) $f'(x)=3x^2-4x-1$, which exists in (0,1).
Hence, $f(x)$ is differentiable in (0,1).
Since, conditions of mean value theorem are satisfied.
Therefore, by mean value theorem $\exists\, c \in (0,1)$, such that

$$f'(c)=\frac{f(1)-f(0)}{1-0}$$

$$\Rightarrow \quad 3c^2 - 4c - 1 = \frac{[1-2-1+3]-[0+3]}{1-0}$$

$$\Rightarrow \quad 3c^2 - 4c - 1 = \frac{-2}{1}$$

$$\Rightarrow \quad 3c^2 - 4c + 1 = 0$$

$$\Rightarrow \quad 3c^2 - 3c - c + 1 = 0$$

$$\Rightarrow \quad 3c(c-1) - 1(c-1) = 0$$

$$\Rightarrow \quad (3c-1)(c-1) = 0$$

$$\Rightarrow \quad c = 1/3,\ 1, \text{ where } \frac{1}{3} \in (0, 1)$$

Hence, the mean value theorem has been verified.

Q. 75 $f(x) = \sin x - \sin 2x$ in $[0, \pi]$

Sol. We have, $f(x) = \sin x - \sin 2x$ in $[0, \pi]$

(i) Since, we know that sine functions are continuous functions hence $f(x) = \sin x - \sin 2x$ is a continuous function in $[0, \pi]$.

(ii) $f'(x) = \cos x - \cos 2x \cdot 2 = \cos x - 2\cos 2x$, which exists in $(0, \pi)$.

So, $f(x)$ is differentiable in $(0, \pi)$. Conditions of mean value theorem are satisfied.

Hence, $\exists\, c \in (0, \pi)$ such that, $f'(c) = \dfrac{f(\pi) - f(0)}{\pi - 0}$

$$\Rightarrow \quad \cos c - 2\cos 2c = \frac{\sin \pi - \sin 2\pi - \sin 0 + \sin 2 \cdot 0}{\pi - 0}$$

$$\Rightarrow \quad 2\cos 2c - \cos c = \frac{0}{\pi}$$

$$\Rightarrow \quad 2 \cdot (2\cos^2 c - 1) - \cos c = 0$$

$$\Rightarrow \quad 4\cos^2 c - 2 - \cos c = 0$$

$$\Rightarrow \quad 4\cos^2 c - \cos c - 2 = 0$$

$$\Rightarrow \quad \cos c = \frac{1 \pm \sqrt{1+32}}{8} = \frac{1 \pm \sqrt{33}}{8}$$

$$\therefore \quad c = \cos^{-1}\left(\frac{1 \pm \sqrt{33}}{8}\right)$$

Also, $\cos^{-1}\left(\dfrac{1 \pm \sqrt{33}}{8}\right) \in (0, \pi)$

Hence, mean value theorem has been verified.

Q. 76 $f(x) = \sqrt{25 - x^2}$ in $[1, 5]$

Sol. We have, $f(x) = \sqrt{25 - x^2}$ in $[1, 5]$

(i) Since, $f(x) = (25 - x^2)^{1/2}$, where $25 - x^2 \geq 0$

$$\Rightarrow \quad x^2 \leq \pm 5 \Rightarrow -5 \leq x \leq 5$$

Hence, $f(x)$ is continuous in $[1, 5]$.

(ii) $f'(x) = \dfrac{1}{2}(25 - x^2)^{-1/2} \cdot -2x = \dfrac{-x}{\sqrt{25 - x^2}}$, which exists in $(1, 5)$.

Hence, $f'(x)$ is differentiable in $(1, 5)$.

Since, conditions of mean value theorem are satisfied.
By mean value theorem $\exists c \in (1, 5)$ such that

$$f'(c) = \frac{f(5) - f(1)}{5 - 1} \Rightarrow \frac{-c}{\sqrt{25 - c^2}} = \frac{0 - \sqrt{24}}{4}$$

$$\Rightarrow \quad \frac{c^2}{25 - c^2} = \frac{24}{16}$$

$$\Rightarrow \quad 16c^2 = 600 - 24c^2$$

$$\Rightarrow \quad c^2 = \frac{600}{40} = 15$$

$$\therefore \quad c = \pm\sqrt{15}$$

Also, $c = \sqrt{15} \in (1, 5)$

Hence, the mean value theorem has been verified.

Q. 77 Find a point on the curve $y = (x - 3)^2$, where the tangent is parallel to the chord joining the points (3, 0) and (4, 1).

Thinking Process

We know that, if $y = f(x)$ be a function defined on $[a, b]$ which follows mean value theorem, then there exists atleast one point c in (a, b) such that the tangent at the point $[c, f(c)]$ is parallel to the secant joining the points $[a, f(a)]$ and $[b, f(b)]$. So, we shall use this concept.

Sol. We have, $y = (x - 3)^2$, which is continuous in $x_1 = 3$ and $x_2 = 4$ *i.e.,* [3, 4].
Also, $y' = 2(x - 3) \cdot 1 = 2(x - 3)$ which exists in (3, 4).
Hence, by mean value theorem there exists a point on the curve at which tangent drawn is parallel to the chord joining the points (3,0) and (4,1).

Thus, $$f'(c) = \frac{f(4) - f(3)}{4 - 3}$$

$$\Rightarrow \quad 2(c - 3) = \frac{(4 - 3)^2 - (3 - 3)^2}{4 - 3}$$

$$\Rightarrow \quad 2c - 6 = \frac{1 - 0}{1} \Rightarrow c = \frac{7}{2}$$

For $x = \frac{7}{2}$, $$y = \left(\frac{7}{2} - 3\right)^2 = \left(\frac{1}{2}\right)^2 = \frac{1}{4}$$

So, $\left(\frac{7}{2}, \frac{1}{4}\right)$ is the point on the curve at which tangent drawn is parallel to the chord joining the points (3, 0) and (4, 1).

Q. 78 Using mean value theorem, prove that there is a point on the curve $y = 2x^2 - 5x + 3$ between the points $A(1, 0)$ and $B(2, 1)$, where tangent is parallel to the chord AB. Also, find that point.

Sol. We have, $y = 2x^2 - 5x + 3$, which is continuous in [1, 2] as it is a polynomial function.
Also, $y' = 4x - 5$, which exists in (1, 2).
By mean value theorem, $\exists c \in (1, 2)$ at which drawn tangent is parallel to the chord AB, where A and B are (1, 0) and (2,1), respectively.

$$\therefore \quad f'(c) = \frac{f(2) - f(1)}{2 - 1}$$

$$\Rightarrow \quad 4c - 5 = \frac{(8 - 10 + 3) - (2 - 5 + 3)}{1}$$

$$\Rightarrow \quad 4c - 5 = 1$$

$$\therefore \quad c = \frac{6}{4} = \frac{3}{2} \in (1, 2)$$

For $x = \frac{3}{2}$,

$$y = 2\left(\frac{3}{2}\right)^2 - 5\left(\frac{3}{2}\right) + 3$$

$$= 2 \times \frac{9}{4} - \frac{15}{2} + 3 = \frac{9 - 15 + 6}{2} = 0$$

Hence, $\left(\frac{3}{2}, 0\right)$ is the point on the curve $y = 2x^2 - 5x + 3$ between the points A (1, 0) and B (2, 1), where tangent is parallel to the chord AB.

Long Answer Type Questions

Q. 79 Find the values of p and q, so that $f(x) = \begin{cases} x^2 + 3x + p, & \text{if } x \le 1 \\ qx + 2, & \text{if } x > 1 \end{cases}$ is differentiable at $x = 1$.

Sol. We have, $f(x) = \begin{cases} x^2 + 3x + p, & \text{if } x \le 1 \\ qx + 2, & \text{if } x > 1 \end{cases}$ is differentiable at $x = 1$.

$$\therefore \quad Lf'(1) = \lim_{x \to 1^-} \frac{f(x) - f(1)}{x - 1}$$

$$= \lim_{x \to 1^-} \frac{(x^2 + 3x + p) - (1 + 3 + p)}{x - 1}$$

$$= \lim_{h \to 0} \frac{[(1 - h)^2 + 3(1 - h) + p] - [1 + 3 + p]}{(1 - h) - 1}$$

$$= \lim_{h \to 0} \frac{[1 + h^2 - 2h + 3 - 3h + p] - [4 + p]}{-h}$$

$$= \lim_{h \to 0} \frac{[h^2 - 5h + p + 4 - 4 - p]}{-h} = \lim_{h \to 0} \frac{h[h - 5]}{-h}$$

$$= \lim_{h \to 0} -[h - 5] = 5$$

$$Rf'(1) = \lim_{x \to 1^+} \frac{f(x) - f(1)}{x - 1} = \lim_{x \to 1^+} \frac{(qx + 2) - (1 + 3 + p)}{x - 1}$$

$$= \lim_{h \to 0} \frac{[q(1 + h) + 2] - (4 + p)}{1 + h - 1}$$

$$= \lim_{h \to 0} \frac{[q + qh + 2 - 4 - p]}{h} = \lim_{h \to 0} \frac{qh + (q - 2 - p)}{h}$$

$\Rightarrow \quad q - 2 - p = 0 \Rightarrow p - q = -2$ ...(i)

$\Rightarrow \quad \lim_{h \to 0} \frac{qh + 0}{h} = q$ [for existing the limit]

If $Lf'(1) = Rf'(1)$, then $5 = q$

$\Rightarrow \quad p - 5 = -2 \Rightarrow p = 3$

$\therefore \quad p = 3$ and $q = 5$

Q. 80 If $x^m \cdot y^n = (x+y)^{m+n}$, prove that

(i) $\dfrac{dy}{dx} = \dfrac{y}{x}$ and (ii) $\dfrac{d^2y}{dx^2} = 0$

Sol. We have, $x^m \cdot y^n = (x+y)^{m+n}$ ...(i)

(i) Differentiating Eq. (i) w.r.t. x, we get

$$\frac{d}{dx}(x^m \cdot y^n) = \frac{d}{dx}(x+y)^{m+n}$$

$$\Rightarrow \quad x^m \cdot \frac{d}{dy} y^n \cdot \frac{dy}{dx} + y^n \cdot \frac{d}{dx} x^m = (m+n)(x+y)^{m+n-1} \frac{d}{dx}(x+y)$$

$$\Rightarrow \quad x^m \cdot ny^{n-1} \frac{dy}{dx} + y^n \cdot mx^{m-1} = (m+n)(x+y)^{m+n-1}\left(1 + \frac{dy}{dx}\right)$$

$$\Rightarrow \quad \frac{dy}{dx}[x^m \cdot ny^{n-1} - (m+n)\cdot(x+y)^{m+n-1}] = (m+n)(x+y)^{m+n-1} - y^n m x^{m-1}$$

$$\Rightarrow \quad \frac{dy}{dx}[nx^m y^{n-1} - (m+n)(x+y)^{m+n-1}] = (m+n)\cdot(x+y)^{m+n-1} - \frac{y^{n-1}\cdot y \cdot mx^m}{x}$$

$$\therefore \quad \frac{dy}{dx} = \frac{\dfrac{(m+n)(x+y)^{m+n}}{(x+y)} - \dfrac{y^{n-1}\cdot y \cdot mx^m}{x}}{\dfrac{n x^m y^n}{y} - (m+n)(x+y)^{m+n}\dfrac{1}{(x+y)}}$$

$$= \frac{\dfrac{x(m+n)(x+y)^{m+n} - (x+y)\cdot y \cdot {}^{n-1} y \cdot mx^m}{(x+y)\cdot x}}{\dfrac{(x+y)\,n\,x^m y^n - y(m+n)(x+y)^{m+n}}{(x+y)\cdot y}}$$

$$= \frac{\dfrac{x(m+n)\cdot x^m \cdot y^n - m(x+y)\,y^n x^m}{(x+y)\cdot x}}{\dfrac{(x+y)\,nx^m \cdot y^n - y(m+n)\cdot x^m \cdot y^n}{(x+y)\cdot y}} \quad [\because (x+y)^{m+n} = x^m \cdot y^n]$$

$$= \frac{x^m y^n [mx + nx - mx - my]\cdot(x+y)\,y}{x^m y^n [nx + ny - my - ny]\cdot(x+y)\cdot x}$$

$$= \frac{y}{x} \quad \text{...(ii)}$$

Hence proved.

(ii) Further, differentiating Eq. (ii) *i.e.*, $\dfrac{dy}{dx} = \dfrac{y}{x}$ on both the sides w.r.t. x, we get

$$\frac{d^2y}{dx^2} = \frac{x \cdot \dfrac{dy}{dx} - y \cdot 1}{x^2}$$

$$= \frac{x \cdot \dfrac{y}{x} - y}{x^2} \quad \left[\because \frac{dy}{dx} = \frac{y}{x}\right]$$

$$= 0$$

Hence proved.

Q. 81 If $x = \sin t$ and $y = \sin pt$, then prove that

$$(1 - x^2)\frac{d^2y}{dx^2} - x\frac{dy}{dx} + p^2y = 0.$$

Sol. We have, $x = \sin t$ and $y = \sin pt$

$$\therefore \quad \frac{dx}{dt} = \cos t \text{ and } \frac{dy}{dt} = \cos pt \cdot p$$

$$\Rightarrow \quad \frac{dy}{dx} = \frac{dy/dt}{dx/dt} = \frac{p \cdot \cos pt}{\cos t} \quad \text{...(i)}$$

Again, differentiating both sides w.r.t. x, we get

$$\frac{d^2y}{dx^2} = \frac{\cos t \cdot \frac{d}{dt}(p \cdot \cos pt)\frac{dt}{dx} - p\cos pt \cdot \frac{d}{dt}\cos t \cdot \frac{dt}{dx}}{\cos^2 t}$$

$$= \frac{[\cos t \cdot p \cdot (-\sin pt) \cdot p - p\cos pt \cdot (-\sin t)]\frac{dt}{dx}}{\cos^2 t}$$

$$= \frac{[-p^2 \sin pt \cdot \cos t + p\sin t \cdot \cos pt] \cdot \frac{1}{\cos t}}{\cos^2 t}$$

$$\Rightarrow \quad \frac{d^2y}{dx^2} = \frac{-p^2 \sin pt \cdot \cos t + p\cos pt \cdot \sin t}{\cos^3 t} \quad \text{...(ii)}$$

Since, we have to prove

$$(1 - x^2)\frac{d^2y}{dx^2} - x\frac{dy}{dx} + p^2y = 0$$

$$\therefore \quad \text{LHS} = (1 - \sin^2 t)\frac{[-p^2 \sin pt \cdot \cos t + p\cos pt \cdot \sin t]}{\cos^3 t}$$

$$- \sin t \cdot \frac{p\cos pt}{\cos t} + p^2 \sin pt$$

$$= \frac{1}{\cos^3 t}\begin{bmatrix}(1 - \sin^2 t)(-p^2 \sin pt \cdot \cos t + p\cos pt \cdot \sin t) \\ - p\cos pt \cdot \sin t \cdot \cos^2 t + p^2 \sin pt \cdot \cos^3 t\end{bmatrix}$$

$$= \frac{1}{\cos^3 t}\begin{bmatrix}-p^2 \sin pt \cdot \cos^3 t + p\cos pt \cdot \sin t \cdot \cos^2 t \\ - p\cos pt \cdot \sin t \cdot \cos^2 t + p^2 \sin pt \cdot \cos^3 t\end{bmatrix} \quad [\because 1 - \sin^2 t = \cos^2 t]$$

$$= \frac{1}{\cos^3 t} \cdot 0$$

$$= 0$$

Hence proved.

Q. 82 Find the value of $\frac{dy}{dx}$, if $y = x^{\tan x} + \sqrt{\frac{x^2 + 1}{2}}$.

Sol. We have,

$$y = x^{\tan x} + \sqrt{\frac{x^2 + 1}{2}} \quad \text{...(i)}$$

Taking $u = x^{\tan x}$ and $v = \sqrt{\frac{x^2 + 1}{2}}$,

$$\log u = \tan x \log x \quad \text{...(ii)}$$

and

$$v^2 = \frac{x^2 + 1}{2} \quad \text{...(iii)}$$

On, differentiating Eq. (ii) w.r.t. x, we get

$$\frac{1}{u}\cdot\frac{du}{dx}=\tan x\cdot\frac{1}{x}+\log x\cdot\sec^2 x$$

$$\Rightarrow \quad \frac{du}{dx}=u\left[\frac{\tan x}{x}+\log x\cdot\sec^2 x\right]$$

$$=x^{\tan x}\left[\frac{\tan x}{x}+\log x\cdot\sec^2 x\right] \quad \ldots\text{(iv)}$$

Also, differentiating Eq. (iii) w.r.t. x, we get

$$2v\cdot\frac{dv}{dx}=\frac{1}{2}(2x)\Rightarrow\frac{dv}{dx}=\frac{1}{4v}\cdot(2x)$$

$$\Rightarrow \quad \frac{dv}{dx}=\frac{1}{4\cdot\sqrt{\frac{x^2+1}{2}}}\cdot 2x=\frac{x\cdot\sqrt{2}}{2\sqrt{x^2+1}}$$

$$\Rightarrow \quad \frac{dv}{dx}=\frac{x}{\sqrt{2(x^2+1)}} \quad \ldots\text{(v)}$$

Now, $\quad y=u+v$

$\therefore \quad \dfrac{dy}{dx}=\dfrac{du}{dx}+\dfrac{dv}{dx}$

$$=x^{\tan x}\left[\frac{\tan x}{x}+\log x\cdot\sec^2 x\right]+\frac{x}{\sqrt{2(x^2+1)}}$$

Objective Type Questions

Q. 83 **If $f(x)=2x$ and $g(x)=\dfrac{x^2}{2}+1$, then which of the following can be a discontinuous function?**

(a) $f(x)+g(x)$ (b) $f(x)-g(x)$

(c) $f(x)\cdot g(x)$ (d) $\dfrac{g(x)}{f(x)}$

Sol. *(d)* We know that, if f and g be continuous functions, then

(a) $f+g$ is continuous **(b)** $f-g$ is continuous.

(c) fg is continuous **(d)** $\dfrac{f}{g}$ is continuous at these points, where $g(x)\neq 0$.

Here, $$\frac{g(x)}{f(x)}=\frac{\frac{x^2}{2}+1}{2x}=\frac{x^2+2}{4x}$$

which is discontinuous at $x=0$.

Q. 84 The function $f(x)=\dfrac{4-x^2}{4x-x^3}$ is

(a) discontinuous at only one point
(b) discontinuous at exactly two points
(c) discontinuous at exactly three points
(d) None of the above

Sol. *(c)* We have,

$$f(x)=\frac{4-x^2}{4x-x^3}=\frac{(4-x^2)}{x\,(4-x^2)}$$

$$=\frac{(4-x^2)}{x\,(2^2-x^2)}=\frac{4-x^2}{x\,(2+x)\,(2-x)}$$

Clearly, $f(x)$ is discontinuous at exactly three points $x=0$, $x=-2$ and $x=2$.

Q. 85 The set of points where the function f given by $f(x)=|2x-1|\sin x$ is differentiable is

(a) R
(b) $R-\left(\frac{1}{2}\right)$
(c) $(0,\infty)$
(d) None of these

Sol. *(b)* We have, $f(x)=|2x-1|\sin x$

At $x=\frac{1}{2}$, $f(x)$ is not differentiable.

Hence, $f(x)$ is differentiable in $R-\left(\frac{1}{2}\right)$.

$\because$

$$Rf'\left(\frac{1}{2}\right)=\lim_{h\to 0}\frac{f\left(\frac{1}{2}+h\right)-f\left(\frac{1}{2}\right)}{h}$$

$$=\lim_{h\to 0}\frac{\left|2\left(\frac{1}{2}+h\right)-1\right|\sin\left(\frac{1}{2}+h\right)-0}{h}$$

$$=\lim_{h\to 0}\frac{|2h|\cdot\sin\left(\frac{1+2h}{2}\right)}{h}=2\cdot\sin\frac{1}{2}$$

and

$$Lf'\left(\frac{1}{2}\right)=\lim_{h\to 0}\frac{f\left(\frac{1}{2}-h\right)-f\left(\frac{1}{2}\right)}{-h}$$

$$=\lim_{h\to 0}\frac{\left|2\left(\frac{1}{2}-h\right)^{-1}\right|-\sin\left(\frac{1}{2}-h\right)-0}{-h}$$

$$=\lim_{h\to 0}\frac{|0-2h|-\sin\left(\frac{1}{2}-h\right)}{-h}=-2\sin\left(\frac{1}{2}\right)$$

$\because$

$$Rf'\left(\frac{1}{2}\right)\neq Lf'\left(\frac{1}{2}\right)$$

So, $f(x)$ is not differentiable at $x=\frac{1}{2}$.

Q. 86 The function $f(x) = \cot x$ is discontinuous on the set

(a) $\{x = n\pi : n \in Z\}$
(b) $\{x = 2n\pi : n \in Z\}$
(c) $\left\{x = (2n+1)\frac{\pi}{2}; n \in Z\right\}$
(d) $\left\{x = \frac{n\pi}{2}; n \in Z\right\}$

Sol. *(a)* We know that, $f(x) = \cot x$ is continuous in $R - \{n\pi : n \in Z\}$.

Since, $f(x) = \cot x = \dfrac{\cos x}{\sin x}$ [since, $\sin x = 0$ at $n\pi$, $n \in Z$]

Hence, $f(x) = \cot x$ is discontinuous on the set $\{x = n\pi : n \in Z\}$.

Q. 87 The function $f(x) = e^{|x|}$ is

(a) continuous everywhere but not differentiable at $x = 0$
(b) continuous and differentiable everywhere
(c) not continuous at $x = 0$
(d) None of the above

Sol. *(a)* Let $u(x) = |x|$ and $v(x) = e^x$

$$\therefore \quad f(x) = vou(x) = v[u(x)]$$
$$= v|x| = e^{|x|}$$

Since, $u(x)$ and $v(x)$ are both continuous functions.

So, $f(x)$ is also continuous function but $u(x) = |x|$ is not differentiable at $x = 0$, whereas $v(x) = e^x$ is differentiable at everywhere.

Hence, $f(x)$ is continuous everywhere but not differentiable at $x = 0$.

Q. 88 If $f(x) = x^2 \sin\frac{1}{x}$, where $x \neq 0$, then the value of the function f at $x = 0$, so that the function is continuous at $x = 0$, is

(a) 0
(b) -1
(c) 1
(d) None of these

Sol. *(a)* $\because$ $f(x) = x^2 \sin\left(\frac{1}{x}\right)$, where $x \neq 0$

Hence, value of the function f at $x = 0$, so that it is continuous at $x = 0$ is 0.

Q. 89 If $f(x) = \begin{cases} mx + 1, & \text{if } x \le \frac{\pi}{2} \\ \sin x + n, & \text{if } x > \frac{\pi}{2} \end{cases}$ is continuous at $x = \frac{\pi}{2}$, then

(a) $m = 1, n = 0$
(b) $m = \frac{n\pi}{2} + 1$
(c) $n = \frac{m\pi}{2}$
(d) $m = n = \frac{\pi}{2}$

Sol. *(c)* We have, $f(x) = \begin{cases} mx + 1, & \text{if } x \le \frac{\pi}{2} \\ (\sin x + n), & \text{if } x > \frac{\pi}{2} \end{cases}$ is continuous at $x = \frac{\pi}{2}$

$\therefore$ $\quad \text{LHL} = \lim_{x \to \frac{\pi^-}{2}} (mx + 1) = \lim_{h \to 0} \left[m\left(\frac{\pi}{2} - h\right) + 1 \right] = \frac{m\pi}{2} + 1$

and $\quad \text{RHL} = \lim_{x \to \frac{\pi^+}{2}} (\sin x + n) = \lim_{h \to 0} \left[\sin\left(\frac{\pi}{2} + h\right) + n \right]$

$$= \lim_{h \to 0} \cos h + n = 1 + n$$

$\therefore$ $\quad \text{LHL} = \text{RHL}$ $\quad \left[\text{to be continuous at } x = \frac{\pi}{2}\right]$

$\Rightarrow \quad m \cdot \frac{\pi}{2} + 1 = n + 1$

$\therefore \quad n = m \cdot \frac{\pi}{2}$

Q. 90 If $f(x) = |\sin x|$, then

(a) f is everywhere differentiable

(b) f is everywhere continuous but not differentiable at $x = n\pi, n \in Z$

(c) f is everywhere continuous but not differentiable at $x = (2n + 1)\frac{\pi}{2}, n \in Z$

(d) None of the above

Sol. *(b)* We have, $\quad f(x) = |\sin x|$

Let $\quad f(x) = vou\,(x) = v\,[u(x)]$ $\quad$ [where, $u(x) = \sin x$ and $v(x) = |x|$]

$= v(\sin x) = |\sin x|$

where, $u(x)$ and $v(x)$ are both continuous.

Hence, $f(x) = vo\,u(x)$ is also a continuous function but $v(x)$ is not differentiable at $x = 0$.

So, $f(x)$ is not differentiable where $\sin x = 0 \Rightarrow x = n\pi,\ n \in Z$

Hence, $f(x)$ is continuous everywhere but not differentiable at $x = n\pi$, $n \in Z$.

Q. 91 If $y = \log\left(\frac{1 - x^2}{1 + x^2}\right)$, then $\frac{dy}{dx}$ is equal to

(a) $\frac{4x^3}{1 - x^4}$ $\quad$ (b) $\frac{-4x}{1 - x^4}$ $\quad$ (c) $\frac{1}{4 - x^4}$ $\quad$ (d) $\frac{-4x^3}{1 - x^4}$

Sol. *(b)* We have, $\quad y = \log\left(\frac{1 - x^2}{1 + x^2}\right)$

$$\therefore \quad \frac{dy}{dx} = \frac{1}{\frac{1 - x^2}{1 + x^2}} \cdot \frac{d}{dx}\left(\frac{1 - x^2}{1 + x^2}\right)$$

$$= \frac{(1 + x^2)}{(1 - x^2)} \cdot \frac{(1 + x^2)\cdot(-2x) - (1 - x^2)\cdot 2x}{(1 + x^2)^2}$$

$$= \frac{-2x[1 + x^2 + 1 - x^2]}{(1 - x^2)\cdot(1 + x^2)} = \frac{-4x}{1 - x^4}$$

Q. 92 If $y = \sqrt{\sin x + y}$, then $\frac{dy}{dx}$ is equal to

(a) $\frac{\cos x}{2y-1}$ (b) $\frac{\cos x}{1-2y}$ (c) $\frac{\sin x}{1-2y}$ (d) $\frac{\sin x}{2y-1}$

Sol. *(a)* $\because$ $y = (\sin x + y)^{1/2}$

$$\therefore \quad \frac{dy}{dx} = \frac{1}{2}(\sin x + y)^{-1/2} \cdot \frac{d}{dx}(\sin x + y)$$

$$\Rightarrow \quad \frac{dy}{dx} = \frac{1}{2} \cdot \frac{1}{(\sin x + y)^{1/2}} \cdot \left(\cos x + \frac{dy}{dx}\right)$$

$$\Rightarrow \quad \frac{dy}{dx} = \frac{1}{2y}\left(\cos x + \frac{dy}{dx}\right) \qquad [\because (\sin x + y)^{1/2} = y]$$

$$\Rightarrow \quad \frac{dy}{dx}\left(1 - \frac{1}{2y}\right) = \frac{\cos x}{2y}$$

$$\therefore \quad \frac{dy}{dx} = \frac{\cos x}{2y} \cdot \frac{2y}{2y-1} = \frac{\cos x}{2y-1}$$

Q. 93 The derivative of $\cos^{-1}(2x^2 - 1)$ w.r.t. $\cos^{-1} x$ is

(a) 2 (b) $\frac{-1}{2\sqrt{1-x^2}}$

(b) $\frac{2}{x}$ (d) $1 - x^2$

Sol. *(a)* Let $u = \cos^{-1}(2x^2 - 1)$ and $v = \cos^{-1} x$

$$\therefore \quad \frac{dv}{dx} = \frac{+-1}{\sqrt{1-(2x^2-1)^2}} \cdot 4x = \frac{-4x}{\sqrt{1-(4x^4+1-4x^2)}}$$

$$= \frac{-4x}{\sqrt{-4x^4+4x^2}} = \frac{-4x}{\sqrt{4x^2(1-x^2)}}$$

$$= \frac{-2}{\sqrt{1-x^2}}$$

and $$\frac{du}{dx} = \frac{-1}{\sqrt{1-x^2}}$$

$$\therefore \quad \frac{dx}{dv} = \frac{du/dx}{dv/dx} = \frac{-2/\sqrt{1-x^2}}{-1/\sqrt{1-x^2}} = 2$$

Q. 94 If $x = t^2$ and $y = t^3$, then $\frac{d^2y}{dx^2}$ is equal to

(a) $\frac{3}{2}$ (b) $\frac{3}{4t}$ (c) $\frac{3}{2t}$ (d) $\frac{3}{2t}$

Sol. *(b)* We have, $x = t^2$ and $y = t^3$

$$\therefore \quad \frac{dx}{dt} = 2t \text{ and } \frac{dy}{dt} = 3t^2$$

$$\therefore \quad \frac{dy}{dx} = \frac{dy/dt}{dx/dt} = \frac{3t^2}{2t} = \frac{3}{2}t$$

On further differentiating w.r.t. x, we get

$$\frac{d^2y}{dx^2} = \frac{3}{2} \cdot \frac{d}{dt} t \cdot \frac{dt}{dx}$$

$$= \frac{3}{2} \cdot \frac{1}{2t} \qquad \left[\because \frac{dt}{dx} = \frac{1}{2t}\right]$$

$$= \frac{3}{4t}$$

Q. 95 The value of c in Rolle's theorem for the function $f(x) = x^3 - 3x$ in the interval $[0, \sqrt{3}]$ is

(a) 1 (b) -1 (c) $\frac{3}{2}$ (d) $\frac{1}{3}$

Sol. *(a)* $\because$ $f'(c) = 0$ $\quad [\because f'(x) = 3x^2 - 3]$

$\Rightarrow$ $3c^2 - 3 = 0$

$\Rightarrow$ $c^2 = \frac{3}{3} = 1$

$\Rightarrow$ $c = \pm 1$, where $1 \in (0, \sqrt{3})$

$\therefore$ $c = 1$

Q. 96 For the function $f(x) = x + \frac{1}{x}$, $x \in [1, 3]$, the value of c for mean value theorem is

(a) 1 (b) $\sqrt{3}$

(c) 2 (d) None of these

Sol. *(b)* $\because$ $f'(c) = \frac{f(b) - f(a)}{b - a}$

$\Rightarrow$ $1 - \frac{1}{c^2} = \frac{\left[3 + \frac{1}{3}\right] - \left[1 + \frac{1}{1}\right]}{3 - 1}$ $\quad \left[\because f'(x) = 1 - \frac{1}{x^2} \text{ and } b = 3, a = 1\right]$

$\Rightarrow$ $\frac{c^2 - 1}{c^2} = \frac{\frac{10}{3} - 2}{2}$

$\Rightarrow$ $\frac{c^2 - 1}{c^2} = \frac{4}{3 \times 2} = \frac{2}{3}$

$\Rightarrow$ $3(c^2 - 1) = 2c^2$

$\Rightarrow$ $3c^2 - 2c^2 = 3$

$\Rightarrow$ $c^2 = 3 \Rightarrow c = \pm \sqrt{3}$

$\because$ $c = \sqrt{3} \in (1, 3)$

Fillers

Q. 97 An example of a function which is continuous everywhere but fails to be differentiable exactly at two points is ....

Sol. $|x| + |x-1|$ is continuous everywhere but fails to be differentiable exactly at two points $x = 0$ and $x = 1$.
So, there can be more such examples of functions.

Q. 98 Derivative of x^2 w.r.t. x^3 is ....

Sol. Derivative of x^2 w.r.t. x^3 is $\frac{2}{3x}$.

Let $u = x^2$ and $v = x^3$

$\therefore \quad \frac{du}{dx} = 2x$ and $\frac{dv}{dx} = 3x^2$

$\Rightarrow \quad \frac{du}{dv} = \frac{2x}{3x^2} = \frac{2}{3x}$

Q. 99 If $f(x) = |\cos x|$, then $f'\left(\frac{\pi}{4}\right)$ is equal to ....

Sol. If $f(x) = |\cos x|$, then $f'\left(\frac{\pi}{4}\right)$

$\because \quad 0 < x < \frac{\pi}{2}, \cos x > 0.$

$f(x) = +\cos x$

$\therefore \quad f'(x) = (-\sin x)$

$\Rightarrow \quad f'\left(\frac{\pi}{4}\right) = -\sin\frac{\pi}{4} = \frac{-1}{\sqrt{2}} \quad \left[\because \sin\frac{\pi}{4} = \frac{1}{\sqrt{2}}\right]$

Q. 100 If $f(x) = |\cos x - \sin x|$, then $f'\left(\frac{\pi}{3}\right)$ is equal to ....

Sol. $\because \quad f(x) = |\cos x - \sin x|,$

$\therefore \quad f'\left(\frac{\pi}{3}\right) = \frac{\sqrt{3}+1}{2}$

We know that, $\frac{\pi}{4} < x < \frac{\pi}{2}, \sin x > \cos x$

$\therefore \cos x - \sin x \le 0$ *i.e.*, $\quad f(x) = -(\cos x - \sin x)$

$f'(x) = -[-\sin x - \cos x]$

$\therefore \quad f'\left(\frac{\pi}{3}\right) = -\left(\frac{-\sqrt{3}}{2} - \frac{1}{2}\right) = \left(\frac{\sqrt{3}+1}{2}\right)$

Q. 101 For the curve $\sqrt{x}+\sqrt{y}=1$, $\frac{dy}{dx}$ at $\left(\frac{1}{4}, \frac{1}{4}\right)$ is ....

Sol. For the curve $\sqrt{x}+\sqrt{y}=1$, $\frac{dy}{dx}$ at $\left(\frac{1}{4}, \frac{1}{4}\right)$ is -1.

We have, $\sqrt{x}+\sqrt{y}=1$

$$\Rightarrow \quad \frac{1}{2\sqrt{x}}+\frac{1}{2\sqrt{y}}\frac{dy}{dx}=0$$

$$\Rightarrow \quad \frac{dy}{dx}=-\frac{\sqrt{y}}{\sqrt{x}}$$

$$\therefore \quad \left(\frac{dy}{dx}\right)_{\left(\frac{1}{4}, \frac{1}{4}\right)}=\frac{-\frac{1}{2}}{\frac{1}{2}}=-1$$

True/False

Q. 102 Rolle's theorem is applicable for the function $f(x)=|x-1|$ in [0, 2].

Sol. ***False***

Hence, $f(x)=|x-1|$ in $[0, 2]$ is not differentiable at $x=1 \in (0, 2)$.

Q. 103 If f is continuous on its domain D, then $|f|$ is also continuous on D.

Sol. ***True***

Q. 104 The composition of two continuous function is a continuous function.

Sol. ***True***

Q. 105 Trigonometric and inverse trigonometric functions are differentiable in their respective domain.

Sol. ***True***

Q. 106 If $f \cdot g$ is continuous at $x=a$, then f and g are separately continuous at $x=a$.

Sol. ***False***

Let $f(x)=\sin x$ and $g(x)=\cot x$

$$\therefore \quad f(x)\cdot g(x)=\sin x \cdot \frac{\cos x}{\sin x}=\cos x$$

which is continuous at $x=0$ but $\cot x$ is not continuous at $x=0$.

6

Application *of* Derivatives

Short Answer Type Questions

Q. 1 **A spherical ball of salt is dissolving in water in such a manner that the rate of decrease of the volume at any instant is propotional to the surface. Prove that the radius is decreasing at a constant rate.**

Thinking Process

First, let V be the volume of the ball and S be the surface area of the ball and then by using $\frac{dV}{dt} \propto S$, we can prove the required result.

Sol. We have, rate of decrease of the volume of spherical ball of salt at any instant is $\propto$ surface.

Let the radius of the spherical ball of the salt be r.

$\therefore$ Volume of the ball $(V) = \frac{4}{3}\pi r^3$

and surface area $(S) = 4\pi r^2$

$\because$ $\frac{dV}{dt} \propto S \Rightarrow \frac{d}{dt}\left(\frac{4}{3}\pi r^3\right) \propto 4\pi r^2$

$\Rightarrow$ $\frac{4}{3}\pi \cdot 3r^2 . \frac{dr}{dt} \propto 4\pi r^2 \Rightarrow \frac{dr}{dt} \propto \frac{4\pi r^2}{4\pi r^2}$

$\Rightarrow$ $\frac{dr}{dt} = k \cdot 1$ [where, k is the proportionality constant]

$\Rightarrow$ $\frac{dr}{dt} = k$

Hence, the radius of ball is decreasing at a constant rate.

Q. 2 **If the area of a circle increases at a uniform rate, then prove that perimeter varies inversely as the radius.**

Sol. Let the radius of circle $= r$ And area of the circle, $A = \pi r^2$

$\therefore$ $\frac{d}{dt}A = \frac{d}{dt}\pi r^2$

$\Rightarrow$ $\frac{dA}{dt} = 2\pi r \cdot \frac{dr}{dt}$ ...(i)

Since, the area of a circle increases at a uniform rate, then

$$\frac{dA}{dt} = k \qquad \text{...(ii)}$$

where, k is a constant.

From Eqs. (i) and (ii), $$2\pi r \cdot \frac{dr}{dt} = k$$

$$\Rightarrow \quad \frac{dr}{dt} = \frac{k}{2\pi r} = \frac{k}{2\pi} \cdot \left(\frac{1}{r}\right) \qquad \text{...(iii)}$$

Let the perimeter, $$P = 2\pi r$$

$$\therefore \quad \frac{dP}{dt} = \frac{d}{dt} \cdot 2\pi r \Rightarrow \frac{dP}{dt} = 2\pi \cdot \frac{dr}{dt}$$

$$= 2\pi \cdot \frac{k}{2\pi} \cdot \frac{1}{r} = \frac{k}{r} \qquad \text{[using Eq. (iii)]}$$

$$\Rightarrow \quad \frac{dP}{dt} \propto \frac{1}{r}$$

Hence proved.

Q. 3 A kite is moving horizontally at a height of 151.5 m. If the speed of kite is 10 m/s, how fast is the string being let out, when the kite is 250 m away from the boy who is flying the kite, if the height of boy is 1.5 m?

Sol. We have , height (h) = 151.5 m, speed of kite (v) = 10 m/s

Let CD be the height of kite and AB be the height of boy.

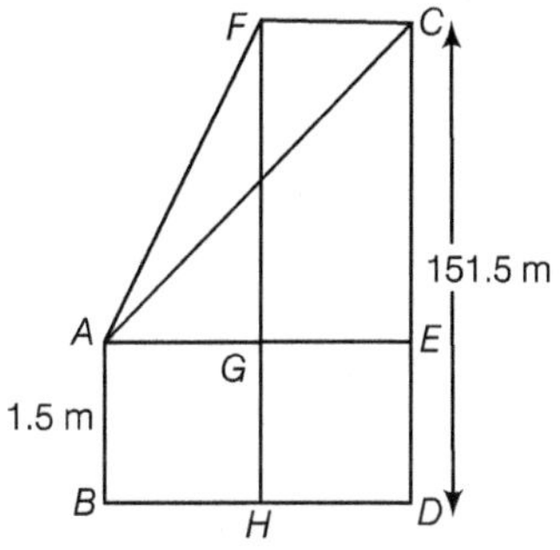

Let $DB = x \text{ m} = EA$ and $AC = 250 \text{ m}$

$$\therefore \quad \frac{dx}{dt} = 10 \text{ m/s}$$

From the figure, we see that

$$EC = 151.5 - 1.5 = 150 \text{ m}$$

and $AE = x$

Also, $AC = 250 \text{ m}$

In right angled ΔCEA,

$$AE^2 + EC^2 = AC^2$$

$$\Rightarrow \quad x^2 + (150)^2 = y^2 \qquad \text{... (i)}$$

$$\Rightarrow \quad x^2 + (150)^2 = (250)^2$$

$$\Rightarrow \quad x^2 = (250)^2 - (150)^2$$

$$= (250 + 150)(250 - 150)$$

$$= 400 \times 100$$

$$\therefore \quad x = 20 \times 10 = 200$$

From Eq. (i), on differentiating w.r.t. t, we get

$$2x \cdot \frac{dx}{dt} + 0 = 2y\frac{dy}{dt}$$

$$\Rightarrow \quad 2y\frac{dy}{dt} = 2x\frac{dx}{dt}$$

$$\therefore \quad \frac{dy}{dt} = \frac{x}{y} \cdot \frac{dx}{dt}$$

$$= \frac{200}{250} \cdot 10 = 8 \text{ m/s} \qquad \left[\because \frac{dx}{dt} = 10 \text{ m/s}\right]$$

So, the required rate at which the string is being let out is 8 m/s.

Q. 4 Two men A and B start with velocities v at the same time from the junction of two roads inclined at 45° to each other. If they travel by different roads, then find the rate at which they are being separated.

Thinking Process

By drawing figure such that men start moving at a point C, A and B are separating points, then draw perpendicular from that point C to AB to get D. Now, get the value of $\angle ACD$ in terms of x and y, then by using $\frac{dy}{dt}$ get desired result. [let $AC = BC = x$ and $AB = y$]

Sol. Let two men start from the point C with velocity v each at the same time.

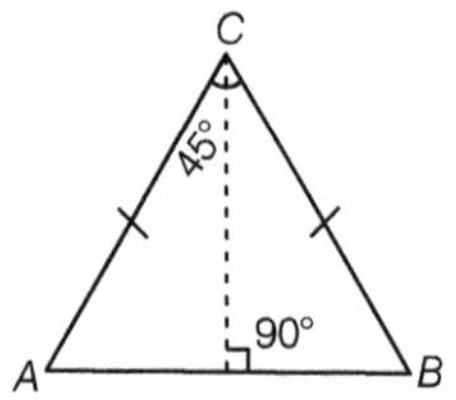

Also, $\angle BCA = 45°$

Since, A and B are moving with same velocity v, so they will cover same distance in same time.

Therefore, ΔABC is an isosceles triangle with $AC = BC$.

Now, draw $CD \perp AB$.

Let at any instant t, the distance between them is AB.

Let $AC = BC = x$ and $AB = y$

In ΔACD and ΔDCB,

$$\angle CAD = \angle CBD \quad [\because AC = BC]$$

$$\angle CDA = \angle CDB = 90°$$

$$\therefore \quad \angle ACD = \angle DCB$$

$$\text{or} \quad \angle ACD = \frac{1}{2} \times \angle ACB$$

$$\Rightarrow \quad \angle ACD = \frac{1}{2} \times 45°$$

$$\Rightarrow \quad \angle ACD = \frac{\pi}{8}$$

$$\therefore \quad \sin\frac{\pi}{8} = \frac{AD}{AC}$$

$$\Rightarrow \quad \sin\frac{\pi}{8} = \frac{y/2}{x} \quad [\because AD = y/2]$$

$$\Rightarrow \quad \frac{y}{2} = x\sin\frac{\pi}{8}$$

$$\Rightarrow \quad y = 2x \cdot \sin\frac{\pi}{8}$$

Now, differentiating both sides w.r.t. t, we get

$$\frac{dy}{dt} = 2 \cdot \sin\frac{\pi}{8} \cdot \frac{dx}{dt}$$

$$= 2 \cdot \sin\frac{\pi}{8} \cdot v \quad \left[\because v = \frac{dx}{dt}\right]$$

$$= 2v \cdot \frac{\sqrt{2-\sqrt{2}}}{2} \quad \left[\because \sin\frac{\pi}{8} = \frac{\sqrt{2-\sqrt{2}}}{2}\right]$$

$$= \sqrt{2-\sqrt{2}}\, v \text{ unit/s}$$

which is the rate at which A and B are being separated.

Q. 5 Find an angle θ, where $0 < \theta < \frac{\pi}{2}$, which increases twice as fast as its sine.

Sol. Let θ increases twice as fast as its sine.

$$\Rightarrow \quad \theta = 2\sin\theta$$

Now, on differentiating both sides w.r.t. t, we get

$$\frac{d\theta}{dt} = 2\cdot\cos\theta\cdot\frac{d\theta}{dt} \Rightarrow 1 = 2\cos\theta$$

$$\Rightarrow \quad \frac{1}{2} = \cos\theta \Rightarrow \cos\theta = \cos\frac{\pi}{3}$$

$$\therefore \quad \theta = \frac{\pi}{3}$$

So, the required angle is $\frac{\pi}{3}$.

Q. 6 Find the approximate value of $(1.999)^5$.

Sol. Let $x = 2$

and $\Delta x = -0.001$ $\quad [\because 2 - 0.001 = 1.999]$

Let $y = x^5$

On differentiating both sides w.r.t. x, we get

$$\frac{dy}{dx} = 5x^4$$

Now,
$$\Delta y = \frac{dy}{dx}\cdot\Delta x = 5x^4 \times \Delta x$$
$$= 5 \times 2^4 \times [-0.001]$$
$$= -80 \times 0.001 = -0.080$$

$$\therefore \quad (1.999)^5 = y + \Delta y$$
$$= 2^5 + (-0.080)$$
$$= 32 - 0.080 = 31.920$$

Q. 7 Find the approximate volume of metal in a hollow spherical shell whose internal and external radii are 3 cm and 3.0005 cm, respectively.

Sol. Let internal radius $= r$ and external radius $= R$

$\therefore$ Volume of hollow spherical shell, $V = \frac{4}{3}\pi(R^3 - r^3)$

$$\Rightarrow \quad V = \frac{4}{3}\pi[(3.0005)^3 - (3)^3] \quad \ldots(i)$$

Now, we shall use differentiation to get approximate value of $(3.0005)^3$.

Let $(3.0005)^3 = y + \Delta y$

and $x = 3, \Delta x = 0.0005$

Also, let $y = x^3$

On differentiating both sides w.r.t. x, we get

$$\frac{dy}{dx} = 3x^2$$

$$\therefore \quad \Delta y = \frac{dy}{dx} \times \Delta x = 3x^2 \times 0.0005$$
$$= 3 \times 3^2 \times 0.0005$$
$$= 27 \times 0.0005 = 0.0135$$

Also, $(3.0005)^3 = y + \Delta y$

$$= 3^3 + 0.0135 = 27.0135$$

$\therefore$ $V = \frac{4}{3}\pi\,[27.0135 - 27.000]$ [using Eq. (i)]

$$= \frac{4}{3}\pi\,[0.0135] = 4\pi \times (0.0045)$$

$$= 0.0180\pi \text{ cm}^3$$

Q. 8 A man, 2 m tall, walks at the rate of $1\frac{2}{3}$ m/s towards a street light which is $5\frac{1}{3}$ m above the ground. At what rate is the tip of his shadow moving and at what rate is the length of the shadow changing when he is $3\frac{1}{3}$ m from the base of the light?

Sol. Let AB be the street light post and CD be the height of man *i.e.*, $CD = 2$ m.

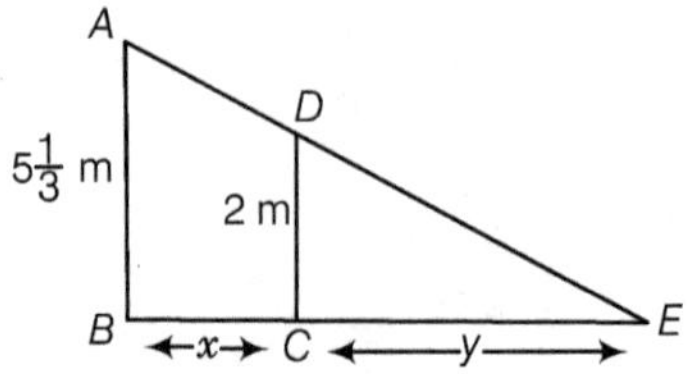

Let $BC = x$ m, $CE = y$ m and $\frac{dx}{dt} = \frac{-5}{3}$ m/s

From ΔABE and ΔDCE, we see that

$\Delta ABE \sim \Delta DCE$ [by AAA similarity]

$\therefore$ $\frac{AB}{DC} = \frac{BE}{CE} \Rightarrow \frac{\frac{16}{3}}{2} = \frac{x+y}{y}$

$\Rightarrow$ $\frac{16}{6} = \frac{x+y}{y}$

$\Rightarrow$ $16y = 6x + 6y \Rightarrow 10y = 6x$

$\Rightarrow$ $y = \frac{3}{5}x$

On differentiating both sides w.r.t. t, we get

$$\frac{dy}{dt} = \frac{3}{5}\cdot\frac{dx}{dt} = \frac{3}{5}\cdot\left(-1\frac{2}{3}\right)$$

[since, man is moving towards the light post]

$$= \frac{3}{5}\cdot\left(\frac{-5}{3}\right) = -1 \text{ m/s}$$

Let $z = x + y$

Now, differentiating both sides w.r.t. t, we get

$$\frac{dz}{dt} = \frac{dx}{dt} + \frac{dy}{dt} = -\left(\frac{5}{3} + 1\right)$$

$$= -\frac{8}{3} = -2\frac{2}{3} \text{ m/s}$$

Hence, the tip of shadow is moving at the rate of $2\frac{2}{3}$ m/s towards the light source and length of the shadow is decreasing at the rate of 1 m/s.

Q. 9 A swimming pool is to be drained for cleaning. If L represents the number of litres of water in the pool t seconds after the pool has been plugged off to drain and $L = 200\,(10 - t)^2$. How fast is the water running out at the end of 5 s and what is the average rate at which the water flows out during the first 5 s?

Sol. Let L represents the number of litres of water in the pool t seconds after the pool has been plugged off to drain, then

$$L = 200\,(10 - t)^2$$

$\therefore$ Rate at which the water is running out $= -\dfrac{dL}{dt}$

$$\frac{dL}{dt} = -200 \cdot 2\,(10 - t) \cdot (-1)$$
$$= 400\,(10 - t)$$

Rate at which the water is running out at the end of 5 s

$$= 400\,(10 - 5)$$
$$= 2000 \text{ L/s} = \text{Final rate}$$

Since, initial rate $= -\left(\dfrac{dL}{dt}\right)_{t=0} = 4000$ L/s

$\therefore$ Average rate during 5 s $= \dfrac{\text{Initial rate} + \text{Final rate}}{2}$

$$= \frac{4000 + 2000}{2}$$
$$= 3000 \text{ L/s}$$

Q. 10 The volume of a cube increases at a constant rate. Prove that the increase in its surface area varies inversely as the length of the side.

Sol. Let the side of a cube be x unit.

$\therefore$ Volume of cube $(V) = x^3$

On differentiating both side w.r.t. t, we get

$$\frac{dV}{dt} = 3x^2 \frac{dx}{dt} = k \quad \text{[constant]}$$

$$\Rightarrow \quad \frac{dx}{dt} = \frac{k}{3x^2} \quad \text{... (i)}$$

Also, surface area of cube, $S = 6x^2$

On differentiating w.r.t. t, we get

$$\frac{dS}{dt} = 12x \cdot \frac{dx}{dt}$$

$$\Rightarrow \quad \frac{dS}{dt} = 12\,x \cdot \frac{k}{3x^2} \quad \text{[using Eq. (i)]}$$

$$\Rightarrow \quad \frac{dS}{dt} = \frac{12k}{3x} = 4\left(\frac{k}{x}\right)$$

$$\Rightarrow \quad \frac{dS}{dt} \propto \frac{1}{x}$$

Hence, the surface area of the cube varies inversely as the length of the side.

Q. 11 If x and y are the sides of two squares such that $y = x - x^2$, then find the rate of change of the area of second square with respect to the area of first square.

Thinking Process

First, let A_1 and A_2 be the areas of two squares and get their values in one variable and then by using dA_1/dt and dA_2/dt get the value of dA_2/dA_1

Sol. Since, x and y are the sides of two squares such that $y = x - x^2$.

$\therefore$ Area of the first square $(A_1) = x^2$

and area of the second square $(A_2) = y^2 = (x - x^2)^2$

$$\therefore \quad \frac{dA_2}{dt} = \frac{d}{dt}(x - x^2)^2 = 2(x - x^2)\left(\frac{dx}{dt} - 2x \cdot \frac{dx}{dt}\right)$$

$$= \frac{dx}{dt}(1 - 2x)\,2(x - x^2)$$

and
$$\frac{dA_1}{dt} = \frac{d}{dt}x^2 = 2x \cdot \frac{dx}{dt}$$

$$\therefore \quad \frac{dA_2}{dA_1} = \frac{dA_2/dt}{dA_1/dt} = \frac{\frac{dx}{dt} \cdot (1 - 2x)(2x - 2x^2)}{2x \cdot \frac{dx}{dt}}$$

$$= \frac{(1 - 2x)\,2x(1 - x)}{2x}$$

$$= (1 - 2x)(1 - x)$$

$$= 1 - x - 2x + 2x^2$$

$$= 2x^2 - 3x + 1$$

Q. 12 Find the condition that curves $2x = y^2$ and $2xy = k$ intersect orthogonally.

Thinking Process

First, get the intersection point of the curve and then get the slopes of both the curves at that point. Then, by using $m_1 \cdot m_2 = -1$, get the required condition.

Sol. Given, equation of curves are $\quad 2x = y^2 \quad$ ... (i)

and $\quad 2xy = k \quad$ ... (ii)

$\Rightarrow \quad y = \dfrac{k}{2x} \quad$ [from Eq. (ii)]

From Eq. (i), $\quad 2x = \left(\dfrac{k}{2x}\right)^2$

$\Rightarrow \quad 8x^3 = k^2$

$\Rightarrow \quad x^3 = \dfrac{1}{8}k^2$

$\Rightarrow \quad x = \dfrac{1}{2}k^{2/3}$

$\therefore \quad y = \dfrac{k}{2x} = \dfrac{k}{2 \cdot \frac{1}{2}k^{2/3}} = k^{1/3}$

Thus, we get point of intersection of curves which is $\left(\dfrac{1}{2}k^{2/3}, k^{1/3}\right)$.

From Eqs. (i) and (ii),

$$2 = 2y\frac{dy}{dx}$$

and $$2\left[x \cdot \frac{dy}{dx} + y \cdot 1\right] = 0$$

$\Rightarrow$ $$\frac{dy}{dx} = \frac{1}{y}$$

and $$\left(\frac{dy}{dx}\right) = \frac{-2y}{2x} = -\frac{y}{x}$$

$\Rightarrow$ $$\left(\frac{dy}{dx}\right)_{\left(\frac{1}{2}k^{2/3},\, k^{1/3}\right)} = \frac{1}{k^{1/3}} \quad \text{[say } m_1\text{]}$$

and $$\left(\frac{dy}{dx}\right)_{\left(\frac{1}{2}k^{2/3},\, k^{1/3}\right)} = \frac{-k^{1/3}}{\frac{1}{2}k^{2/3}} = -2k^{-1/3} \quad \text{[say } m_2\text{]}$$

Since, the curves intersect orthogonally.

i.e., $$m_1 \cdot m_2 = -1$$

$\Rightarrow$ $$\frac{1}{k^{1/3}} \cdot (-2k^{-1/3}) = -1$$

$\Rightarrow$ $$-2\,k^{-2/3} = -1$$

$\Rightarrow$ $$\frac{2}{k^{2/3}} = 1$$

$\Rightarrow$ $$k^{2/3} = 2$$

$\therefore$ $$k^2 = 8$$

which is the required condition.

Q. 13 Prove that the curves $xy = 4$ and $x^2 + y^2 = 8$ touch each other.

Thinking Process

First, find the intersection points of curves and then equate the slopes of both the curves at the obtained point.

Sol. Given equation of curves are

$$xy = 4 \quad \text{...(i)}$$

and $$x^2 + y^2 = 8 \quad \text{...(ii)}$$

$\Rightarrow$ $$x \cdot \frac{dy}{dx} + y = 0$$

and $$2x + 2y\frac{dy}{dx} = 0$$

$\Rightarrow$ $$\frac{dy}{dx} = \frac{-y}{x}$$

and $$\frac{dy}{dx} = \frac{-2x}{2y}$$

$\Rightarrow$ $$\frac{dy}{dx} = \frac{-y}{x} = m_1 \quad \text{[say]}$$

and $$\frac{dy}{dx} = \frac{-x}{y} = m_2 \quad \text{[say]}$$

Since, both the curves should have same slope.

$\therefore$ $$\frac{-y}{x} = \frac{-x}{y} \Rightarrow -y^2 = -x^2$$

$\Rightarrow$ $$x^2 = y^2 \quad \text{...(iii)}$$

Using the value of x^2 in Eq. (ii), we get

$$y^2 + y^2 = 8$$

$$\Rightarrow \quad y^2 = 4 \Rightarrow y = \pm 2$$

For $y = 2,\ x = \frac{4}{2} = 2$

and for $y = -2,\ x = \frac{4}{-2} = -2$

Thus, the required points of intersection are (2, 2) and (– 2, – 2).

For (2, 2), $\quad m_1 = \frac{-y}{x} = \frac{-2}{2} = -1$

and $\quad m_2 = \frac{-x}{y} = \frac{-2}{2} = -1$

$\because \quad m_1 = m_2$

For (–2,–2), $\quad m_1 = \frac{-y}{x} = \frac{-(-2)}{-2} = -1$

and $\quad m_2 = \frac{-x}{y} = \frac{-(-2)}{-2} = -1$

Thus, for both the intersection points, we see that slope of both the curves are same. Hence, the curves touch each other.

Q. 14 Find the coordinates of the point on the curve $\sqrt{x} + \sqrt{y} = 4$ at which tangent is equally inclined to the axes.

Sol. We have, $\quad \sqrt{x} + \sqrt{y} = 4 \quad$ ...(i)

$$\Rightarrow \quad x^{1/2} + y^{1/2} = 4$$

$$\Rightarrow \quad \frac{1}{2}\cdot\frac{1}{x^{1/2}} + \frac{1}{2}\cdot\frac{1}{y^{1/2}}\cdot\frac{dy}{dx} = 0$$

$$\therefore \quad \frac{dy}{dx} = -\frac{1}{2}\cdot x^{-1/2}\ 2\cdot y^{1/2}$$

$$= -\sqrt{\frac{y}{x}}$$

Since, tangent is equally inclined to the axes.

$$\therefore \quad \frac{dy}{dx} = \pm 1$$

$$\Rightarrow \quad -\sqrt{\frac{y}{x}} = \pm 1$$

$$\Rightarrow \quad \frac{y}{x} = 1 \Rightarrow y = x$$

From Eq. (i), $\quad \sqrt{y} + \sqrt{y} = 4$

$$\Rightarrow \quad 2\sqrt{y} = 4$$

$$\Rightarrow \quad 4y = 16$$

$$\therefore \quad y = 4 \text{ and } x = 4$$

When y=4, then $x = 4$

So, the required coordinates are (4, 4).

Q. 15 Find the angle of intersection of the curves $y = 4 - x^2$ and $y = x^2$.

Sol. We have,
$$y = 4 - x^2 \quad \text{...(i)}$$
and
$$y = x^2 \quad \text{...(ii)}$$
$$\Rightarrow \quad \frac{dy}{dx} = -2x$$
and
$$\frac{dy}{dx} = 2x$$
$$\Rightarrow \quad m_1 = -2x$$
and
$$m_2 = 2x$$
From Eqs. (i) and (ii),
$$x^2 = 4 - x^2$$
$$\Rightarrow \quad 2x^2 = 4$$
$$\Rightarrow \quad x^2 = 2$$
$$\Rightarrow \quad x = \pm\sqrt{2}$$
$$\therefore \quad y = x^2 = (\pm\sqrt{2})^2 = 2$$
So, the points of intersection are $(\sqrt{2}, 2)$ and $(-\sqrt{2}, 2)$.

For point $(+\sqrt{2}, 2)$,
$$m_1 = -2x = -2 \cdot \sqrt{2} = -2\sqrt{2}$$
and
$$m_2 = 2x = 2\sqrt{2}$$
and for point $(\sqrt{2}, 2)$,
$$\tan\theta = \left|\frac{m_1 - m_2}{1 + m_1 m_2}\right| = \left|\frac{-2\sqrt{2} - 2\sqrt{2}}{1 - 2\sqrt{2} \cdot 2\sqrt{2}}\right| = \left|\frac{-4\sqrt{2}}{-7}\right|$$
$$\therefore \quad \theta = \tan^{-1}\left(\frac{4\sqrt{2}}{7}\right)$$

Q. 16 Prove that the curves $y^2 = 4x$ and $x^2 + y^2 - 6x + 1 = 0$ touch each other at the point (1, 2).

Sol. We have, $y^2 = 4x$ and $x^2 + y^2 - 6x + 1 = 0$

Since, both the curves touch each other at (1, 2) *i.e.*, curves are passing through (1, 2).
$$\therefore \quad 2y \cdot \frac{dy}{dx} = 4$$
and
$$2x + 2y\frac{dy}{dx} = 6$$
$$\Rightarrow \quad \frac{dy}{dx} = \frac{4}{2y}$$
and
$$\frac{dy}{dx} = \frac{6 - 2x}{2y}$$
$$\Rightarrow \quad \left(\frac{dy}{dx}\right)_{(1,2)} = \frac{4}{4} = 1$$
and
$$\left(\frac{dy}{dx}\right)_{(1,2)} = \frac{6 - 2 \cdot 1}{2 \cdot 2} = \frac{4}{4} = 1$$
$$\Rightarrow \quad m_1 = 1 \text{ and } m_2 = 1$$
Thus, we see that slope of both the curves are equal to each other *i.e.*, $m_1 = m_2 = 1$ at the point (1, 2).

Hence, both the curves touch each other.

Q. 17 Find the equation of the normal lines to the curve $3x^2 - y^2 = 8$ which are parallel to the line $x + 3y = 4$.

Sol. Given equation of the curve is

$$3x^2 - y^2 = 8 \quad \text{...(i)}$$

On differentiating both sides w.r.t. x, we get

$$6x - 2y\frac{dy}{dx} = 0$$

$$\Rightarrow \quad \frac{dy}{dx} = \frac{6x}{2y} = \frac{3x}{y}$$

$$\Rightarrow \quad m_1 = \frac{3x}{y} \quad \text{[say]}$$

and slope of normal $(m_2) = \frac{-1}{m_1} = \frac{-y}{3x}$ ...(ii)

Since, slope of normal to the curve should be equal to the slope of line $x + 3y = 4$, which is parallel to curve.

For line, $y = \frac{4 - x}{3} = \frac{-x}{3} + \frac{4}{3}$

$\Rightarrow$ Slope of the line $(m_3) = \frac{-1}{3}$

$$\therefore \quad m_2 = m_3$$

$$\Rightarrow \quad \frac{-y}{3x} = -\frac{1}{3}$$

$$\Rightarrow \quad -3y = -3x$$

$$\Rightarrow \quad y = x \quad \text{...(iii)}$$

On substituting the value of y in Eq. (i), we get

$$3x^2 - x^2 = 8$$

$$\Rightarrow \quad x^2 = 4$$

$$\Rightarrow \quad x = \pm 2$$

For $x = 2$, $y = 2$ [using Eq. (iii)]

and for $x = -2$, $y = -2$ [using Eq. (iii)]

Thus,the points at which normal to the curve are parallel to the line $x + 3y = 4$ are (2, 2) and (− 2, − 2).

Required equations of normal are

$$y - 2 = m_2(x - 2) \text{ and } y + 2 = m_2(x + 2)$$

$$\Rightarrow \quad y - 2 = \frac{-2}{6}(x - 2) \text{ and } y + 2 = \frac{-2}{6}(x + 2)$$

$$\Rightarrow \quad 3y - 6 = -x + 2 \text{ and } 3y + 6 = -x - 2$$

$$\Rightarrow \quad 3y + x = +8 \text{ and } 3y + x = -8$$

So, the required equations are $3y + x = \pm 8$.

Q. 18 At what points on the curve $x^2 + y^2 - 2x - 4y + 1 = 0$, the tangents are parallel to the Y-axis?

Sol. Given, equation of curve which is

$$x^2 + y^2 - 2x - 4y + 1 = 0 \quad \text{... (i)}$$

$$\Rightarrow \quad 2x + 2y\frac{dy}{dx} - 2 - 4\frac{dy}{dx} = 0$$

$$\Rightarrow \quad \frac{dy}{dx}(2y-4)=2-2x$$

$$\Rightarrow \quad \frac{dy}{dx}=\frac{2(1-x)}{2(y-2)}$$

Since, the tangents are parallel to the Y-axis *i.e.*, $\tan\theta = \tan 90° = \frac{dy}{dx}$.

$$\therefore \quad \frac{1-x}{y-2}=\frac{1}{0}$$

$$\Rightarrow \quad y-2=0$$

$$\Rightarrow \quad y=2$$

For $y=2$ from Eq. (i), we get

$$x^2+2^2-2x-4\times 2+1=0$$

$$\Rightarrow \quad x^2-2x-3=0$$

$$\Rightarrow \quad x^2-3x+x-3=0$$

$$\Rightarrow \quad x(x-3)+1(x-3)=0$$

$$\Rightarrow \quad (x+1)(x-3)=0$$

$$\therefore \quad x=-1,\ x=3$$

So, the required points are $(-1, 2)$ and $(3, 2)$.

Q. 19 Show that the line $\frac{x}{a}+\frac{y}{b}=1$, touches the curve $y=b\cdot e^{-x/a}$ at the point, where the curve intersects the axis of Y.

Sol. We have the equation of line given by $\frac{x}{a}+\frac{y}{b}=1$, which touches the curve $y=b\cdot e^{-x/a}$ at the point, where the curve intersects the axis of Y *i.e.*, $x=0$.

$$\therefore \quad y=b\cdot e^{-0/a}=b \qquad [\because e^0=1]$$

So, the point of intersection of the curve with Y-axis is $(0, b)$.

Now, slope of the given line at $(0, b)$ is given by

$$\frac{1}{a}\cdot 1+\frac{1}{b}\cdot\frac{dy}{dx}=0$$

$$\Rightarrow \quad \frac{dy}{dx}=\frac{-1}{a}\cdot b$$

$$\Rightarrow \quad \frac{dy}{dx}=-\frac{1}{a}\cdot b=\frac{-b}{a}=m_1 \qquad \text{[say]}$$

Also, the slope of the curve at $(0, b)$ is

$$\frac{dy}{dx}=b\cdot e^{-x/a}\cdot\frac{-1}{a}$$

$$\frac{dy}{dx}=\frac{-b}{a}e^{-x/a}$$

$$\left(\frac{dy}{dx}\right)_{(0,\,b)}=\frac{-b}{a}e^{-0}=\frac{-b}{a}=m_2 \qquad \text{[say]}$$

Since, $\quad m_1=m_2=\frac{-b}{a}$

Hence, the line touches the curve at the point, where the curve intersects the axis of Y.

Q. 20 Show that $f(x) = 2x + \cot^{-1} x + \log(\sqrt{1 + x^2} - x)$ is increasing in R.

Thinking Process

If $f'(x) \geq 0$, then we can say that $f(x)$ is increasing function. Use this condition to show the desired result.

Sol. We have,

$$f(x) = 2x + \cot^{-1} x + \log(\sqrt{1 + x^2} - x)$$

$\therefore$

$$f'(x) = 2 + \left(\frac{-1}{1 + x^2}\right) + \frac{1}{(\sqrt{1 + x^2} - x)}\left(\frac{1}{2\sqrt{1 + x^2}} \cdot 2x - 1\right)$$

$$= 2 - \frac{1}{1 + x^2} + \frac{1}{(\sqrt{1 + x^2} - x)} \cdot \frac{(x - \sqrt{1 + x^2})}{\sqrt{1 + x^2}}$$

$$= 2 - \frac{1}{1 + x^2} - \frac{1}{\sqrt{1 + x^2}}$$

$$= \frac{2 + 2x^2 - 1 - \sqrt{1 + x^2}}{1 + x^2} = \frac{1 + 2x^2 - \sqrt{1 + x^2}}{1 + x^2}$$

For increasing function, $f'(x) \geq 0$

$\Rightarrow$ $$\frac{1 + 2x^2 - \sqrt{1 + x^2}}{1 + x^2} \geq 0$$

$\Rightarrow$ $$1 + 2x^2 \geq \sqrt{1 + x^2}$$

$\Rightarrow$ $$(1 + 2x^2)^2 \geq 1 + x^2$$

$\Rightarrow$ $$1 + 4x^4 + 4x^2 \geq 1 + x^2$$

$\Rightarrow$ $$4x^4 + 3x^2 \geq 0$$

$\Rightarrow$ $$x^2(4x^2 + 3) \geq 0$$

which is true for any real value of x.

Hence, $f(x)$ is increasing in R.

Q. 21 Show that for $a \geq 1$, $f(x) = \sqrt{3}\sin x - \cos x - 2ax + b$ is decreasing in R.

Thinking Process

If $f'(x) \leq 0$, then we can say that $f(x)$ is a decreasing function. So, use this condition to show the result.

Sol. We have, $a \geq 1$,

$$f(x) = \sqrt{3}\sin x - \cos x - 2ax + b$$

$\therefore$

$$f'(x) = \sqrt{3}\cos x - (-\sin x) - 2a$$

$$= \sqrt{3}\cos x + \sin x - 2a$$

$$= 2\left[\frac{\sqrt{3}}{2} \cdot \cos x + \frac{1}{2} \cdot \sin x\right] - 2a$$

$$= 2\left[\cos\frac{\pi}{6} \cdot \cos x + \sin\frac{\pi}{6} \cdot \sin x\right] - 2a$$

$$= 2\left(\cos\frac{\pi}{6} - x\right) - 2a$$

$[\because \cos(A - B) = \cos A \cdot \cos B + \sin A \cdot \sin B]$

$$= 2\left[\left(\cos\frac{\pi}{6} - x\right) - a\right]$$

We know that, $\cos x \in [-1, 1]$

and $a \geq 1$

So, $2\left[\cos\left(\frac{\pi}{6} - x\right) - a\right] \leq 0$

$\therefore$ $f'(x) \leq 0$

Hence, $f(x)$ is a decreasing function in R.

Q. 22 Show that $f(x) = \tan^{-1}(\sin x + \cos x)$ is an increasing function in $\left(0, \frac{\pi}{4}\right)$.

Sol. We have, $f(x) = \tan^{-1}(\sin x + \cos x)$

$$\therefore \quad f'(x) = \frac{1}{1 + (\sin x + \cos x)^2} \cdot (\cos x - \sin x)$$

$$= \frac{1}{1 + \sin^2 x + \cos^2 x + 2\sin x \cdot \cos x}(\cos x - \sin x)$$

$$= \frac{1}{(2 + \sin 2x)}(\cos x - \sin x)$$

$[\because \sin 2x = 2\sin x \cos x \text{ and } \sin^2 x + \cos^2 x = 1]$

For $f'(x) \geq 0$,

$$\frac{1}{(2 + \sin 2x)} \cdot (\cos x - \sin x) \geq 0$$

$\Rightarrow$ $\cos x - \sin x \geq 0$ $\quad \left[\because (2 + \sin 2x) \geq 0 \text{ in } \left(0, \frac{\pi}{4}\right)\right]$

$\Rightarrow$ $\cos x \geq \sin x$

which is true, if $x \in \left(0, \frac{\pi}{4}\right)$.

Hence, $f(x)$ is an increasing function in $\left(0, \frac{\pi}{4}\right)$.

Q. 23 At what point, the slope of the curve $y = -x^3 + 3x^2 + 9x - 27$ is maximum? Also, find the maximum slope.

Sol. We have, $y = -x^3 + 3x^2 + 9x - 27$

$\therefore$ $\frac{dy}{dx} = -3x^2 + 6x + 9 =$ Slope of tangent to the curve

Now, $\frac{d^2y}{dx^2} = -6x + 6$

For $\frac{d}{dx}\left(\frac{dy}{dx}\right) = 0$,

$$-6x + 6 = 0$$

$\Rightarrow$ $x = \frac{-6}{-6} = 1$

$\therefore$ $\frac{d}{dx}\left(\frac{d^2y}{dx^2}\right) = -6 < 0$

So, the slope of tangent to the curve is maximum, when $x = 1$.

For $x = 1$, $\left(\frac{dy}{dx}\right)_{(x=1)} = -3 \cdot 1^2 + 6 \cdot 1 + 9 = 12$,

which is maximum slope.

Also, for $x = 1, y = -1^3 + 3\cdot 1^2 + 9\cdot 1 - 27$

$$= -1 + 3 + 9 - 27$$
$$= -16$$

So, the required point is (1, – 16).

Q. 24 Prove that $f(x) = \sin x + \sqrt{3}\cos x$ has maximum value at $x = \frac{\pi}{6}$.

Sol. We have, $f(x) = \sin x + \sqrt{3}\cos x$

$\therefore$ $f'(x) = \cos x + \sqrt{3}(-\sin x)$

$$= \cos x - \sqrt{3}\sin x$$

For $f'(x) = 0$, $\cos x = \sqrt{3}\sin x$

$\Rightarrow$ $\tan x = \frac{1}{\sqrt{3}} = \tan\frac{\pi}{6}$

$\Rightarrow$ $x = \frac{\pi}{6}$

Again, differentiating $f'(x)$, we get

$$f''(x) = -\sin x - \sqrt{3}\cos x$$

At $x = \frac{\pi}{6}$, $f''(x) = -\sin\frac{\pi}{6} - \sqrt{3}\cos\frac{\pi}{6}$

$$= -\frac{1}{2} - \sqrt{3}\cdot\frac{\sqrt{3}}{2}$$
$$= -\frac{1}{2} - \frac{3}{2} = -2 < 0$$

Hence, at $x = \frac{\pi}{6}$, $f(x)$ has maximum value at $\frac{\pi}{6}$ is the point of local maxima.

Long Answer Type Questions

Q. 25 If the sum of lengths of the hypotenuse and a side of a right angled triangle is given, then show that the area of triangle is maximum, when the angle between them is $\frac{\pi}{3}$.

Sol. Let ABC be a triangle with $AC = h$, $AB = x$ and $BC = y$.

Also, $\angle CAB = \theta$

Let $h + x = k$ ...(i)

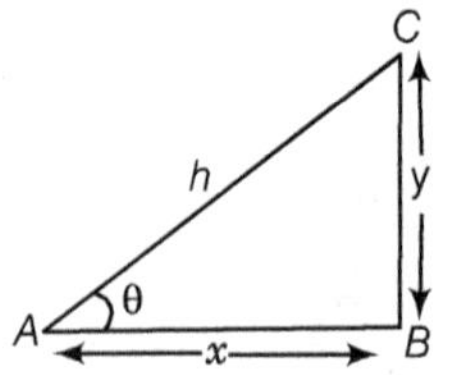

$\therefore$ $\cos\theta = \frac{x}{h}$

$\Rightarrow$ $x = h\cos\theta$

$\Rightarrow$ $h + h\cos\theta = k$ [using Eq. (i)]

$$\Rightarrow \quad h(1+\cos\theta) = k$$

$$\Rightarrow \quad h = \frac{k}{(1+\cos\theta)} \quad \text{...(ii)}$$

Also,

$$\text{area of } \Delta ABC = \frac{1}{2}(AB \cdot BC)$$

$$A = \frac{1}{2} \cdot x \cdot y$$

$$= \frac{1}{2} h\cos\theta \cdot h\sin\theta \qquad \left[\because \sin\theta = \frac{y}{h}\right]$$

$$= \frac{1}{2} h^2 \sin\theta \cdot \cos\theta$$

$$= \frac{2h^2}{4} \sin\theta \cdot \cos\theta$$

$$= \frac{1}{4} h^2 \sin 2\theta \quad \text{...(iii)}$$

Since,

$$h = \frac{k}{1+\cos\theta}$$

$$\therefore \quad A = \frac{1}{4}\left(\frac{k}{1+\cos\theta}\right)^2 \cdot \sin 2\theta$$

$$\Rightarrow \quad A = \frac{k^2}{4} \cdot \frac{\sin 2\theta}{(1+\cos\theta)^2} \quad \text{...(iv)}$$

$$\therefore \quad \frac{dA}{d\theta} = \frac{k^2}{4}\left[\frac{(1+\cos\theta)^2 \cdot \cos 2\theta \cdot 2 - \sin 2\theta \cdot 2(1+\cos\theta) \cdot (0 - \sin\theta)}{(1+\cos\theta)^4}\right]$$

$$= \frac{k^2}{4}\left\{\frac{2(1+\cos\theta)[(1+\cos\theta) \cdot \cos 2\theta + \sin 2\theta(\sin\theta)}{(1+\cos\theta)^4}\right\}$$

$$= \frac{k^2}{4} \cdot \frac{2}{(1+\cos\theta)^3}[(1+\cos\theta) \cdot \cos 2\theta + 2\sin^2\theta \cdot \cos\theta]$$

$$= \frac{k^2}{2(1+\cos\theta)^3}[(1+\cos\theta)(1-2\sin^2\theta) + 2\sin^2\theta \cdot \cos\theta]$$

$$= \frac{k^2}{2(1+\cos\theta)^3}[1+\cos\theta - 2\sin^2\theta - 2\sin^2\theta \cdot \cos\theta + 2\sin^2\theta \cdot \cos\theta]$$

$$= \frac{k^2}{2(1+\cos\theta)^3}[(1+\cos\theta) - 2\sin^2\theta]$$

$$= \frac{k^2}{2(1+\cos\theta)^3}[1+\cos\theta - 2 + 2\cos^2\theta]$$

$$= \frac{k^2}{2(1+\cos\theta)^3}(2\cos^2\theta + \cos\theta - 1) \quad \text{...(v)}$$

For $\frac{dA}{d\theta} = 0$,

$$\frac{k^2}{2(1+\cos\theta)^3}(2\cos^2\theta + \cos\theta - 1) = 0$$

$$\Rightarrow \quad 2\cos^2\theta + \cos\theta - 1 = 0$$

$$\Rightarrow \quad 2\cos^2\theta + 2\cos\theta - \cos\theta - 1 = 0$$

$$\Rightarrow \quad 2\cos\theta(\cos\theta + 1) - 1(\cos\theta + 1) = 0$$

$$\Rightarrow \quad (2\cos\theta - 1)(\cos\theta + 1) = 0$$

$$\Rightarrow \quad \cos\theta = \frac{1}{2} \text{ or } \cos\theta = -1$$

$$\Rightarrow \quad \theta = \frac{\pi}{3} \quad \text{[possible]}$$

$$\text{or} \quad \theta = 2n\pi \pm \pi \quad \text{[not possible]}$$

$$\therefore \quad \theta = \frac{\pi}{3}$$

Again, differentiating w.r.t. θ in Eq. (v), we get

$$\frac{d}{d\theta}\left(\frac{dA}{d\theta}\right) = \frac{d}{d\theta}\left[\frac{k^2}{2(1+\cos\theta)^3}(2\cos^2\theta + \cos\theta - 1)\right]$$

$$\therefore \quad \frac{d^2A}{d\theta^2} = \frac{d}{d\theta}\left[\frac{k^2(2\cos\theta - 1)(1+\cos\theta)}{2(1+\cos\theta)^3}\right] = \frac{d}{d\theta}\left[\frac{k^2}{2}\cdot\frac{(2\cos\theta - 1)}{(1+\cos\theta)^2}\right]$$

$$= \frac{k^2}{2}\left[\frac{(1+\cos\theta)^2\cdot(-2\sin\theta) - 2(1+\cos\theta)\cdot(-\sin\theta)(2\cos\theta - 1)}{(1+\cos\theta)^4}\right]$$

$$= \frac{k^2}{2}\left[\frac{(1+\cos\theta)\cdot[1+\cos\theta](-2\sin\theta) + 2\sin\theta\,(2\cos\theta - 1)}{(1+\cos\theta)^4}\right]$$

$$= \frac{k^2}{2}\left[\frac{-2\sin\theta - 2\sin\theta\cdot\cos\theta + 4\sin\theta\cdot\cos\theta - 2\sin\theta}{(1+\cos\theta)^3}\right]$$

$$= \frac{k^2}{2}\left[\frac{-4\sin\theta - \sin 2\theta + 2\sin 2\theta}{(1+\cos\theta)^3}\right] = \frac{k^2}{2}\left[\frac{\sin 2\theta - 4\sin\theta}{(1+\cos\theta)^3}\right]$$

$$\therefore \quad \left(\frac{d^2A}{d\theta^2}\right)_{\text{at }\theta = \frac{\pi}{3}} = \frac{k^2}{2}\left[\frac{\sin\frac{2\pi}{3} - 4\sin\frac{\pi}{3}}{\left(1+\cos\frac{\pi}{3}\right)^3}\right] = \frac{k^2}{2}\left[\frac{\frac{\sqrt{3}}{2} - \frac{4\sqrt{3}}{2}}{\left(1+\frac{1}{2}\right)^3}\right]$$

$$= \frac{k^2}{2}\left[\frac{-3\sqrt{3}\cdot 8}{2\cdot 27}\right] = -k^2\left(\frac{2\sqrt{3}}{9}\right)$$

which is less than zero.

Hence, area of the right angled triangle is maximum, when the angle between them is $\frac{\pi}{3}$.

Q. 26 Find the points of local maxima, local minima and the points of inflection of the function $f(x) = x^5 - 5x^4 + 5x^3 - 1$. Also, find the corresponding local maximum and local minimum values.

Sol. Given that, $f(x) = x^5 - 5x^4 + 5x^3 - 1$

On differentiating w.r.t. x, we get

$$f'(x) = 5x^4 - 20x^3 + 15x^2$$

For maxima or minima, $f'(x) = 0$

$$\Rightarrow \quad 5x^4 - 20x^3 + 15x^2 = 0$$

$$\Rightarrow \quad 5x^2(x^2 - 4x + 3) = 0$$

$$\Rightarrow \quad 5x^2(x^2 - 3x - x + 3) = 0$$

$$\Rightarrow \quad 5x^2[x(x-3) - 1(x-3)] = 0$$

$$\Rightarrow \quad 5x^2[(x-1)(x-3)] = 0$$

$$\therefore \quad x = 0, 1, 3$$

Sign scheme for $\frac{dy}{dx} = 5x^2(x-1)(x-3)$

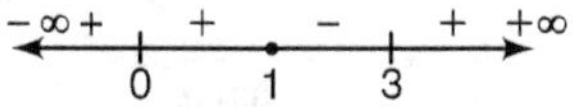

So, y has maximum value at $x = 1$ and minimum value at $x = 3$.

At $x = 0$, y has neither maximum nor minimum value.

$\therefore$ Maximum value of $y = 1 - 5 + 5 - 1 = 0$

and minimum value $= (3)^5 - 5(3)^4 + 5(3)^3 - 1$

$$= 243 - 81 \times 5 - 27 \times 5 - 1 = -298$$

Q. 27 A telephone company in a town has 500 subscribers on its list and collects fixed charges of ₹ 300 per subscriber per year. The company proposes to increase the annual subscription and it is believed that for every increase of ₹ 1 per one subscriber will discontinue the service. Find what increase will bring maximum profit?

Sol. Consider that company increases the annual subscription by ₹ x.

So, x subscribes will discontinue the service.

$\therefore$ Total revenue of company after the increment is given by

$$R(x) = (500 - x)(300 + x)$$
$$= 15 \times 10^4 + 500x - 300x - x^2$$
$$= -x^2 + 200x + 150000$$

On differentiating both sides w.r.t. x, we get

$$R'(x) = -2x + 200$$

Now, $R'(x) = 0$

$\Rightarrow$ $2x = 200 \Rightarrow x = 100$

$\therefore$ $R''(x) = -2 < 0$

So, $R(x)$ is maximum when $x = 100$.

Hence, the company should increase the subscription fee by ₹ 100, so that it has maximum profit.

Q. 28 If the straight line $x\cos\alpha + y\sin\alpha = p$ touches the curve $\frac{x^2}{a^2} + \frac{y^2}{b^2} = 1$, then prove that $a^2\cos^2\alpha + b^2\sin^2\alpha = p^2$.

Sol. Given, line is $x\cos\alpha + y\sin\alpha = p$ ... (i)

and curve is $\frac{x^2}{a^2} + \frac{y^2}{b^2} = 1$

$\Rightarrow$ $b^2x^2 + a^2y^2 = a^2b^2$ ...(ii)

Now, differentiating Eq. (ii) w.r.t. x, we get

$$b^2 \cdot 2x + a^2 \cdot 2y \cdot \frac{dy}{dx} = 0$$

$\Rightarrow$ $\frac{dy}{dx} = \frac{-2b^2x}{2a^2y} = \frac{-xb^2}{ya^2}$ ... (iii)

From Eq. (i), $y\sin\alpha = p - x\cos\alpha$

$\Rightarrow$ $y = -x\cot\alpha + \frac{p}{\sin\alpha}$

Thus, slope of the line is $(-\cot\alpha)$.

So, the given equation of line will be tangent to the Eq. (ii), if $\left(-\frac{x}{y}\cdot\frac{b^2}{a^2}\right)=(-\cot\alpha)$

$$\Rightarrow \quad \frac{x}{a^2\cos\alpha}=\frac{y}{b^2\sin\alpha}=k \quad \text{[say]}$$

$$\Rightarrow \quad x = ka^2\cos\alpha$$

and
$$y = b^2 k\sin\alpha$$

So, the line $x\cos\alpha + y\sin\alpha = p$ will touch the curve $\frac{x^2}{a^2}+\frac{y^2}{b^2}$ at point $(ka^2\cos\alpha, kb^2\sin\alpha)$.

From Eq. (i),
$$ka^2\cos^2\alpha + kb^2\sin^2\alpha = p$$

$$\Rightarrow \quad a^2\cos^2\alpha + b^2\sin^2\alpha = \frac{p}{k}$$

$$\Rightarrow \quad (a^2\cos^2\alpha + b^2\sin^2\alpha)^2 = \frac{p^2}{k^2} \quad \text{...(iv)}$$

From Eq. (ii),
$$b^2k^2a^4\cos^2\alpha + a^2k^2b^4\sin^2\alpha = a^2b^2$$

$$\Rightarrow \quad k^2(a^2\cos^2\alpha + b^2\sin^2\alpha) = 1$$

$$\Rightarrow \quad (a^2\cos^2\alpha + b^2\sin^2\alpha) = \frac{1}{k^2} \quad \text{... (v)}$$

On dividing Eq. (iv) by Eq. (v), we get

$$a^2\cos^2\alpha + b^2\sin^2\alpha = p^2$$

Hence proved.

Alternate Method

We know that, if a line $y = mx + c$ touches ellipse $\frac{x^2}{a^2}+\frac{y^2}{b^2}=1$, then

the required condition is $c^2 = a^2m^2 + b^2$

Here, given equation of the line is

$$x\cos\alpha + y\sin\alpha = p$$

$$\Rightarrow \quad y = \frac{p - x\cos\alpha}{\sin\alpha}$$

$$= -x\cot\alpha + \frac{p}{\sin\alpha}$$

$$\Rightarrow \quad c = \frac{p}{\sin\alpha}$$

and
$$m = -\cot\alpha$$

$$\therefore \quad \left(\frac{p}{\sin\alpha}\right)^2 = a^2(-\cot\alpha)^2 + b^2$$

$$\Rightarrow \quad \frac{p^2}{\sin^2\alpha} = a^2\frac{\cos^2\alpha}{\sin^2\alpha} + b^2$$

$$\Rightarrow \quad p^2 = a^2\cos^2\alpha + b^2\sin^2\alpha$$

Hence proved.

Q. 29 If an open box with square base is to be made of a given quantity of card board of area c^2, then show that the maximum volume of the box is $\frac{c^3}{6\sqrt{3}}$ cu units.

Thinking Process

First, let the sides of box in x and y then find $\frac{dV}{dx}$ in terms c and x. Also, for $\frac{dV}{dx}=0$ get the value of x and if $\frac{d^2V}{dx^2} < 0$ at the value of x, then by putting that value of x in the equation of V, get the desired result.

Sol. Let the length of side of the square base of open box be x units and its height be y units.

$\therefore$ Area of the metal used $= x^2 + 4xy$

$\Rightarrow$ $x^2 + 4xy = c^2$ [given]

$\Rightarrow$ $y = \frac{c^2 - x^2}{4x}$ ...(i)

Now, volume of the box $(V) = x^2 y$

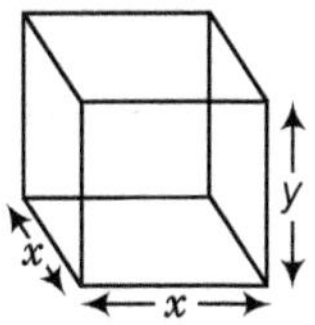

$\Rightarrow$ $V = x^2 \cdot \left(\frac{c^2 - x^2}{4x}\right)$

$= \frac{1}{4} x (c^2 - x^2)$

$= \frac{1}{4} (c^2 x - x^3)$

On differentiating both sides w.r.t. x, we get

$$\frac{dV}{dx} = \frac{1}{4}(c^2 - 3x^2) \quad \text{... (ii)}$$

Now, $\frac{dV}{dx} = 0 \Rightarrow c^2 = 3x^2$

$\Rightarrow$ $x^2 = \frac{c^2}{3}$

$\Rightarrow$ $x = \frac{c}{\sqrt{3}}$ [using positive sign]

Again, differentiating Eq. (ii) w.r.t. x, we get

$$\frac{d^2V}{dx^2} = \frac{1}{4}(-6x) = \frac{-3}{2} x < 0$$

$$\therefore \left(\frac{d^2V}{dx^2}\right)_{\text{at } x = \frac{c}{\sqrt{3}}} = -\frac{3}{2} \cdot \left(\frac{c}{\sqrt{3}}\right) < 0$$

Thus, we see that volume (V) is maximum at $x = \frac{c}{\sqrt{3}}$.

$\therefore$ Maximum volume of the box, $(V)_{x = \frac{c}{\sqrt{3}}} = \frac{1}{4}\left(c^2 \cdot \frac{c}{\sqrt{3}} - \frac{c^3}{3\sqrt{3}}\right)$

$$= \frac{1}{4} \cdot \frac{(3c^3 - c^3)}{3\sqrt{3}} = \frac{1}{4} \cdot \frac{2c^3}{3\sqrt{3}}$$

$$= \frac{c^3}{6\sqrt{3}} \text{ cu units}$$

Q. 30 Find the dimensions of the rectangle of perimeter 36 cm which will sweep out a volume as large as possible, when revolved about one of its sides. Also, find the maximum volume.

Sol. Let breadth and length of the rectangle be x and y, respectively.

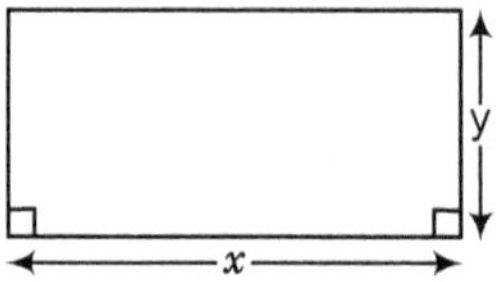

$\because$ Perimeter of the rectangle = 36 cm

$\Rightarrow \quad 2x + 2y = 36$

$\Rightarrow \quad x + y = 18$

$\Rightarrow \quad y = 18 - x \quad \text{... (i)}$

Let the rectangle is being revolved about its length y.

Then, volume (V) of resultant cylinder = $\pi x^2 \cdot y$

$\Rightarrow \quad V = \pi x^2 \cdot (18 - x) \quad [\because V = \pi r^2 h]$ [using Eq. (i)]

$= 18\pi x^2 - \pi x^3 = \pi [18x^2 - x^3]$

On differentiating both sides w.r.t. x, we get

$$\frac{dV}{dx} = \pi (36x - 3x^2)$$

Now, $\dfrac{dV}{dx} = 0$

$\Rightarrow \quad 36x = 3x^2$

$\Rightarrow \quad 3x^2 - 36x = 0$

$\Rightarrow \quad 3(x^2 - 12x) = 0$

$\Rightarrow \quad 3x(x - 12) = 0$

$\Rightarrow \quad x = 0, x = 12$

$\therefore \quad x = 12 \quad [\because, x \neq 0]$

Again, differentiating w.r.t. x, we get

$$\frac{d^2V}{dx^2} = \pi (36 - 6x)$$

$$\Rightarrow \quad \left(\frac{d^2V}{dx^2}\right)_{x=12} = \pi(36 - 6 \times 12) = -36\pi < 0$$

At $x = 12$, volume of the resultant cylinder is the maximum.

So, the dimensions of rectangle are 12 cm and 6 cm, respectively. [using Eq. (i)]

$\therefore$ Maximum volume of resultant cylinder,

$$(V)_{x=12} = \pi [18 \cdot (12)^2 - (12)^3]$$

$$= \pi [12^2 (18 - 12)]$$

$$= \pi \times 144 \times 6$$

$$= 864 \pi \text{ cm}^3$$

Q. 31 I the sum of the surface areas of cube and a sphere is constant, what is the ratio of an edge of the cube to the diameter of the sphere, when the sum of their volumes is minimum?

Sol. Let length of one edge of cube be x units and radius of sphere be r units.

$\therefore$ Surface area of cube $= 6x^2$

and surface area of sphere $= 4\pi r^2$

Also, $6x^2 + 4\pi r^2 = k$ [constant, given]

$$\Rightarrow \quad 6x^2 = k - 4\pi r^2$$

$$\Rightarrow \quad x^2 = \frac{k - 4\pi r^2}{6}$$

$$\Rightarrow \quad x = \left[\frac{k - 4\pi r^2}{6}\right]^{1/2} \quad \text{... (i)}$$

Now, volume of cube $= x^3$

and volume of sphere $= \frac{4}{3}\pi r^3$

Let sum of volume of the cube and volume of the sphere be given by

$$S = x^3 + \frac{4}{3}\pi r^3 = \left[\frac{k - 4\pi r^2}{6}\right]^{3/2} + \frac{4}{3}\pi r^3$$

On differentiating both sides w.r.t. r, we get

$$\frac{dS}{dr} = \frac{3}{2}\left[\frac{k - 4\pi r^2}{6}\right]^{1/2} \cdot \left(\frac{-8\pi r}{6}\right) + \frac{12}{3}\pi r^2$$

$$= -2\pi r\left[\frac{k - 4\pi r^2}{6}\right]^{1/2} + 4\pi r^2 \quad \text{... (ii)}$$

$$= -2\pi r\left[\left\{\frac{k - 4\pi r^2}{6}\right\}^{1/2} - 2r\right]$$

Now, $\frac{dS}{dr} = 0$

$$\Rightarrow \quad r = 0 \text{ or } 2r = \left(\frac{k - 4\pi r^2}{6}\right)^{1/2}$$

$$\Rightarrow \quad 4r^2 = \frac{k - 4\pi r^2}{6} \Rightarrow 24r^2 = k - 4\pi r^2$$

$$\Rightarrow \quad 24r^2 + 4\pi r^2 = k \Rightarrow r^2[24 + 4\pi] = k$$

$$\therefore \quad r = 0 \text{ or } r = \sqrt{\frac{k}{24 + 4\pi}} = \frac{1}{2}\sqrt{\frac{k}{6 + \pi}}$$

We know that, $r \neq 0$

$$\therefore \quad r = \frac{1}{2}\sqrt{\frac{k}{6 + \pi}}$$

Again, differentiating w.r.t. r in Eq. (ii), we get

$$\frac{d^2S}{dr^2} = \frac{d}{dr}\left[-2\pi r\left\{\left(\frac{k - 4\pi r^2}{6}\right)^{1/2} + 4\pi r^2\right\}\right]$$

$$= -2\pi\left[r\cdot\frac{1}{2}\left(\frac{k-4\pi r^2}{6}\right)^{-1/2}\cdot\left(\frac{-8\pi r}{6}\right)+\left(\frac{k-4\pi r^2}{6}\right)^{1/2}\cdot 1\right]+4\pi\cdot 2r$$

$$= -2\pi\left[r\cdot\frac{1}{2\sqrt{\frac{k-4\pi r^2}{6}}}\cdot\left(\frac{-8\pi r}{6}\right)+\sqrt{\frac{k-4\pi r^2}{6}}\right]+8\pi r$$

$$= -2\pi\left[\frac{-8\pi r^2+12\left(k-\frac{4\pi r^2}{6}\right)}{12\sqrt{\frac{k-4\pi r^2}{6}}}\right]+8\pi r$$

$$= -2\pi\left[\frac{-48\pi r^2+72k-48\pi r^2}{72\sqrt{\frac{k-4\pi r^2}{6}}}\right]+8\pi r = -2\pi\left[\frac{-96\pi r^2+72k}{72\sqrt{\frac{k-4\pi r^2}{6}}}\right]+8\pi r>0$$

For $r=\frac{1}{2}\sqrt{\frac{k}{6+\pi}}$, then the sum of their volume is minimum.

For $r=\frac{1}{2}\sqrt{\frac{k}{6+\pi}}$,
$$x=\left[\frac{k-4\pi\cdot\frac{1}{4}\frac{k}{(6+\pi)}}{6}\right]^{1/2}$$
$$=\left[\frac{(6+\pi)k-\pi k}{6(6+\pi)}\right]^{1/2}=\left[\frac{k}{6+\pi}\right]^{1/2}=2r$$

Since, the sum of their volume is minimum when $x=2r$.
Hence, the ratio of an edge of cube to the diameter of the sphere is 1:1.

Q. 32 If *AB* is a diameter of a circle and *C* is any point on the circle, then show that the area of ΔABC is maximum, when it is isosceles.

Sol. We have, $AB=2r$

and $\angle ACB=90^\circ$ [since, angle in the semi-circle is always 90°]

Let $AC=x$ and $BC=y$

$\therefore$ $(2r)^2=x^2+y^2$

$\Rightarrow$ $y^2=4r^2-x^2$

$\Rightarrow$ $y=\sqrt{4r^2-x^2}$ ... (i)

Now, area of ΔABC, $A=\frac{1}{2}\times x\times y$

$=\frac{1}{2}\times x\times(4r^2-x^2)^{1/2}$ [using Eq. (i)]

Now, differentiating both sides w.r.t. x, we get

$$\frac{dA}{dx}=\frac{1}{2}\left[x\cdot\frac{1}{2}(4r^2-x^2)^{-1/2}\cdot(0-2x)+(4r^2-x^2)^{1/2}\cdot 1\right]$$

$$=\frac{1}{2}\left[\frac{-2x^2}{2\sqrt{4r^2-x^2}}+(4r^2-x^2)^{1/2}\right]$$

$$= \frac{1}{2}\left[\frac{-x^2}{\sqrt{4r^2 - x^2}} + \sqrt{4r^2 - x^2}\right]$$

$$= \frac{1}{2}\left[\frac{-x^2 + 4r^2 - x^2}{\sqrt{4r^2 - x^2}}\right] = \frac{1}{2}\left[\frac{-2x^2 + 4r^2}{\sqrt{4r^2 - x^2}}\right]$$

$\Rightarrow \quad \dfrac{dA}{dx} = \left[\dfrac{(-x^2 + 2r^2)}{\sqrt{4r^2 - x^2}}\right]$

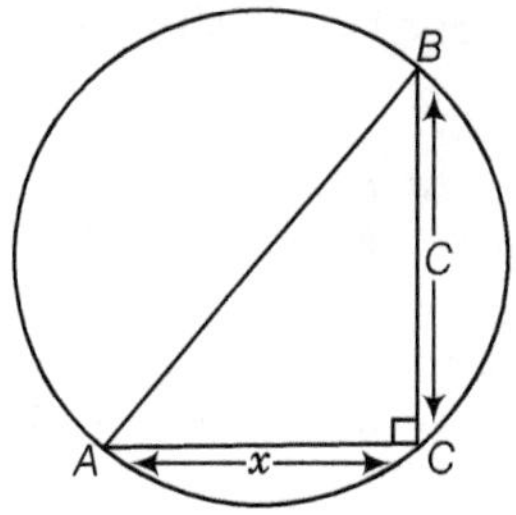

Now, $\quad \dfrac{dA}{dx} = 0$

$\Rightarrow \quad -x^2 + 2r^2 = 0$

$\Rightarrow \quad r^2 = \dfrac{1}{2}x^2$

$\Rightarrow \quad r = \dfrac{1}{\sqrt{2}}x$

$\therefore \quad x = r\sqrt{2}$

Again, differentiating both sides w.r.t. x, we get

$$\frac{d^2A}{dx^2} = \frac{\sqrt{4r^2 - x^2}\cdot(-2x) + (2r^2 - x^2)\cdot\frac{1}{2}(4r^2 - x^2)^{-1/2}(-2x)}{(\sqrt{4r^2 - x^2})^2}$$

$$= \frac{-2x\left[\sqrt{4r^2 - x^2} + (2r^2 - x^2)\cdot\dfrac{1}{2\sqrt{4r^2 - x^2}}\right]}{(\sqrt{4r^2 - x^2})^2}$$

$$= \frac{-4x\cdot\left(\sqrt{4r^2 - x^2}\right)^2 + (2r^2 - x^2)(-2x)}{2\cdot(4r^2 - x^2)^{3/2}}$$

$$= \frac{-4x(4r^2 - x^2) + (2r^2 - x^2)\cdot(-2x)}{2\cdot(4r^2 - x^2)^{3/2}}$$

$$= \frac{-16xr^2 + 4x^3 + (2r^2 - x^2)(-2x)}{2\cdot(4r^2 - x^2)^{3/2}}$$

$$\left(\frac{d^2A}{dx^2}\right)_{x = r\sqrt{2}} = \frac{-16\cdot r\sqrt{2}\cdot r^2 + 4\cdot(r\sqrt{2})^3 + [2r^2 - (r\sqrt{2})^2]\cdot(-2\cdot r\sqrt{2})}{2\cdot(4r^2 - 2r^2)^{3/2}} \quad [\because x = r\sqrt{2}]$$

$$= \frac{-16\sqrt{2}\cdot r^3 + 8\sqrt{2}r^3}{2(2r^2)^{3/2}} = \frac{8\sqrt{2}\,r^2\,[r - 2r]}{4r^3}$$

$$= \frac{-8\sqrt{2}\,r^3}{4r^3} = -2\sqrt{2} < 0$$

For $x = r\sqrt{2}$, the area of triangle is maximum.

For $x = r\sqrt{2}$, $\quad y = \sqrt{4r^2 - (r\sqrt{2})^2} = \sqrt{2r^2} = r\sqrt{2}$

Since, $\quad x = r\sqrt{2} = y$

Hence, the triangle is isosceles.

Q. 33 A metal box with a square base and vertical sides is to contain $1024\ cm^3$. If the material for the top and bottom costs ₹ 5per cm^2 and the material for the sides costs ₹ 2.50 per cm^2. Then, find the least cost of the box.

Sol. Since, volume of the box = $1024\ cm^3$

Let length of the side of square base be x cm and height of the box be y cm.

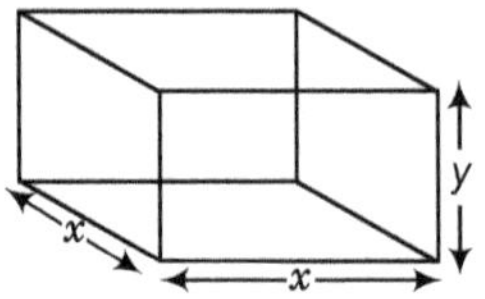

$\therefore$ Volume of the box $(V) = x^2 \cdot y = 1024$

Since, $x^2 y = 1024 \Rightarrow y = \dfrac{1024}{x^2}$

Let C denotes the cost of the box.

$$\therefore \quad C = 2x^2 \times 5 + 4xy \times 2.50$$
$$= 10x^2 + 10xy = 10x(x + y)$$
$$= 10x\left(x + \frac{1024}{x^2}\right)$$
$$= \frac{10x}{x^2}(x^3 + 1024)$$
$$\Rightarrow \quad C = 10x^2 + \frac{10240}{x} \quad \ldots \text{(i)}$$

On differentiating both sides w.r.t. x, we get

$$\frac{dC}{dx} = 20x + 10240(-x)^{-2}$$
$$= 20x - \frac{10240}{x^2} \quad \ldots \text{(ii)}$$

Now, $\dfrac{dC}{dx} = 0$

$$\Rightarrow \quad 20x = \frac{10240}{x^2}$$
$$\Rightarrow \quad 20x^3 = 10240$$
$$\Rightarrow \quad x^3 = 512 = 8^3 \Rightarrow x = 8$$

Again, differentiating Eq. (ii) w.r.t. x, we get

$$\frac{d^2C}{dx^2} = 20 - 10240(-2) \cdot \frac{1}{x^3}$$
$$= 20 + \frac{20480}{x^3} > 0$$
$$\therefore \quad \left(\frac{d^2C}{dx^2}\right)_{x=8} = 20 + \frac{20480}{512} = 60 > 0$$

For $x = 8$, cost is minimum and the corresponding least cost of the box,

$$C(8) = 10 \cdot 8^2 + \frac{10240}{8}$$
$$= 640 + 1280 = 1920$$
$$\therefore \quad \text{Least cost} = ₹\ 1920$$

Q. 34 The sum of surface areas of a rectangular parallelopiped with sides x, $2x$ and $\frac{x}{3}$ and a sphere is given to be constant. Prove that the sum of their volumes is minimum, if x is equal to three times the radius of the sphere. Also, find the minimum value of the sum of their volumes.

Sol. We have given that, the sum of the surface areas of a rectangular parallelopiped with sides x, $2x$ and $\frac{x}{3}$ and a sphere is constant.

Let S be the sum of both the surface area.

$$\therefore \quad S = 2\left(x \cdot 2x + 2x \cdot \frac{x}{3} + \frac{x}{3} \cdot x\right) + 4\pi r^2 = k$$

$$k = 2\left[2x^2 + \frac{2x^2}{3} + \frac{x^2}{3}\right] + 4\pi r^2$$

$$= 2\,[3x^2] + 4\pi r^2 = 6x^2 + 4\pi r^2$$

$$\Rightarrow \quad 4\pi r^2 = k - 6x^2$$

$$\Rightarrow \quad r^2 = \frac{k - 6x^2}{4\pi}$$

$$\Rightarrow \quad r = \sqrt{\frac{k - 6x^2}{4\pi}} \quad \text{... (i)}$$

Let V denotes the volume of both the parallelopiped and the sphere.

Then,
$$V = 2x \cdot x \cdot \frac{x}{3} + \frac{4}{3}\pi r^3 = \frac{2}{3}x^3 + \frac{4}{3}\pi r^3$$

$$= \frac{2}{3}x^3 + \frac{4}{3}\pi\left(\frac{k - 6x^2}{4\pi}\right)^{3/2}$$

$$= \frac{2}{3}x^3 + \frac{4}{3}\pi \cdot \frac{1}{8\pi^{3/2}}(k - 6x^2)^{3/2}$$

$$= \frac{2}{3}x^3 + \frac{1}{6\sqrt{\pi}}(k - 6x^2)^{3/2} \quad \text{...(ii)}$$

On differentiating both sides w.r.t. x, we get

$$\frac{dV}{dx} = \frac{2}{3} \cdot 3x^2 + \frac{1}{6\sqrt{\pi}} \cdot \frac{3}{2}(k - 6x^2)^{1/2} \cdot (-12x)$$

$$= 2x^2 - \frac{12x}{4\sqrt{\pi}}\sqrt{k - 6x^2}$$

$$= 2x^2 - \frac{3x}{\sqrt{\pi}}(k - 6x^2)^{1/2} \quad \text{...(iii)}$$

$$\because \quad \frac{dV}{dx} = 0$$

$$\Rightarrow \quad 2x^2 = \frac{3x}{\sqrt{\pi}}(k - 6x^2)^{1/2}$$

$$\Rightarrow \quad 4x^4 = \frac{9x^2}{\pi}(k - 6x^2)$$

$$\Rightarrow \quad 4\pi x^4 = 9kx^2 - 54x^4$$

$$\Rightarrow \quad 4\pi x^4 + 54x^4 = 9kx^2$$

$$\Rightarrow \quad x^4\,[4\pi + 54] = 9 \cdot k \cdot x^2$$

$$\Rightarrow \quad x^2 = \frac{9k}{4\pi + 54}$$

$$\Rightarrow \quad x = 3 \cdot \sqrt{\frac{k}{4\pi + 54}} \quad \text{...(iv)}$$

Again, differentiating Eq. (iii) w.r.t. x, we get

$$\frac{d^2V}{dx^2} = 4x - \frac{3}{\sqrt{\pi}}\left[x \cdot \frac{1}{2}(k - 6x^2)^{-1/2} \cdot (-12x) + (k - 6x^2)^{1/2} \cdot 1\right]$$

$$= 4x - \frac{3}{\sqrt{\pi}}[-6x^2 \cdot (k - 6x^2)^{-1/2} + (k - 6x^2)^{1/2}]$$

$$= 4x - \frac{3}{\sqrt{\pi}}\left[\frac{-6x^2 + k - 6x^2}{\sqrt{k - 6x^2}}\right]$$

$$= 4x - \frac{3}{\sqrt{\pi}}\left[\frac{k - 12x^2}{\sqrt{k - 6x^2}}\right]$$

Now,
$$\left(\frac{d^2V}{dx^2}\right)_{x = 3\cdot\sqrt{\frac{k}{4\pi + 54}}} = 4 \cdot 3\sqrt{\frac{k}{4\pi + 54}} - \frac{3}{\sqrt{\pi}}\left[\frac{k - 12 \cdot 9 \cdot \frac{k}{4\pi + 54}}{\sqrt{k - \frac{6 \cdot 9 \cdot k}{4\pi + 54}}}\right]$$

$$= 12\sqrt{\frac{k}{4\pi + 54}} - \frac{3}{\sqrt{\pi}}\left[\frac{k - \frac{108k}{4\pi + 54}}{\sqrt{k - \frac{54k}{4\pi + 54}}}\right]$$

$$= 12\sqrt{\frac{k}{4\pi + 54}} - \frac{3}{\sqrt{\pi}}\left[\frac{4k\pi + 54k - 108k/4\pi + 54}{\sqrt{4k\pi + 54k - 54k/4\pi + 54}}\right]$$

$$= 12\sqrt{\frac{k}{4\pi + 54}} - \frac{3}{\sqrt{\pi}}\left[\frac{4k\pi - 54k}{\sqrt{4k\pi}\sqrt{4\pi + 54}}\right]$$

$$= 12\sqrt{\frac{k}{4\pi + 54}} - \frac{6}{\sqrt{\pi}}\left[\frac{k(2\pi - 27)}{\sqrt{k}\sqrt{16\pi^2 + 216\pi}}\right]$$

$$\left[\text{since, } (2\pi - 27) < 0 \Rightarrow \frac{d^2V}{dx^2} > 0; k > 0\right]$$

For $x = 3\sqrt{\frac{k}{4\pi + 54}}$, the sum of volumes is minimum.

For $x = 3\sqrt{\frac{k}{4\pi + 54}}$, then $r = \sqrt{\frac{k - 6x^2}{4\pi}}$ [using Eq. (i)]

$$= \frac{1}{2\sqrt{\pi}}\sqrt{k - 6 \cdot \frac{9k}{4\pi + 54}}$$

$$= \frac{1}{2\sqrt{\pi}} \cdot \sqrt{\frac{4k\pi + 54k - 54k}{4\pi + 54}}$$

$$= \frac{1}{2\sqrt{\pi}}\sqrt{\frac{4k\pi}{4\pi + 54}} = \frac{\sqrt{k}}{\sqrt{4\pi + 54}} = \frac{1}{3}x$$

$\Rightarrow$ $x = 3r$ **Hence proved.**

$\therefore$ Minimum sum of volume,

$$V_{\left(x = 3\cdot\sqrt{\frac{k}{4\pi + 54}}\right)} = \frac{2}{3}x^3 + \frac{4}{3}\pi r^3 = \frac{2}{3}x^3 + \frac{4}{3}\pi \cdot \left(\frac{1}{3}x\right)^3$$

$$= \frac{2}{3}x^3 + \frac{4}{3}\pi \cdot \frac{x^3}{27} = \frac{2}{3}x^3\left(1 + \frac{2\pi}{27}\right)$$

Objective Type Questions

Q. 35 If the sides of an equilateral triangle are increasing at the rate of 2 cm/s then the rate at which the area increases, when side is 10 cm, is

(a) $10 \text{ cm}^2/\text{s}$ (b) $\sqrt{3} \text{ cm}^2/\text{s}$

(c) $10\sqrt{3} \text{ cm}^2/\text{s}$ (d) $\frac{10}{3} \text{ cm}^2/\text{s}$

Sol. *(c)* Let the side of an equilateral triangle be x cm.

$\therefore$ Area of equilateral triangle, $A = \frac{\sqrt{3}}{4}x^2$ ...(i)

Also, $\frac{dx}{dt} = 2\text{cm/s}$

On differentiating Eq. (i) w.r.t. t, we get

$$\frac{dA}{dt} = \frac{\sqrt{3}}{4} \cdot 2x \cdot \frac{dx}{dt}$$

$$= \frac{\sqrt{3}}{4} \cdot 2 \cdot 10 \cdot 2 \quad \left[\because x = 10 \text{ and } \frac{dx}{dt} = 2\right]$$

$$= 10\sqrt{3} \text{ cm}^2/\text{s}$$

Q. 36 A ladder, 5 m long, standing on a horizontal floor, leans against a vertical wall. If the top of the ladder slides downwards at the rate of 10 cm/s, then the rate at which the angle between the floor and the ladder is decreasing when lower end of ladder is 2 m from the wall is

(a) $\frac{1}{10}$ rad/s (b) $\frac{1}{20}$ rad/s

(c) 20 rad/s (d) 10 rad/s

Sol. *(b)* Let the angle between floor and the ladder be θ.

Let $AB = x$ cm and $BC = y$ cm

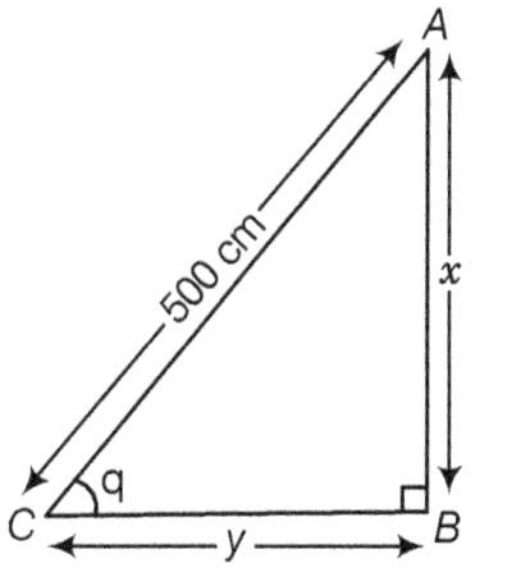

$\therefore$ $\sin\theta = \frac{x}{500}$ and $\cos\theta = \frac{y}{500}$

$\Rightarrow$ $x = 500\sin\theta$ and $y = 500\cos\theta$

Also, $\frac{dx}{dt} = 10$ cm/s

$\Rightarrow$ $500 \cdot \cos\theta \cdot \frac{d\theta}{dt} = 10$ cm/s

$\Rightarrow$ $\frac{d\theta}{dt} = \frac{10}{500\cos\theta} = \frac{1}{50\cos\theta}$

For $y = 2$ m $= 200$ cm,

$$\frac{d\theta}{dt} = \frac{1}{50 \cdot \frac{y}{500}} = \frac{10}{y}$$

$$= \frac{10}{200} = \frac{1}{20} \text{ rad/s}$$

Q. 37 The curve $y = x^{1/5}$ has at (0, 0)

(a) a vertical tangent (parallel to Y-axis)
(b) a horizontal tangent (parallel to X-axis)
(c) an oblique tangent
(d) no tangent

Sol. *(a)* We have,

$$y = x^{1/5}$$

$$\Rightarrow \quad \frac{dy}{dx} = \frac{1}{5}x^{\frac{1}{5}-1} = \frac{1}{5}x^{-4/5}$$

$$\therefore \quad \left(\frac{dy}{dx}\right)_{(0,0)} = \frac{1}{5} \times (0)^{-4/5} = \infty$$

So, the curve $y = x^{1/5}$ has a vertical tangent at (0, 0), which is parallel to Y-axis.

Q. 38 The equation of normal to the curve $3x^2 - y^2 = 8$ which is parallel to the line $x + 3y = 8$ is

(a) $3x - y = 8$
(b) $3x + y + 8 = 0$
(c) $x + 3y \pm 8 = 0$
(d) $x + 3y = 0$

Sol. *(c)* We have, the equation of the curve is $3x^2 - y^2 = 8$ ...(i)

Also, the given equation of the line is $x + 3y = 8$.

$$\Rightarrow \quad 3y = 8 - x$$

$$\Rightarrow \quad y = -\frac{x}{3} + \frac{8}{3}$$

Thus, slope of the line is $-\frac{1}{3}$ which should be equal to slope of the equation of normal to the curve.

On differentiating Eq. (i) w.r.t. x, we get

$$6x - 2y\frac{dy}{dx} = 0$$

$$\Rightarrow \quad \frac{dy}{dx} = \frac{6x}{2y} = \frac{3x}{y} = \text{Slope of the curve}$$

Now, slope of normal to the curve $= -\dfrac{1}{\left(\dfrac{dy}{dx}\right)}$

$$= -\frac{1}{\left(\frac{3x}{y}\right)} = -\frac{y}{3x}$$

$$\therefore \quad -\left(\frac{y}{3x}\right) = -\frac{1}{3}$$

$$\Rightarrow \quad -3y = -3x$$

$$\Rightarrow \quad y = x$$

On substituting the value of the given equation of the curve, we get

$$3x^2 - x^2 = 8$$

$$\Rightarrow \quad x^2 = \frac{8}{2}$$

$$\Rightarrow \quad x = \pm 2$$

For $x = 2$, $3(2)^2 - y^2 = 8$

$\Rightarrow$ $y^2 = 4$

$\Rightarrow$ $y = \pm 2$

and for $x = -2$, $3(-2)^2 - y^2 = 8$

$\Rightarrow$ $y = \pm 2$

So, the points at which normals are parallel to the given line are $(\pm 2, \pm 2)$.

Hence, the equation of normal at $(\pm 2, \pm 2)$ is

$$y - (\pm 2) = -\frac{1}{3}[x - (\pm 2)]$$

$$\Rightarrow \quad 3[y - (\pm 2)] = -[x - (\pm 2)]$$

$$\Rightarrow \quad x + 3y \pm 8 = 0$$

Q. 39 If the curve $ay + x^2 = 7$ and $x^3 = y$, cut orthogonally at (1, 1), then the value of a is

(a) 1 (b) 0 (c) -6 (d) 6

Sol. *(d)* We have, $ay + x^2 = 7$ and $x^3 = y$

On differentiating w.r.t. x in both equations, we get

$$a \cdot \frac{dy}{dx} + 2x = 0 \quad \text{and } 3x^2 = \frac{dy}{dx}$$

$$\Rightarrow \quad \frac{dy}{dx} = -\frac{2x}{a} \text{ and } \frac{dy}{dx} = 3x^2$$

$$\Rightarrow \quad \left(\frac{dy}{dx}\right)_{(1,1)} = \frac{-2}{a} = m_1$$

and $$\left(\frac{dy}{dx}\right)_{(1,1)} = 3 \cdot 1 = 3 = m_2$$

Since, the curves cut orthogonally at (1, 1).

$$\therefore \quad m_1 \cdot m_2 = -1$$

$$\Rightarrow \quad \left(\frac{-2}{a}\right) \cdot 3 = -1$$

$$\therefore \quad a = 6$$

Q. 40 If $y = x^4 - 10$ and x changes from 2 to 1.99, then what is the change in y?

(a) 0.32 (b) 0.032 (c) 5.68 (d) 5.968

Sol. *(a)* We have, $y = x^4 - 10 \Rightarrow \frac{dy}{dx} = 4x^3$

and $$\Delta x = 2.00 - 1.99 = 0.01$$

$$\therefore \quad \Delta y = \frac{dy}{dx} \times \Delta x$$

$$= 4x^3 \times \Delta x$$

$$= 4 \times 2^3 \times 0.01$$

$$= 32 \times 0.01 = 0.32$$

So, the approximate change in y is 0.32.

Q. 41 The equation of tangent to the curve $y(1+x^2)=2-x$, where it crosses X-axis, is

(a) $x+5y=2$ (b) $x-5y=2$

(c) $5x-y=2$ (d) $5x+y=2$

Sol. *(a)* We have, equation of the curve $y(1+x^2)=2-x$ ...(i)

$\therefore \quad y\cdot(0+2x)+(1+x^2)\cdot\frac{dy}{dx}=0-1$ [on differentiating w.r.t. x]

$\Rightarrow \quad 2xy+(1+x^2)\frac{dy}{dx}=-1$

$\Rightarrow \quad \frac{dy}{dx}=\frac{-1-2xy}{1+x^2}$ ...(ii)

Since, the given curve passes through X-axis *i.e.*, $y=0$.

$\therefore \quad 0\,(1+x^2)=2-x$ [using Eq. (i)]

$\Rightarrow \quad x=2$

So, the curve passes through the point (2, 0).

$\therefore \quad \left(\frac{dy}{dx}\right)_{(2,\,0)}=\frac{-1-2\times 0}{1+2^2}=-\frac{1}{5}=$ Slope of the curve

$\therefore$ Slope of tangent to the curve $=-\frac{1}{5}$

$\therefore$ Equation of tangent of the curve passing through (2, 0) is

$$y-0=-\frac{1}{5}(x-2)$$

$\Rightarrow \quad y+\frac{x}{5}=+\frac{2}{5}$

$\Rightarrow \quad 5y+x=2$

Q. 42 The points at which the tangents to the curve $y=x^3-12x+18$ are parallel to X-axis are

(a) $(2,-2),(-2,-34)$ (b) $(2,34),(-2,0)$

(c) $(0,34),(-2,0)$ (d) $(2,2),(-2,34)$

Sol. *(d)* The given equation of curve is

$$y=x^3-12x+18$$

$\therefore \quad \frac{dy}{dx}=3x^2-12$ [on differentiating w.r.t. x]

So, the slope of line parallel to the X-axis.

$\therefore \quad \left(\frac{dy}{dx}\right)=0$

$\Rightarrow \quad 3x^2-12=0$

$\Rightarrow \quad x^2=\frac{12}{3}=4$

$\therefore \quad x=\pm 2$

For $x=2$, $\quad y=2^3-12\times 2+18=2$

and for $x=-2$, $y=(-2)^3-12(-2)+18=34$

So, the points are (2, 2) and (– 2, 34).

Q. 43 The tangent to the curve $y = e^{2x}$ at the point (0, 1) meets X-axis at

(a) (0, 1) (b) $\left(-\frac{1}{2}, 0\right)$ (c) (2, 0) (d) (0, 2)

Sol. *(b)* The equation of curve is $y = e^{2x}$

Since, it passes through the point (0, 1).

$$\therefore \quad \frac{dy}{dx} = e^{2x} \cdot 2 = 2 \cdot e^{2x}$$

$$\Rightarrow \quad \left(\frac{dy}{dx}\right)_{(0,\,1)} = 2 \cdot e^{2 \cdot 0} = 2 = \text{Slope of tangent to the curve}$$

$\therefore$ Equation of tangent is $y - 1 = 2(x - 0)$

$$\Rightarrow \quad y = 2x + 1$$

Since, tangent to curve $y = e^{2x}$ at the point (0, 1) meets X-axis *i.e.*, $y = 0$.

$$\therefore \quad 0 = 2x + 1 \Rightarrow x = -\frac{1}{2}$$

So, the required point is $\left(\frac{-1}{2}, 0\right)$.

Q. 44 The slope of tangent to the curve $x = t^2 + 3t - 8$ and $y = 2t^2 - 2t - 5$ at the point (2, – 1) is

(a) $\frac{22}{7}$ (b) $\frac{6}{7}$ (c) $-\frac{6}{7}$ (d) -6

Sol. *(b)* Equation of curve is given by

$$x = t^2 + 3t - 8 \quad \text{and} \quad y = 2t^2 - 2t - 5.$$

$$\therefore \quad \frac{dx}{dt} = 2t + 3 \quad \text{and} \quad \frac{dy}{dt} = 4t - 2$$

$$\Rightarrow \quad \frac{dy}{dx} = \frac{\frac{dy}{dt}}{\frac{dx}{dt}} = \frac{4t - 2}{2t + 3} \quad \text{...(i)}$$

Since, the curve passes through the point (2, – 1).

$$\therefore \quad 2 = t^2 + 3t - 8$$

$$\text{and} \quad -1 = 2t^2 - 2t - 5$$

$$\Rightarrow \quad t^2 + 3t - 10 = 0$$

$$\text{and} \quad 2t^2 - 2t - 4 = 0$$

$$\Rightarrow \quad t^2 + 5t - 2t - 10 = 0$$

$$\text{and} \quad 2t^2 + 2t - 4t - 4 = 0$$

$$\Rightarrow \quad t(t + 5) - 2(t + 5) = 0$$

$$\text{and} \quad 2t(t + 1) - 4(t + 1) = 0$$

$$\Rightarrow \quad (t - 2)(t + 5) = 0$$

$$\text{and} \quad (2t - 4)(t + 1) = 0$$

$$\Rightarrow \quad t = 2, -5 \text{ and } t = -1, 2$$

$$\Rightarrow \quad t = 2$$

$\therefore$ Slope of tangent,

$$\left(\frac{dy}{dx}\right)_{\text{at } t = 2} = \frac{4 \times 2 - 2}{2 \times 2 + 3} = \frac{6}{7} \quad \text{[using Eq. (i)]}$$

Q. 45 Two curves $x^3 - 3xy^2 + 2 = 0$ and $3x^2y - y^3 - 2 = 0$ intersect at an angle of

(a) $\frac{\pi}{4}$ (b) $\frac{\pi}{3}$ (c) $\frac{\pi}{2}$ (d) $\frac{\pi}{6}$

Sol. *(c)* Equation of two curves are given by

$$x^3 - 3xy^2 + 2 = 0$$

and $$3x^2y - y^3 - 2 = 0$$ [on differentiating w.r.t. x]

$\Rightarrow$ $$3x^2 - 3\left[x \cdot 2y\frac{dy}{dx} + y^2 \cdot 1\right] + 0 = 0$$

and $$3\left[x^2\frac{dy}{dx} + y \cdot 2x\right] - 3y^2\frac{dy}{dx} - 0 = 0$$

$\Rightarrow$ $$3x \cdot 2y\frac{dy}{dx} + 3y^2 = 3x^2$$

and $$3y^2\frac{dy}{dx} = 3x^2\frac{dy}{dx} + 6xy$$

$\Rightarrow$ $$\frac{dy}{dx} = \frac{3x^2 - 3y^2}{6xy}$$

and $$\frac{dy}{dx} = \frac{6xy}{3y^2 - 3x^2}$$

$\Rightarrow$ $$\left(\frac{dy}{dx}\right) = \frac{3(x^2 - y^2)}{6xy}$$

and $$\left(\frac{dy}{dx}\right) = \frac{-6xy}{3(x^2 - y^2)}$$

$\Rightarrow$ $$m_1 = \frac{(x^2 - y^2)}{2xy}$$

and $$m_2 = \frac{-2xy}{x^2 - y^2}$$

$\therefore$ $$m_1m_2 = \frac{x^2 - y^2}{2xy} \cdot \frac{-(2xy)}{x^2 - y^2} = -1$$

Hence, both the curves are intersecting at right angle *i.e.*, making $\frac{\pi}{2}$ with each other.

Q. 46 The interval on which the function $f(x) = 2x^3 + 9x^2 + 12x - 1$ is decreasing is

(a) $[-1, \infty)$ (b) $[-2, -1]$ (c) $(-\infty, -2]$ (d) $[-1, 1]$

Sol. *(b)* We have, $$f(x) = 2x^3 + 9x^2 + 12x - 1$$

$\therefore$ $$f'(x) = 6x^2 + 18x + 12$$
$$= 6(x^2 + 3x + 2) = 6(x + 2)(x + 1)$$

So, $f'(x) \le 0$, for decreasing.

On drawing number lines as below

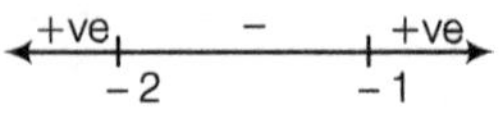

We see that $f'(x)$ is decreasing in $[-2, -1]$.

Q. 47 If $f : R \to R$ be defined by $f(x) = 2x + \cos x$, then f

(a) has a minimum at $x = \pi$ (b) has a maximum at $x = 0$

(c) is a decreasing function (d) is an increasing function

Sol. *(d)* We have, $f(x) = 2x + \cos x$

$\therefore$ $f'(x) = 2 + (-\sin x) = 2 - \sin x$

Since, $f'(x) > 0, \forall x$

Hence, $f(x)$ is an increasing function.

Q. 48 If $y = x(x-3)^2$ decreases for the values of x given by

(a) $1 < x < 3$ (b) $x < 0$ (c) $x > 0$ (d) $0 < x < \frac{3}{2}$

Sol. *(a)* We have, $y = x(x-3)^2$

$\therefore$ $\frac{dy}{dx} = x \cdot 2(x-3) \cdot 1 + (x-3)^2 \cdot 1$

$= 2x^2 - 6x + x^2 + 9 - 6x = 3x^2 - 12x + 9$

$= 3(x^2 - 3x - x + 3) = 3(x-3)(x-1)$

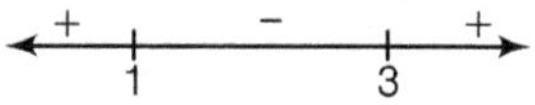

So, $y = x(x-3)^2$ decreases for (1, 3).

[since, $y' < 0$ for all $x \in (1, 3)$, hence y is decreasing on (1, 3)]

Q. 49 The function $f(x) = 4\sin^3 x - 6\sin^2 x + 12\sin x + 100$ is strictly

(a) increasing in $\left(\pi, \frac{3\pi}{2}\right)$ (b) decreasing in $\left(\frac{\pi}{2}, \pi\right)$

(c) decreasing in $\left[\frac{-\pi}{2}, \frac{\pi}{2}\right]$ (d) decreasing in $\left[0, \frac{\pi}{2}\right]$

Sol. *(b)* We have, $f(x) = 4\sin^3 x - 6\sin^2 x + 12\sin x + 100$

$\therefore$ $f'(x) = 12\sin^2 x \cdot \cos x - 12\sin x \cdot \cos x + 12\cos x$

$= 12[\sin^2 x \cdot \cos x - \sin x \cdot \cos x + \cos x]$

$= 12\cos x[\sin^2 x - \sin x + 1]$

$\Rightarrow$ $f'(x) = 12\cos x[\sin^2 x + (1 - \sin x)]$ ...(i)

$\because$ $1 - \sin x \ge 0$ and $\sin^2 x \ge 0$

$\therefore$ $\sin^2 x + 1 - \sin x \ge 0$

Hence, $f'(x) > 0$, when $\cos x > 0$ *i.e.*, $x \in \left(-\frac{\pi}{2}, \frac{\pi}{2}\right)$.

So, $f(x)$ is increasing when $x \in \left(-\frac{\pi}{2}, \frac{\pi}{2}\right)$ and $f'(x) < 0$, when $\cos x < 0$ *i.e.*, $x \in \left(\frac{\pi}{2}, \frac{3\pi}{2}\right)$

Hence, $f(x)$ is decreasing when $x \in \left(\frac{\pi}{2}, \frac{3\pi}{2}\right)$

Since, $\left(\frac{\pi}{2}, \pi\right) \in \left(\frac{\pi}{2}, \frac{3\pi}{2}\right)$

Hence, $f(x)$ is decreasing in $\left(\frac{\pi}{2}, \pi\right)$.

Q. 50 Which of the following functions is decreasing on $\left(0, \frac{\pi}{2}\right)$?

(a) $\sin 2x$ (b) $\tan x$ (c) $\cos x$ (d) $\cos 3x$

Sol. *(c)* In the interval $\left(0, \frac{\pi}{2}\right)$, $f(x) = \cos x$

$\Rightarrow$ $f'(x) = -\sin x$

which gives $f'(x) < 0$ in $\left(0, \frac{\pi}{2}\right)$

Hence, $f(x) = \cos x$ is decreasing in $\left(0, \frac{\pi}{2}\right)$.

Q. 51 The function $f(x) = \tan x - x$

(a) always increases
(b) always decreases
(c) never increases
(d) sometimes increases and sometimes decreases

Sol. *(a)* We have, $f(x) = \tan x - x$

$\therefore$ $f'(x) = \sec^2 x - 1$

$\Rightarrow$ $f'(x) > 0, \forall x \in R$

So, $f(x)$ always increases.

Q. 52 If x is real, then the minimum value of $x^2 - 8x + 17$ is

(a) -1 (b) 0 (c) 1 (d) 2

Sol. *(c)* Let $f(x) = x^2 - 8x + 17$

$\therefore$ $f'(x) = 2x - 8$

So, $f'(x) = 0$, gives $x = 4$

Now, $f''(x) = 2 > 0, \forall x$

So, $x = 4$ is the point of local minima.

$\therefore$ Minimum value of $f(x)$ at $x = 4$,

$$f(4) = 4 \times 4 - 8 \times 4 + 17 = 1$$

Q. 53 The smallest value of polynomial $x^3 - 18x^2 + 96x$ in $[0, 9]$ is

(a) 126 (b) 0 (c) 135 (d) 160

Sol. *(b)* We have, $f(x) = x^3 - 18x^2 + 96x$

$\therefore$ $f'(x) = 3x^2 - 36x + 96$

So, $f'(x) = 0$

Gives, $3x^2 - 36x + 96 = 0$

$\Rightarrow$ $3(x^2 - 12x + 32) = 0$

$\Rightarrow$ $(x - 8)(x - 4) = 0$

$\Rightarrow$ $x = 8, 4 \in [0, 9]$

We shall now evaluate the value of f at these points and at the end points of the interval $[0, 9]$ *i.e.*, at $x = 4$ and $x = 8$ and at $x = 0$ and at $x = 9$.

$$\therefore \quad f(4) = 4^3 - 18 \cdot 4^2 + 96 \cdot 4$$
$$= 64 - 288 + 384 = 160$$
$$f(8) = 8^3 - 18 \cdot 8^2 + 96 \cdot 8 = 128$$
$$f(9) = 9^3 - 18 \cdot 9^2 + 96 \cdot 9$$
$$= 729 - 1458 + 864 = 135$$

and
$$f(0) = 0^3 - 18 \cdot 0^2 + 96 \cdot 0 = 0$$

Thus, we conclude that absolute minimum value of f on $[0, 9]$ is 0 occurring at $x = 0$.

Q. 54 The function $f(x) = 2x^3 - 3x^2 - 12x + 4$, has

(a) two points of local maximum
(b) two points of local minimum
(c) one maxima and one minima
(d) no maxima or minima

Sol. *(c)* We have
$$f(x) = 2x^3 - 3x^2 - 12x + 4$$
$$\therefore \quad f'(x) = 6x^2 - 6x - 12$$

Now,
$$f'(x) = 0 \Rightarrow 6(x^2 - x - 2) = 0$$
$$\Rightarrow \quad 6(x + 1)(x - 2) = 0$$
$$\Rightarrow \quad x = -1 \text{ and } x = +2$$

On number line for $f'(x)$, we get

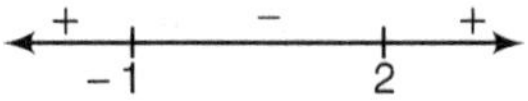

Hence $x = -1$ is point of local maxima and $x = 2$ is point of local minima.
So, $f(x)$ has one maxima and one minima.

Q. 55 The maximum value of $\sin x \cdot \cos x$ is

(a) $\frac{1}{4}$ (b) $\frac{1}{2}$ (c) $\sqrt{2}$ (d) $2\sqrt{2}$

Sol. *(b)* We have,
$$f(x) = \sin x \cdot \cos x = \frac{1}{2}\sin 2x$$
$$\therefore \quad f'(x) = \frac{1}{2} \cdot \cos 2x \cdot 2 = \cos 2x$$

Now,
$$f'(x) = 0 \Rightarrow \cos 2x = 0$$
$$\Rightarrow \quad \cos 2x = \cos\frac{\pi}{2} \Rightarrow x = \frac{\pi}{4}$$

Also
$$f''(x) = \frac{d}{dx}\cos 2x = -\sin 2x \cdot 2 = -2\sin 2x$$
$$\therefore \quad [f''(x)]_{\text{at } x = \pi/4} = -2 \cdot \sin 2 \cdot \frac{\pi}{4} = -2\sin\frac{\pi}{2} = -2 < 0$$

At $\frac{\pi}{4}$, $f(x)$ is maximum and $\frac{\pi}{4}$ is point of maxima.

$$\therefore \quad f\left(\frac{\pi}{4}\right) = \frac{1}{2} \cdot \sin 2 \cdot \frac{\pi}{4} = \frac{1}{2}$$

Q. 56 At $x = \frac{5\pi}{6}$, $f(x) = 2\sin 3x + 3\cos 3x$ is

(a) maximum (b) minimum
(c) zero (d) neither maximum nor minimum

Sol. *(d)* We have, $f(x) = 2\sin 3x + 3\cos 3x$

$\therefore$ $f'(x) = 2\cdot\cos 3x \cdot 3 + 3(-\sin 3x)\cdot 3$

$\Rightarrow$ $f'(x) = 6\cos 3x - 9\sin 3x$ ...(i)

Now, $f''(x) = -18\sin 3x - 27\cos 3x$

$= -9(2\sin 3x + 3\cos 3x)$

$\therefore$ $f'\left(\frac{5\pi}{6}\right) = 6\cos\left(3\cdot\frac{5\pi}{6}\right) - 9\sin\left(3\cdot\frac{5\pi}{6}\right)$

$= 6\cos\frac{5\pi}{2} - 9\sin\frac{5\pi}{2}$

$= 6\cos\left(2\pi + \frac{\pi}{2}\right) - 9\sin\left(2\pi + \frac{\pi}{2}\right)$

$= 0 - 9 \neq 0$

So, $x = \frac{5\pi}{6}$ cannot be point of maxima or minima.

Hence, $f(x)$ at $x = \frac{5\pi}{6}$ is neither maximum nor minimum.

Q. 57 The maximum slope of curve $y = -x^3 + 3x^2 + 9x - 27$ is

(a) 0 (b) 12 (c) 16 (d) 32

Sol. *(b)* We have, $y = -x^3 + 3x^2 + 9x - 27$

$\therefore$ $\frac{dy}{dx} = -3x^2 + 6x + 9 =$ Slope of the curve

and $\frac{d^2y}{dx^2} = -6x + 6 = -6(x-1)$

$\therefore$ $\frac{d^2y}{dx^2} = 0$

$\Rightarrow$ $-6(x-1) = 0 \Rightarrow x = 1 > 0$

Now, $\frac{d^3y}{dx^3} = -6 < 0$

So, the maximum slope of given curve is at $x = 1$.

$\therefore$ $\left(\frac{dy}{dx}\right)_{(x=1)} = -3\cdot 1^2 + 6\cdot 1 + 9 = 12$

Q. 58 The functin $f(x) = x^x$ has a stationary point at

(a) $x = e$ (b) $x = \frac{1}{e}$ (c) $x = 1$ (d) $x = \sqrt{e}$

Sol. *(b)* We have, $f(x) = x^x$

Let $y = x^x$

and $\log y = x\log x$

$\therefore$ $\frac{1}{y}\cdot\frac{dy}{dx} = x\cdot\frac{1}{x} + \log x \cdot 1$

$$\Rightarrow \quad \frac{dy}{dx} = (1+\log x)\cdot x^x$$

$$\therefore \quad \frac{dy}{dx} = 0$$

$$\Rightarrow \quad (1+\log x)\cdot x^x = 0$$

$$\Rightarrow \quad \log x = -1$$

$$\Rightarrow \quad \log x = \log e^{-1}$$

$$\Rightarrow \quad x = e^{-1}$$

$$\Rightarrow \quad x = \frac{1}{e}$$

Hence, $f(x)$ has a stationary point at $x = \frac{1}{e}$.

Q. 59 The maximum value of $\left(\frac{1}{x}\right)^x$ is

(a) e (b) e^e (c) $e^{1/e}$ (d) $\left(\frac{1}{e}\right)^{1/e}$

Sol. *(c)* Let
$$y = \left(\frac{1}{x}\right)^x$$

$$\Rightarrow \quad \log y = x\cdot\log\frac{1}{x}$$

$$\therefore \quad \frac{1}{y}\cdot\frac{dy}{dx} = x\cdot\frac{1}{\frac{1}{x}}\cdot\left(-\frac{1}{x^2}\right) + \log\frac{1}{x}\cdot 1$$

$$= -1 + \log\frac{1}{x}$$

$$\therefore \quad \frac{dy}{dx} = \left(\log\frac{1}{x} - 1\right)\cdot\left(\frac{1}{x}\right)^x$$

Now,
$$\frac{dy}{dx} = 0$$

$$\Rightarrow \quad \log\frac{1}{x} = 1 = \log e$$

$$\Rightarrow \quad \frac{1}{x} = e$$

$$\therefore \quad x = \frac{1}{e}$$

Hence, the maximum value of $f\left(\frac{1}{e}\right) = (e)^{1/e}$.

Fillers

Q. 60 The curves $y = 4x^2 + 2x - 8$ and $y = x^3 - x + 13$ touch each other at the point ....

Sol. The curves $y = 4x^2 + 2x - 8$ and $y = x^3 - x + 13$ touch each other at the point (3, 34).

Given, equation of curves are $y = 4x^2 + 2x - 8$ and $y = x^3 - x + 13$

$$\therefore \quad \frac{dy}{dx} = 8x + 2$$

and $$\frac{dy}{dx} = 3x^2 - 1$$

So, the slope of both curves should be same

$$\therefore \quad 8x + 2 = 3x^2 - 1$$

$$\Rightarrow \quad 3x^2 - 8x - 3 = 0$$

$$\Rightarrow \quad 3x^2 - 9x + x - 3 = 0$$

$$\Rightarrow \quad 3x(x - 3) + 1(x - 3) = 0$$

$$\Rightarrow \quad (3x + 1)(x - 3) = 0$$

$$\therefore \quad x = -\frac{1}{3} \text{ and } x = 3,$$

For $x = -\frac{1}{3}$,

$$y = 4\cdot\left(-\frac{1}{3}\right)^2 + 2\cdot\left(\frac{-1}{3}\right) - 8$$

$$= \frac{4}{9} - \frac{2}{3} - 8 = \frac{4 - 6 - 72}{9}$$

$$= -\frac{74}{9}$$

and for $x = 3$, $y = 4\cdot(3)^2 + 2\cdot(3) - 8$

$$= 36 + 6 - 8 = 34$$

So, the required points are (3, 34) and $\left(-\frac{1}{3}, \frac{-74}{9}\right)$.

Q. 61 The equation of normal to the curve $y = \tan x$ at (0, 0) is ....

Sol. The equation of normal to the curve $y = \tan x$ at (0, 0) is $x + y = 0$.

$$\because \quad y = \tan x \Rightarrow \frac{dy}{dx} = \sec^2 x$$

$$\Rightarrow \quad \left(\frac{dy}{dx}\right)_{(0,0)} = \sec^2 0 = 1 \text{ and } -\frac{1}{\left(\frac{dy}{dx}\right)} = -\frac{1}{1}$$

$\therefore$ Equation of normal to the curve $y = \tan x$ at (0, 0) is

$$y - 0 = -1(x - 0)$$

$$\Rightarrow \quad y + x = 0$$

Q. 62 The values of a for which the function $f(x) = \sin x - ax + b$ increases on R are ....

Sol. The values of a for which the function $f(x) = \sin x - ax + b$ increases on R are $(-\infty, -1)$.

$\because$ $$f'(x) = \cos x - a$$

and $$f'(x) > 0 \Rightarrow \cos x > a$$

Since, $$\cos x \in [-1, 1]$$

$\Rightarrow$ $$a < -1 \Rightarrow a \in (-\infty, -1)$$

Q. 63 The function $f(x) = \dfrac{2x^2 - 1}{x^4}$, (where, $x > 0$) decreases in the interval ....

Sol. The function $f(x) = \dfrac{2x^2 - 1}{x^4}$, where $x > 0$, decreases in the interval $(1, \infty)$.

$\because$ $$f'(x) = \frac{x^4 \cdot 4x - (2x^2 - 1) \cdot 4x^3}{x^8} = \frac{4x^5 - 8x^5 + 4x^3}{x^8}$$

$$= \frac{-4x^5 + 4x^3}{x^8} = \frac{4x^3(-x^2 + 1)}{x^8}$$

Also, $$f'(x) < 0$$

$\Rightarrow$ $$\frac{4x^3(1 - x^2)}{x^8} < 0 \Rightarrow x^2 > 1$$

$\Rightarrow$ $$x > \pm 1$$

$\therefore$ $$x \in (1, \infty)$$

Q. 64 The least value of function $f(x) = ax + \dfrac{b}{x}$ (where, $a > 0$, $b > 0$, $x > 0$) is ....

Sol. The least value of function $f(x) = ax + \dfrac{b}{x}$ (where, $a > 0, b > 0, x > 0$) is $2\sqrt{ab}$.

$\because$ $$f'(x) = a - \frac{b}{x^2} \text{ and } f'(x) = 0$$

$\Rightarrow$ $$a = \frac{b}{x^2}$$

$\Rightarrow$ $$x^2 = \frac{b}{a} \Rightarrow x = \pm\sqrt{\frac{b}{a}}$$

Now, $$f''(x) = -b \cdot \frac{(-2)}{x^3} = +\frac{2b}{x^3}$$

At $x = \sqrt{\dfrac{b}{a}}$, $$f''(x) = +\frac{2b}{\left(\dfrac{b}{a}\right)^{3/2}} = \frac{+2b \cdot a^{3/2}}{b^{3/2}}$$

$$= +2b^{-1/2} \cdot a^{3/2} = +2\sqrt{\frac{a^3}{b}} > 0 \qquad [\because a, b > 0]$$

$\therefore$ Least value of $f(x)$, $$f\left(\sqrt{\frac{b}{a}}\right) = a \cdot \sqrt{\frac{b}{a}} + \frac{b}{\sqrt{\dfrac{b}{a}}}$$

$$= a \cdot a^{-1/2} \cdot b^{1/2} + b \cdot b^{-1/2} \cdot a^{1/2}$$

$$= \sqrt{ab} + \sqrt{ab} = 2\sqrt{ab}$$

7

Integrals

Short Answer Type Questions

Verify the following

Q. 1 $\int \frac{2x-1}{2x+3}dx = x - \log|(2x+3)^2| + C$

Sol. Let
$$I = \int \frac{2x-1}{2x+3}dx = \int \frac{2x+3-3-1}{2x+3}dx$$
$$= \int 1dx - 4\int \frac{1}{2x+3}dx = x - \int \frac{4}{2\left(x+\frac{3}{2}\right)}dx$$
$$= x - 2\log + \left|\left(x+\frac{3}{2}\right)\right| C' = x - 2\log\left|\left(\frac{2x+3}{2}\right)\right| + C'$$
$$= x - 2\log|(2x+3)| + 2\log 2 + C' \qquad \left[\because \log\frac{m}{n} = \log m - \log n\right]$$
$$= x - \log|(2x+3)^2| + C \qquad [\because C = 2\log 2 + C']$$

Q. 2 $\int \frac{2x+3}{x^2+3x}dx = \log|x^2+3x| + C$

Sol. Let
$$I = \int \frac{2x+3}{x^2+3x}dx$$

Put $x^2 + 3x = t$

$\Rightarrow$ $(2x+3)\,dx = dt$

$\therefore$
$$I = \int \frac{1}{t}\,dt = \log|t| + C$$
$$= \log|(x^2+3x)| + C$$

Q. 3 $\int \frac{(x^2+2)d}{x+1} x$

Thinking Process

First of all divided numerator by denominator, then use the formula $\int \frac{1}{x} dx = \log |x|$ *to get the solution.*

Sol. Let

$$I = \int \frac{x^2+2}{x+1} dx$$
$$= \int \left(x - 1 + \frac{3}{x+1} \right) dx$$
$$= \int (x-1)\, dx + 3\int \frac{1}{x+1} dx$$
$$= \frac{x^2}{2} - x + 3\log|(x+1)| + C$$

Q. 4 $\int \frac{e^{6\log x} - e^{5\log x}}{e^{4\log x} - e^{3\log x}} dx$

Sol. Let

$$I = \int \left(\frac{e^{6\log x} - e^{5\log x}}{e^{4\log x} - e^{3\log x}} \right) dx$$
$$= \int \left(\frac{e^{\log x^6} - e^{\log x^5}}{e^{\log x^4} - e^{\log x^3}} \right) dx \qquad [\because a\log b = \log b^a]$$
$$= \int \left(\frac{x^6 - x^5}{x^4 - x^3} \right) dx \qquad [\because e^{\log x} = x]$$
$$= \int \left(\frac{x^3 - x^2}{x-1} \right) dx = \int \frac{x^2(x-1)}{x-1} dx$$
$$= \int x^2 dx = \frac{x^3}{3} + C$$

Q. 5 $\int \frac{(1+\cos x)}{x+\sin x} dx$

Sol. Consider that,

$$I = \int \frac{(1+\cos x)}{(x+\sin x)} dx$$

Let $x + \sin x = t \Rightarrow (1+\cos x) dx = dt$

$\therefore$

$$I = \int \frac{1}{t} dt = \log|t| + C$$
$$= \log|(x+\sin x)| + C$$

Q. 6 $\int \frac{dx}{1+\cos x}$

Thinking Process

$\cos x = 2\cos^2\frac{x}{2} - 1$ and also use formula i.e., $\int \sec^2 x = \tan x + C$ to solve the above problem.

Sol. Let
$$I = \int \frac{dx}{1+\cos x} = \int \frac{dx}{1 + 2\cos^2\frac{x}{2} - 1}$$
$$= \frac{1}{2}\int \frac{1}{\cos^2\frac{x}{2}}\,dx = \frac{1}{2}\int \sec^2\frac{x}{2}dx$$
$$= \frac{1}{2}\cdot\tan\frac{x}{2}\cdot 2 + C = \tan\frac{x}{2} + C \qquad \left[\because \int \sec^2 x\,dx = \tan x\right]$$

Q. 7 $\int \tan^2 x \sec^4 x\,dx$

Thinking Process

Use the formula $\sec^2 x = 1 + \tan^2 x$ and put $\tan x = t$ to solve this problem.

Sol. Let $\quad I = \int \tan^2 x \sec^4 x\,dx$

Put $\quad \tan x = t \Rightarrow \sec^2 x dx = dt$

$\therefore$
$$I = \int t^2(1+t^2)dt = \int (t^2 + t^4)dt$$
$$= \frac{t^3}{3} + \frac{t^5}{5} + C = \frac{\tan^5 x}{5} + \frac{\tan^3 x}{3} + C$$

Q. 8 $\int \frac{\sin x + \cos x}{\sqrt{1+\sin 2x}}dx$

Sol. Let $\quad I = \int \frac{\sin x + \cos x}{\sqrt{1+\sin 2x}}dx = \int \frac{(\sin x + \cos x)}{\sqrt{\sin^2 x + \cos^2 x + 2\sin x\cos x}}dx$
$$= \int \frac{\sin x + \cos x}{\sqrt{(\sin x + \cos x)^2}}dx = \int 1\,dx = x + C$$

Q. 9 $\int \sqrt{1+\sin x}\,dx$

Sol. Let
$$I = \int \sqrt{1+\sin x}\,dx$$
$$= \int \sqrt{\sin^2\frac{x}{2} + \cos^2\frac{x}{2} + 2\sin\frac{x}{2}\cos\frac{x}{2}}\,dx \qquad \left[\because \sin^2\frac{x}{2} + \cos^2\frac{x}{2} = 1\right]$$
$$= \int \sqrt{\left(\sin\frac{x}{2} + \cos\frac{x}{2}\right)^2}dx = \int\left(\sin\frac{x}{2} + \cos\frac{x}{2}\right)dx$$
$$= -\cos\frac{x}{2}\cdot 2 + \sin\frac{x}{2}\cdot 2 + C = -2\cos\frac{x}{2} + 2\sin\frac{x}{2} + C$$

Q. 10 $\int \frac{x}{\sqrt{x}+1}dx$

Sol. Let $$I = \int \frac{x}{\sqrt{x}+1}dx$$

Put $$\sqrt{x} = t \Rightarrow \frac{1}{2\sqrt{x}}dx = dt$$

$\Rightarrow$ $$dx = 2\sqrt{x}\,dt$$

$\therefore$ $$I = 2\int\left(\frac{x\sqrt{x}}{t+1}\right)dt = 2\int\frac{t^2\cdot t}{t+1}dt = 2\int\frac{t^3}{t+1}dt$$

$$= 2\int\frac{t^3+1-1}{t+1}dt = 2\int\frac{(t+1)(t^2-t+1)}{t+1}dt - 2\int\frac{1}{t+1}dt$$

$$= 2\int(t^2-t+1)\,dt - 2\int\frac{1}{t+1}dt$$

$$= 2\left[\frac{t^3}{3} - \frac{t^2}{2} + t - \log|(t+1)|\right] + C$$

$$= 2\left[\frac{x\sqrt{x}}{3} - \frac{x}{2} + \sqrt{x} - \log|(\sqrt{x}+1)|\right] + C$$

Q. 11 $\int\sqrt{\frac{a+x}{a-x}}\,dx$

Thinking Process

Here, put $x = a\cos 2\theta$ and also use the formula i.e., $\cos 2\theta = 2\cos^2\theta - 1 = 1 - 2\sin^2\theta$, to get the solution.

Sol. Let $$I = \int\sqrt{\frac{a+x}{a-x}}\,dx$$

Put $$x = a\cos 2\theta$$

$\Rightarrow$ $$dx = -a\cdot\sin 2\theta\cdot 2\cdot d\theta$$

$\therefore$ $$I = -2\int\sqrt{\frac{a+a\cos 2\theta}{a-a\cos 2\theta}}\cdot a\sin 2\theta\, d\theta$$

$$\left[\because \cos 2\theta = \frac{x}{a} \Rightarrow 2\theta = \cos^{-1}\frac{x}{a} \Rightarrow \theta = \frac{1}{2}\cos^{-1}\frac{x}{a}\right]$$

$$= -2a\int\sqrt{\frac{1+\cos 2\theta}{1-\cos 2\theta}}\sin 2\theta\, d\theta = -2a\int\sqrt{\frac{2\cos^2\theta}{2\sin^2\theta}}\sin 2\theta\, d\theta$$

$$= -2a\int\cot\theta\cdot\sin 2\theta\, d\theta = -2a\int\frac{\cos\theta}{\sin\theta}\cdot 2\sin\theta\cdot\cos\theta\, d\theta$$

$$= -4a\int\cos^2\theta\, d\theta = -2a\int(1+\cos 2\theta)\,d\theta$$

$$= -2a\left[\theta + \frac{\sin 2\theta}{2}\right] + C$$

$$= -2a\left[\frac{1}{2}\cos^{-1}\frac{x}{a} + \frac{1}{2}\sqrt{1-\frac{x^2}{a^2}}\right] + C$$

$$= -a\left[\cos^{-1}\left(\frac{x}{a}\right) + \sqrt{1-\frac{x^2}{a^2}}\right] + C$$

Alternate Method

Let $$I=\int\sqrt{\frac{a+x}{a-x}}\,dx=\int\sqrt{\frac{(a+x)(a+x)}{(a-x)(a+x)}}\,dx$$

$$=\int\frac{(a+x)}{\sqrt{a^2-x^2}}dx$$

$$I=\int\frac{a}{\sqrt{a^2-x^2}}+\int\frac{x}{\sqrt{a^2-x^2}}dx$$

$\therefore$ $$I=I_1+I_2 \quad \ldots(i)$$

Now, $$I_1=\int\frac{a}{\sqrt{a^2-x^2}}=a\sin^{-1}\left(\frac{x}{a}\right)+C_1$$

and $$I_2=\int\frac{x}{\sqrt{a^2-x^2}}dx$$

Put $$a^2-x^2=t^2 \Rightarrow -2x\,dx=2t\,dt$$

$\therefore$ $$I_2=-\int\frac{t}{t}dte=-\int 1dt$$

$$=-t+C_2=-\sqrt{a^2-x^2}+C_2$$

$\therefore$ $$I=a\sin^{-1}\left(\frac{x}{a}\right)+C_1-\sqrt{a^2-x^2}+C_2 \quad [\because t^2=a^2-x^2]$$

$$I=a\sin^{-1}\left(\frac{x}{a}\right)-\sqrt{a^2-x^2}+C \quad [\because C=C_1+C_2]$$

Q. 12 $\int\frac{x^{1/2}}{1+x^{3/4}}dx$

Sol. Let $$I=\int\frac{x^{1/2}}{1+x^{3/4}}dx$$

Put $$x=t^4 \Rightarrow dx=4t^3dt$$

$\therefore$ $$I=4\int\frac{t^2(t^3)}{1+t^3}dt=4\int\left(t^2-\frac{t^2}{1+t^3}\right)dt$$

$$I=4\int t^2dt-4\int\frac{t^2}{1+t^3}dt$$

$$I=I_1-I_2$$

$$I_1=4\int t^2dt=4\cdot\frac{t^3}{3}+C_1=\frac{4}{3}x^{3/4}+C_1$$

Now, $$I_2=4\int\frac{t^2}{1+t^3}dt$$

Again, put $$1+t^3=z \Rightarrow 3t^2dt=dz$$

$\Rightarrow$ $$t^2dt=\frac{1}{3}dz=\frac{4}{3}\int\frac{1}{z}dz$$

$$=\frac{4}{3}\log|z|+C_2=\frac{4}{3}\log|(1+t^3)|+C_2$$

$$=\frac{4}{3}\log|(1+x^{3/4})|+C_2$$

$\therefore$ $$I=\frac{4}{3}x^{3/4}+C_1-\frac{4}{3}\log|(1+x^{3/4})|-C_2$$

$$=\frac{4}{3}x^{3/4}-\log|(1+x^{3/4})+C \quad [\because C=C_1-C_2]$$

Q. 13 $\int \frac{\sqrt{1+x^2}}{x^4} dx$

Sol. Let
$$I = \int \frac{\sqrt{1+x^2}}{x^4} dx = \int \frac{\sqrt{1+x^2}}{x} \cdot \frac{1}{x^3} dx$$
$$= \int \sqrt{\frac{1+x^2}{x^2}} \cdot \frac{1}{x^3} dx = \int \sqrt{\frac{1}{x^2}+1} \cdot \frac{1}{x^3} dx$$

Put $1+\frac{1}{x^2} = t^2 \Rightarrow \frac{-2}{x^3} dx = 2t\,dt$

$\Rightarrow$ $-\frac{1}{x^3} = t\,dt$

$\therefore$
$$I = -\int t^2 dt = -\frac{t^3}{3} + C = -\frac{1}{3}\left(1+\frac{1}{x^2}\right)^{3/2} + C$$

Q. 14 $\int \frac{dx}{\sqrt{16-9x^2}}$

Thinking Process

First of all concert the expression in form of $\frac{1}{\sqrt{a^2-x^2}}$, *then use the formula,*
$$\int \frac{1}{\sqrt{a^2-x^2}} dx = \sin^{-1}\left(\frac{x}{a}\right) + C.$$

Sol. Let $I = \int \frac{dx}{\sqrt{16-9x^2}} = \int \frac{dx}{\sqrt{(4)^2-(3x)^2}} dx = \frac{1}{3}\sin^{-1}\left(\frac{3x}{4}\right) + C$

Q. 15 $\int \frac{dt}{\sqrt{3t-2t^2}}$

Sol. Let
$$I = \int \frac{dt}{\sqrt{3t-2t^2}} = \frac{1}{\sqrt{2}} \int \frac{dt}{\sqrt{-\left(t^2-\frac{3}{2}t\right)}}$$
$$= \frac{1}{\sqrt{2}} \int \frac{dt}{\sqrt{-\left[\left(t^2-2\cdot\frac{1}{2}\cdot\frac{3}{2}t\right)+\left(\frac{3}{4}\right)^2-\left(\frac{3}{4}\right)^2\right]}}$$
$$= \frac{1}{\sqrt{2}} \int \frac{dt}{\sqrt{-\left[\left(t-\frac{3}{4}\right)^2-\left(\frac{3}{4}\right)^2\right]}}$$
$$= \frac{1}{\sqrt{2}} \int \frac{dt}{\sqrt{\left(\frac{3}{4}\right)^2-\left(t-\frac{3}{4}\right)^2}}$$
$$= \frac{1}{\sqrt{2}}\sin^{-1}\left(\frac{t-\frac{3}{4}}{\frac{3}{4}}\right) + C = \frac{1}{\sqrt{2}}\sin^{-1}\left(\frac{4t-3}{3}\right) + C$$

Q. 16 $\int \frac{3x-1}{\sqrt{x^2+9}}dx$

Thinking Process

First of all convert to the given integral into two parts, then by using formula i.e., $\int \frac{1}{\sqrt{a^2+x^2}} = \log|x+\sqrt{a^2+x^2}|+C$ *get the desired result.*

Sol. Let $$I = \int \frac{3x-1}{\sqrt{x^2+9}}dx$$

$$I = \int \frac{3x}{\sqrt{x^2+9}}dx - \int \frac{1}{\sqrt{x^2+9}}dx$$

$$I = I_1 - I_2$$

Now, $$I_1 = \int \frac{3x}{\sqrt{x^2+9}}$$

Put $$x^2+9=t^2 \Rightarrow 2xdx = 2t\,dt \Rightarrow xdx = tdt$$

$\therefore$ $$I_1 = 3\int \frac{t}{t}dt$$

$$= 3\int dt = 3t + C_1 = 3\sqrt{x^2+9} + C_1$$

and $$I_2 = \int \frac{1}{\sqrt{x^2+9}}dx = \int \frac{1}{\sqrt{x^2+(3)^2}}dx$$

$$= \log|x+\sqrt{x^2+9}| + C_2$$

$\therefore$ $$I = 3\sqrt{x^2+9} + C_1 - \log|x+\sqrt{x^2+9}| - C_2$$

$$= 3\sqrt{x^2+9} - \log|x+\sqrt{x^2+9}| + C \qquad [\because C = C_1 - C_2]$$

Q. 17 $\int \sqrt{5-2x+x^2}dx$

Thinking Process

First of all convert the given expression into $\sqrt{x^2+a^2}$ *form, then use the formula i.e.,* $\int \sqrt{x^2+a^2}dx = \frac{1}{2}x\sqrt{x^2+a^2} + \frac{a^2}{2}\log|x+\sqrt{x^2+a^2}|+C.$

Sol. Let $$I = \int \sqrt{5-2x+x^2}dx = \int \sqrt{x^2-2x+1+4}\,dx$$

$$= \int \sqrt{(x-1)^2+(2)^2}dx = \int \sqrt{(2)^2+(x-1)^2}dx$$

$$= \frac{x-1}{2}\sqrt{2^2+(x-1)^2} + 2\log|x-1+\sqrt{2^2+(x-1)^2}| + C$$

$$= \frac{x-1}{2}\sqrt{5-2x+x^2} + 2\log|x-1+\sqrt{5-2x+x^2}| + C$$

Q. 18 $\int \frac{x}{x^4 - 1} dx$

Sol. Let $I = \int \frac{x}{x^4 - 1} dx$

Put $x^2 = t \Rightarrow 2x dx = dt \Rightarrow x dx = \frac{1}{2} dt$

$\therefore$ $I = \frac{1}{2} \int \frac{dt}{t^2 - 1} = \frac{1}{2} \cdot \frac{1}{2} \log \left| \frac{t-1}{t+1} \right| + C$ $\left[\because \int \frac{dx}{x^2 - a^2} = \frac{1}{2a} \log \left| \frac{x-a}{x+a} \right| + C \right]$

$= \frac{1}{4} [\log |x^2 - 1| - \log |x^2 + 1|] + C$

Q. 19 $\int \frac{x^2}{1 - x^4} dx$

Thinking Process

Here, use $\int \frac{1}{1+x^2} dx = \tan^{-1} x + C$ *and* $\int \frac{1}{a^2 - x^2} dx = \frac{1}{2a} \log \left| \frac{1+x}{1-x} \right| + C$, *to solve this problem.*

Sol. Let $I = \int \frac{x^2}{1 - x^4} dx$

$= \int \frac{\left(\frac{1}{2} + \frac{x^2}{2} - \frac{1}{2} + \frac{x^2}{2} \right)}{(1 - x^2)(1 + x^2)} dx$ $[\because a^2 - b^2 = (a+b)(a-b)]$

$= \int \frac{\frac{1}{2}(1 + x^2) - \frac{1}{2}(1 - x^2)}{(1 - x^2)(1 + x^2)} dx$

$= \int \frac{\frac{1}{2}(1 + x^2)}{(1 - x^2)(1 + x^2)} dx - \frac{1}{2} \int \frac{(1 - x^2)}{(1 - x^2)(1 + x^2)} dx$

$= \frac{1}{2} \int \frac{1}{1 - x^2} dx - \frac{1}{2} \int \frac{1}{1 + x^2} dx = \frac{1}{2} \cdot \frac{1}{2} \log \left| \frac{1+x}{1-x} \right| + C_1 - \frac{1}{2} \tan^{-1} x + C_2$

$= \frac{1}{4} \log \left| \frac{1+x}{1-x} \right| - \frac{1}{2} \tan^{-1} x + C$ $[\because C = C_1 + C_2]$

Q. 20 $\int \sqrt{2ax - x^2} dx$

Sol. Let $I = \int \sqrt{2ax - x^2} dx = \int \sqrt{-(x^2 - 2ax)} dx$

$= \int \sqrt{-(x^2 - 2ax + a^2 - a^2)} dx = \int \sqrt{-(x - a)^2 - a^2} dx$

$= \int \sqrt{a^2 - (x - a)^2} dx$

$= \frac{x - a}{2} \sqrt{a^2 - (x - a)^2} + \frac{a^2}{2} \sin^{-1} \left(\frac{x - a}{a} \right) + C$

$= \frac{x - a}{2} \sqrt{2ax - x^2} + \frac{a^2}{2} \sin^{-1} \left(\frac{x - a}{a} \right) + C$

Q. 21 $\int \frac{\sin^{-1} x}{(1-x^2)^{3/4}} dx$

Sol. Let $I = \int \frac{\sin^{-1} x}{(1-x^2)^{3/4}} dx = \int \frac{\sin^{-1} x}{(1-x^2)\sqrt{1-x^2}} dx$

Put $\sin^{-1} x = t \Rightarrow \frac{1}{\sqrt{1-x^2}} dx = dt$

and $x = \sin t \Rightarrow 1 - x^2 = \cos^2 t$

$\Rightarrow$ $\cos t = \sqrt{1-x^2}$

$\therefore$

$$I = \int \frac{t}{\cos^2 t} dt = \int t \cdot \sec^2 t dt$$

$$= t \cdot \int \sec^2 t dt - \int \left(\frac{d}{dt} t \cdot \int \sec^2 t \, dt \right) dt$$

$$= t \cdot \tan t - \int 1 \cdot \tan t \, dt$$

$$= t \tan t + \log|\cos t| + C \quad \left[\because \int \tan x dx = -\log|\cos x| + C\right]$$

$$= \sin^{-1} x \cdot \frac{x}{\sqrt{1-x^2}} + \log|\sqrt{1-x^2}| + C$$

Q. 22 $\int \frac{(\cos 5x + \cos 4x)}{1 - 2\cos 3x} dx$

Sol. Let $I = \int \frac{\cos 5x + \cos 4x}{1 - 2\cos 3x} dx = \int \frac{2\cos \frac{9x}{2} \cdot \cos \frac{x}{2}}{1 - 2\left(2\cos^2 \frac{3x}{2} - 1\right)} dx$

$$\left[\because \cos C + \cos D = 2\cos \frac{C+D}{2} . \cos \frac{C-D}{2} \text{ and } \cos 2x = 2\cos^2 x - 1\right]$$

$\therefore$

$$I = \int \frac{2\cos \frac{9x}{2} \cdot \cos \frac{x}{2}}{3 - 4\cos^2 \frac{3x}{2}} dx = -\int \frac{2\cos \frac{9x}{2} \cdot \cos \frac{x}{2}}{4\cos^2 \frac{3x}{2} - 3} dx$$

$$= -\int \frac{2\cos \frac{9x}{2} \cdot \cos \frac{x}{2} \cdot \cos \frac{3x}{2}}{4\cos^3 \frac{3x}{2} - 3\cos \frac{3x}{2}} dx \quad \left[\text{multiply and divide by } \cos \frac{3x}{2}\right]$$

$$= -\int \frac{2\cos \frac{9x}{2} \cdot \cos \frac{x}{2} \cdot \cos \frac{3x}{2}}{\cos 3 \cdot \frac{3x}{2}} dx = -\int 2\cos \frac{3x}{2} \cdot \cos \frac{x}{2} dx$$

$$= -\int \left\{ \cos\left(\frac{3x}{2} + \frac{x}{2}\right) + \cos\left(\frac{3x}{2} - \frac{x}{2}\right) \right\} dx$$

$$= -\int (\cos 2x + \cos x) dx$$

$$= -\left[\frac{\sin 2x}{2} + \sin x\right] + C$$

$$= -\frac{1}{2}\sin 2x - \sin x + C$$

Q. 23 $\int \frac{\sin^6 x + \cos^6 x}{\sin^2 x \cos^2 x} dx$

Thinking Process

Use $a^3 + b^3 = (a+b)(a^2 - ab + b^2)$ and $\sec^2 x = 1 + \tan^2 x$, $\text{cosec}^2 x = 1 + \cot^2 x$, to solve the above problem.

Sol. Let

$$I = \int \frac{\sin^6 x + \cos^6 x}{\sin^2 x \cos^2 x} dx = \int \frac{(\sin^2 x)^3 + (\cos^2 x)^3}{\sin^2 x \cdot \cos^2 x} dx$$

$$= \int \frac{(\sin^2 x + \cos^2 x)(\sin^4 x - \sin^2 x \cos^2 x + \cos^4 x)}{\sin^2 x \cdot \cos^2 x} dx$$

$$= \int \frac{\sin^4 x}{\sin^2 x \cos^2 x} dx + \int \frac{\cos^4 x}{\sin^2 x \cdot \cos^2 x} dx - \int \frac{\sin^2 x \cos^2 x}{\sin^2 x \cdot \cos^2 x} dx$$

$$= \int \tan^2 x\, dx + \int \cot^2 x\, dx - \int 1 dx$$

$$= \int (\sec^2 x - 1)\, dx + \int (\text{cosec}^2 x - 1)\, dx - \int 1 dx$$

$$= \int \sec^2 x dx + \int \text{cosec}^2 x dx - 3\int dx$$

$$I = \tan x - \cot x - 3x + C$$

Q. 24 $\int \frac{\sqrt{x}}{\sqrt{a^3 - x^3}} dx$

Sol. Let

$$I = \int \frac{\sqrt{x}}{\sqrt{a^3 - x^3}} dx = \int \frac{\sqrt{x}}{\sqrt{(a^{3/2})^2 - (x^{3/2})^2}}$$

Put $x^{3/2} = t \Rightarrow \frac{3}{2} x^{1/2} dx = dt$

$\therefore$

$$I = \frac{2}{3} \int \frac{dt}{\sqrt{(a^{3/2})^2 - t^2}} = \frac{2}{3} \sin^{-1} \frac{t}{a^{3/2}} + C$$

$$= \frac{2}{3} \sin^{-1} \frac{x^{3/2}}{a^{3/2}} + C = \frac{2}{3} \sin^{-1} \sqrt{\frac{x^3}{a^3}} + C$$

Q. 25 $\int \frac{\cos x - \cos 2x}{1 - \cos x} dx$

Thinking Process

Apply the formula, $\cos C - \cos D = 2 \sin \frac{C+D}{2} \cdot \sin \frac{D-C}{2}$ and $\cos x = 1 - 2\sin^2 \frac{x}{2}$ to solve it.

Sol. Let

$$I = \int \frac{\cos x - \cos 2x}{1 - \cos x} dx = \int \frac{2 \sin \frac{3x}{2} \cdot \sin \frac{x}{2}}{1 - 1 + 2\sin^2 \frac{x}{2}} dx$$

$$= 2\int \frac{\sin \frac{3x}{2} \cdot \sin \frac{x}{2}}{2\sin^2 \frac{x}{2}} dx = \int \frac{\sin \frac{3x}{2}}{\sin \frac{x}{2}} dx$$

$$= \int \frac{3\sin\frac{x}{2} - 4\sin^3\frac{x}{2}}{\sin\frac{x}{2}} dx \qquad [\because \sin 3x = 3\sin x - 4\sin^3 x]$$

$$= 3\int dx - 4\int \sin^2\frac{x}{2} dx = 3\int dx - 4\int \frac{1-\cos x}{2} dx$$

$$= 3\int dx - 2\int dx + 2\int \cos x \, dx$$

$$= \int dx + 2\int \cos x \, dx = x + 2\sin x + C = 2\sin x + x + C$$

Q. 26 $\int \frac{dx}{x\sqrt{x^4 - 1}}$

Sol. Let $I = \int \frac{dx}{x\sqrt{x^4 - 1}}$

Put $x^2 = \sec\theta \Rightarrow \theta = \sec^{-1} x^2$

$\Rightarrow$ $2x\,dx = \sec\theta \cdot \tan\theta \, d\theta$

$\therefore$ $I = \frac{1}{2}\int \frac{\sec\theta \cdot \tan\theta}{\sec\theta \tan\theta} d\theta = \frac{1}{2}\int d\theta = \frac{1}{2}\theta + C$

$= \frac{1}{2}\sec^{-1}(x^2) + C$

Q. 27 $\int_0^2 (x^2 + 3)dx$

Thinking Process

$\int_a^b f(x)dx = \lim_{h\to 0} h[f(a) + f(a+h) + \ldots + f\{a + (n-1)h\}]$, where $h = \frac{b-a}{n} \to 0$ as $n \to \infty$.

Sol. Let $I = \int_0^2 (x^2 + 3)\,dx$

Here, $a = 0, b = 2$ and $h = \frac{b-a}{n} = \frac{2-0}{n}$

$\Rightarrow$ $h = \frac{2}{n} \Rightarrow nh = 2 \Rightarrow f(x) = (x^2 + 3)$

Now, $\int_0^2 (x^2 + 3)\,dx = \lim_{h\to 0} h\,[f(0) + f(0+h) + f(0+2h) + \ldots + f\{0 + (n-1)h\}]$ ...(i)

$\because$ $f(0) = 3$

$\Rightarrow$ $f(0+h) = h^2 + 3, f(0+2h) = 4h^2 + 3 = 2^2h^2 + 3$

$f[0 + (n-1)h] = (n^2 - 2n + 1)h + 3 = (n-1)^2h + 3$

From Eq. (i),

$\int_0^2 (x^2 + 3)dx = \lim_{h\to 0} h[3 + h^2 + 3 + 2^2h^2 + 3 + 3^2h^2 + 3 + \ldots + (n-1)^2h^2 + 3]$

$= \lim_{h\to 0} h[3n + h^2\{1^2 + 2^2 + \ldots + (n-1)^2\}]$

$= \lim_{h\to 0} h\left[3n + h^2\left(\frac{(n-1)(2n-2+1)(n-1+)}{6}\right)\right] \quad \left[\because \Sigma n^2 = \frac{n(n+1)(2n+1)}{6}\right]$

$= \lim_{h\to 0} h\left[3n + h^2\left(\frac{(n^2-n)(2n-1)}{6}\right)\right]$

$$= \lim_{h\to 0} h\left[3n + \frac{h^2}{6}(2n^3 - n^2 - 2n^2 + n)\right]$$

$$= \lim_{h\to 0}\left[3nh + \frac{2n^3h^3 - 3n^2h^2\cdot h + nh\cdot h^2}{6}\right]$$

$$= \lim_{h\to 0}\left[3\cdot 2 + \frac{2\cdot 8 - 3\cdot 2^2\cdot h + 2\cdot h^2}{6}\right] = \lim_{h\to 0}\left[6 + \frac{16 - 12h + 2h^2}{6}\right]$$

$$= 6 + \frac{16}{6} = 6 + \frac{8}{3} = \frac{26}{3}$$

Q. 28 $\int_0^2 e^x dx$

Sol. Let $$I = \int_0^2 e^x\, dx$$

Here, $a = 0$ and $b = 2$

$\therefore$ $$h = \frac{b-a}{n}$$

$\Rightarrow$ $nh = 2$ and $f(x) = e^x$

Now, $$\int_0^2 e^x dx = \lim_{h\to 0} h[f(0) + f(0+h) + f(0+2h) + \dots + f\{0 + (n-1)h\}]$$

$\therefore$ $$I = \lim_{h\to 0} h[1 + e^h + e^{2h} + \dots + e^{(n-1)h}]$$

$$= \lim_{h\to 0} h\left[\frac{1\cdot(e^h)^n - 1}{e^h - 1}\right] = \lim_{h\to 0} h\left(\frac{e^{nh} - 1}{e^h - 1}\right)$$

$$= \lim_{h\to 0} h\left(\frac{e^2 - 1}{e^h - 1}\right)$$

$$= e^2 \lim_{h\to 0}\frac{h}{e^h - 1} - \lim_{h\to 0}\frac{h}{e^h - 1} \qquad \left[\because \lim_{h\to 0}\frac{h}{e^h - 1} = 1\right]$$

$$= e^2 - 1 = e^2 - 1$$

Evaluate the following questions.

Q. 29 $\int_0^1 \frac{dx}{e^x + e^{-x}}$

Sol. Let $$I = \int_0^1 \frac{dx}{e^x + e^{-x}} = \int_0^1 \frac{e^x}{1 + e^{2x}} dx$$

Put $e^x = t$

$\Rightarrow$ $e^x\, dx = dt$

$\therefore$ $$I = \int_1^e \frac{dt}{1 + t^2} = [\tan^{-1} t]_1^e$$

$$= \tan^{-1} e - \tan^{-1} 1$$

$$= \tan^{-1} e - \frac{\pi}{4}$$

Q. 30 $\int_0^{\pi/2} \frac{\tan x}{1+m^2\tan^2 x}\,dx$

Sol. Let

$$I = \int_0^{\pi/2} \frac{\tan x\, dx}{1+m^2\tan^2 x}\,dx$$

$$= \int_0^{\pi/2} \frac{\frac{\sin x}{\cos x}}{1+m^2\cdot\frac{\sin^2 x}{\cos^2 x}}\,dx$$

$$= \int_0^{\pi/2} \frac{\frac{\sin x}{\cos x}}{\frac{\cos^2 x + m^2\sin^2 x}{\cos^2 x}}\,dx$$

$$= \int_0^{\pi/2} \frac{\sin x\cos x\, dx}{1-\sin^2 x + m^2\sin^2 x}\,dx$$

$$= \int_0^{\pi/2} \frac{\sin x\cos x}{1-\sin^2 x(1-m^2)}\,dx$$

Put $\sin^2 x = t$

$\Rightarrow$ $2\sin x\cos x\, dx = dt$

$\therefore$

$$I = \frac{1}{2}\int_0^1 \frac{dt}{1-t(1-m^2)}$$

$$= \frac{1}{2}\left[-\log|1-t(1-m^2)|\cdot\frac{1}{1-m^2}\right]_0^1$$

$$= \frac{1}{2}\left[-\log|1-1+m^2|\cdot\frac{1}{1+m^2} + \log|1|\cdot\frac{1}{1-m^2}\right]$$

$$= \frac{1}{2}\left[-\log|m^2|\cdot\frac{1}{1-m^2}\right] = \frac{2}{2}\cdot\frac{\log m}{(m^2-1)}$$

$$= \log\frac{m}{m^2-1}$$

Q. 31 $\int_1^2 \frac{dx}{\sqrt{(x-1)(2-x)}}$

Thinking Process

First of all convert the given function into $\frac{1}{\sqrt{a^2-x^2}}$ *form, then apply the formula i.e.,*

$$\int \frac{1}{\sqrt{a^2-x^2}}\,dx = \sin^{-1}\frac{x}{a} + C.$$

Sol. Let

$$I = \int_1^2 \frac{dx}{\sqrt{(x-1)(2-x)}} = \int_1^2 \frac{dx}{\sqrt{2x-x^2-2+x}}$$

$$= \int_1^2 \frac{dx}{\sqrt{-(x^2-3x+2)}}$$

$$= \int_1^2 \frac{dx}{\sqrt{-\left[x^2 - 2\cdot\frac{3}{2}x + \left(\frac{3}{2}\right)^2 + 2 - \frac{9}{4}\right]}}$$

$$= \int_1^2 \frac{dx}{\sqrt{-\left\{\left(x - \frac{3}{2}\right)^2 - \left(\frac{1}{2}\right)^2\right\}}}$$

$$= \int_1^2 \frac{dx}{\sqrt{\left(\frac{1}{2}\right)^2 - \left(x - \frac{3}{2}\right)^2}} = \left[\sin^{-1}\left(\frac{x - \frac{3}{2}}{\frac{1}{2}}\right)\right]_1^2$$

$$= [\sin^{-1}(2x - 3)]_1^2 = \sin^{-1}1 - \sin^{-1}(-1)$$

$$= \frac{\pi}{2} + \frac{\pi}{2} \qquad \left[\because \sin\frac{\pi}{2} = 1 \text{ and } \sin(-\theta) = -\sin\theta\right]$$

$$= \pi$$

Q. 32 $\int_0^1 \frac{x}{\sqrt{1 + x^2}}\, dx$

Sol. Let $I = \int_0^1 \frac{x}{\sqrt{1 + x^2}}\, dx$

Put $1 + x^2 = t^2$

$\Rightarrow$ $2x\, dx = 2t dt$

$\Rightarrow$ $x\, dx = t dt$

$\therefore$ $I = \int_1^{\sqrt{2}} \frac{t dt}{t}$

$= [t]_1^{\sqrt{2}} = \sqrt{2} - 1$

Q. 33 $\int_0^\pi x \sin x \cos^2 x\, dx$

Thinking Process

Here, use the property i.e., $\int_0^a f(x)dx = \int_0^a (a - x)dx$ and

$\sin(\pi - x) = \sin x, \cos(\pi - x) = \cos x$.

Sol. Let $I = \int_0^\pi x \sin x \cos^2 x\, dx$ ...(i)

and $I = \int_0^\pi (\pi - x)\sin(\pi - x)\cos^2(\pi - x)dx$

$\Rightarrow$ $I = \int_0^\pi (\pi - x)\sin x \cos^2 x\, dx$ ...(ii)

On adding Eqs. (i) and (ii), we get

$$2I = \int_0^\pi \pi \sin x \cos^2 x\, dx$$

Put $\cos x = t$

$\Rightarrow$ $-\sin x\, dx = dt$

As $x \to 0$, then $t \to 1$
and $x \to \pi$, then $t \to -1$

$\therefore \quad I = -\pi\int_1^{-1} t^2\, dt \Rightarrow I = -\pi\left[\frac{t^3}{3}\right]_1^{-1}$

$\Rightarrow \quad 2I = -\frac{\pi}{3}[-1-1] \Rightarrow 2I = \frac{2\pi}{3}$

$\therefore \quad I = \frac{\pi}{3}$

Q. 34 $\int_0^{1/2} \frac{dx}{(1+x^2)\sqrt{1-x^2}}$

Sol. Let $\quad I = \int_0^{1/2} \frac{dx}{(1+x^2)\sqrt{1-x^2}}$

Put $\quad x = \sin\theta$

$\Rightarrow \quad dx = \cos\theta\, d\theta$

As $x \to 0$, then $\theta \to 0$
and $x \to \frac{1}{2}$, then $\theta \to \frac{\pi}{6}$

$$\therefore \quad I = \int_0^{\pi/6} \frac{\cos\theta}{(1+\sin^2\theta)\cos\theta}\, d\theta = \int_0^{\pi/6} \frac{1}{1+\sin^2\theta}\, d\theta$$

$$= \int_0^{\pi/6} \frac{1}{\cos^2\theta\,(\sec^2\theta + \tan^2\theta)}\, d\theta$$

$$= \int_0^{\pi/6} \frac{\sec^2\theta}{\sec^2\theta + \tan^2\theta}\, d\theta$$

$$= \int_0^{\pi/6} \frac{\sec^2\theta}{1+\tan^2\theta + \tan^2\theta}\, d\theta$$

$$= \int_0^{\pi/6} \frac{\sec^2\theta}{1+2\tan^2\theta}\, d\theta$$

Again, put $\quad \tan\theta = t$

$\Rightarrow \quad \sec^2\theta\, d\theta = dt$

As $\theta \to 0$, then $t \to 0$
and $\theta \to \frac{\pi}{6}$, then $t \to \frac{1}{\sqrt{3}}$

$$\therefore \quad I = \int_0^{1/\sqrt{3}} \frac{dt}{1+2t^2} = \frac{1}{2}\int_0^{1/\sqrt{3}} \frac{dt}{\left(\frac{1}{\sqrt{2}}\right)^2 + t^2}$$

$$= \frac{1}{2}\cdot\frac{1}{1/\sqrt{2}}\left[\tan^{-1}\frac{t}{\frac{1}{\sqrt{2}}}\right]_0^{1/\sqrt{3}} = \frac{1}{\sqrt{2}}[\tan^{-1}(\sqrt{2}t)]_0^{1/\sqrt{3}}$$

$$= \frac{1}{\sqrt{2}}\left[\tan^{-1}\sqrt{\frac{2}{3}} - 0\right] = \frac{1}{\sqrt{2}}\tan^{-1}\left(\sqrt{\frac{2}{3}}\right)$$

Long Answer Type Questions

Q. 35 $\int \frac{x^2}{x^4 - x^2 - 12} dx$

Thinking Process

Use $\frac{px+q}{(x-a)(x-b)} = \frac{A}{(x-a)} + \frac{B}{x-b}$, where $a \neq b$, then compare the coefficient of x to get the value of A and B.

Sol. Let
$$I = \int \frac{x^2}{x^4 - x^2 - 12} dx$$
$$= \int \frac{x^2}{x^4 - 4x^2 + 3x^2 - 12} dx$$
$$= \int \frac{x^2 dx}{x^2(x^2 - 4) + 3(x^2 - 4)}$$
$$= \int \frac{x^2 dx}{(x^2 - 4)(x^2 + 3)}$$

Now, $\frac{x^2}{(x^2 - 4)(x^2 + 3)}$ [let $x^2 = t$]

$\Rightarrow$ $$\frac{t}{(t-4)(t+3)} = \frac{A}{t-4} + \frac{B}{t+3}$$

$\Rightarrow$ $$t = A(t+3) + B(t-4)$$

On comparing the coefficient of t on both sides, we get

$$A + B = 1 \quad \ldots(i)$$
$\Rightarrow$ $$3A - 4B = 0 \quad \ldots(ii)$$
$\Rightarrow$ $$3(1-B) - 4B = 0$$
$\Rightarrow$ $$3 - 3B - 4B = 0$$
$\Rightarrow$ $$7B = 3$$
$\Rightarrow$ $$B = \frac{3}{7}$$

If $B = \frac{3}{7}$, then $A + \frac{3}{7} = 1$

$\Rightarrow$ $$A = 1 - \frac{3}{7} = \frac{4}{7}$$

$$\frac{x^2}{(x^2 - 4)(x^2 + 3)} = \frac{4}{7(x^2 - 4)} + \frac{3}{7(x^2 + 3)}$$

$\therefore$ $$I = \frac{4}{7}\int \frac{1}{x^2 - (2)^2} dx + \frac{3}{7}\int \frac{1}{x^2 + (\sqrt{3})^2} dx$$
$$= \frac{4}{7} \cdot \frac{1}{2 \cdot 2} \log\left|\frac{x-2}{x+2}\right| + \frac{3}{7} \cdot \frac{1}{\sqrt{3}} \tan^{-1}\frac{x}{\sqrt{3}} + C$$
$$= \frac{1}{7}\log\left|\frac{x-2}{x+2}\right| + \frac{\sqrt{3}}{7}\tan^{-1}\frac{x}{\sqrt{3}} + C$$

Q. 36 $\int \frac{x^2}{(x^2+a^2)(x^2+b^2)}dx$

Sol. Let $$I = \int \frac{x^2}{(x^2+a^2)(x^2+b^2)}dx$$

Now, $$\frac{x^2}{(x^2+a^2)(x^2+b^2)} \quad [\text{let } x^2 = t]$$

$$= \frac{t}{(t+a^2)(t+b^2)} = \frac{A}{(t+a^2)} + \frac{B}{(t+b^2)}$$

$$t = A(t+b^2) + B(t+a^2)$$

On comparing the coefficient of t, we get

$$A + B = 1 \quad \ldots(i)$$

$$b^2A + a^2B = 0 \quad \ldots(ii)$$

$$\Rightarrow \quad b^2(1-B) + a^2B = 0$$

$$\Rightarrow \quad b^2 - b^2B + a^2B = 0$$

$$\Rightarrow \quad b^2 + (a^2-b^2)B = 0$$

$$\Rightarrow \quad B = \frac{-b^2}{a^2-b^2} = \frac{b^2}{b^2-a^2}$$

From Eq. (i), $$A + \frac{b^2}{b^2-a^2} = 1$$

$$\Rightarrow \quad A = \frac{b^2-a^2-b^2}{b^2-a^2} = \frac{-a^2}{b^2-a^2}$$

$$\therefore \quad I = \int \frac{-a^2}{(b^2-a^2)(x^2+a^2)}dx + \int \frac{b^2}{b^2-a^2}\cdot\frac{1}{x^2+b^2}dx$$

$$= \frac{-a^2}{(b^2-a^2)}\int \frac{1}{x^2+a^2}dx + \frac{b^2}{b^2-a^2}\int \frac{1}{x^2+b^2}dx$$

$$= \frac{-a^2}{b^2-a^2}\cdot\frac{1}{a}\tan^{-1}\frac{x}{a} + \frac{b^2}{b^2-a^2}\cdot\frac{1}{b}\tan^{-1}\frac{x}{b}$$

$$= \frac{1}{b^2-a^2}\left[-a\tan^{-1}\frac{x}{a} + b\tan^{-1}\frac{x}{b}\right]$$

$$= \frac{1}{a^2-b^2}\left[a\tan^{-1}\frac{x}{a} - b\tan^{-1}\frac{x}{b}\right]$$

Q. 37 $\int_0^{\pi} \frac{x}{1+\sin x}$

Sol. Let $$I = \int_0^{\pi} \frac{x}{1+\sin x}dx \quad \ldots(i)$$

and $$I = \int_0^{\pi} \frac{\pi - x}{1+\sin(\pi - x)}dx = \int_0^{\pi} \frac{\pi - x}{1+\sin x}dx \quad \ldots(ii)$$

On adding Eqs. (i) and (ii), we get

$$2I = \pi\int_0^{\pi} \frac{1}{1+\sin x}dx$$

$$= \pi\int_0^{\pi} \frac{(1-\sin x)\,dx}{(1+\sin x)(1-\sin x)}$$

$$= \pi\int_0^{\pi}\frac{(1-\sin x)\,dx}{\cos^2 x}$$

$$= \pi\int_0^{\pi}(\sec^2 x - \tan x\cdot\sec x)\,dx$$

$$= \pi\int_0^{\pi}\sec^2 x\,dx - \pi\int_0^{\pi}\sec x\,x\cdot\tan x\,dx$$

$$= \pi[\tan x]_0^{\pi} - \pi[\sec x]_0^{\pi}$$

$$= \pi[\tan x - \sec x]_0^{\pi}$$

$$= \pi[\tan\pi - \sec\pi - \tan 0 - \sec 0]$$

$\Rightarrow \quad 2I = \pi[0 + 1 - 0 + 1]$

$2I = 2\pi$

$\therefore \quad I = \pi$

Q. 38 $\int\frac{2x-1}{(x-1)(x+2)(x-3)}dx$

Thinking Process

Apply $\frac{px+q}{(x-a)(x-b)(x-c)} = \frac{A}{(x-a)} + \frac{B}{(x-b)} + \frac{C}{(x-c)}$*, then get the values of A, B and C and use* $\int\frac{1}{x}dx = \log|x| + C$.

Sol. Let $\quad I = \int\frac{(2x-1)}{(x-1)(x+2)(x-3)}dx$

Now, $\quad \frac{2x-1}{(x-1)(x+2)(x-3)} = \frac{A}{(x-1)} + \frac{B}{(x+2)} + \frac{C}{(x-3)}$

$\Rightarrow \quad 2x - 1 = A(x+2)(x-3) + B(x-1)(x-3) + C(x-1)(x+2)$

Put $\quad x = 3$, then

$6 - 1 = C(3-1)(3+2)$

$\Rightarrow \quad 5 = 10C \Rightarrow C = \frac{1}{2}$

Again, put $x = 1$, then

$2 - 1 = A(1+2)(1-3)$

$\Rightarrow \quad 1 = -6A \Rightarrow A = -\frac{1}{6}$

Now, put $x = -2$, then

$-4 - 1 = B(-2-1)(-2-3)$

$\Rightarrow \quad -5 = 15B \Rightarrow B = -\frac{1}{3}$

$\therefore \quad I = -\frac{1}{6}\int\frac{1}{x-1}dx - \frac{1}{3}\int\frac{1}{x+2}dx + \frac{1}{2}\int\frac{1}{x-3}dx$

$$= -\frac{1}{6}\log|(x-1)| - \frac{1}{3}\log|(x+2)| + \frac{1}{2}\log|(x-3)| + C$$

$$= -\log|(x-1)|^{1/6} - \log|(x+2)|^{1/3} + \log|(x-3)|^{1/2} + C$$

$$= \log\left|\frac{\sqrt{x-3}}{(x-1)^{1/6}(x+2)^{1/3}}\right| + C$$

Q. 39 $\int e^{\tan^{-1} x}\left(\frac{1+x+x^2}{1+x^2}\right)dx$

Sol. Let

$$I = \int e^{\tan^{-1} x}\left(\frac{1+x+x^2}{1+x^2}\right)dx$$

$$= \int e^{\tan^{-1} x}\left(\frac{1+x^2}{1+x^2} + \frac{x}{1+x^2}\right)dx$$

$$= \int e^{\tan^{-1} x}dx + \int \frac{x\,e^{\tan^{-1} x}}{1+x^2}dx$$

$$I = I_1 + I_2 \quad \ldots(i)$$

Now, $I_2 = \int \frac{x\,e^{\tan^{-1} x}}{1+x^2}dx$

Put $\tan^{-1} x = t \Rightarrow x = \tan t$

$\Rightarrow \frac{1}{1+x^2}dx = dt$

$\therefore$ $I = \int \underset{\text{I}}{\tan t}\cdot \underset{\text{II}}{e^t}\, dt$

$$= \tan t\cdot e^t - \int \sec^2 t\cdot e^t dt + C$$

$$= \tan t\cdot e^t - \int (1+\tan^2 t)e^t dt + C \quad [\because \sec^2\theta = 1+\tan^2\theta]$$

$$I_2 = \tan t\cdot e^t - \int (1+x^2)\frac{e^{\tan^{-1}x}}{1+x^2}dx + C$$

$$I_2 = \tan t\cdot e^t - \int e^{\tan^{-1} x}dx + C$$

$\therefore$ $I = \int e^{\tan^{-1} x}dx + \tan t\cdot e^t - \int e^{\tan^{-1} x}dx + C$

$$= \tan t\cdot e^t + C$$

$$= x\,e^{\tan^{-1} x} + C$$

Q. 40 $\int \sin^{-1}\sqrt{\frac{x}{a+x}}\, dx$

Thinking Process

First of all put $x = \tan^2\theta$ and convert the given expression into two parts, then use the formulae for integration by part i.e., $\int \text{I}\cdot\text{II}\,dx = \text{I}\int \text{II}\,dx - \int\left(\frac{d}{dx}\text{I}\int \text{II}\,dx\right)dx$

Sol. Let

$$I = \int \sin^{-1}\sqrt{\frac{x}{a+x}}\, dx$$

Put

$$x = a\tan^2\theta$$

$\Rightarrow$ $dx = 2a\tan\theta\sec^2\theta\, d\theta$

$\therefore$ $I = \int \sin^{-1}\sqrt{\frac{a\tan^2\theta}{a+a\tan^2\theta}}(2a\tan\theta\cdot\sec^2\theta)\,d\theta$

$$= 2a\int \sin^{-1}\left(\frac{\tan\theta}{\sec\theta}\right)\tan\theta\cdot\sec^2\theta\, d\theta$$

$$= 2a\int \sin^{-1}(\sin\theta)\tan\theta\cdot\sec^2\theta\, d\theta$$

$$= 2a\int \underset{\text{I}}{\theta}\cdot \underset{\text{II}}{\tan\theta\sec^2\theta}\,d\theta$$

$$= 2a\left[\theta\cdot\int \tan\theta\cdot\sec^2\theta\,d\theta - \int\left(\frac{d}{d\theta}\theta\cdot\int\tan\theta\cdot\sec^2\theta\,d\theta\right)d\theta\right]$$

$$\begin{bmatrix} \text{Put} \quad \tan\theta = t \\ \Rightarrow \quad \sec\theta\cdot\tan\theta\cdot d\theta = dt \\ \Rightarrow \int\tan\theta\,\sec^2\theta\,d\theta = \int t\,dt \end{bmatrix}$$

$$= 2a\left[\theta\cdot\frac{\tan^2\theta}{2} - \int\frac{\tan^2\theta}{2}\,d\theta\right]$$

$$= a\theta\tan^2\theta - a\int(\sec^2\theta - 1)\,d\theta$$

$$= a\theta\cdot\tan^2\theta - a\tan\theta + a\theta + C$$

$$= a\left[\frac{x}{a}\tan^{-1}\sqrt{\frac{x}{a}} + \tan^{-1}\sqrt{\frac{x}{a}}\right] + C$$

Q. 41 $\int_{\pi/3}^{\pi/2}\frac{\sqrt{1+\cos x}}{(1-\cos x)^{5/2}}\,dx$

Sol. Let

$$I = \int_{\pi/3}^{\pi/2}\frac{\sqrt{1+\cos x}}{(1-\cos x)^{5/2}}\,dx$$

$$= \int_{\pi/3}^{\pi/2}\frac{\sqrt{1+\cos x}}{(1-\cos x)^2\sqrt{1+\cos x}}\,dx$$

$$= \int_{\pi3}^{\pi2}\frac{1}{(1-\cos^2 x)}\,dx = \int_{\pi3}^{\pi2}\frac{1}{\sin^2 x}\,dx$$

$$= \int_{\pi3}^{\pi2}\text{cosec}^2 x\,dx = [-\cot x]_{\pi/3}^{\pi/2}$$

$$= -\left[\cot\frac{\pi}{2} - \cot\frac{\pi}{3}\right] = -\left[0 - \frac{1}{\sqrt{3}}\right] = +\frac{1}{\sqrt{3}}$$

Alternate Method

Let

$$I = \int_{\pi/3}^{\pi/2}\frac{\sqrt{1+\cos x}}{(1-\cos x)^{5/2}}\,dx = \int_{\pi/3}^{\pi/2}\frac{\left(2\cos^2\frac{x}{2}\right)^{1/2}}{\left(2\sin^2\frac{x}{2}\right)^{5/2}}\,dx$$

$$= \frac{\sqrt{2}}{4\sqrt{2}}\int_{\pi/3}^{\pi/2}\frac{\cos\left(\frac{x}{2}\right)}{\sin^5\left(\frac{x}{2}\right)}\,dx \quad = \frac{1}{4}\int_{\pi/3}^{\pi/2}\frac{\cos\left(\frac{x}{2}\right)}{\sin^5\left(\frac{x}{2}\right)}\,dx$$

Put $\sin\frac{x}{2} = t$

$\Rightarrow$ $\cos\frac{x}{2}\cdot\frac{1}{2}dx = dt$

$\Rightarrow$ $\cos\frac{x}{2}dx = 2dt$

As $x \to \frac{\pi}{3}$, then $t \to \frac{1}{2}$

and $x \to \frac{\pi}{2}$, then $t \to \frac{1}{\sqrt{2}}$

$$\therefore \qquad I = \frac{2}{4}\int_{1/2}^{1/\sqrt{2}} \frac{dt}{t^5} = \frac{1}{2}\left[\frac{t^{-5+1}}{-5+1}\right]_{1/2}^{1/\sqrt{2}}$$

$$= -\frac{1}{8}\left[\frac{1}{\left(\frac{1}{\sqrt{2}}\right)^4} - \frac{1}{\left(\frac{1}{2}\right)^4}\right]$$

$$= -\frac{1}{8}(4-16) = \frac{12}{8} = \frac{3}{2}$$

Note *If we integrate the trigonometric function in different ways [using different identities] then, we can get different answers.*

Q. 42 $\int e^{-3x} \cos^3 x\,dx$

Sol. Let $I = \int \underset{\text{II}}{e^{-3x}} \underset{\text{I}}{\cos^3 x}\, dx$

$$= \cos^3 x \int e^{-3x}\,dx - \int\left(\frac{d}{dx}\cos^3 x \int e^{-3x}\,dx\right)dx$$

$$= \cos^3 x \cdot \frac{e^{-3x}}{-3} - \int (-3\cos^2 x)\sin x \cdot \frac{e^{-3x}}{-3}dx$$

$$= -\frac{1}{3}\cos^3 x e^{-3x} - \int \cos^2 x \sin x e^{-3x} dx$$

$$= -\frac{1}{3}\cos^3 x\, e^{-3x} - \int (1-\sin^2 x)\sin x\, e^{-3x} dx$$

$$= -\frac{1}{3}\cos^3 x e^{-3x} - \int \sin x\, e^{-3x} dx + \int \underset{\text{I}}{\sin^3 x}\, \underset{\text{II}}{e^{-3x}} dx$$

$$= -\frac{1}{3}\cos^3 x\, e^{-3x} - \int \sin x\, e^{-3x} dx + \sin^3 x \cdot \frac{e^{-3x}}{-3} - \int 3\sin^2 x \cos x \cdot \frac{e^{-3x}}{-3} dx$$

$$= -\frac{1}{3}\cos^3 x\, e^{-3x} - \int \sin x\, e^{-3x} dx - \frac{1}{3}\sin^3 x\, e^{-3x} + \int (1-\cos^2 x)\cos x\, e^{-3x} dx$$

$$I = -\frac{1}{3}\cos^3 x\, e^{-3x} - \int \underset{\text{I}}{\sin x}\, \underset{\text{II}}{e^{-3x}} - \frac{1}{3}\sin^3 x\, e^{-3x} + \int \cos x\, e^{-3x} dx - \int \cos^3 x\, e^{-3x} dx$$

$$2I = \frac{e^{-3x}}{3}[\cos^3 x + \sin^3 x] - \left[\sin x \cdot \frac{e^{-3x}}{-3} - \int \cos x \cdot \frac{e^{-3x}}{-3} dx\right] + \int \cos x\, e^{-3x} dx$$

$$2I = \frac{e^{-3x}}{-3}[\cos^3 x + \sin^3 x] + \frac{1}{3}\sin x \cdot e^{-3x} - \frac{1}{3}\int \cos x \cdot e^{-3x} dx + \int \cos x\, e^{-3x} dx$$

$$2I = \frac{e^{-3x}}{-3}[\cos^3 x + \sin^3 x] + \frac{1}{3}\sin x\, e^{-3x} + \frac{2}{3}\int \cos x\, e^{-3x} dx$$

Now, let $I_1 = \int \underset{\text{I}}{\cos x}\, \underset{\text{II}}{e^{-3x}} dx$

$$I_1 = \cos x \cdot \frac{e^{-3x}}{-3} - \int (-\sin x) \cdot \frac{e^{-3x}}{-3} dx$$

$$I_1 = \frac{-1}{3} \cos x \cdot e^{-3x} - \frac{1}{3} \int \sin x \cdot e^{-3x} dx$$

$$= -\frac{1}{3} \cos x \cdot e^{-3x} - \frac{1}{3}\left[\sin x \cdot \frac{e^{-3x}}{-3} - \int \cos x \cdot \frac{e^{-3x}}{-3} dx\right]$$

$$= -\frac{1}{3} \cos x \cdot e^{-3x} + \frac{1}{9} \sin x \cdot e^{-3x} - \frac{1}{9} \int \cos x \cdot e^{-3x} dx$$

$$I_1 + \frac{1}{9} I_1 = -\frac{1}{3} e^{-3x} \cdot \cos x + \frac{1}{9} \sin x \cdot e^{-3x}$$

$$\left(\frac{10}{9}\right) I_1 = -\frac{1}{3} e^{-3x} \cdot \cos x + \frac{1}{9} \sin x \cdot e^{-3x}$$

$$I_1 = \frac{-3}{10} e^{-3x} \cdot \cos x + \frac{1}{10} e^{-3x} \sin x$$

$$2I = -\frac{1}{3} e^{-3x} [\sin^3 x + \cos^3 x] + \frac{1}{3} \sin x \cdot e^{-3x} - \frac{3}{10} e^{-3x} \cdot \cos x + \frac{1}{10} e^{-3x} \cdot \sin x + C$$

$\therefore$

$$I = -\frac{1}{6} e^{-3x} [\sin^3 x + \cos^3 x] + \frac{13}{30} e^{-3x} \cdot \sin x - \frac{3}{10} e^{-3x} \cdot \cos x + C$$

$$\left[\begin{array}{l} \because \ \sin 3x = 3\sin x - 4\sin^3 x \\ \text{and } \cos 3x = 4\cos^3 x - 3\cos x \end{array}\right]$$

$$= \frac{e^{-3x}}{24} [\sin 3x - \cos 3x] + \frac{3e^{-3x}}{40} [\sin x - 3\cos x] + C$$

Q. 43 $\int \sqrt{\tan x}\, dx$

Sol. Let $I = \int \sqrt{\tan x}\, dx$

Put $\tan x = t^2 \Rightarrow \sec^2 x\, dx = 2t\, dt$

$\therefore$

$$I = \int t \cdot \frac{2t}{\sec^2 x} dt = 2\int \frac{t^2}{1 + t^4} dt$$

$$= \int \frac{(t^2 + 1) + (t^2 - 1)}{(1 + t^4)} dt$$

$$= \int \frac{t^2 + 1}{1 + t^4} dt + \int \frac{t^2 - 1}{1 + t^4} dt$$

$$= \int \frac{1 + \frac{1}{t^2}}{t^2 + \frac{1}{t^2}} dt + \int \frac{1 - \frac{1}{t^2}}{t^2 + \frac{1}{t^2}} dt$$

$$= \int \frac{1 - \left(-\frac{1}{t^2}\right) dt}{\left(t - \frac{1}{t}\right)^2 + 2} + \int \frac{1 + \left(-\frac{1}{t^2}\right)}{\left(t + \frac{1}{t}\right)^2 - 2} dt$$

Put $u = t - \frac{1}{t} \Rightarrow du = \left(1 + \frac{1}{t^2}\right) dt$

and $v = t + \frac{1}{t} \Rightarrow dv = \left(1 - \frac{1}{t^2}\right) dt$

$\therefore$
$$I = \int \frac{du}{u^2 + (\sqrt{2})^2} + \int \frac{dv}{v^2 - (\sqrt{2})^2}$$
$$= \frac{1}{\sqrt{2}} \tan^{-1} \frac{u}{\sqrt{2}} + \frac{1}{2\sqrt{2}} \log \left| \frac{v - \sqrt{2}}{v + \sqrt{2}} \right| + C$$
$$= \frac{1}{\sqrt{2}} \tan^{-1} \left(\frac{\tan x - 1}{\sqrt{2 \tan x}} \right) + \frac{1}{2\sqrt{2}} \log \left| \frac{\tan x - \sqrt{2 \tan x} + 1}{\tan x + \sqrt{2 \tan x} + 1} \right| + C$$

Q. 44 $\int_0^{\pi/2} \frac{dx}{(a^2 \cos^2 x + b^2 \sin^2 x)^2}$

Sol. Let
$$I = \int_0^{\pi/2} \frac{dx}{(a^2 \cos^2 x + b^2 \sin^2 x)^2}$$

Divide numerator and denominator by $\cos^4 x$, we get
$$I = \int_0^{\pi/2} \frac{\sec^4 x \, dx}{(a^2 + b^2 \tan^2 x)^2}$$
$$= \int_0^{\pi/2} \frac{(1 + \tan^2 x) \sec^2 x \, dx}{(a^2 + b^2 \tan^2 x)^2}$$

Put $\tan x = t$

$\Rightarrow \sec^2 x \, dx = dt$

As $x \to 0$, then $t \to 0$

and $x \to \frac{\pi}{2}$, then $t \to \infty$
$$I = \int_0^{\infty} \frac{(1 + t^2)}{(a^2 + b^2 t^2)^2}$$

Now, $\frac{1 + t^2}{(a^2 + b^2 t^2)^2}$ [let $t^2 = u$]

$$\frac{1 + u}{(a^2 + b^2 u)^2} = \frac{A}{(a^2 + b^2 u)} + \frac{B}{(a^2 + b^2 u)^2}$$

$\Rightarrow 1 + u = A(a^2 + b^2 u) + B$

On comparing the coefficient of x and constant term on both sides, we get

$a^2 A + B = 1$ ...(i)

and $b^2 A = 1$ ...(ii)

$\therefore A = \frac{1}{b^2}$

Now, $\frac{a^2}{b^2} + B = 1$

$\Rightarrow B = 1 - \frac{a^2}{b^2} = \frac{b^2 - a^2}{b^2}$

$\therefore$
$$I = \int_0^{\infty} \frac{(1 + t^2)}{(a^2 + b^2 t^2)^2}$$
$$= \frac{1}{b^2} \int_0^{\infty} \frac{dt}{a^2 + b^2 t^2} + \frac{b^2 - a^2}{b^2} \int_0^{\infty} \frac{dt}{(a^2 + b^2 t^2)^2}$$

$$= \frac{1}{b^2}\int_0^\infty \frac{dt}{b^2\left(\frac{a^2}{b^2}+t^2\right)} + \frac{b^2-a^2}{b^2}\int_0^\infty \frac{dt}{(a^2+b^2t^2)^2}$$

$$= \frac{1}{ab^3}\left[\tan^{-1}\left(\frac{tb}{a}\right)\right]_0^\infty + \frac{b^2-a^2}{b^2}\left(\frac{\pi}{4}\cdot\frac{1}{a^3b}\right)$$

$$= \frac{1}{ab^3}[\tan^{-1}\infty - \tan^{-1}0] + \frac{\pi}{4}\cdot\frac{b^2-a^2}{(a^3b^3)}$$

$$= \frac{\pi}{2ab^3} + \frac{\pi}{4}\cdot\frac{b^2-a^2}{(a^3b^3)}$$

$$= \pi\left(\frac{2a^2+b^2-a^2}{4a^3b^3}\right) = \frac{\pi}{4}\left(\frac{a^2+b^2}{a^3b^3}\right)$$

Q. 45 $\int_0^1 x\log(1+2x)\,dx$

Thinking Process

Use formula for integration by part i.e., $\int \text{I}\cdot\text{II}\,dx = \text{I}\int \text{II}\,dx - \int\left(\frac{d}{dx}\text{I}\int \text{I}\,dx\right)dx$ *and also use* $\int \frac{1}{x} = \log|x| + C$

Sol. Let

$$I = \int_0^1 x\log(1+2x)dx$$

$$= \left[\log(1+2x)\frac{x^2}{2}\right]_0^1 - \int \frac{1}{1+2x}\cdot 2\cdot\frac{x^2}{2}dx$$

$$= \frac{1}{2}[x^2\log(1+2x)]_0^1 - \int \frac{x^2}{1+2x}dx$$

$$= \frac{1}{2}[1\log 3 - 0] - \left[\int_0^1\left(\frac{x}{2} - \frac{\frac{x}{2}}{1+2x}\right)dx\right]$$

$$= \frac{1}{2}\log 3 - \frac{1}{2}\int_0^1 x\,dx + \frac{1}{2}\int_0^1 \frac{x}{1+2x}dx$$

$$= \frac{1}{2}\log 3 - \frac{1}{2}\left[\frac{x^2}{2}\right]_0^1 + \frac{1}{2}\int_0^1 \frac{\frac{1}{2}(2x+1-1)}{(2x+1)}dx$$

$$= \frac{1}{2}\log 3 - \frac{1}{2}\left[\frac{1}{2} - 0\right] + \frac{1}{4}\int_0^1 dx - \frac{1}{4}\int_0^1 \frac{1}{1+2x}dx$$

$$= \frac{1}{2}\log 3 - \frac{1}{4} + \frac{1}{4}[x]_0^1 - \frac{1}{8}[\log|(1+2x)|]_0^1$$

$$= \frac{1}{2}\log 3 - \frac{1}{4} + \frac{1}{4} - \frac{1}{8}[\log 3 - \log 1]$$

$$= \frac{1}{2}\log 3 - \frac{1}{8}\log 3$$

$$= \frac{3}{8}\log 3$$

Q. 46 $\int_0^{\pi} x \log \sin x \, dx$

Thinking Process

First of all use property of definite integral i.e., $\int_0^a f(x)\,dx = \int_0^a f(a-x)\,dx$, *then use* $\int_0^{2a} f(x)\,dx = 2\int_0^a f(x)\,dx$.

Sol. Let

$$I = \int_0^{\pi} x \log \sin x \, dx \quad \text{...(i)}$$

$$I = \int_0^{\pi} (\pi - x) \log \sin(\pi - x)\, dx$$

$$= \int_0^{\pi} (\pi - x) \log \sin x \, dx \quad \text{...(ii)}$$

$$2I = \pi \int_0^{\pi} \log \sin x \, dx \quad \text{...(iii)}$$

$$2I = 2\pi \int_0^{\pi/2} \log \sin x \, dx \quad \left[\because \int_0^{2a} f(x)\,dx = 2\int_0^a f(x)\,dx\right]$$

$$I = \pi \int_0^{\pi/2} \log \sin x \, dx \quad \text{...(iv)}$$

Now,

$$I = \pi \int_0^{\pi/2} \log \sin(\pi/2 - x)\, dx \quad \text{...(v)}$$

On adding Eqs. (iv) and (v), we get

$$2I = \pi \int_0^{\pi/2} (\log \sin x + \log \cos x)\, dx$$

$$2I = \pi \int_0^{\pi/2} \log \sin x \cos x \, dx$$

$$= \pi \int_0^{\pi/22} \log \frac{2 \sin x \cos x}{2} dx$$

$$2I = \pi \int_0^{\pi/2} (\log \sin 2x - \log 2)\, dx$$

$$2I = \pi \int_0^{\pi/2} \log \sin 2x \, dx - \pi \int_0^{\pi/2} \log 2 \, dx$$

Put $2x = t \Rightarrow dx = \frac{1}{2} dt$

As $x \to 0$, then $t \to 0$

and $x \to \frac{\pi}{2}$, then $t \to \pi$

$$\therefore \quad 2I = \frac{\pi}{2} \int_0^{\pi} \log \sin t \, dt - \frac{\pi^2}{2} \log 2$$

$$\Rightarrow \quad 2I = \frac{\pi}{2} \int_0^{\pi} \log \sin x \, dx - \frac{\pi^2}{2} \log 2$$

$$\Rightarrow \quad 2I = I - \frac{\pi^2}{2} \log 2 \quad \text{[from Eq. (iii)]}$$

$$\therefore \quad I = -\frac{\pi^2}{2} \log 2 = \frac{\pi^2}{2} \log\left(\frac{1}{2}\right)$$

Q. 47 $\int_{\pi/4}^{\pi/4} \log(\sin x + \cos x)\, dx$

Sol. Let $I = \int_{-\pi/4}^{\pi/4} \log(\sin x + \cos x)\, dx$ ...(i)

$$I = \int_{-\pi/4}^{\pi/4} \log\left\{\sin\left(\frac{\pi}{4} - \frac{\pi}{4} - x\right) + \cos\left(\frac{\pi}{4} - \frac{\pi}{4} - x\right)\right\} dx$$

$$= \int_{-\pi/4}^{\pi/4} \log\{\sin(-x) + \cos(-x)\}\, dx$$

and $I = \int_{-\pi/4}^{\pi 4} \log(\cos x - \sin x)\, dx$ ...(ii)

From Eqs. (i) and (ii),

$$2I = \int_{-\pi/4}^{\pi 4} \log\cos 2x\, dx$$

$$2I = \int_{0}^{\pi/4} \log\cos 2x\, dx \quad \text{...(iii)}$$

$$\left[\because \int_{-a}^{a} f(x)\, dx = 2\int_0^a f(x), \text{ if } f(-x) = f(x)\right]$$

Put $2x = t \Rightarrow dx = \frac{dt}{2}$

As $x \to 0$, then $t \to 0$

and $x \to \frac{\pi}{4}$, then $t \to \frac{\pi}{2}$

$$2I = \frac{1}{2}\int_0^{\pi/2} \log\cos t\, dt \quad \text{...(iv)}$$

$$2I = \frac{1}{2}\int_0^{\pi/2} \log\cos\left(\frac{\pi}{2} - t\right) dt \quad \left[\because \int_0^a f(x)\, dx = \int_0^a f(a - x)\, dx\right]$$

$$\Rightarrow 2I = \frac{1}{2}\int_0^{\pi/2} \log\sin t\, dx \quad \text{...(v)}$$

On adding Eqs. (iv) and (v), we get

$$4I = \frac{1}{2}\int_0^{\pi/2} \log\sin t \cos t\, dt$$

$$\Rightarrow 4I = \frac{1}{2}\int_0^{\pi/2} \log\frac{\sin 2t}{2}\, dt$$

$$\Rightarrow 4I = \frac{1}{2}\int_0^{\pi/2} \log\sin 2x\, dx - \frac{1}{2}\int_0^{\pi/2} \log 2\, dx$$

$$\Rightarrow 4I = \frac{1}{2}\int_0^{\pi/2} \log\sin\left(\frac{\pi}{2} - 2x\right) dx - \log 2 \cdot \frac{\pi}{4}$$

$$\Rightarrow 4I = \frac{1}{2}\int_0^{\pi/2} \log\cos 2x\, dx - \frac{\pi}{4}\log 2$$

$$\Rightarrow 4I = \int_0^{\pi/4} \log\cos 2x\, dx - \frac{\pi}{4}\log 2 \quad \left[\because \int_0^{2a} f(x)\, dx = 2\int_0^a f(x)\, dx\right]$$

$$\Rightarrow 4I = 2I - \frac{\pi}{4}\log 2 \quad \text{[from Eq. (iii)]}$$

$$\therefore I = -\frac{\pi}{8}\log 2 = \frac{\pi}{8}\log\left(\frac{1}{2}\right)$$

Objective Type Questions

Q. 48 $\int \frac{\cos 2x - \cos 2\theta}{\cos x - \cos\theta} dx$ is equal to

(a) $2(\sin x + x\cos\theta) + C$ (b) $2(\sin x - x\cos\theta) + C$

(c) $2(\sin x + 2x\cos\theta) + C$ (d) $2(\sin x - 2x\cos\theta) + C$

Thinking Process

Use formula $\cos 2\theta = 2\cos^2\theta - 1$ *to get simplest form, then apply* $\int \cos x\, dx = \sin x + C$.

Sol. *(a)* Let

$$I = \int \frac{\cos 2x - \cos 2\theta}{\cos x - \cos\theta} dx$$

$$= \int \frac{(2\cos^2 x - 1 - 2\cos^2\theta + 1)}{\cos x - \cos\theta} dx$$

$$= 2\int \frac{(\cos x + \cos\theta)(\cos x - \cos\theta)}{(\cos x - \cos\theta)} dx$$

$$= 2\int (\cos x + \cos\theta)\, dx$$

$$= 2(\sin x + x\cos\theta) + C$$

Q. 49 $\frac{dx}{\sin(x-a)\sin(x-b)}$ is equal to

(a) $\sin(b-a)\log\left|\frac{\sin(x-b)}{\sin(x-a)}\right| + C$ (b) $\operatorname{cosec}(b-a)\log\left|\frac{\sin(x-a)}{\sin(x-b)}\right| + C$

(c) $\operatorname{cosec}(b-a)\log\left|\frac{\sin(x-b)}{\sin(x-a)}\right| + C$ (d) $\sin(b-a)\log\left|\frac{\sin(x-a)}{\sin(x-b)}\right| + C$

Sol. *(c)* Let

$$I = \int \frac{dx}{\sin(x-a)\sin(x-b)}$$

$$= \frac{1}{\sin(b-a)}\int \frac{\sin(b-a)}{\sin(x-a)\sin(x-b)} dx$$

$$= \frac{1}{\sin(b-a)}\int \frac{\sin(x-a-x+b)}{\sin(x-a)\sin(x-b)} dx$$

$$= \frac{1}{\sin(b-a)}\int \frac{\sin\{(x-a)-(x-b)\}}{\sin(x-a)\sin(x-b)} dx$$

$$= \frac{1}{\sin(b-a)}\int \frac{\sin(x-a)\cos(x-b) - \cos(x-a)\sin(x-b)}{\sin(x-a)\sin(x-b)} dx$$

$$= \frac{1}{\sin(b-a)}\int [\cot(x-b) - \cot(x-a)]\, dx$$

$$= \frac{1}{\sin(b-a)}[\log|\sin(x-b)| - \log|\sin(x-a)|] + C$$

$$= \operatorname{cosec}(b-a)\log\left|\frac{\sin(x-b)}{\sin(x-a)}\right| + C$$

Q. 50 $\int \tan^{-1}\sqrt{x}\,dx$ is equal to

(a) $(x+1)\tan^{-1}\sqrt{x}-\sqrt{x}+C$ (b) $x\tan^{-1}\sqrt{x}-\sqrt{x}+C$

(c) $\sqrt{x}-x\tan^{-1}\sqrt{x}+C$ (d) $\sqrt{x}-(x+1)\tan^{-1}\sqrt{x}+C$

Thinking Process

Use formula for integration by part i.e., $\int \text{I}\cdot\text{II}\,dx=\text{I}\int\text{II}\,dx-\int\left(\frac{d}{dx}\text{I}\int\text{II}\,dx\right)dx$

Sol. *(a)* Let

$$I=\int 1\cdot\tan^{-1}\sqrt{x}\,dx$$
$$=\tan^{-1}\sqrt{x}\cdot x-\frac{1}{2}\int\frac{1}{(1+x)}\cdot\frac{2}{\sqrt{x}}\,dx$$
$$=x\tan^{-1}\sqrt{x}-\frac{1}{2}\int\frac{2}{\sqrt{x}(1+x)}dx$$

Put $x=t^2\Rightarrow dx=2t\,dt$

$$\therefore\quad I=x\tan^{-1}\sqrt{x}-\int\frac{t}{t(1+t^2)}dt$$
$$=x\tan^{-1}\sqrt{x}-\int\frac{t^2}{1+t^2}\,dt$$
$$=x\tan^{-1}\sqrt{x}-\int\left(1-\frac{1}{1+t^2}\right)dt$$
$$=x\tan^{-1}\sqrt{x}-\sqrt{x}+\tan^{-1}t+C$$
$$=x\tan^{-1}\sqrt{x}-\sqrt{x}+\tan^{-1}\sqrt{x}+C$$
$$=(x+1)\tan^{-1}\sqrt{x}-\sqrt{x}+C$$

Q. 51 $\int\frac{x^9}{(4x^2+1)^6}\,dx$ is equal to

(a) $\frac{1}{5x}\left(4+\frac{1}{x^2}\right)^{-5}+C$ (b) $\frac{1}{5}\left(4+\frac{1}{x^2}\right)^{-5}+C$

(c) $\frac{1}{10x}(1+4)^{-5}+C$ (d) $\frac{1}{10}\left(\frac{1}{x^2}+4\right)^{-5}+C$

Sol. *(d)* Let

$$I=\int\frac{x^9}{(4x^2+1)^6}dx=\int\frac{x^9}{x^{12}\left(4+\frac{1}{x^2}\right)^6}dx$$
$$=\int\frac{dx}{x^3\left(4+\frac{1}{x^2}\right)^6}$$

Put $4+\frac{1}{x^2}=t\Rightarrow\frac{-2}{x^3}dx=dt$

$\Rightarrow\quad\frac{1}{x^3}dx=-\frac{1}{2}dt$

$$\therefore\quad I=-\frac{1}{2}\int\frac{dt}{t^6}=-\frac{1}{2}\left[\frac{t^{-6+1}}{-6+1}\right]+C$$
$$=\frac{1}{10}\left[\frac{1}{t^5}\right]+C=\frac{1}{10}\left(4+\frac{1}{x^2}\right)^{-5}+C$$

Q. 52 If $\int \frac{dx}{(x+2)(x^2+1)} = a\log|1+x^2| + b\tan^{-1}x + \frac{1}{5}\log|x+2| + C$, then

(a) $a = \frac{-1}{10}, b = \frac{-2}{5}$ (b) $a = \frac{1}{10}, b = -\frac{2}{5}$

(c) $a = \frac{-1}{10}, b = \frac{2}{5}$ (d) $a = \frac{1}{10}, b = \frac{2}{5}$

Thinking Process

Use method of partial fraction i.e., $\frac{1}{(x-a)(x^2+bx+c)} = \frac{A}{(x-a)} + \frac{Bx+C}{(x^2+bx+c)}$

to solve the above problem.

Sol. ***(c)*** Given that, $\int \frac{dx}{(x+2)(x^2+1)} = a\log|1+x^2| + b\tan^{-1}x + \frac{1}{5}\log|x+2| + C$

Now, $$I = \int \frac{dx}{(x+2)(x^2+1)}$$

$$\frac{1}{(x+2)(x^2+1)} = \frac{A}{x+2} + \frac{Bx+C}{x^2+1}$$

$\Rightarrow$ $$1 = A(x^2+1) + (Bx+C)(x+2)$$

$\Rightarrow$ $$1 = Ax^2 + A + Bx^2 + 2Bx + Cx + 2C$$

$\Rightarrow$ $$1 = (A+B)x^2 + (2B+C)x + A + 2C$$

$\Rightarrow$ $$A + B = 0,\ A + 2C = 1,\ 2B + C = 0$$

We have, $A = \frac{1}{5}, B = -\frac{1}{5}$ and $C = \frac{2}{5}$

$\therefore$ $$\int \frac{dx}{(x+2)(x^2+1)} = \frac{1}{5}\int \frac{1}{x+2}dx + \int \frac{-\frac{1}{5}x + \frac{2}{5}}{x^2+1}dx$$

$$= \frac{1}{5}\int \frac{1}{x+2}dx - \frac{1}{5}\int \frac{x}{1+x^2}dx + \frac{1}{5}\int \frac{2}{1+x^2}dx$$

$$= \frac{1}{5}\log|x+2| - \frac{1}{10}\log|1+x^2| + \frac{2}{5}\tan^{-1}x + C$$

$\therefore$ $$b = \frac{2}{5} \text{ and } a = \frac{-1}{10}$$

Q. 53 $\int \frac{x^3}{x+1}$ is equal to

(a) $x + \frac{x^2}{2} + \frac{x^3}{3} - \log|1-x| + C$ (b) $x + \frac{x^2}{2} - \frac{x^3}{3} - \log|1-x| + C$

(c) $x - \frac{x^2}{2} - \frac{x^3}{3} - \log|1+x| + C$ (d) $x - \frac{x^2}{2} + \frac{x^3}{3} - \log|1+x| + C$

Sol. ***(d)*** Let $$I = \int \frac{x^3}{x+1}dx$$

$$= \int \left((x^2 - x + 1) - \frac{1}{(x+1)}\right)dx$$

$$= \frac{x^3}{3} - \frac{x^2}{2} + x - \log|x+1| + C$$

Q. 54 $\int \frac{x+\sin x}{1+\cos x}\, dx$ is equal to

(a) $\log|1+\cos x|+C$ (b) $\log|x+\sin x|+C$
(c) $x-\tan\frac{x}{2}+C$ (d) $x\cdot\tan\frac{x}{2}+C$

Sol. *(d)* Let

$$I=\int\frac{x+\sin x}{1+\cos x}dx$$
$$=\int\frac{x}{1+\cos x}dx+\int\frac{\sin x}{1+\cos x}dx$$
$$=\int\frac{x}{2\cos^2 x/2}dx+\int\frac{2\sin x/2\cos x/2}{2\cos^2 x/2}dx$$
$$=\frac{1}{2}\int x\sec^2 x/2\,dx+\int\tan x/2\,dx$$
$$=\frac{1}{2}\left[x\cdot\tan x/2\cdot 2-\int\tan\frac{x}{2}\cdot 2\,dx\right]+\int\tan\frac{x}{2}dx$$
$$=x\cdot\tan\frac{x}{2}+C$$

Q. 55 If $\frac{x^3dx}{\sqrt{1+x^2}}=a(1+x^2)^{3/2}+b\sqrt{1+x^2}+C$, then

(a) $a=\frac{1}{3}, b=1$ (b) $a=\frac{-1}{3}, b=1$
(c) $a=\frac{-1}{3}, b=-1$ (d) $a=\frac{1}{3}, b=-1$

Sol. *(d)* Let $I=\int\frac{x^3}{\sqrt{1+x^2}}dx=a(1+x^2)^{3/2}+b\sqrt{1+x^2}+C$

$\because$ $$I=\int\frac{x^3}{\sqrt{1+x^2}}dx=\int\frac{x^2\cdot x}{\sqrt{1+x^2}}dx$$

Put $1+x^2=t^2$

$\Rightarrow$ $2x\,dx=2t\,dt$

$\therefore$ $$I=\int\frac{t(t^2-1)}{t}dt=\frac{t^3}{3}-t+C$$
$$=\frac{1}{3}(1+x^2)^{3/2}-\sqrt{1+x^2}+C$$

$\therefore$ $a=\frac{1}{3}$ and $b=-1$

Q. 56 $\int_{-\pi/4}^{\pi/4}\frac{dx}{1+\cos 2x}$ is equal to

(a) 1 (b) 2 (c) 3 (d) 4

Sol. *(a)* Let

$$I=\int_{-\pi/4}^{\pi/4}\frac{dx}{1+\cos 2x}=\int_{-\pi/4}^{\pi/4}\frac{dx}{2\cos^2 x}$$
$$=\frac{1}{2}\int_{-\pi/4}^{\pi/4}\sec^2 x\,dx=\int_0^{\pi/4}\sec^2 x\,dx=[\tan x]_0^{\pi/4}=1$$

Q. 57 $\int_0^{\pi/2} \sqrt{1-\sin 2x}\, dx$ is equal to

(a) $2\sqrt{2}$ (b) $2(\sqrt{2}+1)$

(c) 2 (d) $2(\sqrt{2}-1)$

Sol. *(d)* Let

$$I = \int_0^{\pi/2} \sqrt{1-\sin 2x}\, dx$$
$$= \int_0^{\pi/4} \sqrt{(\cos x - \sin x)^2}\, dx + \int_{\pi/4}^{\pi/2} \sqrt{(\sin x - \cos x)^2}\, dx$$
$$= [\sin x + \cos x]_0^{\pi/4} + [-\cos x - \sin x]_{\pi/4}^{\pi/2}$$
$$= \frac{1}{\sqrt{2}} + \frac{1}{\sqrt{2}} - 0 - 1 + \left(-0 - 1 + \frac{1}{\sqrt{2}} + \frac{1}{\sqrt{2}}\right)$$
$$= 2\sqrt{2} - 2 = 2(\sqrt{2}-1)$$

Q. 58 $\int_0^{\pi/4} \cos x e^{\sin x} dx$ is equal to

(a) e + 1 (b) e − 1 (c) e (d) − e

Sol. *(b)* Let

$$I = \int_0^{\pi/2} \cos x\, e^{\sin x} dx$$

Put $\sin x = t \Rightarrow \cos x\, dx = dt$

As $x \to 0$, then $t \to 0$

and $x \to \pi/2$, then $t \to 1$

$\therefore$

$$I = \int_0^1 e^t dt = [e^t]_0^1$$
$$= e^1 - e^0 = e - 1$$

Q. 59 $\int \frac{x+3}{(x+4)^2} e^x dx$ is equal to

(a) $e^x \left(\frac{1}{x+4}\right) + C$ (b) $e^{-x}\left(\frac{1}{x+4}\right) + C$

(c) $e^{-x}\left(\frac{1}{x-4}\right) + C$ (d) $e^{2x}\left(\frac{1}{x-4}\right) + C$

Sol. *(a)* Let

$$I = \int \frac{x+3}{(x+4)^2} e^x\, dx$$
$$= \int \frac{e^x}{(x+4)} - \int \frac{e^x}{(x+4)^2} dx$$
$$= \int e^x \left(\frac{1}{(x+4)} - \frac{1}{(x+4)^2}\right) dx$$
$$= e^x\left(\frac{1}{x+4}\right) + C \qquad \left[\because \int e^x \{f(x) + f'(x)\}\, dx = e^x f(x) + C\right]$$

Fillers

Q. 60 If $\int_0^a \frac{1}{1+4x^2}\,dx = \frac{\pi}{8}$, then $a =$ ....

Sol. Let $I = \int_0^a \frac{1}{1+4x^2}\,dx = \frac{\pi}{8}$

Now, $\int_0^a \frac{1}{4\left(\frac{1}{4}+x^2\right)}\,dx = \frac{2}{4}[\tan^{-1} 2x]_0^a$

$$= \frac{1}{2}\tan^{-1} 2a - 0 = \pi/8$$

$$\frac{1}{2}\tan^{-1} 2a = \frac{\pi}{8}$$

$\Rightarrow$ $\tan^{-1} 2a = \pi/4$

$\Rightarrow$ $2a = 1$

$\therefore$ $a = \frac{1}{2}$

Q. 61 $\int \frac{\sin x}{3+4\cos^2 x}\,dx =$ ....

Sol. Let $I = \int \frac{\sin x}{3+4\cos^2 x}\,dx$

Put $\cos x = t \Rightarrow -\sin x\,dx = dt$

$\therefore$ $I = -\int \frac{dt}{3+4t^2} = -\frac{1}{4}\int \frac{dt}{\left(\frac{\sqrt{3}}{2}\right)^2 + t^2}$

$$= -\frac{1}{4}\cdot\frac{2}{\sqrt{3}}\tan^{-1}\frac{2t}{\sqrt{3}} + C$$

$$= -\frac{1}{2\sqrt{3}}\tan^{-1}\left(\frac{2\cos x}{\sqrt{3}}\right) + C$$

Q. 62 The value of $\int_{-\pi}^{\pi} \sin^3 x \cos^2 x\,dx$ is ....

Sol. We have, $f(x) = \int_{-\pi}^{\pi} \sin^3 x \cos^2 x\,dx$

$$f(-x) = \int_{-\pi}^{\pi} \sin^3(-2) - \cos^2(-x)\,dx$$

$$= -f(x)$$

Since, $f(x)$ is an odd function.

$\therefore$ $\int_{-\pi}^{\pi} \sin^3 x \cos^2 x\,dx = 0$

8

Application *of* Integrals

Short Answer Type Questions

Q. 1 Find the area of the region bounded by the curves $y^2 = 9x$ and $y = 3x$.

Thinking Process

On solving both the equation of curves, get the values of x and then at those values, find the area of the shaded region.

Sol. We have, $y^2 = 9x$ and $y = 3x$

$\Rightarrow \quad (3x)^2 = 9x$

$\Rightarrow \quad 9x^2 - 9x = 0$

$\Rightarrow \quad 9x(x - 1) = 0$

$\Rightarrow \quad x = 1, 0$

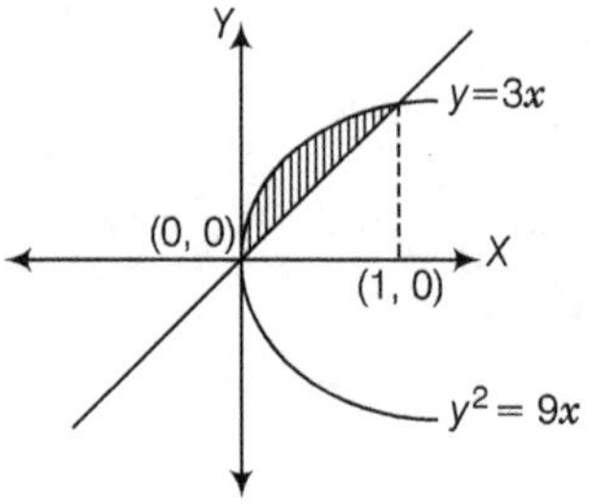

$\therefore$ Required area, $A = \int_0^1 \sqrt{9x}\,dx - \int_0^1 3x\,dx$

$= 3\int_0^1 x^{1/2}\,dx - 3\int_0^1 x\,dx$

$= 3\left[\frac{x^{3/2}}{3/2}\right]_0^1 - 3\left[\frac{x^2}{2}\right]_0^1$

$= 3\left(\frac{2}{3} - 0\right) - 3\left(\frac{1}{2} - 0\right)$

$= 2 - \frac{3}{2} = \frac{1}{2}$ sq units

Q. 2 Find the area of the region bounded by the parabola $y^2 = 2px$ $x^2 = 2py$.

Sol. We have, $y^2 = 2px$ and $x^2 = 2py$

$\therefore \quad y = \sqrt{2px}$

$\Rightarrow \quad x^2 = 2p \cdot \sqrt{2px}$

$\Rightarrow \quad x^4 = 4p^2 \cdot (2px)$

$\Rightarrow \quad x^4 = 8p^3 x$

$\Rightarrow \quad x^4 - 8p^3 x = 0$

$\Rightarrow \quad x^3(x - 8p^3) = 0$

$\Rightarrow \quad x = 0, 2p$

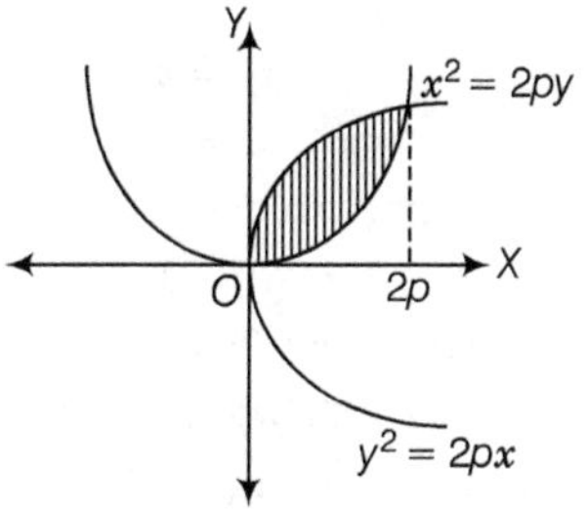

$$\therefore \quad \text{Required area} = \int_0^{2p} \sqrt{2px}\, dx - \int_0^{2p} \frac{x^2}{2p} dx$$

$$= \sqrt{2p}\int_0^{2p} x^{1/2} dx - \frac{1}{2p}\int_0^{2p} x^2 dx$$

$$= \sqrt{2p}\left[\frac{2(x)^{3/2}}{3}\right]_0^{2p} - \frac{1}{2p}\left[\frac{x^3}{3}\right]_0^{2p}$$

$$= \sqrt{2p}\left[\frac{2}{3}\cdot(2p)^{3/2} - 0\right] - \frac{1}{2p}\left[\frac{1}{3}(2p)^3 - 0\right]$$

$$= \sqrt{2p}\left(\frac{2}{3}\cdot 2\sqrt{2}p^{3/2}\right) - \frac{1}{2p}\left(\frac{1}{3}8p^3\right)$$

$$= \sqrt{2}p\left(\frac{4\sqrt{2}}{3}p^{3/2}\right) - \frac{1}{2p}\left(\frac{8}{3}p^3\right)$$

$$= \frac{4\sqrt{2}}{3}\cdot\sqrt{2}p^2 - \frac{8}{6}p^2$$

$$= \frac{(16-8)p^2}{6} = \frac{8p^2}{6}$$

$$= \frac{4p^2}{3} \text{ sq units}$$

Q. 3 **Find the area of the region bounded by the curve $y = x^3$, $y = x + 6$ and $x = 0$.**

Sol. We have, $y = x^3$, $y = x + 6$ and $x = 0$

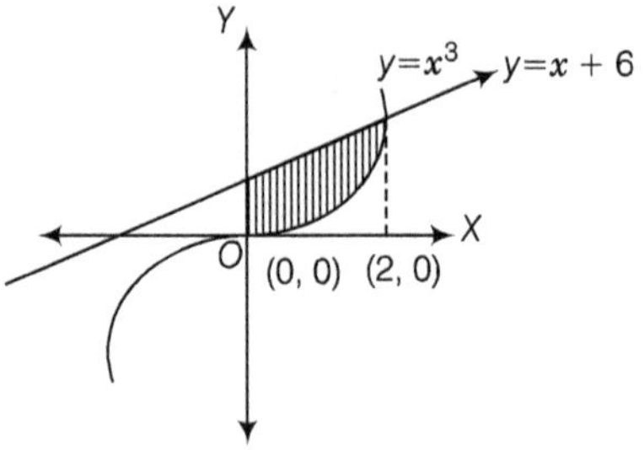

$$\therefore \quad x^3 = x + 6$$
$$\Rightarrow \quad x^3 - x = 6$$
$$\Rightarrow \quad x^3 - x - 6 = 0$$
$$\Rightarrow \quad x^2(x-2) + 2x(x-2) + 3(x-2) = 0$$
$$\Rightarrow \quad (x-2)(x^2+2x+3) = 0$$
$$\Rightarrow \quad x = 2, \text{ with two imaginary points}$$

$\therefore$ Required area of shaded region $= \int_0^2 (x + 6 - x^3)\,dx$

$$= \left[\frac{x^2}{2} + 6x - \frac{x^4}{4}\right]_0^2$$
$$= \left[\frac{4}{2} + 12 - \frac{16}{4} - 0\right]$$
$$= [2 + 12 - 4] = 10 \text{ sq units}$$

Q. 4 **Find the area of the region bounded by the curve $y^2 = 4x$ and $x^2 = 4y$.**

Thinking Process

First, by using both the equation get the values of x and then find the shaded region by using these value of x in the equation of curve in x only.

Sol. Given equation of curves are

$$y^2 = 4x \quad \ldots(i)$$

and

$$x^2 = 4y \quad \ldots(ii)$$

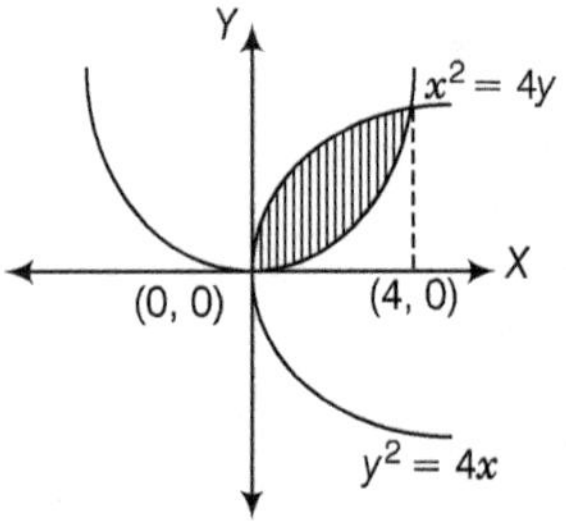

$$\Rightarrow \quad \left(\frac{x^2}{4}\right)^2 = 4x$$
$$\Rightarrow \quad \frac{x^4}{4 \cdot 4} = 4x$$
$$\Rightarrow \quad x^4 = 64x$$
$$\Rightarrow \quad x^4 - 64x = 0$$
$$\Rightarrow \quad x(x^3 - 4^3) = 0$$
$$\Rightarrow \quad x = 4, 0$$

$\therefore$ Area of shaded region, $A = \int_0^4 \left(\sqrt{4x} - \frac{x^2}{4}\right) dx$

$$= \int_0^4 \left(2\sqrt{x} - \frac{x^2}{4}\right) dx = \left[\frac{2x^{3/2}\cdot 2}{3} - \frac{1}{4}\cdot\frac{x^3}{3}\right]_0^4$$

$$= \frac{2\cdot 2}{3}\cdot 8 - \frac{1}{4}\cdot\frac{64}{3} - 0 = \frac{32}{3} - \frac{16}{3} = \frac{16}{3} \text{ sq units}$$

Q. 5 Find the area of the region included between $y^2 = 9x$ and $y = x$.

Sol. We have, $y^2 = 9x$ and $y = x$

$\Rightarrow$ $x^2 = 9x$

$\Rightarrow$ $x^2 - 9x = 0$

$\Rightarrow$ $x(x - 9) = 0$

$\Rightarrow$ $x = 0, 9$

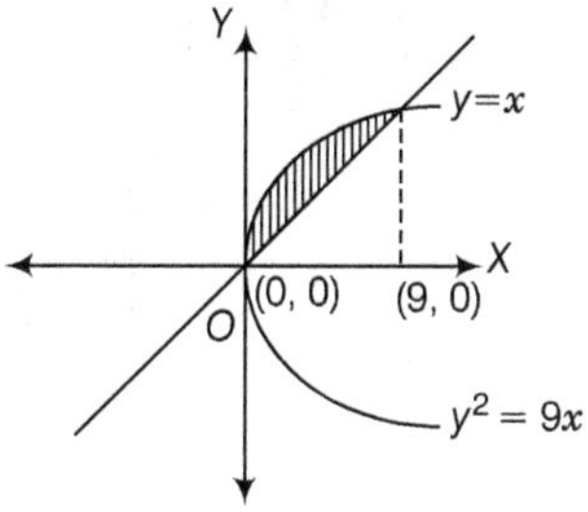

$\therefore$ Area of shaded region, $A = \int_0^9 (\sqrt{9x} - x)\, dx = \int_0^9 3x^{1/2} dx - \int_0^9 x\, dx$

$$= \left[3\cdot\frac{x^{3/2}}{3}\cdot 2\right]_0^9 - \left[\frac{x^2}{2}\right]_0^9$$

$$= \left[\frac{3\cdot 3^{\frac{3}{2}\times 2}}{3}\cdot 2 - 0\right] - \left[\frac{81}{2} - 0\right]$$

$$= 54 - \frac{81}{2} = \frac{108 - 81}{2} = \frac{27}{2} \text{ sq units}$$

Q. 6 Find the area of the region enclosed by the parabola $x^2 = y$ and the line $y = x + 2$.

Sol. We have, $x^2 = y$ and $y = x + 2$

$\Rightarrow$ $x^2 = x + 2$

$\Rightarrow$ $x^2 - x - 2 = 0$

$\Rightarrow$ $x^2 - 2x + x - 2 = 0$

$\Rightarrow$ $x(x - 2) + 1(x - 2) = 0$

$\Rightarrow$ $(x + 1)(x - 2) = 0$

$\Rightarrow$ $x = -1, 2$

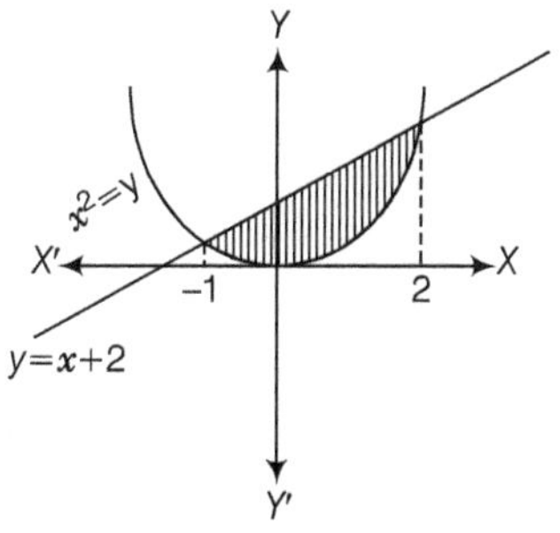

$\therefore$ Required area of shaded region $= \int_{-1}^{2} (x + 2 - x^2)\,dx = \left[\dfrac{x^2}{2} + 2x - \dfrac{x^3}{3}\right]_{-1}^{2}$

$$= \left[\frac{4}{2} + 4 - \frac{8}{3} - \frac{1}{2} + 2 - \frac{1}{3}\right]$$

$$= 6 + \frac{3}{2} - \frac{9}{3} = \frac{36 + 9 - 18}{6} = \frac{27}{6} = \frac{9}{2} \text{ sq units}$$

Q. 7 Find the area of the region bounded by line $x = 2$ and parabola $y^2 = 8x$.

Sol. We have, $y^2 = 8x$ and $x = 2$

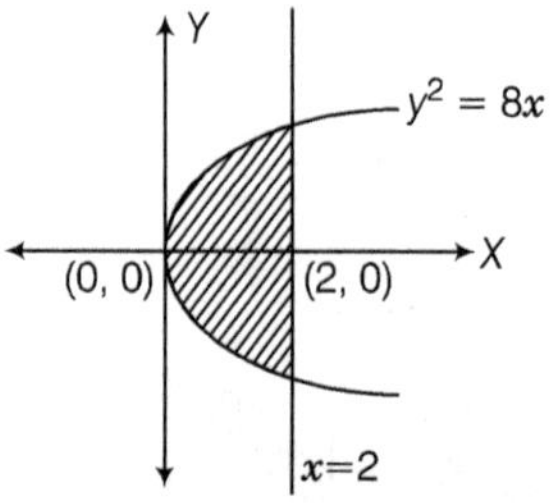

$\therefore$ Area of shaded region, $A = 2\int_0^2 \sqrt{8x}\,dx = 2\cdot 2\sqrt{2}\int_0^2 x^{1/2}dx$

$$= 4\cdot\sqrt{2}\cdot\left[2\cdot\frac{x^{3/2}}{3}\right]_0^2 = 4\sqrt{2}\left[\frac{2}{3}\cdot 2\sqrt{2} - 0\right]$$

$$= \frac{32}{3} \text{ sq units}$$

Q. 8 Sketch the region $\{(x, 0) : y = \sqrt{4 - x^2}\}$ and X-axis. Find the area of the region using integration.

Sol. Given region is $\{(x, 0) : y = \sqrt{4 - x^2}\}$ and X-axis.

We have, $\quad y = \sqrt{4 - x^2} \Rightarrow y^2 = 4 - x^2 \Rightarrow x^2 + y^2 = 4$

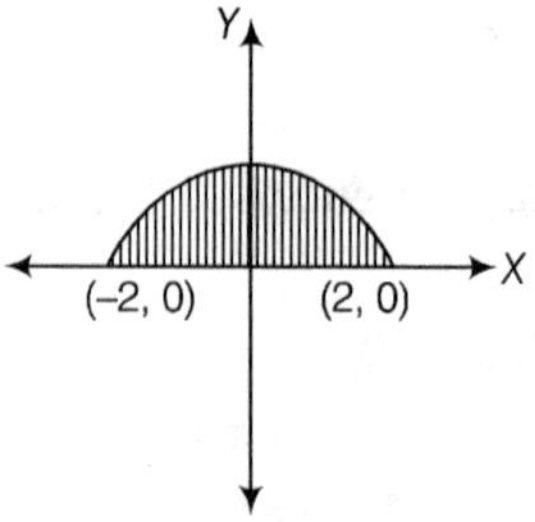

$\therefore$ Area of shaded region, $A = \int_{-2}^{2} \sqrt{4 - x^2}\,dx = \int_{-2}^{2} \sqrt{2^2 - x^2}\,dx$

$$= \left[\frac{x}{2}\sqrt{2^2 - x^2} + \frac{2^2}{2}\cdot\sin^{-1}\frac{x}{2}\right]_{-2}^{2}$$

$$= \frac{2}{2}\cdot 0 + 2.\frac{\pi}{2} + \frac{2}{2}\cdot 0 - 2\sin^{-1}(-1) = 2.\frac{\pi}{2} + 2.\frac{\pi}{2}$$

$$= 2\pi \text{ sq units}$$

Q. 9 Calculate the area under the curve $y = 2\sqrt{x}$ included between the lines $x = 0$ and $x = 1$.

Sol. We have, $y = 2\sqrt{x}$, $x = 0$ and $x = 1$

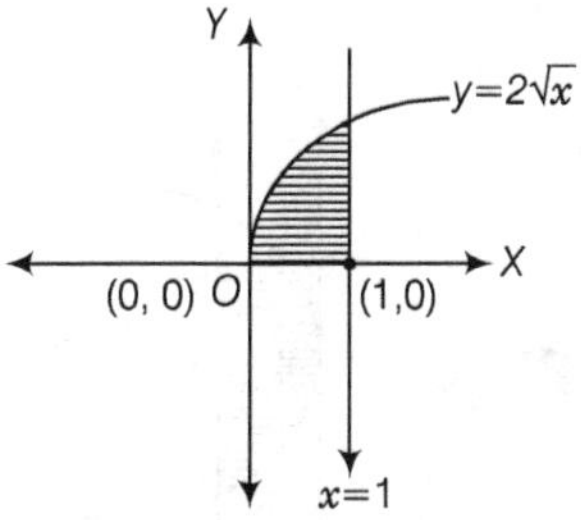

$\therefore$ Area of shaded region, $A = \int_0^1 (2\sqrt{x})\, dx$

$$= 2 \cdot \left[\frac{x^{3/2}}{3} \cdot 2 \right]_0^1$$

$$= 2\left(\frac{2}{3} \cdot 1 - 0 \right) = \frac{4}{3} \text{ sq units}$$

Q. 10 Using integration, find the area of the region bounded by the line $2y = 5x + 7$, X-axis and the lines $x = 2$ and $x = 8$.

Sol. We have, $2y = 5x + 7$

$\Rightarrow$ $y = \frac{5x}{2} + \frac{7}{2}$

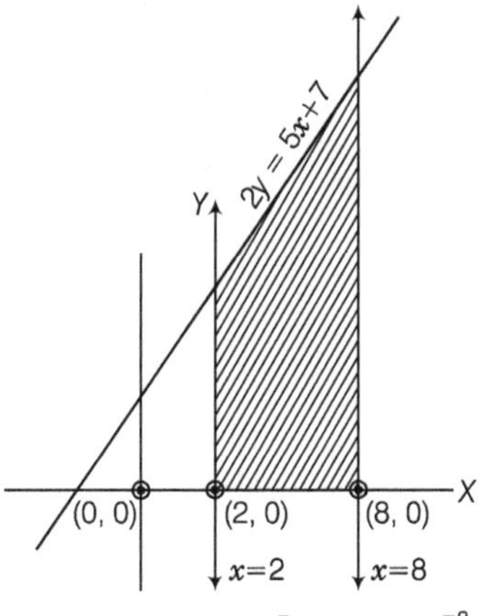

$\therefore$ Area of shaded region $= \frac{1}{2}\int_2^8 (5x + 7)\, dx = \frac{1}{2}\left[5 \cdot \frac{x^2}{2} + 7x \right]_2^8$

$$= \frac{1}{2}[5 \cdot 32 + 7 \cdot 8 - 10 - 14] = \frac{1}{2}[160 + 56 - 24]$$

$$= \frac{192}{2} = 96 \text{ sq units}$$

Q. 11 Draw a rough sketch of the curve $y = \sqrt{x-1}$ in the interval [1, 5]. Find the area under the curve and between the lines $x = 1$ and $x = 5$.

Sol. Given equation of the curve is $y = \sqrt{x-1}$.

$$\Rightarrow \quad y^2 = x - 1$$

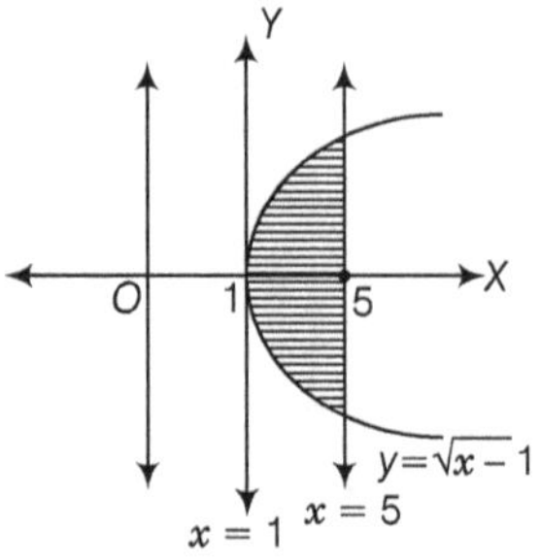

$\therefore$ Area of shaded region, $A = \int_1^5 (x-1)^{1/2}\, dx = \left[\dfrac{2 \cdot (x-1)^{3/2}}{3}\right]_1^5$

$$= \left[\frac{2}{3} \cdot (5-1)^{3/2} - 0\right] = \frac{16}{3} \text{ sq units}$$

Q. 12 Determine the area under the curve $y = \sqrt{a^2 - x^2}$ included between the lines $x = 0$ and $x = a$.

Sol. Given equation of the curve is $y = \sqrt{a^2 - x^2}$.

$$\Rightarrow \quad y^2 = a^2 - x^2 \Rightarrow y^2 + x^2 = a^2$$

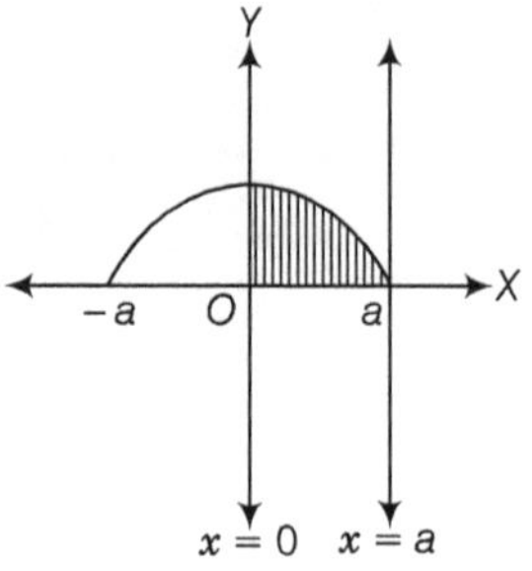

$\therefore$ Required area of shaded region, $A = \int_0^a \sqrt{a^2 - x^2}\, dx$

$$= \left[\frac{x}{2}\sqrt{a^2 - x^2} + \frac{a^2}{2}\sin^{-1}\frac{x}{a}\right]_0^a$$

$$= \left[0 + \frac{a^2}{2}\sin^{-1}(1) - 0 - \frac{a^2}{2}\sin^{-1} 0\right]$$

$$= \frac{a^2}{2} \cdot \frac{\pi}{2} = \frac{\pi a^2}{4} \text{ sq units}$$

Q. 13 Find the area of the region bounded by $y = \sqrt{x}$ and $y = x$.

Sol. Given equation of curves are $y = \sqrt{x}$ and $y = x$.

$\Rightarrow \quad x = \sqrt{x} \Rightarrow x^2 = x$

$\Rightarrow \quad x^2 - x = 0 \Rightarrow x(x-1) = 0$

$\Rightarrow \quad x = 0, 1$

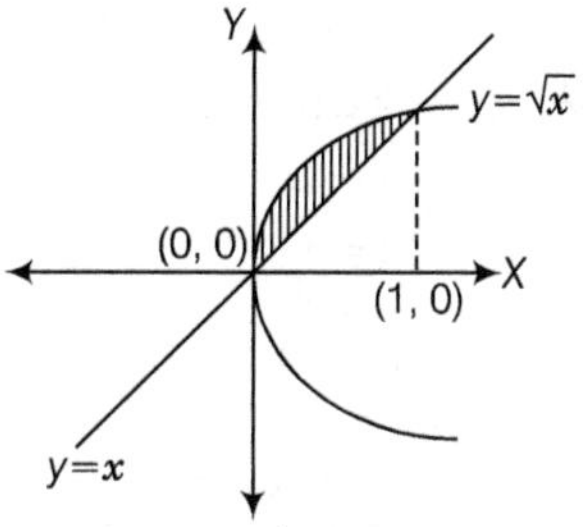

$\therefore$ Required area of shaded region, $A = \int_0^1 (\sqrt{x})dx - \int_0^1 x dx$

$$= \left[2 \cdot \frac{x^{3/2}}{3}\right]_0^1 - \left[\frac{x^2}{2}\right]_0^1$$

$$= \frac{2}{3} \cdot 1 - \frac{1}{2} = \frac{2}{3} - \frac{1}{2} = \frac{1}{6} \text{ sq units}$$

Q. 14 Find the area enclosed by the curve $y = -x^2$ and the straight line $x + y + 2 = 0$.

Sol. We have, $y = -x^2$ and $x + y + 2 = 0$

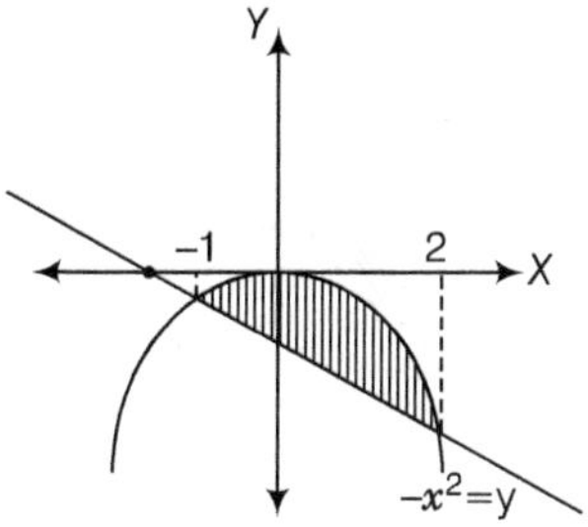

$\Rightarrow \quad -x - 2 = -x^2 \Rightarrow x^2 - x - 2 = 0$

$\Rightarrow \quad x^2 + x - 2x - 2 = 0 \Rightarrow x(x+1) - 2(x+1) = 0$

$\Rightarrow \quad (x-2)(x+1) = 0 \Rightarrow x = 2, -1$

$\therefore$ Area of shaded region, $A = \left|\int_{-1}^2 (-x - 2 + x^2)\, dx\right| = \left|\int_{-1}^2 (x^2 - x - 2)\, dx\right|$

$$= \left|\left[\frac{x^3}{3} - \frac{x^2}{2} - 2x\right]_{-1}^2\right| = \left|\left[\frac{8}{3} - \frac{4}{2} - 4 + \frac{1}{3} + \frac{1}{2} - 2\right]\right|$$

$$= \left|\frac{16 - 12 - 24 + 2 + 3 - 12}{6}\right| = \left|-\frac{27}{6}\right| = \frac{9}{2} \text{ sq units}$$

Q. 15 Find the area bounded by the curve $y=\sqrt{x}$, $x=2y+3$ in the first quadrant and X-axis.

Sol. Given equation of the curves are $y=\sqrt{x}$ and $x=2y+3$ in the first quadrant.

On solving both the equations for y, we get

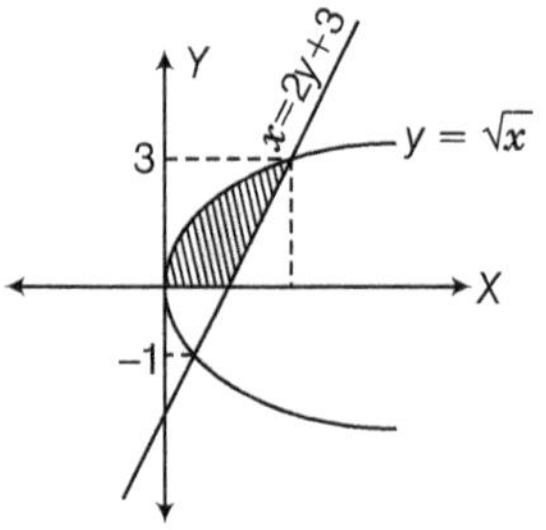

$$y=\sqrt{2y+3}$$

$$\Rightarrow \quad y^2=2y+3$$

$$\Rightarrow \quad y^2-2y-3=0$$

$$\Rightarrow \quad y^2-3y+y-3=0$$

$$\Rightarrow \quad y(y-3)+1(y-3)=0$$

$$\Rightarrow \quad (y+1)(y-3)=0$$

$$\Rightarrow \quad y=-1,3$$

$\therefore$ Required area of shaded region,

$$A=\int_0^3(2y+3-y^2)dy=\left[\frac{2y^2}{2}+3y-\frac{y^3}{3}\right]_0^3$$

$$=\left[\frac{18}{2}+9-9-0\right]=9 \text{ sq units}$$

Long Answer Type Questions

Q. 16 Find the area of the region bounded by the curve $y^2=2x$ and $x^2+y^2=4x$.

Sol. We have, $y^2=2x$ and $x^2+y^2=4x$

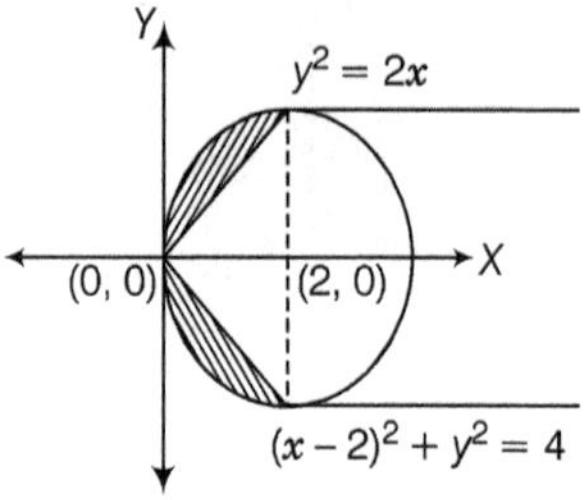

$$\Rightarrow \quad x^2+2x=4x$$

$$\Rightarrow \quad x^2-2x=0$$

$$\Rightarrow \quad x(x-2)=0$$

$$\Rightarrow \quad x=0,2$$

Also, $$x^2+y^2=4x$$

$$\Rightarrow \quad x^2-4x=-y^2$$

$$\Rightarrow \quad x^2-4x+4=-y^2+4$$

$$\Rightarrow \quad (x-2)^2-2^2=-y^2$$

$\therefore$ Required area $= 2\cdot\int_0^2 \left[\sqrt{2^2-(x-2)^2}-\sqrt{2x}\right]dx$

$$= 2\left[\left[\frac{x-2}{2}\cdot\sqrt{2^2-(x-2)^2}+\frac{2^2}{2}\sin^{-1}\left(\frac{x-2}{2}\right)\right]_0^2-\left[\sqrt{2}\cdot\frac{x^{3/2}}{3/2}\right]_0^2\right]$$

$$= 2\left[\left(0+0-1\cdot 0+2\cdot\frac{\pi}{2}\right)-\frac{2\sqrt{2}}{3}(2^{3/2}-0)\right]$$

$$= \frac{4\pi}{2}-\frac{8\cdot 2}{3}=2\pi-\frac{16}{3}=2\left(\pi-\frac{8}{3}\right)\text{ sq units}$$

Q. 17 Find the area bounded by the curve $y=\sin x$ between $x=0$ and $x=2\pi$.

Thinking Process

We know that, $\sin x$ curve has positive region from $[0,\pi]$ and negative region in $[\pi,2\pi]$.

Sol. Required area $=\int_0^{2\pi}\sin x\,dx=\int_0^{\pi}\sin x\,dx+\left|\int_{\pi}^{2\pi}\sin x\,dx\right|$

$$=-[\cos x]_0^{\pi}+\left|[-\cos x]_{\pi}^{2\pi}\right|$$

$$=-[\cos\pi-\cos 0]+\left|-[\cos 2\pi-\cos\pi]\right|$$

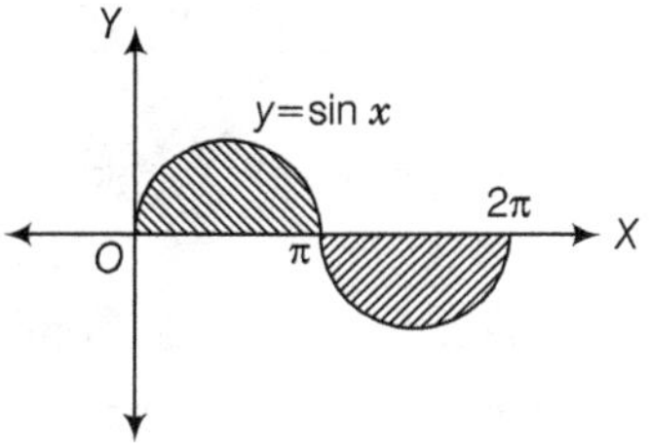

$$=-[-1-1]+|-(1+1)|$$

$$=2+2=4\text{ sq units}$$

Q. 18 Find the area of region bounded by the triangle whose vertices are (– 1, 1), (0, 5) and (3, 2), using integration.

Sol. Let we have the vertices of a ΔABC as $A(-1, 1)$, $B(0, 5)$ and $C(3, 2)$.

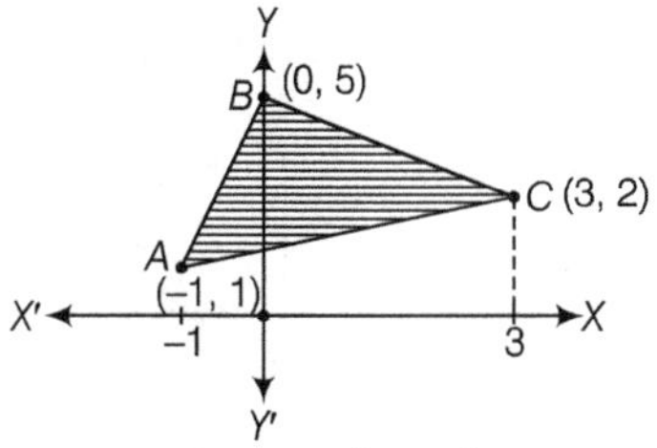

$\therefore$ Equation of AB is $y-1=\left(\frac{5-1}{0+1}\right)(x+1)$

$\Rightarrow$ $y-1=4x+4$

$\Rightarrow$ $y=4x+5$ ...(i)

and equation of BC is $y-5=\left(\frac{2-5}{3-0}\right)(x-0)$

$$\Rightarrow \quad y - 5 = \frac{-3}{3}(x)$$

$$\Rightarrow \quad y = 5 - x \qquad \ldots\text{(ii)}$$

Similarly, equation of AC is $y - 1 = \left(\frac{2-1}{3+1}\right)(x+1)$

$$\Rightarrow \quad y - 1 = \frac{1}{4}(x+1)$$

$$\Rightarrow \quad 4y = x + 5 \qquad \ldots\text{(iii)}$$

$\therefore$ Area of shaded region $= \int_{-1}^{0}(y_1 - y_2)dx + \int_{0}^{3}(y_1 - y_2)dx$

$$= \int_{-1}^{0}\left[4x + 5 - \frac{x+5}{4}\right]dx + \int_{0}^{3}\left[5 - x - \frac{x+5}{4}\right]dx$$

$$= \left[\frac{4x^2}{2} + 5x - \frac{x^2}{8} - \frac{5x}{4}\right]_{-1}^{0} + \left[5x - \frac{x^2}{2} - \frac{x^2}{8} - \frac{5x}{4}\right]_{0}^{3}$$

$$= \left[0 - \left(4\cdot\frac{1}{2} + 5(-1) - \frac{1}{8} + \frac{5}{4}\right)\right] + \left[\left(15 - \frac{9}{2} - \frac{9}{8} - \frac{15}{4}\right) - 0\right]$$

$$= \left[-2 + 5 + \frac{1}{8} - \frac{5}{4} + 15 - \frac{9}{2} - \frac{9}{8} - \frac{15}{4}\right]$$

$$= 18 + \left(\frac{1 - 10 - 36 - 9 - 30}{8}\right)$$

$$= 18 + \left(-\frac{84}{8}\right) = 18 - \frac{21}{2} = \frac{15}{2} \text{ sq units}$$

Q. 19 Draw a rough sketch of the region $\{(x, y) : y^2 \le 6ax$ and $x^2 + y^2 \le 16a^2\}$. Also, find the area of the region sketched using method of integration.

Sol. We have, $y^2 = 6ax$ and $x^2 + y^2 = 16a^2$

$$\Rightarrow \quad x^2 + 6ax = 16a^2$$

$$\Rightarrow \quad x^2 + 6ax - 16a^2 = 0$$

$$\Rightarrow \quad x^2 + 8ax - 2ax - 16a^2 = 0$$

$$\Rightarrow \quad x(x + 8a) - 2a(x + 8a) = 0$$

$$\Rightarrow \quad (x - 2a)(x + 8a) = 0$$

$$\Rightarrow \quad x = 2a, -8a$$

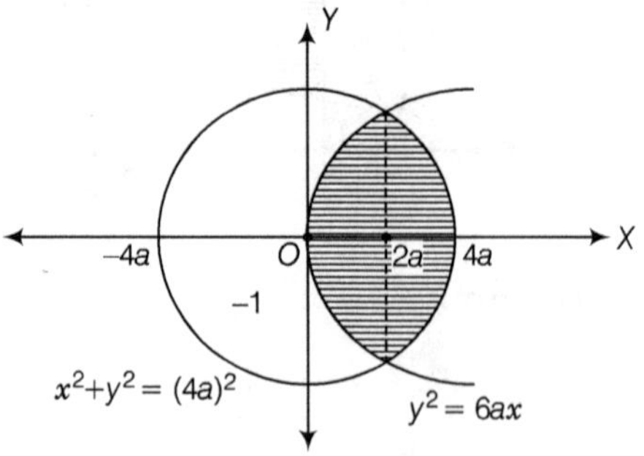

$\therefore$ Area of required region $= 2\left[\int_0^{2a}\sqrt{6ax}\,dx + \int_{2a}^{4a}\sqrt{(4a)^2 - x^2}dx\right]$

$$= 2\left[\int_0^{2a}\sqrt{6a}\,x^{1/2}dx + \int_{2a}^{4a}\sqrt{(4a)^2 - x^2}dx\right]$$

$$= 2\left[\sqrt{6a}\left[\frac{x^{3/2}}{3/2}\right]_0^{2a} + \left(\frac{x}{2}\sqrt{(4a)^2 - x^2} + \frac{(4a)^2}{2}\sin^{-1}\frac{x}{4a}\right)_{2a}^{4a}\right]$$

$$= 2\left[\sqrt{6a}\cdot\frac{2}{3}((2a)^{3/2} - 0) + \frac{4a}{2}\cdot 0 + \frac{16a^2}{2}\cdot\frac{\pi}{2} - \frac{2a}{2}\sqrt{16a^2 - 4a^2} - \frac{16a^2}{2}\cdot\sin^{-1}\frac{2a}{4a}\right]$$

$$= 2\left[\sqrt{6a}\;\frac{2}{3}\cdot 2\sqrt{2}\,a^{3/2} + 0 + 4\pi a^2 - \frac{2a}{2}\cdot 2\sqrt{3}a - 8a^2\cdot\frac{\pi}{6}\right]$$

$$= 2\left[\sqrt{12}\cdot\frac{4}{3}a^2 + 4\pi a^2 - 2\sqrt{3}a^2 - \frac{4a^2\pi}{3}\right]$$

$$= 2\left[\frac{8\sqrt{3}a^2 + 12\pi a^2 - 6\sqrt{3}a^2 - 4a^2\pi}{3}\right]$$

$$= \frac{2}{3}a^2[8\sqrt{3} + 12\pi - 6\sqrt{3} - 4\pi]$$

$$= \frac{2}{3}a^2[2\sqrt{3} + 8\pi] = \frac{4}{3}a^2[\sqrt{3} + 4\pi]$$

Q. 20 Compute the area bounded by the lines $x + 2y = 2$, $y - x = 1$ and $2x + y = 7$.

Sol. We have, $x + 2y = 2$ ...(i)

$y - x = 1$ ...(ii)

and $2x + y = 7$ ...(iii)

On solving Eqs. (i) and (ii), we get

$$y - (2 - 2y) = 1 \Rightarrow 3y - 2 = 1 \Rightarrow y = 1$$

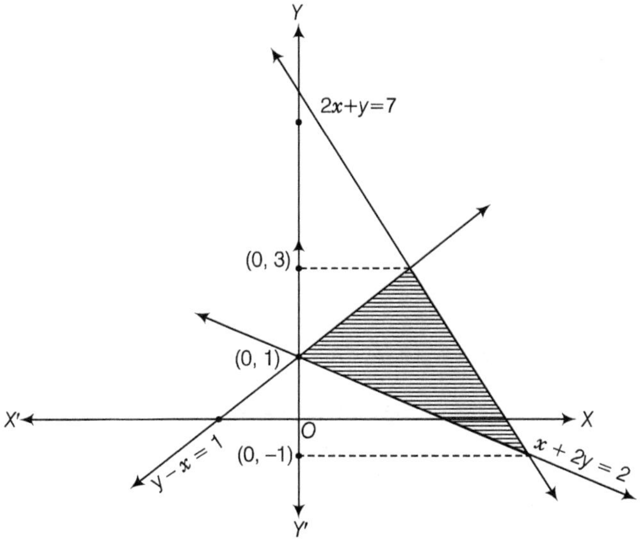

$$2(y - 1) + y = 7$$

On solving Eqs. (ii) and (iii), we get

$$\Rightarrow \quad 2y - 2 + y = 7$$

$$\Rightarrow \quad y = 3$$

On solving Eqs. (i) and (iii), we get

$$2(2-2y) + y = 7$$

$$\Rightarrow \quad 4 - 4y + y = 7$$

$$\Rightarrow \quad -3y = 3$$

$$\Rightarrow \quad y = -1$$

$$\therefore \text{ Required area} = \int_{-1}^{1} (2-2y)\,dy + \int_{-1}^{3} \frac{(7-y)}{2}\,dy - \int_{1}^{3} (y-1)\,dy$$

$$= \left[-2y + \frac{2y^2}{2}\right]_{-1}^{1} + \left[\frac{7y}{2} - \frac{y^2}{2\cdot 2}\right]_{-1}^{3} - \left[\frac{y^2}{2} - y\right]_{1}^{3}$$

$$= \left[-2 + \frac{2}{2} - 2 - \frac{2}{2}\right] + \left[\frac{21}{2} - \frac{9}{4} + \frac{7}{2} + \frac{1}{4}\right] - \left[\frac{9}{2} - 3 - \frac{1}{2} + 1\right]$$

$$= [-4] + \left[\frac{42 - 9 + 14 + 1}{4}\right] - \left[\frac{9 - 6 - 1 + 2}{2}\right]$$

$$= -4 + 12 - 2 = 6 \text{ sq units}$$

Q. 21 Find the area bounded by the lines $y = 4x + 5$, $y = 5 - x$ and $4y = x + 5$.

Sol.

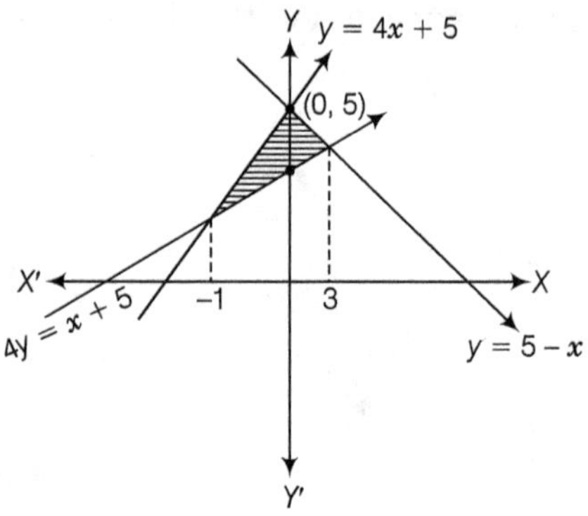

Given equations of lines are

$$y = 4x + 5 \quad \ldots(i)$$

$$y = 5 - x \quad \ldots(ii)$$

and

$$4y = x + 5 \quad \ldots(iii)$$

On solving Eqs. (i) and (ii), we get

$$4x + 5 = 5 - x$$

$$\Rightarrow \quad x = 0$$

On solving Eqs. (i) and (iii), we get

$$4(4x+5) = x + 5$$

$$\Rightarrow \quad 16x + 20 = x + 5$$

$$\Rightarrow \quad 15x = -15$$

$$\Rightarrow \quad x = -1$$

On solving Eqs. (ii) and (iii), we get

$$4(5 - x) = x + 5$$

$$\Rightarrow \quad 20 - 4x = x + 5$$

$$\Rightarrow \quad x = 3$$

$\therefore$ Required area $= \int_{-1}^{0}(4x+5)dx + \int_{0}^{3}(5-x)dx - \frac{1}{4}\int_{-1}^{3}(x+5)dx$

$$= \left[\frac{4x^2}{2}+5x\right]_{-1}^{0} + \left[5x-\frac{x^2}{2}\right]_{0}^{3} - \frac{1}{4}\left[\frac{x^2}{2}+5x\right]_{-1}^{3}$$

$$= [0-2+5] + \left[15-\frac{9}{2}-0\right] - \frac{1}{4}\left[\frac{9}{2}+15-\frac{1}{2}+5\right]$$

$$= 3+\frac{21}{2}-\frac{1}{4}\cdot 24$$

$$= -3+\frac{21}{2}=\frac{15}{2} \text{ sq units}$$

Q. 22 Find the area bounded by the curve $y = 2\cos x$ and the X-axis from $x = 0$ to $x = 2\pi$.

Sol. Required area of shaded region $= \int_0^{2\pi} 2\cos x dx$

$$= \int_0^{\pi/2} 2\cos x\, dx + \left|\int_{\pi/2}^{3\pi/2} 2\cos x dx\right| + \int_{3\pi/2}^{2\pi} 2\cos x\, dx$$

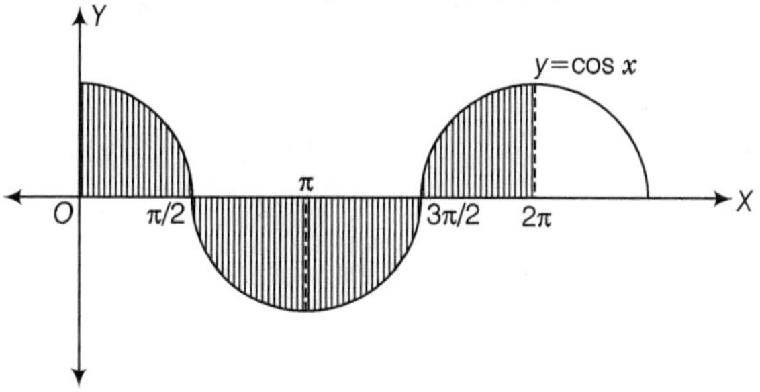

$$= 2[\sin x]_0^{\pi/2} + \left|2(\sin x)_{\pi/2}^{3\pi/2}\right| + 2[\sin x]_{3\pi/2}^{2\pi}$$

$$= 2+4+2 = 8 \text{ sq units}$$

Q. 23 Draw a rough sketch of the given curve $y = 1+|x+1|$, $x=-3$, $x=3$, $y=0$ and find the area of the region bounded by them, using integration.

Sol. We have, $y = 1+|x+1|$, $x=-3$, $x=3$ and $y=0$

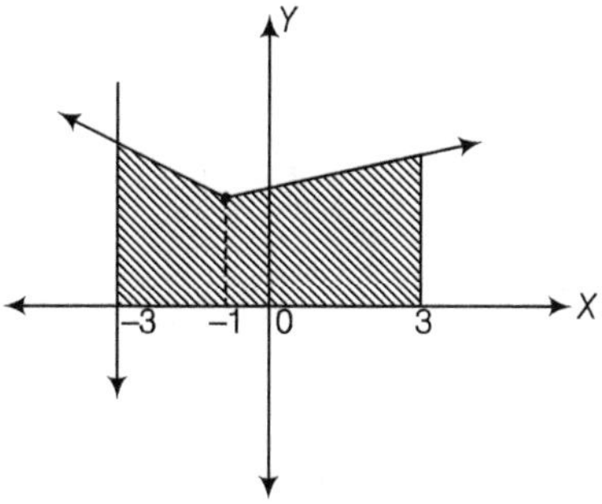

$\because$ $$y = \begin{cases} -x, & \text{if } x < -1 \\ x+2, & \text{if } x \geq -1 \end{cases}$$

$\therefore$ Area of shaded region, $A = \int_{-3}^{-1} -x\,dx + \int_{-1}^{3}(x+2)\,dx$

$$= -\left[\frac{x^2}{2}\right]_{-3}^{-1} + \left[\frac{x^2}{2} + 2x\right]_{-1}^{3}$$

$$= -\left[\frac{1}{2} - \frac{9}{2}\right] + \left[\frac{9}{2} + 6 - \frac{1}{2} + 2\right]$$

$$= -[-4] + [8+4]$$

$$= 12 + 4 = 16 \text{ sq units}$$

Objective Type Questions

Q. 24 The area of the region bounded by the Y-axis $y = \cos x$ and $y = \sin x$, where $0 \leq x \leq \frac{\pi}{2}$, is

(a) $\sqrt{2}$ sq units (b) $(\sqrt{2}+1)$ sq units

(c) $(\sqrt{2}-1)$ sq units (d) $(2\sqrt{2}-1)$ sq units

Sol. *(c)* We have, Y-axis *i.e.*, $x = 0$, $y = \cos x$ and $y = \sin x$, where $0 \leq x \leq \frac{\pi}{2}$.

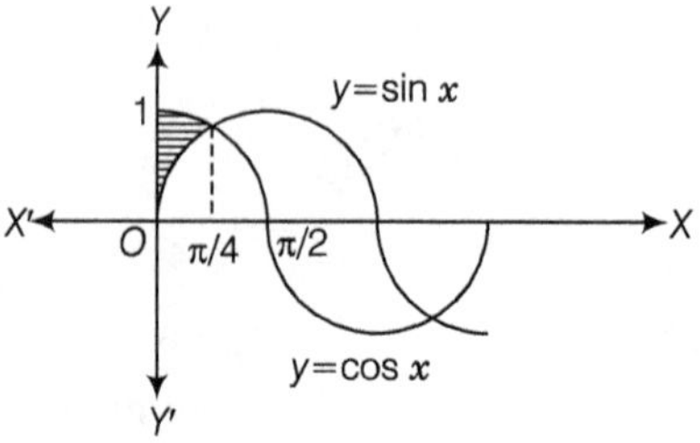

$\therefore$ Required area $= \int_0^{\pi/4} (\cos x - \sin x)dx$

$$= [\sin x]_0^{\pi/4} + [\cos x]_0^{\pi/4}$$

$$= \left(\sin\frac{\pi}{4} - \sin 0\right) + \left(\cos\frac{\pi}{4} - \cos 0\right)$$

$$= \left(\frac{1}{\sqrt{2}} - 0\right) + \left(\frac{1}{\sqrt{2}} - 1\right)$$

$$= \frac{1}{\sqrt{2}} + \frac{1}{\sqrt{2}} - 1$$

$$= -1 + \frac{2}{\sqrt{2}} = \frac{-\sqrt{2}+2}{\sqrt{2}}$$

$$= \frac{-2+2\sqrt{2}}{2} = (\sqrt{2}-1) \text{ sq units}$$

Q. 25 The area of the region bounded by the curve $x^2 = 4y$ and the straight line $x = 4y - 2$ is

(a) $\frac{3}{8}$ sq unit (b) $\frac{5}{8}$ sq unit

(c) $\frac{7}{8}$ sq unit (d) $\frac{9}{8}$ sq units

Sol. *(d)* Given equation of curve is $x^2 = 4y$ and the straight line $x = 4y - 2$.

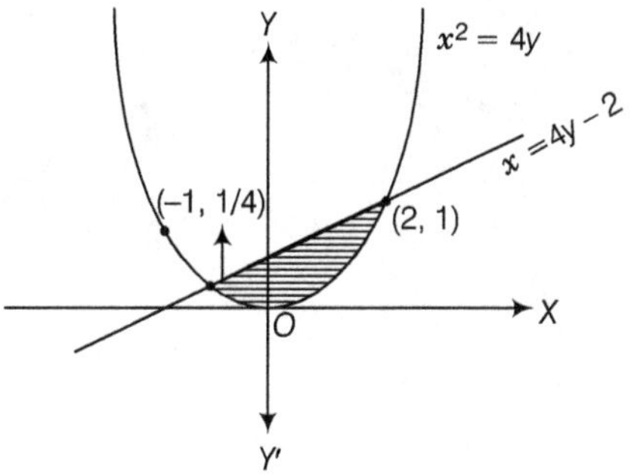

For intersection point, put $x = 4y - 2$ in equation of curve, we get

$$(4y - 2)^2 = 4y$$

$$\Rightarrow \quad 16y^2 + 4 - 16y = 4y$$

$$\Rightarrow \quad 16y^2 - 20y + 4 = 0$$

$$\Rightarrow \quad 4y^2 - 5y + 1 = 0$$

$$\Rightarrow \quad 4y^2 - 4y - y + 1 = 0$$

$$\Rightarrow \quad 4y(y-1) - 1(y-1) = 0$$

$$\Rightarrow \quad (4y - 1)(y - 1) = 0$$

$$\therefore \quad y = 1, \frac{1}{4}$$

For $y = 1$, $x = \sqrt{4 \cdot 1} = 2$ [since, negative value does not satisfy the equation of line]

For $y = \frac{1}{4}$, $x = \sqrt{4 \cdot \frac{1}{4}} = -1$ [positive value does not satisfy the equation of line]

So, the intersection points are (2, 1) and $\left(-1, \frac{1}{4}\right)$.

$$\therefore \text{ Area of shaded region} = \int_{-1}^{2}\left(\frac{x+2}{4}\right)dx - \int_{-1}^{2}\frac{x^2}{4}dx$$

$$= \frac{1}{4}\left[\frac{x^2}{2} + 2x\right]_{-1}^{2} - \frac{1}{4}\left|\frac{x^3}{3}\right|_{-1}^{2}$$

$$= -\frac{1}{4}\left[\frac{4}{2} + 4 - -\frac{1}{2} + 2\right] - \frac{1}{4}\left[\frac{8}{3} + \frac{1}{3}\right]$$

$$= \frac{1}{4} \cdot \frac{15}{2} - \frac{1}{4} \cdot \frac{9}{3} = \frac{45 - 18}{24}$$

$$= \frac{27}{24} = \frac{9}{8} \text{ sq units}$$

Q. 26 The area of the region bounded by the curve $y = \sqrt{16 - x^2}$ and X-axis is

(a) 8π sq units (b) 20π sq units
(c) 16π sq units (d) 256π sq units

Sol. *(a)* Given equation of curve is $y = \sqrt{16 - x^2}$ and the equation of line is X-axis *i.e.*, $y = 0$.

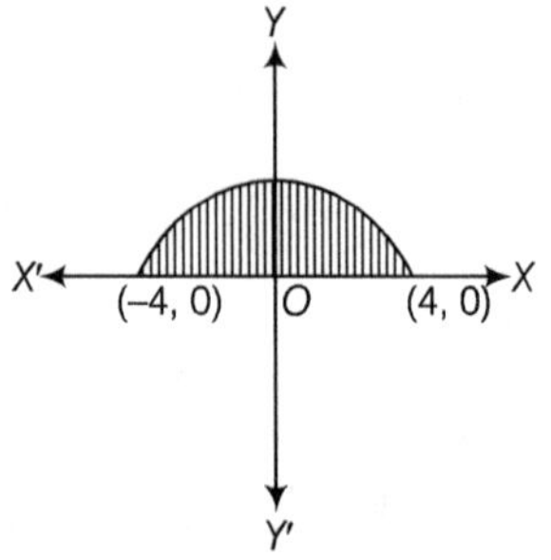

$$\therefore \quad \sqrt{16 - x^2} = 0 \quad \quad \ldots(\text{i})$$
$$\Rightarrow \quad 16 - x^2 = 0$$
$$\Rightarrow \quad x^2 = 16$$
$$\Rightarrow \quad x = \pm 4$$

So, the intersection points are (4, 0) and (–4, 0).

$$\therefore \text{ Area of curve, } A = \int_{-4}^{4} (16 - x^2)^{1/2} dx$$
$$= \int_{-4}^{4} \sqrt{(4^2 - x^2)}\, dx$$
$$= \left[\frac{x}{2}\sqrt{4^2 - x^2} + \frac{4^2}{2}\sin^{-1}\frac{x}{4}\right]_{-4}^{4}$$
$$= \left[\frac{4}{2}\sqrt{4^2 - 4^2} + 8\sin^{-1}\frac{4}{4}\right] - \left[-\frac{4}{2}\sqrt{4^2 - (-4)^2} + 8\sin^{-1}\left(-\frac{4}{4}\right)\right]$$
$$= \left[2 \cdot 0 + 8 \cdot \frac{\pi}{2} - 0 + 8 \cdot \frac{\pi}{2}\right] = 8\pi \text{ sq units}$$

Q. 27 Area of the region in the first quadrant enclosed by the X-axis, the line $y = x$ and the circle $x^2 + y^2 = 32$ is

(a) 16π sq units (b) 4π sq units (c) 32π sq units (d) 24π sq units

Sol. *(b)* We have, area enclosed by X-axis *i.e.*, $y = 0$, $y = x$ and the circle $x^2 + y^2 = 32$ in first quadrant.

$$\text{Since,} \quad x^2 + (x)^2 = 32 \quad \quad [\because y = x]$$
$$\Rightarrow \quad 2x^2 = 32$$
$$\Rightarrow \quad x = \pm 4$$

So, the intersection point of circle $x^2 + y^2 = 32$ and line $y = x$ are (4, 4) or (– 4, 4).

$$\text{and} \quad x^2 + y^2 = (4\sqrt{2})^2$$
$$\text{Since,} \quad y = 0$$
$$\therefore \quad x^2 + (0)^2 = 32$$
$$\Rightarrow \quad x = \pm 4\sqrt{2}$$

So, the circle intersects the X-axis at $(\pm 4\sqrt{2}, 0)$.

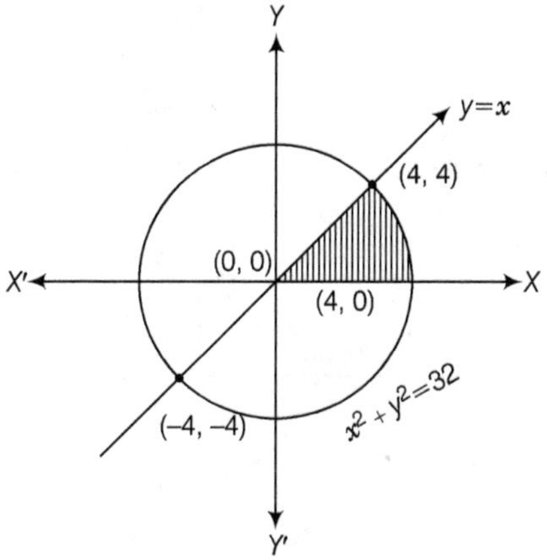

$$\text{Area of shaded region} = \int_0^4 x\,dx + \int_4^{4\sqrt{2}} \sqrt{(4\sqrt{2})^2 - x^2}\,dx$$

$$= \left|\frac{x^2}{2}\right|_0^4 + \left|\frac{x}{2}\sqrt{(4\sqrt{2})^2 - x^2} + \frac{(4\sqrt{2})^2}{2}\sin^{-1}\frac{x}{4\sqrt{2}}\right|_4^{4\sqrt{2}}$$

$$= \frac{16}{2} + \left[\frac{4\sqrt{2}}{2}\cdot 0 + 16\sin^{-1}\frac{(4\sqrt{2})}{(4\sqrt{2})} - \frac{4}{2}\sqrt{(4\sqrt{2})^2 - 16} - 16\sin^{-1}\frac{4}{4\sqrt{2}}\right]$$

$$= 8 + \left[16\cdot\frac{\pi}{2} - 2\cdot\sqrt{16} - 16\cdot\frac{\pi}{4}\right]$$

$$= 8 + [8\pi - 8 - 4\pi] = 4\pi \text{ sq units}$$

Q. 28 Area of the region bounded by the curve $y = \cos x$ between $x = 0$ and $x = \pi$ is

(a) 2 sq units (b) 4 sq units

(c) 3 sq units (d) 1 sq unit

Sol. ***(a)*** Required area enclosed by the curve $y = \cos x$, $x = 0$ and $x = \pi$ is

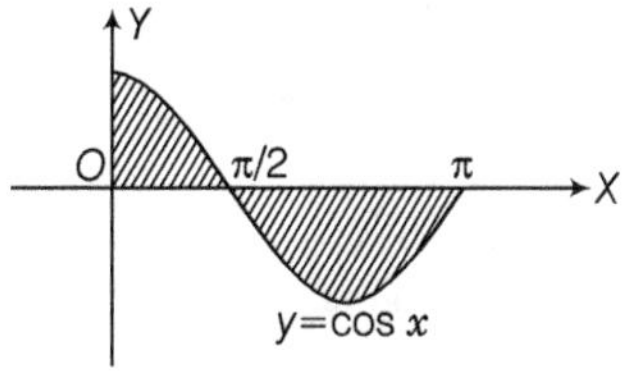

$$A = \int_0^{\pi/2} \cos x\,dx + \left|\int_{\pi/2}^{\pi} \cos x\,dx\right|$$

$$= \left[\sin\frac{\pi}{2} - \sin 0\right] + \left|\sin\frac{\pi}{2} - \sin\pi\right|$$

$$= 1 + 1 = 2 \text{ sq units}$$

Q. 29 The area of the region bounded by parabola $y^2 = x$ and the straight line $2y = x$ is

(a) $\frac{4}{3}$ sq units (b) 1 sq unit (c) $\frac{2}{3}$ sq unit (d) $\frac{1}{3}$ sq unit

Sol. *(a)* We have to find the area enclosed by parabola $y^2 = x$ and the straight line $2y = x$.

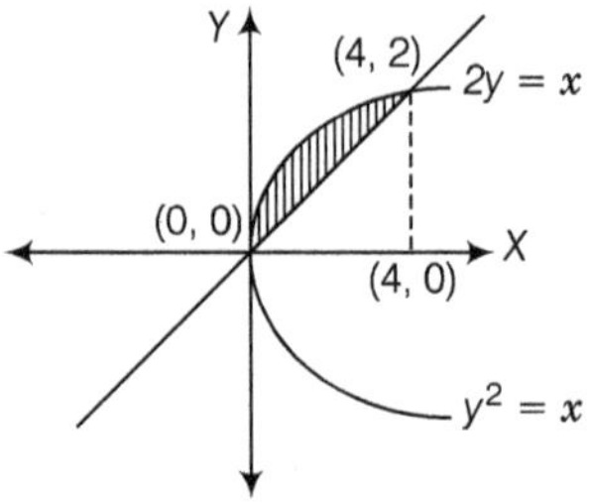

$$\therefore \quad \left(\frac{x}{2}\right)^2 = x$$

$$\Rightarrow \quad x^2 = 4x \Rightarrow x(x-4) = 0$$

$$\Rightarrow \quad x = 4 \Rightarrow y = 2 \text{ and } x = 0 \Rightarrow y = 0$$

So, the intersection points are (0, 0) and (4, 2).

Area enclosed by shaded region,

$$A = \int_0^4 \left[\sqrt{x} - \frac{x}{2}\right] dx$$

$$= \left[\frac{x^{\frac{1}{2}+1}}{\frac{1}{2}+1} - \frac{1}{2}\cdot\frac{x^2}{2}\right]_0^4 = \left[2\cdot\frac{x^{3/2}}{3} - \frac{x^2}{4}\right]_0^4$$

$$= \frac{2}{3}4^{3/2} - \frac{16}{4} - \frac{2}{3}\cdot 0 + \frac{1}{4}\cdot 0$$

$$= \frac{16}{3} - \frac{16}{4} = \frac{64-48}{12} = \frac{16}{12} = \frac{4}{3} \text{ sq units}$$

Q. 30 The area of the region bounded by the curve $y = \sin x$ between the ordinates $x = 0$, $x = \frac{\pi}{2}$ and the X-axis is

(a) 2 sq units (b) 4 sq units (c) 3 sq units (d) 1 sq unit

Sol. *(d)* Area of the region bounded by the curve $y = \sin x$ between the ordinates $x = 0$, $x = \frac{\pi}{2}$ and the X-axis is

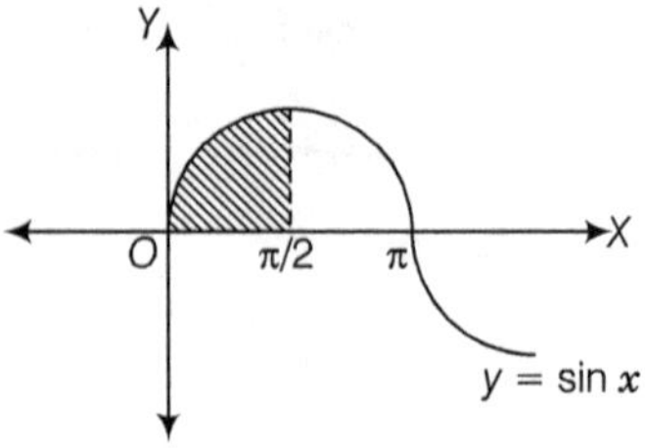

$$A = \int_0^{\pi/2} \sin x\,dx$$

$$= -[\cos x]_0^{\pi/2} = -\left[\cos\frac{\pi}{2} - \cos 0\right]$$

$$= -[0 - 1] = 1 \text{ sq unit}$$

Q. 31 The area of the region bounded by the ellipse $\frac{x^2}{25} + \frac{y^2}{16} = 1$ is

(a) 20π sq units (b) $20\pi^2$ sq units (c) $16\pi^2$ sq units (d) 25π sq units

Sol. *(a)* We have, $\frac{x^2}{5^2} + \frac{y^2}{4^2} = 1$

Here, $a = \pm 5$ and $b = \pm 4$

and $\frac{y^2}{4^2} = 1 - \frac{x^2}{5^2}$

$\Rightarrow$ $y^2 = 16\left(1 - \frac{x^2}{25}\right)$

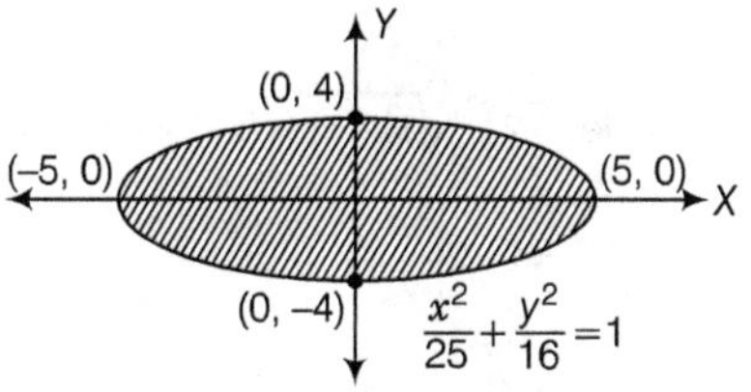

$\Rightarrow$ $y = \sqrt{\frac{16}{25}(25 - x^2)}$

$\Rightarrow$ $y = \frac{4}{5}\sqrt{(5^2 - x^2)}$

$\therefore$ Area enclosed by ellipse, $A = 2 \cdot \frac{4}{5}\int_{-5}^{5} \sqrt{5^2 - x^2}\,dx$

$$= 2 \cdot \frac{8}{5}\int_0^5 \sqrt{5^2 - x^2}\,dx$$

$$= 2 \cdot \frac{8}{5}\left[\frac{x}{2}\sqrt{5^2 - x^2} + \frac{5^2}{2}\sin^{-1}\frac{x}{5}\right]_0^5$$

$$= 2 \cdot \frac{8}{5}\left[\frac{5}{2}\sqrt{5^2 - 5^2} + \frac{5^2}{2}\sin^{-1}\frac{5}{5} - 0 - \frac{25}{2}\cdot 0\right]$$

$$= 2 \cdot \frac{8}{5}\left[\frac{25}{2}\cdot\frac{\pi}{2}\right]$$

$$= \frac{16}{5}\cdot\frac{25\pi}{4}$$

$$= 20\pi \text{ sq units}$$

Q. 32 The area of the region bounded by the circle $x^2 + y^2 = 1$ is

(a) 2π sq units (b) π sq units
(c) 3π sq units (d) 4π sq units

Sol. *(b)* We have, $x^2 + y^2 = 1^2$ $[\because r = \pm 1]$

$\Rightarrow \quad y^2 = 1 - x^2 \Rightarrow y = \sqrt{1 - x^2}$

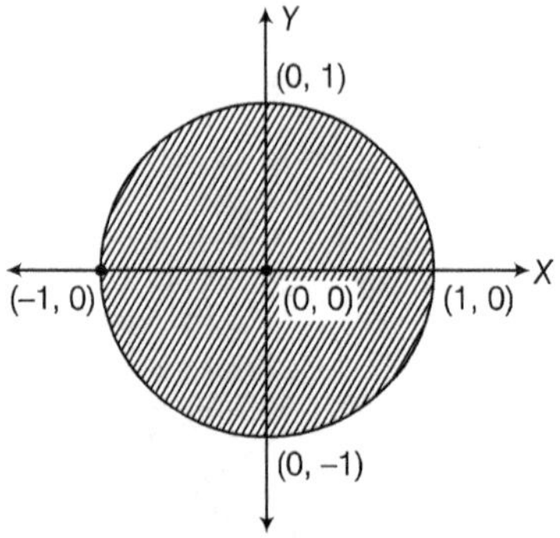

$\therefore$ Area enclosed by circle $= 2\int_{-1}^{1}\sqrt{1^2 - x^2}\,dx = 2 \cdot 2\int_{0}^{1}\sqrt{1^2 - x^2}\,dx$

$$= 2 \cdot 2\left[\frac{x}{2}\sqrt{1^2 - x^2} + \frac{1^2}{2}\sin^{-1}\frac{x}{1}\right]_0^1$$

$$= 4\left[\frac{1}{2} \cdot 0 + \frac{1}{2} \cdot \frac{\pi}{2} - 0 - \frac{1}{2} \cdot 0\right]$$

$$= 4 \cdot \frac{\pi}{4} = \pi \text{ sq units}$$

Q. 33 The area of the region bounded by the curve $y = x + 1$ and the lines $x = 2$, $x = 3$, is

(a) $\frac{7}{2}$ sq units (b) $\frac{9}{2}$ sq units (c) $\frac{11}{2}$ sq units (d) $\frac{13}{2}$ sq units

Sol. *(a)* Required area, $A = \int_2^3 (x + 1)dx = \left[\frac{x^2}{2} + x\right]_2^3$

$$= \left[\frac{9}{2} + 3 - \frac{4}{2} - 2\right] = \left[\frac{5}{2} + 1\right] = \frac{7}{2} \text{ sq units}$$

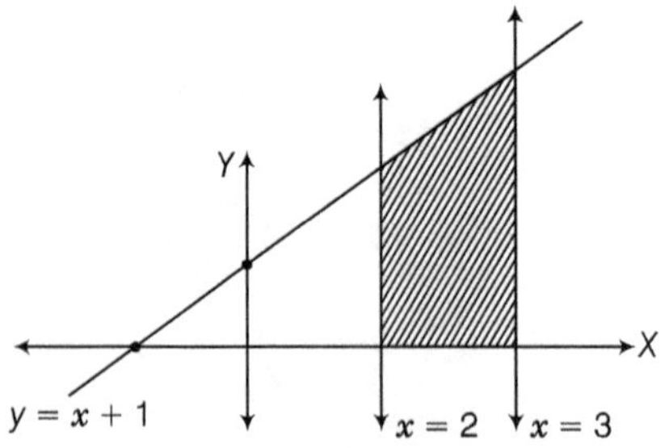

Q. 34 The area of the region bounded by the curve $x = 2y + 3$ and the lines $y = 1,\ y = -1$ is

(a) 4 sq units (b) $\frac{3}{2}$ sq units

(c) 6 sq units (d) 8 sq units

Sol. *(c)* Required area, $A = \int_{-1}^{1} (2y + 3)dy$

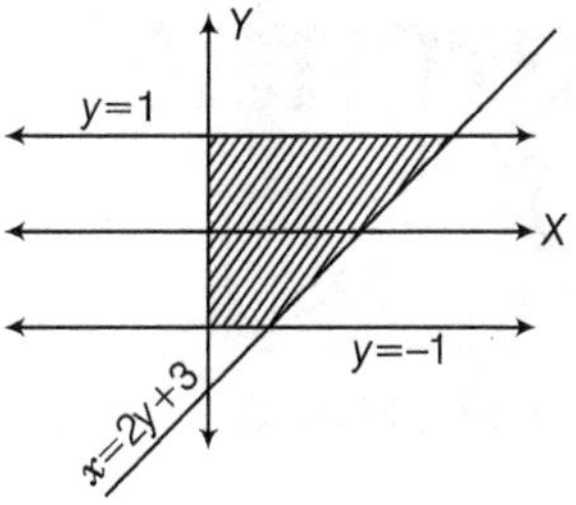

$$= \left[\frac{2y^2}{2} + 3y\right]_{-1}^{1}$$

$$= [y^2 + 3y]_{-1}^{1}$$

$$= [1 + 3 - 1 + 3] \quad = 6 \text{ sq units}$$

9

Differential Equations

Short Answer Type Questions

Q. 1 Find the solution of $\frac{dy}{dx} = 2^{y-x}$.

Sol. Given that,
$$\frac{dy}{dx} = 2^{y-x}$$
$$\Rightarrow \quad \frac{dy}{dx} = \frac{2^y}{2^x} \qquad \left[\because a^{m-n} = \frac{a^m}{a^n}\right]$$
$$\Rightarrow \quad \frac{dy}{2^y} = \frac{dx}{2^x}$$
On integrationg both sides, we get
$$\int 2^{-y} dy = \int 2^{-x} dx$$
$$\Rightarrow \quad \frac{-2^{-y}}{\log 2} = \frac{-2^{-x}}{\log 2} + C$$
$$\Rightarrow \quad -2^{-y} + 2^{-x} = +C \log 2$$
$$\Rightarrow \quad 2^{-x} - 2^{-y} = -C \log 2$$
$$\Rightarrow \quad 2^{-x} - 2^{-y} = K \qquad [\text{where, } K = +C \log 2]$$

Q. 2 Find the differential equation of all non-vertical lines in a plane.

Sol. Since, the family of all non-vertical line is $y = mx + c$, where $m \neq \tan \frac{\pi}{2}$.

On differentiating w.r.t. x, we get
$$\frac{dy}{dx} = m$$
Again, differentiating w.r.t. x, we get
$$\frac{d^2y}{dx^2} = 0$$

Q. 3 If $\frac{dy}{dx} = e^{-2y}$ and $y = 0$ when $x = 5$, then find the value of x when $y = 3$.

Sol. Given that, $\frac{dy}{dx} = e^{-2y} \Rightarrow \frac{dy}{e^{-2y}} = dx$
$$\Rightarrow \quad \int e^{2y} dy = \int dx \Rightarrow \frac{e^{2y}}{2} = x + C \qquad \dots \text{(i)}$$

When $x = 5$ and $y = 0$, then substituting these values in Eq. (i), we get

$$\frac{e^0}{2} = 5 + C$$

$$\Rightarrow \quad \frac{1}{2} = 5 + C \quad \Rightarrow \quad C = \frac{1}{2} - 5 = -\frac{9}{2}$$

Eq. (i) becomes $\quad e^{2y} = 2x - 9$

When $y = 3$, then $\quad e^6 = 2x - 9 \quad \Rightarrow \quad 2x = e^6 + 9$

$$\therefore \quad x = \frac{(e^6 + 9)}{2}$$

Q. 4 Solve $(x^2 - 1)\dfrac{dy}{dx} + 2xy = \dfrac{1}{x^2 - 1}$.

Sol. Given differential equation is

$$(x^2 - 1)\frac{dy}{dx} + 2xy = \frac{1}{x^2 - 1}$$

$$\Rightarrow \quad \frac{dy}{dx} + \left(\frac{2x}{x^2 - 1}\right) y = \frac{1}{(x^2 - 1)^2}$$

which is a linear differential equation.

On comparing it with $\quad \dfrac{dy}{dx} + Py = Q$, we get

$$P = \frac{2x}{x^2 - 1}, Q = \frac{1}{(x^2 - 1)^2}$$

$$\text{IF} = e^{\int P dx} = e^{\int \left(\frac{2x}{x^2 - 1}\right) dx}$$

Put $\quad x^2 - 1 = t \Rightarrow 2x dx = dt$

$$\therefore \quad \text{IF} = e^{\int \frac{dt}{t}} = e^{\log t} = t = (x^2 - 1)$$

The complete solution is

$$y \cdot \text{IF} = \int Q \cdot \text{IF} + K$$

$$\Rightarrow \quad y \cdot (x^2 - 1) = \int \frac{1}{(x^2 - 1)^2} \cdot (x^2 - 1) dx + K$$

$$\Rightarrow \quad y \cdot (x^2 - 1) = \int \frac{dx}{(x^2 - 1)} + K$$

$$\Rightarrow \quad y \cdot (x^2 - 1) = \frac{1}{2} \log \left(\frac{x - 1}{x + 1}\right) + K$$

Q. 5 Solve $\dfrac{dy}{dx} + 2xy = y$.

Sol. Given that, $\quad \dfrac{dy}{dx} + 2xy = y$

$$\Rightarrow \quad \frac{dy}{dx} + 2xy - y = 0$$

$$\Rightarrow \quad \frac{dy}{dx} + (2x - 1) y = 0$$

which is a linear differential equation.

On comparing it with $\frac{dy}{dx} + Py = Q$, we get

$$P = (2x - 1), Q = 0$$

$$\text{IF} = e^{\int P dx} = e^{\int (2x-1)dx}$$

$$= e^{\left(\frac{2x^2}{2} - x\right)} = e^{x^2 - x}$$

The complete solution is

$$y \cdot e^{x^2 - x} = \int Q \cdot e^{x^2 - x} dx + C$$

$\Rightarrow$ $$y . e^{x^2 - x} = 0 + C$$

$\Rightarrow$ $$y = C e^{x - x^2}$$

Q. 6 Find the general solution of $\frac{dy}{dx} + ay = e^{mx}$.

Sol. Given differential equation is

$$\frac{dy}{dx} + ay = e^{mx}$$

which is a linear differential equation.

On comparing it with $\frac{dy}{dx} + Py = Q$, we get

$$P = a, Q = e^{mx}$$

$$\text{IF} = e^{\int P dx} = e^{\int a dx} = e^{ax}$$

The general solution is $$y \cdot e^{ax} = \int e^{mx} \cdot e^{ax} dx + C$$

$\Rightarrow$ $$y \cdot e^{ax} = \int e^{(m+a)x} dx + C$$

$\Rightarrow$ $$y \cdot e^{ax} = \frac{e^{(m+a)x}}{(m+a)} + C$$

$\Rightarrow$ $$(m + a)\, y = \frac{e^{(m+a)x}}{e^{ax}} + \frac{(m+a)C}{e^{ax}}$$

$\Rightarrow$ $$(m + a)\, y = e^{mx} + K e^{-ax}$$ $[\because K = (m+a)C]$

Q. 7 Solve the differential equation $\frac{dy}{dx} + 1 = e^{x+y}$.

Sol. Given differential equation is $$\frac{dy}{dx} + 1 = e^{x+y} \quad \dots \text{(i)}$$

On substituting $x + y = t$, we get

$$1 + \frac{dy}{dx} = \frac{dt}{dx}$$

Eq. (i) becomes $$\frac{dt}{dx} = e^t$$

$\Rightarrow$ $$e^{-t} dt = dx$$

$\Rightarrow$ $$-e^{-t} = x + C$$

$\Rightarrow$ $$\frac{-1}{e^{x+y}} = x + C$$

$\Rightarrow$ $$-1 = (x + C)e^{x+y}$$

$\Rightarrow$ $$(x + C)e^{x+y} + 1 = 0$$

Q. 8 Solve $ydx - xdy = x^2ydx$.

Sol. Given that, $$ydx - xdy = x^2ydx$$

$$\Rightarrow \quad \frac{1}{x^2} - \frac{1}{xy}.\frac{dy}{dx} = 1 \qquad \text{[dividing throughout by } x^2ydx]$$

$$\Rightarrow \quad -\frac{1}{xy}.\frac{dy}{dx} + \frac{1}{x^2} - 1 = 0$$

$$\Rightarrow \quad \frac{dy}{dx} - \frac{xy}{x^2} + xy = 0$$

$$\Rightarrow \quad \frac{dy}{dx} - \frac{y}{x} + xy = 0$$

$$\Rightarrow \quad \frac{dy}{dx} + \left(x - \frac{1}{x}\right)y = 0$$

which is a linear differential equation.

On comparing it with $\frac{dy}{dx} + Py = Q$, we get

$$P = \left(x - \frac{1}{x}\right), Q = 0$$

$$\text{IF} = e^{\int Pdx}$$

$$= e^{\int\left(x - \frac{1}{x}\right)dx}$$

$$= e^{\frac{x^2}{2} - \log x}$$

$$= e^{\frac{x^2}{x}}, e^{-\log x}$$

$$= \frac{1}{x}e^{\frac{x^2}{2}}$$

The general solution is

$$y \cdot \frac{1}{x}e^{x^2/2} = \int 0 \cdot \frac{1}{x}e^{x^2/2}\,dx + C$$

$$\Rightarrow \quad y \cdot \frac{1}{x}e^{x^2/2} = C$$

$$\Rightarrow \quad y = C\,x\,e^{-x^2/2}$$

Q. 9 Solve the differential equation $\frac{dy}{dx} = 1 + x + y^2 + xy^2$, when $y = 0$ and $x = 0$.

Sol. Given that, $$\frac{dy}{dx} = 1 + x + y^2 + xy^2$$

$$\Rightarrow \quad \frac{dy}{dx} = (1 + x) + y^2(1 + x)$$

$$\Rightarrow \quad \frac{dy}{dx} = (1 + y^2)(1 + x)$$

$$\Rightarrow \quad \frac{dy}{1 + y^2} = (1 + x)\,dx$$

On integrating both sides, we get

$$\tan^{-1} y = x + \frac{x^2}{2} + K \qquad \text{... (i)}$$

When $y = 0$ and $x = 0$, then substituting these values in Eq. (i), we get

$$\tan^{-1}(0) = 0 + 0 + K$$

$$\Rightarrow \quad K = 0$$

$$\Rightarrow \quad \tan^{-1} y = x + \frac{x^2}{2}$$

$$\Rightarrow \quad y = \tan\left(x + \frac{x^2}{2}\right)$$

Q. 10 **Find the general solution of $(x + 2y^3)\dfrac{dy}{dx} = y$.**

Sol. Given that,

$$(x + 2y^3)\frac{dy}{dx} = y$$

$$\Rightarrow \quad y \cdot \frac{dx}{dy} = x + 2y^3$$

$$\Rightarrow \quad \frac{dx}{dy} = \frac{x}{y} + 2y^2 \quad \text{[dividing throughout by } y]$$

$$\Rightarrow \quad \frac{dx}{dy} - \frac{x}{y} = 2y^2$$

which is a linear differential equation.

On comparing it with $\dfrac{dx}{dy} + Px = Q$, we get

$$P = -\frac{1}{y}, Q = 2y^2$$

$$\text{IF} = e^{\int -\frac{1}{y} dy} = e^{-\int \frac{1}{y} dy}$$

$$\therefore \quad = e^{-\log y} = \frac{1}{y}$$

The general solution is

$$x \cdot \frac{1}{y} = \int 2y^2 \cdot \frac{1}{y} dy + C$$

$$\Rightarrow \quad \frac{x}{y} = \frac{2y^2}{2} + C$$

$$\Rightarrow \quad \frac{x}{y} = y^2 + C$$

$$\Rightarrow \quad x = y^3 + Cy$$

Q. 11 **If $y(x)$ is a solution of $\left(\dfrac{2 + \sin x}{1 + y}\right)\dfrac{dy}{dx} = -\cos x$ and $y(0) = 1$, then find the value of $y\left(\dfrac{\pi}{2}\right)$.**

Sol. Given that,

$$\left(\frac{2 + \sin x}{1 + y}\right)\frac{dy}{dx} = -\cos x$$

$$\Rightarrow \quad \frac{dy}{1 + y} = -\frac{\cos x}{2 + \sin x} dx$$

On integrating both sides, we get

$$\int \frac{1}{1 + y} dy = -\int \frac{\cos x}{2 + \sin x} dx$$

$$\Rightarrow \quad \log(1 + y) = -\log(2 + \sin x) + \log C$$

$$\Rightarrow \quad \log(1+y)+\log(2+\sin x)=\log C$$
$$\Rightarrow \quad \log(1+y)(2+\sin x)=\log C$$
$$\Rightarrow \quad (1+y)(2+\sin x)=C$$
$$\Rightarrow \quad 1+y=\frac{C}{2+\sin x}$$
$$\Rightarrow \quad y=\frac{C}{2+\sin x}-1 \quad \text{... (i)}$$

When $x=0$ and $y=1$, then

$$1=\frac{C}{2}-1$$
$$\Rightarrow \quad C=4$$

On putting $C=4$ in Eq. (i), we get

$$y=\frac{4}{2+\sin x}-1$$
$$\therefore \quad y\left(\frac{\pi}{2}\right)=\frac{4}{2+\sin\frac{\pi}{2}}-1=\frac{4}{2+1}-1$$
$$=\frac{4}{3}-1=\frac{1}{3}$$

Q. 12 If $y(t)$ is a solution of $(1+t)\frac{dy}{dt}-ty=1$ and $y(0)=-1$, then show that $y(1)=-\frac{1}{2}$.

Sol. Given that,

$$(1+t)\frac{dy}{dt}-ty=1$$
$$\Rightarrow \quad \frac{dy}{dt}-\left(\frac{t}{1+t}\right)y=\frac{1}{1+t}$$

which is a linear differential equation.

On comparing it with $\frac{dy}{dt}+Py=Q$, we get

$$P=-\left(\frac{t}{1+t}\right), Q=\frac{1}{1+t}$$
$$\text{IF}=e^{-\int\frac{t}{1+t}dt}=e^{-\int\left(1-\frac{1}{1+t}\right)dt}=e^{-[t-\log(1+t)]}$$
$$=e^{-t}\cdot e^{\log(1+t)}$$
$$=e^{-t}(1+t)$$

The general solution is

$$y(t)\cdot\frac{(1+t)}{e^t}=\int\frac{(1+t)\cdot e^{-t}}{(1+t)}dt+C$$
$$\Rightarrow \quad y(t)=\frac{e^{-t}}{(-1)}\cdot\frac{e^t}{1+t}+C', \text{ where } C'=\frac{Ce^t}{1+t}$$
$$\Rightarrow \quad y(t)=-\frac{1}{1+t}+C'$$

When $t=0$ and $y=-1$, then

$$-1=-1+C' \Rightarrow C'=0$$
$$y(t)=-\frac{1}{1+t} \Rightarrow y(1)=-\frac{1}{2}$$

Q. 13 Form the differential equation having $y = (\sin^{-1} x)^2 + A\cos^{-1} x + B$, where A and B are arbitrary constants, as its general solution.

Sol. Given that, $$y = (\sin^{-1} x)^2 + A\cos^{-1} x + B$$

On differentiating w.r.t. x, we get

$$\frac{dy}{dx} = \frac{2\sin^{-1} x}{\sqrt{1-x^2}} + \frac{(-A)}{\sqrt{1-x^2}}$$

$$\Rightarrow \quad \sqrt{1-x^2}\frac{dy}{dx} = 2\sin^{-1} x - A$$

Again, differentiating w.r.t. x, we get

$$\sqrt{1-x^2}\frac{d^2y}{dx^2} + \frac{dy}{dx}\cdot\frac{-2x}{2\sqrt{1+x^2}} = \frac{2}{\sqrt{1-x^2}}$$

$$\Rightarrow \quad (1-x^2)\frac{d^2y}{dx^2} - \frac{x}{\sqrt{1-x^2}}\cdot\sqrt{1-x^2}\frac{dy}{dx} = 2$$

$$\Rightarrow \quad (1-x^2)\frac{d^2y}{dx^2} - x\frac{dy}{dx} = 2$$

$$\Rightarrow \quad (1-x^2)\frac{d^2y}{dx^2} - x\frac{dy}{dx} - 2 = 0$$

which is the required differential equation.

Q. 14 Form the differential equation of all circles which pass through origin and whose centres lie on Y-axis.

Sol. It is given that, circles pass through origin and their centreslie on Y-axis. Let $(0, k)$ be the centre of the circle and radius is k.

So, the equation of circle is

$$(x-0)^2 + (y-k)^2 = k^2$$

$$\Rightarrow \quad x^2 + (y-k)^2 = k^2$$

$$\Rightarrow \quad x^2 + y^2 - 2ky = 0$$

$$\Rightarrow \quad \frac{x^2+y^2}{2y} = k \qquad \text{... (i)}$$

On differentiating Eq. (i) w.r.t. x, we get

$$\frac{2y\left(2x + 2y\frac{dy}{dx}\right) - (x^2+y^2)\frac{2dy}{dx}}{4y^2} = 0$$

$$\Rightarrow \quad 4y\left(x + y\frac{dy}{dx}\right) - 2(x^2+y^2)\frac{dy}{dx} = 0$$

$$\Rightarrow \quad 4xy + 4y^2\frac{dy}{dx} - 2(x^2+y^2)\frac{dy}{dx} = 0$$

$$\Rightarrow \quad [4y^2 - 2(x^2+y^2)]\frac{dy}{dx} + 4xy = 0$$

$$\Rightarrow \quad (4y^2 - 2x^2 - 2y^2)\frac{dy}{dx} + 4xy = 0$$

$$\Rightarrow \quad (2y^2 - 2x^2)\frac{dy}{dx} + 4xy = 0$$

$$\Rightarrow \quad (y^2 - x^2)\frac{dy}{dx} + 2xy = 0$$

$$\Rightarrow \quad (x^2 - y^2)\frac{dy}{dx} - 2xy = 0$$

Q. 15 Find the equation of a curve passing through origin and satisfying the differential equation $(1+x^2)\frac{dy}{dx}+2xy=4x^2$.

Sol. Given that, $$(1+x^2)\frac{dy}{dx}+2xy=4x^2$$

$$\Rightarrow \quad \frac{dy}{dx}+\frac{2x}{1+x^2}\cdot y=\frac{4x^2}{1+x^2}$$

which is a linear differential equation.

On comparing it with $\frac{dy}{dx}+Py=Q$, we get

$$P=\frac{2x}{1+x^2}, Q=\frac{4x^2}{1+x^2}$$

$$\therefore \quad IF=e^{\int P\,dx}=e^{\int \frac{2x}{1+x^2}dx}$$

Put $1+x^2=t \Rightarrow \quad 2x\,dx=dt$

$$IF=1+x^2=e^{\int \frac{dt}{t}}=e^{\log t}=e^{\log(1+x^2)}$$

The general solution is

$$y\cdot(1+x^2)=\int\frac{4x^2}{1+x^2}(1+x^2)\,dx+C$$

$$\Rightarrow \quad y\cdot(1+x^2)=\int 4x^2\,dx+C$$

$$\Rightarrow \quad y\cdot(1+x^2)=4\frac{x^3}{3}+C \quad \text{... (i)}$$

Since, the curve passes through origin, then substituting

$x=0$ and $y=0$ in Eq. (i), we get

$C=0$

The required equation of curve is

$$y(1+x^2)=\frac{4x^3}{3}$$

$$\Rightarrow \quad y=\frac{4x^3}{3(1+x^2)}$$

Q. 16 Solve $x^2\frac{dy}{dx}=x^2+xy+y^2$.

Sol. Given that, $$x^2\frac{dy}{dx}=x^2+xy+y^2$$

$$\Rightarrow \quad \frac{dy}{dx}=1+\frac{y}{x}+\frac{y^2}{x^2} \quad \text{... (i)}$$

Let $$f(x,y)=1+\frac{y}{x}+\frac{y^2}{x^2}$$

$$f(\lambda x,\lambda y)=1+\frac{\lambda y}{\lambda x}+\frac{\lambda^2 y^2}{\lambda^2 x^2}$$

$$f(\lambda x,\lambda y)=\lambda^0\left(1+\frac{y}{x}+\frac{y^2}{x^2}\right)$$

$$=\lambda^0 f(x,y)$$

which is homogeneous expression of degree 0.

Put $$y = vx \Rightarrow \frac{dy}{dx} = v + x\frac{dv}{dx}$$

On substituting these values in Eq.(i), we get

$$\left(v + x\frac{dv}{dx}\right) = 1 + v + v^2$$

$$\Rightarrow \quad x\frac{dv}{dx} = 1 + v + v^2 - v$$

$$\Rightarrow \quad x\frac{dv}{dx} = 1 + v^2$$

$$\Rightarrow \quad \frac{dv}{1+v^2} = \frac{dx}{x}$$

On integrating both sides, we get

$$\tan^{-1} v = \log|x| + C$$

$$\Rightarrow \quad \tan^{-1}\left(\frac{y}{x}\right) = \log|x| + C$$

Q. 17 Find the general solution of the differential equation $(1 + y^2) + (x - e^{\tan^{-1} y})\dfrac{dy}{dx} = 0.$

Sol. Given, differential equation is

$$(1 + y^2) + (x - e^{\tan^{-1} y})\frac{dy}{dx} = 0$$

$$\Rightarrow \quad (1 + y^2) = -(x - e^{\tan^{-1} y})\frac{dy}{dx}$$

$$(1 + y^2)\frac{dx}{dy} = -x + e^{\tan^{-1} y}$$

$$\Rightarrow \quad (1 + y^2)\frac{dx}{dy} + x = e^{\tan^{-1} y}$$

$$\Rightarrow \quad \frac{dx}{dy} + \frac{x}{1+y^2} = \frac{e^{\tan^{-1} y}}{1+y^2} \qquad \text{[dividing throughout by } (1+y^2)]$$

which is a linear differential equation.

On comparing it with $\dfrac{dx}{dy} + Px = Q$, we get

$$P = \frac{1}{1+y^2},\ Q = \frac{e^{\tan^{-1} y}}{1+y^2}$$

$$\text{IF} = e^{\int P dy} = e^{\int \frac{1}{1+y^2} dy} = e^{\tan^{-1} y}$$

The general solution is $$x \cdot e^{\tan^{-1} y} = \int \frac{e^{\tan^{-1} y}}{1+y^2} \cdot e^{\tan^{-1} y}\, dy + C$$

$$\Rightarrow \quad x \cdot e^{\tan^{-1} y} = \int \frac{(e^{\tan^{-1} y})^2}{1+y^2} \cdot dy + C$$

Put $\tan^{-1} y = t \Rightarrow$ $$\frac{1}{1+y^2}dy = dt$$

$$\therefore \quad x \cdot e^{\tan^{-1} y} = \int e^{2t}\, dt + C$$

$$\Rightarrow \quad x \cdot e^{\tan^{-1} y} = \frac{1}{2} e^{2 \tan^{-1} y} + C$$

$$\Rightarrow \quad 2x\, e^{\tan^{-1} y} = e^{2 \tan^{-1} y} + 2C$$

$$\Rightarrow \quad 2x\, e^{\tan^{-1} y} = e^{2 \tan^{-1} y} + K \qquad [\because K = 2C]$$

Q. 18 Find the general solution of $y^2 dx + (x^2 - xy + y^2)\, dy = 0$.

Sol. Given, differential equation is

$$y^2 dx + (x^2 - xy + y^2) dy = 0$$

$$\Rightarrow \quad y^2 dx = -(x^2 - xy + y^2) dy$$

$$\Rightarrow \quad y^2 \frac{dx}{dy} = -(x^2 - xy + y^2)$$

$$\Rightarrow \quad \frac{dx}{dy} = -\left(\frac{x^2}{y^2} - \frac{x}{y} + 1\right) \qquad \text{... (i)}$$

which is a homogeneous differential equation.

Put $\quad \frac{x}{y} = v$ or $x = vy$

$$\Rightarrow \quad \frac{dx}{dy} = v + y\frac{dv}{dy}$$

On substituting these values in Eq. (i), we get

$$v + y\frac{dv}{dy} = -[v^2 - v + 1]$$

$$\Rightarrow \quad y\frac{dv}{dy} = -v^2 + v - 1 - v$$

$$\Rightarrow \quad y\frac{dv}{dy} = -v^2 - 1 \Rightarrow \frac{dv}{v^2 + 1} = -\frac{dy}{y}$$

On integrating both sides, we get

$$\tan^{-1}(v) = -\log y + C$$

$$\Rightarrow \quad \tan^{-1}\left(\frac{x}{y}\right) + \log y = C \qquad \left[\because v = \frac{x}{y}\right]$$

Q. 19 Solve $(x + y)(dx - dy) = dx + dy$.

Sol. Given differential equation is

$$(x + y)(dx - dy) = dx + dy$$

$$\Rightarrow \quad (x + y)\left(1 - \frac{dy}{dx}\right) = 1 + \frac{dy}{dx} \qquad \text{...(i)}$$

Put $\quad x + y = z$

$$\Rightarrow \quad 1 + \frac{dy}{dx} = \frac{dz}{dx}$$

On substituting these values in Eq. (i), we get

$$z\left(1 - \frac{dz}{dx} + 1\right) = \frac{dz}{dx}$$

$$\Rightarrow \quad z\left(2 - \frac{dz}{dx}\right) = \frac{dz}{dx}$$

$$\Rightarrow \quad 2z - z\frac{dz}{dx} - \frac{dz}{dx} = 0$$

$$\Rightarrow \quad 2z-(z+1)\frac{dz}{dx}=0$$

$$\Rightarrow \quad \frac{dz}{dx}=\frac{2z}{z+1}$$

$$\Rightarrow \quad \left(\frac{z+1}{z}\right)dz=2\,dx$$

On integrating both sides, we get

$$\int\left(1+\frac{1}{z}\right)dz=2\int dx$$

$$\Rightarrow \quad z+\log z=2x-\log C$$

$$\Rightarrow \quad (x+y)+\log(x+y)=2x-\log C \qquad [\because z=x+y]$$

$$\Rightarrow \quad 2x-x-y=\log C+\log(x+y)$$

$$\Rightarrow \quad x-y=\log|C(x+y)|$$

$$\Rightarrow \quad e^{x-y}=C(x+y)$$

$$\Rightarrow \quad (x+y)=\frac{1}{C}e^{x-y}$$

$$\Rightarrow \quad x+y=Ke^{x-y} \qquad \left[\because K=\frac{1}{C}\right]$$

Q. 20 Solve $2(y+3)-xy\dfrac{dy}{dx}=0$, given that $y(1)=-2$.

Sol. Given that, $$2(y+3)-xy\frac{dy}{dx}=0$$

$$\Rightarrow \quad 2(y+3)=xy\frac{dy}{dx}$$

$$\Rightarrow \quad 2\frac{dx}{x}=\left(\frac{y}{y+3}\right)dy$$

$$\Rightarrow \quad 2\cdot\frac{dx}{x}=\left(\frac{y+3-3}{y+3}\right)dy$$

$$\Rightarrow \quad 2\cdot\frac{dx}{x}=\left(1-\frac{3}{y+3}\right)dy$$

On integrating both sides, we get

$$2\log x=y-3\log(y+3)+C \qquad \text{... (i)}$$

When $x=1$ and $y=-2$, then

$$2\log 1=-2-3\log(-2+3)+C$$

$$\Rightarrow \quad 2\cdot 0=-2-3\cdot 0+C$$

$$\Rightarrow \quad C=2$$

On substituting the value of C in Eq. (i), we get

$$2\log x=y-3\log(y+3)+2$$

$$\Rightarrow \quad 2\log x+3\log(y+3)=y+2$$

$$\Rightarrow \quad \log x^2+\log(y+3)^3=(y+2)$$

$$\Rightarrow \quad \log x^2(y+3)^3=y+2$$

$$\Rightarrow \quad x^2(y+3)^3=e^{y+2}$$

Q. 21 Solve the differential equation $dy = \cos x\,(2 - y \text{ cosec } x)\,dx$ given that $y = 2$, when $x = \frac{\pi}{2}$.

Sol. Given differential equation,

$$dy = \cos x\,(2 - y\,\text{cosec}\,x)dx$$

$$\Rightarrow \quad \frac{dy}{dx} = \cos x\,(2 - y\,\text{cosec}\,x)$$

$$\Rightarrow \quad \frac{dy}{dx} = 2\cos x - y\,\text{cosec}\,x \cdot \cos x$$

$$\Rightarrow \quad \frac{dy}{dx} = 2\cos x - y\cot x$$

$$\Rightarrow \quad \frac{dy}{dx} + y\cot x = 2\cos x$$

which is a linear differential equation.

On comparing it with $\frac{dy}{dx} + Py = Q$, we get

$$P = \cot x,\ Q = 2\cos x$$

$$\text{IF} = e^{\int P dx} = e^{\int \cot x\, dx} = e^{\log \sin x} = \sin x$$

The general solution is

$$y \cdot \sin x = \int 2\cos x \cdot \sin x\, dx + C$$

$$\Rightarrow \quad y \cdot \sin x = \int \sin 2x\, dx + C \qquad [\because \sin 2x = 2\sin x \cos x]$$

$$\Rightarrow \quad y \cdot \sin x = -\frac{\cos 2x}{2} + C \qquad \text{... (i)}$$

When $x = \frac{\pi}{2}$ and $y = 2$, then

$$2 . \sin\frac{\pi}{2} = -\frac{\cos\left(2 \times \frac{\pi}{2}\right)}{2} + C$$

$$\Rightarrow \quad 2 \cdot 1 = +\frac{1}{2} + C$$

$$\Rightarrow \quad 2 - \frac{1}{2} = C \Rightarrow \frac{4-1}{2} = C$$

$$\Rightarrow \therefore \quad C = \frac{3}{2}$$

On substituting the value of C in Eq. (i), we get

$$y\sin x = -\frac{1}{2}\cos 2x + \frac{3}{2}$$

Q. 22 Form the differential equation by eliminating A and B in $Ax^2 + By^2 = 1$.

Sol. Given differential equation is $\quad Ax^2 + By^2 = 1$

On differentiating both sides w.r.t. x, we get

$$2Ax + 2By\frac{dy}{dx} = 0$$

$$\Rightarrow \quad 2By\frac{dy}{dx} = -2Ax$$

$$\Rightarrow \quad By\frac{dy}{dx} = -Ax \Rightarrow \frac{y}{x} \cdot \frac{dy}{dx} = -\frac{A}{B}$$

Again, differentiating w.r.t. x, we get

$$\frac{y}{x}\cdot\frac{d^2y}{dx^2}+\frac{dy}{dx}\cdot\left(\frac{x\frac{dy}{dx}-y}{x^2}\right)=0$$

$$\Rightarrow \quad \frac{y}{x}\cdot\frac{d^2y}{dx^2}+\frac{x\left(\frac{dy}{dx}\right)^2-y\left(\frac{dy}{dx}\right)}{x^2}=0$$

$$\Rightarrow \quad xy\frac{d^2y}{dx^2}+x\left(\frac{dy}{dx}\right)^2-y\left(\frac{dy}{dx}\right)=0$$

$$\Rightarrow \quad xy\,y''+x\,(y')^2-y\,y'=0$$

Q. 23 **Solve the differential equation $(1+y^2)\tan^{-1}x\,dx+2y\,(1+x^2)\,dy=0$.**

Sol. Given differential equation is

$$(1+y^2)\tan^{-1}x dx+2y\,(1+x^2)\,dy=0$$

$$\Rightarrow \quad (1+y^2)\tan^{-1}x dx=-2\,y\,(1+x^2)\,dy$$

$$\Rightarrow \quad \frac{\tan^{-1}x dx}{1+x^2}=-\frac{2\,y}{1+y^2}dy$$

On integrating both sides, we get

$$\int\frac{\tan^{-1}x}{1+x^2}dx=-\int\frac{2y}{1+y^2}dy$$

Put $\tan^{-1}x=t$ in LHS, we get

$$\frac{1}{1+x^2}dx=dt$$

and put $1+y^2=u$ in RHS, we get

$$2\,y\,dy=du$$

$$\Rightarrow \quad \int t\,dt=-\int\frac{1}{u}du\Rightarrow\frac{t^2}{2}=-\log u+C$$

$$\Rightarrow \quad \frac{1}{2}(\tan^{-1}x)^2=-\log(1+y^2)+C$$

$$\Rightarrow \quad \frac{1}{2}(\tan^{-1}x)^2+\log(1+y^2)=C$$

Q. 24 **Find the differential equation of system of concentric circles with centre (1, 2).**

Sol. The family of concentric circles with centre (1, 2) and radius a is given by

$$(x-1)^2+(y-2)^2=a^2$$

$$\Rightarrow \quad x^2+1-2x+y^2+4-4y=a^2$$

$$\Rightarrow \quad x^2+y^2-2x-4y+5=a^2 \qquad \text{...(i)}$$

On differentiating Eq. (i) w.r.t. x, we get

$$2x+2y\frac{dy}{dx}-2-4\frac{dy}{dx}=0$$

$$\Rightarrow \quad (2y-4)\frac{dy}{dx}+2x-2=0$$

$$\Rightarrow \quad (y-2)\frac{dy}{dx}+(x-1)=0$$

Long Answer Type Questions

Q. 25 Solve $y + \frac{d}{dx}(xy) = x(\sin x + \log x)$.

Sol. Given differential equation is

$$y + \frac{d}{dx}(xy) = x(\sin x + \log x)$$

$$\Rightarrow \quad y + x\frac{dy}{dx} + y = x(\sin x + \log x)$$

$$\Rightarrow \quad x\frac{dy}{dx} + 2y = x(\sin x + \log x)$$

$$\Rightarrow \quad \frac{dy}{dx} + \frac{2}{x}y = \sin x + \log x$$

which is a linear differential equation.

On comparing it with $\frac{dy}{dx} + Py = Q$, we get

$$P = \frac{2}{x}, Q = \sin x + \log x$$

$$\text{IF} = e^{\int \frac{2}{x}dx} = e^{2\log x} = x^2$$

The general solution is

$$y \cdot x^2 = \int (\sin x + \log x)\, x^2 dx + C$$

$$\Rightarrow \quad y \cdot x^2 = \int (x^2 \sin x + x^2 \log x)\, dx + C$$

$$\Rightarrow \quad y \cdot x^2 = \int x^2 \sin x\, dx + \int x^2 \log x\, dx + C$$

$$\Rightarrow \quad y \cdot x^2 = I_1 + I_2 + C \quad \text{...(i)}$$

Now,

$$I_1 = \int x^2 \sin x\, dx$$

$$= x^2(-\cos x) + \int 2x \cos x\, dx$$

$$= -x^2 \cos x + [2x(\sin x) - \int 2\sin x\, dx]$$

$$I_1 = -x^2 \cos x + 2x \sin x + 2\cos x \quad \text{... (ii)}$$

and

$$I_2 = \int x^2 \log x\, dx$$

$$= \log x \cdot \frac{x^3}{3} - \int \frac{1}{x} \cdot \frac{x^3}{3} dx$$

$$= \log x \cdot \frac{x^3}{3} - \frac{1}{3}\int x^2 dx$$

$$= \log x \cdot \frac{x^3}{3} - \frac{1}{3} \cdot \frac{x^3}{3} \quad \text{... (iii)}$$

On substituting the value of I_1 and I_2 in Eq. (i), we get

$$y \cdot x^2 = -x^2 \cos x + 2x \sin x + 2\cos x + \frac{x^3}{3}\log x - \frac{1}{9}x^3 + C$$

$$\therefore \quad y = -\cos x + \frac{2\sin x}{x} + \frac{2\cos x}{x^2} + \frac{x}{3}\log x - \frac{x}{9} + Cx^{-2}$$

Q. 26 Find the general solution of $(1+\tan y)(dx-dy)+2x\,dy=0$.

Sol. Given differential equation is $(1+\tan y)(dx-dy)+2x\,dy=0$
on dividing throughout by dy, we get

$$(1+\tan y)\left(\frac{dx}{dy}-1\right)+2x=0$$

$$\Rightarrow \quad (1+\tan y)\frac{dx}{dy}-(1+\tan y)+2x=0$$

$$\Rightarrow \quad (1+\tan y)\frac{dx}{dy}+2x=(1+\tan y)$$

$$\Rightarrow \quad \frac{dx}{dy}+\frac{2x}{1+\tan y}=1$$

which is a linear differential equation.

On comparing it with $\frac{dx}{dy}+Px=Q$, we get

$$P=\frac{2}{1+\tan y}, Q=1$$

$$\text{IF}=e^{\int\frac{2}{1+\tan y}dy}=e^{\int\frac{2\cos y}{\cos y+\sin y}dy}$$

$$=e^{\int\frac{\cos y+\sin y+\cos y-\sin y}{\cos y+\sin y}dy}$$

$$=e^{\int\left(1+\frac{\cos y-\sin y}{\cos y+\sin y}\right)dy}=e^{y+\log(\cos y+\sin y)}$$

$$=e^{y}\cdot(\cos y+\sin y) \qquad [\because e^{\log x}=x]$$

The general solution is

$$x\cdot e^{y}(\cos y+\sin y)=\int 1\cdot e^{y}(\cos y+\sin y)dy+C$$

$$\Rightarrow \quad x\cdot e^{y}(\cos y+\sin y)=\int e^{y}(\sin y+\cos y)dy+C$$

$$\Rightarrow \quad x\cdot e^{y}(\cos y+\sin y)=e^{y}\sin y+C \qquad [\because \int e^{x}\{f(x)+f'(x)\}dx=e^{x}f(x)]$$

$$\Rightarrow \quad x(\sin y+\cos y)=\sin y+Ce^{-y}$$

Q. 27 Solve $\frac{dy}{dx}=\cos(x+y)+\sin(x+y)$.

Sol. Given,

$$\frac{dy}{dx}=\cos(x+y)+\sin(x+y) \qquad \ldots(\text{i})$$

Put $x+y=z$

$$\Rightarrow \quad 1+\frac{dy}{dx}=\frac{dz}{dx}$$

On substituting these values in Eq. (i), we get

$$\left(\frac{dz}{dx}-1\right)=\cos z+\sin z$$

$$\Rightarrow \quad \frac{dz}{dx}=(\cos z+\sin z+1)$$

$$\Rightarrow \quad \frac{dz}{\cos z+\sin z+1}=dx$$

On integrating both sides, we get

$$\int \frac{dz}{\cos z + \sin z + 1} = \int 1 d x$$

$$\Rightarrow \quad \int \frac{dz}{\frac{1-\tan^2 z/2}{1+\tan^2 z/2} + \frac{2\tan z/2}{1+\tan^2 z/2} + 1} = \int dx$$

$$\Rightarrow \quad \int \frac{dz}{\frac{1-\tan^2 z/2 + 2\tan z/2 + 1 + \tan^2 z/2}{(1+\tan^2 z/2)}} = \int dx$$

$$\Rightarrow \quad \int \frac{(1+\tan^2 z/2)\,dz}{2+2\tan^2 z/2} = \int dx$$

$$\Rightarrow \quad \int \frac{\sec^2 z/2\,dz}{2\,(1+\tan z/2)} = \int dx$$

Put $1+\tan z/2 = t \Rightarrow \quad \left(\frac{1}{2}\sec^2 z/2\right) d z = dt$

$$\Rightarrow \quad \int \frac{dt}{t} = \int dx$$

$$\Rightarrow \quad \log|t| = x + C$$

$$\Rightarrow \quad \log|1+\tan z/2| = x + C$$

$$\Rightarrow \quad \log\left|1+\tan\frac{(x+y)}{2}\right| = x + C$$

Q. 28 Find the general solution of $\dfrac{dy}{dx} - 3y = \sin 2x$.

Sol. Given, $\dfrac{dy}{dx} - 3y = \sin 2x$

which is a linear differential equation.

On comparing it with $\dfrac{dy}{dx} + Py = Q$, we get

$$P = -3, Q = \sin 2x$$

$$\text{IF} = e^{-3\int dx} = e^{-3x}$$

The general solution is

$$y\,.\,e^{-3x} = \int \underset{\text{I}}{\sin 2x}\, \underset{\text{II}}{e^{-3x}}\, dx$$

Let $\quad y \cdot e^{-3x} = I$ ... (i)

$$\therefore \quad I = \int \underset{\text{II}}{e^{-3x}}\, \underset{\text{I}}{\sin 2x}$$

$$\Rightarrow \quad I = \sin 2\,x\left(.\frac{e^{-3x}}{-3}\right) - \int 2\cos 2x\left(\frac{e^{-3x}}{-3}\right) dx + C_1$$

$$\Rightarrow \quad I = -\frac{1}{3}e^{-3x}\sin 2x + \frac{2}{3}\int \underset{\text{II}}{e^{-3x}}\, \underset{\text{I}}{\cos 2x}\, dx + C_1$$

$$\Rightarrow \quad I = -\frac{1}{3}e^{-3x}\sin 2x + \frac{2}{3}\left(\cos 2x\,\frac{e^{-3x}}{-3} - \int (-2\sin 2x)\,\frac{e^{-3x}}{-3}\,dx\right) + C_1 + C_2$$

$$\Rightarrow \quad I = -\frac{1}{3}e^{-3x}\sin 2x - \frac{2}{9}\cos 2x\, e^{-3x} - \frac{4}{9}I + C' \qquad [\text{where, } C' = C_1 + C_2]$$

$$\Rightarrow \quad I + \frac{4I}{9}2 = + e^{-3x}\left(-\frac{1}{3}\sin 2\,x - \frac{2}{9}\cos 2\,x\right) + C'$$

$$\Rightarrow \quad \frac{13}{9} I = e^{-3x}\left(-\frac{1}{3}\sin 2x - \frac{2}{9}\cos 2x\right) + C'$$

$$\Rightarrow \quad I = \frac{9}{13} e^{-3x}\left(-\frac{1}{3}\sin 2x - \frac{2}{9}\cos 2x\right) + C \qquad \left[\text{where } C = \frac{9C'}{13}\right]$$

$$\Rightarrow \quad I = \frac{3}{13} e^{-3x}\left(-\sin 2x - \frac{2}{3}\cos 2x\right) + C$$

$$\Rightarrow \quad = \frac{3}{13} e^{-3x} \frac{(-3\sin 2x - 2\cos 2x)}{3} + C$$

$$\Rightarrow \quad = \frac{e^{-3x}}{13}(-3\sin 2x - 2\cos 2x) + C$$

$$\Rightarrow \quad I = -\frac{e^{-3x}}{13}(2\cos 2x + 3\sin 2x) + C$$

On substituting the value of I in Eq. (i), we get

$$y \cdot e^{-3x} = -\frac{e^{-3x}}{13}(2\cos 2x + 3\sin 2x) + C$$

$$\Rightarrow \quad y = -\frac{1}{13}(2\cos 2x + 3\sin 2x) + Ce^{3x}$$

Q. 29 Find the equation of a curve passing through (2, 1), if the slope of the tangent to the curve at any point (x, y) is $\frac{x^2 + y^2}{2xy}$.

Sol. It is given that, the slope of tangent to the curve at point (x, y) is $\frac{x^2 + y^2}{2xy}$.

$$\therefore \quad \left(\frac{dy}{dx}\right)_{(x,\, y)} = \frac{x^2 + y^2}{2xy}$$

$$\Rightarrow \quad \frac{dy}{dx} = \frac{1}{2}\left(\frac{x}{y} + \frac{y}{x}\right) \qquad \ldots \text{(i)}$$

which is homogeneous differential equation.

Put $\quad y = vx$

$$\Rightarrow \quad \frac{dy}{dx} = v + x\frac{dv}{dx}$$

On substituting these values in Eq. (i), we get

$$v + x\frac{dv}{dx} = \frac{1}{2}\left(\frac{1}{v} + v\right)$$

$$\Rightarrow \quad v + x\frac{dv}{dx} = \frac{1}{2}\left(\frac{1 + v^2}{v}\right)$$

$$\Rightarrow \quad x\frac{dv}{dx} = \frac{1 + v^2}{2v} - v$$

$$\Rightarrow \quad x\frac{dv}{dx} = \frac{1 + v^2 - 2v^2}{2v}$$

$$\Rightarrow \quad x\frac{dv}{dx} = \frac{1 - v^2}{2v}$$

$$\Rightarrow \quad \frac{2v}{1 - v^2}\,dv = \frac{dx}{x}$$

On integrating both sides, we get

$$\int \frac{2v}{1-v^2}\,dv = \int \frac{dx}{x}$$

Put $1 - v^2 = t$ in LHS, we get

$$-2\,v dv = dt$$

$$\Rightarrow \quad -\int \frac{dt}{t} = \int \frac{dx}{x}$$

$$\Rightarrow \quad -\log t = \log x + \log C$$

$$\Rightarrow \quad -\log(1 - v^2) = \log x + \log C$$

$$\Rightarrow \quad -\log\left(1 - \frac{y^2}{x^2}\right) = \log x + \log C$$

$$\Rightarrow \quad -\log\left(\frac{x^2 - y^2}{x^2}\right) = \log x + \log C$$

$$\Rightarrow \quad \log\left(\frac{x^2}{x^2 - y^2}\right) = \log x + \log C$$

$$\Rightarrow \quad \frac{x^2}{x^2 - y^2} = C\,x \qquad \ldots\text{(ii)}$$

Since, the curve passes through the point (2, 1).

$$\therefore \quad \frac{(2)^2}{(2)^2 - (1)^2} = C\,(2) \Rightarrow C = \frac{2}{3}$$

So, the required solution is $2\,(x^2 - y^2) = 3x$.

Q. 30 Find the equation of the curve through the point (1, 0), if the slope of the tangent to the curve at any point (x, y) is $\dfrac{y-1}{x^2+x}$.

Sol. It is given that, slope of tangent to the curve at any point (x, y) is $\dfrac{y-1}{x^2+x}$.

$$\therefore \quad \left(\frac{dy}{dx}\right)_{(x,\,y)} = \frac{y-1}{x^2+x}$$

$$\Rightarrow \quad \frac{dy}{dx} = \frac{y-1}{x^2+x}$$

$$\Rightarrow \quad \frac{dy}{y-1} = \frac{dx}{x^2+x}$$

On integrating both sides, we get

$$\int \frac{dy}{y-1} = \int \frac{dx}{x^2+x}$$

$$\Rightarrow \quad \int \frac{dy}{y-1} = \int \frac{dx}{x\,(x+1)}$$

$$\Rightarrow \quad \int \frac{dy}{y-1} = \int \left(\frac{1}{x} - \frac{1}{x+1}\right) dx$$

$$\Rightarrow \quad \log(y-1) = \log x - \log(x+1) + \log C$$

$$\Rightarrow \quad \log(y-1) = \log\left(\frac{x\,C}{x+1}\right)$$

Since, the given curve passes through point (1, 0).

$$\therefore \quad 0-1=\frac{1\cdot C}{1+1} \Rightarrow C=-2$$

The particular solution is $\quad y-1=\frac{-2x}{x+1}$

$$\Rightarrow \quad (y-1)(x+1)=-2x$$

$$\Rightarrow \quad (y-1)(x+1)+2x=0$$

Q. 31 Find the equation of a curve passing through origin, if the slope of the tangent to the curve at any point (x, y) is equal to the square of the difference of the abcissa and ordinate of the point.

Sol. Slope of tangent to the curve $=\frac{dy}{dx}$

and difference of abscissa and ordinate $= x - y$

According to the question, $\quad \frac{dy}{dx}=(x-y)^2 \quad \ldots$(i)

Put $\quad x-y=z$

$$\Rightarrow \quad 1-\frac{dy}{dx}=\frac{dz}{dx}$$

$$\Rightarrow \quad \frac{dy}{dx}=1-\frac{dz}{dx}$$

On substituting these values in Eq. (i), we get

$$1-\frac{dz}{dx}=z^2$$

$$\Rightarrow \quad 1-z^2=\frac{dz}{dx}$$

$$\Rightarrow \quad dx=\frac{dz}{1-z^2}$$

On integrating both sides, we get

$$\int dx=\int\frac{dz}{1-z^2}$$

$$\Rightarrow \quad x=\frac{1}{2}\log\left|\frac{1+z}{1-z}\right|+C$$

$$\Rightarrow \quad tx=\frac{1}{2}\log\left|\frac{1+x-y}{1-x+y}\right|+C \quad \ldots \text{(ii)}$$

Since, the curve passes through the origin.

$$\therefore \quad 0=\frac{1}{2}\log\left|\frac{1+0-0}{1-0+0}\right|+C$$

$$\Rightarrow \quad C=0$$

On substituting the value of C in Eq. (ii), we get

$$x=\frac{1}{2}\log\left|\frac{1+x-y}{1-x+y}\right|$$

$$\Rightarrow \quad 2x=\log\left|\frac{1+x-y}{1-x+y}\right|$$

$$\Rightarrow \quad e^{2x}=\left|\frac{1+x-y}{1-x+y}\right|$$

$$\Rightarrow \quad (1-x+y)e^{2x}=1+x-y$$

Q. 32 Find the equation of a curve passing through the point (1, 1), if the tangent drawn at any point $P(x, y)$ on the curve meets the coordinate axes at A and B such that P is the mid-point of AB.

Sol. The below figure obtained by the given information

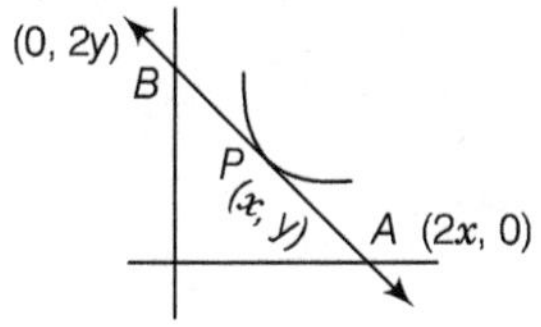

Let the coordinate of the point P is (x, y). It is given that, P is mid-point of AB.
So, the coordinates of points A and B are $(2x, 0)$ and $(0, 2y)$, respectively.

$$\therefore \quad \text{Slope of } AB = \frac{0-2y}{2x-0} = -\frac{y}{x}$$

Since, the segment AB is a tangent to the curve at P.

$$\therefore \quad \frac{dy}{dx} = -\frac{y}{x}$$

$$\Rightarrow \quad \frac{dy}{y} = -\frac{dx}{x}$$

On integrating both sides, we get

$$\log y = -\log x + \log C$$

$$\log y = \log \frac{C}{x} \qquad \text{...(i)}$$

Since, the given curve passes through (1, 1).

$$\therefore \quad \log 1 = \log \frac{C}{1}$$

$$\Rightarrow \quad 0 = \log C$$

$$\Rightarrow \quad c = 1$$

$$\therefore \quad \log y = \log \frac{1}{x}$$

$$\Rightarrow \quad y = \frac{1}{x}$$

$$\Rightarrow \quad xy = 1$$

Q. 33 Solve $x\dfrac{dy}{dx} = y(\log y - \log x + 1)$

Sol. Given,

$$x\frac{dy}{dx} = y(\log y - \log x + 1)$$

$$\Rightarrow \quad x\frac{dy}{dx} = y\log\left(\frac{y}{x} + 1\right)$$

$$\Rightarrow \quad \frac{dy}{dx} = \frac{y}{x}\left(\log\frac{y}{x} + 1\right) \qquad \text{...(i)}$$

which is a homogeneous equation.

Put $\quad \dfrac{y}{x} = v$ or $y = vx$

$$\therefore \quad \frac{dy}{dx} = v + x\frac{dv}{dx}$$

On substituting these values in Eq.(i), we get

$$v + x\frac{dv}{dx} = v(\log v + 1)$$

$$\Rightarrow \quad x\frac{dv}{dx} = v(\log v + 1 - 1)$$

$$\Rightarrow \quad x\frac{dv}{dx} = v(\log v)$$

$$\Rightarrow \quad \frac{dv}{v\log v} = \frac{dx}{x}$$

On integrating both sides, we get

$$\int \frac{dv}{v\log v} = \int \frac{dx}{x}$$

On putting $\log v = u$ in LHS integral, we get

$$\frac{1}{v}\cdot dv = du$$

$$\int \frac{du}{u} = \int \frac{dx}{x}$$

$$\Rightarrow \quad \log u = \log x + \log C$$

$$\Rightarrow \quad \log u = \log C x$$

$$\Rightarrow \quad u = Cx$$

$$\Rightarrow \quad \log v = Cx$$

$$\Rightarrow \quad \log\left(\frac{y}{x}\right) = Cx$$

Objective Type Questions

Q. 34 The degree of the differential equation $\left(\frac{d^2y}{dx^2}\right)^2 + \left(\frac{dy}{dx}\right)^2 = x\sin\left(\frac{dy}{dx}\right)$ is

(a) 1 (b) 2 (c) 3 (d) not defined

Sol. *(d)* The degree of above differential equation is not defined because when we expand $\sin\left(\frac{dy}{dx}\right)$ we get an infinite series in the increasing powers of $\frac{dy}{dx}$. Therefore its degree is not defined.

Q. 35 The degree of the differential equation $\left[1 + \left(\frac{dy}{dx}\right)^2\right]^{3/2} = \frac{d^2y}{dx^2}$ is

(a) 4 (b) $\frac{3}{2}$ (c) not defined (d) 2

Sol. *(d)* Given that $\left[1 + \left(\frac{dy}{dx}\right)^2\right]^{3/2} = \frac{d^2y}{dx^2}$

On squaring both sides, we get

$$\left[1 + \left(\frac{dy}{dx}\right)^2\right]^3 = \left(\frac{d^2y}{dx^2}\right)^2$$

So, the degree of differential equation is 2.

Q. 36 The order and degree of the differential equation $\frac{d^2y}{dx^2}+\left(\frac{dy}{dx}\right)^{1/4}+x^{1/5}=0$ respectively, are

(a) 2 and 4
(b) 2 and 2
(c) 2 and 3
(d) 3 and 3

Sol. *(a)* Given that,
$$\frac{d^2y}{dx^2}+\left(\frac{dy}{dx}\right)^{1/4}=-x^{1/5}$$
$$\Rightarrow \frac{d^2y}{dx^2}+\left(\frac{dy}{dx}\right)^{1/4}=-x^{1/5}$$
$$\Rightarrow \left(\frac{dy}{dx}\right)^{1/4}=-\left(x^{1/5}+\frac{d^2y}{dx^2}\right)$$

On squaring both sides, we get
$$\left(\frac{dy}{dx}\right)^{1/2}=\left(x^{1/5}+\frac{d^2y}{dx^2}\right)^2$$

Again, on squaring both sides, we have
$$\frac{dy}{dx}=\left(x^{1/5}+\frac{d^2y}{dx^2}\right)^4$$
order = 2, degree = 4

Q. 37 If $y=e^{-x}(A\cos x+B\sin x)$, then y is a solution of

(a) $\frac{d^2y}{dx^2}+2\frac{dy}{dx}=0$
(b) $\frac{d^2y}{dx^2}-2\frac{dy}{dx}+2y=0$
(c) $\frac{d^2y}{dx^2}+2\frac{dy}{dx}+2y=0$
(d) $\frac{d^2y}{dx^2}+2y=0$

Sol. *(c)* Given that, $y=e^{-x}(A\cos x+B\sin x)$

On differentiating both sides w.r.t., x we get
$$\frac{dy}{dx}=-e^{-x}(A\cos x+B\sin x)+e^{-x}(-A\sin x+B\cos x)$$
$$\frac{dy}{dx}=-y+e^{-x}(-A\sin x+B\cos x)$$

Again, differentiating both sides w.r.t. x, we get
$$\frac{d^2y}{dx^2}=\frac{-dy}{dx}+e^{-x}(-\cos x-B\sin x)-e^{-x}(-A\sin x+B\cos x)$$
$$\Rightarrow \frac{d^2y}{dx^2}=-\frac{dy}{dx}-y-\left[\frac{dy}{dx}+y\right]$$
$$\Rightarrow \frac{d^2y}{dx^2}=-\frac{dy}{dx}-y-\frac{dy}{dx}-y$$
$$\Rightarrow \frac{d^2y}{dx^2}=-2\frac{dy}{dx}-2y$$
$$\Rightarrow \frac{d^2y}{dx^2}+2\frac{dy}{dx}+2y=0$$

Q. 38 The differential equation for $y = A\cos\alpha x + B\sin\alpha x$, where A and B are arbitrary constants is

(a) $\frac{d^2y}{dx^2} - \alpha^2 y = 0$ (b) $\frac{d^2y}{dx^2} + \alpha^2 y = 0$

(c) $\frac{d^2y}{dx^2} + \alpha y = 0$ (d) $\frac{d^2y}{dx^2} - \alpha y = 0$

Sol. *(b)* Given, $y = A\cos\alpha + B\sin\alpha$

$$\Rightarrow \quad \frac{dy}{dx} = -\alpha A\sin\alpha x + \alpha B\cos\alpha x$$

Again, differentiating both sides w.r.t. x, we get

$$\frac{d^2y}{dx^2} = -A\alpha^2\cos\alpha x - \alpha^2 B\sin\alpha x$$

$$\Rightarrow \quad \frac{d^2y}{dx^2} = -\alpha^2(A\cos\alpha x + B\sin\alpha x)$$

$$\Rightarrow \quad \frac{d^2y}{dx^2} = -\alpha^2 y$$

$$\Rightarrow \quad \frac{d^2y}{dx^2} + \alpha^2 y = 0$$

Q. 39 The solution of differential equation $xdy - ydx = 0$ represents

(a) a rectangular hyperbola
(b) parabola whose vertex is at origin
(c) straight line passing through origin
(d) a circle whose centre is at origin

Sol. *(c)* Given that, $xdy - ydx = 0$

$$\Rightarrow \quad xdy = ydx$$

$$\Rightarrow \quad \frac{dy}{y} = \frac{dx}{x}$$

On integrating both sides, we get

$$\log y = \log x + \log C$$

$$\Rightarrow \quad \log y = \log Cx$$

$$\Rightarrow \quad y = Cx$$

which is a straight line passing through origin.

Q. 40 The integrating factor of differential equation $\cos x\frac{dy}{dx} + y\sin x = 1$ is

(a) $\cos x$ (b) $\tan x$ (c) $\sec x$ (d) $\sin x$

Sol. *(c)* Given that, $\cos x\frac{dy}{dx} + y\sin x = 1$

$$\Rightarrow \quad \frac{dy}{dx} + y\tan x = \sec x$$

Here, $P = \tan x$ and $Q = \sec x$

$$IF = e^{\int P dx} = e^{\int \tan x dx} = e^{\log \sec x}$$

$$\therefore \quad = \sec x$$

Q. 41 The solution of differential equation $\tan y \sec^2 x dx + \tan x \sec^2 y dy = 0$ is

(a) $\tan x + \tan y = k$
(b) $\tan x - \tan y = k$
(c) $\frac{\tan x}{\tan y} = k$
(d) $\tan x \cdot \tan y = k$

Sol. *(d)* Given that, $\tan y \sec^2 x dx + \tan x \sec^2 y dy = 0$

$\Rightarrow \tan \sec^2 x dx = - \tan x \sec^2 y dy$

$\Rightarrow \frac{\sec^2 x}{\tan x} dx = \frac{-\sec^2 y}{\tan y} dy$ ...(i)

On integrating both sides, we have

$$\int \frac{\sec^2 x}{\tan x} dx = - \int \frac{\sec^2 y}{\tan y} dy$$

Put $\tan x = t$ in LHS integral, we get

$$\sec^2 x \, dx = dt \Rightarrow \sec^2 x \, dx = dt$$

and $\tan y = u$ in RHS integral, we get

$$\sec^2 y dy = du$$

On substituting these values in Eq. (i), we get

$$\int \frac{dt}{t} = - \int \frac{du}{u}$$

$$\log t = - \log u + \log k$$

$\Rightarrow \log(t \cdot u) = \log k$

$\Rightarrow \log(\tan x \tan y) = \log k$

$\Rightarrow \tan x \tan y = k$

Q. 42 The family $y = Ax + A^3$ of curves is represented by differential equation of degree

(a) 1 (b) 2 (c) 3 (d) 4

Sol. *(a)* Given that, $y = Ax + A^3$

$\Rightarrow \frac{dy}{dx} = A$

[we can differential above equation only once because it has only one arbitrary constant]

$\therefore$ Degree = 1

Q. 43 The integrating factor of $\frac{xdy}{dx} - y = x^4 - 3x$ is

(a) x (b) $\log x$ (c) $\frac{1}{x}$ (d) $-x$

Sol. *(c)* Given that, $x\frac{dy}{dx} - y = x^4 - 3x$

$\Rightarrow \frac{dy}{dx} - \frac{y}{x} = x^3 - 3$

Here, $P = -\frac{1}{x}, Q = x^3 - 3$

$\therefore \text{IF} = e^{\int P dx} = e^{-\int \frac{1}{x} dx} = e^{-\log x}$

$$= \frac{1}{x}$$

Q. 44 The solution of $\frac{dy}{dx} - y = 1$, $y(0) = 1$ is given by

(a) $xy = -e^x$
(b) $xy = -e^{-x}$
(c) $xy = -1$
(d) $y = 2e^x - 1$

Sol. *(b)* Given that,

$$\frac{dy}{dx} - y = 1$$

$$\Rightarrow \quad \frac{dy}{dx} = 1 + y$$

$$\Rightarrow \quad \frac{dy}{1+y} = dx$$

On integrating both sides, we get

$$\log(1 + y) = x + C \quad \text{...(i)}$$

When $x = 0$ and $y = 1$, then

$$\log 2 = 0 + c$$

$$\Rightarrow \quad C = \log 2$$

The required solution is

$$\log(1 + y) = x + \log 2$$

$$\Rightarrow \quad \log\left(\frac{1+y}{2}\right) = x$$

$$\Rightarrow \quad \frac{1+y}{2} = e^x$$

$$\Rightarrow \quad 1 + y = 2e^x$$

$$\Rightarrow \quad y = 2e^x - 1$$

Q. 45 The number of solutions of $\frac{dy}{dx} = \frac{y+1}{x-1}$, when $y(1) = 2$ is

(a) none
(b) one
(c) two
(d) infinite

Sol. *(b)* Given that,

$$\frac{dy}{dx} = \frac{y+1}{x-1}$$

$$\Rightarrow \quad \frac{dy}{y+1} = \frac{dx}{x-1}$$

On integrating both sides, we get

$$\log(y + 1) = \log(x - 1) - \log C$$

$$C(y + 1) = (x - 1)$$

$$\Rightarrow \quad C = \frac{x-1}{y+1}$$

When $x = 1$ and $y = 2$, then $C = 0$

So, the required solution is $x - 1 = 0$.

Hence, only one solution exist.

Q. 46 Which of the following is a second order differential equation?

(a) $(y')^2 + x = y^2$
(b) $y'y'' + y = \sin x$
(c) $y''' + (y'')^2 + y = 0$
(d) $y' = y^2$

Sol. *(b)* The second order differential equation is $y'y'' + y = \sin x$.

Q. 47 The integrating factor of differential equation $(1-x^2)\dfrac{dy}{dx} - xy = 1$ is

(a) $-x$ (b) $\dfrac{x}{1+x^2}$ (c) $\sqrt{1-x^2}$ (d) $\dfrac{1}{2}\log(1-x^2)$

Sol. *(c)* Given that, $$(1-x^2)\frac{dy}{dx} - xy = 1$$

$$\Rightarrow \quad \frac{dy}{dx} - \frac{x}{1-x^2}y = \frac{1}{1-x^2}$$

which is a linear differential equation.

$$\therefore \quad \text{IF} = e^{-\int \frac{x}{1-x^2}dx}$$

Put $$1-x^2 = t \Rightarrow -2xdx = dt \Rightarrow xdx = -\frac{dt}{2}$$

Now, $$\text{IF} = e^{\frac{1}{2}\int \frac{dt}{t}} = e^{\frac{1}{2}\log t} = e^{\frac{1}{2}\log(1-x^2)} = \sqrt{1-x^2}$$

Q. 48 $\tan^{-1} x + \tan^{-1} y = C$ is general solution of the differential equation

(a) $\dfrac{dy}{dx} = \dfrac{1+y^2}{1+x^2}$ (b) $\dfrac{dy}{dx} = \dfrac{1+x^2}{1+y^2}$

(c) $(1+x^2)dy + (1+y^2)dx = 0$ (d) $(1+x^2)dx + (1+y^2)dy = 0$

Sol. *(c)* Given that, $\tan^{-1} x + \tan^{-1} y = C$

On differentiating w.r.t. x, we get

$$\frac{1}{1+x^2} + \frac{1}{1+y^2}\cdot\frac{dy}{dx} = 0$$

$$\Rightarrow \quad \frac{1}{1+y^2}\cdot\frac{dy}{dx} = -\frac{1}{1+x^2}$$

$$\Rightarrow \quad (1+x^2)\,dy + (1+y^2)\,dx = 0$$

Q. 49 The differential equation $y\dfrac{dy}{dx} + x = C$ represents

(a) family of hyperbolas (b) family of parabolas

(c) family of ellipses (d) family of circles

Sol. *(d)* Given that, $$y\frac{dy}{dx} + x = C$$

$$\Rightarrow \quad y\frac{dy}{dx} = C - x$$

$$\Rightarrow \quad y\,dy = (C-x)\,dx$$

On integrating both sides, we get

$$\frac{y^2}{2} = Cx - \frac{x^2}{2} + K$$

$$\Rightarrow \quad \frac{x^2}{2} + \frac{y^2}{2} = Cx + K$$

$$\Rightarrow \quad \frac{x^2}{2} + \frac{y^2}{2} - Cx = K$$

which represent family of circles.

Q. 50 The general solution of $e^x \cos y dx - e^x \sin y dy = 0$ is

(a) $e^x \cos y = k$ (b) $e^x \sin y = k$
(c) $e^x = k \cos y$ (d) $e^x = k \sin y$

Sol. *(a)* Given that, $e^x \cos y dx - e^x \sin y dy = 0$

$$\Rightarrow \quad e^x \cos y dx = e^x \sin y dy$$
$$\Rightarrow \quad \frac{dx}{dy} = \tan y$$
$$\Rightarrow \quad dx = \tan y dy$$

On integrating both sides, we get

$$x = \log \sec y + C$$
$$\Rightarrow \quad x - C = \log \sec y$$
$$\Rightarrow \quad \sec y = e^{x-C}$$
$$\Rightarrow \quad \sec y = e^x e^{-C}$$
$$\Rightarrow \quad \frac{1}{\cos y} = \frac{e^x}{e^C}$$
$$\Rightarrow \quad e^x \cos y = e^C$$
$$\Rightarrow \quad e^x \cos y = K \qquad [\text{where, } K = e^C]$$

Q. 51 The degree of differential equation $\frac{d^2y}{dx^2} + \left(\frac{dy}{dx}\right)^3 + 6y^5 = 0$ is

(a) 1 (b) 2 (c) 3 (d) 5

Sol. *(a)* $\frac{d^2y}{dx^2} + \left(\frac{dy}{dx}\right)^3 + 6y^5 = 0$

We know that, the degree of a differential equation is exponent heighest of order derivative.

$$\therefore \quad \text{Degree} = 1$$

Q. 52 The solution of $\frac{dy}{dx} + y = e^{-x}$, $y(0) = 0$ is

(a) $y = e^x(x - 1)$ (b) $y = xe^{-x}$
(c) $y = xe^{-x} + 1$ (d) $y = (x + 1)e^{-x}$

Sol. *(b)* Given that, $\frac{dy}{dx} + y = e^{-x}$

Here, $P = 1, Q = e^{-x}$

$$\text{IF} = e^{\int P dx} = e^{\int dx} = e^x$$

The general solution is

$$y \cdot e^x = \int e^{-x} e^x dx + C$$
$$\Rightarrow \quad y \cdot e^x = \int dx + C$$
$$\Rightarrow \quad y \cdot e^x = x + C \qquad \text{...(i)}$$

When $x = 0$ and $y = 0$, then

$$0 = 0 + C \Rightarrow C = 0$$

Eq. (i) becomes $y \cdot e^x = x$

$$\Rightarrow \quad y = xe^{-x}$$

Q. 53 The integrating factor of differential equation $\frac{dy}{dx} + y\tan x - \sec x = 0$ is

(a) $\cos x$ (b) $\sec x$ (c) $e^{\cos x}$ (d) $e^{\sec x}$

Sol. *(b)* Given that, $\frac{dy}{dx} + y\tan x - \sec x = 0$

Here, $P = \tan x, Q = \sec x$

$$IF = e^{\int P dx} = e^{\int \tan x dx}$$
$$= e^{(\log \sec x)}$$
$$= \sec x$$

Q. 54 The solution of differential equation $\frac{dy}{dx} = \frac{1 + y^2}{1 + x^2}$ is

(a) $y = \tan^{-1} x$ (b) $y - x = k(1 + xy)$
(c) $x = \tan^{-1} y$ (d) $\tan(xy) = k$

Sol. *(b)* Given that, $\frac{dy}{dx} = \frac{1+y^2}{1+x^2}$

$\Rightarrow \frac{dy}{1+y^2} = \frac{dx}{1+x^2}$

On integrating both sides, we get

$$\tan^{-1} y = \tan^{-1} x + C$$
$\Rightarrow \tan^{-1} y - \tan^{-1} x = C$

$\Rightarrow \tan^{-1}\left(\frac{y - x}{1 + xy}\right) = C$

$\Rightarrow \frac{y - x}{1 + xy} = \tan C$

$\Rightarrow y - x = \tan c(1 + x y)$

$\Rightarrow y - x = K (1 + x y)$

where, $k = \tan C$

Q. 55 The integrating factor of differential equation $\frac{dy}{dx} + y = \frac{1 + y}{x}$ is

(a) $\frac{x}{e^x}$ (b) $\frac{e^x}{x}$ (c) xe^x (d) e^x

Sol. *(b)* Given that, $\frac{dy}{dx} + y = \frac{1+y}{x}$

$\Rightarrow \frac{dy}{dx} = \frac{1+y}{x} - y$

$\Rightarrow \frac{dy}{dx} = \frac{1+y-xy}{x}$

$\Rightarrow \frac{dy}{dx} = \frac{1}{x} + \frac{y(1-x)}{x}$

$\Rightarrow \frac{dy}{dx} - \left(\frac{1-x}{x}\right)y = \frac{1}{x}$

Here, $$P = \frac{-(1-x)}{x}, Q = \frac{1}{x}$$

$$\text{IF} = e^{\int P dx} = e^{-\int \frac{1-x}{x} dx} = e^{\int \frac{x-1}{x} dx}$$

$$= e^{\int \left(1 - \frac{1}{x}\right) dx}$$

$$= e^{\int x - \log x}$$

$$= e^x \cdot e^{\log\left(\frac{1}{x}\right)}$$

$$= e^x \cdot \frac{1}{x}$$

Q. 56 $y = ae^{mx} + be^{-mx}$ **satisfies which of the following differential equation?**

(a) $\frac{dy}{dx} + my = 0$ (b) $\frac{dy}{dx} - my = 0$

(c) $\frac{d^2y}{dx^2} - m^2y = 0$ (d) $\frac{d^2y}{dx^2} + m^2y = 0$

Sol. *(c)* Given that, $y = ae^{mx} + be^{-mx}$

On differentiating both sides w.r.t. x, we get

$$\frac{dy}{dx} = mae^{mx} - bme^{-mx}$$

Again, differentiating both sides w.r.t. x, we get

$$\frac{d^2y}{dx^2} = m^2ae^{mx} + bm^2e^{-mx}$$

$$\Rightarrow \frac{d^2y}{dx^2} = m^2(ae^{mn} + be^{-mn})$$

$$\Rightarrow \frac{d^2y}{dx^2} = m^2y$$

$$\Rightarrow \frac{d^2y}{dx^2} - m^2y = 0$$

Q. 57 The solution of differential equation $\cos x \sin y dx + \sin x \cos y dy = 0$ **is**

(a) $\frac{\sin x}{\sin y} = C$ (b) $\sin x \sin y = C$

(c) $\sin x + \sin y = C$ (d) $\cos x \cos y = C$

Sol. *(b)* Given differential equation is

$$\cos x \sin y dx + \sin x \cos y dy = 0$$

$$\Rightarrow \cos x \sin y dx = -\sin x \cos y dy$$

$$\Rightarrow \frac{\cos x}{\sin x} dx = -\frac{\cos y}{\sin y} dy$$

$$\Rightarrow \cot x \, dx = -\cot y dy$$

On integrating both sides, we get

$$\log \sin x = -\log \sin y + \log C$$

$$\Rightarrow \log \sin x \sin y = \log C$$

$$\Rightarrow \sin x \cdot \sin y = C$$

Q. 58 The solution of $x\frac{dy}{dx} + y = e^x$ is

(a) $y = \frac{e^x}{x} + \frac{k}{x}$ (b) $y = xe^x + Cx$ (c) $y = xe^x + k$ (d) $x = \frac{e^y}{y} + \frac{k}{y}$

Sol. *(a)* Given that, $$x\frac{dy}{dx} + y = e^x$$

$$\Rightarrow \quad \frac{dy}{dx} + \frac{y}{x} = \frac{e^x}{x}$$

which is a linear differential equation.

$$\therefore \quad \text{IF} = e^{\int \frac{1}{x} dx} = e^{(\log x)} = x$$

The general solution is $$y \cdot x = \int \left(\frac{d^x}{x} \cdot x\right) dx$$

$$\Rightarrow \quad y \cdot x = \int e^x dx$$

$$\Rightarrow \quad y \cdot x = e^x + k$$

$$\Rightarrow \quad y = \frac{e^x}{x} + \frac{k}{x}$$

Q. 59 The differential equation of the family of curves $x^2 + y^2 - 2ay = 0$, where a is arbitrary constant, is

(a) $(x^2 - y^2)\frac{dy}{dx} = 2xy$ (b) $2(x^2 + y^2)\frac{dy}{dx} = xy$

(c) $2(x^2 - y^2)\frac{dy}{dx} = xy$ (d) $(x^2 + y^2)\frac{dy}{dx} = 2xy$

Sol. *(a)* Given equation of curve is

$$x^2 + y^2 - 2ay = 0$$

$$\Rightarrow \quad \frac{x^2 + y^2}{y} = 2a$$

On differentiating both sides w.r.t. x, we get

$$\frac{y\left(2x + 2y\frac{dy}{dx}\right) - (x^2 + y^2)\frac{dy}{dx}}{y^2} = 0$$

$$\Rightarrow \quad 2xy + 2y^2\frac{dy}{dx} - (x^2 + y^2)\frac{dy}{dx} = 0$$

$$\Rightarrow \quad (2y^2 - x^2 - y^2)\frac{dy}{dx} = -2xy$$

$$\Rightarrow \quad (y^2 - x^2)\frac{dy}{dx} = -2xy$$

$$\Rightarrow \quad (x^2 - y^2)\frac{dy}{dx} = 2xy$$

Q. 60 The family $Y = Ax + A^3$ of curves will correspond to a differential equation of order

(a) 3 (b) 2

(c) 1 (d) not defined

Sol. *(c)* Given family of curves is $y = Ax + A^3$ ...(i)

$\Rightarrow \quad \dfrac{dy}{dx} = A$

Replacing A by $\dfrac{dy}{dx}$ in Eq. (i), we get

$$y = x\frac{dy}{dx} + \left(\frac{dy}{dx}\right)^3$$

$\therefore$ Order = 1

Q. 61 The general solution of $\dfrac{dy}{dx} = 2x\, e^{x^2 - y}$ is

(a) $e^{x^2 - y} = C$ (b) $e^{-y} + e^{x^2} = C$
(c) $e^{y} = e^{x^2} + C$ (d) $e^{x^2 + y} = C$

Sol. *(c)* Given that, $\dfrac{dy}{dx} = 2x\, e^{x^2 - y} = 2x\, e^{x^2} \cdot e^{-y}$

$\Rightarrow \quad e^y \dfrac{dy}{dx} = 2x\, e^{x^2}$

$\Rightarrow \quad e^y\, dy = 2x\, e^{x^2}\, dx$

On integrating both sides, we get

$$\int e^y\, dy = 2\int x e^{x^2}\, dx$$

Put $x^2 = t$ in RHS integral, we get

$$2x\, dx = dt$$

$$\int e^y\, dy = \int e^t\, dt$$

$\Rightarrow \quad e^y = e^t + C$

$\Rightarrow \quad e^y = e^{x^2} + C$

Q. 62 The curve for which the slope of the tangent at any point is equal to the ratio of the abcissa to the ordinate of the point is

(a) an ellipse (b) parabola
(c) circle (d) rectangular hyperbola

Sol. *(d)* Slope of tangent to the curve $= \dfrac{dy}{dx}$

and ratio of abscissa to the ordinate $= \dfrac{x}{y}$

According to the question, $\dfrac{dy}{dx} = \dfrac{x}{y}$

$$y\,dy = x\,dx$$

On integrating both sides, we get

$$\frac{y^2}{2} = \frac{x^2}{2} + C$$

$\Rightarrow \quad \dfrac{y^2}{2} - \dfrac{x^2}{2} = C \Rightarrow y^2 - x^2 = 2C$

which is an equation of rectangular hyperbola.

Q. 63 The general solution of differential equation $\frac{dy}{dx} = e^{\frac{x^2}{2}} + xy$ is

(a) $y = Ce^{-x^2/2}$ (b) $y = Ce^{x^2/2}$

(c) $y = (x + C)e^{x^2/2}$ (d) $y = (C - x)e^{x^2/2}$

Sol. *(c)* Given that, $\frac{dy}{dx} = e^{x^2/2} + xy$

$\Rightarrow \quad \frac{dy}{dx} - xy = e^{x^2/2}$

Here, $P = -x, Q = e^{x^2/2}$

$\therefore \quad \text{IF} = e^{\int -x\,dx} = e^{-x^2/2}$

The general solution is

$$y \cdot e^{-x^2/2} = \int e^{-x^2/2} - e^{x^2/2}\, dx + C$$

$\Rightarrow \quad ye^{-x^2/2} = \int 1 d\,x + C$

$\Rightarrow \quad y \cdot e^{-x^2/2} = x + C$

$\Rightarrow \quad y = x\,e^{x^2/2} + C\,e^{+x^2/2}$

$\Rightarrow \quad y = (x + C)e^{x^2/2}$

Q. 64 The solution of equation $(2y - 1)\, dx - (2x + 3)\, dy = 0$ is

(a) $\frac{2x - 1}{2y + 3} = k$ (b) $\frac{2y + 1}{2x - 3} = k$

(c) $\frac{2x + 3}{2y - 1} = k$ (d) $\frac{2x - 1}{2y - 1} = k$

Sol. *(c)* Given that, $(2y - 1)dx - (2x + 3)d\,y = 0$

$\Rightarrow \quad (2y - 1)\,dx = (2x + 3)\,dy$

$\Rightarrow \quad \frac{dx}{2x + 3} = \frac{dy}{2y - 1}$

On integrating both sides, we get

$$\frac{1}{2}\log(2x + 3) = \frac{1}{2}\log(2y - 1) + \log C$$

$\Rightarrow \quad \frac{1}{2}[\log \cdot (2x + 3) - \log(2y - 1)] = \log C$

$\Rightarrow \quad \frac{1}{2}\log\left(\frac{2x + 3}{2y - 1}\right) = \log C$

$\Rightarrow \quad \left(\frac{2x + 3}{2y - 1}\right)^{1/2} = C$

$\Rightarrow \quad \frac{2x + 3}{2y - 1} = C^2$

$\Rightarrow \quad \frac{2x + 3}{2y - 1} = k$, where $K = C^2$

Q. 65 The differential equation for which $y = a\cos x + b\sin x$ is a solution, is

(a) $\frac{d^2y}{dx^2} + y = 0$ (b) $\frac{d^2y}{dx^2} - y = 0$

(c) $\frac{d^2y}{dx^2} + (a + b)y = 0$ (d) $\frac{d^2y}{dx^2} + (a - b)y = 0$

Sol. *(a)* Given that, $y = a\cos x + b\sin x$

On differentiating both sides w.r.t. x, we get

$$\frac{dy}{dx} = -a\sin x + b\cos x$$

Again, differentiating w.r.t. x, we get

$$\frac{d^2y}{dx^2} = -a\sin x + b\cos x$$

$$\Rightarrow \quad \frac{d^2y}{dx^2} = -y$$

$$\Rightarrow \quad \frac{d^2y}{dx^2} + y = 0$$

Q. 66 The solution of $\frac{dy}{dx} + y = e^{-x}$, $y(0) = 0$ is

(a) $y = e^{-x}(x - 1)$ (b) $y = xe^{x}$

(c) $y = xe^{-x} + 1$ (d) $y = xe^{-x}$

Sol. *(d)* Given that, $\frac{dy}{dx} + y = e^{-x}$

which is a linear differential equation.

Here, $P = 1$ and $Q = e^{-x}$

$$\text{IF} = e^{\int dx} = e^{x}$$

The general solution is

$$y \cdot e^{x} = \int e^{-x} \cdot e^{x}\, dx + C$$

$$\Rightarrow \quad ye^{x} = \int dx + C$$

$$\Rightarrow \quad ye^{x} = x + C \qquad \text{...(i)}$$

When $x = 0$ and $y = 0$ then, $0 = 0 + C \Rightarrow C = 0$

Eq. (i) becomes $y \cdot e^{x} = x \Rightarrow y = x\,e^{-x}$

Q. 67 The order and degree of differential equation

$$\left(\frac{d^3y}{dx^3}\right)^2 - 3\frac{d^2y}{dx^2} + 2\left(\frac{dy}{dx}\right)^4 = y^4 \text{ are}$$

(a) 1, 4 (b) 3, 4 (c) 2, 4 (d) 3, 2

Sol. *(d)* Given that, $\left(\frac{d^3y}{dx^3}\right)^2 - 3\frac{d^2y}{dx^2} + 2\left(\frac{dy}{dx}\right)^4 = y^4$

$\therefore$ Order = 3

and degree = 2

Q. 68 The order and degree of differential equation $\left[1+\left(\frac{dy}{dx}\right)^2\right]=\frac{d^2y}{dx^2}$ are

(a) $2, \frac{3}{2}$ (b) 2, 3 (c) 2, 1 (d) 3, 4

Sol. *(c)* Given that, $\left[1+\left(\frac{dy}{dx}\right)^2\right]=\frac{d^2y}{dx^2}$

$\therefore$ Order = 2 and degree = 1

Q. 69 The differential equation of family of curves $y^2 = 4a(x+a)$ is

(a) $y^2 = 4\frac{dy}{dx}\left(x+\frac{dy}{dx}\right)$ (b) $2y\frac{dy}{dx} = 4a$

(c) $y\frac{d^2y}{dx^2}+\left(\frac{dy}{dx}\right)^2 = 0$ (d) $2x\frac{dy}{dx}+y\left(\frac{dy}{dx}\right)^2 - y = 0$

Sol. *(d)* Given that, $y^2 = 4a(x+a)$ .. (i)

On differentiating both sides w.r.t. x, we get

$$2y\frac{dy}{dx} = 4a \Rightarrow 2y\frac{dy}{dx} = 4a$$

$$\Rightarrow \quad y\frac{dy}{dx} = 2a \Rightarrow a = \frac{1}{2}y\frac{dy}{dx} \quad ...(ii)$$

On putting the value of a from Eq. (ii) in Eq. (i), we get

$$y^2 = 2y\frac{dy}{dx}\left(x+\frac{1}{2}y\frac{dy}{dx}\right)$$

$$\Rightarrow \quad y^2 = 2xy\frac{dy}{dx} + y^2\left(\frac{dy}{dx}\right)^2$$

$$\Rightarrow \quad 2x\frac{dy}{dx} + y\left(\frac{dy}{dx}\right)^2 - y = 0$$

Q. 70 Which of the following is the general solution of $\frac{d^2y}{dx^2} - 2\frac{dy}{dx} + y = 0$?

(a) $y = (Ax+B)e^x$ (b) $y = (Ax+B)e^{-x}$

(c) $y = Ae^x + Be^{-x}$ (d) $y = A\cos x + B\sin x$

Sol. *(a)* Given that, $\frac{d^2y}{dx^2} - 2\frac{dy}{dx} + y = 0$

$$D^2y - 2Dy + y = 0,$$

where $D = \frac{d}{dx}$

$$(D^2 - 2D + 1)y = 0$$

The auxiliary equation is $m^2 - 2m + 1 = 0$

$$(m-1)^2 = 0 \Rightarrow m = 1, 1$$

Since, the roots are real and equal.

$\therefore$ $CF = (Ax+B)e^x \Rightarrow y = (Ax+B)e^x$

[since, if roots of Auxilliary equation are real and equal say (m), then $CF = (C_1x + C_2)e^{mx}$]

Q. 71 **The general solution of $\frac{dy}{dx} + y \tan x = \sec x$ is**

(a) $y \sec x = \tan x + C$
(b) $y \tan x = \sec x + C$
(c) $\tan x = y \tan x + C$
(d) $x \sec x = \tan y + C$

Sol. *(a)* Given differential equation is

$$\frac{dy}{dx} + y \tan x = \sec x$$

which is a linear differential equation

Here, $P = \tan x$, $Q = \sec x$,

$\therefore$ $\text{IF} = e^{\int \tan x \, dx} = e^{\log|\sec x|} = \sec x$

The general solution is

$$y \cdot \sec x = \int \sec x \cdot \sec x + C$$

$\Rightarrow$ $y \cdot \sec x = \int \sec^2 x \, dx + C$

$\Rightarrow$ $y \cdot \sec x = \tan x + C$

Q. 72 **The solution of differential equation $\frac{dy}{dx} + \frac{y}{x} = \sin x$ is**

(a) $x(y + \cos x) = \sin x + C$
(b) $x(y - \cos x) = \sin x + C$
(c) $xy \cos x = \sin x + C$
(d) $x(y + \cos x) = \cos x + C$

Sol. *(a)* Given differential equation is

$$\frac{dy}{dx} + y\frac{1}{x} = \sin x$$

which is linear differential equation.

Here, $P = \frac{1}{x}$ and $Q = \sin x$

$\therefore$ $\text{IF} = e^{\int \frac{1}{x} dx} = e^{\log x} = x$

The general solution is

$$y \cdot x = \int x \cdot \sin x \, dx + C \quad \text{...(i)}$$

Take $I = \int x \sin x \, dx$

$$- x \cos x - \int - \cos x \, dx$$

$$= -x \cos x + \sin x$$

Put the value of I in Eq. (i), we get

$$xy = - x \cos x + \sin x + C$$

$\Rightarrow$ $x(y + \cos x) = \sin x + C$

Q. 73 **The general solution of differential equation $(e^x + 1) ydy = (y + 1) e^x dx$ is**

(a) $(y + 1) = k(e^x + 1)$
(b) $y + 1 = e^x + 1 + k$
(c) $y = \log \{k(y + 1)(e^x + 1)\}$
(d) $y = \log \left\{\frac{e^x + 1}{y + 1}\right\} + k$

Sol. *(c)* Given differential equation

$$(e^x + 1)\, y dy = (y + 1) e^x\, dx$$

$$\Rightarrow \quad \frac{dy}{dx} = \frac{e^x(1+y)}{(e^x+1)y} \Rightarrow \frac{dx}{dy} = \frac{(e^x+1)\,y}{e^x(1+y)}$$

$$\Rightarrow \quad \frac{dx}{dy} = \frac{e^x\, y}{e^x(1+y)} + \frac{y}{e^x(1+y)}$$

$$\Rightarrow \quad \frac{dx}{dy} = \frac{y}{1+y} + \frac{y}{(1+y)e^x}$$

$$\Rightarrow \quad \frac{dx}{dy} = \frac{y}{1+y}\left(1 + \frac{1}{e^x}\right)$$

$$\Rightarrow \quad \frac{dx}{dy} = \frac{y}{1+y}\left(\frac{e^x+1}{e^x}\right)$$

$$\Rightarrow \quad \left(\frac{y}{1+y}\right) dy = \left(\frac{e^x}{e^x+1}\right) dx$$

On integrating both sides, we get

$$\int \frac{y}{1+y}\, dy = \int \frac{e^x}{1+e^x}\, dx$$

$$\Rightarrow \quad \int \frac{1+y-1}{1+y}\, dy = \int \frac{e^x}{1+e^x}\, dx$$

$$\Rightarrow \quad \int 1\, dy - \int \frac{1}{1+y}\, dy = \int \frac{e^x}{1+e^x}\, dx$$

$$\Rightarrow \quad y - \log|(1+y) = \log|(1+e^x) + \log k$$

$$\Rightarrow \quad y = \log(1+y) + \log(1+e^x) + \log(k)$$

$$\Rightarrow \quad y = \log\{k(1+y)(1+e^x)\}$$

Q. 74 The solution of differential equation $\dfrac{dy}{dx} = e^{x-y} + x^2 e^{-y}$ is

(a) $y = e^{x-y} - x^2 e^{-y} + C$

(b) $e^y - e^x = \dfrac{x^3}{3} + C$

(c) $e^x + e^y = \dfrac{x^3}{3} + C$

(d) $e^x - e^y = \dfrac{x^3}{3} + C$

Sol. *(b)* Given that,

$$\frac{dy}{dx} = e^{x-y} + x^2 e^{-y}$$

$$\Rightarrow \quad \frac{dy}{dx} = e^x e^{-y} + x^2 e^{-y}$$

$$\Rightarrow \quad \frac{dy}{dx} = \frac{e^x + x^2}{e^y}$$

$$\Rightarrow \quad e^y\, dy = (e^x + x^2)\, dx$$

On integrating both sides, we get

$$\int e^y\, dy = \int (e^x + x^2)\, dx$$

$$\Rightarrow \quad e^y = e^x + \frac{x^3}{3} + C$$

$$\Rightarrow \quad e^y - e^x = \frac{x^3}{3} + C$$

Q. 75 The solution of differential equation $\frac{dy}{dx}+\frac{2xy}{1+x^2}=\frac{1}{(1+x^2)^2}$ is

(a) $y(1+x^2)=C+\tan^{-1}x$ (b) $\frac{y}{1+x^2}=C+\tan^{-1}x$

(c) $y\log(1+x^2)=C+\tan^{-1}x$ (d) $y(1+x^2)=C+\sin^{-1}x$

Sol. *(a)* Given that, $\frac{dy}{dx}+\frac{2xy}{1+x^2}=\frac{1}{(1+x^2)^2}$

Here, $P=\frac{2x}{1+x^2}$ and $Q=\frac{1}{(1+x^2)^2}$

which is a linear differential equation.

$\therefore$ $\text{IF}=e^{\int\frac{2x}{1+x^2}dx}$

Put $1+x^2=t\Rightarrow 2x\,dx=dt$

$\therefore$ $\text{IF}=e^{\int\frac{dt}{t}}=e^{\log t}=e^{\log(1+x^2)}=1+x^2$

The general solution is

$$y\cdot(1+x^2)=\int(1+x^2)\frac{1}{(1+x^2)^2}+C$$

$$\Rightarrow\quad y(1+x^2)=\int\frac{1}{1+x^2}dx+C$$

$$\Rightarrow\quad y(1+x^2)=\tan^{-1}x+C$$

Fillers

Q. 76 (i) The degree of the differential equation $\frac{d^2y}{dx^2}+e^{dy/dx}=0$ is ....

(ii) The degree of the differential equation $\sqrt{1+\left(\frac{dy}{dx}\right)^2}=x$ is ....

(iii) The number of arbitrary constants in the general solution of a differential equation of order three is ....

(iv) $\frac{dy}{dx}+\frac{y}{x\log x}=\frac{1}{x}$ is an equation of the type ....

(v) General solution of the differential equation of the type is given by ....

(vi) The solution of the differential equation $\frac{xdy}{dx}+2y=x^2$ is ....

(vii) The solution of $(1+x^2)\frac{dy}{dx}+2xy-4x^2=0$ is ....

(viii) The solution of the differential equation $ydx + (x + xy)\, dy = 0$ is ....

(ix) General solution of $\dfrac{dy}{dx} + y = \sin x$ is ....

(x) The solution of differential equation $\cot y\, dx = xdy$ is ....

(xi) The integrating factor of $\dfrac{dy}{dx} + y = \dfrac{1+y}{x}$ is ....

Sol. **(i)** Given differential equation is

$$\frac{d^2y}{dx^2} + e^{\frac{dy}{dx}} = 0$$

Degree of this equation is not defined.

(ii) Given differential equation is $\sqrt{1 + \left(\dfrac{dy}{dx}\right)^2} = x$

So, degree of this equation is two.

(iii) There are three arbitrary constants.

(iv) Given differential equation is $\dfrac{dy}{dx} + \dfrac{y}{x \log x} = \dfrac{1}{x}$

The equation is of the type $\dfrac{dy}{dx} + Py = Q$

(v) Given differential equation is

$$\frac{dx}{dy} + P_1\, x = Q_1$$

The general solution is

$$x \cdot \text{IF} = \int Q\,(\text{IF})\, dy + C \;\; i.e., x\, e^{\int P dy} = \int Q\,\{e^{\int P_1 dy}\}\, dy + C$$

(vi) Given differential equation is

$$x\frac{dy}{dx} + 2y = x^2 \Rightarrow \frac{dy}{dx} + \frac{2y}{x} = x$$

This equation of the form $\dfrac{dy}{dx} + Py = Q$.

$$\therefore \qquad \text{IF} = e^{\int \frac{2}{x} dx} = e^{2 \log x} = x^2$$

The general solution is

$$yx^2 = \int x \cdot x^2\, dx + C$$

$$\Rightarrow \qquad yx^2 = \frac{x^4}{4} + C$$

$$\Rightarrow \qquad y = \frac{x^2}{4} + Cx^{-2}$$

(vii) Given differential equation is

$$(1 + x^2)\frac{dy}{dx} + 2xy - 4x^2 = 0$$

$$\Rightarrow \qquad \frac{dy}{dx} + \frac{2xy}{1+x^2} - \frac{4x^2}{1+x^2} = 0$$

$$\Rightarrow \quad \frac{dy}{dx} + \frac{2x}{1+x^2} y = \frac{4x^2}{1+x^2}$$

$$\therefore \quad \text{IF} = e^{\int \frac{2x}{1+x^2} dx}$$

Put $\quad 1 + x^2 = t \Rightarrow 2xdx = dt$

$$\therefore \quad \text{IF} = e^{\int \frac{dt}{t}} = e^{\log t} = e^{\log(1+x^2)} = 1 + x^2$$

The general solution is

$$y \cdot (1 + x^2) = \int (1 + x^2) \frac{.4x^2}{(1 + x^2)} dx + C$$

$$\Rightarrow \quad (1 + x^2)\, y = \int 4x^2\, dx + C$$

$$\Rightarrow \quad (1 + x^2) y = 4 \frac{x^3}{3} + C$$

$$\Rightarrow \quad y = \frac{4x^3}{3(1 + x^2)} + C\,(1 + x^2)^{-1}$$

(viii) Given differential equation is

$$\Rightarrow \quad ydx + (x + xy)\, dy = 0$$

$$\Rightarrow \quad ydx + x\,(1 + y)\, d\,y = 0$$

$$\Rightarrow \quad \frac{dx}{-x} = \left(\frac{1+y}{y}\right) dy$$

$$\Rightarrow \quad \int \frac{1}{x} dx = -\int \left(\frac{1}{y} + 1\right) dy \qquad \text{[on integrating]}$$

$$\Rightarrow \quad \log(x) = -\log(y) - y + \log A$$

$$\log(x) + \log(y) + y = \log A$$

$$\log(xy) + y = \log A$$

$$\Rightarrow \quad \log xy + \log e^y = \log A$$

$$\Rightarrow \quad xy\, e^y = A$$

$$\Rightarrow \quad xy = Ae^{-y}$$

(ix) Given differential equation is

$$\frac{dy}{dx} + y = \sin x$$

$$\text{IF} = \int e^{1dx} = e^x$$

The general solution is

$$y \cdot e^x = \int e^x \sin x\, dx + C \qquad \text{...(i)}$$

Let $\quad I = \int e^x \sin x\, dx$

$$I = \sin x\, e^x - \int \cos x\, e^x\, dx$$

$$= \sin x\, e^x - \cos x\, e^x + \int (-\sin x) e^x\, dx$$

$$2I = e^x (\sin x - \cos x)$$

$$I = \frac{1}{2} e^x (\sin x - \cos x)$$

From Eq. (i),

$$y \cdot e^x = \frac{x}{2}(\sin x - \cos x) + C$$

$$\Rightarrow \quad y = \frac{1}{2}(\sin x - \cos x) + C \cdot e^{-x}$$

(x) Given differential equation is

$$\cot y\, dx = x dy$$

$$\Rightarrow \quad \frac{1}{x} dx = \tan y\, dy$$

On integrating both sides, we get

$$\Rightarrow \quad \int \frac{1}{x} dx = \int \tan y\, d\, y$$

$$\Rightarrow \quad \log(x) = \log(\sec y) + \log C$$

$$\Rightarrow \quad \log\left(\frac{x}{\sec y}\right) = \log C$$

$$\Rightarrow \quad \frac{x}{\sec y} = C$$

$$\Rightarrow \quad x = C \sec y$$

(xi) Given differential equation is

$$\frac{dy}{dx} + y = \frac{1+y}{x}$$

$$\frac{dy}{dx} + y = \frac{1}{x} + \frac{y}{x}$$

$$\Rightarrow \quad \frac{dy}{dx} + y\left(1 - \frac{1}{x}\right) = \frac{1}{x}$$

$$\therefore \quad \text{IF} = e^{\int \left(1 - \frac{1}{x}\right) dx}$$

$$= e^{x - \log x}$$

$$= e^x \cdot e^{-\log x} = \frac{e^x}{x}$$

True/False

Q. 77 State True or False for the following

(i) Integrating factor of the differential of the form $\frac{dx}{dy} + P_1\, x = Q_1$ is given by $e^{\int P_1 dy}$.

(ii) Solution of the differential equation of the type $\frac{dx}{dy} + P_1 x = Q_1$ is given by $x \cdot \text{IF} = \int (\text{IF}) \times Q_1\, dy$.

(iii) Correct substitution for the solution of the differential equation of the type $\frac{dy}{dx} = f(x, y)$, where $f(x, y)$ is a homogeneous function of zero degree is $y = vx$.

(iv) Correct substitution for the solution of the differential equation of the type $\frac{dy}{dx} = g(x, y)$, where $g(x, y)$ is a homogeneous function of the degree zero is $x = vy$.

(v) Number of arbitrary constants in the particular solution of a differential equation of order two is two.

(vi) The differential equation representing the family of circles $x^2 + (y - a)^2 = a^2$ will be of order two.

(vii) The solution of $\frac{dy}{dx} = \left(\frac{y}{x}\right)^{1/3}$ is $y^{2/3} - x^{2/3} = c$

(viii) Differential equation representing the family of curves $y = e^x(A \cos x + B \sin x)$ is $\frac{d^2y}{dx^2} - 2\frac{dy}{dx} + 2y = 0$.

(ix) The solution of the differential equation $\frac{dy}{dx} = \frac{x + 2y}{x}$ is $x + y = kx^2$.

(x) Solution of $\frac{xdy}{dx} = y + x \tan \frac{y}{x}$ is $\sin\left(\frac{y}{x}\right) = cx$

(xi) The differential equation of all non horizontal lines in a plane is $\frac{d^2x}{dy^2} = 0$.

Sol. (i) ***True***

Given differential equation,

$$\frac{dx}{dy} + P_1 x = Q_1$$

$$\therefore \quad \text{IF} = e^{\int P_1 dy}$$

(ii) ***True***

(iii) ***True***

(iv) ***True***

(v) ***False***

There is no arbitrary constant in the particular solution of a differential equation.

(vi) ***False***

We know that, order of the differential equation = number of arbitrary constant

Here, number of arbitrary constant = 1.

So order is one.

(vii) ***True***

Given differential equation, $$\frac{dy}{dx}=\left(\frac{y}{x}\right)^{1/3}$$

$$\Rightarrow \quad \frac{dy}{dx}=\frac{y^{1/3}}{x^{1/3}}$$

$$\Rightarrow \quad y^{-1/3}\,dy=x^{-1/3}\,dx$$

On integrating both sides, we get

$$\int y^{-1/3}\,dy=\int x^{-1/3}dx$$

$$\Rightarrow \quad \frac{y^{-1/3+1}}{\frac{-1}{3}+1}=\frac{x^{-1/3+1}}{\frac{-1}{3}+1}+C'$$

$$\Rightarrow \quad \frac{3}{2}y^{2/3}=\frac{3}{2}x^{2/3}+C'$$

$$\Rightarrow \quad y^{2/3}-x^{2/3}=C' \qquad \left[\text{where, } \frac{2}{3}C'=C\right]$$

(viii) ***True***

Given that, $y=e^{x}\,(A\cos x+B\sin x)$

On differentiating w.r.t. x, we get

$$\frac{dy}{dx}=e^{x}\,(-A\sin x+B\cos x)+e^{x}(A\cos x+B\sin x)$$

$$\Rightarrow \quad \frac{dy}{dx}-y=e^{x}\,(-A\sin x+B\cos x)$$

Again differentiating w.r.t. x, we get

$$\frac{d^2y}{dx^2}-\frac{dy}{dx}=e^{x}\,(-A\cos x-B\sin x)+e^{x}(-A\sin x+B\cos x)$$

$$\Rightarrow \quad \frac{d^2y}{dx^2}-\frac{dy}{dx}+y=\frac{dy}{dx}-y$$

$$\Rightarrow \quad \frac{d^2y}{dx^2}-2\frac{dy}{dx}+2y=0$$

(ix) ***True***

Given that, $$\frac{dy}{dx}=\frac{x+2y}{x}\Rightarrow\frac{dy}{dx}=1+\frac{2}{x}.y$$

$$\Rightarrow \quad \frac{dy}{dx}-\frac{2}{x}y=1$$

$$\text{IF}=e^{\int\frac{-2}{x}dx}=e^{-2\log x}=x^{-2}$$

The differential solution,

$$y\cdot x^{-2}=\int x^{-2}\cdot 1dx+k$$

$$\Rightarrow \quad \frac{y}{x^2}=\frac{x^{-2+1}}{-2+1}+k$$

$$\Rightarrow \quad \frac{y}{x^2}=\frac{-1}{x}+k$$

$$\Rightarrow \quad y=-x+kx^2$$

$$\Rightarrow \quad x+y=kx^2$$

(x) ***True***

Given differential equation,

$$\frac{xdy}{dx} = y + x\tan\left(\frac{y}{x}\right)$$

$$\Rightarrow \quad \frac{dy}{dx} = \frac{y}{x} + \tan\left(\frac{y}{x}\right). \quad \ldots\text{(i)}$$

Put $\frac{y}{x} = v$ *i.e.*, $y = vx$

$$\Rightarrow \quad \frac{dy}{dx} = v + \frac{xdv}{dx}$$

On substituting these values in Eq. (i), we get

$$\frac{xdv}{dx} + v = v + \tan v$$

$$\Rightarrow \quad \frac{dx}{x} = \frac{dv}{\tan v}$$

On integrating both sides, we get

$$\int \frac{1}{x}dx = \int \frac{1}{\tan v}dx$$

$$\Rightarrow \quad \log(x) = \log(\sin v) + \log C'$$

$$\Rightarrow \quad \log\left(\frac{x}{\sin v}\right) = \log C'$$

$$\Rightarrow \quad \frac{x}{\sin v} = C'$$

$$\Rightarrow \quad \sin v = Cx \quad \left[\text{where, } C = \frac{1}{C'}\right]$$

$$\Rightarrow \quad \sin\frac{y}{x} = Cx$$

(xi) ***True***

Let any non-horizontal line in a plane is given by

$$y = mx + c$$

On differentiating w.r.t. x, we get

$$\frac{dy}{dx} = m$$

Again, differentiating w.r.t. x, we get

$$\frac{d^2y}{dx^2} = 0$$

10

Vector Algebra

Short Answer Type Questions

Q. 1 Find the unit vector in the direction of sum of vectors $\vec{\mathbf{a}} = 2\hat{\mathbf{i}} - \hat{\mathbf{j}} + \hat{\mathbf{k}}$ and $\vec{\mathbf{b}} = 2\hat{\mathbf{j}} + \hat{\mathbf{k}}$.

Thinking Process

We know that, unit vector in the direction of a vector $\vec{\mathbf{a}}$ is $\dfrac{\vec{\mathbf{a}}}{|\vec{\mathbf{a}}|}$. So, first we will find the sum of vectors and then we will use this concept.

Sol. Let $\vec{c}$ denote the sum of $\vec{a}$ and $\vec{b}$.

We have,
$$\vec{c} = \vec{a} + \vec{b}$$
$$= 2\hat{i} - \hat{j} + \hat{k} + 2\hat{j} + \hat{k} = 2\hat{i} + \hat{j} + 2\hat{k}$$

$\therefore$ Unit vector in the direction of $\vec{c} = \dfrac{\vec{c}}{|\vec{c}|} = \dfrac{2\hat{i} + \hat{j} + 2\hat{k}}{\sqrt{2^2 + 1^2 + 2^2}} = \dfrac{2\hat{i} + \hat{j} + 2\hat{k}}{\sqrt{9}}$

$$\hat{c} = \frac{2\hat{i} + \hat{j} + 2\hat{k}}{3}$$

Q. 2 If $\vec{\mathbf{a}} = \hat{\mathbf{i}} + \hat{\mathbf{j}} + 2\hat{\mathbf{k}}$ and $\vec{\mathbf{b}} = 2\hat{\mathbf{i}} + \hat{\mathbf{j}} + 2\hat{\mathbf{k}}$, then find the unit vector in the direction of

(i) $6\vec{\mathbf{b}}$ (ii) $2\vec{\mathbf{a}} - \vec{\mathbf{b}}$

Sol. Here, $\vec{a} = \hat{i} + \hat{j} + 2\hat{k}$ and $\vec{b} = 2\hat{i} + \hat{j} - 2\hat{k}$

(i) Since,
$$6\vec{b} = 12\hat{i} + 6\hat{j} - 12\hat{k}$$

$\therefore$ Unit vector in the direction of $6\vec{b} = \dfrac{6\vec{b}}{|6\vec{b}|}$

$$= \frac{12\hat{i} + 6\hat{j} - 12\hat{k}}{\sqrt{12^2 + 6^2 + 12^2}} = \frac{6(2\hat{i} + \hat{j} - 2\hat{k})}{\sqrt{324}}$$

$$= \frac{6(2\hat{i} + \hat{j} - 2\hat{k})}{18} = \frac{2\hat{i} + \hat{j} - 2\hat{k}}{3}$$

(ii) Since, $2\vec{a}-\vec{b}=2(\hat{i}+\hat{j}+2\hat{k})-(2\hat{i}+\hat{j}-2\hat{k})$
$=2\hat{i}+2\hat{j}+4\hat{k}-2\hat{i}-\hat{j}+2\hat{k}=\hat{j}+6\hat{k}$

$\therefore$ Unit vector in the direction of $2\vec{a}-\vec{b}=\dfrac{2\vec{a}-\vec{b}}{|2\vec{a}-\vec{b}|}=\dfrac{\hat{j}+6\hat{k}}{\sqrt{1+36}}=\dfrac{1}{\sqrt{37}}(\hat{j}+6\hat{k})$

Q. 3 Find a unit vector in the direction of $\overrightarrow{PQ}$, where P and Q have coordinates (5, 0, 8) and (3, 3, 2), respectively.

Sol. Since, the coordinates of P and Q are (5, 0, 8) and (3, 3, 2), respectively.

$$\therefore \quad \overrightarrow{PQ}=\overrightarrow{OQ}-\overrightarrow{OP}$$
$$=(3\hat{i}+3\hat{j}+2\hat{k})-(5\hat{i}+0\hat{j}+8\hat{k})$$
$$=-2\hat{i}+3\hat{j}-6\hat{k}$$

$\therefore$ Unit vector in the direction of $\overrightarrow{PQ}=\dfrac{\overrightarrow{PQ}}{|\overrightarrow{PQ}|}=\dfrac{-2\hat{i}+3\hat{j}-6\hat{k}}{\sqrt{2^2+3^2+6^2}}$

$$=\frac{-2\hat{i}+3\hat{j}-6\hat{k}}{\sqrt{49}}=\frac{-2\hat{i}+3\hat{j}-6\hat{k}}{7}$$

Q. 4 If $\vec{a}$ and $\vec{b}$ are the position vectors of $\vec{A}$ and $\vec{B}$ respectively, then find the position vector of a point $\vec{C}$ in $\overrightarrow{BA}$ produced such that $\overrightarrow{BC}=1.5\overrightarrow{BA}$.

Sol. Since, $\overrightarrow{OA}=\vec{a}$ and $\overrightarrow{OB}=\vec{b}$

$\therefore \quad \overrightarrow{BA}=\overrightarrow{OA}-\overrightarrow{OB}=\vec{a}-\vec{b}$

and $\quad 1.5\overrightarrow{BA}=1.5(\vec{a}-\vec{b})$

Since, $\quad \overrightarrow{BC}=1.5\overrightarrow{BA}=1.5(\vec{a}-\vec{b})$

$$\overrightarrow{OC}-\overrightarrow{OB}=1.5\vec{a}-1.5\vec{b}$$
$$\overrightarrow{OC}=1.5\vec{a}-1.5\vec{b}+\vec{b} \qquad [\because \overrightarrow{OB}=\vec{b}]$$
$$=1.5\vec{a}-0.5\vec{b}$$
$$=\frac{3\vec{a}-\vec{b}}{2}$$

Graphically, explanation of the above solution is given below

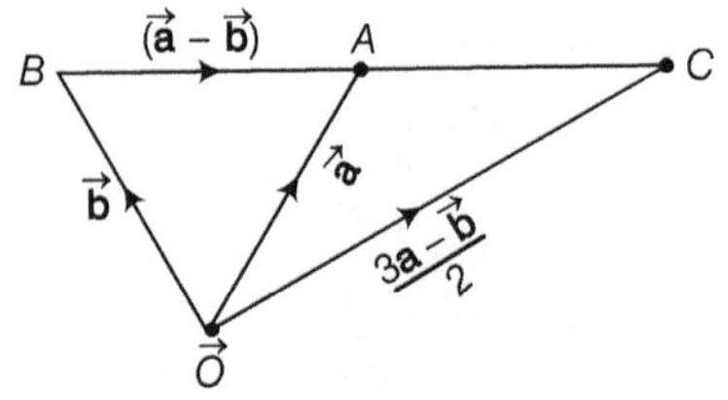

Q. 5 Using vectors, find the value of k, such that the points $(k, -10, 3)$, $(1, -1, 3)$ and $(3, 5, 3)$ are collinear.

Thinking Process

Here, use the following stepwise approach first, get the values of $|\vec{\mathbf{AB}}|, |\vec{\mathbf{BC}}|$ *and* $|\vec{\mathbf{AC}}|$ *and then use the concept that three points are collinear, if* $|\vec{\mathbf{AB}}| + |\vec{\mathbf{BC}}| = |\vec{\mathbf{AC}}|$ *such that.*

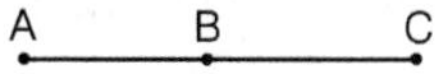

Sol. Let the points are $A(k, -10, 3)$, $B(1, -1, 3)$ and $C(3, 5, 3)$.

So,
$$\vec{AB} = \vec{OB} - \vec{OA}$$
$$= (\hat{\mathbf{i}} - \hat{\mathbf{j}} + 3\hat{\mathbf{k}}) - (k\hat{\mathbf{i}} - 10\hat{\mathbf{j}} + 3\hat{\mathbf{k}})$$
$$= (1-k)\hat{\mathbf{i}} + (-1+10)\hat{\mathbf{j}} + (3-3)\hat{\mathbf{k}}$$
$$= (1-k)\hat{\mathbf{i}} + 9\hat{\mathbf{j}} + 0\hat{\mathbf{k}}$$
$$\therefore \quad |\vec{AB}| = \sqrt{(1-k)^2 + (9)^2 + 0} = \sqrt{(1-k)^2 + 81}$$

Similarly,
$$\vec{BC} = \vec{OC} - \vec{OB}$$
$$= (3\hat{\mathbf{i}} + 5\hat{\mathbf{j}} + 3\hat{\mathbf{k}}) - (\hat{\mathbf{i}} - \hat{\mathbf{j}} + 3\hat{\mathbf{k}})$$
$$= 2\hat{\mathbf{i}} + 6\hat{\mathbf{j}} + 0\hat{\mathbf{k}}$$
$$\therefore \quad |\vec{BC}| = \sqrt{2^2 + 6^2 + 0} = 2\sqrt{10}$$

and
$$\vec{AC} = \vec{OC} - \vec{OA}$$
$$= (3\hat{\mathbf{i}} + 5\hat{\mathbf{j}} + 3\hat{\mathbf{k}}) - (k\hat{\mathbf{i}} - 10\hat{\mathbf{j}} + 3\hat{\mathbf{k}})$$
$$= (3-k)\hat{\mathbf{i}} + 15\hat{\mathbf{j}} + 0\hat{\mathbf{k}}$$
$$\therefore \quad |\vec{AC}| = \sqrt{(3-k)^2 + 225}$$

If A, B and C are collinear, then sum of modulus of any two vectors will be equal to the modulus of third vectors

For $|\vec{AB}| + |\vec{BC}| = |\vec{AC}|$,
$$\sqrt{(1-k)^2 + 81} + 2\sqrt{10} = \sqrt{(3-k)^2 + 225}$$
$$\Rightarrow \quad \sqrt{(3-k)^2 + 225} - \sqrt{(1-k)^2 + 81} = 2\sqrt{10}$$
$$\Rightarrow \quad \sqrt{9 + k^2 - 6k + 225} - \sqrt{1 + k^2 - 2k + 81} = 2\sqrt{10}$$
$$\Rightarrow \quad \sqrt{k^2 - 6k + 234} - 2\sqrt{10} = \sqrt{k^2 - 2k + 82}$$
$$\Rightarrow \quad k^2 - 6k + 234 + 40 - 2\sqrt{k^2 - 6k + 234} \cdot 2\sqrt{10} = k^2 - 2k + 82$$
$$\Rightarrow \quad k^2 - 6k + 234 + 40 - k^2 + 2k - 82 = 4\sqrt{10}\sqrt{k^2 + 234 - 6k}$$
$$\Rightarrow \quad -4k + 192 = 4\sqrt{10}\sqrt{k^2 + 234 - 6k}$$
$$\Rightarrow \quad -k + 48 = \sqrt{10}\sqrt{k^2 + 234 - 6k}$$

On squaring both sides, we get
$$48 \times 48 + k^2 - 96k = 10(k^2 + 234 - 6k)$$
$$\Rightarrow \quad k^2 - 96k - 10k^2 + 60k = -48 \times 48 + 2340$$
$$\Rightarrow \quad -9k^2 - 36k = -48 \times 48 + 2340$$

$$\Rightarrow \quad (k^2 + 4k) = + 16 \times 16 - 260 \quad \text{[dividing by 9 in both sides]}$$
$$\Rightarrow \quad k^2 + 4k = -4$$
$$k^2 + 4k + 4 = 0$$
$$\Rightarrow \quad (k+2)^2 = 0$$
$$\therefore \quad k = -2$$

Q. 6 A vector $\vec{r}$ is inclined at equal angles to the three axes. If the magnitude of $\vec{r}$ is $2\sqrt{3}$ units, then find the value of $\vec{r}$.

Thinking Process

If a vector $\vec{r}$ is inclined at equal angles to the three axes, then direction cosines of vector, $\vec{r}$ will be same and then use, $\vec{r} = \vec{r} \cdot |\vec{r}|$.

Sol. We have, $|\vec{r}| = 2\sqrt{3}$

Since, $\vec{r}$ is equally inclined to the three axes, $\vec{r}$ so direction cosines of the unit vector $\vec{r}$ will be same. *i.e.*, $l = m = n$.

We know that,

$$l^2 + m^2 + n^2 = 1$$
$$\Rightarrow \quad l^2 + l^2 + l^2 = 1$$
$$\Rightarrow \quad l^2 = \frac{1}{3}$$
$$\Rightarrow \quad l = \pm\left(\frac{1}{\sqrt{3}}\right)$$

So, $$\hat{\mathbf{r}} = \pm\frac{1}{\sqrt{3}}\hat{\mathbf{i}} \pm \frac{1}{\sqrt{3}}\hat{\mathbf{j}} \pm \frac{1}{\sqrt{3}}\hat{\mathbf{k}}$$

$$\therefore \quad \vec{r} = \hat{r}|\vec{r}| \quad \left[\because \hat{r} = \frac{\vec{r}}{|\vec{r}|}\right]$$
$$= \left[\pm\frac{1}{\sqrt{3}}\hat{\mathbf{i}} \pm \frac{1}{\sqrt{3}}\hat{\mathbf{j}} \pm \frac{1}{\sqrt{3}}\hat{\mathbf{k}}\right] 2\sqrt{3} \quad [\because |r| = 2\sqrt{3}]$$
$$= \pm 2\hat{\mathbf{i}} \pm 2\hat{\mathbf{j}} \pm 2\hat{\mathbf{k}} = \pm 2(\hat{\mathbf{i}} + \hat{\mathbf{j}} + \hat{\mathbf{k}})$$

Q. 7 If a vector $\vec{r}$ has magnitude 14 and direction ratios 2, 3 and − 6. Then, find the direction cosines and components of $\vec{r}$, given that $\vec{r}$ makes an acute angle with X-axis.

Sol. Here, $|\vec{r}| = 14$, $\vec{a} = 2k$, $\vec{b} = 3k$ and $\vec{c} = -6k$

$\therefore$ Direction cosines l, m and n are

$$l = \frac{\vec{a}}{|\vec{r}|} = \frac{2k}{14} = \frac{k}{7}$$
$$m = \frac{\vec{b}}{|\vec{r}|} = \frac{3k}{14}$$
and $$n = \frac{\vec{c}}{|\vec{r}|} = \frac{-6k}{14} = \frac{-3k}{7}$$

Also, we know that

$$l^2 + m^2 + n^2 = 1$$

$$\Rightarrow \quad \frac{k^2}{49} + \frac{9k^2}{196} + \frac{9k^2}{49} = 1$$

$$\Rightarrow \quad \frac{4k^2 + 9k^2 + 36k^2}{196} = 1$$

$$\Rightarrow \quad k^2 = \frac{196}{49} = 4$$

$$\Rightarrow \quad k = \pm 2$$

So, the direction cosines (l, m, n) are $\frac{2}{7}, \frac{3}{7}$ and $\frac{-6}{7}$.

[since, $\vec{\mathbf{r}}$ makes an acute angle with X-axis]

$$\because \quad \vec{\mathbf{r}} = \hat{\mathbf{r}} \cdot |\vec{\mathbf{r}}|$$

$$\therefore \quad \vec{\mathbf{r}} = (l\hat{\mathbf{i}} + m\hat{\mathbf{j}} + n\hat{\mathbf{k}})|\vec{\mathbf{r}}|$$

$$= \left(\frac{+2}{7}\hat{\mathbf{i}} + \frac{3}{7}\hat{\mathbf{j}} - \frac{6}{7}\hat{\mathbf{k}}\right) \cdot 14$$

$$= +4\hat{\mathbf{i}} + 6\hat{\mathbf{j}} - 12\hat{\mathbf{k}}$$

Q. 8 Find a vector of magnitude 6, which is perpendicular to both the vectors $2\hat{\mathbf{i}} - \hat{\mathbf{j}} + 2\hat{\mathbf{k}}$ and $4\hat{\mathbf{i}} - \hat{\mathbf{j}} + 3\hat{\mathbf{k}}$.

Thinking Process

First, we will use this concept any vector perpendicular to both the vectors $\vec{\mathbf{a}}$ and $\vec{\mathbf{b}}$ is given by $\vec{\mathbf{a}} \times \vec{\mathbf{b}} = \begin{vmatrix} \hat{\mathbf{i}} & \hat{\mathbf{j}} & \hat{\mathbf{k}} \\ a_1 & a_2 & a_3 \\ b_1 & b_2 & b_3 \end{vmatrix}$ *and then we will find the vector with magnitude 6.*

Sol. Let $\vec{\mathbf{a}} = 2\hat{\mathbf{i}} - \hat{\mathbf{j}} + 2\hat{\mathbf{k}}$ and $\vec{\mathbf{b}} = 4\hat{\mathbf{i}} - \hat{\mathbf{j}} + 3\hat{\mathbf{k}}$

So, any vector perpendicular to both the vectors $\vec{\mathbf{a}}$ and $\vec{\mathbf{b}}$ is given by

$$\vec{\mathbf{a}} \times \vec{\mathbf{b}} = \begin{vmatrix} \hat{\mathbf{i}} & \hat{\mathbf{j}} & \hat{\mathbf{k}} \\ 2 & -1 & 2 \\ 4 & -1 & 3 \end{vmatrix}$$

$$= \hat{\mathbf{i}}(-3 + 2) - \hat{\mathbf{j}}(6 - 8) + \hat{\mathbf{k}}(-2 + 4)$$

$$= -\hat{\mathbf{i}} + 2\hat{\mathbf{j}} + 2\hat{\mathbf{k}} = \vec{\mathbf{r}} \quad \text{[say]}$$

A vector of magnitude 6 in the direction of $\vec{r}$

$$= \frac{\vec{\mathbf{r}}}{|\vec{\mathbf{r}}|} . 6 = \frac{-\hat{\mathbf{i}} + 2\hat{\mathbf{j}} + 2\hat{\mathbf{k}}}{\sqrt{1^2 + 2^2 + 2^2}} . 6$$

$$= \frac{-6}{3}\hat{\mathbf{i}} + \frac{12}{3}\hat{\mathbf{j}} + \frac{12}{3}\hat{\mathbf{k}}$$

$$= -2\hat{\mathbf{i}} + 4\hat{\mathbf{j}} + 4\hat{\mathbf{k}}$$

Q. 9 Find the angle between the vectors $2\hat{i} - \hat{j} + \hat{k}$ and $3\hat{i} + 4\hat{j} - \hat{k}$.

Thinking Process

If $\vec{a}$ and $\vec{b}$ are two vectors, making angle θ with each other, then $\cos\theta = \dfrac{\vec{a}\cdot\vec{b}}{|\vec{a}||\vec{b}|}$, using this concept we will find θ

Sol. Let $\vec{a} = 2\hat{i} - \hat{j} + \hat{k}$ and $\vec{b} = 3\hat{i} + 4\hat{j} - \hat{k}$

We know that, angle between two vectors $\vec{a}$ and $\vec{b}$ is given by

$$\cos\theta = \frac{\vec{a}\cdot\vec{b}}{|\vec{a}||\vec{b}|}$$

$$= \frac{(2\hat{i} - \hat{j} + \hat{k})(3\hat{i} + 4\hat{j} - \hat{k})}{\sqrt{4+1+1}\sqrt{9+16+1}}$$

$$= \frac{6-4-1}{\sqrt{6}\sqrt{26}} = \frac{1}{2\sqrt{39}}$$

$$\therefore \quad \theta = \cos^{-1}\left(\frac{1}{2\sqrt{39}}\right)$$

Q. 10 If $\vec{a} + \vec{b} + \vec{c} = 0$, then show that $\vec{a} \times \vec{b} = \vec{b} \times \vec{c} = \vec{c} \times \vec{a}$. Interpret the result geometrically.

Sol. Since, $\quad \vec{a} + \vec{b} + \vec{c} = 0$

$\Rightarrow \quad \vec{b} = -\vec{c} - \vec{a}$

Now, $\quad \vec{a} \times \vec{b} = \vec{a} \times (-\vec{c} - \vec{a})$

$= \vec{a} \times (-\vec{c}) + \vec{a} \times (-\vec{a}) = -\vec{a} \times \vec{c}$

$\Rightarrow \quad \vec{a} \times \vec{b} = \vec{c} \times \vec{a} \quad$ ...(i)

Also, $\quad \vec{b} \times \vec{c} = (-\vec{c} - \vec{a}) \times \vec{c}$

$= (-\vec{c} \times \vec{c}) + (-\vec{a} \times \vec{c}) = -\vec{a} \times \vec{c}$

$\Rightarrow \quad \vec{b} \times \vec{c} = \vec{c} \times \vec{a} \quad$ ...(ii)

From Eqs. (i) and (ii), $\quad \vec{a} \times \vec{b} = \vec{b} \times \vec{c} = \vec{c} \times \vec{a}$

Geometrical interpretation of the result

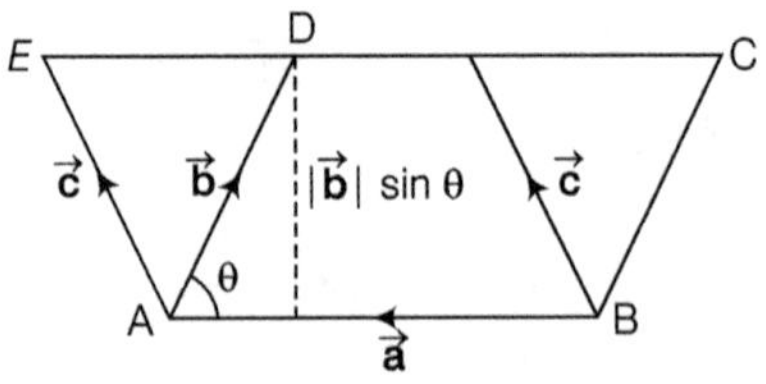

If *ABCD* is a parallelogram such that $\vec{AB} = \vec{a}$ and $\vec{AD} = \vec{b}$ and these adjacent sides are making angle θ between each other, then we say that

Area of parallelogram $ABCD = |\vec{a}||\vec{b}||\sin\theta| = |\vec{a} \times \vec{b}|$

Since, parallelogram on the same base and between the same parallels are equal in area.

We can say that, $|\vec{a} \times \vec{b}| = |\vec{a} \times \vec{c}| = |\vec{b} \times \vec{c}|$

This also implies that, $\vec{a} \times \vec{b} = \vec{a} \times \vec{c} = \vec{b} \times \vec{c}$

So, area of the parallelograms formed by taking any two sides represented by $\vec{a}$, $\vec{b}$ and $\vec{c}$ as adjacent are equal.

Q. 11 Find the sine of the angle between the vectors $\vec{a} = 3\hat{i} + \hat{j} + 2\hat{k}$ and $\vec{b} = 2\hat{i} - 2\hat{j} + 4\hat{k}$.

Thinking Process

We know that, if $\vec{a}$ and $\vec{b}$ are in their component form, then $\cos\theta = \dfrac{a_1b_1 + a_2b_2 + a_3b_3}{\sqrt{a_1^2 + a_2^2 + a_3^2}\sqrt{b_1^2 + b_2^2 + b_3^2}}$. After getting $\cos\theta$, we shall find the sine of the angle.

Sol. Here, $a_1 = 3, a_2 = 1, a_3 = 2$ and $b_1 = 2, b_2 = -2, b_3 = 4$

We know that,

$$\cos\theta = \frac{a_1b_1 + a_2b_2 + a_3b_3}{\sqrt{a_1^2 + a_2^2 + a_3^2}\sqrt{b_1^2 + b_2^2 + b_3^2}}$$

$$= \frac{3 \times 2 + 1 \times (-2) + 2 \times 4}{\sqrt{3^2 + 1^2 + 2^2}\sqrt{2^2 + (-2)^2 + 4^2}}$$

$$= \frac{6 - 2 + 8}{\sqrt{14}\sqrt{24}} = \frac{12}{2\sqrt{14}\sqrt{6}} = \frac{6}{\sqrt{84}} = \frac{6}{2\sqrt{21}} = \frac{3}{\sqrt{21}}$$

$\therefore$
$$\sin\theta = \sqrt{1 - \cos^2\theta}$$

$$= \sqrt{1 - \frac{9}{21}} = \sqrt{\frac{12}{21}} = \frac{2\sqrt{3}}{\sqrt{3}\sqrt{7}} = \frac{2}{\sqrt{7}}$$

Q. 12 If A, B, C and D are the points with position vectors $\hat{i} - \hat{j} + \hat{k}$, $2\hat{i} - \hat{j} + 3\hat{k}$, $2\hat{i} - 3\hat{k}$ and $3\hat{i} - 2\hat{j} + \hat{k}$ respectively, then find the projection of $\vec{AB}$ along $\vec{CD}$.

Thinking Process

We shall use the concept that projection of $\vec{a}$ along $\vec{b}$ is $\dfrac{\vec{a} \cdot \vec{b}}{|\vec{b}|}$.

Sol. Here, $\vec{OA} = \hat{i} + \hat{j} - \hat{k}$, $\vec{OB} = 2\hat{i} - \hat{j} + 3\hat{k}$, $\vec{OC} = 2\hat{i} - 3\hat{k}$ and $\vec{OD} = 3\hat{i} - 2\hat{j} + \hat{k}$

$\therefore$
$$\vec{AB} = \vec{OB} - \vec{OA} = (2 - 1)\hat{i} + (-1 - 1)\hat{j} + (3 + 1)\hat{k}$$
$$= \hat{i} - 2\hat{j} + 4\hat{k}$$

and
$$\vec{CD} = \vec{OD} - \vec{OC} = (3 - 2)\hat{i} + (-2 - 0)\hat{j} + (1 + 3)\hat{k}$$
$$= \hat{i} - 2\hat{j} + 4\hat{k}$$

So, the projection of $\vec{AB}$ along $\vec{CD} = \vec{AB} \cdot \dfrac{\vec{CD}}{|\vec{CD}|}$

$$= \frac{(\hat{i} - 2\hat{j} + 4\hat{k})\cdot(\hat{i} - 2\hat{j} + 4\hat{k})}{\sqrt{1^2 + 2^2 + 4^2}}$$

$$= \frac{1 + 4 + 16}{\sqrt{21}} = \frac{21}{\sqrt{21}}$$

$$= \sqrt{21} \text{ units}$$

Q.13 Using vectors, find the area of the ΔABC with vertices $A(1, 2, 3)$, $B(2, -1, 4)$ and $C(4, 5, -1)$.

Thinking Process

We know that,

Area of $\Delta ABC = \frac{1}{2}|\vec{AB} \times \vec{AC}|$. *So, here we shall use this concept.*

Sol. Here,
$$\vec{AB} = (2 - 1)\hat{i} + (-1 - 2)\hat{j} + (4 - 3)\hat{k}$$
$$= \hat{i} - 3\hat{j} + \hat{k}$$

and
$$\vec{AC} = (4 - 1)\hat{i} + (5 - 2)\hat{j} + (-1 - 3)\hat{k}$$
$$= 3\hat{i} + 3\hat{j} - 4\hat{k}$$

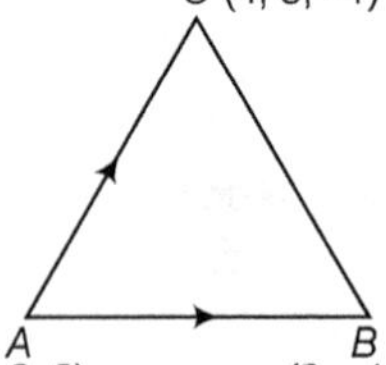

$$\therefore \quad \vec{AB} \times \vec{AC} = \begin{vmatrix} \hat{i} & \hat{j} & \hat{k} \\ 1 & -3 & 1 \\ 3 & 3 & -4 \end{vmatrix}$$
$$= \hat{i}(12 - 3) - \hat{j}(-4 - 3) + \hat{k}(3 + 9)$$
$$= 9\hat{i} + 7\hat{j} + 12\hat{k}$$

and
$$|\vec{AB} \times \vec{AC}| = \sqrt{9^2 + 7^2 + 12^2}$$
$$= \sqrt{81 + 49 + 144}$$
$$= \sqrt{274}$$

$$\therefore \quad \text{Area of } \Delta ABC = \frac{1}{2}|\vec{AB} \times \vec{AC}|$$
$$= \frac{1}{2}\sqrt{274} \text{ sq units}$$

Q. 14 **Using vectors, prove that the parallelogram on the same base and between the same parallels are equal in area.**

Sol. Let *ABCD* and *ABFE* are parallelograms on the same base *AB* and between the same parallel lines *AB* and *DF*.

Here, $AB \parallel CD$ and $AE \parallel BF$

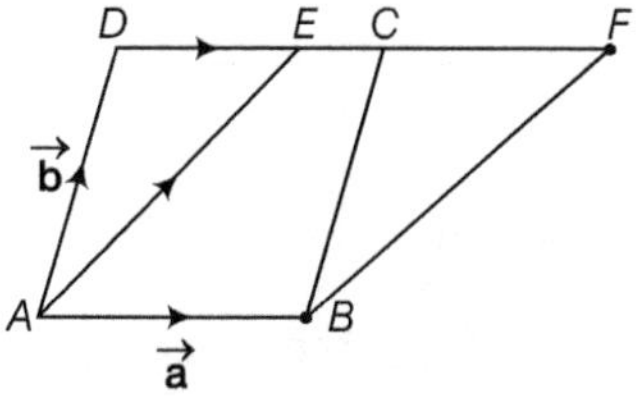

Let $\vec{AB} = \vec{a}$ and $\vec{AD} = \vec{b}$

$\therefore$ Area of parallelogram $ABCD = \vec{a} \times \vec{b}$

Now, area of parallelogram $ABFF = \vec{AB} \times \vec{AE}$

$= \vec{AB} \times (\vec{AD} + \vec{DE})$

$= \vec{AB} \times (\vec{b} + k\vec{a})$ [let $\vec{DE} = k\vec{a}$, where k is a scalar]

$= \vec{a} \times (\vec{b} + k\vec{a})$

$= (\vec{a} \times \vec{b}) + (\vec{a} \times k\vec{a})$

$= (\vec{a} \times \vec{b}) + k(\vec{a} \times \vec{a})$

$= (\vec{a} \times \vec{b})$ [$\because \vec{a} \times \vec{a} = 0$]

= Area of parallelogram *ABCD*

Hence proved.

Long Answer Type Questions

Q. 15 **Prove that in any ΔABC, $\cos A = \dfrac{b^2 + c^2 - a^2}{2bc}$, where a, b and c are the magnitudes of the sides opposite to the vertices A, B and C, respectively.**

Sol. Here, components of C are $c \cos A$ and $c \sin A$ is drawn.

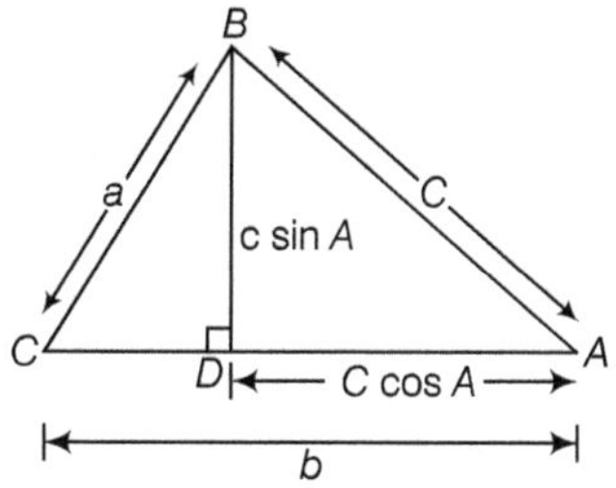

Since, $\quad \vec{CD} = b - c\cos A$

In ΔBDC,

$$a^2 = (b - c\cos A)^2 + (c\sin A)^2$$

$\Rightarrow \quad a^2 = b^2 + c^2\cos^2 A - 2bc\cos A + c^2\sin^2 A$

$\Rightarrow \quad 2bc\cos A = b^2 - a^2 + c^2(\cos^2 A + \sin^2 A)$

$\therefore \quad \cos A = \dfrac{b^2 + c^2 - a^2}{2bc}$

Q. 16 **If $\vec{a}, \vec{b}$ and $\vec{c}$ determine the vertices of a triangle, show that $\frac{1}{2}[\vec{b}\times\vec{c} + \vec{c}\times\vec{a} + \vec{a}\times\vec{b}]$ gives the vector area of the triangle. Hence, deduce the condition that the three points $\vec{a}, \vec{b}$ and $\vec{c}$ are collinear. Also, find the unit vector normal to the plane of the triangle.**

Thinking Process

Here, we shall use the following two concepts.

(i) *If $\vec{a}, \vec{b}$ and $\vec{c}$ are collinear, then the area of the triangle formed by the vectors will be zero.*

(ii) *We know that, $\vec{a}\times\vec{b} = |\vec{a}||\vec{b}|\sin\theta\hat{n}$.*

Sol. Since, $\vec{a}, \vec{b}$ and $\vec{c}$ are the vertices of a ΔABC as shown.

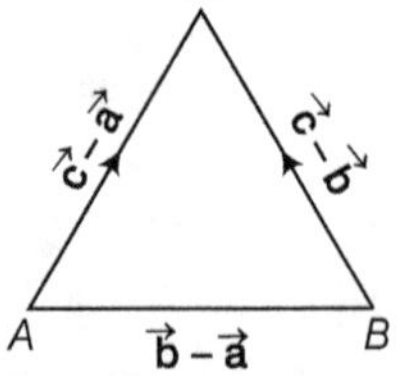

$\therefore \quad$ Area of $\Delta ABC = \frac{1}{2}|\vec{AB}\times\vec{AC}|$

Now, $\quad \vec{AB} = \vec{b} - \vec{a}$ and $\vec{AC} = \vec{c} - \vec{a}$

$\therefore \quad$ Area of $\Delta ABC = \frac{1}{2}|\vec{b} - \vec{a}\times\vec{c} - \vec{a}|$

$$= \frac{1}{2}|\vec{b}\times\vec{c} - \vec{b}\times\vec{a} - \vec{a}\times\vec{c} + \vec{a}\times\vec{a}|$$

$$= \frac{1}{2}|\vec{b}\times\vec{c} + \vec{a}\times\vec{b} + \vec{c}\times\vec{a} + \vec{0}|$$

$$= \frac{1}{2}|\vec{b}\times\vec{c} + \vec{a}\times\vec{b} + \vec{c}\times\vec{a}| \quad \text{...(i)}$$

For three points to be collinear, area of the $\Delta\ ABC$ should be equal to zero.

$\Rightarrow \quad \frac{1}{2}[\vec{b}\times\vec{c} + \vec{c}\times\vec{a} + \vec{a}\times\vec{b}] = 0$

$\Rightarrow \quad \vec{b}\times\vec{c} + \vec{c}\times\vec{a} + \vec{a}\times\vec{b} = 0 \quad \text{...(ii)}$

This is the required condition for collinearity of three points $\vec{a}, \vec{b}$ and $\vec{c}$.

Let $\hat{n}$ be the unit vector normal to the plane of the ΔABC.

$$\therefore \quad \hat{n} = \frac{\vec{AB} \times \vec{AC}}{|\vec{AB} \times \vec{AC}|}$$

$$= \frac{\vec{a} \times \vec{b} + \vec{b} \times \vec{c} + \vec{c} \times \vec{a}}{|\vec{a} \times \vec{b} + \vec{b} \times \vec{c} + \vec{c} \times \vec{a}|}$$

Q. 17 Show that area of the parallelogram whose diagonals are given by $\vec{a}$ and $\vec{b}$ is $\frac{|\vec{a} \times \vec{b}|}{2}$. Also, find the area of the parallelogram, whose diagonals are $2\hat{i} - \hat{j} + k$ and $\hat{i} + 3\hat{j} - \hat{k}$.

Thinking Process

If $\vec{p}$ and $\vec{q}$ are adjacent sides of a parallelogram, then the area formed by parallelogram $= |\vec{p} \times \vec{q}|$ and then we shall obtained the desired result.

Sol. Let $ABCD$ be a parallelogram such that

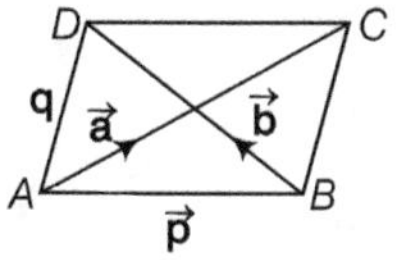

$$\vec{AB} = \vec{p}, \ \vec{AD} = \vec{q} \Rightarrow \vec{BC} = \vec{q}$$

By triangle law of addition, we get

$$\vec{AC} = \vec{p} + \vec{q} = \vec{a} \quad \text{[say]} \ldots\text{(i)}$$

Similarly,

$$\vec{BD} = -\vec{p} + \vec{q} = \vec{b} \quad \text{[say]} \ldots\text{(ii)}$$

On adding Eqs. (i) and (ii), we get

$$\vec{a} + \vec{b} = 2\vec{q} \Rightarrow \vec{q} = \frac{1}{2}(\vec{a} + \vec{b})$$

On subtracting Eq. (ii) from Eq. (i), we get

$$\vec{a} - \vec{b} = 2\vec{p} \Rightarrow \vec{p} = \frac{1}{2}(\vec{a} - \vec{b})$$

Now,

$$\vec{p} \times \vec{q} = \frac{1}{4}(\vec{a} - \vec{b}) \times (\vec{a} + \vec{b})$$

$$= \frac{1}{4}(\vec{a} \times \vec{a} + \vec{a} \times \vec{b} - \vec{b} \times \vec{a} - \vec{b} \times \vec{b})$$

$$= \frac{1}{4}[\vec{a} \times \vec{b} + \vec{a} \times \vec{b}]$$

$$= \frac{1}{2}(\vec{a} \times \vec{b})$$

So, area of a parallelogram $ABCD = |\vec{p} \times \vec{q}| = \frac{1}{2}|\vec{a} \times \vec{b}|$

Now, area of a parallelogram, whose diagonals are $2\hat{\mathbf{i}} - \hat{\mathbf{j}} + \hat{\mathbf{k}}$ and $\hat{\mathbf{i}} + 3\hat{\mathbf{j}} - \hat{\mathbf{k}}$.

$$= \frac{1}{2}|(2\hat{\mathbf{i}} - \hat{\mathbf{j}} + \hat{\mathbf{k}}) \times (\hat{\mathbf{i}} + 3\hat{\mathbf{j}} - \hat{\mathbf{k}})|$$

$$= \frac{1}{2}\left\|\begin{matrix} \hat{\mathbf{i}} & \hat{\mathbf{j}} & \hat{\mathbf{k}} \\ 2 & -1 & 1 \\ 1 & 3 & -1 \end{matrix}\right\|$$

$$= \frac{1}{2}|[\hat{\mathbf{i}}(1-3) - \hat{\mathbf{j}}(-2-1) + \hat{\mathbf{k}}(6+1)]|$$

$$= \frac{1}{2}|-2\hat{\mathbf{i}} + 3\hat{\mathbf{j}} + 7\hat{\mathbf{k}}|$$

$$= \frac{1}{2}\sqrt{4+9+49}$$

$$= \frac{1}{2}\sqrt{62} \text{ sq units}$$

Q. 18 If $\vec{\mathbf{a}} = \hat{\mathbf{i}} - \hat{\mathbf{j}} + \hat{\mathbf{k}}$ and $\vec{\mathbf{b}} = \hat{\mathbf{j}} - \hat{\mathbf{k}}$, then find a vector $\vec{\mathbf{c}}$ such that $\vec{\mathbf{a}} \times \vec{\mathbf{c}} = \vec{\mathbf{b}}$ and $\vec{\mathbf{a}} \cdot \vec{\mathbf{c}} = 3$.

Thinking Process

We know that, for any two vectors

$$\vec{\mathbf{a}} \times \vec{\mathbf{b}} = \begin{vmatrix} \hat{\mathbf{i}} & \hat{\mathbf{j}} & \hat{\mathbf{k}} \\ a_1 & a_2 & a_3 \\ b_1 & b_2 & b_3 \end{vmatrix}$$

and $\vec{\mathbf{a}} \cdot \vec{\mathbf{b}} = a_1b_1 + a_2b_2 + a_3b_3$, *where* $\vec{\mathbf{a}} = a_1\hat{\mathbf{i}} + a_2\hat{\mathbf{j}} + a_3\hat{\mathbf{k}}$ *and* $\vec{\mathbf{b}} = b_1\hat{\mathbf{i}} + b_2\hat{\mathbf{j}} + b_3\hat{\mathbf{k}}$.

So, we shall use this concept.

Sol. Let $\vec{\mathbf{c}} = x\hat{\mathbf{i}} + y\hat{\mathbf{j}} + z\hat{\mathbf{k}}$

Also, $\vec{\mathbf{a}} = \hat{\mathbf{i}} + \hat{\mathbf{j}} + \hat{\mathbf{k}}$ and $\vec{\mathbf{b}} = \hat{\mathbf{j}} - \hat{\mathbf{k}}$

For $\vec{\mathbf{a}} \times \vec{\mathbf{c}} = \vec{\mathbf{b}}$,

$$\begin{vmatrix} \hat{\mathbf{i}} & \hat{\mathbf{j}} & \hat{\mathbf{k}} \\ 1 & 1 & 1 \\ x & y & z \end{vmatrix} = \hat{\mathbf{j}} - \hat{\mathbf{k}}$$

$\Rightarrow$ $\hat{\mathbf{i}}(z-y) - \hat{\mathbf{j}}(z-x) + \hat{\mathbf{k}}(y-x) = \hat{\mathbf{j}} - \hat{\mathbf{k}}$

$\therefore$ $z - y = 0$ ...(i)

$x - z = 1$ ...(ii)

$x - y = 1$ ...(iii)

Also, $\vec{\mathbf{a}} \cdot \vec{\mathbf{c}} = 3$

$(\hat{\mathbf{i}} + \hat{\mathbf{j}} + \hat{\mathbf{k}}) \cdot (x\hat{\mathbf{i}} + y\hat{\mathbf{j}} + z\hat{\mathbf{k}}) = 3$

$\Rightarrow$ $x + y + z = 3$ ...(iv)

On adding Eqs. (ii) and (iii), we get

$2x - y - z = 2$ ...(v)

On solving Eqs. (iv) and (v), we get

$$x = \frac{5}{3}$$

$$\therefore \quad y = \frac{5}{3} - 1 = \frac{2}{3} \text{ and } z = \frac{2}{3}$$

Now,

$$\vec{c} = \frac{5}{3}\hat{i} + \frac{2}{3}\hat{j} + \frac{2}{3}\hat{k}$$

$$= \frac{1}{3}(5\hat{i} + 2\hat{j} + 2\hat{k})$$

Objective Type Questions

Q. 19 The vector in the direction of the vector $\hat{i} - 2\hat{j} + 2\hat{k}$ that has magnitude 9 is

(a) $\hat{i} - 2\hat{j} + 2\hat{k}$
(b) $\frac{\hat{i} - 2\hat{j} + 2\hat{k}}{3}$
(c) $3(\hat{i} - 2\hat{j} + 2\hat{k})$
(d) $9(\hat{i} - 2\hat{j} + 2\hat{k})$

Sol. *(c)* Let $\vec{a} = \hat{i} - 2\hat{j} + 2\hat{k}$

Any vector in the direction of a vector $\vec{a}$ is given by $\frac{\vec{a}}{|\vec{a}|}$.

$$= \frac{\hat{i} - 2\hat{j} + 2\hat{k}}{\sqrt{1^2 + 2^2 + 2^2}} = \frac{\hat{i} - 2\hat{j} + 2\hat{k}}{3}$$

$\therefore$ Vector in the direction of $\vec{a}$ with magnitude $9 = 9 \cdot \frac{\hat{i} - 2\hat{j} + 2\hat{k}}{3}$

$$= 3(\hat{i} - 2\hat{j} + 2\hat{k})$$

Q. 20 The position vector of the point which divides the join of points $2\vec{a} - 3\vec{b}$ and $\vec{a} + \vec{b}$ in the ratio 3 : 1, is

(a) $\frac{3\vec{a} - 2\vec{b}}{2}$
(b) $\frac{7\vec{a} - 8\vec{b}}{4}$
(c) $\frac{3\vec{a}}{4}$
(d) $\frac{5\vec{a}}{4}$

Sol. *(d)* Let the position vector of the point R divides the join of points $2\vec{a} - 3\vec{b}$ and $\vec{a} + \vec{b}$.

$$\therefore \quad \text{Position vector } R = \frac{3(\vec{a} + \vec{b}) + 1(2\vec{a} - 3\vec{b})}{3 + 1}$$

Since, the position vector of a point R dividing the line segment joining the points P and Q, whose position vectors are $\vec{p}$ and $\vec{q}$ in the ratio $m : n$ internally, is given by $\frac{m\vec{q} + n\vec{p}}{m + n}$.

$$\therefore \quad R = \frac{5\vec{a}}{4}$$

Q. 21 The vector having initial and terminal points as (2, 5, 0) and (−3, 7, 4), respectively is

(a) $-\hat{i}+12\hat{j}+4\hat{k}$ (b) $5\hat{i}+2\hat{j}-4\hat{k}$

(c) $-5\hat{i}+2\hat{j}+4\hat{k}$ (d) $\hat{i}+\hat{j}+\hat{k}$

Sol. *(c)* Required vector $=(-3-2)\hat{i}+(7-5)\hat{j}+(4-0)\hat{k}$

$$=-5\hat{i}+2\hat{j}+4\hat{k}$$

Similarly, we can say that for having initial and terminal points as

(i) (4, 1, 1) and (3, 13, 5), respectively.

(ii) (1, 1, 9) and (6, 3, 5), respectively.

(iii) (1, 2, 3) and (2, 3, 4), respectively, we shall get (a), (b) and (d) as its correct options.

Q. 22 The angle between two vectors $\vec{a}$ and $\vec{b}$ with magnitudes $\sqrt{3}$ and 4, respectively and $\vec{a}\cdot\vec{b}=2\sqrt{3}$ is

(a) $\frac{\pi}{6}$ (b) $\frac{\pi}{3}$ (c) $\frac{\pi}{2}$ (d) $\frac{5\pi}{2}$

Sol. *(b)* Here, $|\vec{a}|=\sqrt{3}, |\vec{b}|=4$ and $\vec{a}\cdot\vec{b}=2\sqrt{3}$ [given]

We know that, $\vec{a}\cdot\vec{b}=|\vec{a}||\vec{b}|\cos\theta$

$\Rightarrow$ $2\sqrt{3}=\sqrt{3}\cdot 4\cdot\cos\theta$

$\Rightarrow$ $\cos\theta=\frac{2\sqrt{3}}{4\sqrt{3}}=\frac{1}{2}$

$\therefore$ $\theta=\frac{\pi}{3}$

Q. 23 Find the value of λ such that the vectors $\vec{a}=2\hat{i}+\lambda\hat{j}+\hat{k}$ and $\vec{b}=\hat{i}+2\hat{j}+3\hat{k}$ are orthogonal.

(a) 0 (b) 1 (c) $\frac{3}{2}$ (d) $\frac{-5}{2}$

Thinking Process

Two non-zero vectors are orthogonal, if their dot product is zero. So, by using this concept, we shall get the value of λ.

Sol. *(d)* Since, two non-zero vectors $\vec{a}$ and $\vec{b}$ are orthogonal *i.e.*, $\vec{a}\cdot\vec{b}=0$.

$\therefore$ $(2\hat{i}+\lambda\hat{j}+\hat{k})\cdot(\hat{i}+2\hat{j}+3\hat{k})=0$

$\Rightarrow$ $2+2\lambda+3=0$

$\therefore$ $\lambda=\frac{-5}{2}$

Q. 24 The value of λ for which the vectors $3\hat{\mathbf{i}} - 6\hat{\mathbf{j}} + \hat{\mathbf{k}}$ and $2\hat{\mathbf{i}} - 4\hat{\mathbf{j}} + \lambda\hat{\mathbf{k}}$ are parallel, is

(a) $\frac{2}{3}$ (b) $\frac{3}{2}$ (c) $\frac{5}{2}$ (d) $\frac{2}{5}$

Sol. *(a)* Since, two vectors are parallel *i.e.*, angle between them is zero.

$\therefore \quad (3\hat{i} - 6\hat{j} + \hat{k})\cdot(2\hat{i} - 4\hat{j} + \lambda\hat{k}) = |3\hat{i} - 6\hat{j} + \hat{k}| \cdot |2\hat{i} - 4\hat{j} + \lambda\hat{k}|$

$[\because \vec{a}\cdot\vec{b} = |\mathbf{a}||\mathbf{b}|\cos 0° \Rightarrow \vec{a}\cdot\vec{b} = |\vec{a}||\vec{b}|]$

$\Rightarrow \quad 6 + 24 + \lambda = \sqrt{9 + 36 + 1}\sqrt{4 + 16 + \lambda^2}$

$\Rightarrow \quad 30 + \lambda = \sqrt{46}\sqrt{20 + \lambda^2}$

$\Rightarrow \quad 900 + \lambda^2 + 60\lambda = 46(20 + \lambda^2)$ [on squaring both sides]

$\Rightarrow \quad \lambda^2 + 60\lambda - 46\lambda^2 = 920 - 900$

$\Rightarrow \quad -45\lambda^2 + 60\lambda - 20 = 0$

$\Rightarrow \quad -45\lambda^2 + 30\lambda + 30\lambda - 20 = 0$

$\Rightarrow \quad -15\lambda(3\lambda - 2) + 10(3\lambda - 2) = 0$

$\Rightarrow \quad (10 - 15\lambda)(3\lambda - 2) = 0$

$\therefore \quad \lambda = \frac{2}{3}, \frac{2}{3}$

Alternate Method

Let $\quad \vec{a} = 3\hat{i} - 6\hat{j} + \hat{k}$ and $\vec{b} = 2\hat{i} - 4\hat{j} + \lambda\hat{k}$

Since, $\quad \vec{a} \parallel \vec{b}$

$\Rightarrow \quad \frac{3}{2} = \frac{-6}{-4} = \frac{1}{\lambda} \Rightarrow \lambda = \frac{2}{3}$

Q. 25 The vectors from origin to the points A and B are $\vec{\mathbf{a}} = 2\hat{\mathbf{i}} - 3\hat{\mathbf{j}} + 2\hat{\mathbf{k}}$ and $\vec{\mathbf{b}} = 2\hat{\mathbf{i}} + 3\hat{\mathbf{j}} + \hat{\mathbf{k}}$ respectively, then the area of ΔOAB is equal to

(a) 340 (b) $\sqrt{25}$

(c) $\sqrt{229}$ (d) $\frac{1}{2}\sqrt{229}$

Sol. *(d)* $\therefore \quad$ Area of $\Delta OAB = \frac{1}{2}|\vec{OA} \times \vec{OB}|$

$= \frac{1}{2}|(2\hat{i} - 3\hat{j} + 2\hat{k}) \times (2\hat{i} + 3\hat{j} + \hat{k})|$

$= \frac{1}{2}\begin{vmatrix} \hat{i} & \hat{j} & \hat{k} \\ 2 & -3 & 2 \\ 2 & 3 & 1 \end{vmatrix}$

$= \frac{1}{2}|[\hat{i}(-3 - 6) - \hat{j}(2 - 4) + \hat{k}(6 + 6)]|$

$= \frac{1}{2}|-9i + 2\hat{j} + 12\hat{k}|$

$\therefore \quad$ Area of $\Delta OAB = \frac{1}{2}\sqrt{(81 + 4 + 144)} = \frac{1}{2}\sqrt{229}$

Q. 26 For any vector $\vec{a}$, the value of $(\vec{a} \times \hat{i})^2 + (\vec{a} \times \hat{j})^2 + (\vec{a} \times \hat{k})^2$ is

(a) $\vec{a}^2$ (b) $3\vec{a}^2$

(c) $4\vec{a}^2$ (d) $2\vec{a}^2$

Sol. *(d)* Let $\vec{a} = x\hat{i} + y\hat{j} + z\hat{k}$

$$\therefore \quad \vec{a}^2 = x^2 + y^2 + z^2$$

$$\therefore \quad \vec{a} \times \hat{i} = \begin{vmatrix} \hat{i} & \hat{j} & \hat{k} \\ x & y & z \\ 1 & 0 & 0 \end{vmatrix}$$

$$= \hat{i}[0] - \hat{j}[-z] + \hat{k}[-y]$$

$$= z\hat{j} - y\hat{k}$$

$$\therefore \quad (\vec{a} \times \hat{i})^2 = (z\hat{j} - y\hat{k})(z\hat{j} - y\hat{k})$$

$$= y^2 + z^2$$

Similarly, $(\vec{a} \times \hat{j})^2 = x^2 + z^2$

and $(\vec{a} \times \hat{k})^2 = x^2 + y^2$

$$\therefore \quad (\vec{a} \times \hat{i})^2 + (\vec{a} \times \hat{j})^2 + (\vec{a} \times \hat{k})^2 = y^2 + z^2 + x^2 + z^2 + x^2 + y^2$$

$$= 2(x^2 + y^2 + z^2) = 2\vec{a}^2$$

Q. 27 If $|\vec{a}| = 10$, $|\vec{b}| = 2$ and $\vec{a} \cdot \vec{b} = 12$, then the value of $|\vec{a} \times \vec{b}|$ is

(a) 5 (b) 10 (c) 14 (d) 16

Thinking Process

We know that, $|\vec{a} \times \vec{b}| = |\vec{a}||\vec{b}||\sin\theta|\hat{n}$ and $\vec{a} \cdot \vec{b} = |\vec{a}||\vec{b}|\cos\theta$. So, we shall use these formulae to get the value of $|\vec{a} \times \vec{b}|$.

Sol. *(d)* Here, $|\vec{a}| = 10, |\vec{b}| = 2$ and $\vec{a} \cdot \vec{b} = 12$ [given]

$$\therefore \quad \vec{a} \cdot \vec{b} = |\vec{a}||\vec{b}|\cos\theta$$

$$12 = 10 \times 2\cos\theta$$

$$\Rightarrow \quad \cos\theta = \frac{12}{20} = \frac{3}{5}$$

$$\Rightarrow \quad \sin\theta = \sqrt{1 - \cos^2\theta} = \sqrt{1 - \frac{9}{25}}$$

$$\sin\theta = \pm\frac{4}{5}$$

$$\therefore \quad |\vec{a} \times \vec{b}| = |\vec{a}||\vec{b}||\sin\theta|$$

$$= 10 \times 2 \times \frac{4}{5}$$

$$= 16$$

Q. 28 The vectors $\lambda\hat{i}+\hat{j}+2\hat{k}$, $\hat{i}+\lambda\hat{j}-\hat{k}$ and $2\hat{i}-\hat{j}+\lambda\hat{k}$ are coplanar, if

(a) $\lambda=-2$ (b) $\lambda=0$
(c) $\lambda=1$ (d) $\lambda=-1$

Sol. *(a)* Let $\vec{a}=\lambda\hat{i}+\hat{j}+2\hat{k}$, $\vec{b}=\hat{i}+\lambda\hat{j}-\hat{k}$ and $\vec{c}=2\hat{i}-\hat{j}+\lambda\hat{k}$

For $\vec{a}$, $\vec{b}$ and $\vec{c}$ to be coplanar,

$$\begin{vmatrix} \lambda & 1 & 2 \\ 1 & \lambda & -1 \\ 2 & -1 & \lambda \end{vmatrix}=0$$

$$\Rightarrow \lambda(\lambda^2-1)-1(\lambda+2)+2(-1-2\lambda)=0$$

$$\Rightarrow \lambda^3-\lambda-\lambda-2-2-4\lambda=0$$

$$\Rightarrow \lambda^3-6\lambda-4=0$$

$$\Rightarrow (\lambda+2)(\lambda^2-2\lambda-2)=0$$

$$\Rightarrow \lambda=-2 \text{ or } \lambda=\frac{2\pm\sqrt{12}}{2}$$

$$\Rightarrow \lambda=-2 \text{ or } \lambda=\frac{2\pm2\sqrt{3}}{2}=1\pm\sqrt{3}$$

Q. 29 If $\vec{a}$, $\vec{b}$ and $\vec{c}$ are unit vectors such that $\vec{a}+\vec{b}+\vec{c}=\vec{0}$, then the value of $\vec{a}\cdot\vec{b}+\vec{b}\cdot\vec{c}+\vec{c}\cdot\vec{a}$ is

(a) 1 (b) 3
(c) $-\frac{3}{2}$ (d) None of these

Sol. *(c)* We have, $\vec{a}+\vec{b}+\vec{c}=0$ and $\vec{a}^2=1$, $\vec{b}^2=1$, $\vec{c}^2=1$

$$\because (\vec{a}+\vec{b}+\vec{c})(\vec{a}+\vec{b}+\vec{c})=0$$

$$\Rightarrow \vec{a}^2+\vec{a}\cdot\vec{b}+\vec{a}\cdot\vec{c}+\vec{b}\cdot\vec{a}+\vec{b}^2+\vec{b}\cdot\vec{c}+\vec{c}\cdot\vec{a}+\vec{c}\cdot\vec{b}+\vec{c}^2=0$$

$$\Rightarrow \vec{a}^2+\vec{b}^2+\vec{c}^2+2(\vec{a}\cdot\vec{b}+\vec{b}\cdot\vec{c}+\vec{c}\cdot\vec{a})=0$$

$[\because \vec{a}\cdot\vec{b}=\vec{b}\cdot\vec{a},\ \vec{b}\cdot\vec{c}=\vec{c}\cdot\vec{b} \text{ and } \vec{c}\cdot\vec{a}=\vec{a}\cdot\vec{c}]$

$$\Rightarrow 1+1+1+2(\vec{a}\cdot\vec{b}+\vec{b}\cdot\vec{c}+\vec{c}\cdot\vec{a})=0$$

$$\Rightarrow \vec{a}\cdot\vec{b}+\vec{b}\cdot\vec{c}+\vec{c}\cdot\vec{a}=-\frac{3}{2}$$

Q. 30 The projection vector of $\vec{a}$ on $\vec{b}$ is

(a) $\left(\frac{\vec{a}\cdot\vec{b}}{|\vec{b}|}\right)\vec{b}$ (b) $\frac{\vec{a}\cdot\vec{b}}{|\vec{b}|}$ (c) $\frac{\vec{a}\cdot\vec{b}}{|\vec{a}|}$ (d) $\left(\frac{\vec{a}\cdot\vec{b}}{|\vec{a}|^2}\right)\hat{b}$

Sol. *(a)* Projection vector of $\vec{a}$ on $\vec{b}$ is given by $=\vec{a}\cdot\frac{\vec{b}}{|\vec{b}|}\vec{b}=\left(\vec{a}\cdot\frac{\vec{b}}{|\vec{b}|}\right)\cdot\vec{b}$

Q. 31 If $\vec{a}$, $\vec{b}$ and $\vec{c}$ are three vectors such that $\vec{a}+\vec{b}+\vec{c}=\vec{0}$ and $|\vec{a}|=2$, $|\vec{b}|=3$ and $|\vec{c}|=5$, then the value of $\vec{a}\cdot\vec{b}+\vec{b}\cdot\vec{c}+\vec{c}\cdot\vec{a}$ is

(a) 0 (b) 1 (c) −19 (d) 38

Sol. *(c)* Here, $\vec{a}+\vec{b}+\vec{c}=\vec{0}$ and $\vec{a}^2=4, \vec{b}^2=9, \vec{c}^2=25$

$\therefore \quad (\vec{a}+\vec{b}+\vec{c})\cdot(\vec{a}+\vec{b}+\vec{c})=\vec{0}$

$\Rightarrow \vec{a}^2+\vec{a}\cdot\vec{b}+\vec{a}\cdot\vec{c}+\vec{b}\cdot\vec{a}+\vec{b}^2+\vec{b}\cdot\vec{c}+\vec{c}\cdot\vec{a}+\vec{c}\cdot\vec{b}+\vec{c}^2=\vec{0}$

$\Rightarrow \quad \vec{a}^2+\vec{b}^2+\vec{c}^2+2(\vec{a}\cdot\vec{b}+\vec{b}\cdot\vec{c}+\vec{c}\cdot\vec{a})=0 \qquad [\because \vec{a}\cdot\vec{b}=\vec{b}\cdot\vec{a}]$

$\Rightarrow \quad 4+9+25+2(\vec{a}\cdot\vec{b}+\vec{b}\cdot\vec{c}+\vec{c}\cdot\vec{a})=0$

$\Rightarrow \quad \vec{a}\cdot\vec{b}+\vec{b}\cdot\vec{c}+\vec{c}\cdot\vec{a}=\frac{-38}{2}=-19$

Q. 32 If $|\vec{a}|=4$ and $-3\le\lambda\le 2$, then the range of $|\lambda\vec{a}|$ is

(a) [0, 8] (b) [−12, 8]

(c) [0, 12] (d) [8, 12]

Sol. *(c)* We have, $|\vec{a}|=4$ and $-3\le\lambda\le 2$

$\therefore \quad |\lambda\vec{a}|=|\lambda||\vec{a}|=\lambda|4|$

$\Rightarrow \quad |\lambda\vec{a}|=|-3|4=12$, at $\lambda=-3$

$|\lambda\vec{a}|=|0|4=0$, at $\lambda=0$

and $\quad |\lambda\vec{a}|=|2|4=8$, at $\lambda=2$

So, the range of $|\lambda\vec{a}|$ is [0, 12].

Alternate Method

Since, $\quad -3\le\lambda\le 2$

$0\le|\lambda|\le 3$

$\Rightarrow \quad 0\le 4|\lambda|\le 12$

$|\lambda\vec{a}|\in[0,12]$

Q. 33 The number of vectors of unit length perpendicular to the vectors $\vec{a}=2\hat{i}+\hat{j}+2\hat{k}$ and $\vec{b}=\hat{j}+\hat{k}$ is

(a) one (b) two

(c) three (d) infinite

Sol. *(b)* The number of vectors of unit length perpendicular to the vectors $\vec{a}$ and $\vec{b}$ is $\vec{c}$ (say)

i.e., $\quad \vec{c}=\pm(\vec{a}\times\vec{b})$.

So, there will be two vectors of unit length perpendicular to the vectors $\vec{a}$ and $\vec{b}$.

Fillers

Q. 34 The vector $\vec{\mathbf{a}} + \vec{\mathbf{b}}$ bisects the angle between the non-collinear vectors $\vec{\mathbf{a}}$ and $\vec{\mathbf{b}}$, if...... .

Sol. If vector $\vec{a} + \vec{b}$ bisects the angle between the non-collinear vectors, then

$$\vec{a}\cdot(\vec{a} + \vec{b}) = |\vec{a}||\vec{a} + \vec{b}|\cos\theta$$

$$\vec{a}\cdot(\vec{a} + \vec{b}) = a\sqrt{a^2 + b^2}\cos\theta$$

$$\Rightarrow \quad \cos\theta = \frac{\vec{a}\cdot(\vec{a} + \vec{b})}{a\sqrt{a^2 + b^2}} \quad \text{...(i)}$$

and

$$\vec{b}\cdot(\vec{a} + \vec{b}) = |\vec{b}|\cdot|\vec{a} + \vec{b}|\cos\theta$$

$$\vec{b}\cdot(\vec{a} + \vec{b}) = b\sqrt{a^2 + b^2}\cos\theta \quad \text{[since, } \theta \text{ should be same]}$$

$$\Rightarrow \quad \cos\theta = \frac{\vec{b}\cdot(\vec{a} + \vec{b})}{b\sqrt{a^2 + b^2}} \quad \text{...(ii)}$$

From Eqs. (i) and (ii),

$$\frac{\vec{a}\cdot(\vec{a} + \vec{b})}{a\sqrt{a^2 + b^2}} = \frac{\vec{b}\cdot(\vec{a} + \vec{b})}{b\sqrt{a^2 + b^2}} \Rightarrow \frac{\vec{a}}{|\vec{a}|} = \frac{\vec{b}}{|\vec{b}|}$$

$\therefore \quad \hat{a} = \hat{b} \Rightarrow \vec{a}$ and $\vec{b}$ are equal vectors.

Q. 35 If $\vec{\mathbf{r}}\cdot\vec{\mathbf{a}} = 0$, $\vec{\mathbf{r}}\cdot\vec{\mathbf{b}} = 0$ and $\vec{\mathbf{r}}\cdot\vec{\mathbf{c}} = 0$ for some non-zero vector $\vec{\mathbf{r}}$, then the value of $\vec{\mathbf{a}}\cdot(\vec{\mathbf{b}} \times \vec{\mathbf{c}})$ is...... .

Sol. Since, $\vec{r}$ is a non-zero vector. So, we can say that $\vec{a}$, $\vec{b}$ and $\vec{c}$ are in a same plane.

$$\therefore \quad \vec{a}\cdot(\vec{b} \times \vec{c}) = 0$$

[since, angle between $\vec{a}$, $\vec{b}$ and $\vec{c}$ are zero *i.e.*, $\theta = 0$]

Q. 36 The vectors $\vec{\mathbf{a}} = 3\hat{\mathbf{i}} - 2\hat{\mathbf{j}} + 2\hat{\mathbf{k}}$ and $\vec{\mathbf{b}} = -\hat{\mathbf{i}} - 2\hat{\mathbf{k}}$ are the adjacent sides of a parallelogram. The angle between its diagonals is...... .

Sol. We have, $\vec{a} = 3\hat{i} - 2\hat{j} + 2\hat{k}$ and $\vec{b} = -\hat{i} - 2\hat{k}$

$$\therefore \quad \vec{a} + \vec{b} = 2\hat{i} - 2\hat{j} \text{ and } \vec{a} - \vec{b} = 4\hat{i} - 2\hat{j} + 4\hat{k}$$

Now, let θ is the acute angle between the diagonals $\vec{a} + \vec{b}$ and $\vec{a} - \vec{b}$.

$$\therefore \quad \cos\theta = \frac{(\vec{a} + \vec{b})\cdot(\vec{a} - \vec{b})}{|\vec{a} + \vec{b}||\vec{a} - \vec{b}|}$$

$$= \frac{(2\hat{i} - 2\hat{j})\cdot(4\hat{i} - 2\hat{j} + 4\hat{k})}{\sqrt{8}\sqrt{16 + 4 + 16}} = \frac{8 + 4}{2\sqrt{2}\cdot 6} = \frac{1}{\sqrt{2}}$$

$$\therefore \quad \theta = \frac{\pi}{4} \quad \left[\because \cos\frac{\pi}{4} = \frac{1}{\sqrt{2}}\right]$$

Q. 37 The values of k, for which $|k\vec{\mathbf{a}}| < |\vec{\mathbf{a}}|$ and $k\vec{\mathbf{a}} + \frac{1}{2}\vec{\mathbf{a}}$ is parallel to $\vec{\mathbf{a}}$ holds true are ....

Sol. We have, $|k\vec{\mathbf{a}}| < |\vec{\mathbf{a}}|$ and $k\vec{\mathbf{a}} + \frac{1}{2}\vec{\mathbf{a}}$ is parallel to $\vec{\mathbf{a}}$.

$\therefore \quad |k\vec{\mathbf{a}}| < |\vec{\mathbf{a}}| \Rightarrow |k||\vec{\mathbf{a}}| < |\vec{\mathbf{a}}|$

$\Rightarrow \quad |k| < 1 \Rightarrow -1 < k < 1$

Also, since $k\vec{\mathbf{a}} + \frac{1}{2}\vec{\mathbf{a}}$ is parallel to $\vec{\mathbf{a}}$, then we see that at $k = \frac{-1}{2}$, $k\vec{\mathbf{a}} + \frac{1}{2}\vec{\mathbf{a}}$ becomes a null vector and then it will not be parallel to $\vec{\mathbf{a}}$.

So, $k\vec{\mathbf{a}} + \frac{1}{2}\vec{\mathbf{a}}$ is parallel to $\vec{\mathbf{a}}$ holds true when $k \in]-1, 1[\ k \neq \frac{-1}{2}$.

Q. 38 The value of the expression $|\vec{\mathbf{a}} \times \vec{\mathbf{b}}|^2 + (\vec{\mathbf{a}} \cdot \vec{\mathbf{b}})^2$ is ....

Sol.

$$\begin{aligned}|\vec{\mathbf{a}} \times \vec{\mathbf{b}}|^2 + (\vec{\mathbf{a}} \cdot \vec{\mathbf{b}})^2 &= |\vec{\mathbf{a}}|^2|\vec{\mathbf{b}}|^2\sin^2\theta + (\vec{\mathbf{a}} \cdot \vec{\mathbf{b}})^2 \\ &= |\vec{\mathbf{a}}|^2|\vec{\mathbf{b}}|^2(1-\cos^2\theta) + (\vec{\mathbf{a}} \cdot \vec{\mathbf{b}})^2 \\ &= |\vec{\mathbf{a}}|^2|\vec{\mathbf{b}}|^2 - |\vec{\mathbf{a}}|^2|\vec{\mathbf{b}}|^2\cos^2\theta + (\vec{\mathbf{a}} \cdot \vec{\mathbf{b}})^2 \\ &= |\vec{\mathbf{a}}|^2|\vec{\mathbf{b}}|^2 - (\vec{\mathbf{a}} \cdot \vec{\mathbf{b}})^2 + (\vec{\mathbf{a}} \cdot \vec{\mathbf{b}})^2\end{aligned}$$

$$|\vec{\mathbf{a}} \times \vec{\mathbf{b}}|^2 + (\vec{\mathbf{a}} \cdot \vec{\mathbf{b}})^2 = |\vec{\mathbf{a}}|^2|\vec{\mathbf{b}}|^2$$

Q. 39 If $|\vec{\mathbf{a}} \times \vec{\mathbf{b}}|^2 + |\vec{\mathbf{a}} \cdot \vec{\mathbf{b}}|^2 = 144$ and $|\vec{\mathbf{a}}| = 4$, then $|\vec{\mathbf{b}}|$ is equal to ......

Thinking Process

We know that, $|\vec{\mathbf{a}} \times \vec{\mathbf{b}}|^2 + |\vec{\mathbf{a}} \cdot \vec{\mathbf{a}}|^2 = |\vec{\mathbf{a}}|^2|\vec{\mathbf{b}}|^2$. So, we shall use this concept here to find the value of $|\vec{\mathbf{b}}|$.

Sol. $\because \quad |\vec{\mathbf{a}} \times \vec{\mathbf{b}}|^2 + |\vec{\mathbf{a}} \cdot \vec{\mathbf{b}}|^2 = 144 = |\vec{\mathbf{a}}|^2 \cdot |\vec{\mathbf{b}}|^2$

$\Rightarrow \quad |\vec{\mathbf{a}}|^2|\vec{\mathbf{b}}|^2 = 144$

$\Rightarrow \quad |\vec{\mathbf{b}}|^2 = \frac{144}{|\vec{\mathbf{a}}|^2} = \frac{144}{16} = 9$

$\therefore \quad |\vec{\mathbf{b}}| = 3$

Q. 40 If $\vec{\mathbf{a}}$ is any non-zero vector, then $(\vec{\mathbf{a}} \cdot \hat{\mathbf{i}}) \cdot \hat{\mathbf{i}} + (\vec{\mathbf{a}} \cdot \hat{\mathbf{j}}) \cdot \hat{\mathbf{j}} + (\vec{\mathbf{a}} \cdot \hat{\mathbf{k}})\hat{\mathbf{k}}$ is equal to ......

Sol. Let $\quad \vec{\mathbf{a}} = a_1\hat{\mathbf{i}} + a_2\hat{\mathbf{j}} + a_3\hat{\mathbf{k}}$

$\therefore \quad \vec{\mathbf{a}} \cdot \hat{\mathbf{i}} = a_1, \vec{\mathbf{a}} \cdot \hat{\mathbf{j}} = a_2$ and $\vec{\mathbf{a}} \cdot \hat{\mathbf{k}} = a_3$

$\therefore \quad (\vec{\mathbf{a}} \cdot \hat{\mathbf{i}})\hat{\mathbf{i}} + (\vec{\mathbf{a}} \cdot \hat{\mathbf{j}})\hat{\mathbf{j}} + (\vec{\mathbf{a}} \cdot \hat{\mathbf{k}})\hat{\mathbf{k}} = a_1\hat{\mathbf{i}} + a_2\hat{\mathbf{j}} + a_3\hat{\mathbf{k}} = \vec{\mathbf{a}}$

True/False

Q. 41 If $|\vec{a}| = |\vec{b}|$, then necessarily it implies $\vec{a} = \pm\vec{b}$.

Sol. ***True***

If $\quad |\vec{a}| = |\vec{b}| \Rightarrow \vec{a} = \pm\vec{b}$

So, it is a true statement.

Q. 42 Position vector of a point $\vec{P}$ is a vector whose initial point is origin.

Sol. ***True***

Since, $\vec{P} = \overrightarrow{OP}$ = displacement of vector $\vec{P}$ from origin

Q. 43 If $|\vec{a} + \vec{b}| = |\vec{a} - \vec{b}|$, then the vectors $\vec{a}$ and $\vec{b}$ are orthogonal

Sol. ***True***

Since, $\quad |\vec{a} + \vec{b}| = |\vec{a} - \vec{b}|$

$\Rightarrow \quad |\vec{a} + \vec{b}|^2 = |\vec{a} - \vec{b}|^2$

$\Rightarrow \quad 2|\vec{a}||\vec{b}| = -2|\vec{a}||\vec{b}|$

$\Rightarrow \quad 4|\vec{a}||\vec{b}| = 0$

$\Rightarrow \quad |\vec{a}||\vec{b}| = 0$

Hence, $\vec{a}$ and $\vec{b}$ are orthogonal. $\quad [\because \vec{a}\cdot\vec{b} = |\vec{a}|\cdot|\vec{b}|\cos 90° = 0]$

Q. 44 The formula $(\vec{a} + \vec{b})^2 = \vec{a}^2 + \vec{b}^2 + 2\vec{a} \times \vec{b}$ is valid for non-zero vectors $\vec{a}$ and $\vec{b}$.

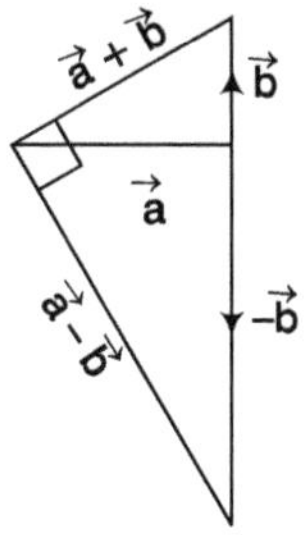

Sol. ***False***

$$(\vec{a} + \vec{b})^2 = (\vec{a} + \vec{b})\cdot(\vec{a} + \vec{b})$$

$$= \vec{a}^2 + \vec{b}^2 + 2\vec{a}\cdot\vec{b}$$

Q. 45 If $\vec{a}$ and $\vec{b}$ are adjacent sides of a rhombus, then $\vec{a}\cdot\vec{b} = 0$.

Sol. ***False***

If $\vec{a}\cdot\vec{b} = 0$, then $\vec{a}\cdot\vec{b} = |\vec{a}||\vec{b}|\cos 90°$

Hence, angle between $\vec{a}$ and $\vec{b}$ is 90°, which is not possible in a rhombus.
Since, angle between adjacent sides in a rhombus is not equal to 90°.

11

Three Dimensional Geometry

Short Answer Type Questions

Q. 1 Find the position vector of a point A in space such that $\vec{\mathbf{OA}}$ is inclined at 60° to OX and at 45° to OY and $|\vec{\mathbf{OA}}| = 10$ units.

Sol. Since, $\vec{\mathbf{OA}}$ is inclined at 60° to OX and at 45° to OY. Let $\vec{\mathbf{OA}}$ makes angle α with OZ.

$$\therefore \quad \cos^2 60° + \cos^2 45° + \cos^2 \alpha = 1$$

$$\Rightarrow \quad \left(\frac{1}{2}\right)^2 + \left(\frac{1}{\sqrt{2}}\right)^2 + \cos^2 \alpha = 1 \qquad [\because l^2 + m^2 + n^2 = 1]$$

$$\Rightarrow \quad \frac{1}{4} + \frac{1}{2} + \cos^2 \alpha = 1$$

$$\Rightarrow \quad \cos^2 \alpha = 1 - \left(\frac{1}{2} + \frac{1}{4}\right)$$

$$\Rightarrow \quad \cos^2 \alpha = 1 - \left(\frac{6}{8}\right)$$

$$\Rightarrow \quad \cos^2 \alpha = \frac{1}{4}$$

$$\Rightarrow \quad \cos \alpha = \frac{1}{2} = \cos 60°$$

$$\therefore \quad \alpha = 60°$$

$$\therefore \quad \vec{\mathbf{OA}} = |\vec{\mathbf{OA}}| \left(\frac{1}{2}\hat{\mathbf{i}} + \frac{1}{\sqrt{2}}\hat{\mathbf{j}} + \frac{1}{2}\hat{\mathbf{k}}\right)$$

$$= 10\left(\frac{1}{2}\hat{\mathbf{i}} + \frac{1}{\sqrt{2}}\hat{\mathbf{j}} + \frac{1}{2}\hat{\mathbf{k}}\right) \qquad [\because |\vec{\mathbf{OA}}| = 10]$$

$$= 5\hat{\mathbf{i}} + 5\sqrt{2}\,\hat{\mathbf{j}} + 5\,\hat{\mathbf{k}}$$

Q. 2 Find the vector equation of the line which is parallel to the vector $3\hat{i} - 2\hat{j} + 6\hat{k}$ and which passes through the point $(1, -2, 3)$.

Thinking Process

Here, we use the formula $\vec{r} = \vec{b} + \lambda\vec{a}$, where $\vec{r}$ is the equation of the line which passes through $\vec{b}$ and parallel to $\vec{a}$.

Sol. Let $\vec{a} = 3\hat{i} - 2\hat{j} + 6\hat{k}$ and $\vec{b} = \hat{i} - 2\hat{j} + 3\hat{k}$

So, vector equation of the line, which is parallel to the vector $\vec{a} = 3\hat{i} - 2\hat{j} + 6\hat{k}$ and passes through the vector $\vec{b} = \hat{i} - 2\hat{j} + 3\hat{k}$ is $\vec{r} = \vec{b} + \lambda\vec{a}$.

$$\therefore \quad \vec{r} = (\hat{i} - 2\hat{j} + 3\hat{k}) + \lambda(3\hat{i} - 2\hat{j} + 6\hat{k})$$

$$\Rightarrow \quad (x\hat{i} + y\hat{j} + z\hat{k}) - (\hat{i} - 2\hat{j} + 3\hat{k}) = \lambda(3\hat{i} - 2\hat{j} + 6\hat{k})$$

$$\Rightarrow \quad (x-1)\hat{i} + (y+2)\hat{j} + (z-3)\hat{k} = \lambda(3\hat{i} - 2\hat{j} + 6\hat{k})$$

Q. 3 Show that the lines $\frac{x-1}{2} = \frac{y-2}{3} = \frac{z-3}{4}$ and $\frac{x-4}{5} = \frac{y-1}{2} = z$ intersect. Also, find their point of intersection.

Thinking Process

If shortest distance between the lines is zero, then they intersect.

Sol. We have, $x_1 = 1, y_1 = 2, z_1 = 3$ and $a_1 = 2, b_1 = 3, c_1 = 4$

Also, $x_2 = 4, y_2 = 1, z_2 = 0$ and $a_2 = 5, b_2 = 2, c_2 = 1$

If two lines intersect, then shortest distance between them should be zero.

$\therefore$ Shortest distance between two given lines

$$= \frac{\begin{vmatrix} x_2 - x_1 & y_2 - y_1 & z_2 - z_1 \\ a_1 & b_1 & c_1 \\ a_2 & b_2 & c_2 \end{vmatrix}}{\sqrt{(b_1c_2 - b_2c_1)^2 + (c_1a_2 - c_2a_1)^2 + (a_1b_2 - a_2b_1)^2}}$$

$$= \frac{\begin{vmatrix} 4-1 & 1-2 & 0-3 \\ 2 & 3 & 4 \\ 5 & 2 & 1 \end{vmatrix}}{\sqrt{(3\cdot1 - 2\cdot4)^2 + (4\cdot5 - 1\cdot2)^2 + (2\cdot2 - 5\cdot3)^2}}$$

$$= \frac{\begin{vmatrix} 3 & -1 & -3 \\ 2 & 3 & 4 \\ 5 & 2 & 1 \end{vmatrix}}{\sqrt{25 + 324 + 121}}$$

$$= \frac{3(3-8) + 1(2-20) - 3(4-15)}{\sqrt{470}}$$

$$= \frac{-15 - 18 + 33}{\sqrt{470}} = \frac{0}{\sqrt{470}} = 0$$

Therefore, the given two lines are intersecting.

For finding their point of intersection for first line,

$$\frac{x-1}{2}=\frac{y-2}{3}=\frac{z-3}{4}=\lambda$$

$\Rightarrow$ $x=2\lambda+1,\ y=3\lambda+2$ and $z=4\lambda+3$

Since, the lines are intersecting. So, let us put these values in the equation of another line.

Thus, $$\frac{2\lambda+1-4}{5}=\frac{3\lambda+2-1}{2}=\frac{4\lambda+3}{1}$$

$$\Rightarrow \quad \frac{2\lambda-3}{5}=\frac{3\lambda+1}{2}=\frac{4\lambda+3}{1}$$

$$\Rightarrow \quad \frac{2\lambda-3}{5}=\frac{4\lambda+3}{1}$$

$$\Rightarrow \quad 2\lambda-3=20\lambda+15$$

$$\Rightarrow \quad 18\lambda=-18=-1$$

So, the required point of intersection is

$$x=2(-1)+1=-1$$
$$y=3(-1)+2=-1$$
$$z=4(-1)+3=-1$$

Thus, the lines intersect at $(-1,-1,-1)$.

Q. 4 Find the angle between the lines
$\vec{r}=3\hat{i}-2\hat{j}+6\hat{k}+\lambda(2\hat{i}+\hat{j}+2\hat{k})$ and $\vec{r}=(2\hat{j}-5\hat{k})+\mu(6\hat{i}+3\hat{j}+2\hat{k})$.

Thinking Process

We know that, $\cos\theta=\frac{|\vec{b}_1\cdot\vec{b}_2|}{|\vec{b}_1|\cdot|\vec{b}_2|}$*, where, θ is the angle between the lines* $\vec{a}_1+\lambda\vec{b}_1$ *and* $\vec{a}_2+\mu\vec{b}_2$.

Sol. We have, $\vec{r}=3\hat{i}-2\hat{j}+6\hat{k}+\lambda(2\hat{i}+\hat{j}+2\hat{k})$

and $\vec{r}=(2\hat{j}-5\hat{k})+\mu(6\hat{i}+3\hat{j}+2\hat{k})$

where, $\vec{a}_1=3\hat{i}-2\hat{j}+6\hat{k},\ \vec{b}_1=2\hat{i}+\hat{j}+2\hat{k}$

and $\vec{a}_2=2\hat{j}-5\hat{k},\ \vec{b}_2=6\hat{i}+3\hat{j}+2\hat{k}$

If θ is angle between the lines, then

$$\cos\theta=\frac{|\vec{b}_1\cdot\vec{b}_2|}{|\vec{b}_1|\cdot|\vec{b}_2|}$$
$$=\frac{|(2\hat{i}+\hat{j}+2\hat{k})\cdot(6\hat{i}+3\hat{j}+2\hat{k})|}{|2\hat{i}+\hat{j}+2\hat{k}||6\hat{i}+3\hat{j}+2\hat{k}|}$$
$$=\frac{|12+3+4|}{\sqrt{9}\sqrt{49}}=\frac{19}{21}$$

$$\therefore \quad \theta=\cos^{-1}\frac{19}{21}$$

Q. 5 Prove that the line through $A(0, -1, -1)$ and $B(4, 5, 1)$ intersects the line through $C(3, 9, 4)$ and $D(-4, 4, 4)$.

Sol. We know that,the cartesian equation of a line that passes through two points (x_1, y_1, z_1) and (x_2, y_2, z_2) is

$$\frac{x - x_1}{x_2 - x_1} = \frac{y - y_1}{y_2 - y_1} = \frac{z - z_1}{z_2 - z_1}$$

Hence, the cartesian equation of line passes through $A(0, -1, -1)$ and $B(4, 5, 1)$ is

$$\frac{x - 0}{4 - 0} = \frac{y + 1}{5 + 1} = \frac{z + 1}{1 + 1}$$

$$\Rightarrow \quad \frac{x}{4} = \frac{y + 1}{6} = \frac{z + 1}{2} \quad \text{...(i)}$$

and cartesian equation of the line passes through $C(3, 9, 4)$ and $D(-4, 4, 4)$ is

$$\frac{x - 3}{-4 - 3} = \frac{y - 9}{4 - 9} = \frac{z - 4}{4 - 4}$$

$$\Rightarrow \quad \frac{x - 3}{-7} = \frac{y - 9}{-5} = \frac{z - 4}{0} \quad \text{...(ii)}$$

If the lines intersect, then shortest distance between both of them should be zero.

$\therefore$ Shortest distance between the lines

$$= \frac{\begin{vmatrix} x_2 - x_1 & y_2 - y_1 & z_2 - z_1 \\ a_1 & b_1 & c_1 \\ a_2 & b_2 & c_2 \end{vmatrix}}{\sqrt{(b_1c_2 - b_2c_1)^2 + (c_1a_2 - c_2a_1)^2 + (a_1b_2 - a_2b_1)^2}}$$

$$= \frac{\begin{vmatrix} 3 - 0 & 9 + 1 & 4 + 1 \\ 4 & 6 & 2 \\ -7 & -5 & 0 \end{vmatrix}}{\sqrt{(6 \cdot 0 + 10)^2 + (-14 - 0)^2 + (-20 + 42)^2}}$$

$$= \frac{\begin{vmatrix} 3 & 10 & 5 \\ 4 & 6 & 2 \\ -7 & -5 & 0 \end{vmatrix}}{\sqrt{100 + 196 + 484}}$$

$$= \frac{3(0 + 10) - 10(14) + 5(-20 + 42)}{\sqrt{780}}$$

$$= \frac{30 - 140 + 110}{\sqrt{780}} = 0$$

So, the given lines intersect.

Q. 6 Prove that the lines $x = py + q$, $z = ry + s$ and $x = p'y + q'$, $z = r'y + s'$ are perpendicular, if $pp' + rr' + 1 = 0$.

Sol. We have, $\quad x = py + q \Rightarrow y = \frac{x - q}{p} \quad$ ..(i)

and $\quad z = ry + s \Rightarrow y = \frac{z - s}{r} \quad$ ...(ii)

$$\Rightarrow \quad \frac{x - q}{p} = \frac{y}{1} = \frac{z - s}{r} \quad \text{[using Eqs. (i) and (ii)] ...(iii)}$$

Similarly, $\quad \frac{x - q'}{p'} = \frac{y}{1} = \frac{z - s'}{r'} \quad$ ...(iv)

From Eqs. (iii) and (iv),

$$a_1 = p, b_1 = 1, c_1 = r$$

and $$a_2 = p', b_2 = 1, c_2 = r'$$

If these given lines are perpendicular to each other, then

$$a_1 a_2 + b_1 b_2 + c_1 c_2 = 0$$

$\Rightarrow$ $$pp' + 1 + rr' = 0$$

which is the required condition.

Q. 7 Find the equation of a plane which bisects perpendicularly the line joining the points $A(2, 3, 4)$ and $B(4, 5, 8)$ at right angles.

Sol. Since, the equation of a plane is bisecting perpendicular the line joining the points $A(2, 3, 4)$ and $B(4, 5, 8)$ at right angles.

So, mid-point of AB is $\left(\frac{2+4}{2}, \frac{3+5}{2}, \frac{4+8}{2}\right)$ *i.e.*, $(3, 4, 6)$.

Also, $$\vec{N} = (4-2)\hat{i} + (5-3)\hat{j} + (8-4)\hat{k} = 2\hat{i} + 2\hat{j} + 4\hat{k}$$

So, the required equation of the plane is $(\vec{r} - \vec{a})\cdot\vec{N} = 0$.

$\Rightarrow$ $[(x-3)\hat{i} + (y-4)\hat{j} + (z-6)\hat{k}]\cdot(2\hat{i} + 2\hat{j} + 4\hat{k}) = 0$ $[\because \vec{a} = 3\hat{i} + 4\hat{j} + 6\hat{k}]$

$\Rightarrow$ $$2x - 6 + 2y - 8 + 4z - 24 = 0$$

$\Rightarrow$ $$2x + 2y + 4z = 38$$

$\therefore$ $$x + y + 2z = 19$$

Q. 8 Find the equation of a plane which is at a distance $3\sqrt{3}$ units from origin and the normal to which is equally inclined to coordinate axis.

Sol. Since, normal to the plane is equally inclined to the coordinate axis.

Therefore, $$\cos\alpha = \cos\beta = \cos\gamma = \frac{1}{\sqrt{3}}$$

So, the normal is $\vec{N} = \frac{1}{\sqrt{3}}\hat{i} + \frac{1}{\sqrt{3}}\hat{j} + \frac{1}{\sqrt{3}}\hat{k}$ and plane is at a distance of $3\sqrt{3}$ units from origin.

The equation of plane is $\vec{r}\cdot\hat{N} = 3\sqrt{3}$ $\left[\because \hat{N} = \frac{\vec{N}}{|\vec{N}|}\right]$

[since, vector equation of the plane at a distance p from the origin is $\vec{r}\cdot\hat{N} = p$]

$\Rightarrow$ $$(x\hat{i} + y\hat{j} + z\hat{k})\cdot\frac{\left(\frac{1}{\sqrt{3}}\hat{i} + \frac{1}{\sqrt{3}}\hat{j} + \frac{1}{\sqrt{3}}\hat{k}\right)}{1} = 3\sqrt{3}$$

$\Rightarrow$ $$\frac{x}{\sqrt{3}} + \frac{y}{\sqrt{3}} + \frac{z}{\sqrt{3}} = 3\sqrt{3}$$

$\therefore$ $$x + y + z = 3\sqrt{3}\cdot\sqrt{3} = 9$$

So, the required equation of plane is $x + y + z = 9$.

Q. 9 If the line drawn from the point (–2, – 1, – 3) meets a plane at right angle at the point (1, – 3, 3), then find the equation of the plane.

Sol. Since, the line drawn from the point (–2, – 1, – 3) meets a plane at right angle at the point (1, – 3, 3). So, the plane passes through the point (1, – 3, 3) and normal to plane is $(-3\hat{i} + 2\hat{j} - 6\hat{k})$.

$$\Rightarrow \quad \vec{a} = \hat{i} - 3\hat{j} + 3\hat{k}$$

$$\text{and} \quad \vec{N} = -3\hat{i} + 2\hat{j} - 6\hat{k}$$

So, the equation of required plane is $(\vec{r} - \vec{a})\cdot\vec{N} = 0$

$$\Rightarrow \quad [(x\hat{i} + y\hat{j} + z\hat{k}) - (\hat{i} - 3\hat{j} + 3\hat{k})]\cdot(-3\hat{i} + 2\hat{j} - 6\hat{k}) = 0$$

$$\Rightarrow \quad [(x-1)\hat{i} + (y+3)\hat{j} + (z-3)\hat{k}]\cdot(-3\hat{i} + 2\hat{j} - 6\hat{k}) = 0$$

$$\Rightarrow \quad -3x + 3 + 2y + 6 - 6z + 18 = 0$$

$$\Rightarrow \quad -3x + 2y - 6z = -27$$

$$\therefore \quad 3x - 2y + 6z - 27 = 0$$

Q. 10 Find the equation of the plane through the points (2, 1, 0), (3, – 2, – 2) and (3, 1, 7).

Thinking Process

Here, apply the equation of the plane passing through the points (x_1, y_1, z_1), (x_2, y_2, z_2) and (x_3, y_3, z_3) is given by $\begin{vmatrix} x-x_1 & y-y_1 & z-z_1 \\ x_2-x_1 & y_2-y_1 & z_2-z_1 \\ x_3-x_1 & y_3-y_1 & z_3-z_1 \end{vmatrix} = 0.$

Sol. We know that, the equation of a plane passing through three non-collinear points (x_1, y_1, z_1), (x_2, y_2, z_2) and (x_3, y_3, z_3) is

$$\begin{vmatrix} x-x_1 & y-y_1 & z-z_1 \\ x_2-x_1 & y_2-y_1 & z_2-z_1 \\ x_3-x_1 & y_3-y_1 & z_3-z_1 \end{vmatrix} = 0$$

$$\Rightarrow \quad \begin{vmatrix} x-2 & y-1 & z-0 \\ 3-2 & -2-1 & -2-0 \\ 3-2 & 1-1 & 7-0 \end{vmatrix} = 0$$

$$\Rightarrow \quad \begin{vmatrix} x-2 & y-1 & z \\ 1 & -3 & -2 \\ 1 & 0 & 7 \end{vmatrix} = 0$$

$$\Rightarrow \quad (x-2)(-21+0) - (y-1)(7+2) + z(3) = 0$$

$$\Rightarrow \quad -21x + 42 - 9y + 9 + 3z = 0$$

$$\Rightarrow \quad -21x - 9y + 3z = -51$$

$$\therefore \quad 7x + 3y - z = 17$$

So, the required equation of plane is $7x + 3y - z = 17$.

Q. 11 Find the equations of the two lines through the origin which intersect the line $\frac{x-3}{2}=\frac{y-3}{1}=\frac{z}{1}$ at angles of $\frac{\pi}{3}$ each.

Sol. Given equation of the line is $\frac{x-3}{2}=\frac{y-3}{1}=\frac{z}{1}=\lambda$ ...(i)

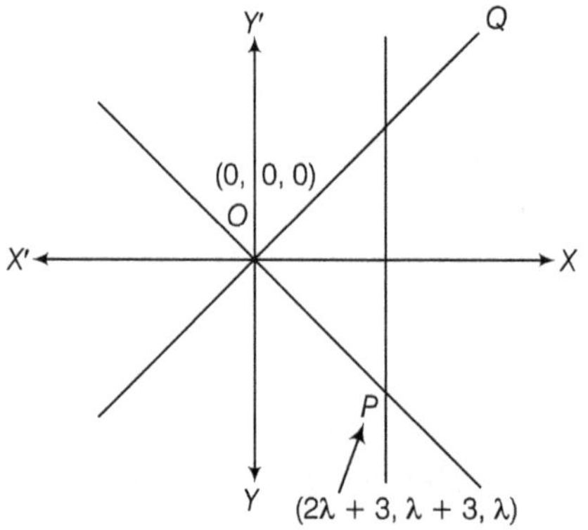

So, DR's of the line are 2, 1, 1 and DC's of the given line are $\frac{2}{\sqrt{6}}, \frac{1}{\sqrt{6}}, \frac{1}{\sqrt{16}}$.

Also, the required lines make angle $\frac{\pi}{3}$ with the given line.

From Eq. (i), $x=(2\lambda+3),\ y=(\lambda+3)$ and $z=\lambda$

$$\because \quad \cos\theta=\frac{a_1a_2+b_1b_2+c_1c_2}{\sqrt{a_1^2+b_1^2+c_1^2}\sqrt{a_2^2+b_2^2+c_2^2}}$$

$$\therefore \quad \cos\frac{\pi}{3}=\frac{(4\lambda+6)+(\lambda+3)+(\lambda)}{\sqrt{6}\sqrt{(2\lambda+3)^2+(\lambda+3)^2+\lambda^2}}$$

$$\Rightarrow \quad \frac{1}{2}=\frac{6\lambda+9}{\sqrt{6}\sqrt{(4\lambda^2+9+12\lambda+\lambda^2+9+6\lambda+\lambda^2)}}$$

$$\Rightarrow \quad \frac{\sqrt{6}}{2}=\frac{6\lambda+9}{\sqrt{6\lambda^2+18\lambda+18}}$$

$$\Rightarrow \quad 6\sqrt{(\lambda^2+3\lambda+3)}=2(6\lambda+9)$$

$$\Rightarrow \quad 36(\lambda^2+3\lambda+3)=36(4\lambda^2+9+12\lambda)$$

$$\Rightarrow \quad \lambda^2+3\lambda+3=4\lambda^2+9+12\lambda$$

$$\Rightarrow \quad 3\lambda^2+9\lambda+6=0$$

$$\Rightarrow \quad \lambda^2+3\lambda+2=0$$

$$\Rightarrow \quad \lambda(\lambda+2)+1(\lambda+2)=0$$

$$\Rightarrow \quad (\lambda+1)(\lambda+2)=0$$

$$\therefore \quad \lambda=-1,-2$$

So, the DC's are 1, 2, −1 and −1, 1, −2.

Also, both the required lines passes through origin.

So, the equations of required lines are $\frac{x}{1}=\frac{y}{2}=\frac{z}{-1}$ and $\frac{x}{-1}=\frac{y}{1}=\frac{z}{-2}$.

Q. 12 **Find the angle between the lines whose direction cosines are given by the equation $l+m+n=0$ and $l^2+m^2-n^2=0$.**

Sol. Eliminating n from both the equations, we have

$$l^2+m^2-(l-m)^2=0$$

$\Rightarrow \quad l^2+m^2-l^2-m^2+2ml=0 \quad \Rightarrow 2lm=0$

$\Rightarrow \quad lm=0 \quad \Rightarrow (-m-n)m=0 \qquad [\because l=-m-n]$

$\Rightarrow \quad (m+n)m=0$

$\Rightarrow \quad m=-n \Rightarrow m=0$

$\Rightarrow \quad l=0, l=-n$

Thus, Dr's two lines are proportional to 0, $-n$, n and $-n$, 0, n *i.e.*, 0, -1, 1 and -1, 0, 1.

So, the vector parallel to these given lines are $\vec{\mathbf{a}}=-\hat{\mathbf{j}}+\hat{\mathbf{k}}$ and $\vec{\mathbf{b}}=-\hat{\mathbf{i}}+\hat{\mathbf{k}}$

Now, $\quad \cos\theta=\dfrac{\vec{\mathbf{a}}\vec{\mathbf{b}}}{|\vec{\mathbf{a}}||\vec{\mathbf{b}}|}=\dfrac{1}{\sqrt{2}}\cdot\dfrac{1}{\sqrt{2}} \Rightarrow \cos\theta=\dfrac{1}{2}$

$\therefore \quad \theta=\dfrac{\pi}{3} \qquad \left[\because \cos\dfrac{\pi}{3}=\dfrac{1}{2}\right]$

Q. 13 **If a variable line in two adjacent positions has direction cosines l, m, n and $l+\delta l, m+\delta m, n+\delta n$, then show that the small angle $\delta\theta$ between the two positions is given by $\delta\theta^2=\delta l^2+\delta m^2+\delta n^2$.**

Sol. We have l, m, n and $l+\delta l, m+\delta m, n+\delta n$ as direction cosines of a variable line in two different positions.

$\therefore \quad l^2+m^2+n^2=1 \qquad \text{... (i)}$

and $\quad (l+\delta l)^2+(m+\delta m)^2+(n+\delta n)^2=1 \qquad \text{...(ii)}$

$\Rightarrow \quad l^2+m^2+n^2+\delta l^2+\delta m^2+\delta n^2+2(l\delta l+m\delta m+n\delta n)=1$

$\Rightarrow \quad \delta l^2+\delta m^2+\delta n^2=-2(l\delta l+m\delta m+n\delta n) \qquad [\because l^2+m^2+n^2=1]$

$\Rightarrow \quad l\delta l+m\delta m+n\delta n=\dfrac{-1}{2}(\delta l^2+\delta m^2+\delta n^2) \qquad \text{...(iii)}$

Now, $\vec{\mathbf{a}}$ and $\vec{\mathbf{b}}$ are unit vectors along a line with direction cosines l, m, n and $(l+\delta l), (m+\delta m), (n+\delta n)$, respectively.

$\therefore \quad \vec{\mathbf{a}}=l\hat{\mathbf{i}}+m\hat{\mathbf{j}}+n\hat{\mathbf{k}}$ and $\vec{\mathbf{b}}=(l+\delta l)\hat{\mathbf{i}}+(m+\delta m)\hat{\mathbf{j}}+(n+\delta n)\hat{\mathbf{k}}$

$\Rightarrow \quad \cos\delta\theta=\dfrac{\vec{\mathbf{a}}\cdot\vec{\mathbf{b}}}{|\vec{\mathbf{a}}||\vec{\mathbf{b}}|}=\vec{\mathbf{a}}\cdot\vec{\mathbf{b}} \qquad [\because |\hat{\mathbf{a}}|=|\hat{\mathbf{b}}|=1]$

$\Rightarrow \quad \cos\delta\theta=l(l+\delta l)+m(m+\delta m)+n(n+\delta n)$

$\quad =(l^2+m^2+n^2)+(l\delta l+m\delta m+n\delta n)$

$\quad =1-\dfrac{1}{2}(\delta l^2+\delta m^2+\delta n^2) \qquad \text{[using Eq. (iii)]}$

$\Rightarrow \quad 2(1-\cos\delta\theta)=(\delta l^2+\delta m^2+\delta n^2)$

$\Rightarrow \quad 2\cdot 2\sin^2\dfrac{\delta\theta}{2}=\delta l^2+\delta m^2+\delta n^2 \qquad \left[\because 1-\cos\theta=2\sin^2\dfrac{\theta}{2}\right]$

$\Rightarrow \quad 4\left(\dfrac{\delta\theta}{2}\right)^2=\delta l^2+\delta m^2+\delta n^2 \qquad \left[\text{since, } \dfrac{\delta\theta}{2} \text{ is small, then } \sin\dfrac{\delta\theta}{2}=\dfrac{\delta\theta}{2}\right]$

$\therefore \quad \delta\theta^2=\delta l^2+\delta m^2+\delta n^2$

Q. 14 **If O is the origin and A is (a, b, c), then find the direction cosines of the line OA and the equation of plane through A at right angle to OA.**

Sol. Since, DC's of line OA are $\frac{a}{\sqrt{a^2+b^2+c^2}}, \frac{b}{\sqrt{a^2+b^2+c^2}}$ and $\frac{c}{\sqrt{a^2+b^2+c^2}}$.

Also, $\vec{n} = \vec{OA} = \vec{a} = a\hat{i} + b\hat{j} + c\hat{k}$

The equation of plane passes through (a, b, c) and perpendicular to OA is given by

$$[\vec{r} - \vec{a}] \cdot \vec{n} = 0$$

$$\Rightarrow \quad \vec{r} \cdot \vec{n} = \vec{a} \cdot \vec{n}$$

$$\Rightarrow \quad [(x\hat{i} + y\hat{j} + z\hat{k}) \cdot (a\hat{i} + b\hat{j} + c\hat{k})] = (a\hat{i} + b\hat{j} + c\hat{k}) \cdot (a\hat{i} + b\hat{j} + c\hat{k})$$

$$\Rightarrow \quad ax + by + cz = a^2 + b^2 + c^2$$

Q. 15 **Two systems of rectangular axis have the same origin. If a plane cuts them at distances a, b, c and a', b', c', respectively from the origin, then prove that $\frac{1}{a^2} + \frac{1}{b^2} + \frac{1}{c^2} = \frac{1}{a'^2} + \frac{1}{b'^2} + \frac{1}{c'^2}$.**

Sol. Consider OX, OY, OZ and ox, oy, oz are two system of rectangular axes.

Let their corresponding equation of plane be

$$\frac{x}{a} + \frac{y}{b} + \frac{z}{c} = 1 \quad \text{...(i)}$$

and

$$\frac{x}{a'} + \frac{y}{b'} + \frac{z}{c'} = 1 \quad \text{...(ii)}$$

Also, the length of perpendicular from origin to Eqs. (i) and (ii) must be same.

$$\therefore \quad \frac{\frac{0}{a} + \frac{0}{b} + \frac{0}{c} - 1}{\sqrt{\frac{1}{a^2} + \frac{1}{b^2} + \frac{1}{c^2}}} = \frac{\frac{0}{a'} + \frac{0}{b'} + \frac{0}{c'} - 1}{\sqrt{\frac{1}{a'^2} + \frac{1}{b'^2} + \frac{1}{c'^2}}}$$

$$\Rightarrow \quad \sqrt{\frac{1}{a'^2} + \frac{1}{b'^2} + \frac{1}{c'^2}} = \sqrt{\frac{1}{a^2} + \frac{1}{b^2} + \frac{1}{c^2}}$$

$$\Rightarrow \quad \frac{1}{a^2} + \frac{1}{b^2} + \frac{1}{c^2} = \frac{1}{a'^2} + \frac{1}{b'^2} + \frac{1}{c'^2}$$

Long Answer Type Questions

Q. 16 **Find the foot of perpendicular from the point $(2, 3, -8)$ to the line $\frac{4-x}{2} = \frac{y}{6} = \frac{1-z}{3}$. Also, find the perpendicular distance from the given point to the line.**

Sol. We have, equation of line as $\frac{4-x}{2} = \frac{y}{6} = \frac{1-z}{3}$

$$\Rightarrow \quad \frac{x-4}{-2} = \frac{y}{6} = \frac{z-1}{-3} = \lambda$$

$$\Rightarrow \quad x = -2\lambda + 4, \; y = 6\lambda \text{ and } z = -3\lambda + 1$$

Let the coordinates of L be $(4-2\lambda, 6\lambda, 1-3\lambda)$ and direction ratios of PL are proportional to $(4-2\lambda-2, 6\lambda-3, 1-3\lambda+8)$ *i.e.*, $(2-2\lambda, 6\lambda-3, 9-3\lambda)$.

Also, direction ratios are proportional to $-2, 6, -3$. Since, PL is perpendicular to give line.

$\therefore \quad -2(2-2\lambda)+6(6\lambda-3)-3(9-3\lambda)=0$

$\Rightarrow \quad -4+4\lambda+36\lambda-18-27+9\lambda=0$

$\Rightarrow \quad 49\lambda=49 \Rightarrow \lambda=1$

So, the coordinates of L are $(4-2\lambda, 6\lambda, 1-3\lambda)$ *i.e.*, $(2, 6, -2)$.

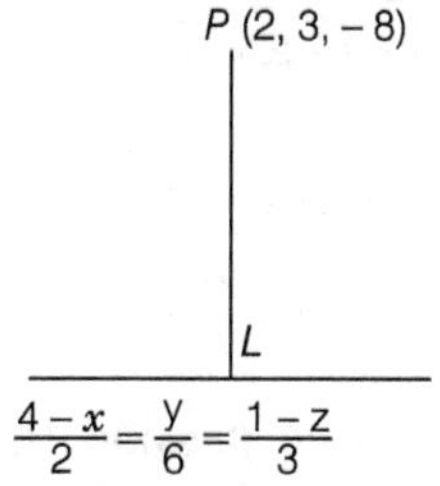

Also, $\quad$ length of $PL=\sqrt{(2-2)^2+(6-3)^2+(-2+8)^2}$

$$=\sqrt{0+9+36}=3\sqrt{5} \text{ units}$$

Q. 17 Find the distance of a point (2, 4, −1) from the line

$$\frac{x+5}{1}=\frac{y+3}{4}=\frac{z-6}{-9}.$$

Sol. We have, equation of the line as $\frac{x+5}{1}=\frac{y+3}{4}=\frac{z-6}{-9}=\lambda$

$\Rightarrow \quad x=\lambda-5, y=4\lambda-3, z=6-9\lambda$

Let the coordinates of L be $(\lambda-5, 4\lambda-3, 6-9\lambda)$, then Dr's of PL are $(\lambda-7, 4\lambda-7, 7-9\lambda)$.

Also, the direction ratios of given line are proportional to 1, 4, –9.

Since, PL is perpendicular to the given line.

$\therefore \quad (\lambda-7)\cdot 1+(4\lambda-7)\cdot 4+(7-9\lambda)\cdot(-9)=0$

$\Rightarrow \quad \lambda-7+16\lambda-28+81\lambda-63=0$

$\Rightarrow \quad 98\lambda=98 \Rightarrow \lambda=1$

So, the coordinates of L are $(-4, 1, -3)$.

$\therefore \quad$ Required distance, $PL=\sqrt{(-4-2)^2+(1-4)^2+(-3+1)^2}$

$$=\sqrt{36+9+4}=7 \text{ units}$$

Q. 18 Find the length and the foot of perpendicular from the point $\left(1, \frac{3}{2}, 2\right)$ to the plane $2x-2y+4z+5=0$.

Sol. Equation of the given plane is $2x-2y+4z+5=0$ $\quad$ ... (i)

$\Rightarrow \quad \vec{n}=2\hat{i}-2\hat{j}+4\hat{k}$

So, the equation of line through $\left(1, \frac{3}{2}, 2\right)$ and parallel to $\vec{n}$ is given by

$$\frac{x-1}{2}=\frac{y-3/2}{-2}=\frac{z-2}{4}=\lambda$$

$\Rightarrow \quad x=2\lambda+1, y=-2\lambda+\frac{3}{2}$ and $z=4\lambda+2$

If this point lies on the given plane, then

$$2(2\lambda+1)-2\left(-2\lambda+\frac{3}{2}\right)+4(4\lambda+2)+5=0 \qquad \text{[using Eq. (i)]}$$

$$\Rightarrow \quad 4\lambda+2+4\lambda-3+16\lambda+8+5=0$$

$$\Rightarrow \quad 24\lambda=-12 \Rightarrow \lambda=\frac{-1}{2}$$

$\therefore$ Required foot of perpendicular

$$=\left[2\times\left(\frac{-1}{2}\right)+1, -2\times\left(\frac{-1}{2}\right)+\frac{3}{2}, 4\times\left(\frac{-1}{2}\right)+2\right] \text{ i.e., } \left(0, \frac{5}{2}, 0\right)$$

$\therefore$ Required length of perpendicular $=\sqrt{(1-0)^2+\left(\frac{3}{2}-\frac{5}{2}\right)^2+(2-0)^2}$

$$=\sqrt{1+1+4}=\sqrt{6} \text{ units}$$

Q. 19 Find the equation of the line passing through the point (3, 0, 1) and parallel to the planes $x+2y=0$ and $3y-z=0$.

Sol. Equation of the two planes are $x+2y=0$ and $3y-z=0$.

Let $\vec{n_1}$ and $\vec{n_2}$ are the normals to the two planes, respectively.

$$\therefore \quad \vec{n_1}=\hat{i}+2\hat{j} \quad \text{and} \quad \vec{n_2}=3\hat{j}-\hat{k}$$

Since, required line is parallel to the given two planes.

Therefore,
$$\vec{b}=\vec{n_1}\times\vec{n_2}=\begin{vmatrix}\hat{i} & \hat{j} & \hat{k}\\ 1 & 2 & 0\\ 0 & 3 & -1\end{vmatrix}$$

$$=\hat{i}(-2)-\hat{j}(-1)+\hat{k}(3)$$

$$=-2\hat{i}+\hat{j}+3\hat{k}$$

So, the equation of the lines through the point (3, 0, 1) and parallel to the given two planes are

$$(x-3)\hat{i}+(y-0)\hat{j}+(z-1)\hat{k}+\lambda(-2\hat{i}+\hat{j}+3\hat{k})$$

$$\Rightarrow \quad (x-3)\hat{i}+y\hat{j}+(z-1)\hat{k}+\lambda(-2\hat{i}+\hat{j}+3\hat{k})$$

Q. 20 Find the equation of the plane through the points (2, 1, − 1), (−1, 3, 4) and perpendicular to the plane $x-2y+4z=10$.

Sol. The equation of the plane passing through (2, 1, − 1) is

$$a(x-2)+b(y-1)+c(z+1)=0 \qquad \text{...(i)}$$

Sicne, this passes through (–1, 3, 4).

$$\therefore \quad a(-1-2)+b(3-1)+c(4+1)=0$$

$$\Rightarrow \quad -3a+2b+5c=0 \qquad \text{... (ii)}$$

Since, the plane (i) is perpendicular to the plane $x-2y+4z=10$.

$$\therefore \quad 1\cdot a-2\cdot b+4\cdot c=0$$

$$\Rightarrow \quad a-2b+4c=0 \qquad \text{...(iii)}$$

On solving Eqs. (ii) and (iii), we get

$$\frac{a}{8+10}=\frac{-b}{-17}=\frac{c}{4}=\lambda$$

$$\Rightarrow \quad a=18\lambda, b=17\lambda, c=4\lambda$$

From Eq. (i),

$$18\lambda(x-2)+17\lambda(y-1)+4\lambda(z+1)=0$$

$$\Rightarrow \quad 18x-36+17y-17+4z+4=0$$

$$\Rightarrow \quad 18x+17y+4z-49=0$$

$$\therefore \quad 18x+17y+4z=49$$

Q. 21 Find the shortest distance between the lines gives by

$$\vec{r}=(8+3\lambda)\hat{i}-(9+16\lambda)\hat{j}+(10+7\lambda)\hat{k}$$

and $$\vec{r}=15\hat{i}+29\hat{j}+5\hat{k}+\mu(3\hat{i}+8\hat{j}-5\hat{k}).$$

Sol. We have, $\vec{r}=(8+3\lambda)\hat{i}-(9+16\lambda)\hat{j}+(10+7\lambda)\hat{k})$

$$=8\hat{i}-9\hat{j}+10\hat{k}+3\lambda\hat{i}-16\lambda\hat{j}+7\lambda\hat{k}$$

$$=8\hat{i}-9\hat{j}+10\hat{k}+\lambda(3\hat{i}-16\hat{j}+7\hat{k})$$

$$\Rightarrow \quad \vec{a}_1=8\hat{i}-9\hat{j}+10\hat{k} \text{ and } \vec{b}_1=3\hat{i}-16\hat{j}+7\hat{k} \quad \text{...(i)}$$

Also $\vec{r}=15\hat{i}+29\hat{j}+5\hat{k}+\mu(3\hat{i}+8\hat{j}-5\hat{k})$

$$\Rightarrow \quad \vec{a}_2=15\hat{i}+29\hat{j}+5\hat{k} \text{ and } \vec{b}_2=3\hat{i}+8\hat{j}-5\hat{k} \quad \text{... (ii)}$$

Now, shortest distance betwen two lines is given by $\left|\dfrac{(\vec{b}_1\times\vec{b}_2)\cdot(\vec{a}_2-\vec{a}_1)}{|\vec{b}_1\times\vec{b}_2|}\right|$

$$\therefore \quad \vec{b}_1\times\vec{b}_2=\begin{vmatrix}\hat{i} & \hat{j} & \hat{k}\\ 3 & -16 & 7\\ 3 & 8 & -5\end{vmatrix}$$

$$=\hat{i}(80-56)-\hat{j}(-15-21)+\hat{k}(24+48)$$

$$=24\hat{i}+36\hat{j}+72\hat{k}$$

Now, $|\vec{b}_1\times\vec{b}_2|=\sqrt{(24)^2+(36)^2+(72)^2}$

$$=12\sqrt{2^2+3^2+6^2}=84$$

and $(\vec{a}_2-\vec{a}_1)=(15-8)\hat{i}+(29+9)\hat{j}+(5-10)\hat{k}$

$$=7\hat{i}+38\hat{j}-5\hat{k}$$

$$\therefore \quad \text{Shortest distance}=\left|\frac{(24\hat{i}+36\hat{j}+72\hat{k})\cdot(7\hat{i}+38\hat{j}-5\hat{k})}{84}\right|$$

$$=\left|\frac{168+1368-360}{84}\right|=\left|\frac{1176}{84}\right|=14\text{ units}$$

Q. 22 Find the equation of the plane which is perpendicular to the plane $5x+3y+6z+8=0$ and which contains the line of intersection of the planes $x+2y+3z-4=0$ and $2x+y-z+5=0$.

Sol. The equation of a plane through the line of intersection of the planes $x+2y+3z-4=0$ and $2x+y-z+5=0$ is

$$(x+2y+3z-4)+\lambda(2x+y-z+5)=0$$

$$\Rightarrow \quad x(1+2\lambda)+y(2+\lambda)+z(-\lambda+3)-4+5\lambda=0 \quad \text{...(i)}$$

Also, this is perpendicular to the plane $5x + 3y + 6z + 8 = 0$.

$\therefore \quad 5(1 + 2\lambda) + 3(2 + \lambda) + 6(3 - \lambda) = 0 \qquad [\because a_1 a_2 + b_1 b_2 + c_1 c_2 = 0]$

$\Rightarrow \quad 5 + 10\lambda + 6 + 3\lambda + 18 - 6\lambda = 0$

$\therefore \quad \lambda = -29/7$

From Eq. (i),

$$x\left[1 + 2\left(\frac{-29}{7}\right)\right] + y\left(2 - \frac{29}{7}\right) + z\left(\frac{29}{7} + 3\right) - 4 + 5\left(\frac{-29}{7}\right) = 0$$

$\Rightarrow \quad x(7 - 58) + y(14 - 29) + z(29 + 21) - 28 - 145 = 0$

$\Rightarrow \quad -51x - 15y + 50z - 173 = 0$

So, the required equation of plane is $51x + 15y - 50z + 173 = 0$.

Q. 23 If the plane $ax + by = 0$ is rotated about its line of intersection with the plane $z = 0$ through an angle α, then prove that the equation of the plane in its new position is $ax + by \pm (\sqrt{a^2 + b^2}\tan\alpha)\, z = 0$.

Sol. Equation of the plane is $ax + by = 0$ ... (i)

$\therefore$ Equation of the plane after new position is

$$\frac{ax\cos\alpha}{\sqrt{a^2 + b^2}} + \frac{by\cos\alpha}{\sqrt{b^2 + a^2}} \pm z\sin\alpha = 0$$

$\Rightarrow \quad \dfrac{ax}{\sqrt{a^2 + b^2}} + \dfrac{by}{\sqrt{b^2 + a^2}} \pm z\tan\alpha = 0 \qquad$ [on dividing by $\cos\alpha$]

$\Rightarrow \quad ax + by \pm z\tan\alpha\sqrt{\alpha^2 + b^2} = 0 \qquad$ [on multiplying with $\sqrt{a^2 + b^2}$]

Alternate Method

Given, planes are $\quad ax + by = 0$ ...(i)

and $\quad z = 0$ ...(ii)

Therefore, the equation of any plane passing through the line of intersection of planes (i) and (ii) may be taken as $ax + by + k = 0$. ...(iii)

Then, direction cosines of a normal to the plane (iii) are $\dfrac{a}{\sqrt{a^2 + b^2 + k^2}}, \dfrac{b}{\sqrt{a^2 + b^2 + k^2}}, \dfrac{c}{\sqrt{a^2 + b^2 + k^2}}$ and direction cosines of the normal to the plane (i) are $\dfrac{a}{\sqrt{a^2 + b^2}}, \dfrac{b}{\sqrt{a^2 + b^2}}$, 0.

Since, the angle between the planes (i) and (ii) is α,

$$\therefore \quad \cos\alpha = \frac{a \cdot a + b \cdot b + k \cdot 0}{\sqrt{a^2 + b^2 + k^2}\sqrt{a^2 + b^2}}$$

$$= \sqrt{\frac{a^2 + b^2}{a^2 + b^2 + k^2}}$$

$\Rightarrow \quad k^2\cos^2\alpha = a^2(1 - \cos^2\alpha) + b^2(1 - \cos^2\alpha)$

$\Rightarrow \quad k^2 = \dfrac{(a^2 + b^2)\sin^2\alpha}{\cos^2\alpha}$

$$k = \pm\sqrt{a^2 + b^2}\tan\alpha$$

On putting this value in plane (iii), we get the equation of the plane as

$$ax + by + z\sqrt{a^2 + b^2}\tan\alpha = 0$$

Q. 24 Find the equation of the plane through the intersection of the planes $\vec{r}\cdot(\hat{i}+3\hat{j})-6=0$ and $\vec{r}\cdot(3\hat{i}-\hat{j}-4\hat{k})=0$, whose perpendicular distance from origin is unity.

Sol. We have, $\vec{n_1}=(\hat{i}+3\hat{j}), d_1=6$ and $\vec{n_2}=(3\hat{i}-\hat{j}-4\hat{k}), d_2=0$

Using the relation, $\vec{r}\cdot(\vec{n_1}+\lambda\vec{n_2})=d_1+d_2\lambda$

$$\Rightarrow \quad \vec{r}\cdot[(\hat{i}+3\hat{j})+\lambda(3\hat{i}-\hat{j}-4\hat{k})]=6+0\cdot\lambda$$

$$\Rightarrow \quad \vec{r}\cdot[(1+3\lambda)\hat{i}+(3-\lambda)\hat{j}+\hat{k}(-4\lambda)]=6 \quad \text{...(i)}$$

On dviding both sides by $\sqrt{(1+3\lambda)^2+(3-\lambda)^2+(-4\lambda)^2}$, we get

$$\frac{\vec{r}\cdot[(1+3\lambda)\hat{i}+(3-\lambda)\hat{j}+\hat{k}(-4\lambda)]}{\sqrt{(1+3\lambda)^2+(3-\lambda)^2+(-4\lambda)^2}}=\frac{6}{\sqrt{(1+3\lambda)^2+(3-\lambda)^2+(-4\lambda)^2}}$$

Since, the perpendicular distance from origin is unity.

$$\therefore \quad \frac{6}{\sqrt{(1+3\lambda)^2+(3-\lambda)^2+(-4\lambda)^2}}=1$$

$$\Rightarrow \quad (1+3\lambda)^2+(3-\lambda)^2+(-4\lambda)^2=36$$

$$\Rightarrow \quad 1+9\lambda^2+6\lambda+9+\lambda^2-6\lambda+16\lambda^2=36$$

$$\Rightarrow \quad 26\lambda^2+10=36$$

$$\Rightarrow \quad \lambda^2=1$$

$$\therefore \quad \lambda=\pm 1$$

Using Eq. (i), the required equation of plane is

$$\vec{r}\cdot[(1\pm 3)\hat{i}+(3\mp 1)\hat{j}+(\mp 4)\hat{k}]=6$$

$$\Rightarrow \quad \vec{r}\cdot[(1+3)\hat{i}+(3-1)\hat{j}+(-4)\hat{k}]=6$$

$$\text{and} \quad \vec{r}\cdot[(1-3)\hat{i}+(3+1)\hat{j}+4\hat{k}]=6$$

$$\Rightarrow \quad \vec{r}\cdot(4\hat{i}+2\hat{j}-4\hat{k})=6$$

$$\text{and} \quad \vec{r}\cdot(-2\hat{i}+4\hat{j}+4\hat{k})=6$$

$$\Rightarrow \quad 4x+2y-4z-6=0$$

$$\text{and} \quad -2x+4y+4z-6=0$$

Q. 25 Show that the points $(\hat{i}-\hat{j}+3\hat{k})$ and $3(\hat{i}+\hat{j}+\hat{k})$ are equidistant from the plane $\vec{r}\cdot(5\hat{i}+2\hat{j}-7\hat{k})+9=0$ and lies on opposite side of it.

Sol. To show that these given points $(\hat{i}-\hat{j}+3\hat{k})$ and $3(\hat{i}+\hat{j}+\hat{k})$ are equidistant from the plane $\vec{r}\cdot(5\hat{i}+2\hat{j}-7\hat{k})+9=0$, we first find out the mid- point of the points which is $2\hat{i}+\hat{j}+3\hat{k}$.

On substituting $\vec{r}$ by the mid-point in plane, we get

$$\text{LHS}=(2\hat{i}+\hat{j}+3\hat{k})\cdot(5\hat{i}+2\hat{j}-7\hat{k})+9$$

$$=10+2-21+9=0$$

$$=\text{RHS}$$

Hence, the two points lie on opposite sides of the plane are equidistant from the plane.

Q. 26 $\vec{AB} = 3\hat{i} - \hat{j} + \hat{k}$ and $\vec{CD} = -3\hat{i} + 2\hat{j} + 4\hat{k}$ are two vectors. The position vectors of the points A and C are $6\hat{i} + 7\hat{j} + 4\hat{k}$ and $-9\hat{i} + 2\hat{k}$, respectively. Find the position vector of a point P on the line AB and a point Q on the line CD such that $\vec{PQ}$ is perpendicular to $\vec{AB}$ and $\vec{CD}$ both.

Sol. We have, $\vec{AB} = 3\hat{i} - \hat{j} + \hat{k}$ and $\vec{CD} = -3\hat{i} + 2\hat{j} + 4\hat{k}$

Also, the position vectors of A and C are $6\hat{i} + 7\hat{j} + 4\hat{k}$ and $-9\hat{j} + 2\hat{k}$, respectively. Since, $\vec{PQ}$ is perpendicular to both $\vec{AB}$ and $\vec{CD}$.

So, P and Q will be foot of perpendicular to both the lines through A and C.

Now, equation of the line through A and parallel to the vector $\vec{AB}$ is,

$$\vec{r} = (6\hat{i} + 7\hat{j} + 4\hat{k}) + \lambda(3\hat{i} - \hat{j} + \hat{k})$$

and the line through C and parallel to the vector $\vec{CD}$ is given by

$$\vec{r} = -9\hat{j} + 2\hat{k} + \mu(-3\hat{i} + 2\hat{j} + 4\hat{k}) \quad \text{...(i)}$$

Let $\vec{r} = (6\hat{i} + 7\hat{j} + 4\hat{k}) + \lambda(3\hat{i} - \hat{j} + \hat{k})$

and $\vec{r} = -9\hat{j} + 2\hat{k} + \mu(-3\hat{i} + 2\hat{j} + 4\hat{k}) \quad \text{...(ii)}$

Let $P(6 + 3\lambda, 7 - \lambda, 4 + \lambda)$ is any point on the first line and Q be any point on second line is given by $(-3\mu, -9 + 2\mu, 2 + 4\mu)$.

$$\therefore \quad \vec{PQ} = (-3\mu - 6 - 3\lambda)\hat{i} + (-9 + 2\mu - 7 + \lambda)\hat{j} + (2 + 4\mu - 4 - \lambda)\hat{k}$$
$$= (-3\mu - 6 - 3\lambda)\hat{i} + (2\mu + \lambda - 16)\hat{j} + (4\mu - \lambda - 2)\hat{k}$$

If $\vec{PQ}$ is perpendicular to the first line, then

$$3(-3\mu - 6 - 3\lambda) - (2\mu + \lambda - 16) + (4\mu - \lambda - 2) = 0$$
$$\Rightarrow \quad -9\mu - 18 - 9\lambda - 2\mu - \lambda + 16 + 4\mu - \lambda - 2 = 0$$
$$\Rightarrow \quad -7\mu - 11\lambda - 4 = 0 \quad \text{...(iii)}$$

If $\vec{PQ}$ is perpendicular to the second line, then

$$-3(-3\mu - 6 - 3\lambda) + 2(2\mu + \lambda - 16) + 4(4\mu - \lambda - 2) = 0$$
$$\Rightarrow \quad 9\mu + 18 + 9\lambda + 4\mu + 2\lambda - 32 + 16\mu - 4\lambda - 8 = 0$$
$$\Rightarrow \quad 29\mu + 7\lambda - 22 = 0 \quad \text{...(iv)}$$

On solving Eqs. (iii) and (iv), we get

$$-49\mu - 77\lambda - 28 = 0$$
$$\Rightarrow \quad 319\mu + 77\lambda - 242 = 0$$
$$\Rightarrow \quad 270\mu - 270 = 0$$
$$\Rightarrow \quad \mu = 1$$

Using μ in Eq. (iii), we get

$$-7(1) - 11\lambda - 4 = 0$$
$$\Rightarrow \quad -7 - 11\lambda - 4 = 0$$
$$\Rightarrow \quad -11 - 11\lambda = 0$$
$$\Rightarrow \quad \lambda = -1$$

$$\therefore \quad \vec{PQ} = [-3(1) - 6 - 3(-1)]\hat{i} + [2(1) + (-1) - 16]\hat{j} + [4(1) - (-1) - 2]\hat{k}$$
$$= -6\hat{i} - 15\hat{j} + 3\hat{k}$$

Q. 27 Show that the straight lines whose direction cosines are given by $2l + 2m - n = 0$ and $mn + nl + lm = 0$ are at right angles.

Sol. We have, $2l + 2m - n = 0$ ...(i)

and $mn + nl + lm = 0$ ...(ii)

Eliminating m from the both equations, we get

$$m = \frac{n - 2l}{2} \quad \text{[from Eq. (i)]}$$

$$\Rightarrow \left(\frac{n-2l}{2}\right)n + nl + l\left(\frac{n-2l}{2}\right) = 0$$

$$\Rightarrow \frac{n^2 - 2nl + 2nl + nl - 2l^2}{2} = 0$$

$$\Rightarrow n^2 + nl - 2l^2 = 0$$

$$\Rightarrow n^2 + 2nl - nl - 2l^2 = 0$$

$$\Rightarrow (n + 2l)(n - l) = 0$$

$$\Rightarrow n = -2l \text{ and } n = l$$

$$\therefore m = \frac{-2l - 2l}{2}, m = \frac{l - 2l}{2}$$

$$\Rightarrow m = -2l, m = \frac{-l}{2}$$

Thus, the direction ratios of two lines are proportional to $l, -2l, -2$ and $l, \frac{-l}{2}, l$.

$$\Rightarrow 1, -2, -2 \text{ and } 1, \frac{-1}{2}, 1$$

$$\Rightarrow 1, -2, -2 \text{ and } 2, -1, 2$$

Also, the vectors parallel to these lines are $\vec{a} = \hat{i} - 2\hat{j} - 2\hat{k}$ and $\vec{b} = 2\hat{i} - \hat{j} + 2\hat{k}$, respectively.

$$\therefore \cos\theta = \frac{\vec{a}.\vec{b}}{|\vec{a}||\vec{b}|} = \frac{(\hat{i} - 2\hat{j} - 2\hat{k})\cdot(2\hat{i} - \hat{j} + 2\hat{k})}{3\cdot 3}$$

$$= \frac{2 + 2 - 4}{9} = 0$$

$$\therefore \theta = \frac{\pi}{2} \quad \left[\because \cos\frac{\pi}{2} = 0\right]$$

Q. 28 If $l_1, m_1, n_1, l_2, m_2, n_2$ and l_3, m_3, n_3 are the direction cosines of three mutually perpendicular lines, then prove that the line whose direction cosines are proportional to $l_1 + l_2 + l_3, m_1 + m_2 + m_3$ and $n_1 + n_2 + n_3$ makes equal angles with them.

Sol. Let

$$\vec{a} = l_1\hat{i} + m_1\hat{j} + n_1\hat{k}$$

$$\vec{b} = l_2\hat{i} + m_2\hat{j} + n_2\hat{k}$$

$$\vec{c} = l_3\hat{i} + m_3\hat{j} + n_3\hat{k}$$

$$\vec{d} = (l_1 + l_2 + l_3)\hat{i} + (m_1 + m_2 + m_2)\hat{j} + (n_1 + n_2 + n_3)\hat{k}$$

Also, let α, β and γ are the angles between $\vec{a}$ and $\vec{d}$, $\vec{b}$ and $\vec{d}$, $\vec{c}$ and $\vec{d}$.

$$\therefore \cos\alpha = l_1(l_1 + l_2 + l_3) + m_1(m_1 + m_2 + m_3) + n_1(n_1 + n_2 + n_3)$$

$$= l_1^2 + l_1 l_2 + l_1 l_3 + m_1^2 + m_1 m_2 + m_1 m_3 + n_1^2 + n_1 n_2 + n_1 n_3$$

$= (l_1^2 + m_1^2 + n_1^2) + (l_1 l_2 + l_1 l_3 + m_1 m_2 + m_1 m_3 + n_1 n_2 + n_1 n_3)$

$= 1 + 0 = 1$

$[\because l_1^2 + m_1^2 + n_1^2 = 1 \text{ and } l_1 \perp l_2, l_1 \perp l_3, m_1 \perp m_2, m_1 \perp m_3, n_1 \perp n_2, n_1 \perp n_3]$

Similarly, $\cos\beta = l_2 (l_1 + l_2 + l_3) + m_2 (m_1 + m_2 + m_3) + n_2 (n_1 + n_2 + n_3)$

$= 1 + 0$ and $\cos\gamma = 1 + 0$

$\Rightarrow \quad \cos\alpha = \cos\beta = \cos\gamma$

$\Rightarrow \quad \alpha = \beta = \gamma$

So, the line whose direction cosines are proportional to $l_1 + l_2 + l_3, m_1 + m_2 + m_3, n_1 + n_2 + n_3$ makes equal angles with the three mutually perpendicular lines whose direction cosines are $l_1, m_1, n_1, l_2, m_2, n_2$ and l_3, m_3, n_3 respectively.

Objective Type Questions

Q. 29 Distance of the point (α, β, γ) from Y-axis is

(a) β (b) $|\beta|$

(c) $|\beta| + |\gamma|$ (d) $\sqrt{\alpha^2 + \gamma^2}$

Sol. *(d)* Required distance $= \sqrt{(\alpha - 0)^2 + (\beta - \beta)^2 + (\gamma - 0)^2} = \sqrt{\alpha^2 + \gamma^2}$

Q. 30 If the direction cosines of a line are k, k and k, then

(a) $k > 0$ (b) $0 < k < 1$

(c) $k = 1$ (d) $k = \frac{1}{\sqrt{3}}$ or $-\frac{1}{\sqrt{3}}$

Sol. *(d)* Since, direction cosines of a line are k, k and k.

$\therefore \quad l = k, m = k$ and $n = k$

We know that, $\quad l^2 + m^2 + n^2 = 1$

$\Rightarrow \quad k^2 + k^2 + k^2 = 1$

$\Rightarrow \quad k^2 = \frac{1}{3}$

$\therefore \quad k = \pm \frac{1}{\sqrt{3}}$

Q. 31 The distance of the plane $\vec{r}\left(\frac{2}{7}\hat{i} + \frac{3}{7}\hat{j} - \frac{6}{7}\hat{k}\right) = 1$ from the origin is

(a) 1 (b) 7

(c) $\frac{1}{7}$ (d) None of these

Sol. *(a)* The distance of the plane $\vec{r}\left(\frac{2}{7}\hat{i} + \frac{3}{7}\hat{j} - \frac{6}{7}\hat{k}\right) = 1$ from the origin is 1.

[since, $\vec{r} \cdot \vec{n} = d$ is the form of above equation, where d represents the distance of plane from the origin *i.e.*, $d = 1$]

Q. 32 The sine of the angle between the straight line $\frac{x-2}{3}=\frac{y-3}{4}=\frac{z-4}{5}$ and the plane $2x-2y+z=5$ is

(a) $\frac{10}{6\sqrt{5}}$ (b) $\frac{4}{5\sqrt{2}}$ (c) $\frac{2\sqrt{3}}{5}$ (d) $\frac{\sqrt{2}}{10}$

Sol. *(d)* We have, the equation of line as

$$\frac{x-2}{3}=\frac{y-3}{4}=\frac{z-4}{5}$$

Now, the line passes through point (2, 3, 4) and having direction ratios (3, 4, 5).

Since, the line passes through point (2, 3, 4) and parallel to the vector $(3\hat{i}+4\hat{j}+5\hat{k})$.

$\therefore$ $$\vec{b}=3\hat{i}+4\hat{j}+5\hat{k}$$

Also, the cartesian form of the given plane is $2x-2y+z=5$.

$\Rightarrow$ $(x\hat{i}+y\hat{j}+z\hat{k})(2\hat{i}-2\hat{j}+\hat{k})=5$

$\therefore$ $$\vec{n}=(2\hat{i}-2\hat{j}+\hat{k})$$

We know that, $\sin\theta=\frac{|\vec{b}\,.\,\vec{n}|}{|\vec{b}|\,.\,|\vec{n}|}=\frac{|(3\hat{i}+4\hat{j}+5\hat{k}).(2\hat{i}-2\hat{j}+\hat{k})|}{\sqrt{3^2+4^2+5^2}\cdot\sqrt{4+4+1}}$

$$=\frac{|6-8+5|}{\sqrt{50}\cdot 3}=\frac{3}{15\sqrt{2}}=\frac{1}{5\sqrt{2}}$$

$$\sin\theta=\frac{\sqrt{2}}{10}$$

Q. 33 The reflection of the point (α,β,γ) in the XY-plane is

(a) $(\alpha,\beta,0)$ (b) $(0,0,\gamma)$ (c) $(-\alpha,-\beta,\gamma)$ (d) $(\alpha,\beta,-\gamma)$

Sol. *(d)* In XY-plane, the reflection of the point (α,β,γ) is $(\alpha,\beta,-\gamma)$.

Q. 34 The area of the quadrilateral $ABCD$ where A (0,4,1), B (2, 3, −1), C (4, 5, 0), and D (2, 6, 2) is equal to

(a) 9 sq units (b) 18 sq units

(c) 27 sq units (d) 81 sq units

Sol. *(a)* We have,

$$\vec{AB}=(2-0)\hat{i}+(3-4)\hat{j}+(-1-1)\hat{k}=2\hat{i}-\hat{j}-2\hat{k}$$

$$\vec{BC}=(4-2)\hat{i}+(5-3)\hat{j}+(0+1)\hat{k}=2\hat{i}+2\hat{j}+\hat{k}$$

$$\vec{CD}=(2-4)\hat{i}+(6-5)\hat{j}+(2-0)\hat{k}=-2\hat{i}+\hat{j}+2\hat{k}$$

$$\vec{DA}=(0-2)\hat{i}+(4-6)\hat{j}+(1-2)\hat{k}=-2\hat{i}-2\hat{j}-\hat{k}$$

$\therefore$ Area of quadrilateral $ABCD=|\vec{AB}\times\vec{BC}|=\begin{vmatrix}\hat{i} & \hat{j} & \hat{k}\\ 2 & -1 & -2\\ 2 & 2 & 1\end{vmatrix}$

$$=|\hat{i}(-1+4)-\hat{j}(2+4)+\hat{k}(4+2)|$$

$$=|3\hat{i}-6\hat{j}+6\hat{k}|$$

$$=\sqrt{9+36+36}=9\text{ sq units}$$

Q. 35 The locus represented by $xy + yz = 0$ is

(a) a pair of perpendicular lines
(b) a pair of parallel lines
(c) a pair of parallel planes
(d) a pair of perpendicular planes

Sol. *(d)* We have, $xy + yz = 0$

$\Rightarrow \quad xy = -yz$

So, a pair of perpendicular planes.

Q. 36 If the plane $2x - 3y + 6z - 11 = 0$ makes an angle $\sin^{-1} \alpha$ with X-axis, then the value of α is

(a) $\frac{\sqrt{3}}{2}$ (b) $\frac{\sqrt{2}}{3}$

(c) $\frac{2}{7}$ (d) $\frac{3}{7}$

Sol. *(c)* Since, $2x - 3y + 6z - 11 = 0$ makes an angle $\sin^{-1} \alpha$ with X-axis.

$$\vec{b} = (1\hat{i} + 0\hat{j} + 0\hat{k}) \text{ and } \vec{n} = 2\hat{i} - 3\hat{j} + 6\hat{k}$$

We know that, $$\sin \theta = \frac{|\vec{b} \cdot \vec{n}|}{|\vec{b}| \cdot |\vec{n}|}$$

$$= \frac{|(1\hat{i}) \cdot (2\hat{i} - 3\hat{j} + 6\hat{k})|}{\sqrt{1}\sqrt{4 + 9 + 36}} = \frac{2}{7}$$

Fillers

Q. 37 If a plane passes through the points (2, 0,0) (0, 3, 0) and (0, 0, 4) the equation of plane is ....

Sol. We know that, equation of a the plane that cut the coordinate axes at $(a, 0, 0)$ $(0, b, 0)$ and $(0, 0, c)$ is $\frac{x}{a} + \frac{y}{b} + \frac{z}{c} = 1$.

Hence, the equation of plane passes through the points (2, 0, 0), (0, 3, 0) and (0, 0, 4) is $\frac{x}{2} + \frac{y}{3} + \frac{z}{4} = 1$.

Q. 38 The direction cosines of the vector $(2\hat{i} + 2\hat{j} - \hat{k})$ are ....

Sol. Direction cosines of $(2\hat{i} + 2\hat{j} - \hat{k})$ are $\frac{2}{\sqrt{4+4+1}}, \frac{2}{\sqrt{4+4+1}}, \frac{-1}{\sqrt{4+4+1}}$ *i.e.*, $\frac{2}{3}, \frac{2}{3}, \frac{-1}{3}$.

Q. 39 The vector equation of the line $\frac{x-5}{3}=\frac{y+4}{7}=\frac{z-6}{2}$ is ....

Sol. We have, $\vec{a} = 5\hat{i} - 4\hat{j} + 6\hat{k}$ and $\vec{b} = 3\hat{i} + 7\hat{j} + 2\hat{k}$

So, the vector equation will be

$$\vec{r} = (5\hat{i} - 4\hat{j} + 6\hat{k}) + \lambda(3\hat{i} + 7\hat{j} + 2\hat{k}$$

$$\Rightarrow \quad (x\hat{i} + y\hat{j} + z\hat{k}) - (5\hat{i} - 4\hat{j} + 6\hat{k}) = \lambda(3\hat{i} + 7\hat{j} + 2\hat{k})$$

$$\Rightarrow \quad (x-5)\hat{i} + (y+4)\hat{j} + (z-6)\hat{k} = \lambda(3\hat{i} + 7\hat{j} + 2\hat{k})$$

Q. 40 The vector equation of the line through the points (3, 4, −7) and (1, −1, 6) is ....

Sol. We know that, vector equation of a line passes through two points is represented by $\vec{r} = \vec{a} + \lambda(\vec{b} - \vec{a})$

Here, $\vec{r} = x\hat{i} + y\hat{j} + 3\hat{k}$, $\vec{a} = 3\hat{i} + 4\hat{j} - 7\hat{k}$

and $\vec{b} = \hat{i} - \hat{j} + 6\hat{k}$

$$\Rightarrow \quad (\vec{b} - \vec{a}) = -2\hat{i} - 5\hat{j} + 13\hat{k}$$

So, the required equation is

$$x\hat{i} + y\hat{j} + z\hat{k} = 3\hat{i} + 4\hat{j} - 7\hat{k} + \lambda(-2\hat{i} - 5\hat{j} + 13\hat{k})$$

$$\Rightarrow \quad (x-3)\hat{i} + (y-4)\hat{j} + (z+7)\hat{k} = \lambda(-2\hat{i} - 5\hat{j} + 13\hat{k})$$

Q. 41 The cartesian equation of the plane $\vec{r} \cdot (\hat{i} + \hat{j} - \hat{k}) = 2$ is ....

Sol. We have, $\vec{r} \cdot (\hat{i} + \hat{j} - \hat{k}) = 2$

$$\Rightarrow \quad (x\hat{i} + y\hat{j} + z\hat{k}) \cdot (\hat{i} + \hat{j} - \hat{k}) = 2$$

$$\Rightarrow \quad x + y - z = 2$$

which is the required form

True/False

Q. 42 The unit vector normal to the plane $x + 2y + 3z - 6 = 0$ is $\frac{1}{\sqrt{14}}\hat{i} + \frac{2}{\sqrt{14}}\hat{j} + \frac{3}{\sqrt{14}}\hat{k}$.

Sol. *True*

We have, $\vec{n} = \hat{i} + 2\hat{j} + 3\hat{k}$

$$\therefore \quad \hat{n} = \frac{\hat{i} + 2\hat{j} + 3\hat{k}}{\sqrt{1^2 + 2^2 + 3^2}} = \frac{\hat{i}}{\sqrt{14}} + \frac{2\hat{j}}{\sqrt{14}} + \frac{3\hat{k}}{\sqrt{14}}$$

Q. 43 The intercepts made by the plane $2x - 3y + 5z + 4 = 0$ on the coordinate axis are $-2, \frac{4}{3}$ and $-\frac{4}{5}$.

Sol. ***True***

We have, $2x - 3y + 5z + 4 = 0$

$$\Rightarrow \quad 2x - 3y + 5z = -4$$

$$\Rightarrow \quad \frac{2x}{-4} - \frac{3y}{-4} + \frac{5z}{-4} = 1$$

$$\Rightarrow \quad \frac{x}{-2} + \frac{y}{\frac{4}{3}} - \frac{z}{\frac{4}{5}} = 1$$

$$\Rightarrow \quad \frac{x}{-2} + \frac{y}{\frac{4}{3}} + \frac{z}{\left(-\frac{4}{5}\right)} = 1$$

So, the intercepts are $-2, \frac{4}{3}$ and $-\frac{4}{5}$.

Q. 44 The angle between the line $\vec{r} = (5\hat{i} - \hat{j} - 4\hat{k}) + \lambda(2\hat{i} - \hat{j} + \hat{k})$ and the plane $\vec{r}(3\hat{i} - 4\hat{j} - \hat{k}) + 5 = 0$ is $\sin^{-1}\left(\frac{5}{2\sqrt{91}}\right)$.

Sol. ***False***

We have, $\vec{b} = 2\hat{i} - \hat{j} + \hat{k}$ and $\vec{n} = 3\hat{i} - 4\hat{j} - \hat{k}$

Let θ is the angle between line and plane.

Then,
$$\sin\theta = \frac{|\vec{b} \cdot \vec{n}|}{|\vec{b}| \cdot |\vec{n}|} = \frac{|(2\hat{i} - \hat{j} + \hat{k}) \cdot (3\hat{i} - 4\hat{j} - \hat{k})|}{\sqrt{6} \cdot \sqrt{26}}$$

$$= \frac{|6 + 4 - 1|}{\sqrt{156}} = \frac{9}{2\sqrt{39}}$$

$$\therefore \quad \theta = \sin^{-1}\frac{9}{2\sqrt{39}}$$

Q. 45 The angle between the planes $\vec{r}(2\hat{i} - 3\hat{j} + \hat{k}) = 1$ and $\vec{r}(\hat{i} - \hat{j}) = 4$ is $\cos^{-1}\left(\frac{-5}{\sqrt{58}}\right)$.

Sol. ***False***

We know that, the angle between two planes is given by $\cos\theta = \frac{|\vec{n_1} \cdot \vec{n_2}|}{|\vec{n_1}||\vec{n_2}|}$

Here, $\vec{n_1} = (2\hat{i} - 3\hat{j} + \hat{k})$ and $\vec{n_2} = (\hat{i} - \hat{j})$

$$\therefore \quad \cos\theta = \frac{|(2\hat{i} - 3\hat{j} + \hat{k})\ (\hat{i} - \hat{j})|}{\sqrt{4 + 9 + 1}\ \sqrt{1 + 1}}$$

$$\Rightarrow \quad \cos\theta = \frac{|2 + 3|}{\sqrt{14} \cdot \sqrt{2}} = \frac{5}{2\sqrt{7}}$$

$$\therefore \quad \theta = \cos^{-1}\left(\frac{5}{2\sqrt{7}}\right)$$

Q. 46 The line $\vec{r} = 2\hat{i} - 3\hat{j} - \hat{k} + \lambda(\hat{i} - \hat{j} + 2\hat{k})$ lies in the plane $\vec{r}\,(3\hat{i} + \hat{j} - \hat{k}) + 2 = 0$.

Sol. ***False***

We have, $\vec{r} = 2\hat{i} - 3\hat{j} - \hat{k} + \lambda(\hat{i} - \hat{j} + 2\hat{k})$

$\Rightarrow \quad (x\hat{i} + y\hat{j} + z\hat{k}) = \hat{i}(2+\lambda) + \hat{j}(-3-\lambda) + \hat{k}(-1+2\lambda)$

Since, $x = (2+\lambda)$, $y = (-3-\lambda)$ and $z = (-1+2\lambda)$ are coordinates of general point which should satisfy the equation of the given plane.

$\therefore \quad [(2+\lambda)\hat{i} + (-3-\lambda)\hat{j} + (2\lambda - 1)\hat{k}]\cdot[\hat{i} + \hat{j} - \hat{k}] = 2$

$\Rightarrow \quad (2+\lambda) - 3 - \lambda - 2\lambda + 1 = 2$

$\Rightarrow \quad -2\lambda = 2$

$\Rightarrow \quad \lambda = -1$

$\therefore \quad \vec{r} = (2-1)\hat{i} + (-3+1)\hat{j} + (-2-1)\hat{k}$

$= \hat{i} - 2\hat{j} - 3\hat{k}$

Again, from the equation of the plane

$\vec{r}\cdot(3\hat{i} + \hat{j} - \hat{k}) + 2 = 0$

$\Rightarrow \quad (\hat{i} - 2\hat{j} - 3\hat{k})\,(3\hat{i} + \hat{j} - \hat{k}) + 2 = 0$

$\Rightarrow \quad (3 - 2 + 3) + 2 = 0$

$\Rightarrow \quad 6 \neq 0$

which is not true.

So, the line $\vec{r} = 2\hat{i} - 3\hat{j} - \hat{k} + \lambda(\hat{i} - \hat{j} + 2\hat{k})$ does not lie in a plane.

Q. 47 The vector equation of the line $\frac{x-5}{3} = \frac{y+4}{7} = \frac{z-6}{2}$ is

$$\vec{r} = 5\hat{i} - 4\hat{j} + 6\hat{k} + \lambda(3\hat{i} + 7\hat{j} + 2\hat{k})$$

Sol. ***True***

We have, $x = 5, y = -4, z = 6$

and $a = 3, b = 7, c = 2$

$\therefore \quad \vec{r} = (5\hat{i} - 4\hat{j} + 6\hat{k}) + \lambda(3\hat{i} + 7\hat{j} + 2\hat{k})$

Q. 48 The equation of a line, which is parallel to $2\hat{i} + \hat{j} + 3\hat{k}$ and which passes through the point $(5, -2, 4)$ is $\frac{x-5}{2} = \frac{y+2}{-1} = \frac{z-4}{3}$.

Sol. ***False***

Here, $x_1 = 5, y_1 = -2, z_1 = 4$

and $a = 2, b = 1, c = 3$

$$\Rightarrow \quad \frac{x-5}{2} = \frac{y+2}{1} = \frac{z-4}{3}$$

Q. 49 If the foot of perpendicular drawn from the origin to a plane is $(5, -3, -2)$, then the equation of plane is $\vec{r} \cdot (5\hat{i} - 3\hat{j} - 2\hat{k}) = 38$.

Sol. *True*

Since, the required plane passes through the point $P(5, -3, -2)$ and is perpendicular to $\overrightarrow{OP}$.

$\therefore \quad \vec{a} = 5\hat{i} - 3\hat{j} - 2\hat{k}$

and $\quad \vec{n} = \overrightarrow{OP} = 5\hat{i} - 3\hat{j} - 2\hat{k}$

Now, the equation of the plane is

$$(\vec{r} - \vec{a}) \cdot \vec{n} = 0$$

$$\Rightarrow \quad \vec{r} \cdot \vec{n} = \vec{a} \cdot \vec{n}$$

$$\Rightarrow \quad \vec{r} \cdot (5\hat{i} - 3\hat{j} - 2\hat{k}) = (5\hat{i} - 3\hat{j} - 2\hat{k}) \cdot (5\hat{i} - 3\hat{j} - 2\hat{k})$$

$$\Rightarrow \quad \vec{r} \cdot (5\hat{i} - 3\hat{j} - 2\hat{k}) = 25 + 9 + 4$$

$$\Rightarrow \quad \vec{r} \cdot (5\hat{i} - 3\hat{j} - 2\hat{k}) = 38$$

12

Linear Programming

Short Answer Type Questions

Q. 1 Determine the maximum value of $Z = 11x + 7y$ subject to the constraints $2x + y \leq 6$, $x \leq 2$, $x \geq 0$, $y \geq 0$.

Thinking Process

Using constraints, get the corner points for the bounded region and then for each corner point check the corresponding value of Z.

Sol. We have, maximise $Z = 11x + 7y$ ...(i)

Subject to the constraints

$$2x + y \leq 6 \quad ...(ii)$$

$$x \leq 2 \quad ...(iii)$$

$$x \geq 0, y \geq 0 \quad ...(iv)$$

We see that, the feasible region as shaded determined by the system of constraints (ii) to (iv) is $OABC$ and is bounded. So, now we shall use corner point method to determine the maximum value of Z.

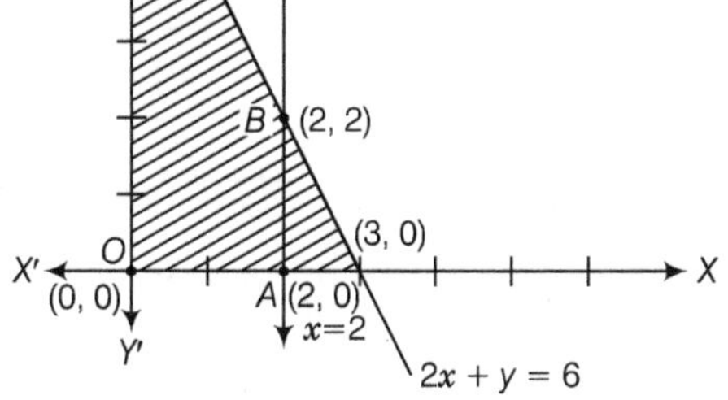

Corner points	Corresponding value of Z
(0, 0)	0
(2, 0)	22
(2, 2)	36
(0, 6)	42 ← Maximum

Hence, the maximum value of Z is 42 at (0, 6).

Q. 2 Maximise $Z = 3x + 4y$, subject to the constraints $x + y \le 1$, $x \ge 0$, $y \ge 0$.

Sol. Maximise $Z = 3x + 4y$, Subject to the constraints

$$x + y \le 1,\ x \ge 0,\ y \ge 0.$$

The shaded region shown in the figure as OAB is bounded and the coordinates of corner points O, A and B are (0, 0), (1, 0) and (0, 1), respectively.

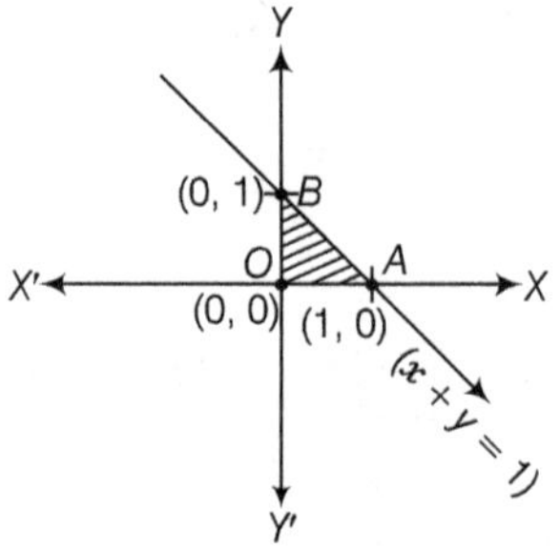

Corner points	Corresponding value of Z
(0, 0)	0
(1, 0)	3
(0, 1)	4 ← Maximum

Hence, the maximum value of Z is 4 at (0, 1).

Q. 3 Maximise the function $Z = 11x + 7y$, subject to the constraints $x \le 3$, $y \le 2$, $x \ge 0$ and $y \ge 0$.

Sol. Maximise $Z = 11x + 7y$, subject to the constraints $x \le 3$, $y \le 2$, $x \ge 0$, $y \ge 0$.

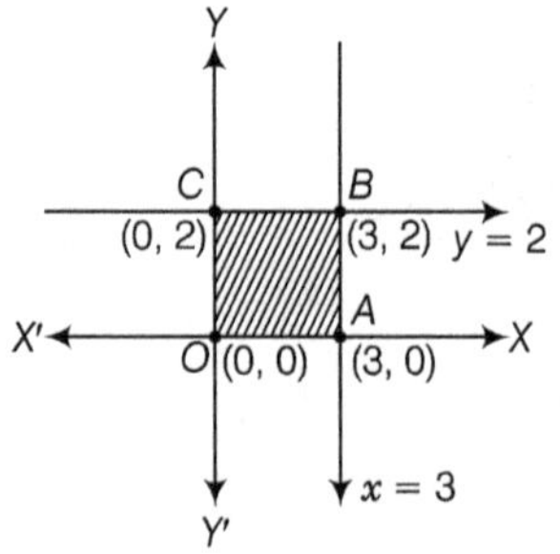

The shaded region as shown in the figure as $OABC$ is bounded and the coordinates of corner points are (0, 0), (3, 0), (3, 2) and (0, 2), respectively.

Corner points	Corresponding value of Z
(0, 0)	0
(3, 0)	33
(3, 2)	47 ← Maximum
(0, 2)	14

Hence, Z is maximum at (3, 2) and its maximum value is 47.

Q. 4 Minimise $Z = 13x - 15y$ subject to the constraints $x + y \le 7$, $2x - 3y + 6 \ge 0$, $x \ge 0$ and $y \ge 0$.

Sol. Minimise $Z = 13x - 15y$ subject to the constraints $x + y \le 7$, $2x - 3y + 6 \ge 0$, $x \ge 0$, $y \ge 0$.

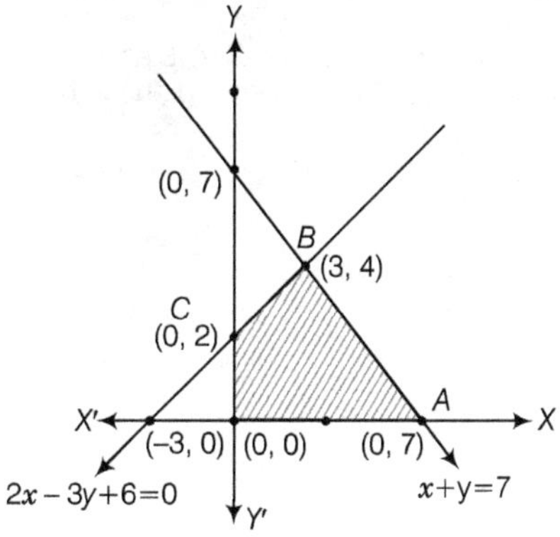

Shaded region shown as $OABC$ is bounded and coordinates of its corner points are (0, 0), (7, 0), (3, 4) and (0, 2), respectively.

Corner points	Corresponding value of Z
(0, 0)	0
(7, 0)	91
(3, 4)	–21
(0, 2)	–30 ← Minimum

Hence, the minimum value of Z is (– 30) at (0, 2).

Q. 5 Determine the maximum value of $Z = 3x + 4y$, if the feasible region (shaded) for a LPP is shown in following figure.

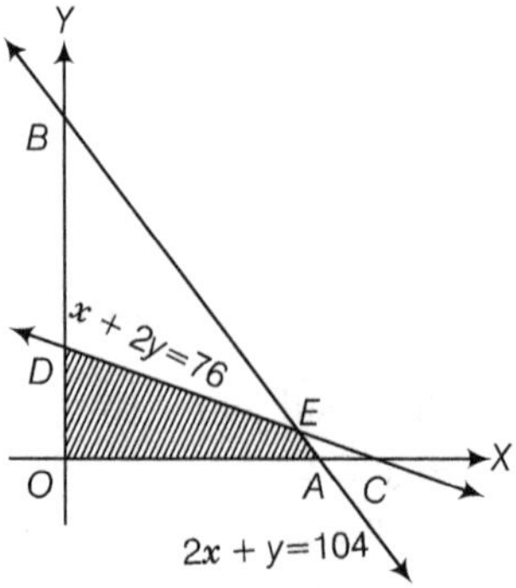

Sol. As clear from the graph, corner points are O, A, E and D with coordinates (0, 0), (52, 0), (144, 16) and (0, 38), respectively. Also, given region is bounded.

Here, $Z = 3x + 4y$

$\because$ $2x + y = 104$ and $2x + 4y = 152$

$\Rightarrow$ $-3y = -48$

$\Rightarrow$ $y = 16$ and $x = 44$

Corner points	Corresponding value of Z
(0, 0)	0
(52, 0)	156
(44, 16)	196 ← Maximum
(0, 38)	152

Hence, Z is at (44, 16) is maximum and its maximum value is 196.

Q. 6 Feasible region (shaded) for a LPP is shown in following figure. Maximise $Z = 5x + 7y$.

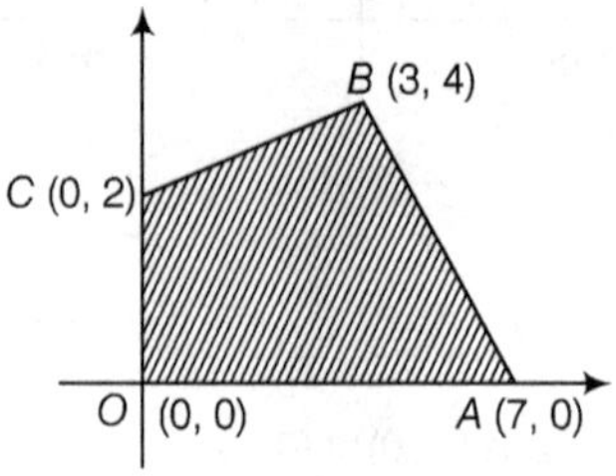

Sol. The shaded region is bounded and has coordinates of corner points as (0, 0), (7, 0), (3, 4) and (0, 2). Also, $Z = 5x + 7y$.

Corner points	Corresponding value of Z
(0, 0)	0
(7, 0)	35
(3, 4)	43 ← Maximum
(0, 2)	14

Hence, the maximum value of Z is 43 at (3, 4).

Q. 7 The feasible region for a LPP is shown in following figure. Find the minimum value of $Z = 11x + 7y$.

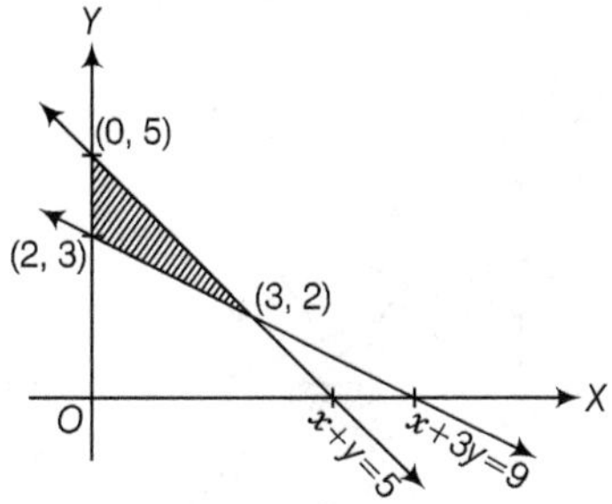

Sol. From the figure, it is clear that feasible region is bounded with coordinates of corner points as (0, 3), (3, 2) and (0, 5). Here, $Z = 11x + 7y$.

$\because \quad x + 3y = 9$ and $x + y = 5$

$\Rightarrow \quad 2y = 4$

$\therefore \quad y = 2$ and $x = 3$

So, intersection points of $x + y = 5$ and $x + 3y = 9$ is (3, 2).

Corner points	Corresponding value of Z
(0, 3)	21 ← Minimum
(3, 2)	47
(0, 5)	35

Hence, the minimum value of Z is 21 at (0, 3).

Q. 8 Refer to question 7 above. Find the maximum value of Z.

Sol. From question 7, above, it is clear that Z is maximum at (3, 2) and its maximum value is 47.

Q. 9 The feasible region for a LPP is shown in the following figure. Evaluate $Z = 4x + y$ at each of the corner points of this region. Find the minimum value of Z, if it exists.

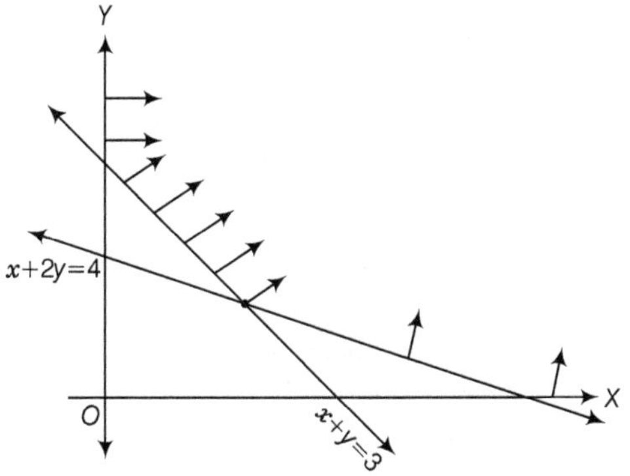

Sol. From the shaded region, it is clear that feasible region is unbounded with the corner points A (4, 0), B (2, 1) and C (0, 3).

Also, we have $Z = 4x + y$.

[since, $x + 2y = 4$ and $x + y = 3 \Rightarrow y = 1$ and $x = 2$]

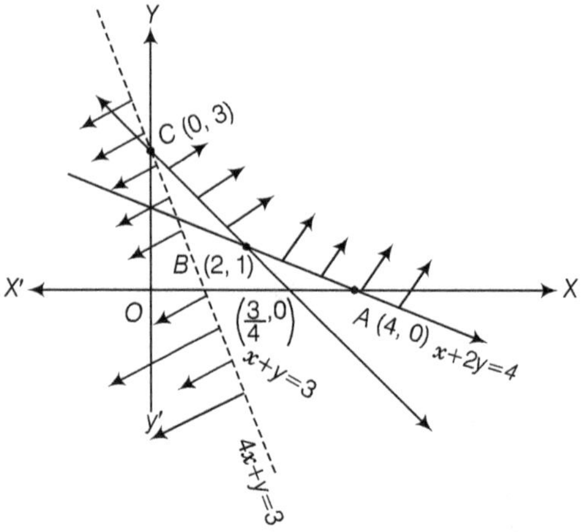

Corner points	Corresponding value of Z
(4, 0)	16
(2, 1)	9
(0, 3)	3 ← Minimum

Now, we see that 3 is the smallest value of Z at the corner point (0, 3). Note that here we see that, the region is unbounded, therefore 3 may or may not be the minimum value of Z.

To decide this issue, we graph the inequality $4x + y < 3$ and check whether the resulting open half plan has no point in common with feasible region otherwise, Z has no minimum value.

From the shown graph above, it is clear that there is no point in common with feasible region and hence Z has minimum value 3 at (0, 3).

Q. 10 In following figure, the feasible region (shaded) for a LPP is shown. Determine the maximum and minimum value of $Z = x + 2y$.

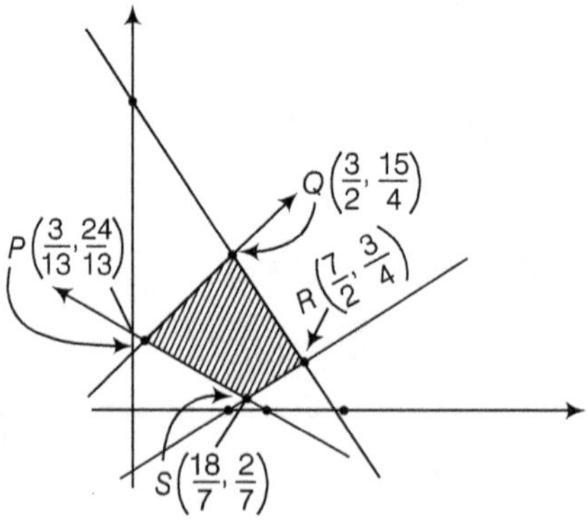

Sol. From the shaded bounded region, it is clear that the coordinates of corner points are $\left(\frac{3}{13}, \frac{24}{13}\right)$, $\left(\frac{18}{7}, \frac{2}{7}\right)$, $\left(\frac{7}{2}, \frac{3}{4}\right)$ and $\left(\frac{3}{2}, \frac{15}{4}\right)$.

Also, we have to determine maximum and minimum value of $Z = x + 2y$.

Corner points	Corresponding value of Z
$\left(\frac{3}{13}, \frac{24}{13}\right)$	$\frac{3}{13} + \frac{48}{13} = \frac{51}{13} = 3\frac{12}{13}$
$\left(\frac{18}{7}, \frac{2}{7}\right)$	$\frac{18}{7} + \frac{4}{7} = \frac{22}{7} = 3\frac{1}{7}$ Minimum
$\left(\frac{7}{2}, \frac{3}{4}\right)$	$\frac{7}{2} + \frac{6}{4} = \frac{20}{4} = 5$
$\left(\frac{3}{2}, \frac{15}{4}\right)$	$\frac{3}{2} + \frac{30}{4} = \frac{36}{4} = 9$ Maximum

Hence, the maximum and minimum values of Z are 9 and $3\frac{1}{7}$, respectively.

Q. 11 A manufacturer of electronic circuits has a stock of 200 resistors, 120 transistors and 150 capacitors and is required to produce two types of circuits *A* and *B*. Type *A* requires 20 resistors, 10 transistors and 10 capacitors. Type *B* requires 10 resistors, 20 transistors and 30 capacitors. If the profit on type *A* circuit is ₹ 50 and that on type *B* circuit is ₹ 60, formulate this problem as a LPP, so that the manufacturer can maximise his profit.

Thinking Process

For maximising the profit, use resistor constraint, transistor constraint, capacitor constraint and non-negative constraint.

Sol. Let the manufacturer produces x units of type A circuits and y units of type B circuits.

Form the given information, we have following corresponding constraint table.

	Type A (x)	Type B (y)	Maximum stock
Resistors	20	10	200
Transistors	10	20	120
Capacitors	10	30	150
Profit	₹ 50	₹ 60	

Thus, we see that total profit $Z = 50x + 60y$ (in ₹).

Now, we have the following mathematical model for the given problem.

Maximise $Z = 50x + 60y$ ...(i)

Subject to the constraints.

$20x + 10y \le 200$ [resistors constraint]

$\Rightarrow$ $2x + y \le 20$ ...(ii)

and $10x + 20y \le 120$ [transistor constraint]

$\Rightarrow$ $x + 2y \le 12$ ...(iii)

and $10x + 30y \le 150$ [capacitor constraint]

$\Rightarrow$ $x + 3y \le 15$ ...(iv)

and $x \ge 0, y \ge 0$ [non-negative constraint] ...(v)

So, maximise $Z = 50x + 60y$, subject to $2x + y \le 20$, $x + 2y \le 12$, $x + 3y \le 15$, $x \ge 0$, $y \ge 0$.

Q. 12 A firm has to transport 1200 packages using large vans which can carry 200 packages each and small vans which can take 80 packages each. The cost for engaging each large van is ₹ 400 and each small van is ₹ 200. Not more than ₹ 3000 is to be spent on the job and the number of large vans cannot exceed the number of small vans. Formulate this problem as a LPP given that the objective is to minimise cost.

Sol. Let the firm has x number of large vans and y number of small vans. From the given information, we have following corresponding constraint table.

	Large vans (x)	**Small vans** (y)	**Maximum / Minimum**
Packages	200	80	1200
Cost	400	200	3000

Thus, we see that objective function for minimum cost is $Z = 400x + 200y$.
Subject to constraints

$$200x + 80y \geq 1200 \quad \text{[package constraint]}$$
$$\Rightarrow \quad 5x + 2y \geq 30 \quad \text{...(i)}$$
$$\text{and} \quad 400x + 200y \leq 3000 \quad \text{[cost constraint]}$$
$$\Rightarrow \quad 2x + y \leq 15 \quad \text{...(ii)}$$
$$\text{and} \quad x \leq y \quad \text{[van constraint] ...(iii)}$$
$$\text{and} \quad x \geq 0, y \geq 0 \quad \text{[non-negative constraints] ...(iv)}$$

Thus, required LPP to minimise cost is minimise $Z = 400x + 200y$, subject to $5x + 2y \geq 30$.

$$2x + y \leq 15$$
$$x \leq y$$
$$x \geq 0, y \geq 0$$

Q. 13 A company manufactures two types of screws A and B. All the screws have to pass through a threading machine and a slotting machine. A box of type A screws requires 2 min on the threading machine and 3 min on the slotting machine. A box of type B screws requires 8 min on the threading machine and 2 min on the slotting machine. In a week, each machine is available for 60 h. On selling these screws, the company gets a profit of ₹ 100 per box on type A screws and ₹ 170 per box on type B screws.

Formulate this problem as a LPP given that the objective is to maximise profit.

Sol. Let the company manufactures x boxes of type A screws and y boxes of type B screws. From the given information, we have following corresponding constraint table

	Type *A* (x)	**Type *B*** (y)	**Maximum time available on each machine in a week**
Time required for screws on threading machine	2	8	60×60 (min)
Time required for screws on slotting machine	3	2	60×60 (min)
Profit	₹ 100	₹ 170	

Thus, we see that objective function for maximum profit is $Z = 100x + 170y$.

Subject to constraints

$$2x + 8y \le 60 \times 60 \quad \text{[time constraint for threading machine]}$$

$\Rightarrow$ $$x + 4y \le 1800 \quad \text{...(i)}$$

and $$3x + 2y \le 60 \times 60 \quad \text{[time constraint for slotting machine]}$$

$\Rightarrow$ $$3x + 2y \le 3600 \quad \text{... (ii)}$$

Also, $$x \ge 0, y \ge 0 \quad \text{[non-negative constraints] ...(iii)}$$

$\therefore$ Required LPP is,

Maximise $$Z = 100x + 170y$$

Subject to constraints $x + 4y \le 1800$, $3x + 2y \le 3600$, $x \ge 0$, $y \ge 0$.

Q. 14 A company manufactures two types of sweaters type *A* and type *B*. It costs ₹ 360 to make a type *A* sweater and ₹ 120 to make a type *B* sweater. The company can make atmost 300 sweaters and spend atmost ₹ 72000 a day. The number of sweaters of type *B* cannot exceed the number of sweaters of type *A* by more than 100. The company makes a profit of ₹ 200 for each sweater of type A and ₹ 120 for every sweater of type *B*.

Formulate this problem as a LPP to maximise the profit to the company.

Sol. Let the company manufactures x number of type *A* sweaters and y number of type *B* sweaters.

From the given information we see that cost to make a type *A* sweater is ₹360 and cost to make a type *B* sweater is ₹ 120.

Also, the company spend atmost ₹ 72000 a day.

$\therefore$ $$360x + 120y \le 72000$$

$\Rightarrow$ $$3x + y \le 600 \quad \text{...(i)}$$

Also, company can make atmost 300 sweaters.

$\therefore$ $$x + y \le 300 \quad \text{...(ii)}$$

Further, the number of sweaters of type *B* cannot exceed the number of sweaters of type *A* by more than 100 *i.e.*,

$$x + 100 \ge y$$

$\Rightarrow$ $$x - y \ge -100 \quad \text{...(iii)}$$

Also, we have non-negative constraints for x and y *i.e.*, $x \ge 0$, $y \ge 0$ ...(iv)

Hence, the company makes a profit of ₹200 for each sweater of type *A* and ₹120 for each sweater of type *B i.e.*,

$$\text{Profit } (Z) = 200x + 120y$$

Thus, the required LPP to maximise the profit is

Maximise $Z = 200x + 120y$ is subject to constraints.

$$3x + y \le 600$$
$$x + y \le 300$$
$$x - y \ge -100$$
$$x \ge 0, y \ge 0$$

Q. 15 A man rides his motorcycle at the speed of 50 km/h. He has to spend ₹ 2 per km on petrol. If he rides it at a faster speed of 80 km/h, the petrol cost increases to ₹ 3 per km. He has atmost ₹ 120 to spend on petrol and one hour's time. He wishes to find the maximum distance that he can travel. Express this problem as a linear programming problem.

Sol. Let the man rides to his motorcycle to a distance x km at the speed of 50 km/h and to a distance y km at the speed of 80 km/h.

Therefore, cost on petrol is $2x + 3y$.

Since, he has to spend ₹ 120 atmost on petrol.

$\therefore \quad 2x + 3y \le 120 \quad$ ...(i)

Also, he has atmost one hour's time.

$\therefore \quad \frac{x}{50} + \frac{y}{80} \le 1$

$\Rightarrow \quad 8x + 5y \le 400 \quad$ ...(ii)

Also, we have $x \ge 0$, $y \ge 0$ [non-negative constraints]

Thus, required LPP to travel maximum distance by him is

Maximise $Z = x + y$, subject to $2x + 3y \le 120$, $8x + 5y \le 400$, $x \ge 0$, $y \ge 0$

Q. 16 Refer to question 11. How many of circuits of type *A* and of type *B*, should be produced by the manufacturer, so as to maximise his profit? Determine the maximum profit.

Thinking Process

Using the constraints draw the graph to get the corner points and find the maximum value of possible corner points (as asked).

Sol. Referring to solution 11, we have

Maximise $Z = 50x + 60y$, subject to

$$2x + y \le 20,\ x + 2y \le 12,\ x + 3y \le 15,\ x \ge 0,\ y \ge 0$$

From the shaded region it is clear that the feasible region determined by the system of constraints is *OABCD* and is bounded and the coordinates of corner points are (0, 0), (10, 0), $\left(\frac{28}{3}, \frac{4}{3}\right)$, (6, 3) and (0, 5), respectively.

[since, $x + 2y = 12$ and $2x + y = 20 \Rightarrow x = \frac{28}{3}$, $y = \frac{4}{3}$ and $x + 3y = 15$ and $x + 2y = 12 \Rightarrow y = 3$ and $x = 6$]

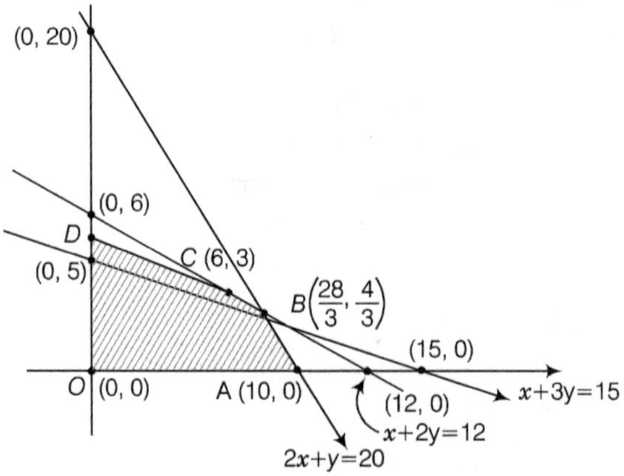

Corner points	Corresponding value of $Z = 50x + 60y$
(0, 0)	0
(10, 0)	500
$\left(\frac{28}{3}, \frac{4}{3}\right)$	$\frac{1400}{3} + \frac{240}{3} = \frac{1640}{3} = 546.66 \leftarrow$ Maximum
(6,3)	480
(0,5)	300

Since, the manufacturer is required to produce two types of circuits A and B and it is clear that parts of resistor, transistor and capacitor cannot be in fraction, so the required maximum profit is 480 where circuits of type A is 6 and circuits of type B is 3.

Q. 17 Refer to question 12. What will be the minimum cost?

Sol. Referring to solution 12, we have minimise $Z = 400x + 200y$, subject to $5x + 2y \geq 30$,

$$2x + y \leq 15,\ x \leq y,\ x \geq 0,\ y \geq 0.$$

On solving $x - y = 0$ and $5x + 2y = 30$, we get

$$y = \frac{30}{7},\ x = \frac{30}{7}$$

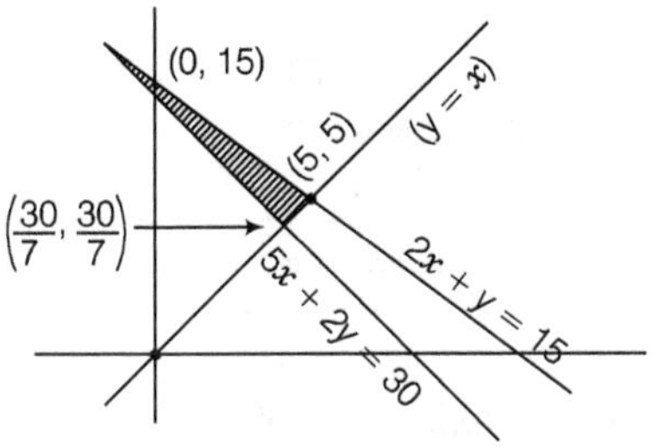

On solving $x - y = 0$ and $2x + y = 15$, we get $x = 5$, $y = 5$

So, from the shaded feasible region it is clear that coordinates of corner points are (0, 15), (5, 5) and $\left(\frac{30}{7}, \frac{30}{7}\right)$.

Corner points	Corresponding value of $Z = 400x + 200y$
(0, 15)	3000
(5, 5)	3000
$\left(\frac{30}{7}, \frac{30}{7}\right)$	$400 \times \frac{30}{7} + 200 \times \frac{30}{7} = \frac{18000}{7}$ $= 2571.43 \leftarrow$ Minimum

Hence, the minimum cost is ₹ 2571.43.

Q. 18 Refer to question 13. Solve the linear programming problem and determine the maximum profit to the manufacturer.

Sol. Referring to solution 13, we have

Maximise $Z = 100x + 170y$ subject to

$$3x + 2y \le 3600,\ x + 4y \le 1800,\ x \ge 0,\ y \ge 0$$

From the shaded feasible region it is clear that the coordinates of corner points are (0, 0), (1200, 0), (1080, 180) and (0, 450).

On solving $x + 4y = 1800$ and $3x + 2y = 3600$, we get $x = 1080$ and $y = 180$

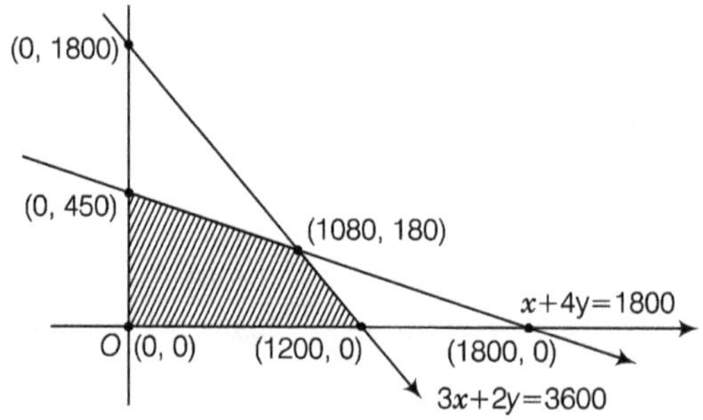

Corner points	Corresponding value of $Z = 100x + 170y$
(0, 0)	0
(1200, 0)	$1200 \times 100 = 120000$
(1080, 180)	$100 \times 1080 + 170 \times 180 = 138600 \leftarrow$ Maximum
(0, 450)	$0 + 170 \times 450 = 76500$

Hence, the maximum profit to the manufacturer is 138600.

Q. 19 Refer to question 14. How many sweaters of each type should the company make in a day to get a maximum profit? What is the maximum profit?

Sol. Referring to solution 14, we have maximise $Z = 200x + 120y$

subject to $x + y \le 300,\ 3x + y \le 600,\ x - y \ge -100,\ x \ge 0,\ y \ge 0.$

On solving $x + y = 300$ and $3x + y = 600$, we get

$$x = 150,\ y = 150$$

On solving $x - y = -100$ and $x + y = 300$, we get

$$x = 100,\ y = 200$$

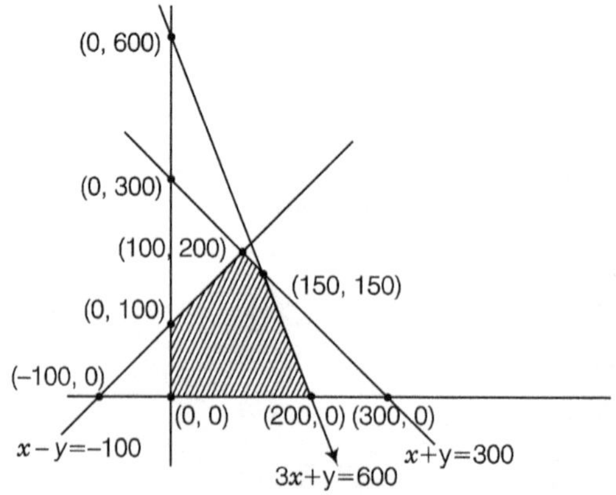

From the shaded feasible region it is clear that coordinates of corner points are (0, 0), (200, 0), (150, 150), (100, 200) and (0, 100).

Corner points	Corresponding value of $Z = 200x + 120y$
(0, 0)	0
(200, 0)	40000
(150, 150)	$150 \times 200 + 120 \times 150 = 48000 \leftarrow$ Maximum
(100, 200)	$100 \times 200 + 120 \times 200 = 44000$
(0, 100)	$120 \times 100 = 12000$

Hence, 150 sweaters of each type made by company and maximum profit = ₹ 48000.

Q. 20 Refer to question 15. Determine the maximum distance that the man can travel.

Sol. Referring to solution 15, we have

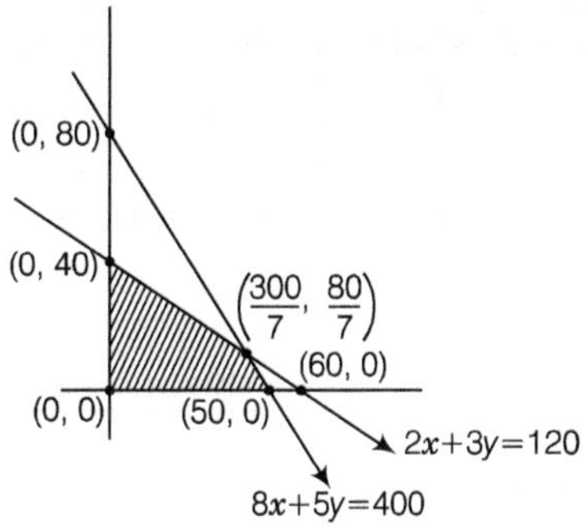

Maximise $Z = x + y$, subject to

$$2x + 3y \le 120,\ 8x + 5y \le 400,\ x \ge 0, y \ge 0$$

On solving, we get

$$8x + 5y = 400 \text{ and } 2x + 3y = 120, \text{ we get}$$

$$x = \frac{300}{7},\ y = \frac{80}{7}$$

From the shaded feasible region, it is clear that coordinates of corner points are (0, 0), (50, 0), $\left(\frac{300}{7}, \frac{80}{7}\right)$ and (0, 40).

Corner points	Corresponding value of $Z = x + y$
(0, 0)	0
(50, 0)	50
$\frac{300}{7}, \frac{80}{7}$	$\frac{380}{7} = 54\frac{2}{7}$ km $\leftarrow$ Maximum
(0, 40)	40

Hence, the maximum distance that the man can travel is $54\frac{2}{7}$ km.

Q. 21 Maximise $Z = x + y$ subject to $x + 4y \le 8$, $2x + 3y \le 12$, $3x + y \le 9$, $x \ge 0$ and $y \ge 0$.

Sol. Here, the given LPP is,

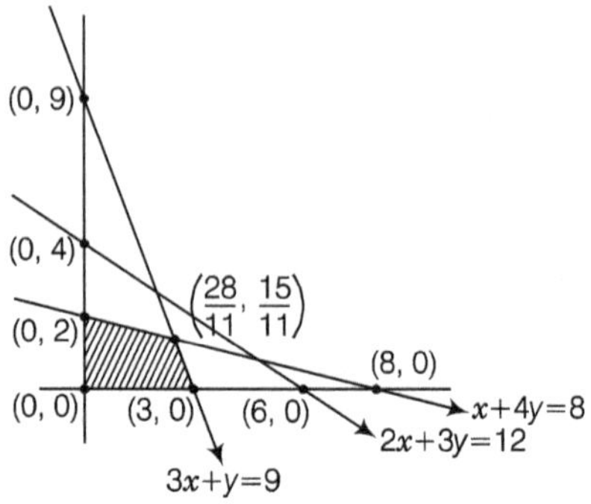

Maximise $Z = x + y$ subject to,

$$x + 4y \le 8, 2x + 3y \le 12, 3x + y \le 9, x \ge 0, y \ge 0.$$

On solving $x + 4y = 8$ and $3x + y = 9$, we get

$$x = \frac{28}{11}, y = \frac{15}{11}.$$

From the feasible region, it is clear that coordinates of corner points are (0, 0), (3, 0), $\left(\frac{28}{11}, \frac{15}{11}\right)$ and (0, 2).

Corner points	Value of $Z = x + y$
(0, 0)	0
(3, 0)	3
$\left(\frac{28}{11}, \frac{15}{11}\right)$	$\frac{43}{11} = 3\frac{10}{11}$ ← Maximum
(0, 2)	2

Hence, the maximum value is $3\frac{10}{11}$.

Q. 22 A manufacturer produces two models of bikes-model X and model Y. Model X takes a 6 man-hours to make per unit, while model Y takes 10 man hours per unit. There is a total of 450 man-hour available per week. Handling and marketing costs are ₹ 2000 and ₹ 1000 per unit for models X and Y, respectively. The total funds available for these purposes are ₹ 80000 per week. Profits per unit for models X and Y are ₹ 1000 and ₹ 500, respectively. How many bikes of each model should the manufacturer produce, so as to yield a maximum profit? Find the maximum profit.

Thinking Process

First check whether the drawn graph (by using constraints) gives bounded region or not and then get the maximised profit on corresponding corner points.

Sol. Let the manufacturer produces x number of models X and y number of model Y bikes. Model X takes a 6 man-hours to make per unit and model Y takes a 10 man-hours to make per unit.

There is total of 450 man-hour available per week.

$$\therefore 6x + 10y \le 450$$

$\Rightarrow$ $$3x + 5y \le 225 \qquad \text{...(i)}$$

For models X and Y, handling and marketing costs are ₹ 2000 and ₹1000, respectively, total funds available for these purposes are ₹ 80000 per week.

$\therefore$ $$2000x + 1000y \le 80000$$

$\Rightarrow$ $$2x + y \le 80 \qquad \text{...(ii)}$$

Also, $$x \ge 0,\ y \ge 0$$

Hence, the profits per unit for models X and Y are ₹ 1000 and ₹ 500, respectively.

$\therefore$ Required LPP is

Maximise $Z = 1000x + 500y$

Subject to, $3x + 5y \le 225$, $2x + y \le 80$, $x \ge 0$, $y \ge 0$

From the shaded feasible region, it is clear that coordinates of corner points are (0, 0), (40, 0), (25, 30) and (0, 45).

On solving $3x + 5y = 225$ and $2x + y = 80$, we get

$$x = 25,\ y = 30$$

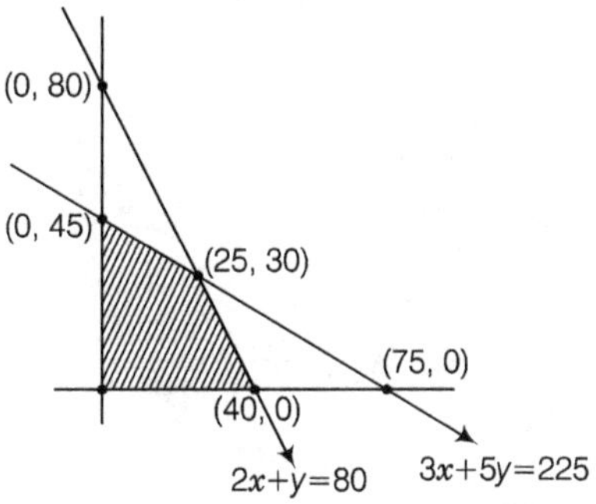

Corner points	Value of $Z = 1000x + 500y$
(0, 0)	0
(40, 0)	40000 ← Maximum
(25, 30)	25000 + 15000 = 40000 ← Maximum
(0, 45)	22500

So, the manufacturer should produce 25 bikes of model X and 30 bikes of model Y to get a maximum profit of ₹ 40000.

Since, in question it is asked that each model bikes should be produced.

Q. 23 In order to supplement daily diet, a person wishes to take some X and some wishes Y tablets. The contents of iron, calcium and vitamins in X and Y (in mg/tablet) are given as below

Tablets	Iron	Calcium	Vitamin
X	6	3	2
Y	2	3	4

The person needs atleast 18 mg of iron, 21 mg of calcium and 16 mg of vitamins. The price of each tablet of X and Y is ₹ 2 and ₹1, respectively. How many tablets of each should the person take in order to satisfy the above requirement at the minimum cost?

Sol. Let the person takes x units of tablet X and y units of tablet Y.

So, from the given information, we have

$$6x + 2y \geq 18 \Rightarrow 3x + y \geq 9 \quad \text{...(i)}$$

$$3x + 3y \geq 21 \Rightarrow x + y \geq 7 \quad \text{...(ii)}$$

and $$2x + 4y \geq 16 \Rightarrow x + 2y \geq 8 \quad \text{...(iii)}$$

Also, we know that here, $x \geq 0$, $y \geq 0$ ...(iv)

The price of each tablet of X and Y is ₹ 2 and ₹ 1, respectively.

So, the corresponding LPP is minimise $Z = 2x + y$, subject to $3x + y \geq 9$, $x + y \geq 7$, $x + 2y \geq 8$, $x \geq 0$, $y \geq 0$

From the shaded graph, we see that for the shown unbounded region, we have coordinates of corner points A, B, C and D as (8, 0), (6, 1), (1, 6), and (0, 9), respectively.

[on solving $x + 2y = 8$ and $x + y = 7$, we get $x = 6$, $y = 1$ and on solving $3x + y = 9$ and $x + y = 7$, we get $x = 1$, $y = 6$]

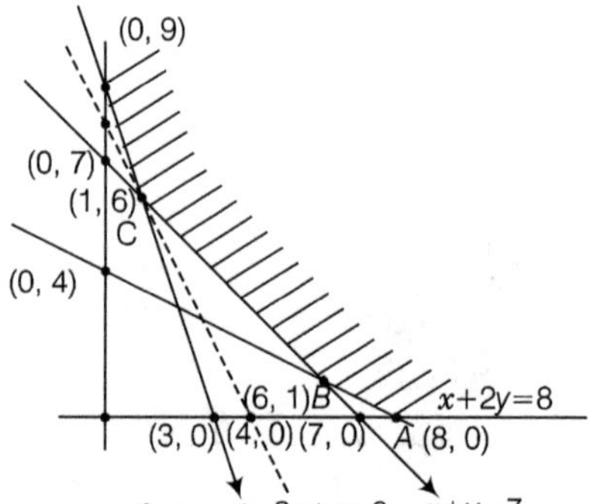

Corner points	Value of $Z = 2x + y$
(8, 0)	16
(6, 1)	13
(1, 6)	8 ← Minimum
(0, 9)	9

Thus, we see that 8 is the minimum value of Z at the corner point (1, 6). Here, we see that the feasible region is unbounded. Therefore, 8 may or may not be the minimum value of Z. To decide this issue, we graph the inequality

$$2x + y < 8 \quad \text{...(v)}$$

and check whether the resulting open half has points in common with feasible region or not. If it has common point, then 8 will not be the minimum value of Z, otherwise 8 will be the minimum value of Z.

Thus, from the graph it is clear that, it has no common point.

Therefore, $Z = 2x + y$ has 8 as minimum value subject to the given constraints.

Hence, the person should take 1 unit of X tablet and 6 units of Y tablets to satisfy the given requirements and at the minimum cost of ₹ 8.

Q. 24 A company makes 3 model of calculators; *A*, *B* and *C* at factory I and factory II. The company has orders for atleast 6400 calculators of model *A*, 4000 calculators of model *B* and 4800 calculators of model *C*. At factory I, 50 calculators of model *A*, 50 of model *B* and 30 of model *C* are made everyday; at factory II, 40 calculators of model *A*, 20 of model *B* and 40 of model *C* are made everyday. It costs ₹ 12000 and ₹ 15000 each day to operate factory I and II, respectively. Find the number of days each factory should operate to minimise the operating costs and still meet the demand.

Sol. Let the factory I operate for x days and the factory II operate for y days.

At factory I, 50 calculators of model *A* and at factory II, 40 calculators of model *A* are made everyday. Also, company has ordered for atleast 6400 calculators of model *A*.

$\therefore \quad 50x + 40y \geq 6400 \Rightarrow 5x + 4y \geq 640 \quad \ldots(i)$

Also, at factory I, 50 calculators of model *B* and at factory II, 20 calculators of modal *B* are made everyday.

Since, the company has ordered atleast 4000 calculators of model *B*.

$\therefore \quad 50x + 20y \geq 4000 \Rightarrow 5x + 2y \geq 400 \quad \ldots(ii)$

Similarly, for model *C*, $\quad 30x + 40y \geq 4800$

$\Rightarrow \quad 3x + 4y \geq 480 \quad \ldots(iii)$

Also, $\quad x \geq 0, y \geq 0 \quad \ldots(iv)$

[since, x and y are non-negative]

It costs ₹ 12000 and ₹ 15000 each day to operate factories I and II, respectively.

$\therefore$ Corresponding LPP is,

Minimise $Z = 12000x + 15000y$, subject to

$$5x + 4y \geq 640$$
$$5x + 2y \geq 400$$
$$3x + 4y \geq 480$$
$$x \geq 0, y \geq 0$$

On solving $3x + 4y = 480$ and $5x + 4y = 640$, we get $x = 80$, $y = 60$.

On solving $5x + 4y = 640$ and $5x + 2y = 400$, we get $x = 32$, $y = 120$

Thus, from the graph, it is clear that feasible region is unbounded and the coordinates of corner points *A*, *B*, *C* and *D* are (160, 0), (80, 60), (32, 120) and (0, 200), respectively.

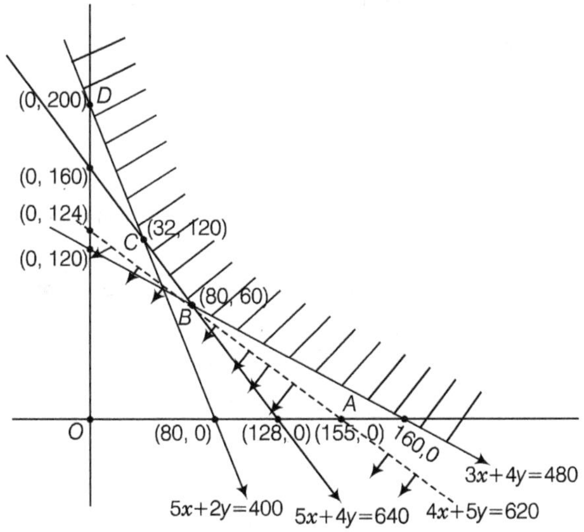

Corner points	Value of $Z = 12000x + 15000y$
(160, 0)	$160 \times 12000 = 1920000$
(80, 60)	$(80 \times 12 + 60 \times 15) \times 1000 = 1860000$ ← Minimum
(32, 120)	$(32 \times 12 + 120 \times 15) \times 1000 = 2184000$
(0, 200)	$0 + 200 \times 15000 = 3000000$

From the above table, it is clear that for given unbounded region the minimum value of Z may or may not be 1860000.

Now, for deciding this, we graph the inequality

$$12000x + 15000y < 1860000$$

$$\Rightarrow \quad 4x + 5y < 620$$

and check whether the resulting open half plane has points in common with feasible region or not.

Thus, as shown in the figure, it has no common points so, $Z = 12000x + 15000y$ has minimum value 1860000.

So, number of days factory I should be operated is 80 and number of days factory II should be operated is 60 for the minimum cost and satisfying the given constraints.

Q. 25 Maximise and minimise $Z = 3x - 4y$ subject to $x - 2y \le 0$, $-3x + y \le 4$, $x - y \le 6$ and $x, y \ge 0$.

Sol. Given LPP is,

maximise and minimise $Z = 3x - 4y$ subject to $x - 2y \le 0$, $-3x + y \le 4$, $x - y \le 6$, $x, y \ge 0$.

[on solving $x - y = 6$ and $x - 2y = 0$, we get $x = 12$, $y = 6$]

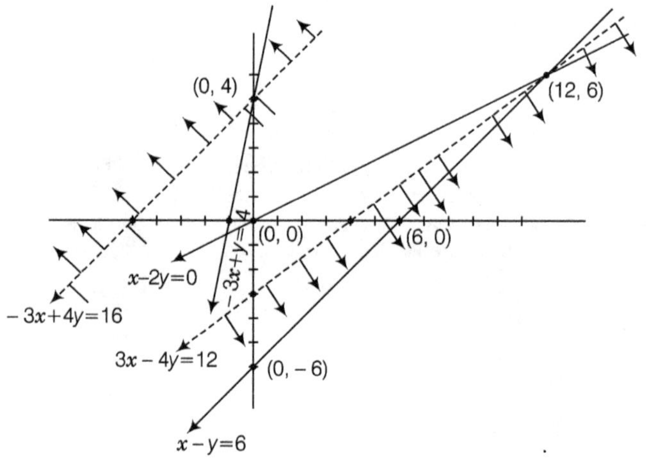

From the shown graph, for the feasible region, we see that it is unbounded and coordinates of corner points are (0, 0), (12, 6) and (0, 4).

Corner points	Corresponding value of $Z = 3x - 4y$
(0, 0)	0
(0, 4)	−16 ← Minimum
(12, 6)	12 ← Maximum

For given unbounded region the minimum value of Z may or may not be -16. So, for deciding this, we graph the inequality.

$$3x - 4y < -16$$

and check whether the resulting open half plane has common points with feasible region or not.

Thus, from the figure it shows it has common points with feasible region, so it does not have any minimum value.

Also, similarly for maximum value, we graph the inequality $3x - 4y > 12$

and see that resulting open half plane has no common points with the feasible region and hence maximum value 12 exist for $Z = 3x - 4y$.

Objective Type Questions

Q. 26 The corner points of the feasible region determined by the system of linear constraints are (0, 0), (0, 40), (20, 40), (60, 20), (60, 0). The objective function is $Z = 4x + 3y$. Compare the quantity in column A and column B.

Column A	Column B
Maximum of Z	325

(a) The quantity in column A is greater

(b) The quantity in column B is greater

(c) The two quantities are equal

(d) The relationship cannot be determined on the basis of the information supplied.

Sol. *(b)*

Corner points	Corresponding value of $Z = 4x + 3y$
(0, 0)	0
(0, 40)	120
(20, 40)	200
(60, 20)	300 ← Maximum
(60, 0)	240

Hence, maximum value of $Z = 300 < 325$

So, the quantity in column B is greater.

Q. 27 The feasible solution for a LPP is shown in following figure. Let $Z = 3x - 4y$ be the objective function. Minimum of Z occurs at

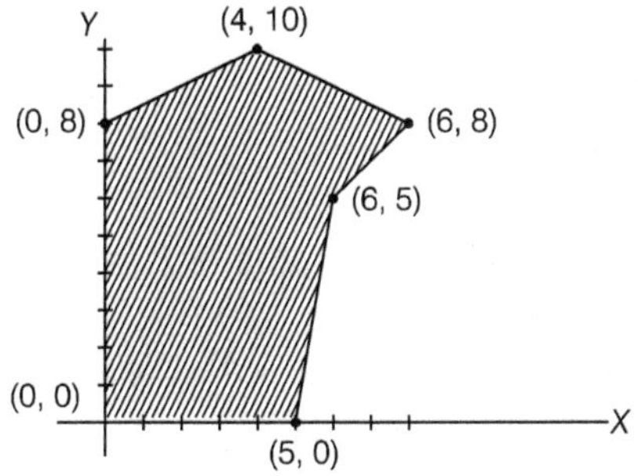

(a) (0, 0) (b) (0, 8) (c) (5, 0) (d) (4, 10)

Sol. *(b)*

Corner points	Corresponding value of $Z = 3x - 4y$
(0, 0)	0
(5, 0)	15←Maximum
(6, 5)	−2
(6, 8)	−14
(4, 10)	−28
(0, 8)	−32←Minimum

Hence, the minimum of Z occurs at (0, 8) and its minimum value is (−32).

Q. 28 Refer to question 27. Maximum of Z occurs at

(a) (5, 0) (b) (6, 5) (c) (6, 8) (d) (4, 10)

Sol. *(a)* Refer to solution 27, maximum of Z occurs at (5, 0).

Q. 29 Refer to question 7, maximum value of Z + minimum value of Z is equal to

(a) 13 (b) 1 (c) −13 (d) −17

Sol. *(d)* Refer to solution 27, maximum value of Z + minimum value of Z

$$= 15 - 32 = -17$$

Q. 30 The feasible region for an LPP is shown in the following figure. Let $F = 3x - 4y$ be the objective function. Maximum value of F is

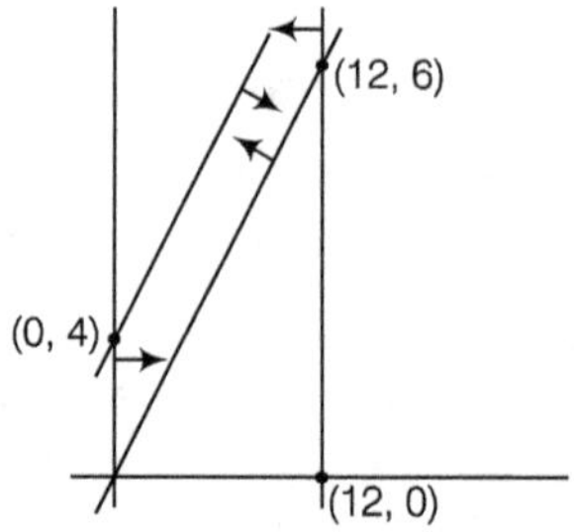

(a) 0 (b) 8 (c) 12 (d) −18

Sol. *(c)* The feasible region as shown in the figure, has objective function $F = 3x - 4y$.

Corner points	Corresponding value of $F = 3x - 4y$
(0, 0)	0
(12, 6)	12 ←Maximum
(0, 4)	−16 ←Minimum

Hence, the maximum value of F is 12.

Q. 31 Refer to question 30. Minimum value of F is

(a) 0 (b) −16 (c) 12 (d) Does not exist

Sol. *(b)* Referring to solution 30, minimum value of F is −16 at (0, 4).

Q. 32 Corner points of the feasible region for an LPP are (0, 2), (3, 0), (6, 0), (6, 8) and (0, 5). Let $F = 4x + 6y$ be the objective function. The minimum value of F occurs at

(a) Only (0, 2)
(b) Only (3, 0)
(c) the mid-point of the line segment joining the points (0, 2) and (3, 0)
(d) any point on the line segment joining the points (0, 2) and (3, 0)

Sol. *(d)*

Corner points	Corresponding value of $F = 4x + 6y$
(0, 2)	12←Minimum
(3, 0)	12←Minimum
(6, 0)	24
(6, 8)	72←Maximum
(0, 5)	30

Hence, minimum value of F occurs at any points on the line segment joining the points (0, 2) and (3, 0).

Q. 33 Refer to question 32, maximum of F– minimum of F is equal to

(a) 60 (b) 48 (c) 42 (d) 18

Sol. *(a)* Referring to the solution 32, maximum of F – minimum of $F = 72 - 12 = 60$

Q. 34 Corner points of the feasible region determined by the system of linear constraints are (0, 3), (1, 1) and (3, 0). Let $Z = px + qy$, where $p, q > 0$. Condition on p and q, so that the minimum of Z occurs at (3, 0) and (1, 1) is

(a) $p = 2q$ (b) $p = \frac{q}{2}$ (c) $p = 3q$ (d) $p = q$

Sol. *(b)*

Corner points	Corresponding value of $Z = px + qy; p, q > 0$
(0, 3)	$3q$
(1, 1)	$p + q$
(3, 0)	$3p$

So, condition of p and q, so that the minimum of Z occurs at (3, 0) and (1, 1) is

$$p + q = 3p \Rightarrow 2p = q$$

$$\therefore \quad p = \frac{q}{2}$$

Fillers

Q. 35 In a LPP, the linear inequalities or restrictions on the variables are called... .

Sol. In a LPP, the linear inequalities or restrictions on the variables are called linear constraints.

Q. 36 In a LPP, the objective function is always... .

Sol. In a LPP, objective function is always linear.

Q. 37 In the feasible region for a LPP is ..., then the optimal value of the objective function $Z = ax + by$ may or may not exist.

Sol. If the feasible region for a LPP is unbounded, then the optimal value of the objective function $Z = ax + by$ may or may not exist.

Q. 38 In a LPP, if the objective function $Z = ax + by$ has the same maximum value on two corner points of the feasible region, then every point on the line segment joining these two points give the same ... value.

Sol. In a LPP, if the objective function $Z = ax + by$ has the same maximum value on two corner points of the feasible region, then every point on the line segment joining these two points give the same maximum value.

Q. 39 A feasible region of a system of linear inequalities is said to be ..., if it can be enclosed within a circle.

Sol. A feasible region of a system of linear inequalities is said to be bounded, if it can be enclosed within a circle.

Q. 40 A corner point of a feasible region is a point in the region which is the ... of two boundary lines.

Sol. A corner point of a feasible region is a point in the region which is the intersection of two boundary lines.

Q. 41 The feasible region for an LPP is always a ... polygon.

Sol. The feasible region for an LPP is always a **convex** polygon.

True/False

Q. 42 If the feasible region for a LPP is unbounded, maximum or minimum of the objective function $Z = ax + by$ may or may not exist.

Sol. *True*

Q. 43 Maximum value of the objective function $Z = ax + by$ in a LPP always occurs at only one corner point of the feasible region.

Sol. *False*

Q. 44 In a LPP, the minimum value of the objective function $Z = ax + by$ is always 0, if origin is one of the corner point of the feasible region.

Sol. *False*

Q. 45 In a LPP, the maximum value of the objective function $Z = ax + by$ is always finite.

Sol. *True*

13

Probability

Short Answer Type Questions

Q. 1 For a loaded die, the probabilities of outcomes are given as under

$$P(1) = P(2) = 0.2,\ P(3) = P(5) = P(6) = 0.1 \text{ and } P(4) = 0.3.$$

The die is thrown two times. Let A and B be the events, 'same number each time' and 'a total score is 10 or more', respectively. Determine whether or not A and B are independent.

Thinking Process

First, find $P(A), P(B)$ and $P(A \cap B)$ and then use the concept that two events A and B are called independent events, if $P(A \cap B) = P(A) \cdot P(B)$.

Sol. For a loaded die, it is given that

$$P(1) = P(2) = 0.2,$$
$$P(3) = P(5) = P(6) = 0.1 \text{ and } P(4) = 0.3$$

Also, die is thrown two times.

Here, A = Same number each time and B = Total score is 10 or more

$\therefore$ $A = \{(1, 1), (2, 2), (3, 3), (4, 4), (5, 5), (6, 6)\}$

So,
$$\begin{aligned} P(A) &= [P(1, 1) + P(2, 2) + P(3, 3) + P(4, 4) + P(5, 5) + P(6, 6)] \\ &= [P(1) \cdot P(1) + P(2) \cdot P(2) + P(3) \cdot P(3) + P(4) \cdot P(4) + P(5) \cdot P(5) + P(6) \cdot P(6)] \\ &= [0.2 \times 0.2 + 0.2 \times 0.2 + 0.1 \times 0.1 + 0.3 \times 0.3 + 0.1 \times 0.1 + 0.1 \times 0.1] \\ &= 0.04 + 0.04 + 0.01 + 0.09 + 0.01 + 0.01 = 0.20 \end{aligned}$$

and $B = \{(4, 6), (6, 4), (5, 5), (5, 6), (6, 5), (6, 6)\}$

$\therefore$
$$\begin{aligned} P(B) &= P(4, 6) + P(6, 4) + P(5, 5) + P(5, 6) + P(6, 5) + P(6, 6) \\ &= P(4) \cdot P(6) + P(6) \cdot P(4) + P(5) \cdot P(5) + P(5) \cdot P(6) + P(6) \cdot P(5) + P(6) \cdot P(6) \\ &= 0.3 \times 0.1 + 0.1 \times 0.3 + 0.1 \times 0.1 + 0.1 \times 0.1 + 0.1 \times 0.1 + 0.1 \times 0.1 \\ &= 0.03 + 0.03 + 0.01 + 0.01 + 0.01 + 0.01 = 0.10 \end{aligned}$$

Also, $A \cap B = \{(5, 5), (6, 6)\}$

$\therefore$
$$\begin{aligned} P(A \cap B) &= P(5, 5) + P(6, 6) = P(5) \cdot P(5) + P(6) \cdot P(6) \\ &= 0.1 \times 0.1 + 0.1 \times 0.1 = 0.01 + 0.01 = 0.02 \end{aligned}$$

We know that, for two events A and B, if $P(A \cap B) = P(A) \cdot P(B)$, then both are independent events.

Here, $P(A \cap B) = 0.02$ and $P(A) \cdot P(B) = 0.20 \times 0.10 = 0.02$

Thus, $P(A \cap B) = P(A) \cdot P(B) = 0.02$

Hence, A and B are independent events.

Q. 2 Refer to question 1 above. If the die were fair, determine whether or not the events A and B are independent.

Thinking Process

In a fair die, we have equally likely outcomes. So, with the given events A and B, we first find P(A), P(B) and P(A ∩ B) and then check whether they are dependent or independent.

Sol. Referring to the above solution, we have

$$A = \{(1, 1), (2, 2), (3, 3), (4, 4), (5, 5), (6, 6)\}$$

$\Rightarrow$ $n(A) = 6$ and $n(S) = 6^2 = 36$ [where, S is sample space]

$\therefore$ $P(A) = \dfrac{n(A)}{n(S)} = \dfrac{6}{36} = \dfrac{1}{6}$

and $B = \{(4, 6), (6, 4), (5, 5), (6, 5), (5, 6), (6, 6)\}$

$\Rightarrow$ $n(B) = 6$ and $n(S) = 6^2 = 36$

$\therefore$ $P(B) = \dfrac{n(B)}{n(S)} = \dfrac{6}{36} = \dfrac{1}{6}$

Also, $A \cap B = \{(5, 5), (6, 6)\}$

$\Rightarrow$ $n(A \cap B) = 2$ and $n(S) = 36$

$\therefore$ $P(A \cap B) = \dfrac{2}{36} = \dfrac{1}{18}$

Also, $P(A) \cdot P(B) = \dfrac{1}{36}$

Thus, $P(A \cap B) \neq P(A) \cdot P(B)$ $\left[\because \dfrac{1}{18} \neq \dfrac{1}{36}\right]$

So, we can say that both A and B are not independent events.

Q. 3 The probability that atleast one of the two events A and B occurs is 0.6. If A and B occur simultaneously with probability 0.3, evaluate $P(\bar{A}) + P(\bar{B})$.

Sol. We know that, $A \cup B$ denotes the occurrence of atleast one of A and B and $A \cap B$ denotes the occurrence of both A and B, simultaneously.

Thus, $P(A \cup B) = 0.6$ and $P(A \cap B) = 0.3$

Also, $P(A \cup B) = P(A) + P(B) - P(A \cap B)$

$\Rightarrow$ $0.6 = P(A) + P(B) - 0.3$

$\Rightarrow$ $P(A) + P(B) = 0.9$

$\Rightarrow$ $[1 - P(\bar{A})] + [1 - P(\bar{B})] = 0.9$ $[\because P(A) = 1 - P(\bar{A})$ and $P(B) = 1 - P(\bar{B})]$

$\Rightarrow$ $P(\bar{A}) + P(\bar{B}) = 2 - 0.9 = 1.1$

Q. 4 A bag contains 5 red marbles and 3 black marbles. Three marbles are drawn one by one without replacement. What is the probability that atleast one of the three marbles drawn be black, if the first marble is red?

Sol. Let $R = \{5 \text{ red marbles}\}$ and $B = \{3 \text{ black marbles}\}$

For atleast one of the three marbles drawn be black, if the first marble is red, then the following three conditions will be followed

(i) Second ball is black and third is red (E_1).

(ii) Second ball is black and third is also black (E_2).

(iii) Second ball is red and third is black (E_3).

$\therefore \quad P(E_1) = P(R_1) \cdot P(B_1 / R_1) \cdot P(R_2 / R_1 B_1) = \frac{5}{8} \cdot \frac{3}{7} \cdot \frac{4}{6} = \frac{60}{336} = \frac{5}{28}$

$P(E_2) = P(R_1) \cdot P(B_1 / R_1) \cdot P(B_2 / R_1 B_1) = \frac{5}{8} \cdot \frac{3}{7} \cdot \frac{2}{6} = \frac{30}{336} = \frac{5}{56}$

and $\quad P(E_3) = P(R_1) \cdot P(R_2 / R_1) \cdot P(B_1 / R_1 R_2) = \frac{5}{8} \cdot \frac{4}{7} \cdot \frac{3}{6} = \frac{60}{336} = \frac{5}{28}$

$\therefore \quad P(E) = P(E_1) + P(E_2) + P(E_3) = \frac{5}{28} + \frac{5}{56} + \frac{5}{28}$

$= \frac{10 + 5 + 10}{56} = \frac{25}{56}$

Q. 5 Two dice are thrown together and the total score is noted. The events *E*, *F* and *G* are 'a total of 4', 'a total of 9 or more' and 'a total divisible by 5', respectively. Calculate *P*(*E*), *P*(*F*) and *P*(*G*) and decide which pairs of events, if any are independent.

Sol. Two dice are thrown together *i.e.*, sample space $(S) = 36 \Rightarrow n(S) = 36$

$E = \text{A total of } 4 = \{(2, 2), (3, 1), (1, 3)\}$

$\Rightarrow \quad n(E) = 3$

$F = \text{A total of 9 or more}$

$= \{(3, 6), (6, 3), (4, 5), (4, 6), (5, 4), (6, 4), (5, 5), (5, 6), (6, 5), (6, 6)\}$

$\Rightarrow \quad n(F) = 10$

$G = \text{a total divisible by } 5 = \{(1, 4), (4, 1), (2, 3), (3, 2), (4, 6), (6, 4), (5, 5)\}$

$\Rightarrow \quad n(G) = 7$

Here, $\quad (E \cap F) = \phi$ and $(E \cap G) = \phi$

Also, $\quad (F \cap G) = \{(4, 6), (6, 4), (5, 5)\}$

$\Rightarrow \quad n(F \cap G) = 3$ and $(E \cap F \cap G) = \phi$

$\therefore \quad P(E) = \frac{n(E)}{n(S)} = \frac{3}{36} = \frac{1}{12}$

$P(F) = \frac{n(F)}{n(S)} = \frac{10}{36} = \frac{5}{18}$

$P(G) = \frac{n(G)}{n(S)} = \frac{7}{36}$

$P(F \cap G) = \frac{3}{36} = \frac{1}{12}$

and $\quad P(F) \cdot P(G) = \frac{5}{18} \cdot \frac{7}{36} = \frac{35}{648}$

Here, we see that $P(F \cap G) \neq P(F) \cdot P(G)$

[since, only *F* and *G* have common events, so only *F* and *G* are used here]

Hence, there is no pair which is independent.

Q. 6 Explain why the experiment of tossing a coin three times is said to have Binomial distribution.

Sol. We know that, a random variable *X* taking values 0, 1, 2, ..., *n* is said to have a binomial distribution with parameters *n* and *P*, if its probability distribution is given by

$$P(X = r) = {}^nC_r p^r q^{n-r}$$

where, $\quad q = 1 - p$

and $\quad r = 0, 1, 2, \ldots, n$

Similarly, in an experiment of tossing a coin three times, we have $n = 3$ and random variable X can take values $r = 0, 1, 2$ and 3 with $p = \frac{1}{2}$ and $q = \frac{1}{2}$

X	0	1	2	3
P(X)	${}^3C_0\, q^3$	${}^3C_1\, Pq^2$	${}^3C_2\, P^2q$	${}^3C_3\, P^3$

So, we see that in the experiment of tossing a coin three times, we have random variable X which can take values 0, 1, 2 and 3 with parameters $n = 3$ and $P = \frac{1}{2}$.

Therefore, it is said to have a Binomial distribution.

Q. 7 If A and B are two events such that

$$P(A) = \frac{1}{2},\ P(B) = \frac{1}{3} \text{ and } P(A \cap B) = \frac{1}{4}, \text{ then find}$$

(i) $P(A / B)$.
(ii) $P(B / A)$.
(iii) $P(A' / B)$.
(iv) $P(A' / B')$.

Sol. Here, $P(A) = \frac{1}{2},\ P(B) = \frac{1}{3}$ and $P(A \cap B) = \frac{1}{4}$

(i) $P(A/B) = \dfrac{P(A \cap B)}{P(B)} = \dfrac{1/4}{1/3} = \dfrac{3}{4}$

(ii) $P(B/A) = \dfrac{P(A \cap B)}{P(A)} = \dfrac{1/4}{1/2} = \dfrac{1}{2}$

(iii) $P(A'/B) = 1 - P(A/B) = 1 - \dfrac{3}{4} = \dfrac{1}{4}$

or $P(A'/B) = \dfrac{P(A' \cap B)}{P(B)} = \dfrac{P(B) - P(A \cap B)}{P(B)} = \dfrac{\frac{1}{3} - \frac{1}{4}}{\frac{1}{3}} = \dfrac{\frac{1}{12}}{\frac{1}{3}} = \dfrac{1}{4}$

(iv) $P(A'/B') = \dfrac{P(A' \cap B')}{P(B')} = \dfrac{1 - P(A \cup B)}{1 - P(B)} = \dfrac{1 - [P(A) + P(B) - P(A \cap B)]}{1 - P(B)}$

$$= \frac{1 - \left[\frac{1}{2} + \frac{1}{3} - \frac{1}{4}\right]}{1 - \frac{1}{3}} = \frac{1 - \left(\frac{5}{6} - \frac{1}{4}\right)}{\frac{2}{3}}$$

$$= \frac{1 - 14/24}{2/3} = \frac{10/24}{2/3} = \frac{30}{48} = \frac{5}{8}$$

Q. 8 Three events A, B and C have probabilities $\frac{2}{5}, \frac{1}{3}$ and $\frac{1}{2}$, respectively. If, $P(A \cap C) = \frac{1}{5}$ and $P(B \cap C) = \frac{1}{4}$, then find the values of $P(C/B)$ and $P(A' \cap C')$.

Sol. Here, $P(A) = \frac{2}{5},\ P(B) = \frac{1}{3},\ P(C) = \frac{1}{2},\ P(A \cap C) = \frac{1}{5}$ and $P(B \cap C) = \frac{1}{4}$

$\therefore$ $P(C/B) = \dfrac{P(B \cap C)}{P(B)} = \dfrac{1/4}{1/3} = \dfrac{3}{4}$

and $P(A' \cap C') = 1 - P(A \cup C) = 1 - [P(A) + P(C) - P(A \cap C)]$

$$= 1 - \left[\frac{2}{5} + \frac{1}{2} - \frac{1}{5}\right] = 1 - \left[\frac{4 + 5 - 2}{10}\right] = 1 - \frac{7}{10} = \frac{3}{10}$$

Q. 9 Let E_1 and E_2 be two independent events such that $P(E_1) = P_1$ and $P(E_2) = P_2$. Describe in words of the events whose probabilities are

(i) P_1P_2 (ii) $(1 - P_1)P_2$

(iii) $1 - (1 - P_1)(1 - P_2)$ (iv) $P_1 + P_2 - 2P_1P_2$

Sol. $P(E_1) = P_1$ and $P(E_2) = P_2$

(i) $P_1P_2 \Rightarrow P(E_1) \cdot P(E_2) = P(E_1 \cap E_2)$

So, E_1 and E_2 occur.

(ii) $(1 - P_1)P_2 = P(E_1)' \cdot P(E_2) = P(E_1' \cap E_2)$

So, E_1 does not occur but E_2 occurs.

(iii) $1 - (1 - P_1)(1 - P_2) = 1 - P(E_1)'P(E_2)' = 1 - P(E_1' \cap E_2')$

$= 1 - [1 - P(E_1 \cup E_2)] = P(E_1 \cup E_2)$

So, either E_1 or E_2 or both E_1 and E_2 occurs.

(iv) $P_1 + P_2 - 2P_1P_2 = P(E_1) + P(E_2) - 2P(E_1) \cdot P(E_2)$

$= P(E_1) + P(E_2) - 2P(E_1 \cap E_2)$

$= P(E_1 \cup E_2) - P(E_1 \cap E_2)$

So, either E_1 or E_2 occurs but not both.

Q. 10 A discrete random variable X has the probability distribution as given below

X	0.5	1	1.5	2
P(X)	k	k^2	$2k^2$	k

(i) Find the value of k.

(ii) Determine the mean of the distribution.

Sol. We have,

X	0.5	1	1.5	2
P(X)	k	k^2	$2k^2$	k

(i) We know that, $\sum_{i=1}^{n} P_i = 1$, where $P_i \geq 0$

$\Rightarrow \quad P_1 + P_2 + P_3 + P_4 = 1$

$\Rightarrow \quad k + k^2 + 2k^2 + k = 1$

$\Rightarrow \quad 3k^2 + 2k - 1 = 0$

$\Rightarrow \quad 3k^2 + 3k - k - 1 = 0$

$\Rightarrow \quad 3k(k + 1) - 1(k + 1) = 0$

$\Rightarrow \quad (3k - 1)(k + 1) = 0$

$\Rightarrow \quad k = 1/3 \Rightarrow k = -1$

Since, k is $\geq 0 \Rightarrow k = 1/3$

(ii) Mean of the distribution $(\mu) = E(X) = \sum_{i=1_i}^{n} x_i P_i$

$= 0.5(k) + 1(k^2) + 1.5(2k^2) + 2(k) = 4k^2 + 2.5k$

$= 4 \cdot \frac{1}{9} + 2.5 \cdot \frac{1}{3}$ $\quad \left[\because k = \frac{1}{3}\right]$

$= \frac{4 + 7.5}{9} = \frac{23}{18}$

Q. 11 Prove that

(i) $P(A) = P(A \cap B) + P(A \cap \bar{B})$

(ii) $P(A \cup B) = P(A \cap B) + P(A \cap \bar{B}) + P(\bar{A} \cap B)$

Sol. (i) $\because \quad P(A) = P(A \cap B) + P(A \cap \bar{B})$

$\therefore \quad \text{RHS} = P(A \cap B) + P(A \cap \bar{B})$

$= P(A) \cdot P(B) + P(A) \cdot P(\bar{B})$

$= P(A)[P(B) + P(\bar{B})]$

$= P(A)[P(B) + 1 - P(B)]$ $\quad [\because P(\bar{B}) = 1 - P(B)]$

$= P(A) = \text{LHS}$ **Hence proved.**

(ii) $\because P(A \cup B) = P(A \cap B) + P(A \cap \bar{B}) + P(\bar{A} \cap B)$

$\therefore \quad \text{RHS} = P(A) \cdot P(B) + P(A) \cdot P(\bar{B}) + P(\bar{A}) \cdot P(B)$

$= P(A) \cdot P(B) + P(A) \cdot [1 - P(B)] + [1 - P(A)]\, P(B)$

$= P(A) \cdot P(B) + P(A) - P(A) \cdot P(B) + P(B) - P(A) \cdot P(B)$

$= P(A) + P(B) - P(A) \cdot P(B)$

$= P(A) + P(B) - P(A \cap B)$

$= P(A \cup B) = \text{LHS}$ **Hence proved.**

Q. 12 If X is the number of tails in three tosses of a coin, then determine the standard deviation of X.

Thinking Process

First get the values of $P(X)$ at $x = 0, 1, 2, 3$ and then use the formula of standard deviation of $X = \sqrt{\text{Var}(X)}$, where $\text{Var}(X) = E(X^2) - [E(X)]^2 = \Sigma X^2 P(X) - [\Sigma XP(X)]^2$

Sol. Given that, random variable X is the number of tails in three tosses of a coin.

So, $\quad X = 0, 1, 2, 3.$

$\Rightarrow \quad P(X = x) = {}^nC_x (p)^x q^{n-x},$

where $\quad n = 3, p = 1/2, q = 1/2$ and $x = 0, 1, 2, 3$

X	0	1	2	3
$P(X)$	$\frac{1}{8}$	$\frac{3}{8}$	$\frac{3}{8}$	$\frac{1}{8}$
$XP(X)$	0	$\frac{3}{8}$	$\frac{3}{4}$	$\frac{3}{8}$
$X^2P(X)$	0	$\frac{3}{8}$	$\frac{3}{2}$	$\frac{9}{8}$

We know that, $\text{Var}(X) = E(X^2) - [E(X)]^2$ ...(i)

where, $E(X^2) = \sum_{i=1}^{n} x_i^2 P(x_i)$ and $E(X) = \sum_{i=1}^{n} x_i P(x_i)$

$$\therefore \quad E(X^2) = \sum_{i=1}^{n} x_i^2 P(X_i) = 0 + \frac{3}{8} + \frac{3}{2} + \frac{9}{8} = \frac{24}{8} = 3$$

and $$[E(X)]^2 = \left[\sum_{i=0}^{n} x_i^2 P(x_i)\right]^2 = \left[0 + \frac{3}{8} + \frac{3}{4} + \frac{3}{8}\right]^2 = \left[\frac{12}{8}\right]^2 = \frac{9}{4}$$

$$\therefore \quad \text{Var}(X) = 3 - \frac{9}{4} = \frac{3}{4} \quad \text{[using Eq. (i)]}$$

and standard deviation of $X = \sqrt{\text{Var}(X)} = \sqrt{\frac{3}{4}} = \frac{\sqrt{3}}{2}$

Q. 13 **In a dice game, a player pays a stake of ₹ 1 for each throw of a die. She receives ₹ 5, if the die shows a 3, ₹ 2, if the die shows a 1 or 6 and nothing otherwise, then what is the player's expected profit per throw over a long series of throws?**

Thinking Process

Take X as the random variable of profit per throw and at $X = -1, 1$ and 4 get the values of P(X) and use the formula expected profit $E(X) = \Sigma X P(X)$ to get the desired result.

Sol. Let X is the random variable of profit per throw.

X	-1	1	4
$P(X)$	$\frac{1}{2}$	$\frac{1}{3}$	$\frac{1}{6}$

Since, she loss ₹ 1 on getting any of 2, 4 or 5.

So, at $X = -1$, $P(X) = \frac{1}{6} + \frac{1}{6} + \frac{1}{6} = \frac{3}{6} = \frac{1}{2}$

Similarly, at $X = 1$, $P(X) = \frac{1}{6} + \frac{1}{6} = \frac{1}{3}$ [if die shows of either 1 or 6]

and at $X = 4$, $P(X) = \frac{1}{6}$ [if die shows a 3]

$\therefore$ Player's expected profit $= E(X) = \Sigma X P(X)$

$$= -1 \times \frac{1}{2} + 1 \times \frac{1}{3} + 4 \times \frac{1}{6}$$

$$= \frac{-3 + 2 + 4}{6} = \frac{3}{6} = \frac{1}{2} = ₹\,0.50$$

Q. 14 **Three dice are thrown at the same time. Find the probability of getting three two's, if it is known that the sum of the numbers on the dice was six.**

Sol. On a throw of three dice, we have sample space $[n(S)] = 6^3 = 216$

Let E_1 is the event when the sum of numbers on the dice was six and E_2 is the event when three two's occurs.

$\Rightarrow$ $E_1 = \{(1, 1, 4), (1, 2, 3), (1, 3, 2), (1, 4, 1), (2, 1, 3), (2, 2, 2), (2, 3, 1), (3, 1, 2), (3, 2, 1), (4, 1, 1)\}$

$\Rightarrow$ $n(E_1) = 10$ and $E_2 = \{2, 2, 2\}$

$\Rightarrow$ $n(E_2) = 1$

Also, $(E_1 \cap E_2) = 1$

$\therefore$ $P(E_2 / E_1) = \frac{P \cdot (E_1 \cap E_2)}{P(E_1)} = \frac{1/216}{10/216} = \frac{1}{10}$

Q. 15 **Suppose 10000 tickets are sold in a lottery each for ₹ 1. First prize is of ₹ 3000 and the second prize is of ₹ 2000. There are three third prizes of ₹ 500 each. If you buy one ticket, then what is your expectation?**

Thinking Process

Take X is the random variable for the prize, so at $X = 0$, 500, 2000 and 3000, get P(X) for each X and then use the formula of $E(X) = \Sigma X P(X)$ to get the answer.

Sol. Let X is the random variable for the prize.

X	0	500	2000	3000
$P(X)$	$\frac{9995}{10000}$	$\frac{3}{10000}$	$\frac{1}{10000}$	$\frac{1}{10000}$

Since, $E(X) = \Sigma X\, P(X)$

$$\therefore \quad E(X) = 0 \times \frac{9995}{10000} + \frac{1500}{10000} + \frac{2000}{10000} + \frac{3000}{10000}$$

$$= \frac{1500 + 2000 + 3000}{10000}$$

$$= \frac{6500}{10000} = \frac{13}{20} = ₹\,0.65$$

Q. 16 **A bag contains 4 white and 5 black balls. Another bag contains 9 white and 7 black balls. A ball is transferred from the first bag to the second and then a ball is drawn at random from the second bag. Find the probability that the ball drawn is white.**

Sol. Here, $W_1 = \{4 \text{ white balls}\}$ and $B_1 = \{5 \text{ black balls}\}$
and $W_2 = \{9 \text{ white balls}\}$ and $B_2 = \{7 \text{ black balls}\}$
Let E_1 is the event that ball transferred from the first bag is white and E_2 is the event that the ball transferred from the first bag is black.
Also, E is the event that the ball drawn from the second bag is white.

$$\therefore \quad P(E/E_1) = \frac{10}{17},\ P(E/E_2) = \frac{9}{17}$$

and $$P(E_1) = \frac{4}{9} \text{ and } P(E_2) = \frac{5}{9}$$

$$\therefore \quad P(E) = P(E_1)\cdot P(E/E_1) + P(E_2)\cdot P(E/E_2)$$

$$= \frac{4}{9}\cdot\frac{10}{17} + \frac{5}{9}\cdot\frac{9}{17}$$

$$= \frac{40+45}{153} = \frac{85}{153} = \frac{5}{9}$$

Q. 17 **Bag I contains 3 black and 2 white balls, bag II contains 2 black and 4 white balls. A bag and a ball is selected at random. Determine the probability of selecting a black ball.**

Sol. Bag I = $\{3B, 2W\}$, Bag II = $\{2B, 4W\}$

Let E_1 = Event that bag I is selected
E_2 = Event that bag II is selected
and E = Event that a black ball is selected

$$\Rightarrow \quad P(E_1) = 1/2,\ P(E_2) = \frac{1}{2},\ P(E/E_1) = \frac{3}{5},\ P(E/E_2) = \frac{2}{6} = \frac{1}{3}$$

$$\therefore \quad P(E) = P(E_1)\cdot P(E/E_1) + P(E_2)\cdot P(E/E_2)$$

$$= \frac{1}{2}\cdot\frac{3}{5} + \frac{1}{2}\cdot\frac{2}{6} = \frac{3}{10} + \frac{2}{12}$$

$$= \frac{18+10}{60} = \frac{28}{60} = \frac{7}{15}$$

Q. 18 A box has 5 blue and 4 red balls. One ball is drawn at random and not replaced. Its colour is also not noted. Then, another ball is drawn at random. What is the probability of second ball being blue?

Sol. A box = {5 blue, 4 red}

Let E_1 is the event that first ball drawn is blue, E_2 is the event that first ball drawn is red and E is the event that second ball drawn is blue.

$$\therefore \quad P(E) = P(E_1)\cdot P(E/E_1) + P(E_2)\cdot P(E/E_2)$$

$$= \frac{5}{9}\cdot\frac{4}{8} + \frac{4}{9}\cdot\frac{5}{8} = \frac{20}{72} + \frac{20}{72} = \frac{40}{72} = \frac{5}{9}$$

Q. 19 Four cards are successively drawn without replacement from a deck of 52 playing cards. What is the probability that all the four cards are king?

Sol. Let E_1, E_2, E_3 and E_4 are the events that the first, second, third and fourth card is king, respectively.

$$\therefore \quad P(E_1 \cap E_2 \cap E_3 \cap E_4) = P(E_1)\cdot P(E_2/E_1)\cdot P(E_3/E_1 \cap E_2)\cdot P[E_4/(E_1 \cap E_2 \cap E_3 \cap E_4)]$$

$$= \frac{4}{52}\cdot\frac{3}{51}\cdot\frac{2}{50}\cdot\frac{1}{49} = \frac{24}{52\cdot 51\cdot 50\cdot 49}$$

$$= \frac{1}{13\cdot 17\cdot 25\cdot 49} = \frac{1}{270725}$$

Q. 20 If a die is thrown 5 times, then find the probability that an odd number will come up exactly three times.

Sol. Here, $n = 5,\ p = \left(\frac{1}{6}+\frac{1}{6}+\frac{1}{6}\right) = \frac{1}{2}$ and $q = 1 - p = 1 - \frac{1}{2} = \frac{1}{2}$

Also, $r = 3$

$$\therefore \quad P(X = r) = {}^nC_r (p)^r (q)^{n-r} = {}^5C_3\left(\frac{1}{2}\right)^3\left(\frac{1}{2}\right)^{5-3}$$

$$= \frac{5!}{3!2!}\cdot\frac{1}{8}\cdot\frac{1}{4} = \frac{10}{32} = \frac{5}{16}$$

Q. 21 If ten coins are tossed, then what is the probability of getting atleast 8 heads?

Thinking Process

For getting atleast 8 heads, take random variable X for getting head on tossing a coin. So, get sum of P(8), P(9) and P(10) to get the answer.

Sol. In this case, we have to find out the probability of getting atleast 8 heads. Let X is the random variable for getting a head.

Here, $n = 10,\ r \ge 8,$

i.e., $r = 8, 9, 10,\ p = \frac{1}{2}, q = \frac{1}{2}$

We know that, $P(X = r) = {}^nC_r p^r q^{n-r}$

$\therefore \quad P(X = r) = P(r = 8) + P(r = 9) + P(r = 10)$

$$= {}^{10}C_8\left(\frac{1}{2}\right)^8\left(\frac{1}{2}\right)^{10-8} + {}^{10}C_9\left(\frac{1}{2}\right)^9\left(\frac{1}{2}\right)^{10-9} + {}^{10}C_{10}\left(\frac{1}{2}\right)^{10}\left(\frac{1}{2}\right)^{10-10}$$

$$= \frac{10!}{8!2!}\left(\frac{1}{2}\right)^{10} + \frac{10!}{9!1!}\left(\frac{1}{2}\right)^{10} + \frac{10!}{0!10!}\left(\frac{1}{2}\right)^{10}$$

$$= \left(\frac{1}{2}\right)^{10}\left[\frac{10 \times 9}{2} + 10 + 1\right]$$

$$= \left(\frac{1}{2}\right)^{10} \cdot 56 = \frac{1}{2^7 \cdot 2^3} \cdot 56 = \frac{7}{128}$$

Q. 22 The probability of a man hitting a target is 0.25. If he shoots 7 times, then what is the probability of his hitting atleast twice?

Thinking Process

Using Binomial distribution $P(X = r)$ to get the answer. Here,

$$P(X = r) = 1 - [P(r = 0) + P(r = 1)]$$

Sol. Here, $\quad n = 7\ p = 0.25 = \frac{1}{4}, q = 1 - \frac{1}{4} = \frac{3}{4} r \geq 2,$

where, $\quad P(X) = {}^nC_r(p)^r(q)^{n-r}$

In this case for easy approach we shall first find out the probability of his hitting atmost once (*i.e.*, $r = 0, 1$) and then subtract this probability from 1 to get the desired probability.

$\therefore \quad P(X = r) = 1 - [P(r = 0) + P(r = 1)]$

$$= 1 - \left[{}^7C_0\left(\frac{1}{4}\right)^0\left(\frac{3}{4}\right)^{7-0} + {}^7C_1\left(\frac{1}{4}\right)^1\left(\frac{3}{4}\right)^{7-1}\right]$$

$$= 1 - \left[\frac{7!}{0!7!}\left(\frac{3}{4}\right)^7 + \frac{7!}{1!6!}\left(\frac{1}{4}\right)\left(\frac{3}{4}\right)^6\right]$$

$$= 1 - \left[\left(\frac{3}{4}\right)^6\left(\frac{3}{4} \cdot 1 + \frac{1}{4} \cdot 7\right)\right]$$

$$= 1 - \left[\frac{3^6}{4^6}\left(\frac{10}{4}\right)\right] = 1 - \left[\frac{3^6 \times 10}{4^7}\right] = 1 - \left[\frac{27 \cdot 27 \cdot 10}{64 \cdot 256}\right]$$

$$= 1 - \left[\frac{7290}{16384}\right] = 1 - \frac{3645}{8192} = \frac{4547}{8192}$$

Q. 23 A lot of 100 watches is known to have 10 defective watches. If 8 watches are selected (one by one with replacement) at random, then what is the probability that there will be atleast one defective watch?

Sol. Probability of defective watch from a lot of 100 watches $= \frac{10}{100} = \frac{1}{10}$

$\therefore \quad p = 1/10, q = \frac{9}{10}, n = 8$ and $r \geq 1$

$\therefore \quad P(r \geq 1) = 1 - P(r = 0) = 1 - {}^8C_0\left(\frac{1}{10}\right)^0\left(\frac{9}{10}\right)^{8-0}$

$$= 1 - \frac{8!}{0!8!} \cdot \left(\frac{9}{10}\right)^8 = 1 - \left(\frac{9}{10}\right)^8$$

Q. 24 Consider the probability distribution of a random variable X.

X	0	1	2	3	4
$P(X)$	0.1	0.25	0.3	0.2	0.15

Calculate

(i) $V\left(\frac{X}{2}\right)$. (ii) Variance of X.

Sol. We have,

X	**0**	**1**	**2**	**3**	**4**
$P(X)$	0.1	0.25	0.3	0.2	0.15
$XP(X)$	0	0.25	0.6	0.6	0.60
$X^2P(X)$	0	0.25	1.2	1.8	2.40

$$\text{Var}(X) = E(X^2) - [E(X)]^2$$

where, $$E(X) = \mu = \sum_{i=1}^{n} x_i P_i(xi)$$

and $$E(X^2) = \sum_{i=1}^{n} x_i^2 P(x_i)$$

$\therefore$ $$E(X) = 0 + 0.25 + 0.6 + 0.6 + 0.60 = 2.05$$
$$E(X^2) = 0 + 0.25 + 1.2 + 1.8 + 2.40 = 5.65$$

(i) $$V\left(\frac{X}{2}\right) = \frac{1}{4}V(X) = \frac{1}{4}[5.65 - (2.05)^2]$$
$$= \frac{1}{4}[5.65 - 4.2025] = \frac{1}{4} \times 1.4475 = 0.361875$$

(ii) $V(X) = 1.4475$

Q. 25 The probability distribution of a random variable X is given below

X	0	1	2	3
$P(X)$	k	$\frac{k}{2}$	$\frac{k}{4}$	$\frac{k}{8}$

(i) Determine the value of k.
(ii) Determine $P(X \le 2)$ and $P(X > 2)$.
(iii) Find $P(X \le 2) + P(X > 2)$.

Sol. We have,

X	0	1	2	3
$P(X)$	k	$\frac{k}{2}$	$\frac{k}{4}$	$\frac{k}{8}$

(i) Since, $$\sum_{i=1}^{n} P_i = 1, i = 1, 2, \ldots, n \text{ and } P_i \ge 0$$

$\therefore$ $$k + \frac{k}{2} + \frac{k}{4} + \frac{k}{8} = 1$$

$\Rightarrow$ $$8k + 4k + 2k + k = 8$$

$\therefore$ $$k = \frac{8}{15}$$

(ii) $P(X \le 2) = P(0) + P(1) + P(2) = k + \frac{k}{2} + \frac{k}{4}$

$$= \frac{(4k + 2k + k)}{4} = \frac{7k}{4} = \frac{7}{4} \cdot \frac{8}{15} = \frac{14}{15}$$

and $$P(X > 2) = P(3) = \frac{k}{8} = \frac{1}{8} \cdot \frac{8}{15} = \frac{1}{15}$$

(iii) $P(X \le 2) + P(X > 2) = \frac{14}{15} + \frac{1}{15} = 1$

Q. 26 **For the following probability distribution determine standard deviation of the random variable *X*.**

X	2	3	4
P(X)	0.2	0.5	0.3

Sol. We have,

X	**2**	**3**	**4**
P(X)	0.2	0.5	0.3
XP(X)	0.4	1.5	1.2
$X^2P(X)$	0.8	4.5	4.8

We know that, standard deviation of $X = \sqrt{\text{Var} X}$

where, $$\text{Var} X = E(X^2) - [E(X)]^2$$

$$= \sum_{i=1}^{n} x_i^2 \, P(x_i) - \left[\sum_{i=1}^{n} x_i P_i\right]^2$$

$\therefore$ $$\text{Var } X = [0.8 + 4.5 + 4.8] - [0.4 + 1.5 + 1.2]^2$$

$$= 10.1 - (3.1)^2 = 10.1 - 9.61 = 0.49$$

$\therefore$ Standard deviation of $X = \sqrt{\text{Var} X} = \sqrt{0.49} = 0.7$

Q. 27 **A biased die is such that $P(4) = \frac{1}{10}$ and other scores being equally likely. The die is tossed twice. If *X* is the 'number of fours seen', then find the variance of the random variable *X*.**

Sol. Since, X = Number of fours seen

On tossing two die, $X = 0, 1, 2$.

Also, $$P_{(4)} = \frac{1}{10} \text{ and } P_{(\text{not } 4)} = \frac{9}{10}$$

So, $$P(X = 0) = P_{(\text{not } 4)} \cdot P_{(\text{not } 4)} = \frac{9}{10} \cdot \frac{9}{10} = \frac{81}{100}$$

$$P(X = 1) = P_{(\text{not } 4)} \cdot P_{(4)} + P_{(4)} \cdot P_{(\text{not } 4)} = \frac{9}{10} \cdot \frac{1}{10} + \frac{1}{10} \cdot \frac{9}{10} = \frac{18}{100}$$

$$P(X = 2) = P_{(4)} \cdot P_{(4)} = \frac{1}{10} \cdot \frac{1}{10} = \frac{1}{100}$$

Thus, we get following table

X	**0**	**1**	**2**
P(X)	$\frac{81}{100}$	$\frac{18}{100}$	$\frac{1}{100}$
XP(X)	0	18/100	2/100
$X^2P(X)$	0	18/100	4/100

$$\therefore \quad \text{Var}(X) = E(X^2) - [E(X)]^2 = \Sigma X^2 P(X) - [\Sigma XP(X)]^2$$
$$= \left[0 + \frac{18}{100} + \frac{4}{100}\right] - \left[0 + \frac{18}{100} + \frac{2}{100}\right]^2$$
$$= \frac{22}{100} - \left(\frac{20}{100}\right)^2 = \frac{11}{50} - \frac{1}{25}$$
$$= \frac{11-2}{50} = \frac{9}{50} = \frac{18}{100} = 0.18$$

Q. 28 A die is thrown three times. Let X be the 'number of twos seen', find the expectation of X.

Sol. We have, $X =$ number of twos seen

So, on throwing a die three times, we will have $X = 0, 1, 2, 3$.

$$\therefore \quad P(X=0) = P_{(\text{not } 2)} \cdot P_{(\text{not } 2)} \cdot P_{(\text{not } 2)} = \frac{5}{6} \cdot \frac{5}{6} \cdot \frac{5}{6} = \frac{125}{216}$$
$$P(X=1) = P_{((\text{not } 2)} \cdot P_{(\text{not } 2)} \cdot P_{(2)} + P_{(\text{not } 2)} \cdot P_{(2)} \cdot P_{(\text{not } 2)} + P_{(2)} \cdot P_{(\text{not } 2)} \cdot P_{(\text{not } 2)}$$
$$= \frac{5}{6} \cdot \frac{5}{6} \cdot \frac{1}{6} + \frac{5}{6} \cdot \frac{1}{6} \cdot \frac{5}{6} + \frac{1}{6} \cdot \frac{5}{6} \cdot \frac{5}{6} = \frac{25}{36} \cdot \frac{3}{6} = \frac{25}{72}$$
$$P(X=2) = P_{(\text{not } 2)} \cdot P_{(2)} \cdot P_{(2)} + P_{(2)} \cdot P_{(2)} \cdot P_{(\text{not } 2)} + P_{(2)} \cdot P_{(\text{not } 2)} + P_{(2)}$$
$$= \frac{5}{6} \cdot \frac{1}{6} \cdot \frac{1}{6} + \frac{1}{6} \cdot \frac{1}{6} \cdot \frac{5}{6} + \frac{1}{6} \cdot \frac{5}{6} \cdot \frac{1}{6}$$
$$= \frac{1}{36} \cdot \left[\frac{15}{6}\right] = \frac{15}{216}$$
$$P(X=3) = P_{(2)} \cdot P_{(2)} \cdot P_{(2)} = \frac{1}{6} \cdot \frac{1}{6} \cdot \frac{1}{6} = \frac{1}{216}$$

We know that, $E(X) = \Sigma X\,P(X) = 0 \cdot \frac{125}{216} + 1 \cdot \frac{25}{72} + 2 \cdot \frac{15}{216} + 3 \cdot \frac{1}{216}$
$$= \frac{75 + 30 + 3}{216} = \frac{108}{216} = \frac{1}{2}$$

Q. 29 Two biased dice are thrown together. For the first die $P(6) = \frac{1}{2}$, the other scores being equally likely while for the second die $P(1) = \frac{2}{5}$ and the other scores are equally likely. Find the probability distribution of 'the number of one's seen'.

Sol. For first die, $P(6) = \frac{1}{2}$ and $P(6') = \frac{1}{2}$

$$\Rightarrow \quad P(1) + P(2) + P(3) + P(4) + P(5) = \frac{1}{2}$$
$$\Rightarrow \quad P(1) = \frac{1}{10} \text{ and } P(1') = \frac{9}{10} \qquad [\because P(1) = P(2) = P(3) = P(4) = P(5)]$$

For second die, $P(1) = \frac{2}{5}$ and $P(1') = 1 - \frac{2}{5} = \frac{3}{5}$

Let X = Number of one's seen

For $X = 0$, $P(X = 0) = P(1') \cdot P(1') = \frac{9}{10} \cdot \frac{3}{5} = \frac{27}{50} = 0.54$

$$P(X = 1) = P(1') \cdot P(1') + P(1') \cdot P(1') = \frac{9}{10} \cdot \frac{2}{5} + \frac{1}{10} \cdot \frac{3}{5}$$

$$= \frac{18}{50} + \frac{3}{50} = \frac{21}{50} = 0.42$$

$$P(X = 2) = P(1) \cdot P(1) = \frac{1}{10} \cdot \frac{2}{5} = \frac{2}{50} = 0.04$$

Hence, the required probability distribution is as below

X	0	1	2
P (X)	0.54	0.42	0.04

Q. 30 Two probability distributions of the discrete random variables X and Y are given below.

X	0	1	2	3
P(X)	$\frac{1}{5}$	$\frac{2}{5}$	$\frac{1}{5}$	$\frac{1}{5}$

Y	0	1	2	3
P (Y)	$\frac{1}{5}$	$\frac{3}{10}$	$\frac{2}{5}$	$\frac{1}{10}$

Prove that $E(Y^2) = 2E(X)$.

Sol.

X	0	1	2	3
P (X)	$\frac{1}{5}$	$\frac{2}{5}$	$\frac{1}{5}$	$\frac{1}{5}$

Y	0	1	2	3
P (Y)	$\frac{1}{5}$	$\frac{3}{10}$	$\frac{2}{5}$	$\frac{1}{10}$

Since, we have to prove that, $E(Y^2) = 2E(X)$

$$\therefore \quad E(X) = \Sigma X\, P(X)$$

$$= 0 \cdot \frac{1}{5} + 1 \cdot \frac{2}{5} + 2 \cdot \frac{1}{5} + 3 \cdot \frac{1}{5} = \frac{7}{5}$$

$$\Rightarrow \quad 2E(X) = \frac{14}{5} \quad \text{...(i)}$$

$$E(Y)^2 = \Sigma Y^2 P(Y)$$

$$= 0 \cdot \frac{1}{5} + 1 \cdot \frac{3}{10} + 4 \cdot \frac{2}{5} + 9 \cdot \frac{1}{10}$$

$$= \frac{3}{10} + \frac{8}{5} + \frac{9}{10} = \frac{28}{10} = \frac{14}{5}$$

$$\Rightarrow \quad E(Y^2) = \frac{14}{5} \quad \text{...(ii)}$$

From Eqs. (i) and (ii),

$$E(Y^2) = 2E(X)$$ **Hence proved.**

Q. 31 **A factory produces bulbs. The probability that any one bulb is defective is $\frac{1}{50}$ and they are packed in 10 boxes. From a single box, find the probability that**

(i) none of the bulbs is defective.

(ii) exactly two bulbs are defective.

(iii) more than 8 bulbs work properly.

Sol. Let X is the random variable which denotes that a bulb is defective.

Also, $n = 10, p = \frac{1}{50}$ and $q = \frac{49}{50}$ and $P(X = r) = {}^nC_r\, p^r q^{n-r}$

(i) None of the bulbs is defective *i.e.*, $r = 0$

$$\therefore \quad p(X = r) = P_{(0)} = {}^{10}C_0\left(\frac{1}{50}\right)^0\left(\frac{49}{50}\right)^{10-0} = \left(\frac{49}{50}\right)^{10}$$

(ii) Exactly two bulbs are defective *i.e.*, $r = 2$

$$\therefore \quad P(X = r) = P_{(2)} = {}^{10}C_2\left(\frac{1}{50}\right)^2\left(\frac{49}{50}\right)^8$$

$$= \frac{10!}{8!2!}\left(\frac{1}{50}\right)^2 \cdot \left(\frac{49}{50}\right)^8 = 45 \times \left(\frac{1}{50}\right)^{10} \times (49)^8$$

(iii) More than 8 bulbs work properly *i.e.*, there is less than 2 bulbs which are defective.

So, $\quad r < 2 \Rightarrow r = 0, 1$

$$\therefore \quad P(X = r) = P(r < 2) = P(0) + P(1)$$

$$= {}^{10}C_0\left(\frac{1}{50}\right)^0\left(\frac{49}{50}\right)^{10-0} + {}^{10}C_1\left(\frac{1}{50}\right)^1\left(\frac{49}{50}\right)^{10-1}$$

$$= \left(\frac{49}{50}\right)^{10} + \frac{10!}{1!9!}\cdot\frac{1}{50}\cdot\left(\frac{49}{50}\right)^9$$

$$= \left(\frac{49}{50}\right)^{10} + \frac{1}{5}\cdot\left(\frac{49}{50}\right)^9 = \left(\frac{49}{50}\right)^9\left(\frac{49}{50} + \frac{1}{5}\right)$$

$$= \left(\frac{49}{50}\right)^9\left(\frac{59}{50}\right) = \frac{59\,(49)^9}{(50)^{10}}$$

Q. 32 **Suppose you have two coins which appear identical in your pocket. You know that, one is fair and one is 2 headed. If you take one out, toss it and get a head, what is the probability that it was a fair coin?**

Sol. Let E_1 = Event that fair coin is drawn

E_2 = Event that 2 headed coin is drawn

E = Event that tossed coin get a head

$$\therefore \quad P(E_1) = 1/2, P(E_2) = 1/2,\ P(E/E_1) = 1/2 \text{ and } P(E/E_2) = 1$$

Now, using Baye's theorem $P(E_1/E) = \dfrac{P(E_1)\cdot P(E/E_1)}{P(E_1)\cdot P(E/E_1) + P(E_2)\cdot P(E/E_2)}$

$$= \frac{\frac{1}{2}\cdot\frac{1}{2}}{\frac{1}{2}\cdot\frac{1}{2} + \frac{1}{2}\cdot 1} = \frac{\frac{1}{4}}{\frac{1}{4} + \frac{1}{2}} = \frac{\frac{1}{4}}{\frac{3}{4}} = \frac{1}{3}$$

Q. 33 Suppose that 6% of the people with blood group O are left handed and 10% of those with other blood groups are left handed, 30% of the people have blood group O. If a left handed person is selected at random, what is the probability that he/she will have blood group O?

Sol.

		Blood group 'O'	Other than blood group 'O'
I.	Number of people	30 %	70 %
II.	Percentage of left handed people	6 %	10 %

E_1 = Event that the person selected is of blood group O

E_2 = Event that the person selected is of other than blood group O

(E_3) = Event that selected person is left handed

$$\therefore \quad P(E_1) = 0.30,\ P(E_2) = 0.70$$

$$P(E_3/E_1) = 0.06 \text{ and } P(E_3/E_2) = 0.10$$

By using Baye's theorem, $P(E_1/E_3) = \dfrac{P(E_1)\cdot P(E_3/E_1)}{P(E_1)\cdot P(E_3/E_1) + P(E_2)\cdot P(E_3/E_2)}$

$$= \frac{0.30 \times 0.06}{0.30 \cdot 0.06 + 0.70 \cdot 0.10}$$

$$= \frac{0.0180}{0.0180 + 0.0700}$$

$$= \frac{0.0180}{0.0880} = \frac{180}{880} = \frac{9}{44}$$

Q. 34 If two natural numbers r and s are drawn one at a time, without replacement from the set $S = \{1, 2, 3, \ldots n\}$, then find $P(r \leq p / s \leq p)$, where $p \in S$.

Sol. $\because$ Set $S = \{1, 2, 3, \ldots, n\}$

$$\therefore \quad P(r \leq p/s \leq p) = \frac{P(p \cap S)}{P(S)}$$

$$= \frac{p-1}{n} \times \frac{n}{n-1} = \frac{p-1}{n-1}$$

Q. 35 Find the probability distribution of the maximum of the two scores obtained when a die is thrown twice. Determine also the mean of the distribution.

Sol. Let X is the random variable score obtained when a die is thrown twice.

$\therefore \quad X = 1, 2, 3, 4, 5, 6$

Here, $\quad S = \{(1, 1), (1, 2), (2, 1), (2, 2), (1, 3), (2, 3), (3, 1), (3, 2), (3, 3), \ldots, (6, 6)\}$

$$\therefore \quad P(X = 1) = \frac{1}{6}\cdot\frac{1}{6} = \frac{1}{36}$$

$$P(X = 2) = \frac{1}{6}\cdot\frac{1}{6} + \frac{1}{6}\cdot\frac{1}{6} + \frac{1}{6}\cdot\frac{1}{6} = \frac{3}{36}$$

$$P(X = 3) = \frac{1}{6}\cdot\frac{1}{6} + \frac{1}{6}\cdot\frac{1}{6} + \frac{1}{6}\cdot\frac{1}{6} + \frac{1}{6}\cdot\frac{1}{6} + \frac{1}{6}\cdot\frac{1}{6} = \frac{5}{36}$$

Similarly, $P(X = 4) = \frac{7}{36}$

$P(X = 5) = \frac{9}{36}$

$P(X = 6) = \frac{11}{36}$

So, the required distribution is,

X	1	2	3	4	5	6
P(x)	1/36	3/36	5/36	7/36	9/36	11/36

Also, we know that, Mean $\{E(X)\} = \Sigma X\, P(X)$

$$= \frac{1}{36} + \frac{6}{36} + \frac{15}{36} + \frac{28}{36} + \frac{45}{36} + \frac{66}{36} = \frac{161}{36}$$

Q. 36 **The random variable X can take only the values 0, 1, 2. If**

$$P(X = 0) = P(X = 1) = p \text{ and } E(X^2) = E[X],$$

then find the value of p.

Sol. Since, $X = 0, 1, 2$ and $P(X)$ at $X = 0$ and 1 is p, let at $X = 2$, $P(X)$ is x.

$\Rightarrow \quad p + p + x = 1$

$\Rightarrow \quad x = 1 - 2p$

We get, the following distribution.

X	0	1	2
P (X)	p	p	$1-2p$

$\therefore \quad E[X] = \Sigma X\, P(X)$

$= 0 \cdot p + 1 \cdot p + 2(1 - 2p)$

$= p + 2 - 4p = 2 - 3p$

and $\quad E(X^2) = \Sigma X^2\, P(X)$

$= 0 \cdot p + 1 \cdot p + 4 \cdot (1 - 2p)$

$= p + 4 - 8p = 4 - 7p$

Also, given that $E(X^2) = E[X]$

$\Rightarrow \quad 4 - 7p = 2 - 3p$

$\Rightarrow \quad 4p = 2 \Rightarrow p = \frac{1}{2}$

Q. 37 **Find the variance of the following distribution.**

X	0	1	2	3	4	5
P (X)	$\frac{1}{6}$	$\frac{5}{18}$	$\frac{2}{9}$	$\frac{1}{6}$	$\frac{1}{9}$	$\frac{1}{18}$

Sol. We have,

X	**0**	**1**	**2**	**3**	**4**	**5**
P (X)	$\frac{1}{6}$	$\frac{5}{18}$	$\frac{2}{9}$	$\frac{1}{6}$	$\frac{1}{9}$	$\frac{1}{18}$
X P (X)	0	$\frac{5}{18}$	$\frac{4}{9}$	$\frac{1}{2}$	$\frac{4}{9}$	$\frac{5}{18}$
X^2 P (X)	0	$\frac{5}{18}$	$\frac{8}{9}$	$\frac{3}{2}$	$\frac{16}{9}$	$\frac{25}{18}$

$\therefore$ Variance $= E(X^2) - [E(X)]^2 = \Sigma X^2 P(X) - [\Sigma X P(X)]^2$

$$= \left[0 + \frac{5}{18} + \frac{8}{9} + \frac{3}{2} + \frac{16}{9} + \frac{25}{18}\right] - \left[0 + \frac{5}{18} + \frac{4}{9} + \frac{1}{2} + \frac{4}{9} + \frac{5}{18}\right]^2$$

$$= \left[\frac{5 + 16 + 27 + 32 + 25}{18}\right] - \left[\frac{5 + 8 + 9 + 8 + 5}{18}\right]^2$$

$$= \frac{105}{18} - \frac{35 \cdot 35}{18 \cdot 18} = \frac{18 \cdot 105 - 35 \cdot 35}{18 \cdot 18}$$

$$= \frac{35}{18 \cdot 18}[54 - 35] = \frac{19 \cdot 35}{324} = \frac{665}{324}$$

Q. 38 **A and B throw a pair of dice alternately. A wins the game, if he gets a total of 6 and B wins, if she gets a total of 7. If A starts the game, then find the probability of winning the game by A in third throw of the pair of dice.**

Sol. Let A_1 = A total of 6 = {(2, 4), (1, 5), (5, 1), (4, 2), (3, 3)}

and B_1 = A total of 7 = {(2, 5), (1, 6), (6, 1), (5, 2), (3, 4), (4, 3)}

Let $P(A)$ is the probability, if A wins in a throw $\Rightarrow P(A) = \frac{5}{36}$

and $P(B)$ is the probability, if B wins in a throw $\Rightarrow P(B) = \frac{1}{6}$

$\therefore$ Required probability $= P(\bar{A}) \cdot P(\bar{B}) \cdot P(A) = \frac{31}{36} \cdot \frac{5}{6} \cdot \frac{5}{36} = \frac{775}{216 \cdot 36} = \frac{775}{7776}$

Q. 39 **Two dice are tossed. Find whether the following two events A and B are independent $A = \{(x, y) : x + y = 11\}$ and $B = \{(x, y): x \neq 5\}$, where (x, y) denotes a typical sample point.**

Sol. We have, $A = \{(x, y) : x + y = 11\}$ and $B = \{(x, y): x \neq 5\}$

$\therefore$ A = {(5, 6), (6, 5)}, B = {(1,1), (1,2), (1,3), (1,4), (1,5) (1,6), (2,1), (2,2), (2,3), (2,4), (2,5) (2,6), (3,1), (3,2), (3,3), (3,4), (3,5) (3,6), (4,1), (4,2), (4,3), (4,4), (4,5) (4,6), (6,1), (6,2), (6,3), (6,4), (6,5), (6,6)}

$\Rightarrow$ $n(A) = 2$, $n(B) = 30$ and $n(A \cap B) = 1$

$\therefore$ $P(A) = \frac{2}{36} = \frac{1}{18}$ and $P(B) = \frac{30}{36} = \frac{5}{6}$

$\Rightarrow$ $P(A) \cdot P(B) = \frac{5}{108}$ and $P(A \cap B) = \frac{1}{36} \neq P(A) \cdot P(B)$

So, A and B are not independent.

Q. 40 **An urn contains m white and n black balls. A ball is drawn at random and is put back into the urn along with k additional balls of the same colour as that of the ball drawn. A ball is again drawn at random. Show that the probability of drawing a white ball now does not depend on k.**

Sol. Let U = {m white, n black balls}

E_1 = {First ball drawn of white colour}

E_2 = {First ball drawn of black colour}

and E_3 = {Second ball drawn of white colour}

$\therefore \quad P(E_1) = \dfrac{m}{m+n}$ and $P(E_2) = \dfrac{n}{m+n}$

Also, $\quad P(E_3/E_1) = \dfrac{m+k}{m+n+k}$ and $P(E_3/E_2) = \dfrac{m}{m+n+k}$

$$\therefore \quad P(E_3) = P(E_1)\cdot P(E_3/E_1) + P(E_2)\cdot P(E_3/E_2)$$
$$= \frac{m}{m+n}\cdot\frac{m+k}{m+n+k} + \frac{n}{m+n}\cdot\frac{m}{m+n+k}$$
$$= \frac{m(m+k)+nm}{(m+n+k)(m+n)} = \frac{m^2+mk+nm}{(m+n+k)(m+n)}$$
$$= \frac{m(m+k+n)}{(m+n+k)(m+n)} = \frac{m}{m+n}$$

Hence, the probability of drawing a white ball does not depend on k.

Long Answer Type Questions

Q. 41 Three bags contain a number of red and white balls as follows Bag I : 3 red balls, Bag II : 2 red balls and 1 white ball and Bag III : 3 white balls. The probability that bag i will be chosen and a ball is selected from it is $\frac{i}{6}$, where $i = 1, 2, 3$. What is the probability that

(i) a red ball will be selected? (ii) a white ball is selected?

Sol. Bag I : 3 red balls and 0 white ball.
Bag II : 2 red balls and 1 white ball.
Beg III : 0 red ball and 3 white balls.
Let E_1, E_2 and E_3 be the events that bag I , bag II and bag III is selected and a ball is chosen from it.

$$P(E_1) = \frac{1}{6},\ P(E_2) = \frac{2}{6} \text{ and } P(E_3) = \frac{3}{6}$$

(i) Let E be the event that a red ball is selected. Then, probability that red ball will be selected

$$P(E) = P(E_1)\cdot P(E/E_1) + P(E_2)\cdot P(E/E_2) + P(E_3)\cdot P(E/E_3)$$
$$= \frac{1}{6}\cdot\frac{3}{3} + \frac{2}{6}\cdot\frac{2}{3} + \frac{3}{6}\cdot 0$$
$$= \frac{1}{6} + \frac{2}{9} + 0$$
$$= \frac{3+4}{18} = \frac{7}{18}$$

(ii) Let F be the event that a white ball is selected.

$$\therefore \quad P(F) = P(E_1)\cdot P(F/E_1) + P(E_2)\cdot P(F/E_2) + P(E_3)\cdot P(F/E_3)$$
$$= \frac{1}{6}\cdot 0 + \frac{2}{6}\cdot\frac{1}{3} + \frac{3}{6}\cdot 1 = \frac{1}{9} + \frac{3}{6} = \frac{11}{18}$$

Note $P(F) = 1 - P(E) = 1 - \frac{7}{18} = \frac{11}{18}$ *[since, we know that $P(E) + P(F) = 1$]*

Q. 42 Refer to question 41 above. If a white ball is selected, what is the probability that it came from

(i) Bag II? (ii) Bag III?

Sol. Referring to the previous solution, using Bay's theorem, we have

(i) $$P(E_2/F)=\frac{P(E_2)\cdot P(F/E_2)}{P(E_1)\cdot P(F/E_1)+P(E_2)\cdot P(F/E_2)+P(E_3)\cdot P(F/E_3)}$$

$$=\frac{\frac{2}{6}\cdot\frac{1}{3}}{\frac{1}{6}\cdot 0+\frac{2}{6}\cdot\frac{1}{3}+\frac{3}{6}\cdot 1}=\frac{\frac{2}{18}}{\frac{2}{18}+\frac{3}{6}}$$

$$=\frac{2/18}{\frac{2+9}{18}}=\frac{2}{11}$$

(ii) $$P(E_3/F)=\frac{P(E_3)\cdot P(F/E_3)}{P(E_1)\cdot P(F/E_1)+P(E_2)\cdot P(F/E_2)+P(E_3)\cdot P(F/E_3)}$$

$$=\frac{\frac{3}{6}\cdot 1}{\frac{1}{6}\cdot 0+\frac{2}{6}\cdot\frac{1}{3}+\frac{3}{6}\cdot 1}$$

$$=\frac{\frac{3}{6}}{\frac{2}{18}+\frac{3}{6}}=\frac{3/6}{\frac{2}{18}+\frac{9}{18}}=\frac{9}{11}$$

Q. 43 A shopkeeper sells three types of flower seeds A_1, A_2 and A_3. They are sold as a mixture, where the proportions are 4 : 4 : 2, respectively. The germination rates of the three types of seeds are 45%, 60% and 35%. Calculate the probability

(i) of a randomly chosen seed to germinate.

(ii) that it will not germinate given that the seed is of type A_3.

(iii) that it is of the type A_2 given that a randomly chosen seed does not germinate.

Sol. We have, $A_1 : A_2 : A_3 = 4 : 4 : 2$

$$P(A_1)=\frac{4}{10},\ P(A_2)=\frac{4}{10}\text{ and }P(A_3)=\frac{2}{10}$$

where A_1, A_2 and A_3 denote the three types of flower seeds.

Let E be the event that a seed germinates and $\bar{E}$ be the event that a seed does not germinate.

$\therefore$ $$P(E/A_1)=\frac{45}{100},\ P(E/A_2)=\frac{60}{100}\text{ and }P(E/A_3)=\frac{35}{100}$$

and $$P(\bar{E}/A_1)=\frac{55}{100},\ P(\bar{E}/A_2)=\frac{40}{100}\text{ and }P(\bar{E}/A_3)=\frac{65}{100}$$

(i) $\therefore$ $$P(E)=P(A_1)\cdot P(E/A_1)+P(A_2)\cdot P(E/A_2)+P(A_3)\cdot P(E/A_3)$$

$$=\frac{4}{10}\cdot\frac{45}{100}+\frac{4}{10}\cdot\frac{60}{100}+\frac{2}{10}\cdot\frac{35}{100}$$

$$=\frac{180}{1000}+\frac{240}{1000}+\frac{70}{1000}=\frac{490}{1000}=0.49$$

(ii) $P(\bar{E}/A_3) = 1 - P(E/A_3) = 1 - \frac{35}{100} = \frac{65}{100}$ [as given above]

(iii) $P(A_2/\bar{E}) = \dfrac{P(A_2)\cdot P(\bar{E}/A_2)}{P(A_1)\cdot P(\bar{E}/A_1) + P(A_2)\cdot P(\bar{E}/A_2) + P(A_3)\cdot P(\bar{E}/A_3)}$

$$= \dfrac{\frac{4}{10}\cdot\frac{40}{100}}{\frac{4}{10}\cdot\frac{55}{100}+\frac{4}{10}\cdot\frac{40}{100}+\frac{2}{10}\cdot\frac{65}{100}} = \dfrac{\frac{160}{1000}}{\frac{220}{1000}+\frac{160}{1000}+\frac{130}{1000}}$$

$$= \frac{160/1000}{510/1000} = \frac{16}{51} = 0.313725 = 0.314$$

Q. 44 A letter is known to have come either from 'TATA NAGAR' or from 'CALCUTTA'. On the envelope, just two consecutive letters TA are visible. What is the probability that the letter came from 'TATA NAGAR'?

Sol. Let E_1 be the event that letter is from TATA NAGAR and E_2 be the event that letter is from CALCUTTA.

Also, let E_3 be the event that on the letter, two consecutive letters TA are visible.

$\therefore$ $P(E_1) = \frac{1}{2}$ and $P(E_2) = \frac{1}{2}$

and $P(E_3/E_1) = \frac{2}{8}$ and $P(E_3/E_2) = \frac{1}{7}$

[since, if letter is from TATA NAGAR, we see that the events of two consecutive letters visible are {TA, AT, TA, AN, NA, AG, GA , AR }. So, $P(E_3/E_1) = \frac{2}{8}$ and if letter is from CALCUTTA, we see that the events of two consecutive letters to visible are {CA, AL, LC, CU, UT, TT, TA}. So, $P(E_3/E_2) = \frac{1}{7}$]

$\therefore$ $P(E_1/E_3) = \dfrac{P(E_1)\cdot P(E_3/E_1)}{P(E_1)\cdot P(E_3/E_1) + P(E_2)\cdot P(E_3/E_2)}$

$$= \dfrac{\frac{1}{2}\cdot\frac{2}{8}}{\frac{1}{2}\cdot\frac{2}{8}+\frac{1}{2}\cdot\frac{1}{7}} = \dfrac{\frac{1}{8}}{\frac{1}{8}+\frac{1}{14}} = \dfrac{1/8}{\frac{22}{8\times 14}} = \dfrac{\frac{1}{8}}{\frac{11}{56}} = \frac{7}{11}$$

Q. 45 There are two bags, one of which contains 3 black and 4 white balls while the other contains 4 black and 3 white balls. A die is thrown. If it shows up 1 or 3, a ball is taken from the Ist bag but it shows up any other number, a ball is chosen from the II bag. Find the probability of choosing a black ball.

Sol. Since, Bag I = {3 black, 4 white balls}, Bag II = {4 black, 3 white balls}

Let E_1 be the event that bag I is selected and E_2 be the event that bag II is selected.

Let E_3 be the event that black ball is chosen.

$\therefore$ $P(E_1) = \frac{1}{6} + \frac{1}{6} = \frac{1}{3}$ and $P(E_2) = 1 - \frac{1}{3} = \frac{2}{3}$

and $P(E_3/E_1) = \frac{3}{7}$ and $P(E_3/E_2) = \frac{4}{7}$

$\therefore$ $P(E_3) = P(E_1)\cdot P(E_3/E_1) + P(E_2)\cdot P(E_3/E_2)$

$$= \frac{1}{3}\cdot\frac{3}{7} + \frac{2}{3}\cdot\frac{4}{7} = \frac{11}{21}$$

Q. 46 **There are three urns containing 2 white and 3 black balls, 3 white and 2 black balls and 4 white and 1 black balls, respectively. There is an equal probability of each urn being chosen. A ball is drawn at random from the chosen urn and it is found to be white. Find the probability that the ball drawn was from the second urn.**

Sol. Let $U_1 = \{2 \text{ white, } 3 \text{ black balls}\}$

$U_2 = \{3 \text{ white, } 2 \text{ black balls}\}$

and $U_3 = \{4 \text{ white, } 1 \text{ black balls}\}$

$\therefore \quad P(U_1) = P(U_2) = P(U_3) = \frac{1}{3}$

Let E_1 be the event that a ball is chosen from urn U_1, E_2 be the event that a ball is chosen from urn U_2 and E_3 be the event that a ball is chosen from urn U_3.

Also, $P(E_1) = P(E_2) = P(E_3) = 1/3$

Now, let E be the event that white ball is drawn.

$\therefore \quad P(E/E_1) = \frac{2}{5},\ P(E/E_2) = \frac{3}{5},\ P(E/E_3) = \frac{4}{5}$

Now,
$$P(E_2/E) = \frac{P(E_2)\cdot P(E/E_2)}{P(E_1)\cdot P(E/E_1) + P(E_2)\cdot P(E/E_2) + P(E_3)\cdot P(E/E_3)}$$
$$= \frac{\frac{1}{3}\cdot\frac{3}{5}}{\frac{1}{3}\cdot\frac{2}{5} + \frac{1}{3}\cdot\frac{3}{5} + \frac{1}{3}\cdot\frac{4}{5}}$$
$$= \frac{\frac{3}{15}}{\frac{2}{15} + \frac{3}{15} + \frac{4}{15}} = \frac{3}{9} = \frac{1}{3}$$

Q. 47 **By examining the chest X-ray, the probability that TB is detected when a person is actually suffering is 0.99. The probability of an healthy person diagnosed to have TB is 0.001. In a certain city, 1 in 1000 people suffers from TB. A person is selected at random and is diagnosed to have TB. What is the probability that he actually has TB?**

Sol. Let E_1 = Event that person has TB

E_2 = Event that person does not have TB

E = Event that the person is diagnosed to have TB

$\therefore \quad P(E_1) = \frac{1}{1000} = 0.001,\ P(E_2) = \frac{999}{1000} = 0.999$

and $P(E/E_1) = 0.99$ and $P(E/E_2) = 0.001$

$$\therefore \quad P(E_1/E) = \frac{P(E_1)\cdot P(E/E_1)}{P(E_1)\cdot P(E/E_1) + P(E_2)\cdot P(E/E_2)}$$
$$= \frac{0.001 \times 0.99}{0.001 \times 0.99 + 0.999 \times 0.001}$$
$$= \frac{0.000990}{0.000990 + 0.000999}$$
$$= \frac{990}{1989} = \frac{110}{221}$$

Q. 48 An item is manufactured by three machines A, B and C. Out of the total number of items manufactured during a specified period, 50% are manufactured on A, 30% on B and 20% on C. 2% of the items produced on A and 2% of items produced on B are defective and 3% of these produced on C are defective. All the items are stored at one godown. One item is drawn at random and is found to be defective. What is the probability that it was manufactured on machine A?

Sol. Let E_1 = Event that item is manufactured on A,

E_2 = Event that an item is manufactured on B,

E_3 = Event that an item is manufactured on C,

Let E be the event that an item is defective.

$$\therefore \quad P(E_1) = \frac{50}{100} = \frac{1}{2}, P(E_2) = \frac{30}{100} = \frac{3}{10} \text{ and } P(E_3) = \frac{20}{100} = \frac{1}{5}$$

$$P\left(\frac{E}{E_1}\right) = \frac{2}{100} = \frac{1}{50}, P\left(\frac{E}{E_2}\right) = \frac{2}{100} = \frac{1}{50} \text{ and } P\left(\frac{E}{E_3}\right) = \frac{3}{100}$$

$$\therefore \quad P\left(\frac{E_1}{E}\right) = \frac{P(E_1)\cdot P\left(\frac{E}{E_1}\right)}{P(E_1)\cdot P\left(\frac{E}{E_1}\right) + P(E_2)\cdot P\left(\frac{E}{E_2}\right) + P(E_3)\cdot P\left(\frac{E}{E_3}\right)}$$

$$= \frac{\frac{1}{2}\cdot\frac{1}{50}}{\frac{1}{2}\cdot\frac{1}{50} + \frac{3}{10}\cdot\frac{1}{50} + \frac{1}{5}\cdot\frac{3}{100}}$$

$$= \frac{\frac{1}{100}}{\frac{1}{100} + \frac{3}{500} + \frac{3}{500}} = \frac{\frac{1}{100}}{\frac{5+3+3}{500}} = \frac{5}{11}$$

Q. 49 Let X be a discrete random variable whose probability distribution is defined as follows.

$$P(X = x) = \begin{cases} k(x+1), & \text{for } x = 1, 2, 3, 4 \\ 2kx, & \text{for } x = 5, 6, 7 \\ 0, & \text{otherwise} \end{cases}$$

where, k is a constant. Calculate

(i) the value of k. (ii) $E(X)$.

(iii) standard deviation of X.

Sol. $$P(X = x) = \begin{cases} k(x+1), & \text{for } x = 1, 2, 3, 4 \\ 2kx, & \text{for } x = 5, 6, 7 \\ 0, & \text{otherwise} \end{cases}$$

Thus, we have following table

X	1	2	3	4	5	6	7	Otherwise
$P(X)$	$2k$	$3k$	$4k$	$5k$	$10k$	$12k$	$14k$	0
$XP(X)$	$2k$	$6k$	$12k$	$20k$	$50k$	$72k$	$98k$	0
$X^2P(X)$	$2k$	$12k$	$36k$	$80k$	$250k$	$432k$	$686k$	0

(i) Since, $\Sigma P_i = 1$

$\Rightarrow \quad k(2 + 3 + 4 + 5 + 10 + 12 + 14) = 1 \Rightarrow k = \frac{1}{50}$

(ii) $\because \quad E(X) = \Sigma XP(X)$

$\therefore \quad E(X) = 2k + 6k + 12k + 20k + 50k + 72k + 98k + 0 = 260k$

$= 260 \times \frac{1}{50} = \frac{26}{5} = 5.2 \qquad \left[\because k = \frac{1}{50}\right] \quad ...(i)$

(iii) We know that,

$\text{Var}(X) = [E(X^2)] - [E(X)]^2 = \Sigma X^2 P(X) - [\Sigma\{XP(X)\}]^2$

$= [2k + 12k + 36k + 80k + 250k + 432k + 686k + 0] - [5.2]^2 \qquad$ [using Eq. (i)]

$= [1498k] - 27.04 = \left[1498 \times \frac{1}{50}\right] - 27.04 \qquad \left[\because k = \frac{1}{50}\right]$

$= 29.96 - 27.04 = 2.92$

We know that, standard deviation of $X = \sqrt{\text{Var}(X)} = \sqrt{2.92} = 1.7088 = 1.7$ (approx)

Q. 50 The probability distribution of a discrete random variable X is given as under

X	1	2	4	$2A$	$3A$	$5A$
P(X)	$\frac{1}{2}$	$\frac{1}{5}$	$\frac{3}{25}$	$\frac{1}{10}$	$\frac{1}{25}$	$\frac{1}{25}$

Calculate

(i) the value of A, if $E(X) = 2.94$.

(ii) variance of X.

Sol. (i) We have, $\Sigma XP(X) = \frac{1}{2} + \frac{2}{5} + \frac{12}{25} + \frac{2A}{10} + \frac{3A}{25} + \frac{5A}{25}$

$= \frac{25 + 20 + 24 + 10A + 6A + 10A}{50} = \frac{69 + 26A}{50}$

Since, $\quad E(X) = \Sigma XP(X)$

$\Rightarrow \quad 2.94 = \frac{69 + 26A}{50}$

$\Rightarrow \quad 26A = 50 \times 2.94 - 69$

$\Rightarrow \quad A = \frac{147 - 69}{26} = \frac{78}{26} = 3$

(ii) We know that,

$\text{Var}(X) = E(X^2) - [E(X)]^2$

$= \Sigma X^2 P(X) - [\Sigma XP(X)]^2$

$= \frac{1}{2} + \frac{4}{5} + \frac{48}{25} + \frac{4A^2}{10} + \frac{9A^2}{25} + \frac{25A^2}{25} - [E(X)]^2$

$= \frac{25 + 40 + 96 + 20A^2 + 18A^2 + 50A^2}{50} - [E(X)]^2$

$= \frac{161 + 88A^2}{50} - [E(X)]^2 = \frac{161 + 88 \times (3)^2}{50} - [E(X)]^2 \qquad [\because A = 3]$

$= \frac{953}{50} - [2.94]^2 \qquad [\because E(X) = 2.94]$

$= 19.0600 - 8.6436 = 10.4164$

Q. 51 The probability distribution of a random variable x is given as under

$$P(X = x) = \begin{cases} kx^2, & x = 1, 2, 3 \\ 2kx, & x = 4, 5, 6 \\ 0, & \text{otherwise} \end{cases}$$

where, k is a constant. Calculate

(i) $E(X)$ (ii) $E(3X^2)$ (iii) $P(X \geq 4)$

Sol.

X	1	2	3	4	5	6	Otherwise
P(X)	k	$4k$	$9k$	$8k$	$10k$	$12k$	0

We know that, $\Sigma P_i = 1$

$\Rightarrow \quad 44k = 1 \Rightarrow k = \frac{1}{44}$

$\therefore \quad \Sigma XP(X) = k + 8k + 27k + 32k + 50k + 72k + 0$

$= 190k = 190 \times \frac{1}{44} = \frac{95}{22}$

(i) So, $E(X) = \Sigma XP(X) = \frac{95}{22} = 4.32$

(ii) Also, $E(X^2) = \Sigma X^2 P(X) = k + 16k + 81k + 128k + 250k + 432k$

$= 908k = 908 \times \frac{1}{44}$ $\quad \left[\because k = \frac{1}{44}\right]$

$= 20.636 = 20.64$ (approx)

$\therefore \quad E(3X^2) = 3E(X^2) = 3 \times 20.64 = 61.92 = 61.9$

(iii) $P(X \geq 4) = P(X = 4) + P(X = 5) + P(X = 6)$

$= 8k + 10k + 12k = 30k = 30 \cdot \frac{1}{44} = \frac{15}{22}$

Q. 52 A bag contains $(2n + 1)$ coins. It is known that n of these coins have a head on both sides whereas the rest of the coins are fair. A coin is picked up at random from the bag and is tossed. If the probability that the toss results in a head is $\frac{31}{42}$, then determine the value of n.

Sol. Given, n coins have head on both sides and $(n + 1)$ coins are fair coins.

Let E_1 = Event that an unfair coin is selected

E_2 = Event that a fair coin is selected

E = Event that the toss results in a head

$\therefore \quad P(E_1) = \frac{n}{2n + 1}$ and $P(E_2) = \frac{n + 1}{2n + 1}$

Also, $\quad P\left(\frac{E}{E_1}\right) = 1$ and $P\left(\frac{E}{E_2}\right) = \frac{1}{2}$

$\therefore \quad P(E) = P(E_1) \cdot P\left(\frac{E}{E_1}\right) + P(E_2) \cdot P\left(\frac{E}{E_2}\right) = \frac{n}{2n + 1} \cdot 1 + \frac{n + 1}{2n + 1} \cdot \frac{1}{2}$

$\Rightarrow \quad \frac{31}{42} = \frac{2n + n + 1}{2(2n + 1)} \Rightarrow \frac{31}{42} = \frac{3n + 1}{4n + 2}$

$\Rightarrow \quad 124n + 62 = 126n + 42$

$\Rightarrow \quad 2n = 20 \Rightarrow n = 10$

Q. 53 **Two cards are drawn successively without replacement from a well shuffled deck of cards. Find the mean and standard variation of the random variable X, where X is the number of aces.**

Sol. Let X denotes a random variable of number of aces.

$\therefore \quad X = 0, 1, 2$

Now, $\quad P(X = 0) = \frac{48}{52} \cdot \frac{47}{51} = \frac{2256}{2652}$

$$P(X = 1) = \frac{48}{52} \cdot \frac{4}{51} + \frac{4}{52} \cdot \frac{48}{51} = \frac{384}{2652}$$

$$P(X = 2) = \frac{4}{52} \cdot \frac{3}{51} = \frac{12}{2652}$$

X	0	1	2
$P(X)$	$\frac{2256}{2652}$	$\frac{384}{2652}$	$\frac{12}{2652}$
$XP(X)$	0	$\frac{384}{2652}$	$\frac{24}{2652}$
$X^2P(X)$	0	$\frac{384}{2652}$	$\frac{48}{2652}$

We know that, Mean $(\mu) = E(X) = \Sigma XP(X)$

$$= 0 + \frac{384}{2652} + \frac{24}{2652}$$

$$= \frac{408}{2652} = \frac{2}{13}$$

Also, $\quad \text{Var}(X) = E(X^2) - [E(X)]^2 = \Sigma X^2P(X) - [E(X)]^2$

$$= \left[0 + \frac{384}{2652} + \frac{48}{2652}\right] - \left(\frac{2}{13}\right)^2 \quad \left[\because E(X) = \frac{2}{13}\right]$$

$$= \frac{432}{2652} - \frac{4}{169} = 0.1628 - 0.0236 = 0.1391$$

$\therefore \quad$ Standard deviation $= \sqrt{\text{Var}(X)} = \sqrt{0.139} = 0.373$ (approx)

Q. 54 **A die is tossed twice. If a 'success' is getting an even number on a toss, then find the variance of the number of successes.**

Sol. Let X be the random variable for a 'success' for getting an even number on a toss.

$\therefore \quad X = 0, 1, 2, \; n = 2, \; p = \frac{3}{6} = \frac{1}{2}$ and $q = \frac{1}{2}$

At $X = 0$, $\quad P(X = 0) = {}^2C_0\left(\frac{1}{2}\right)^0\left(\frac{1}{2}\right)^{2-0} = \frac{1}{4}$

At $X = 1$, $\quad P(X = 1) = {}^2C_1\left(\frac{1}{2}\right)^1\left(\frac{1}{2}\right)^{2-1} = 2 \cdot \frac{1}{2} \cdot \frac{1}{2} = \frac{1}{2}$

At $X = 2$, $\quad P(X = 2) = {}^2C_2\left(\frac{1}{2}\right)^2\left(\frac{1}{2}\right)^{2-2} = \frac{1}{4}$

Thus,

X	0	1	2
$P(X)$	$\frac{1}{4}$	$\frac{1}{2}$	$\frac{1}{4}$
$XP(X)$	0	$\frac{1}{2}$	$\frac{1}{2}$
$X^2P(X)$	0	$\frac{1}{2}$	1

$\therefore \quad \Sigma XP(X) = 0 + \frac{1}{2} + \frac{1}{2} = 1 \quad \ldots(i)$

and $\quad \Sigma X^2P(X) = 0 + \frac{1}{2} + 1 = \frac{3}{2} \quad \ldots(ii)$

$\because \quad \text{Var}(X) = E(X^2) - [E(X)]^2$

$= \Sigma X^2P(X) - [\Sigma XP(X)]^2 = \frac{3}{2} - (1)^2 = \frac{1}{2}$ [using Eqs. (i) and (ii)]

Q. 55 There are 5 cards numbered 1 to 5, one number on one card. Two cards are drawn at random without replacement. Let X denotes the sum of the numbers on two cards drawn. Find the mean and variance of X.

Sol. Here, $S = \{(1, 2), (2, 1), (1, 3), (3, 1), (2, 3), (3, 2), (1, 4), (4, 1), (1, 5), (5, 1), (2, 4), (4, 2), (2, 5), (5, 2), (3, 4), (4, 3), (3, 5), (5, 3), (5, 4), (4, 5)\}$.

$\Rightarrow n(S) = 20$

Let random variable be X which denotes the sum of the numbers on two cards drawn.

$\therefore \quad X = 3, 4, 5, 6, 7, 8, 9$

At $X = 3$, $P(X) = \frac{2}{20} = \frac{1}{10}$

At $X = 4$, $P(X) = \frac{2}{20} = \frac{1}{10}$

At $X = 5$, $P(X) = \frac{4}{20} = \frac{1}{5}$

At $X = 6$, $P(X) = \frac{4}{20} = \frac{1}{5}$

At $X = 7$, $P(X) = \frac{4}{20} = \frac{1}{5}$

At $X = 8$, $P(X) = \frac{2}{20} = \frac{1}{10}$

At $X = 9$, $P(X) = \frac{2}{20} = \frac{1}{10}$

$\therefore \quad \text{Mean, } E(X) = \Sigma XP(X) = \frac{3}{10} + \frac{4}{10} + \frac{5}{5} + \frac{6}{5} + \frac{7}{5} + \frac{8}{10} + \frac{9}{10}$

$= \frac{3 + 4 + 10 + 12 + 14 + 8 + 9}{10} = 6$

Also, $\quad \Sigma X^2P(X) = \frac{9}{10} + \frac{16}{10} + \frac{25}{5} + \frac{36}{5} + \frac{49}{5} + \frac{64}{10} + \frac{81}{10}$

$= \frac{9 + 16 + 50 + 72 + 98 + 64 + 81}{10} = 39$

$\therefore \quad \text{Var}(X) = \Sigma X^2P(X) - [\Sigma XP(X)]^2$

$= 39 - (6)^2 = 39 - 36 = 3$

Objective Type Questions

Q. 56 If $P(A) = \frac{4}{5}$ and $P(A \cap B) = \frac{7}{10}$, then $P(B/A)$ is equal to

(a) $\frac{1}{10}$ (b) $\frac{1}{8}$ (c) $\frac{7}{8}$ (d) $\frac{17}{20}$

Sol. *(c)* $\because$ $P(A) = \frac{4}{5}, P(A \cap B) = \frac{7}{10}$

$\therefore$ $P(B/A) = \frac{P(A \cap B)}{P(A)} = \frac{7/10}{4/5} = \frac{7}{8}$

Q. 57 If $P(A \cap B) = \frac{7}{10}$ and $P(B) = \frac{17}{20}$, then $P(A/B)$ equals to

(a) $\frac{14}{17}$ (b) $\frac{17}{20}$ (c) $\frac{7}{8}$ (d) $\frac{1}{8}$

Sol. *(a)* Here, $P(A \cap B) = \frac{7}{10}$ and $P(B) = \frac{17}{20}$

$\therefore$ $P(A/B) = \frac{P(A \cap B)}{P(B)} = \frac{7/10}{17/20} = \frac{14}{17}$

Q. 58 If $P(A) = \frac{3}{10}$, $P(B) = \frac{2}{5}$ and $P(A \cup B) = \frac{3}{5}$, then $P(B/A) + P(A/B)$ equals to

(a) $\frac{1}{4}$ (b) $\frac{1}{3}$ (c) $\frac{5}{12}$ (d) $\frac{7}{12}$

Sol. *(d)* Here, $P(A) = \frac{3}{10}$, $P(B) \frac{2}{5}$ and $P(A \cup B) = \frac{3}{5}$

$$P(B/A) + P(A/B) = \frac{P(B \cap A)}{P(A)} + \frac{P(A \cap B)}{P(B)}$$

$$= \frac{P(A) + P(B) - P(A \cup B)}{P(A)} + \frac{P(A) + P(B) - P(A \cup B)}{P(B)}$$

$$\left[\begin{array}{l} \because P(A \cup B) = P(A) + P(B) - P(A \cap B) \\ \text{i.e., } P(A \cap B) = P(A) + P(B) - P(A \cup B) \end{array}\right]$$

$$= \frac{\frac{3}{10} + \frac{2}{5} - \frac{3}{5}}{\frac{3}{10}} + \frac{\frac{3}{10} + \frac{2}{5} - \frac{3}{5}}{\frac{2}{5}}$$

$$= \frac{\frac{1}{10}}{\frac{3}{10}} + \frac{\frac{1}{10}}{\frac{2}{5}} = \frac{1}{3} + \frac{1}{4} = \frac{7}{12}$$

Q. 59 If $P(A)=\frac{2}{5}$, $P(B)=\frac{3}{10}$ and $P(A\cap B)=\frac{1}{5}$, then $P(A'/B')\cdot P(B'/A')$ is equal to

(a) $\frac{5}{6}$ (b) $\frac{5}{7}$ (c) $\frac{25}{42}$ (d) 1

Sol. *(c)* Here, $P(A)=\frac{2}{5}$, $P(B)=\frac{3}{10}$ and $P(A\cap B)=\frac{1}{5}$

$$P(A'/B')=\frac{P(A'\cap B')}{P(B')}=\frac{1-P(A\cup B)}{1-P(B)}$$

$$=\frac{1-[P(A)+P(B)-P(A\cap B)]}{1-P(B)}$$

$$=\frac{1-\left(\frac{2}{5}+\frac{3}{10}-\frac{1}{5}\right)}{1-\frac{3}{10}}$$

$$=\frac{1-\left(\frac{4+3-2}{10}\right)}{\frac{7}{10}}=\frac{1-\frac{1}{2}}{\frac{7}{10}}=\frac{5}{7}$$

and $$P(B'/A')=\frac{P(B'\cap A')}{P(A')}=\frac{1-P(A\cup B)}{1-P(A)}$$

$$=\frac{1-\frac{1}{2}}{1-\frac{2}{5}}=\frac{1/2}{3/5}=\frac{5}{6}\qquad\left[\because P(A\cup B)=\frac{1}{2}\right]$$

$$\therefore\ P(A'/B')\cdot P(B'/A')=\frac{5}{7}\cdot\frac{5}{6}=\frac{25}{42}$$

Q. 60 If A and B are two events such that $P(A)=\frac{1}{2}$, $P(B)=\frac{1}{3}$ and $P(A/B)=\frac{1}{4}$, then $P(A'\cap B')$ equals to

(a) $\frac{1}{12}$ (b) $\frac{3}{4}$

(c) $\frac{1}{4}$ (d) $\frac{3}{16}$

Sol. *(c)* Here, $P(A)=\frac{1}{2}$, $P(B)=\frac{1}{3}$ and $P(A/B)=\frac{1}{4}$

$\because$ $$P(A/B)=\frac{P(A\cap B)}{P(B)}$$

$\Rightarrow$ $$P(A\cap B)=P(A/B)\cdot P(B)=\frac{1}{4}\cdot\frac{1}{3}=\frac{1}{12}$$

Now, $$P(A'\cap B')=1-P(A\cup B)$$

$$=1-[P(A)+P(B)-P(A\cap B)]$$

$$=1-\left[\frac{1}{2}+\frac{1}{3}-\frac{1}{12}\right]=1-\left[\frac{6+4-1}{12}\right]$$

$$=1-\frac{9}{12}=\frac{3}{12}=\frac{1}{4}$$

Q. 61 If $P(A) = 0.4$, $P(B) = 0.8$ and $P(B/A) = 0.6$, then $P(A \cup B)$ is equal to

(a) 0.24 (b) 0.3

(c) 0.48 (d) 0.96

Sol. *(d)* Here, $P(A) = 0.4$, $P(B) = 0.8$ and $P(A/B) = 0.6$

$$\because \quad P(B/A) = \frac{P(B \cap A)}{P(A)}$$

$$\Rightarrow \quad P(B \cap A) = P(B/A) \cdot P(A) = 0.6 \times 0.4 = 0.24$$

$$\because \quad P(A \cup B) = P(A) + P(B) - P(A \cap B) = 0.4 + 0.8 - 0.24 = 1.2 - 0.24 = 0.96$$

Q. 62 If A and B are two events and $A \neq \phi$, $B \neq \phi$, then

(a) $P(A/B) = P(A) \cdot P(B)$ (b) $P(A/B) = \frac{P(A \cap B)}{P(B)}$

(c) $P(A/B) \cdot P(B/A) = 1$ (d) $P(A/B) = P(A)/P(B)$

Sol. *(b)* If $A \neq \phi$ and $B \neq \phi$, then $P(A/B) = \frac{P(A \cap B)}{P(B)}$

Q. 63 If A and B are events such that $P(A) = 0.4$, $P(B) = 0.3$ and $P(A \cup B) = 0.5$, then $P(B' \cap A)$ equals to

(a) $\frac{2}{3}$ (b) $\frac{1}{2}$

(c) $\frac{3}{10}$ (d) $\frac{1}{5}$

Sol. *(d)* Here, $P(A) = 0.4$, $P(B) = 0.3$ and $P(A \cup B) = 0.5$

$$\because \quad P(A \cup B) = P(A) + P(B) - P(A \cap B)$$

$$\Rightarrow \quad P(A \cap B) = 0.4 + 0.3 - 0.5 = 0.2$$

$$\therefore \quad P(B' \cap A) = P(A) - P(A \cap B) = 0.4 - 0.2 = 0.2 = \frac{1}{5}$$

Q. 64 If A and B are two events such that $P(B) = \frac{3}{5}$, $P(A/B) = \frac{1}{2}$ and $P(A \cup B) = \frac{4}{5}$, then $P(A)$ equals to

(a) $\frac{3}{10}$ (b) $\frac{1}{5}$ (c) $\frac{1}{2}$ (d) $\frac{3}{5}$

Sol. *(c)* Here, $P(B) = \frac{3}{5}$, $P(A/B) = \frac{1}{2}$ and $P(A \cup B) = \frac{4}{5}$

$$\because \quad P(A/B) = \frac{P(A \cap B)}{P(B)}$$

$$\Rightarrow \quad \frac{1}{2} = \frac{P(A \cap B)}{3/5}$$

$$\Rightarrow \quad P(A \cap B) = \frac{3}{5} \times \frac{1}{2} = \frac{3}{10}$$

and $$P(A \cup B) = P(A) + P(B) - P(A \cap B)$$

$$\Rightarrow \quad \frac{4}{5} = P(A) + \frac{3}{5} - \frac{3}{10}$$

$$\therefore \quad P(A) = \frac{4}{5} - \frac{3}{5} + \frac{3}{10} = \frac{8-6+3}{10} = \frac{1}{2}$$

Q. 65 In question 64 (above), $P(B/A')$ is equal to

(a) $\frac{1}{5}$ (b) $\frac{3}{10}$ (c) $\frac{1}{2}$ (d) $\frac{3}{5}$

Sol. ***(d)*** $$P(B/A') = \frac{P(B \cap A')}{P(A')} = \frac{P(B) - P(B \cap A)}{1 - P(A)}$$

$$= \frac{\frac{3}{5} - \frac{3}{10}}{1 - \frac{1}{2}} = \frac{\frac{6-3}{10}}{\frac{1}{2}} = \frac{6}{10} = \frac{3}{5}$$

Q. 66 If $P(B) = \frac{3}{5}$, $P(A/B) = \frac{1}{2}$ and $P(A \cup B) = \frac{4}{5}$, then $P(A \cup B)' + P(A' \cup B)$ is equal to

(a) $\frac{1}{5}$ (b) $\frac{4}{5}$ (c) $\frac{1}{2}$ (d) 1

Sol. ***(d)*** Here, $$P(B) = \frac{3}{5}, P(A/B) = \frac{1}{2}$$

and $$P(A \cup B) = \frac{4}{5}$$

Since, $$P(A/B) = \frac{P(A \cap B)}{P(B)}$$

$$\Rightarrow \quad P(A \cap B) = P(A/B) \cdot P(B)$$

$$= \frac{1}{2} \times \frac{3}{5} = \frac{3}{10}$$

Also, $$P(A \cup B) = P(A) + P(B) - P(A \cap B)$$

$$\Rightarrow \quad P(A) = \frac{4}{5} - \frac{3}{5} + \frac{3}{10} = \frac{1}{2}$$

$$\therefore \quad P(A \cup B)' = 1 - P(A \cup B) = 1 - \frac{4}{5} = \frac{1}{5}$$

and $$P(A' \cup B) = 1 - P(A - B) = 1 - P(A \cap B')$$

$$= 1 - P(A) \cdot P(B')$$

$$= 1 - \frac{1}{2} \cdot \frac{2}{5} = \frac{4}{5}$$

$$\Rightarrow \quad P(A \cup B)' + P(A' \cup B) = \frac{1}{5} + \frac{4}{5} = \frac{5}{5} = 1$$

Q. 67 If $P(A)=\frac{7}{13}$, $P(B)=\frac{9}{13}$ and $P(A\cap B)=\frac{4}{13}$, then $P(A'/B)$ is equal to

(a) $\frac{6}{13}$ (b) $\frac{4}{13}$ (c) $\frac{4}{9}$ (d) $\frac{5}{9}$

Sol. *(d)* Here, $P(A)=\frac{7}{13}$, $P(B)=\frac{9}{13}$ and $P(A\cap B)=\frac{4}{13}$

$$\therefore \quad P(A'/B)=\frac{P(A'\cap B)}{P(B)}=\frac{P(B)-P(A\cap B)}{P(B)}$$

$$=\frac{\frac{9}{13}-\frac{4}{13}}{\frac{9}{13}}=\frac{\frac{5}{13}}{\frac{9}{13}}=\frac{5}{9}$$

Q. 68 If A and B are such events that $P(A)>0$ and $P(B)\neq 1$, then $P(A'/B')$ equals to

(a) $1-P(A/B)$ (b) $1-P(A'/B)$ (c) $\frac{1-P(A\cup B)}{P(B')}$ (d) $P(A')/P(B')$

Sol. *(c)* $\because$ $P(A)>0$ and $P(B)\neq 1$

$$P(A'/B')=\frac{P(A'\cap B')}{P(B')}=\frac{1-P(A\cup B)}{P(B')}$$

Q. 69 If A and B are two independent events with $P(A)=\frac{3}{5}$ and $P(B)=\frac{4}{9}$, then $P(A'\cap B')$ equals to

(a) $\frac{4}{15}$ (b) $\frac{8}{45}$ (c) $\frac{1}{3}$ (d) $\frac{2}{9}$

Sol. *(d)*

$$P(A'\cap B')=1-P(A\cup B)$$

$$=1-[P(A)+P(B)-P(A\cap B)]$$

$$=1-\left[\frac{3}{5}+\frac{4}{9}-\frac{3}{5}\times\frac{4}{9}\right] \quad [\because P(A\cap B)=P(A)\cdot P(B)]$$

$$=1-\left[\frac{27+20-12}{45}\right]=1-\frac{35}{45}=\frac{10}{45}=\frac{2}{9}$$

Q. 70 If two events are independent, then

(a) they must be mutually exclusive

(b) the sum of their probabilities must be equal to 1

(c) Both (a) and (b) are correct

(d) None of the above is correct

Sol. *(d)* If two events A and B are independent ,then we know that

$$P(A\cap B)=P(A)\cdot P(B),\ P(A)\neq 0,\ P(B)\neq 0$$

Since, A and B have a common outcome.

Further, mutually exclusive events never have a common outcome.

In other words, two independent events having non-zero probabilities of occurrence cannot be mutually exclusive and conversely, *i.e.*, two mutually exclusive events having non-zero probabilities of outcome cannot be independent.

Q. 71 If A and B be two events such that $P(A)=\frac{3}{8}$, $P(B)=\frac{5}{8}$ and $P(A\cup B)=\frac{3}{4}$, then $P(A/B)\cdot P(A'/B)$ is equal to

(a) $\frac{2}{5}$ (b) $\frac{3}{8}$ (c) $\frac{3}{20}$ (d) $\frac{6}{25}$

Sol. *(d)* Here, $P(A)=\frac{3}{8}, P(B)=\frac{5}{8}$ and $P(A\cup B)=\frac{3}{4}$

$\because$ $P(A\cup B)=P(A)+P(B)-P(A\cap B)$

$\Rightarrow$ $P(A\cap B)=\frac{3}{8}+\frac{5}{8}-\frac{3}{4}=\frac{3+5-6}{8}=\frac{2}{8}=\frac{1}{4}$

$\because$ $P(A/B)=\frac{P(A\cap B)}{P(B)}=\frac{1/4}{5/8}=\frac{8}{20}=\frac{2}{5}$

and $P(A'/B)=\frac{P(A'\cap B)}{P(B)}=\frac{P(B)-P(A\cap B)}{P(B)}$

$$=\frac{\frac{5}{8}-\frac{1}{4}}{\frac{5}{8}}=\frac{\frac{5-2}{8}}{\frac{5}{8}}=\frac{3}{5}$$

$\therefore$ $P(A/B)\cdot P(A'/B)=\frac{2}{5}\cdot\frac{3}{5}=\frac{6}{25}$

Q. 72 If the events A and B are independent, then $P(A\cap B)$ is equal to

(a) $P(A)+P(B)$ (b) $P(A)-P(B)$

(c) $P(A)\cdot P(B)$ (d) $P(A)/P(B)$

Sol. *(c)* If A and B are independent, then $P(A\cap B)=P(A)\cdot P(B)$

Q. 73 Two events E and F are independent. If $P(E)=0.3$ and $P(E\cup F)=0.5$, then $P(E/F)-P(F/E)$ equals to

(a) $\frac{2}{7}$ (b) $\frac{3}{35}$ (c) $\frac{1}{70}$ (d) $\frac{1}{7}$

Sol. *(c)* Here, $P(E)=0.3$ and $P(E\cup F)=0.5$

Let $P(F)=x$

$\because$ $P(E\cup F)=P(E)+P(F)-P(E\cap F)$

$=P(E)+P(F)-P(E)\cdot P(F)$

$\Rightarrow$ $0.5=0.3+x-0.3x$

$\Rightarrow$ $x=\frac{0.5-0.3}{0.7}=\frac{2}{7}=P(F)$

$\therefore$ $P(E/F)-P(F/E)=\frac{P(E\cap F)}{P(F)}-\frac{P(F\cap E)}{P(E)}$

$$=\frac{P(E\cap F)\cdot P(E)-P(F\cap E)\cdot P(F)}{P(E)\cdot P(F)}$$

$$=\frac{P(E\cap F)[P(E)-P(F)]}{P(E\cap F)}=P(E)-P(F)$$

$$=\frac{3}{10}-\frac{2}{7}=\frac{21-20}{70}=\frac{1}{70}$$

Q. 74 A bag contains 5 red and 3 blue balls. If 3 balls are drawn at random without replacement, them the probability of getting exactly one red ball is

(a) $\frac{45}{196}$ (b) $\frac{135}{392}$ (c) $\frac{15}{56}$ (d) $\frac{15}{29}$

Sol. ***(c)*** Probability of getting exactly one red (R) ball $= P_R \cdot P_{\bar{R}} \cdot P_{\bar{R}} + P_{\bar{R}} \cdot P_R \cdot P_{\bar{R}} + P_{\bar{R}} \cdot P_{\bar{R}} \cdot P_R$

$$= \frac{5}{8} \cdot \frac{3}{7} \cdot \frac{2}{6} + \frac{3}{8} \cdot \frac{5}{7} \cdot \frac{2}{6} + \frac{3}{8} \cdot \frac{2}{7} \cdot \frac{5}{6}$$

$$= \frac{15}{4 \cdot 7 \cdot 6} + \frac{15}{4 \cdot 7 \cdot 6} + \frac{15}{4 \cdot 7 \cdot 6}$$

$$= \frac{5}{56} + \frac{5}{56} + \frac{5}{56} = \frac{15}{56}$$

Q. 75 Refer to question 74 above. If the probability that exactly two of the three balls were red, then the first ball being red, is

(a) $\frac{1}{3}$ (b) $\frac{4}{7}$ (c) $\frac{15}{28}$ (d) $\frac{5}{28}$

Sol. ***(b)*** Let E_1 = Event that first ball being red

and E_2 = Event that exactly two of the three balls being red

$$\therefore \quad P(E_1) = P_R \cdot P_R \cdot P_R + P_R \cdot P_R \cdot P_{\bar{R}} + P_R \cdot P_{\bar{R}} \cdot P_R + P_R \cdot P_{\bar{R}} \cdot P_{\bar{R}}$$

$$= \frac{5}{8} \cdot \frac{4}{7} \cdot \frac{3}{6} + \frac{5}{8} \cdot \frac{4}{7} \cdot \frac{3}{6} + \frac{5}{8} \cdot \frac{3}{7} \cdot \frac{4}{6} + \frac{5}{8} \cdot \frac{3}{7} \cdot \frac{2}{6}$$

$$= \frac{60 + 60 + 60 + 30}{336} = \frac{210}{336}$$

$$P(E_1 \cap E_2) = P_R \cdot P_{\bar{R}} \cdot P_R + P_R \cdot P_R \cdot P_{\bar{R}}$$

$$= \frac{5}{8} \cdot \frac{3}{7} \cdot \frac{4}{6} + \frac{5}{8} \cdot \frac{4}{7} \cdot \frac{3}{6} = \frac{120}{336}$$

$$\therefore \quad P(E_2 / E_1) = \frac{P(E_1 \cap E_2)}{P(E_1)} = \frac{120/336}{210/336} = \frac{4}{7}$$

Q. 76 Three persons A, B and C, fire at a target in turn, starting with A. Their probability of hitting the target are 0.4, 0.3 and 0.2, respectively. The probability of two hits is

(a) 0.024 (b) 0.188 (c) 0.336 (d) 0.452

Sol. ***(b)*** Here, $P(A) = 0.4, P(\bar{A}) = 0.6, P(B) = 0.3, P(\bar{B}) = 0.7,$
$P(C) = 0.2$ and $P(\bar{C}) = 0.8$

$\therefore$ Probability of two hits $= P_A \cdot P_B \cdot P_{\bar{C}} + P_A \cdot P_{\bar{B}} \cdot P_C + P_{\bar{A}} \cdot P_B \cdot P_C$

$$= 0.4 \times 0.3 \times 0.8 + 0.4 \times 0.7 \times 0.2 + 0.6 \times 0.3 \times 0.2$$

$$= 0.096 + 0.056 + 0.036 = 0.188$$

Q. 77 Assume that in a family, each child is equally likely to be a boy or a girl. A family with three children is chosen at random. The probability that the eldest child is a girl given that the family has atleast one girl is

(a) $\frac{1}{2}$ (b) $\frac{1}{3}$ (c) $\frac{2}{3}$ (d) $\frac{4}{7}$

Sol. *(d)* Here, $S = \{(B, B, B), (G, G, G), (B, G, G), (G, B, G), (G, G, B), (G, B, B), (B, G, B), (B, B, G)\}$

E_1 = Event that a family has atleast one girl, then

$$E_1 = \{(G, B, B), (B, G, B), (B, B, G), (G, G, B), (B, G, G), (G, B, G), (G, G, G)\}$$

E_2 = Event that the eldest child is a girl, then

$$E_2 = \{(G, B, B), (G, G, B), (G, B, G), (G, G, G)\}$$

$$\therefore \quad E_1 \cap E_2 = \{(G, B, B), (G, G, B), (G, B, G), (G, G, G)\}$$

$$\therefore \quad P(E_2 / E_1) = \frac{P(E_1 \cap E_2)}{P(E_1)} = \frac{4/8}{7/8} = \frac{4}{7}$$

Q. 78 If a die is thrown and a card is selected at random from a deck of 52 playing cards, then the probability of getting an even number on the die and a spade card is

(a) $\frac{1}{2}$ (b) $\frac{1}{4}$ (c) $\frac{1}{8}$ (d) $\frac{3}{4}$

Sol. *(c)* Let E_1 = Event for getting an even number on the die

and E_2 = Event that a spade card is selected

$$\therefore \quad P(E_1) = \frac{3}{6} = \frac{1}{2} \text{ and } P(E_2) = \frac{13}{52} = \frac{1}{4}$$

Then, $P(E_1 \cap E_2) = P(E_1) \cdot P(E_2) = \frac{1}{2} \cdot \frac{1}{4} = \frac{1}{8}$

Q. 79 A box contains 3 orange balls, 3 green balls and 2 blue balls. Three balls are drawn at random from the box without replacement. The probability of drawing 2 green balls and one blue ball is

(a) $\frac{3}{28}$ (b) $\frac{2}{21}$ (c) $\frac{1}{28}$ (d) $\frac{167}{168}$

Sol. *(a)* Probability of drawing 2 green balls and one blue ball

$$= P_G \cdot P_G \cdot P_B + P_B \cdot P_G \cdot P_G + P_G \cdot P_B \cdot P_G$$

$$= \frac{3}{8} \cdot \frac{2}{7} \cdot \frac{2}{6} + \frac{2}{8} \cdot \frac{3}{7} \cdot \frac{2}{6} + \frac{3}{8} \cdot \frac{2}{7} \cdot \frac{2}{6}$$

$$= \frac{1}{28} + \frac{1}{28} + \frac{1}{28} = \frac{3}{28}$$

Q. 80 A flashlight has 8 batteries out of which 3 are dead. If two batteries are selected without replacement and tested, then probability that both are dead is

(a) $\frac{33}{56}$ (b) $\frac{9}{64}$ (c) $\frac{1}{14}$ (d) $\frac{3}{28}$

Sol. *(d)* Required probability $= P_D \cdot P_D = \frac{3}{8} \cdot \frac{2}{7} = \frac{3}{28}$

Q. 81 If eight coins are tossed together, then the probability of getting exactly 3 heads is

(a) $\frac{1}{256}$ (b) $\frac{7}{32}$ (c) $\frac{5}{32}$ (d) $\frac{3}{32}$

Sol. *(b)* We know that, probability distribution $P(X = r) = {}^nC_r\,(p)^r\,q^{n-r}$

Here, $n = 8, r = 3, p = \frac{1}{2}$ and $q = \frac{1}{2}$

$\therefore$ Required probability $= {}^8C_3\left(\frac{1}{2}\right)^3\left(\frac{1}{2}\right)^{8-3} = \frac{8!}{5!3!}\left(\frac{1}{2}\right)^8$

$= \frac{8\cdot 7\cdot 6}{3\cdot 2}\cdot\frac{1}{16\cdot 16} = \frac{7}{32}$

Q. 82 **Two dice are thrown. If it is known that the sum of numbers on the dice was less than 6, the probability of getting a sum 3, is**

(a) $\frac{1}{18}$ (b) $\frac{5}{18}$ (c) $\frac{1}{5}$ (d) $\frac{2}{5}$

Sol. *(c)* Let E_1 = Event that the sum of numbers on the dice was less than 6

and E_2 = Event that the sum of numbers on the dice is 3

$\therefore$ $E_1 = \{(1, 4), (4, 1), (2, 3), (3, 2), (2, 2), (1, 3), (3, 1), (1, 2), (2, 1), (1, 1)\}$

$\Rightarrow$ $n(E_1) = 10$

and $E_2 = \{(1, 2), (2, 1)\} \Rightarrow n(E_2) = 2$

$\therefore$ Required probability $= \frac{2}{10} = \frac{1}{5}$

Q. 83 **Which one is not a requirement of a Binomial distribution?**

(a) There are 2 outcomes for each trial

(b) There is a fixed number of trials

(c) The outcomes must be dependent on each other

(d) The probability of success must be the same for all the trials

Sol. *(c)* We know that, in a Binomial distribution,

(i) There are 2 outcomes for each trial.

(ii) There is a fixed number of trials.

(iii) The probability of success must be the same for all the trials.

Q. 84 **If two cards are drawn from a well shuffled deck of 52 playing cards with replacement, then the probability that both cards are queens, is**

(a) $\frac{1}{13}\cdot\frac{1}{13}$ (b) $\frac{1}{13}+\frac{1}{13}$ (c) $\frac{1}{13}\cdot\frac{1}{17}$ (d) $\frac{1}{13}\cdot\frac{4}{51}$

Sol. *(a)* Required probability $= \frac{4}{52}\cdot\frac{4}{52} = \frac{1}{13}\times\frac{1}{13}$ [with replacement]

Q. 85 **The probability of guessing correctly atleast 8 out of 10 answers on a true false type examination is**

(a) $\frac{7}{64}$ (b) $\frac{7}{128}$ (c) $\frac{45}{1024}$ (d) $\frac{7}{41}$

Sol. *(b)* We know that, $P(X = r) = {}^nC_r\,(p)^r\,(q)^{n-r}$

Here, $n = 10, p = \frac{1}{2}, q = \frac{1}{2}$

and $r \geq 8$ *i.e.*, $r = 8, 9, 10$

$$\Rightarrow \quad P(X=r) = P(r=8) + P(r=9) + P(r=10)$$
$$= {}^{10}C_8 \left(\frac{1}{2}\right)^8 \left(\frac{1}{2}\right)^{10-8} + {}^{10}C_9 \left(\frac{1}{2}\right)^9 \left(\frac{1}{2}\right) + {}^{10}C_{10} \left(\frac{1}{2}\right)^{10} \cdot \left(\frac{1}{2}\right)^0$$
$$= \frac{10!}{8!2!}\left(\frac{1}{2}\right)^{10} + \frac{10!}{9!1!}\left(\frac{1}{2}\right)^{10} + \left(\frac{1}{2}\right)^{10}$$
$$= \left(\frac{1}{2}\right)^{10} \cdot [45 + 10 + 1] = \left(\frac{1}{2}\right)^{10} \cdot 56$$
$$= \frac{1}{16 \cdot 64} \cdot 56 = \frac{7}{128}$$

Q. 86 If the probability that a person is not a swimmer is 0.3, then the probability that out of 5 persons 4 are swimmers is

(a) ${}^5C_4(0.7)^4\,(0.3)$ (b) ${}^5C_1\,(0.7)\,(0.3)^4$

(c) ${}^5C_4\,(0.7)\,(0.3)^4$ (d) $(0.7)^4\,(0.3)$

Sol. *(a)* Here, $\bar{p} = 0.3 \Rightarrow p = 0.7$ and $q = 0.3$, $n = 5$ and $r = 4$

$\therefore$ Required probability $= {}^5C_4\,(0.7)^4\,(0.3)$

Q. 87 The probability distribution of a discrete random variable X is given below

X	2	3	4	5
P(X)	$\frac{5}{k}$	$\frac{7}{k}$	$\frac{9}{k}$	$\frac{11}{k}$

The value of k is

(a) 8 (b) 16 (c) 32 (d) 48

Sol. *(c)* We know that, $\Sigma P(X) = 1$

$$\Rightarrow \quad \frac{5}{k} + \frac{7}{k} + \frac{9}{k} + \frac{11}{k} = 1$$
$$\Rightarrow \quad \frac{32}{k} = 1$$
$$\therefore \quad k = 32$$

Q. 88 For the following probability distribution.

X	−4	−3	−2	−1	0
P(X)	0.1	0.2	0.3	0.2	0.2

$E(X)$ is equal to

(a) 0 (b) −1 (c) −2 (d) −1.8

Sol. *(d)*
$$E(X) = \Sigma X\,P(X)$$
$$= -4 \times (0.1) + (-3 \times 0.2) + (-2 \times 0.3) + (-1 \times 0.2) + (0 \times 0.2)$$
$$= -0.4 - 0.6 - 0.6 - 0.2 = -1.8$$

Q. 89 For the following probability distribution.

X	1	2	3	4
$P(X)$	$\frac{1}{10}$	$\frac{1}{5}$	$\frac{3}{10}$	$\frac{2}{5}$

$E(X^2)$ is equal to

(a) 3 (b) 5 (c) 7 (d) 10

Sol. *(d)*
$$E(X^2) = \Sigma X^2 \, P(X) = 1 \cdot \frac{1}{10} + 4 \cdot \frac{1}{5} + 9 \cdot \frac{3}{10} + 16 \cdot \frac{2}{5}$$
$$= \frac{1}{10} + \frac{4}{5} + \frac{27}{10} + \frac{32}{5}$$
$$= \frac{1 + 8 + 27 + 64}{10} = 10$$

Q. 90 Suppose a random variable X follows the Binomial distribution with parameters n and p, where $0 < p < 1$. If $P(x = r) / P(x = n - r)$ is independent of n and r, then p equals to

(a) $\frac{1}{2}$ (b) $\frac{1}{3}$ (c) $\frac{1}{5}$ (d) $\frac{1}{7}$

Sol. *(a)* $\because$ $P(X = r) = {}^nC_r \, (p)^r (q)^{n-r} = \frac{n!}{(n-r)!r!}(p)^r (1-p)^{n-r}$ $[\because q = 1 - p]$ ...(i)

$P(X = 0) = (1-p)^n$

and $P(X = n - r) = {}^nC_{n-r} \, (p)^{n-r} \, (q)^{n-(n-r)}$

$$= \frac{n!}{(n-r)!r!}(p)^{n-r}(1-p)^{+r}$$ $[\because q = 1 - p]$ $[\because {}^nC_r = {}^nC_{n-r}]$ ...(ii)

Now, $$\frac{P(x = r)}{P(x = n - r)} = \frac{\frac{n!}{(n-r)!r!} p^r (1-p)^{n-r}}{\frac{n!}{(n-r)!\,r!} p^{n-r} (1-p)^{+r}}$$ [using Eqs. (i) and (ii)]

$$= \left(\frac{1-p}{p}\right)^{n-r} \times \frac{1}{\left(\frac{1-p}{p}\right)^r}$$

Above expression is independent of n and r, if $\frac{1-p}{p} = 1 \Rightarrow \frac{1}{p} = 2 \Rightarrow p = \frac{1}{2}$

Q. 91 In a college, 30% students fail in Physics, 25% fail in Mathematics and 10% fail in both. One student is chosen at random. The probability that she fails in Physics, if she has failed in Mathematics is

(a) $\frac{1}{10}$ (b) $\frac{2}{5}$ (c) $\frac{9}{20}$ (d) $\frac{1}{3}$

Sol. *(b)* Here, $P_{(Ph)} = \frac{30}{100} = \frac{3}{10}, \; P_{(M)} = \frac{25}{100} = \frac{1}{4}$

and $P_{(M \cap Ph)} = \frac{10}{100} = \frac{1}{10}$

$\therefore$ $$P\left(\frac{Ph}{M}\right) = \frac{P(Ph \cap M)}{P(M)} = \frac{1/10}{1/4} = \frac{2}{5}$$

Q. 92 *A* and *B* are two students. Their chances of solving a problem correctly are $\frac{1}{3}$ and $\frac{1}{4}$, respectively. If the probability of their making a common error is, $\frac{1}{20}$ and they obtain the same answer, then the probability of their answer to be correct is

(a) $\frac{1}{12}$ (b) $\frac{1}{40}$ (c) $\frac{13}{120}$ (d) $\frac{10}{13}$

Sol. *(d)* Let E_1 = Event that both *A* and *B* solve the problem

$$\therefore \quad P(E_1) = \frac{1}{3} \times \frac{1}{4} = \frac{1}{12}.$$

Let E_2 = Event that both *A* and *B* got incorrect solution of the problem

$$\therefore \quad P(E_2) = \frac{2}{3} \times \frac{3}{4} = \frac{1}{2}$$

Let E = Event that they got same answer

Here, $P(E/E_1) = 1, P(E/E_2) = \frac{1}{20}$

$$\therefore \quad P(E_1/E) = \frac{P(E_1 \cap E)}{P(E)} = \frac{P(E_1) \cdot P(E/E_1)}{P(E_1) \cdot P(E/E_1) + P(E_2)\,P(E/E_2)}$$

$$= \frac{\frac{1}{12} \times 1}{\frac{1}{12} \times 1 + \frac{1}{2} \times \frac{1}{20}} = \frac{1/12}{\frac{10+3}{120}} = \frac{120}{12 \times 13} = \frac{10}{13}$$

Q. 93 If a box has 100 pens of which 10 are defective, then what is the probability that out of a sample of 5 pens drawn one by one with replacement atmost one is defective?

(a) $\left(\frac{9}{10}\right)^5$ (b) $\frac{1}{2}\left(\frac{9}{10}\right)^4$

(c) $\frac{1}{2}\left(\frac{9}{10}\right)^4$ (d) $\left(\frac{9}{10}\right)^5 + \frac{1}{2}\left(\frac{9}{10}\right)^4$

Sol. *(d)* Here, $n = 5, p = \frac{10}{100} = \frac{1}{10}$ and $q = \frac{9}{10}$

$$r \le 1$$

$$\Rightarrow \quad r = 0, 1$$

Also, $P(X = r) = {}^nC_r\, p^r q^{n-r}$

$$\therefore \quad P(X = r) = P(r = 0) + P(r = 1)$$

$$= {}^5C_0\left(\frac{1}{10}\right)^0\left(\frac{9}{10}\right)^5 + {}^5C_1\left(\frac{1}{10}\right)^1\left(\frac{9}{10}\right)^4$$

$$= \left(\frac{9}{10}\right)^5 + 5 \cdot \frac{1}{10} \cdot \left(\frac{9}{10}\right)^4$$

$$= \left(\frac{9}{10}\right)^5 + \frac{1}{2}\left(\frac{9}{10}\right)^4$$

True/False

Q. 94 If $P(A) > 0$ and $P(B) > 0$. Then, A and B can be both mutually exclusive and independent.

Sol. ***False***

Q. 95 If A and B are independent events, then A' and B' are also independent.

Sol. ***True***

Q. 96 If A and B are mutually exclusive events, then they will be independent also.

Sol. ***False***

Q. 97 Two independent events are always mutually exclusive.

Sol. ***False***

Q. 98 If A and B are two independent events, then $P(A \text{ and } B) = P(A) \cdot P(B)$.

Sol. ***True***

Q. 99 Another name for the mean of a probability distribution is expected value.

Sol. ***True***

$$E(X) = \Sigma X\, P(X) = \mu$$

Q. 100 If A and B' are independent events, then $P(A' \cup B) = 1 - P(A)\, P(B')$.

Sol. ***True***

$$P(A' \cup B) = 1 - P(A \cap B') = 1 - P(A)\, P(B')$$

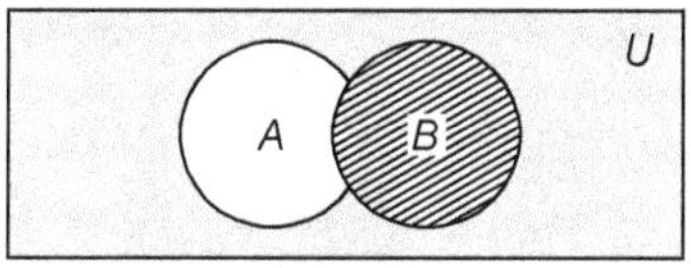

$(A' \cup B)$

Q. 101 If A and B are independent, then P (exactly one of A, B occurs)

$$= P(A)\, P(B') + P(B)\, P(A').$$

Sol. ***True***

Q. 102 If A and B are two events such that $P(A) > 0$ and $P(A) + P(B) > 1$, then $P(B/A) \geq 1 - \dfrac{P(B')}{P(A)}$

Sol. ***False***

$$\because \quad P(B/A) = \frac{P(A \cap B)}{P(A)}$$
$$= \frac{P(A) + P(B) - P(A \cup B)}{P(A)} > \frac{1 - P(A \cup B)}{P(A)}$$

Q. 103 If A, B and C are three independent events such that

$$P(A) = P(B) = P(C) = p,$$

then P (atleast two of A, B and C occur) $= 3p^2 - 2p^3$.

Sol. ***True***

P (atleast two of A, B and C occur)

$$= p \times p \times (1 - p) + (1 - p) \cdot p \cdot p + p(1 - p) \cdot p + p \cdot p \cdot p$$
$$= p^2[1 - p + 1 - p + 1 - p + p]$$
$$= p^2(3 - 3p) + p^3$$
$$= 3p^2 - 3p^3 + p^3 = 3p^2 - 2p^3$$

Fillers

Q. 104 If A and B are two events such that $P(A/B) = p$, $P(A) = p$, $P(B) = \dfrac{1}{3}$ and $P(A \cup B) = \dfrac{5}{9}$, then p is equal to ....

Sol. Here, $\quad P(A) = p, P(B) = \dfrac{1}{3}$ and $P(A \cup B) = \dfrac{5}{9}$

$$\because \quad P(A/B) = \frac{P(A \cap B)}{P(B)} = p \Rightarrow P(A \cap B) = \frac{p}{3}$$

and $\quad P(A \cup B) = P(A) + P(B) - P(A \cap B)$

$$\Rightarrow \quad \frac{5}{9} = p + \frac{1}{3} - \frac{p}{3} \Rightarrow \frac{5}{9} - \frac{1}{3} = \frac{2p}{3}$$

$$\Rightarrow \quad \frac{5 - 3}{9} = \frac{2p}{3} \Rightarrow p = \frac{2}{9} \times \frac{3}{2} = \frac{1}{3}$$

Q. 105 If A and B are such that $P(A' \cup B') = \dfrac{2}{3}$ and $P(A \cup B) = \dfrac{5}{9}$, then $P(A') + P(B')$ is equal to ....

Sol. Here, $\quad P(A' \cup B') = \dfrac{2}{3}$ and $P(A \cup B) = \dfrac{5}{9}$

$$P(A' \cup B') = 1 - P(A \cap B)$$

$$\Rightarrow \quad \frac{2}{3} = 1 - P(A \cap B)$$

$$\Rightarrow \quad P(A \cap B) = 1 - \frac{2}{3} = \frac{1}{3}$$

$\because \quad P(A') + P(B') = 1 - P(A) + 1 - P(B)$

$$= 2 - [P(A) + P(B)]$$

$$= 2 - [P(A \cup B) + P(A \cap B)]$$

$$= 2 - \left(\frac{5}{9} + \frac{1}{3}\right) = 2 - \left(\frac{5+3}{9}\right)$$

$$= \frac{18-8}{9} = \frac{10}{9}$$

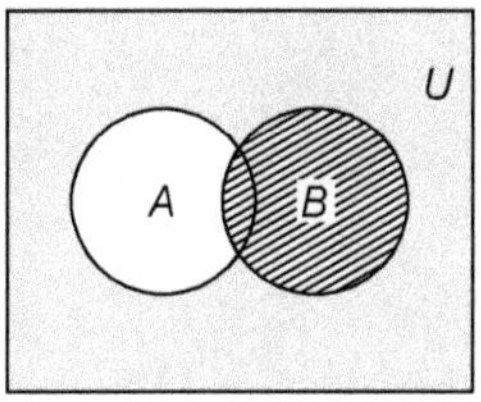

Q. 106 If X follows Binomial distribution with parameters $n = 5$, p and $P(X = 2) = 9P(X = 3)$, then p is equal to ....

Sol. $\because \quad P(X = 2) = 9 \cdot P(X = 3)$ (where, $n = 5$ and $q = 1 - p$)

$\Rightarrow \quad {}^5C_2\, p^2 (1-p)^3 = 9 \cdot {}^5C_3 p^3 (1-p)^2$

$\Rightarrow \quad \frac{5!}{2!3!} p^2 (1-p)^3 = 9 \cdot \frac{5!}{3!2!} p^3 (1-p)^2$

$\Rightarrow \quad \frac{p^2(1-p)^3}{p^3(1-p)^2} = 9$

$\Rightarrow \quad \frac{(1-p)}{p} = 9 \Rightarrow 9p + p = 1$

$\therefore \quad p = \frac{1}{10}$

Q. 107 If X be a random variable taking values $x_1, x_2, x_3, \ldots, x_n$ with probabilities $P_1, P_2, P_3, \ldots, P_n$, respectively. Then, Var (x) is equal to ....

Sol.

$$\text{Var}(X) = E(X)^2 - [E(X)]^2$$

$$= \sum_{i=1}^{n} X^2 P(X) - [\sum_{i=1}^{n} X\, P(X)]^2$$

$$= \Sigma P_i x_i^2 - (\Sigma P_i\, x_i)^2$$

Q. 108 Let A and B be two events. If $P(A/B) = P(A)$, then A is ... of B.

Sol. $\because \quad P(A/B) = \frac{P(A \cap B)}{P(B)}$

$\Rightarrow \quad P(A) = \frac{P(A \cap B)}{P(B)}$

$\Rightarrow \quad P(A) \cdot P(B) = P(A \cap B)$

So, A is independent of B.

CPSIA information can be obtained
at www.ICGtesting.com
Printed in the USA
LVHW071100110623
749338LV00005BA/56

9 789327 197471